Praise for the First Edition

Lucid and engaging—this is without doubt the fun way to learn R!
—Amos A. Folarin, University College London

Be prepared to quickly raise the bar with the sheer quality that R can produce.
—Patrick Breen, Rogers Communications Inc.

An excellent introduction and reference on R from the author of the best R website.
—Christopher Williams, University of Idaho

Thorough and readable. A great R companion for the student or researcher.
—Samuel McQuillin, University of South Carolina

Finally, a comprehensive introduction to R for programmers.
—Philipp K. Janert, Author of *Gnuplot in Action*

Essential reading for anybody moving to R for the first time.
—Charles Malpas, University of Melbourne

One of the quickest routes to R proficiency. You can buy the book on Friday and have a working program by Monday.
—Elizabeth Ostrowski, Baylor College of Medicine

One usually buys a book to solve the problems they know they have. This book solves problems you didn't know you had.
—Carles Fenollosa, Barcelona Supercomputing Center

Clear, precise, and comes with a lot of explanations and examples...the book can be used by beginners and professionals alike, and even for teaching R!
—Atef Ouni, Tunisian National Institute of Statistics

A great balance of targeted tutorials and in-depth examples.
—Landon Cox, 360VL Inc.

R in Action

SECOND EDITION
Data analysis and graphics with R

ROBERT I. KABACOFF

MANNING

SHELTER ISLAND

Manning Publications Co.
20 Baldwin Road
PO Box 761
Shelter Island, NY 11964

Development editor: Jennifer Stout
Copyeditor: Tiffany Taylor
Proofreader: Toma Mulligan
Typesetter: Marija Tudor
Cover designer: Marija Tudor

ISBN: 9781617291388
Printed in the United States of America
1 2 3 4 5 6 7 8 9 10 – EBM – 20 19 18 17 16 15

brief contents

contents

preface

What is the use of a book, without pictures or conversations?

—Alice, *Alice's Adventures in Wonderland*

It's wondrous, with treasures to satiate desires both subtle and gross; but it's not for the timid.

—Q, "Q Who?" *Stark Trek: The Next Generation*

When I began writing this book, I spent quite a bit of time searching for a good quote to start things off. I ended up with two. R is a wonderfully flexible platform and language for exploring, visualizing, and understanding data. I chose the quote from *Alice's Adventures in Wonderland* to capture the flavor of statistical analysis today—an interactive process of exploration, visualization, and interpretation.

The second quote reflects the generally held notion that R is difficult to learn. What I hope to show you is that is doesn't have to be. R is broad and powerful, with so many analytic and graphic functions available (more than 50,000 at last count) that it easily intimidates both novice and experienced users alike. But there is rhyme and reason to the apparent madness. With guidelines and instructions, you can navigate the tremendous resources available, selecting the tools you need to accomplish your work with style, elegance, efficiency—and more than a little coolness.

I first encountered R several years ago, when applying for a new statistical consulting position. The prospective employer asked in the pre-interview material if I was conversant in R. Following the standard advice of recruiters, I immediately said yes, and set off to learn it. I was an experienced statistician and researcher, had 25 years experience as an SAS and SPSS programmer, and was fluent in a half dozen programming languages. How hard could it be? Famous last words.

As I tried to learn the language (as fast as possible, with an interview looming), I found either tomes on the underlying structure of the language or dense treatises on specific advanced statistical methods, written by and for subject-matter experts. The online help was written in a spartan style that was more reference than tutorial. Every time I thought I had a handle on the overall organization and capabilities of R, I found something new that made me feel ignorant and small.

To make sense of it all, I approached R as a data scientist. I thought about what it takes to successfully process, analyze, and understand data, including

- Accessing the data (getting the data into the application from multiple sources)
- Cleaning the data (coding missing data, fixing or deleting miscoded data, transforming variables into more useful formats)
- Annotating the data (in order to remember what each piece represents)
- Summarizing the data (getting descriptive statistics to help characterize the data)
- Visualizing the data (because a picture really is worth a thousand words)
- Modeling the data (uncovering relationships and testing hypotheses)
- Preparing the results (creating publication-quality tables and graphs)

Then I tried to understand how I could use R to accomplish each of these tasks. Because I learn best by teaching, I eventually created a website (www.statmethods.net) to document what I had learned.

Then, about a year later, Marjan Bace, Manning's publisher, called and asked if I would like to write a book on R. I had already written 50 journal articles, 4 technical manuals, numerous book chapters, and a book on research methodology, so how hard could it be? At the risk of sounding repetitive—famous last words.

A year after the first edition came out in 2011, I started working on the second edition. The R platform is evolving, and I wanted to describe these new developments. I also wanted to expand the coverage of predictive analytics and data mining—important topics in the world of big data. Finally, I wanted to add chapters on advanced data visualization, software development, and dynamic report writing.

The book you're holding is the one that I wished I had so many years ago. I have tried to provide you with a guide to R that will allow you to quickly access the power of this great open source endeavor, without all the frustration and angst. I hope you enjoy it.

P.S. I was offered the job but didn't take it. But learning R has taken my career in directions that I could never have anticipated. Life can be funny.

acknowledgments

A number of people worked hard to make this a better book. They include

- Marjan Bace, Manning's publisher, who asked me to write this book in the first place.
- Sebastian Stirling and Jennifer Stout, development editors on the first and second editions, respectively. Each spent many hours helping me organize the material, clarify concepts, and generally make the text more interesting.
- Pablo Domínguez Vaselli, technical proofreader, who helped uncover areas of confusion and provided an independent and expert eye for testing code. I came to rely on his vast knowledge, careful reviews, and considered judgment.
- Olivia Booth, the review editor, who helped obtain reviewers and coordinate the review process.
- Mary Piergies, who helped shepherd this book through the production process, and her team of Tiffany Taylor, Toma Mulligan, Janet Vail, David Novak, and Marija Tudor.
- The peer reviewers who spent hours of their own time carefully reading through the material, finding typos, and making valuable substantive suggestions: Bryce Darling, Christian Theil Have, Cris Weber, Deepak Vohra, Dwight Barry, George Gaines, Indrajit Sen Gupta, Dr. L. Duleep Kumar Samuel, Mahesh Srinivason, Marc Paradis, Peter Rabinovitch, Ravishankar Rajagopalan, Samuel Dale McQuillin, and Zekai Otles.
- The many Manning Early Access Program (MEAP) participants who bought the book before it was finished, asked great questions, pointed out errors, and made helpful suggestions.

Each contributor has made this a better and more comprehensive book.

I would also like to acknowledge the many software authors who have contributed to making R such a powerful data-analytic platform. They include not only the core developers, but also the selfless individuals who have created and maintain contributed packages, extending R's capabilities greatly. Appendix E provides a list of the authors of contributed packages described in this book. In particular, I would like to mention John Fox, Hadley Wickham, Frank E. Harrell, Jr., Deepayan Sarkar, and William Revelle, whose works I greatly admire. I have tried to represent their contributions accurately, and I remain solely responsible for any errors or distortions inadvertently included in this book.

I really should have started this book by thanking my wife and partner, Carol Lynn. Although she has no intrinsic interest in statistics or programming, she read each chapter multiple times and made countless corrections and suggestions. No greater love has any person than to read multivariate statistics for another. Just as important, she suffered the long nights and weekends that I spent writing this book, with grace, support, and affection. There is no logical explanation why I should be this lucky.

There are two other people I would like to thank. One is my father, whose love of science was inspiring and who gave me an appreciation of the value of data. I miss him dearly. The other is Gary K. Burger, my mentor in graduate school. Gary got me interested in a career in statistics and teaching when I thought I wanted to be a clinician. This is all his fault.

about this book

If you picked up this book, you probably have some data that you need to collect, summarize, transform, explore, model, visualize, or present. If so, then R is for you! R has become the worldwide language for statistics, predictive analytics, and data visualization. It offers the widest range of methodologies for understanding data currently available, from the most basic to the most complex and bleeding edge.

As an open source project it's freely available for a range of platforms, including Windows, Mac OS X, and Linux. It's under constant development, with new procedures added daily. Additionally, R is supported by a large and diverse community of data scientists and programmers who gladly offer their help and advice to users.

Although R is probably best known for its ability to create beautiful and sophisticated graphs, it can handle just about any statistical problem. The base installation provides hundreds of data-management, statistical, and graphical functions out of the box. But some of its most powerful features come from the thousands of extensions (packages) provided by contributing authors.

This breadth comes at a price. It can be hard for new users to get a handle on what R is and what it can do. Even the most experienced R user is surprised to learn about features they were unaware of.

R in Action, Second Edition provides you with a guided introduction to R, giving you a 2,000-foot view of the platform and its capabilities. It will introduce you to the most important functions in the base installation and more than 90 of the most useful contributed packages. Throughout the book, the goal is practical application—how you can make sense of your data and communicate that understanding to others. When you finish, you should have a good grasp of how R works and what it can do and where you can go to learn more. You'll be able to apply a variety of techniques for visualizing data, and you'll have the skills to tackle both basic and advanced data analytic problems.

What's new in the second edition

If you want to delve into the use of R more deeply, the second edition offers more than 200 pages of new material. Concentrated in the second half of the book are new chapters on data mining, predictive analytics, and advanced programming. In particular, chapters 15 (time series), 16 (cluster analysis), 17 (classification), 19 (ggplot2 graphics), 20 (advanced programming), 21 (creating a package), and 22 (creating dynamic reports) are new. In addition, chapter 2 (creating a dataset) has more detailed information on importing data from text and SAS files, and appendix F (working with large datasets) has been expanded to include new tools for working with big data problems. Finally, numerous updates and corrections have been made throughout the text.

Who should read this book

R in Action, Second Edition should appeal to anyone who deals with data. No background in statistical programming or the R language is assumed. Although the book is accessible to novices, there should be enough new and practical material to satisfy even experienced R mavens.

Users without a statistical background who want to use R to manipulate, summarize, and graph data should find chapters 1–6, 11, and 19 easily accessible. Chapters 7 and 10 assume a one-semester course in statistics; and readers of chapters 8, 9, and 12–18 will benefit from two semesters of statistics. Chapters 20–22 offer a deeper dive into the R language and have no statistical prerequisites. I've tried to write each chapter in such a way that both beginning and expert data analysts will find something interesting and useful.

Roadmap

This book is designed to give you a guided tour of the R platform, with a focus on those methods most immediately applicable for manipulating, visualizing, and understanding data. The book has 22 chapters and is divided into 5 parts: "Getting Started," "Basic Methods," "Intermediate Methods," "Advanced Methods," and "Expanding Your Skills." Additional topics are covered in seven appendices.

Chapter 1 begins with an introduction to R and the features that make it so useful as a data-analysis platform. The chapter covers how to obtain the program and how to enhance the basic installation with extensions that are available online. The remainder of the chapter is spent exploring the user interface and learning how to run programs interactively and in batch.

Chapter 2 covers the many methods available for getting data into R. The first half of the chapter introduces the data structures R uses to hold data, and how to enter data from the keyboard. The second half discusses methods for importing data into R from text files, web pages, spreadsheets, statistical packages, and databases.

Many users initially approach R because they want to create graphs, so we jump right into that topic in chapter 3. No waiting required. We review methods of creating graphs, modifying them, and saving them in a variety of formats.

Chapter 4 covers basic data management, including sorting, merging, and subsetting datasets, and transforming, recoding, and deleting variables.

Building on the material in chapter 4, chapter 5 covers the use of functions (mathematical, statistical, character) and control structures (looping, conditional execution) for data management. I then discuss how to write your own R functions and how to aggregate data in various ways.

Chapter 6 demonstrates methods for creating common univariate graphs, such as bar plots, pie charts, histograms, density plots, box plots, and dot plots. Each is useful for understanding the distribution of a single variable.

Chapter 7 starts by showing how to summarize data, including the use of descriptive statistics and cross-tabulations. We then look at basic methods for understanding relationships between two variables, including correlations, t-tests, chi-square tests, and nonparametric methods.

Chapter 8 introduces regression methods for modeling the relationship between a numeric outcome variable and a set of one or more numeric predictor variables. Methods for fitting these models, evaluating their appropriateness, and interpreting their meaning are discussed in detail.

Chapter 9 considers the analysis of basic experimental designs through the analysis of variance and its variants. Here we're usually interested in how treatment combinations or conditions affect a numerical outcome. Methods for assessing the appropriateness of the analyses and visualizing the results are also covered.

Chapter 10 provides a detailed treatment of power analysis. Starting with a discussion of hypothesis testing, the chapter focuses on how to determine the sample size necessary to detect a treatment effect of a given size with a given degree of confidence. This can help you to plan experimental and quasi-experimental studies that are likely to yield useful results.

Chapter 11 expands on the material in chapter 6, covering the creation of graphs that help you to visualize relationships among two or more variables. These include various types of 2D and 3D scatter plots, scatter-plot matrices, line plots, correlograms, and mosaic plots.

Chapter 12 presents analytic methods that work well in cases where data are sampled from unknown or mixed distributions, where sample sizes are small, where outliers are a problem, or where devising an appropriate test based on a theoretical distribution is too complex and mathematically intractable. They include both resampling and bootstrapping approaches—computer-intensive methods that are easily implemented in R.

Chapter 13 expands on the regression methods in chapter 8 to cover data that are not normally distributed. The chapter starts with a discussion of generalized linear models and then focuses on cases where you're trying to predict an outcome variable that is either categorical (logistic regression) or a count (Poisson regression).

One of the challenges of multivariate data problems is simplification. Chapter 14 describes methods of transforming a large number of correlated variables into a smaller set of uncorrelated variables (principal component analysis), as well as methods for uncovering the latent structure underlying a given set of variables (factor analysis). The many steps involved in an appropriate analysis are covered in detail.

Chapter 15 describes methods for creating, manipulating, and modeling time series data. It covers visualizing and decomposing time series data, as well as exponential and ARIMA approaches to forecasting future values.

Chapter 16 illustrates methods of clustering observations into naturally occurring groups. The chapter begins with a discussion of the common steps in a comprehensive cluster analysis, followed by a presentation of hierarchical clustering and partitioning methods. Several methods for determining the proper number of clusters are presented.

Chapter 17 presents popular supervised machine-learning methods for classifying observations into groups. Decision trees, random forests, and support vector machines are considered in turn. You'll also learn about methods for evaluating the accuracy of each approach.

In keeping with my attempt to present practical methods for analyzing data, chapter 18 considers modern approaches to the ubiquitous problem of missing data values. R supports a number of elegant approaches for analyzing datasets that are incomplete for various reasons. Several of the best are described here, along with guidance for which ones to use when, and which ones to avoid.

Chapter 19 wraps up the discussion of graphics with a presentation of one of R's most useful and advanced approaches to visualizing data: ggplot2. The ggplot2 package implements a grammar of graphics that provides a powerful and consistent set of tools for graphing multivariate data.

Chapter 20 covers advanced programming techniques. You'll learn about object-oriented programming techniques and debugging approaches. The chapter also presents a variety of tips for efficient programming. This chapter will be particularly helpful if you're seeking a greater understanding of how R works, and it's a prerequisite for chapter 21.

Chapter 21 provides a step-by-step guide to creating R packages. This will allow you to create more sophisticated programs, document them efficiently, and share them with others.

Finally, chapter 22 offers several methods for creating attractive reports from within R. You'll learn how to generate web pages, reports, articles, and even books from your R code. The resulting documents can include your code, tables of results, graphs, and commentary.

The afterword points you to many of the best internet sites for learning more about R, joining the R community, getting questions answered, and staying current with this rapidly changing product.

Last, but not least, the seven appendices (A through G) extend the text's coverage to include such useful topics as R graphic user interfaces, customizing and upgrading an R installation, exporting data to other applications, using R for matrix algebra (à la MATLAB), and working with very large datasets.

We also offer a bonus chapter, which is available online only from the publisher's website at manning.com/RinActionSecondEdition. Online chapter 23 covers the `lattice` package, which is introduced in chapter 19.

Advice for data miners

Data mining is a field of analytics concerned with discovering patterns in large data sets. Many data-mining specialists are turning to R for its cutting-edge analytical capabilities. If you're a data miner making the transition to R and want to access the language as quickly as possible, I recommend the following reading sequence: chapter 1 (introduction), chapter 2 (data structures and those portions of importing data that are relevant to your setting), chapter 4 (basic data management), chapter 7 (descriptive statistics), chapter 8 (sections 1, 2, and 6; regression), chapter 13 (section 2; logistic regression), chapter 16 (clustering), chapter 17 (classification), and appendix F (working with large datasets). Then review the other chapters as needed.

Code examples

In order to make this book as broadly applicable as possible, I've chosen examples from a range of disciplines, including psychology, sociology, medicine, biology, business, and engineering. None of these examples require a specialized knowledge of that field.

The datasets used in these examples were selected because they pose interesting questions and because they're small. This allows you to focus on the techniques described and quickly understand the processes involved. When you're learning new methods, smaller is better. The datasets are provided with the base installation of R or available through add-on packages that are available online.

The source code for each example is available from www.manning.com/RinAction SecondEdition and at www.github.com/kabacoff/RiA2. To get the most out of this book, I recommend that you try the examples as you read them.

Finally, a common maxim states that if you ask two statisticians how to analyze a dataset, you'll get three answers. The flip side of this assertion is that each answer will move you closer to an understanding of the data. I make no claim that a given analysis is the best or only approach to a given problem. Using the skills taught in this text, I invite you to play with the data and see what you can learn. R is interactive, and the best way to learn is to experiment.

Code conventions

The following typographical conventions are used throughout this book:

- A `monospaced font` is used for code listings that should be typed as is.

- A monospaced font is also used within the general text to denote code words or previously defined objects.
- *Italics* within code listings indicate placeholders. You should replace them with appropriate text and values for the problem at hand. For example, *path_to _my_file* would be replaced with the actual path to a file on your computer.
- R is an interactive language that indicates readiness for the next line of user input with a prompt (> by default). Many of the listings in this book capture interactive sessions. When you see code lines that start with >, don't type the prompt.
- Code annotations are used in place of inline comments (a common convention in Manning books). Additionally, some annotations appear with numbered bullets like ❶ that refer to explanations appearing later in the text.
- To save room or make text more legible, the output from interactive sessions may include additional white space or omit text that is extraneous to the point under discussion.

Author Online

Purchase of *R in Action, Second Edition* includes free access to a private web forum run by Manning Publications where you can make comments about the book, ask technical questions, and receive help from the author and from other users. To access the forum and subscribe to it, point your web browser to www.manning.com/RinActionSecond Edition. This page provides information on how to get on the forum once you're registered, what kind of help is available, and the rules of conduct on the forum.

Manning's commitment to our readers is to provide a venue where a meaningful dialog between individual readers and between readers and the author can take place. It isn't a commitment to any specific amount of participation on the part of the author, whose contribution to the AO forum remains voluntary (and unpaid). We suggest you try asking the author some challenging questions, lest his interest stray!

The AO forum and the archives of previous discussions will be accessible from the publisher's website as long as the book is in print.

About the author

Dr. Robert Kabacoff is Vice President of Research for Management Research Group, an international organizational development and consulting firm. He has more than 20 years of experience providing research and statistical consultation to organizations in health care, financial services, manufacturing, behavioral sciences, government, and academia. Prior to joining MRG, Dr. Kabacoff was a professor of psychology at Nova Southeastern University in Florida, where he taught graduate courses in quantitative methods and statistical programming. For the past five years, he has managed Quick-R (www.statmethods.net), a popular R tutorial website.

about the cover illustration

The figure on the cover of *R in Action, Second Edition* is captioned "A man from Zadar."
The illustration is taken from a reproduction of an album of Croatian traditional costumes from the mid-nineteenth century by Nikola Arsenovic, published by the Ethnographic Museum in Split, Croatia, in 2003. The illustrations were obtained from a helpful librarian at the Ethnographic Museum in Split, itself situated in the Roman core of the medieval center of the town: the ruins of Emperor Diocletian's retirement palace from around AD 304. The book includes finely colored illustrations of figures from different regions of Croatia, accompanied by descriptions of the costumes and of everyday life.

Zadar is an old Roman-era town on the northern Dalmatian coast of Croatia. It's over 2,000 years old and served for hundreds of years as an important port on the trading route from Constantinople to the West. Situated on a peninsula framed by small Adriatic islands, the city is picturesque and has become a popular tourist destination with its architectural treasures of Roman ruins, moats, and old stone walls. The figure on the cover wears blue woolen trousers and a white linen shirt, over which he dons a blue vest and jacket trimmed with the colorful embroidery typical for this region. A red woolen belt and cap complete the costume.

Dress codes and lifestyles have changed over the last 200 years, and the diversity by region, so rich at the time, has faded away. It's now hard to tell apart the inhabitants of different continents, let alone of different hamlets or towns separated by only a few miles. Perhaps we have traded this cultural diversity for a more varied personal life—certainly for a more varied and fast-paced technological life.

Manning celebrates the inventiveness and initiative of the computer business with book covers based on the rich diversity of regional life of two centuries ago, brought back to life by illustrations from old books and collections like this one.

Part 1

Getting started

Welcome to *R in Action*! R is one of the most popular platforms for data analysis and visualization currently available. It's free, open source software, available for Windows, Mac OS X, and Linux operating systems. This book will provide you with the skills needed to master this comprehensive software and apply it effectively to your own data.

The book is divided into four sections. Part I covers the basics of installing the software, learning to navigate the interface, importing data, and massaging it into a useful format for further analysis.

Chapter 1 is all about becoming familiar with the R environment. The chapter begins with an overview of R and the features that make it such a powerful platform for modern data analysis. After briefly describing how to obtain and install the software, the user interface is explored through a series of simple examples. Next, you'll learn how to enhance the functionality of the basic installation with extensions (called *contributed packages*), that can be freely downloaded from online repositories. The chapter ends with an example that allows you to test out your new skills.

Once you're familiar with the R interface, the next challenge is to get your data into the program. In today's information-rich world, data can come from many sources and in many formats. Chapter 2 covers the wide variety of methods available for importing data into R. The first half of the chapter introduces the data structures R uses to hold data and describes how to input data manually. The second half discusses methods for importing data from text files, web pages, spreadsheets, statistical packages, and databases.

From a workflow point of view, it would probably make sense to discuss data management and data cleaning next. But many users approach R for the first time out of an interest in its powerful graphics capabilities. Rather than frustrating that interest and keeping you waiting, we dive right into graphics in chapter 3. The chapter reviews methods for creating graphs, customizing them, and saving them in a variety of formats. The chapter describes how to specify the colors, symbols, lines, fonts, axes, titles, labels, and legends used in a graph, and ends with a description of how to combine several graphs into a single plot.

Once you've had a chance to try out R's graphics capabilities, it's time to get back to the business of analyzing data. Data rarely comes in a readily usable format. Significant time must often be spent combining data from different sources, cleaning messy data (miscoded data, mismatched data, missing data), and creating new variables (combined variables, transformed variables, recoded variables) before the questions of interest can be addressed. Chapter 4 covers basic data-management tasks in R, including sorting, merging, and subsetting datasets, and transforming, recoding, and deleting variables.

Chapter 5 builds on the material in chapter 4. It covers the use of numeric (arithmetic, trigonometric, and statistical) and character functions (string subsetting, concatenation, and substitution) in data management. A comprehensive example is used throughout this section to illustrate many of the functions described. Next, control structures (looping, conditional execution) are discussed, and you'll learn how to write your own R functions. Writing custom functions allows you to extend R's capabilities by encapsulating many programming steps into a single, flexible function call. Finally, powerful methods for reorganizing (reshaping) and aggregating data are discussed. Reshaping and aggregation are often useful in preparing data for further analyses.

After having completed part I, you'll be thoroughly familiar with programming in the R environment. You'll have the skills needed to enter or access your data, clean it up, and prepare it for further analyses. You'll also have experience creating, customizing, and saving a variety of graphs.

Introduction to R

How we analyze data has changed dramatically in recent years. With the advent of personal computers and the internet, the sheer volume of data we have available has grown enormously. Companies have terabytes of data about the consumers they interact with, and governmental, academic, and private research institutions have extensive archival and survey data on every manner of research topic. Gleaning information (let alone wisdom) from these massive stores of data has become an industry in itself. At the same time, presenting the information in easily accessible and digestible ways has become increasingly challenging.

The science of data analysis (statistics, psychometrics, econometrics, and machine learning) has kept pace with this explosion of data. Before personal computers and the internet, new statistical methods were developed by academic researchers who published their results as theoretical papers in professional journals. It could take years for these methods to be adapted by programmers and incorporated into the statistical packages widely available to data analysts. Today, new methodologies appear *daily*. Statistical researchers publish new and improved methods, along with the code to produce them, on easily accessible websites.

The advent of personal computers had another effect on the way we analyze data. When data analysis was carried out on mainframe computers, computer time was precious and difficult to come by. Analysts would carefully set up a computer run with all the parameters and options thought to be needed. When the procedure ran, the resulting output could be dozens or hundreds of pages long. The analyst would sift through this output, extracting useful material and discarding the rest. Many popular statistical packages were originally developed during this period and still follow this approach to some degree.

With the cheap and easy access afforded by personal computers, modern data analysis has shifted to a different paradigm. Rather than setting up a complete data analysis all at once, the process has become highly interactive, with the output from each stage serving as the input for the next stage. An example of a typical analysis is shown in figure 1.1. At any point, the cycles may include transforming the data, imputing missing values, adding or deleting variables, and looping back through the whole process again. The process stops when the analyst believes they

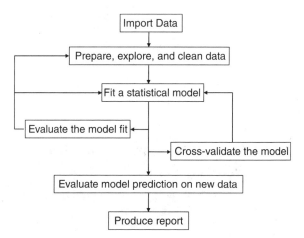

Figure 1.1   Steps in a typical data analysis

understand the data intimately and have answered all the relevant questions that can be answered.

The advent of personal computers (and especially the availability of high-resolution monitors) has also had an impact on how results are understood and presented. A picture *really can* be worth a thousand words, and human beings are adept at extracting useful information from visual presentations. Modern data analysis increasingly relies on graphical presentations to uncover meaning and convey results.

Today's data analysts need to access data from a wide range of sources (database management systems, text files, statistical packages, and spreadsheets), merge the pieces of data together, clean and annotate them, analyze them with the latest methods, present the findings in meaningful and graphically appealing ways, and incorporate the results into attractive reports that can be distributed to stakeholders and the public. As you'll see in the following pages, R is a comprehensive software package that's ideally suited to accomplish these goals.

1.1 Why use R?

R is a language and environment for statistical computing and graphics, similar to the S language originally developed at Bell Labs. It's an open source solution to data analysis that's supported by a large and active worldwide research community. But there are many popular statistical and graphing packages available (such as Microsoft Excel, SAS, IBM SPSS, Stata, and Minitab). Why turn to R?

R has many features to recommend it:

- Most commercial statistical software platforms cost thousands, if not tens of thousands, of dollars. R is free! If you're a teacher or a student, the benefits are obvious.
- R is a comprehensive statistical platform, offering all manner of data-analytic techniques. Just about any type of data analysis can be done in R.
- R contains advanced statistical routines not yet available in other packages. In fact, new methods become available for download on a weekly basis. If you're a SAS user, imagine getting a new SAS PROC every few days.
- R has state-of-the-art graphics capabilities. If you want to visualize complex data, R has the most comprehensive and powerful feature set available.
- R is a powerful platform for interactive data analysis and exploration. From its inception, it was designed to support the approach outlined in figure 1.1. For example, the results of any analytic step can easily be saved, manipulated, and used as input for additional analyses.
- Getting data into a usable form from multiple sources can be a challenging proposition. R can easily import data from a wide variety of sources, including text files, database-management systems, statistical packages, and specialized data stores. It can write data out to these systems as well. R can also access data directly from web pages, social media sites, and a wide range of online data services.
- R provides an unparalleled platform for programming new statistical methods in an easy, straightforward manner. It's easily extensible and provides a natural language for quickly programming recently published methods.
- R functionality can be integrated into applications written in other languages, including C++, Java, Python, PHP, Pentaho, SAS, and SPSS. This allows you to continue working in a language that you may be familiar with, while adding R's capabilities to your applications.
- R runs on a wide array of platforms, including Windows, Unix, and Mac OS X. It's likely to run on any computer you may have. (I've even come across guides for installing R on an iPhone, which is impressive but probably not a good idea.)
- If you don't want to learn a new language, a variety of graphic user interfaces (GUIs) are available, offering the power of R through menus and dialogs.

You can see an example of R's graphic capabilities in figure 1.2. This graph, created with a single line of code, describes the relationships between income, education, and

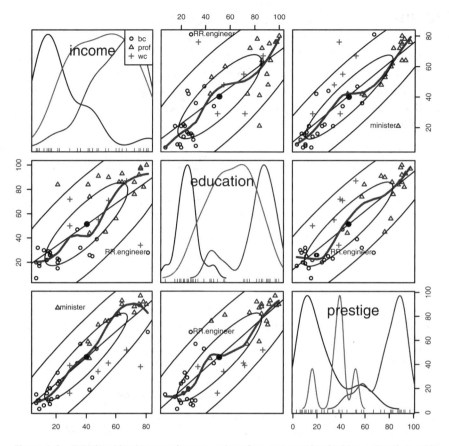

Figure 1.2   Relationships between income, education, and prestige for blue-collar (bc), white-collar (wc), and professional (prof) jobs. Source: car package (`scatterplotMatrix()` function) written by John Fox. Graphs like this are difficult to create in other statistical programming languages but can be created with a line or two of code in R.

prestige for blue-collar, white-collar, and professional jobs. Technically, it's a scatter-plot matrix with groups displayed by color and symbol, two types of fit lines (linear and loess), confidence ellipses, two types of density display (kernel density estimation, and rug plots). Additionally, the largest outlier in each scatter plot has been automatically labeled. If these terms are unfamiliar to you, don't worry. We'll cover them in later chapters. For now, trust me that they're really cool (and that the statisticians reading this are salivating).

Basically, this graph indicates the following:

- Education, income, and job prestige are linearly related.
- In general, blue-collar jobs involve lower education, income, and prestige, whereas professional jobs involve higher education, income, and prestige. White-collar jobs fall in between.

- There are some interesting exceptions. Railroad engineers have high income and low education. Ministers have high prestige and low income.

Chapter 8 will have much more to say about this type of graph. The important point is that R allows you to create elegant, informative, highly customized graphs in a simple and straightforward fashion. Creating similar plots in other statistical languages would be difficult, time-consuming, or impossible.

Unfortunately, R can have a steep learning curve. Because it can do so much, the documentation and help files available are voluminous. Additionally, because much of the functionality comes from optional modules created by independent contributors, this documentation can be scattered and difficult to locate. In fact, getting a handle on all that R can do is a challenge.

The goal of this book is to make access to R quick and easy. We'll tour the many features of R, covering enough material to get you started on your data, with pointers on where to go when you need to learn more. Let's begin by installing the program.

1.2 Obtaining and installing R

R is freely available from the Comprehensive R Archive Network (CRAN) at http://cran.r-project.org. Precompiled binaries are available for Linux, Mac OS X, and Windows. Follow the directions for installing the base product on the platform of your choice. Later we'll talk about adding functionality through optional modules called *packages* (also available from CRAN). Appendix G describes how to update an existing R installation to a newer version.

1.3 Working with R

R is a case-sensitive, interpreted language. You can enter commands one at a time at the command prompt (>) or run a set of commands from a source file. There are a wide variety of data types, including vectors, matrices, data frames (similar to datasets), and lists (collections of objects). We'll discuss each of these data types in chapter 2.

Most functionality is provided through built-in and user-created functions and the creation and manipulation of objects. An *object* is basically anything that can be assigned a value. For R, that is just about everything (data, functions, graphs, analytic results, and more). Every object has a class attribute telling R how to handle it.

All objects are kept in memory during an interactive session. Basic functions are available by default. Other functions are contained in packages that can be attached to a current session as needed.

Statements consist of functions and assignments. R uses the symbol <- for assignments, rather than the typical = sign. For example, the statement

```
x <- rnorm(5)
```

creates a vector object named x containing five random deviates from a standard normal distribution.

NOTE   R allows the = sign to be used for object assignments. But you won't find many programs written that way, because it's not standard syntax, there are some situations in which it won't work, and R programmers will make fun of you. You can also reverse the assignment direction. For instance, `rnorm(5) -> x` is equivalent to the previous statement. Again, doing so is uncommon and isn't recommended in this book.

Comments are preceded by the # symbol. Any text appearing after the # is ignored by the R interpreter.

1.3.1   *Getting started*

If you're using Windows, launch R from the Start menu. On a Mac, double-click the R icon in the Applications folder. For Linux, type R at the command prompt of a terminal window. Any of these will start the R interface (see figure 1.3 for an example).

To get a feel for the interface, let's work through a simple, contrived example. Say that you're studying physical development and you've collected the ages and weights of 10 infants in their first year of life (see table 1.1). You're interested in the distribution of the weights and their relationship to age.

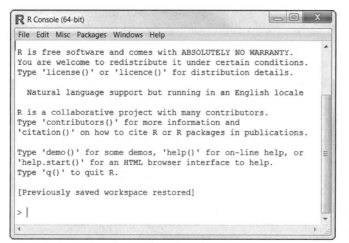

Figure 1.3   Example of the R interface on Windows

Table 1.1   The ages and weights of 10 infants

Age (mo.)	Weight (kg.)	Age (mo.)	Weight (kg.)
01	4.4	09	7.3
03	5.3	03	6.0
05	7.2	09	10.4
02	5.2	12	10.2
11	8.5	03	6.1

Note: These are fictional data.

The analysis is given in listing 1.1. Age and weight data are entered as vectors using the function c(), which combines its arguments into a vector or list. The mean and standard deviation of the weights, along with the correlation between age and weight, are provided by the functions mean(), sd(), and cor(), respectively. Finally, age is plotted against weight using the plot() function, allowing you to visually inspect the trend. The q() function ends the session and lets you quit.

Listing 1.1 A sample R session

```
> age <- c(1,3,5,2,11,9,3,9,12,3)
> weight <- c(4.4,5.3,7.2,5.2,8.5,7.3,6.0,10.4,10.2,6.1)
> mean(weight)
[1] 7.06
> sd(weight)
[1] 2.077498
> cor(age,weight)
[1] 0.9075655
> plot(age,weight)
> q()
```

You can see from listing 1.1 that the mean weight for these 10 infants is 7.06 kilograms, that the standard deviation is 2.08 kilograms, and that there is strong linear relationship between age in months and weight in kilograms (correlation = 0.91). The relationship can also be seen in the scatter plot in figure 1.4. Not surprisingly, as infants get older, they tend to weigh more.

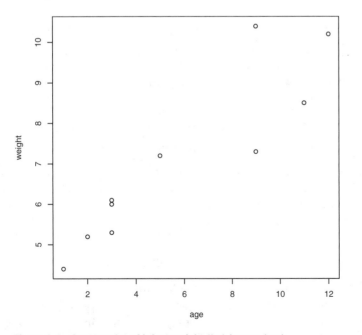

Figure 1.4 Scatter plot of infant weight (kg) by age (mo)

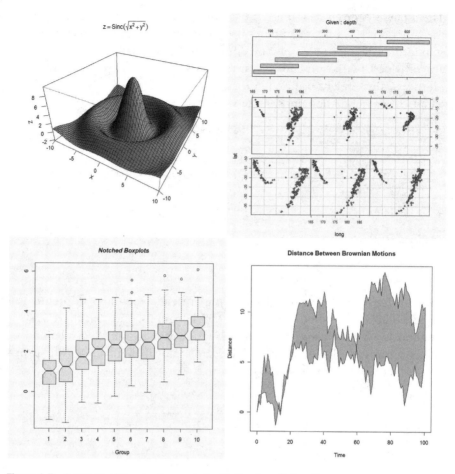

Figure 1.5   A sample of the graphs created with the `demo()` **function**

The scatter plot in figure 1.4 is informative but somewhat utilitarian and unattractive. In later chapters, you'll see how to customize graphs to suit your needs.

> **TIP**   To get a sense of what R can do graphically, enter `demo()` at the command prompt. A sample of the graphs produced is included in figure 1.5. Other demonstrations include `demo(Hershey)`, `demo(persp)`, and `demo(image)`. To see a complete list of demonstrations, enter `demo()` without parameters.

1.3.2   *Getting help*

R provides extensive help facilities, and learning to navigate them will help you significantly in your programming efforts. The built-in help system provides details, references, and examples of any function contained in a currently installed package. You can obtain help using the functions listed in table 1.2.

Table 1.2 R help functions

Function	Action
help.start()	General help
help("*foo*") or ?*foo*	Help on function foo (quotation marks optional)
help.search("*foo*") or ??*foo*	Searches the help system for instances of the string foo
example("*foo*")	Examples of function foo (quotation marks optional)
RSiteSearch("*foo*")	Searches for the string foo in online help manuals and archived mailing lists
apropos("*foo*", mode="function")	Lists all available functions with foo in their name
data()	Lists all available example datasets contained in currently loaded packages
vignette()	Lists all available vignettes for currently installed packages
vignette("*foo*")	Displays specific vignettes for topic foo

The function help.start() opens a browser window with access to introductory and advanced manuals, FAQs, and reference materials. The RSiteSearch() function searches for a given topic in online help manuals and archives of the R-Help discussion list and returns the results in a browser window. The vignettes returned by the vignette() function are practical introductory articles provided in PDF format. Not all packages have vignettes.

As you can see, R provides extensive help facilities, and learning to navigate them will definitely aid your programming efforts. It's a rare session that I don't use ? to look up the features (such as options or return values) of some function.

1.3.3 The workspace

The workspace is your current R working environment and includes any user-defined objects (vectors, matrices, functions, data frames, and lists). At the end of an R session, you can save an image of the current workspace that's automatically reloaded the next time R starts. Commands are entered interactively at the R user prompt. You can use the up and down arrow keys to scroll through your command history. Doing so allows you to select a previous command, edit it if desired, and resubmit it using the Enter key.

The current working directory is the directory from which R will read files and to which it will save results by default. You can find out what the current working directory is by using the getwd() function. You can set the current working directory by using the setwd() function. If you need to input a file that isn't in the current working directory, use the full pathname in the call. Always enclose the names of files and directories from the operating system in quotation marks. Some standard commands for managing your workspace are listed in table 1.3.

Table 1.3   Functions for managing the R workspace

Function	Action
getwd()	Lists the current working directory.
setwd("*mydirectory*")	Changes the current working directory to *mydirectory*.
ls()	Lists the objects in the current workspace.
rm(*objectlist*)	Removes (deletes) one or more objects.
help(*options*)	Provides information about available options.
options()	Lets you view or set current options.
history(*#*)	Displays your last # commands (default = 25).
savehistory("*myfile*")	Saves the commands history to *myfile* (default = .Rhistory).
loadhistory("*myfile*")	Reloads a command's history (default = .Rhistory).
save.image("*myfile*")	Saves the workspace to *myfile* (default = .RData).
save(*objectlist*, file="*myfile*")	Saves specific objects to a file.
load("*myfile*")	Loads a workspace into the current session.
q()	Quits R. You'll be prompted to save the workspace.

To see these commands in action, look at the following listing.

Listing 1.2   An example of commands used to manage the R workspace

```
setwd("C:/myprojects/project1")
options()
options(digits=3)
x <- runif(20)
summary(x)
hist(x)
q()
```

First, the current working directory is set to C:/myprojects/project1, the current option settings are displayed, and numbers are formatted to print with three digits after the decimal place. Next, a vector with 20 uniform random variates is created, and summary statistics and a histogram based on this data are generated. When the q() function is executed, the user is prompted to save their workspace. If they type y, the session history is saved to the file .Rhistory, and the workspace (including vector x) is saved to the file .RData in the current directory. The session is ended, and R closes.

Note the forward slashes in the pathname of the setwd() command. R treats the backslash (\) as an escape character. Even when you're using R on a Windows platform, use forward slashes in pathnames. Also note that the setwd() function won't create a directory that doesn't exist. If necessary, you can use the dir.create() function to create a directory and then use setwd() to change to its location.

It's a good idea to keep your projects in separate directories. You may want to start an R session by issuing the setwd() command with the appropriate path to a project, followed by the load(".RData") command. This lets you start up where you left off in your last session and keeps both your objects and history separate between projects. On Windows and Mac OS X platforms, it's even easier. Just navigate to the project directory and double-click the saved image file. Doing so starts R, loads the saved workspace, and sets the current working directory to this location.

1.3.4   *Input and output*

By default, launching R starts an interactive session with input from the keyboard and output to the screen. But you can also process commands from a *script file* (a file containing R statements) and direct output to a variety of destinations.

INPUT

The source("*filename*") function submits a script to the current session. If the filename doesn't include a path, the file is assumed to be in the current working directory. For example, source("myscript.R") runs a set of R statements contained in the file myscript.R. By convention, script filenames end with an .R extension, but this isn't required.

TEXT OUTPUT

The sink("*filename*") function redirects output to the file *filename*. By default, if the file already exists, its contents are overwritten. Include the option append=TRUE to append text to the file rather than overwriting it. Including the option split=TRUE will send output to both the screen and the output file. Issuing the command sink() without options will return output to the screen alone.

GRAPHIC OUTPUT

Although sink() redirects text output, it has no effect on graphic output. To redirect graphic output, use one of the functions listed in table 1.4. Use dev.off() to return output to the terminal.

Table 1.4   Functions for saving graphic output

Function	Output
bmp("*filename*.bmp")	BMP file
jpeg("*filename*.jpg")	JPEG file
pdf("*filename*.pdf")	PDF file
png("*filename*.png")	PNG file
postscript("*filename*.ps")	PostScript file

Table 1.4   Functions for saving graphic output *(continued)*

Function	Output
`svg("`*`filename.svg`*`")`	SVG file
`win.metafile("`*`filename.wmf`*`")`	Windows metafile

Let's put it all together with an example. Assume that you have three script files containing R code (script1.R, script2.R, and script3.R). Issuing the statement

```
source("script1.R")
```

submits the R code from script1.R to the current session, and the results appear on the screen.

If you then issue the statements

```
sink("myoutput", append=TRUE, split=TRUE)
pdf("mygraphs.pdf")
source("script2.R")
```

the R code from file script2.R is submitted, and the results again appear on the screen. In addition, the text output is appended to the file myoutput, and the graphic output is saved to the file mygraphs.pdf.

Finally, if you issue the statements

```
sink()
dev.off()
source("script3.R")
```

the R code from script3.R is submitted, and the results appear on the screen. This time, no text or graphic output is saved to files. The sequence is outlined in figure 1.6.

R provides quite a bit of flexibility and control over where input comes from and where it goes. In section 1.5, you'll learn how to run a program in batch mode.

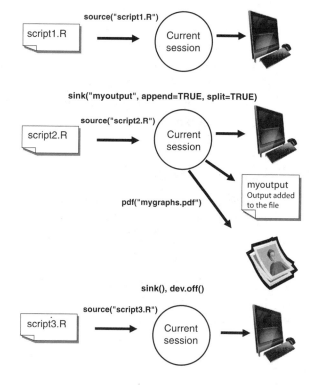

Figure 1.6   **Input with the** `source()` **function and output with the** `sink()` **function**

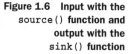

1.4 Packages

R comes with extensive capabilities right out of the box. But some of its most exciting features are available as optional modules that you can download and install. There are more than 5,500 user-contributed modules called *packages* that you can download from http://cran.r-project.org/web/packages. They provide a tremendous range of new capabilities, from the analysis of geospatial data to protein mass spectra processing to the analysis of psychological tests! You'll use many of these optional packages in this book.

1.4.1 What are packages?

Packages are collections of R functions, data, and compiled code in a well-defined format. The directory where packages are stored on your computer is called the *library*. The function .libPaths() shows you where your library is located, and the function library() shows you what packages you've saved in your library.

   R comes with a standard set of packages (including base, datasets, utils, grDevices, graphics, stats, and methods). They provide a wide range of functions and datasets that are available by default. Other packages are available for download and installation. Once installed, they must be loaded into the session in order to be used. The command search() tells you which packages are loaded and ready to use.

1.4.2 Installing a package

A number of R functions let you manipulate packages. To install a package for the first time, use the install.packages() command. For example, install.packages() without options brings up a list of CRAN mirror sites. Once you select a site, you're presented with a list of all available packages. Selecting one downloads and installs it. If you know what package you want to install, you can do so directly by providing it as an argument to the function. For example, the gclus package contains functions for creating enhanced scatter plots. You can download and install the package with the command install.packages("gclus").

   You only need to install a package once. But like any software, packages are often updated by their authors. Use the command update.packages() to update any packages that you've installed. To see details on your packages, you can use the installed.packages() command. It lists the packages you have, along with their version numbers, dependencies, and other information.

1.4.3 Loading a package

Installing a package downloads it from a CRAN mirror site and places it in your library. To use it in an R session, you need to load the package using the library() command. For example, to use the package gclus, issue the command library(gclus).

   Of course, you must have installed a package before you can load it. You'll only have to load the package once in a given session. If desired, you can customize your startup environment to automatically load the packages you use most often. Customizing your startup is covered in appendix B.

1.4.4   *Learning about a package*

When you load a package, a new set of functions and datasets becomes available. Small illustrative datasets are provided along with sample code, allowing you to try out the new functionalities. The help system contains a description of each function (along with examples) and information about each dataset included. Entering `help(package="package_name")` provides a brief description of the package and an index of the functions and datasets included. Using `help()` with any of these function or dataset names provides further details. The same information can be downloaded as a PDF manual from CRAN.

Common mistakes in R programming

Some common mistakes are made frequently by both beginning and experienced R programmers. If your program generates an error, be sure to check for the following:

- *Using the wrong case*—`help()`, `Help()`, and `HELP()` are three different functions (only the first will work).
- *Forgetting to use quotation marks when they're needed*—`install.packages("gclus")` works, whereas `install.packages(gclus)` generates an error.
- *Forgetting to include the parentheses in a function call*—For example, `help()` works, but `help` doesn't. Even if there are no options, you still need the `()`.
- *Using the \ in a pathname on Windows*—R sees the backslash character as an escape character. `setwd("c:\mydata")` generates an error. Use `setwd("c:/mydata")` or `setwd("c:\\mydata")` instead.
- *Using a function from a package that's not loaded*—The function `order.clusters()` is contained in the `gclus` package. If you try to use it before loading the package, you'll get an error.

The error messages in R can be cryptic, but if you're careful to follow these points, you should avoid seeing many of them.

1.5   *Batch processing*

Most of the time, you'll be running R interactively, entering commands at the command prompt and seeing the results of each statement as it's processed. Occasionally, you may want to run an R program in a repeated, standard, and possibly unattended fashion. For example, you may need to generate the same report once a month. You can write your program in R and run it in batch mode.

How you run R in batch mode depends on your operating system. On Linux or Mac OS X systems, you can use the following command in a terminal window

```
R CMD BATCH options infile outfile
```

where `infile` is the name of the file containing R code to be executed, `outfile` is the name of the file receiving the output, and `options` lists options that control execution. By convention, `infile` is given the extension .R, and `outfile` is given the extension .Rout.

For Windows, use

```
"C:\Program Files\R\R-3.1.0\bin\R.exe" CMD BATCH
?--vanilla --slave "c:\my projects\myscript.R"
```

adjusting the paths to match the location of your R.exe binary and your script file. For additional details on how to invoke R, including the use of command-line options, see the "Introduction to R" documentation available from CRAN (http://cran.r-project.org).

1.6   *Using output as input: reusing results*

One of the most useful design features of R is that the output of analyses can easily be saved and used as input to additional analyses. Let's walk through an example, using one of the datasets that comes preinstalled with R. If you don't understand the statistics involved, don't worry. We're focusing on the general principle here.

First, run a simple linear regression predicting miles per gallon (mpg) from car weight (wt), using the automotive dataset mtcars. This is accomplished with the following function call:

```
lm(mpg~wt, data=mtcars)
```

The results are displayed on the screen, and no information is saved.

Next, run the regression, but store the results in an object:

```
lmfit <- lm(mpg~wt, data=mtcars)
```

The assignment creates a list object called lmfit that contains extensive information from the analysis (including the predicted values, residuals, regression coefficients, and more). Although no output is sent to the screen, the results can be both displayed and manipulated further.

Typing summary(lmfit) displays a summary of the results, and plot(lmfit) produces diagnostic plots. The statement cook<-cooks.distance(lmfit) generates and stores influence statistics, and plot(cook) graphs them. To predict miles per gallon from car weight in a new set of data, you'd use predict(lmfit, mynewdata).

To see what a function returns, look at the Value section of the R help page for that function. Here you'd look at help(lm) or ?lm. This tells you what's saved when you assign the results of that function to an object.

1.7   *Working with large datasets*

Programmers frequently ask me if R can handle large data problems. Typically, they work with massive amounts of data gathered from web research, climatology, or genetics. Because R holds objects in memory, you're generally limited by the amount of RAM available. For example, on my 5-year-old Windows PC with 2 GB of RAM, I can easily handle datasets with 10 million elements (100 variables by 100,000 observations). On an iMac with 4 GB of RAM, I can usually handle 100 million elements without difficulty.

But there are two issues to consider: the size of the dataset and the statistical methods that will be applied. R can handle data analysis problems in the gigabyte to terabyte range, but specialized procedures are required. The management and analysis of very large datasets is discussed in appendix F.

1.8 *Working through an example*

We'll finish this chapter with an example that ties together many of these ideas. Here's the task:

1 Open the general help, and look at the "Introduction to R" section.
2 Install the vcd package (a package for visualizing categorical data that you'll be using in chapter 11).
3 List the functions and datasets available in this package.
4 Load the package, and read the description of the dataset Arthritis.
5 Print out the Arthritis dataset (entering the name of an object will list it).
6 Run the example that comes with the Arthritis dataset. Don't worry if you don't understand the results; it basically shows that arthritis patients receiving treatment improved much more than patients receiving a placebo.
7 Quit.

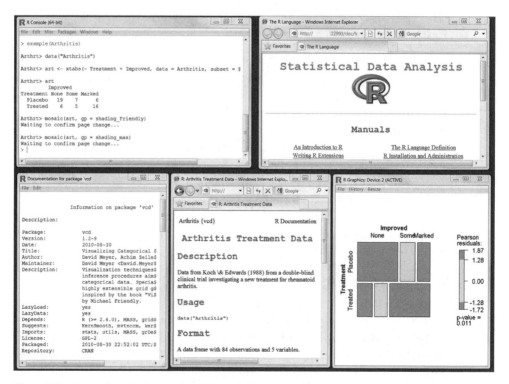

Figure 1.7   Output from listing 1.3, including (left to right) output from the arthritis example, general help, information about the vcd package, information about the Arthritis dataset, and a graph displaying the relationship between arthritis treatment and outcome

The code required is provided in the following listing, with a sample of the results displayed in figure 1.7. As this short exercise demonstrates, you can accomplish a great deal with a small amount of code.

Listing 1.3 Working with a new package

```
help.start()
install.packages("vcd")
help(package="vcd")
library(vcd)
help(Arthritis)
Arthritis
example(Arthritis)
q()
```

1.9 Summary

In this chapter, we looked at some of the strengths that make R an attractive option for students, researchers, statisticians, and data analysts trying to understand the meaning of their data. We walked through the program's installation and talked about how to enhance R's capabilities by downloading additional packages. We explored the basic interface, running programs interactively and in a batch, and produced a few sample graphs. You also learned how to save your work to both text and graphic files. Because R can be a complex program, we spent some time looking at how to access the extensive help that's available. Hopefully you're getting a sense of how powerful this freely available software can be.

Now that you have R up and running, it's time to get your data into the mix. In the next chapter, we'll look at the types of data R can handle and how to import them into R from text files, other programs, and database management systems.

Creating a dataset

2

This chapter covers

- Exploring R data structures
- Using data entry
- Importing data
- Annotating datasets

The first step in any data analysis is the creation of a dataset containing the information to be studied, in a format that meets your needs. In R, this task involves the following:

- Selecting a data structure to hold your data
- Entering or importing your data into the data structure

The first part of this chapter (sections 2.1–2.2) describes the wealth of structures that R can use to hold data. In particular, section 2.2 describes vectors, factors, matrices, data frames, and lists. Familiarizing yourself with these structures (and the notation used to access elements within them) will help you tremendously in understanding how R works. You might want to take your time working through this section.

The second part of this chapter (section 2.3) covers the many methods available for importing data into R. Data can be entered manually or imported from an external source. These data sources can include text files, spreadsheets, statistical packages, and database-management systems. For example, the data that I work with typically comes from SQL databases. On occasion, though, I receive data from legacy DOS systems and from current SAS and SPSS databases. It's likely that you'll only have to use one or two of the methods described in this section, so feel free to choose those that fit your situation.

Once a dataset is created, you'll typically annotate it, adding descriptive labels for variables and variable codes. The third portion of this chapter (section 2.4) looks at annotating datasets and reviews some useful functions for working with datasets (section 2.5). Let's start with the basics.

2.1 Understanding datasets

A dataset is usually a rectangular array of data with rows representing observations and columns representing variables. Table 2.1 provides an example of a hypothetical patient dataset.

Table 2.1 A patient dataset

PatientID	AdmDate	Age	Diabetes	Status
1	10/15/2014	25	Type1	Poor
2	11/01/2014	34	Type2	Improved
3	10/21/2014	28	Type1	Excellent
4	10/28/2014	52	Type1	Poor

Different traditions have different names for the rows and columns of a dataset. Statisticians refer to them as observations and variables, database analysts call them records and fields, and those from the data-mining and machine-learning disciplines call them examples and attributes. We'll use the terms *observations* and *variables* throughout this book.

You can distinguish between the structure of the dataset (in this case, a rectangular array) and the contents or data types included. In the dataset shown in table 2.1, PatientID is a row or case identifier, AdmDate is a date variable, Age is a continuous variable, Diabetes is a nominal variable, and Status is an ordinal variable.

R contains a wide variety of structures for holding data, including scalars, vectors, arrays, data frames, and lists. Table 2.1 corresponds to a data frame in R. This diversity of structures provides the R language with a great deal of flexibility in dealing with data.

The data types or modes that R can handle include numeric, character, logical (TRUE/FALSE), complex (imaginary numbers), and raw (bytes). In R, PatientID, AdmDate, and Age are numeric variables, whereas Diabetes and Status are character variables. Additionally, you need to tell R that PatientID is a case identifier, that AdmDate contains dates, and that Diabetes and Status are nominal and ordinal variables, respectively. R refers to case identifiers as `rownames` and categorical variables (nominal, ordinal) as `factors`. We'll cover each of these in the next section. You'll learn about dates in chapter 3.

2.2   Data structures

R has a wide variety of objects for holding data, including scalars, vectors, matrices, arrays, data frames, and lists. They differ in terms of the type of data they can hold, how they're created, their structural complexity, and the notation used to identify and access individual elements. Figure 2.1 shows a diagram of these data structures. Let's look at each structure in turn, starting with vectors.

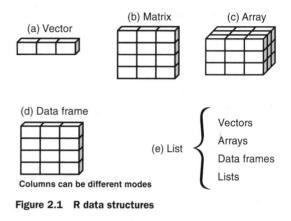

Figure 2.1   R data structures

Some definitions

Several terms are idiosyncratic to R and thus confusing to new users.

In R, an *object* is anything that can be assigned to a variable. This includes constants, data structures, functions, and even graphs. An object has a *mode* (which describes how the object is stored) and a *class* (which tells generic functions like `print` how to handle it).

A data frame is a structure in R that holds data and is similar to the datasets found in standard statistical packages (for example, SAS, SPSS, and Stata). The columns are variables, and the rows are observations. You can have variables of different types (for example, numeric or character) in the same data frame. Data frames are the main structures you use to store datasets.

Factors are nominal or ordinal variables. They're stored and treated specially in R. You'll learn about factors in section 2.2.5.

Most other terms used in R should be familiar to you and follow the terminology used in statistics and computing in general.

2.2.1   Vectors

Vectors are one-dimensional arrays that can hold numeric data, character data, or logical data. The combine function `c()` is used to form the vector. Here are examples of each type of vector:

```
a <- c(1, 2, 5, 3, 6, -2, 4)
b <- c("one", "two", "three")
c <- c(TRUE, TRUE, TRUE, FALSE, TRUE, FALSE)
```

Here, a is a numeric vector, b is a character vector, and c is a logical vector. Note that the data in a vector must be only one type or mode (numeric, character, or logical). You can't mix modes in the same vector.

> **NOTE** *Scalars* are one-element vectors. Examples include f <- 3, g <- "US", and h <- TRUE. They're used to hold constants.

You can refer to elements of a vector using a numeric vector of positions within brackets. For example, a[c(2, 4)] refers to the second and fourth elements of vector a. Here are additional examples:

```
> a <- c("k", "j", "h", "a", "c", "m")
> a[3]
[1] "h"
> a[c(1, 3, 5)]
[1] "k" "h" "c"
> a[2:6]
[1]  "j" "h" "a" "c" "m"
```

The colon operator used in the last statement generates a sequence of numbers. For example, a <- c(2:6) is equivalent to a <- c(2, 3, 4, 5, 6).

2.2.2 Matrices

A *matrix* is a two-dimensional array in which each element has the same mode (numeric, character, or logical). Matrices are created with the matrix() function. The general format is

```
myymatrix <- matrix(vector, nrow=number_of_rows, ncol=number_of_columns,
             byrow=logical_value, dimnames=list(
             char_vector_rownames, char_vector_colnames))
```

where *vector* contains the elements for the matrix, nrow and ncol specify the row and column dimensions, and dimnames contains optional row and column labels stored in character vectors. The option byrow indicates whether the matrix should be filled in by row (byrow=TRUE) or by column (byrow=FALSE). The default is by column. The following listing demonstrates the matrix function.

Listing 2.1 Creating matrices

```
> y <- matrix(1:20, nrow=5, ncol=4)          ◄─┐
> y                                             ❶ Creates a 5 × 4 matrix
     [,1] [,2] [,3] [,4]
[1,]    1    6   11   16
[2,]    2    7   12   17
[3,]    3    8   13   18
[4,]    4    9   14   19
[5,]    5   10   15   20
> cells     <- c(1,26,24,68)
> rnames    <- c("R1", "R2")
> cnames    <- c("C1", "C2")
> mymatrix <- matrix(cells, nrow=2, ncol=2, byrow=TRUE,    ❷ 2 × 2 matrix
              dimnames=list(rnames, cnames))                 filled by rows
```

```
> mymatrix
   C1 C2
R1  1 26
R2 24 68
> mymatrix <- matrix(cells, nrow=2, ncol=2, byrow=FALSE,
                 dimnames=list(rnames, cnames))
> mymatrix
   C1 C2
R1  1 24
R2 26 68
```

❸ 2 × 2 matrix
filled by columns

First you create a 5 × 4 matrix ❶. Then you create a 2 × 2 matrix with labels and fill the matrix by rows ❷. Finally, you create a 2 × 2 matrix and fill the matrix by columns ❸.

You can identify rows, columns, or elements of a matrix by using subscripts and brackets. X[i,] refers to the *i*th row of matrix X, X[,j] refers to the *j*th column, and X[i, j] refers to the *ij*th element, respectively. The subscripts *i* and *j* can be numeric vectors in order to select multiple rows or columns, as shown in the following listing.

Listing 2.2   Using matrix subscripts

```
> x <- matrix(1:10, nrow=2)
> x
     [,1] [,2] [,3] [,4] [,5]
[1,]    1    3    5    7    9
[2,]    2    4    6    8   10
> x[2,]
 [1]  2  4  6  8 10
> x[,2]
[1] 3 4
> x[1,4]
[1] 7
> x[1, c(4,5)]
[1] 7 9
```

First a 2 × 5 matrix is created containing the numbers 1 to 10. By default, the matrix is filled by column. Then the elements in the second row are selected, followed by the elements in the second column. Next, the element in the first row and fourth column is selected. Finally, the elements in the first row and the fourth and fifth columns are selected.

Matrices are two-dimensional and, like vectors, can contain only one data type. When there are more than two dimensions, you use arrays (section 2.2.3). When there are multiple modes of data, you use data frames (section 2.2.4).

2.2.3   Arrays

Arrays are similar to matrices but can have more than two dimensions. They're created with an array function of the following form

```
myarray <- array(vector, dimensions, dimnames)
```

where *vector* contains the data for the array, *dimensions* is a numeric vector giving the maximal index for each dimension, and *dimnames* is an optional list of dimension labels. The following listing gives an example of creating a three-dimensional ($2 \times 3 \times 4$) array of numbers.

Listing 2.3 Creating an array

```
> dim1 <- c("A1", "A2")
> dim2 <- c("B1", "B2", "B3")
> dim3 <- c("C1", "C2", "C3", "C4")
> z <- array(1:24, c(2, 3, 4), dimnames=list(dim1, dim2, dim3))
> z
, , C1
   B1 B2 B3
A1  1  3  5
A2  2  4  6

, , C2
   B1 B2 B3
A1  7  9 11
A2  8 10 12

, , C3
   B1 B2 B3
A1 13 15 17
A2 14 16 18

, , C4
   B1 B2 B3
A1 19 21 23
A2 20 22 24
```

As you can see, arrays are a natural extension of matrices. They can be useful in programming new statistical methods. Like matrices, they must be a single mode. Identifying elements follows what you've seen for matrices. In the previous example, the z[1,2,3] element is 15.

2.2.4 Data frames

A *data frame* is more general than a matrix in that different columns can contain different modes of data (numeric, character, and so on). It's similar to the dataset you'd typically see in SAS, SPSS, and Stata. Data frames are the most common data structure you'll deal with in R.

The patient dataset in table 2.1 consists of numeric and character data. Because there are multiple modes of data, you can't contain the data in a matrix. In this case, a data frame is the structure of choice.

A data frame is created with the data.frame() function

```
mydata <- data.frame(col1, col2, col3,...)
```

where *col1*, *col2*, *col3*, and so on are column vectors of any type (such as character, numeric, or logical). Names for each column can be provided with the names function. The following listing makes this clear.

Listing 2.4   Creating a data frame

```
> patientID <- c(1, 2, 3, 4)
> age <- c(25, 34, 28, 52)
> diabetes <- c("Type1", "Type2", "Type1", "Type1")
> status <- c("Poor", "Improved", "Excellent", "Poor")
> patientdata <- data.frame(patientID, age, diabetes, status)
> patientdata
  patientID age diabetes    status
1         1  25    Type1      Poor
2         2  34    Type2  Improved
3         3  28    Type1 Excellent
4         4  52    Type1      Poor
```

Each column must have only one mode, but you can put columns of different modes together to form the data frame. Because data frames are close to what analysts typically think of as datasets, we'll use the terms *columns* and *variables* interchangeably when discussing data frames.

There are several ways to identify the elements of a data frame. You can use the subscript notation you used before (for example, with matrices), or you can specify column names. Using the `patientdata` data frame created earlier, the following listing demonstrates these approaches.

Listing 2.5   Specifying elements of a data frame

```
> patientdata[1:2]
  patientID age
1         1  25
2         2  34
3         3  28
4         4  52
> patientdata[c("diabetes", "status")]
  diabetes    status
1    Type1      Poor
2    Type2  Improved
3    Type1 Excellent
4    Type1      Poor
 > patientdata$age
[1] 25 34 28 52
```

❶ Indicates the age variable in the patient data frame

The `$` notation in the third example is new ❶. It's used to indicate a particular variable from a given data frame. For example, if you want to cross-tabulate diabetes type by status, you can use the following code:

```
> table(patientdata$diabetes, patientdata$status)

        Excellent Improved Poor
  Type1         1        0    2
  Type2         0        1    0
```

It can get tiresome typing `patientdata$` at the beginning of every variable name, so shortcuts are available. You can use either the `attach()` and `detach()` or `with()` functions to simplify your code.

ATTACH, DETACH, AND WITH

The `attach()` function adds the data frame to the R search path. When a variable name is encountered, data frames in the search path are checked for the variable in order. Using the `mtcars` data frame from chapter 1 as an example, you could use the following code to obtain summary statistics for automobile mileage (`mpg`) and plot this variable against engine displacement (`disp`) and weight (`wt`):

```
summary(mtcars$mpg)
plot(mtcars$mpg, mtcars$disp)
plot(mtcars$mpg, mtcars$wt)
```

This can also be written as follows:

```
attach(mtcars)
  summary(mpg)
  plot(mpg, disp)
  plot(mpg, wt)
detach(mtcars)
```

The `detach()` function removes the data frame from the search path. Note that `detach()` does nothing to the data frame itself. The statement is optional but is good programming practice and should be included routinely. (I'll sometimes ignore this sage advice in later chapters in order to keep code fragments simple and short.)

The limitations with this approach are evident when more than one object can have the same name. Consider the following code:

```
> mpg <- c(25, 36, 47)
> attach(mtcars)
The following object(s) are masked _by_ '.GlobalEnv':    mpg
> plot(mpg, wt)
Error in xy.coords(x, y, xlabel, ylabel, log) :
  'x' and 'y' lengths differ
> mpg
[1] 25 36 47
```

Here you already have an object named `mpg` in your environment when the `mtcars` data frame is attached. In such cases, the original object takes precedence, which isn't what you want. The `plot` statement fails because `mpg` has 3 elements and `disp` has 32 elements. The `attach()` and `detach()` functions are best used when you're analyzing a single data frame and you're unlikely to have multiple objects with the same name. In any case, be vigilant for warnings that say that objects are being masked.

An alternative approach is to use the `with()` function. You can write the previous example as

```
with(mtcars, {
  print(summary(mpg))
  plot(mpg, disp)
  plot(mpg, wt)
})
```

In this case, the statements within the {} brackets are evaluated with reference to the `mtcars` data frame. You don't have to worry about name conflicts. If there's only one statement (for example, `summary(mpg)`), the {} brackets are optional.

The limitation of the `with()` function is that assignments exist only within the function brackets. Consider the following:

```
> with(mtcars, {
    stats <- summary(mpg)
    stats
    })
  Min. 1st Qu.  Median    Mean 3rd Qu.    Max.
  10.40   15.43   19.20   20.09   22.80   33.90
> stats
Error: object 'stats' not found
```

If you need to create objects that will exist outside of the `with()` construct, use the special assignment operator `<<-` instead of the standard one (`<-`). It saves the object to the global environment outside of the `with()` call. This can be demonstrated with the following code:

```
> with(mtcars, {
    nokeepstats <- summary(mpg)
    keepstats <<- summary(mpg)
})
> nokeepstats
Error: object 'nokeepstats' not found
> keepstats
   Min. 1st Qu.  Median    Mean 3rd Qu.    Max.
   10.40   15.43   19.20   20.09   22.80   33.90
```

Most books on R recommend using `with()` instead of `attach()`. I think that ultimately the choice is a matter of preference and should be based on what you're trying to achieve and your understanding of the implications. You'll use both in this book.

CASE IDENTIFIERS

In the patient data example, `patientID` is used to identify individuals in the dataset. In R, case identifiers can be specified with a `rowname` option in the data-frame function. For example, the statement

```
patientdata <- data.frame(patientID, age, diabetes,
                    status, row.names=patientID)
```

specifies `patientID` as the variable to use in labeling cases on various printouts and graphs produced by R.

2.2.5   *Factors*

As you've seen, variables can be described as nominal, ordinal, or continuous. *Nominal variables* are categorical, without an implied order. Diabetes (`Type1`, `Type2`) is an example of a nominal variable. Even if `Type1` is coded as a 1 and `Type2` is coded as a 2 in the data, no order is implied. *Ordinal variables* imply order but not amount. `Status` (`poor`, `improved`, `excellent`) is a good example of an ordinal variable. You know that a patient with a poor status isn't doing as well as a patient with an improved status, but not by how much. *Continuous variables* can take on any value within some range, and both order and amount are implied. Age in years is a continuous variable and can take on values such as 14.5 or 22.8 and any value in between. You know that someone who is 15 is one year older than someone who is 14.

Categorical (nominal) and ordered categorical (ordinal) variables in R are called *factors*. Factors are crucial in R because they determine how data is analyzed and presented visually. You'll see examples of this throughout the book.

The function `factor()` stores the categorical values as a vector of integers in the range $[1... k]$, (where k is the number of unique values in the nominal variable) and an internal vector of character strings (the original values) mapped to these integers.

For example, assume that you have this vector:

```
diabetes <- c("Type1", "Type2", "Type1", "Type1")
```

The statement `diabetes <- factor(diabetes)` stores this vector as (1, 2, 1, 1) and associates it with 1 = Type1 and 2 = Type2 internally (the assignment is alphabetical). Any analyses performed on the vector `diabetes` will treat the variable as nominal and select the statistical methods appropriate for this level of measurement.

For vectors representing ordinal variables, you add the parameter `ordered=TRUE` to the `factor()` function. Given the vector

```
status <- c("Poor", "Improved", "Excellent", "Poor")
```

the statement `status <- factor(status, ordered=TRUE)` will encode the vector as (3, 2, 1, 3) and associate these values internally as 1 = Excellent, 2 = Improved, and 3 = Poor. Additionally, any analyses performed on this vector will treat the variable as ordinal and select the statistical methods appropriately.

By default, factor levels for character vectors are created in alphabetical order. This worked for the `status` factor, because the order "Excellent," "Improved," "Poor" made sense. There would have been a problem if "Poor" had been coded as "Ailing" instead, because the order would have been "Ailing," "Excellent," "Improved." A similar problem would exist if the desired order was "Poor," "Improved," "Excellent." For ordered factors, the alphabetical default is rarely sufficient.

You can override the default by specifying a `levels` option. For example,

```
status <- factor(status, order=TRUE,
            levels=c("Poor", "Improved", "Excellent"))
```

assigns the levels as 1 = Poor, 2 = Improved, 3 = Excellent. Be sure the specified levels match your actual data values. Any data values not in the list will be set to `missing`.

Numeric variables can be coded as factors using the `levels` and `labels` options. If sex was coded as 1 for male and 2 for female in the original data, then

```
sex <- factor(sex, levels=c(1, 2), labels=c("Male", "Female"))
```

would convert the variable to an unordered factor. Note that the order of the labels must match the order of the levels. In this example, sex would be treated as categorical, the labels "Male" and "Female" would appear in the output instead of 1 and 2, and any sex value that wasn't initially coded as a 1 or 2 would be set to `missing`.

The following listing demonstrates how specifying factors and ordered factors impacts data analyses.

Listing 2.6   Using factors

```
> patientID <- c(1, 2, 3, 4)
> age <- c(25, 34, 28, 52)                              ❶ Enter data
> diabetes <- c("Type1", "Type2", "Type1", "Type1")        as vectors.
> status <- c("Poor", "Improved", "Excellent", "Poor")
> diabetes <- factor(diabetes)
> status <- factor(status, order=TRUE)
> patientdata <- data.frame(patientID, age, diabetes, status)
> str(patientdata)                                      Displays
'data.frame':   4 obs. of  4 variables:                  the object
 $ patientID: num  1 2 3 4                             ❷ structure
 $ age      : num  25 34 28 52
 $ diabetes : Factor w/ 2 levels "Type1","Type2": 1 2 1 1
 $ status   : Ord.factor w/ 3 levels "Excellent"<"Improved"<..: 3 2 1 3
> summary(patientdata)                                  Displays
   patientID        age          diabetes      status     the object
 Min.   :1.00   Min.   :25.00   Type1:3   Excellent:1   ❸ summary
 1st Qu.:1.75   1st Qu.:27.25   Type2:1   Improved :1
 Median :2.50   Median :31.00             Poor     :2
 Mean   :2.50   Mean   :34.75
 3rd Qu.:3.25   3rd Qu.:38.50
 Max.   :4.00   Max.   :52.00
```

First you enter the data as vectors ❶. Then you specify that `diabetes` is a factor and `status` is an ordered factor. Finally, you combine the data into a data frame. The function `str(object)` provides information about an object in R (the data frame, in this case) ❷. It clearly shows that `diabetes` is a factor and `status` is an ordered factor, along with how they're coded internally. Note that the `summary()` function treats the variables differently ❸. It provides the minimum, maximum, mean, and quartiles for the continuous variable age, and frequency counts for the categorical variables `diabetes` and `status`.

2.2.6   *Lists*

Lists are the most complex of the R data types. Basically, a *list* is an ordered collection of objects (components). A list allows you to gather a variety of (possibly unrelated) objects under one name. For example, a list may contain a combination of vectors, matrices, data frames, and even other lists. You create a list using the `list()` function

```
mylist <- list(object1, object2, ...)
```

where the objects are any of the structures seen so far. Optionally, you can name the objects in a list:

```
mylist <- list(name1=object1, name2=object2, ...)
```

The following listing shows an example.

```
Listing 2.7   Creating a list
```

```
> g <- "My First List"
> h <- c(25, 26, 18, 39)
> j <- matrix(1:10, nrow=5)
> k <- c("one", "two", "three")                          Creates a list
> mylist <- list(title=g, ages=h, j, k)
> mylist                                                 Prints the entire list
$title
[1] "My First List"

$ages
[1] 25 26 18 39

[[3]]
     [,1] [,2]
[1,]    1    6
[2,]    2    7
[3,]    3    8
[4,]    4    9
[5,]    5   10

[[4]]
[1] "one"    "two"    "three"
                                                         Prints the second component
> mylist[[2]]
[1] 25 26 18 39
> mylist[["ages"]]
[[1] 25 26 18 39
```

In this example, you create a list with four components: a string, a numeric vector, a matrix, and a character vector. You can combine any number of objects and save them as a list.

You can also specify elements of the list by indicating a component number or a name within double brackets. In this example, `mylist[[2]]` and `mylist[["ages"]]` both refer to the same four-element numeric vector. For named components, `mylist$ages` would also work. Lists are important R structures for two reasons. First, they allow you to organize and recall disparate information in a simple way. Second, the results of many R functions return lists. It's up to the analyst to pull out the components that are needed. You'll see numerous examples of functions that return lists in later chapters.

A note for programmers

Experienced programmers typically find several aspects of the R language unusual. Here are some features of the language you should be aware of:

- The period (.) has no special significance in object names. The dollar sign ($) has a somewhat analogous meaning to the period in other object-oriented languages and can be used to identify the parts of a data frame or list. For example, `A$x` refers to variable `x` in data frame `A`.

(continued)

- R doesn't provide multiline or block comments. You must start each line of a multiline comment with #. For debugging purposes, you can also surround code that you want the interpreter to ignore with the statement `if(FALSE){...}`. Changing the `FALSE` to `TRUE` allows the code to be executed.
- Assigning a value to a nonexistent element of a vector, matrix, array, or list expands that structure to accommodate the new value. For example, consider the following:

```
> x <- c(8, 6, 4)
> x[7] <- 10
> x
[1]  8  6  4 NA NA NA 10
```

The vector `x` has expanded from three to seven elements through the assignment. `x <- x[1:3]` would shrink it back to three elements.

- R doesn't have scalar values. Scalars are represented as one-element vectors.
- Indices in R start at 1, not at 0. In the vector earlier, `x[1]` is 8.
- Variables can't be declared. They come into existence on first assignment.

To learn more, see John Cook's excellent blog post, "R Language for Programmers" (http://mng.bz/6NwQ). Programmers looking for stylistic guidance may also want to check out "Google's R Style Guide" (http://mng.bz/i775).

2.3 *Data input*

Now that you have data structures, you need to put some data in them! As a data analyst, you're typically faced with data that comes from a variety of sources and in a variety of formats. Your task is to import the data into your tools, analyze the data, and report on the results. R provides a wide range of tools for importing data. The definitive guide for importing data in R is the *R Data Import/Export* manual available at http://mng.bz/urwn.

As you can see in figure 2.2, R can import data from the keyboard, from text files, from Microsoft Excel and Access, from popular statistical packages, from a variety of

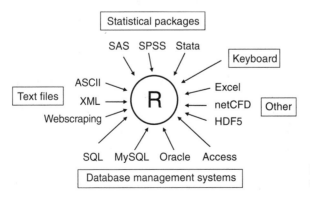

Figure 2.2 Sources of data that can be imported into R

relational database management systems, from specialty databases, and from web sites and online services. Because you never know where your data will come from, we'll cover each of them here. You only need to read about the ones you're going to be using.

2.3.1 Entering data from the keyboard

Perhaps the simplest way to enter data is from the keyboard. There are two common methods: entering data through R's built-in text editor and embedding data directly into your code. We'll consider the editor first.

The `edit()` function in R invokes a text editor that lets you enter data manually. Here are the steps:

1 Create an empty data frame (or matrix) with the variable names and modes you want to have in the final dataset.
2 Invoke the text editor on this data object, enter your data, and save the results to the data object.

The following example creates a data frame named `mydata` with three variables: `age` (numeric), `gender` (character), and `weight` (numeric). You then invoke the text editor, add your data, and save the results:

```
mydata <- data.frame(age=numeric(0),
  gender=character(0), weight=numeric(0))
mydata <- edit(mydata)
```

Assignments like `age=numeric(0)` create a variable of a specific mode, but without actual data. Note that the result of the editing is assigned back to the object itself. The `edit()` function operates on a copy of the object. If you don't assign it a destination, all of your edits will be lost!

The results of invoking the `edit()` function on a Windows platform are shown in figure 2.3. In this figure, I've added some data. If you click a column title, the editor

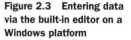

Figure 2.3 Entering data via the built-in editor on a Windows platform

gives you the option of changing the variable name and type (numeric or character). You can add variables by clicking the titles of unused columns. When the text editor is closed, the results are saved to the object assigned (`mydata`, in this case). Invoking `mydata <- edit(mydata)` again allows you to edit the data you've entered and to add new data. A shortcut for `mydata <- edit(mydata)` is `fix(mydata)`.

Alternatively, you can embed the data directly in your program. For example, the code

```
mydatatxt <- "
age gender weight
25 m 166
30 f 115
18 f 120
"
mydata <- read.table(header=TRUE, text=mydatatxt)
```

creates the same data frame as that created with the `edit()` function. A character string is created containing the raw data, and the `read.table()` function is used to process the string and return a data frame. The `read.table()` function is described more fully in the next section.

Keyboard data entry can be convenient when you're working with small datasets. For larger datasets, you'll want to use the methods described next: importing data from existing text files, Excel spreadsheets, statistical packages, or database-management systems.

2.3.2 *Importing data from a delimited text file*

You can import data from delimited text files using `read.table()`, a function that reads a file in table format and saves it as a data frame. Each row of the table appears as one line in the file. The syntax is

```
mydataframe <- read.table(file, options)
```

where *file* is a delimited ASCII file and the *options* are parameters controlling how data is processed. The most common options are listed in table 2.2.

Table 2.2 `read.table()` options

Option	Description
header	A logical value indicating whether the file contains the variable names in the first line.
sep	The delimiter separating data values. The default is `sep=" "`, which denotes one or more spaces, tabs, new lines, or carriage returns. Use `sep=","` to read comma-delimited files, and `sep="\t"` to read tab-delimited files.
row.names	An optional parameter specifying one or more variables to represent row identifiers.
col.names	If the first row of the data file doesn't contain variable names (`header=FALSE`), you can use `col.names` to specify a character vector containing the variable names. If `header=FALSE` and the `col.names` option is omitted, variables will be named V1, V2, and so on.

Table 2.2 `read.table()` **options**

Option	Description
na.strings	Optional character vector indicating missing-values codes. For example, `na.strings =c("-9", "?")` converts each `-9` and `?` value to `NA` as the data is read.
colClasses	Optional vector of classes to be assign to the columns. For example, `colClasses =c("numeric", "numeric", "character", "NULL", "numeric")` reads the first two columns as numeric, reads the third column as character, skips the fourth column, and reads the fifth column as numeric. If there are more than five columns in the data, the values in `colClasses` are recycled. When you're reading large text files, including the `colClasses` option can speed up processing considerably.
quote	Character(s) used to delimit strings that contain special characters. By default this is either double (") or single (') quotes.
skip	The number of lines in the data file to skip before beginning to read the data. This option is useful for skipping header comments in the file.
strings-AsFactors	A logical value indicating whether character variables should be converted to factors. The default is `TRUE` unless this is overridden by `colClasses`. When you're processing large text files, setting `stringsAsFactors=FALSE` can speed up processing.
text	A character string specifying a text string to process. If `text` is specified, leave `file` blank. An example is given in section 2.3.1.

Consider a text file named studentgrades.csv containing students' grades in math, science, and social studies. Each line of the file represents a student. The first line contains the variable names, separated with commas. Each subsequent line contains a student's information, also separated with commas. The first few lines of the file are as follows:

```
StudentID,First,Last,Math,Science,Social Studies
011,Bob,Smith,90,80,67
012,Jane,Weary,75,,80
010,Dan,"Thornton, III",65,75,70
040,Mary,"O'Leary",90,95,92
```

The file can be imported into a data frame using the following code:

```
grades <- read.table("studentgrades.csv", header=TRUE,
    row.names="StudentID", sep=",")
```

The results are as follows:

```
> grades

    First              Last Math Science Social.Studies
11   Bob              Smith   90      80             67
12  Jane              Weary   75      NA             80
10   Dan      Thornton, III   65      75             70
40  Mary            O'Leary   90      95             92

> str(grades)
```

```
'data.frame':    4 obs. of  5 variables:
 $ First         : Factor w/ 4 levels "Bob","Dan","Jane",..: 1 3 2 4
 $ Last          : Factor w/ 4 levels "O'Leary","Smith",..: 2 4 3 1
 $ Math          : int  90 75 65 90
 $ Science       : int  80 NA 75 95
 $ Social.Studies: int  67 80 70 92
```

There are several interesting things to note about how the data is imported. The variable name Social Studies is automatically renamed to follow R conventions. The StudentID column is now the row name, no longer has a label, and has lost its leading zero. The missing science grade for Jane is correctly read as missing. I had to put quotation marks around Dan's last name in order to escape the comma between Thornton and III. Otherwise, R would have seen seven values on that line, rather than six. I also had to put quotation marks around O'Leary. Otherwise, R would have read the single quote as a string delimiter (which isn't what I want). Finally, the first and last names are converted to factors.

By default, read.table() converts character variables to factors, which may not always be desirable. For example, there would be little reason to convert a character variable containing a respondent's comments into a factor. You can suppress this behavior in a number of ways. Including the option stringsAsFactors=FALSE turns off this behavior for all character variables. Alternatively, you can use the colClasses option to specify a class (for example, logical, numeric, character, or factor) for each column.

Importing the same data with

```
grades <- read.table("studentgrades.csv", header=TRUE,
    row.names="StudentID", sep=",",
    colClasses=c("character", "character", "character",
                 "numeric", "numeric", "numeric"))
```

produces the following data frame:

```
> grades

    First             Last Math Science Social.Studies
011   Bob            Smith   90      80             67
012  Jane            Weary   75      NA             80
010   Dan   Thornton, III   65      75             70
040  Mary          O'Leary   90      95             92

> str(grades)

'data.frame':    4 obs. of  5 variables:
 $ First         : chr  "Bob" "Jane" "Dan" "Mary"
 $ Last          : chr  "Smith" "Weary" "Thornton, III" "O'Leary"
 $ Math          : num  90 75 65 90
 $ Science       : num  80 NA 75 95
 $ Social.Studies: num  67 80 70 92
```

Note that the row names retain their leading zero and First and Last are no longer factors. Additionally, the grades are stored as real values rather than integers.

The `read.table()` function has many options for fine-tuning data imports. See `help(read.table)` for details.

Importing data via connections

Many of the examples in this chapter import data from files that exist on your computer. R provides several mechanisms for accessing data via connections as well. For example, the functions `file()`, `gzfile()`, `bzfile()`, `xzfile()`, `unz()`, and `url()` can be used in place of the filename. The `file()` function allows you to access files, the clipboard, and C-level standard input. The `gzfile()`, `bzfile()`, `xzfile()`, and `unz()` functions let you read compressed files.

The `url()` function lets you access internet files through a complete URL that includes http://, ftp://, or file://. For HTTP and FTP, proxies can be specified. For convenience, complete URLs (surrounded by double quotation marks) can usually be used directly in place of filenames as well. See `help(file)` for details.

2.3.3 Importing data from Excel

The best way to read an Excel file is to export it to a comma-delimited file from Excel and import it into R using the method described earlier. Alternatively, you can import Excel worksheets directly using the `xlsx` package. Be sure to download and install it before you first use it. You'll also need the `xlsxjars` and `rJava` packages and a working installation of Java (http://java.com).

The `xlsx` package can be used to read, write, and format Excel 97/2000/XP/ 2003/2007 files. The `read.xlsx()` function imports a worksheet into a data frame. The simplest format is `read.xlsx(file, n)` where `file` is the path to an Excel workbook, `n` is the number of the worksheet to be imported, and the first line of the worksheet contains the variable names. For example, on a Windows platform, the code

```
library(xlsx)
workbook <- "c:/myworkbook.xlsx"
mydataframe <- read.xlsx(workbook, 1)
```

imports the first worksheet from the workbook myworkbook.xlsx stored on the C: drive and saves it as the data frame `mydataframe`.

The `read.xlsx()` function has options that allow you to specify specific rows (`row-Index`) and columns (`colIndex`) of the worksheet, along with the class of each column (`colClasses`). For large worksheets (say, 100,000+ cells), you can also use `read.xlsx2()`. It performs more of the processing work in Java, resulting in significant performance gains. See `help(read.xlsx)` for details.

There are other packages that can help you work with Excel files. Alternatives include the `XLConnect` and `openxlsx` packages; `XLConnect` depends on Java, but `openxlsx` doesn't. All of these package can do more than import worksheets—they can create and manipulate Excel files as well. Programmers who need to develop an interface between R and Excel should check out one or more of these packages.

2.3.4   *Importing data from XML*

Increasingly, data is provided in the form of files encoded in XML. R has several packages for handling XML files. For example, the XML package written by Duncan Temple Lang allows you to read, write, and manipulate XML files. Coverage of XML is beyond the scope of this text; if you're interested in accessing XML documents from within R, see the excellent package documentation at www.omegahat.org/RSXML.

2.3.5   *Importing data from the web*

Data can be obtained from the web via *webscraping* or the use of *application programming interfaces (APIs)*. *Webscraping* is used to extract the information embedded in specific web pages, whereas APIs allow you to interact with web services and online data stores.

Typically, webscraping is used to extract data from a web page and save it into an R structure for further analysis. For example, the text on a web page can be downloaded into an R character vector using the readLines() function and manipulated with functions such as grep() and gsub(). For complex web pages, the RCurl and XML packages can be used to extract the information desired. For more information, including examples, see "Webscraping Using readLines and RCurl," available from the website *Programming with R* (www.programmingr.com).

APIs specify how software components should interact with each other. A number of R packages use this approach to extract data from web-accessible resources. These include data sources in biology, medicine, Earth sciences, physical science, economics and business, finance, literature, marketing, news, and sports.

For example, if you're interested in social media, you can access Twitter data via twitteR, Facebook data via Rfacebook, and Flickr data via Rflickr. Other packages allow you to access popular web services provided by Google, Amazon, Dropbox, Salesforce, and others. For a comprehensive list of R packages that can help you access web-based resources, see the CRAN Task view on *Web Technologies and Services* (http://mng.bz/370r).

2.3.6   *Importing data from SPSS*

IBM SPSS datasets can be imported into R via the read.spss() function in the foreign package. Alternatively, you can use the spss.get() function in the Hmisc package. spss.get() is a wrapper function that automatically sets many parameters of read.spss() for you, making the transfer easier and more consistent with what data analysts expect as a result.

First, download and install the Hmisc package (the foreign package is already installed by default):

```
install.packages("Hmisc")
```

Then use the following code to import the data:

```
library(Hmisc)
mydataframe <- spss.get("mydata.sav", use.value.labels=TRUE)
```

In this code, mydata.sav is the SPSS data file to be imported, `use.value.labels=TRUE` tells the function to convert variables with value labels into R factors with those same levels, and `mydataframe` is the resulting R data frame.

2.3.7 *Importing data from SAS*

A number of functions in R are designed to import SAS datasets, including `read.ssd()` in the `foreign` package, `sas.get()` in the `Hmisc` package, and `read.sas7bdat()` in the `sas7bdat` package. If you have SAS installed, `sas.get()` can be a good option.

Let's say that you want to import an SAS dataset named clients.sas7bdat that resides in the C:/mydata directory on a Windows machine. The following code imports the data and saves it as an R data frame:

```
library(Hmisc)
datadir <- "C:/mydata"
sasexe <- "C:/Program Files/SASHome/SASFoundation/9.4/sas.exe"
mydata <- sas.get(libraryName=datadir, member="clients", sasprog=sasexe)
```

`libraryName` is a directory containing the SAS dataset, `member` is the dataset name (excluding the sas7bdat extension), and `sasprog` is the full path to the SAS executable. Many additional options are available; see `help(sas.get)` for details.

You can also save the SAS dataset as a comma-delimited text file from within SAS using `PROC EXPORT`, and you can read the resulting file into R using the method described in section 2.3.2. Here's an example:

```
SAS program:

libname datadir "C:\mydata";
proc export data=datadir.clients
    outfile="clients.csv"
    dbms=csv;
run;

R program:

mydata <- read.table("clients.csv", header=TRUE, sep=",")
```

The previous two approaches require that you have a fully functional version of SAS installed. If you don't have access to SAS, the `read.sas7bdat()` function may be a good alternative. The function can read an SAS dataset in sas7bdat format directly. The code for this example would be

```
library(sas7bdat)
mydata <- read.sas7bdat("C:/mydata/clients.sas7bdat")
```

Unlike `sas.get()`, the `read.sas7bdat()` function ignores SAS user-defined formats. Additionally, it takes significantly longer to run. Although I've had good luck with this package, it's still considered experimental.

Finally, a commercial product named Stat/Transfer (described in section 2.3.12) does an excellent job of saving SAS datasets (including any existing variable formats) as R data frames. As with `read.sas7dbat()`, access to an SAS installation isn't required.

2.3.8   Importing data from Stata

Importing data from Stata to R is straightforward. The necessary code looks like this:

```
library(foreign)
mydataframe <- read.dta("mydata.dta")
```

Here, mydata.dta is the Stata dataset, and `mydataframe` is the resulting R data frame.

2.3.9   Importing data from NetCDF

Unidata's Network Common Data Form (NetCDF) open source software contains machine-independent data formats for the creation and distribution of array-oriented scientific data. NetCDF is commonly used to store geophysical data. The `ncdf` and `ncdf4` packages provide high-level R interfaces to NetCDF data files.

The `ncdf` package provides support for data files created with Unidata's NetCDF library (version 3 or earlier) and is available for Windows, Mac OS X, and Linux platforms. The `ncdf4` package supports version 4 or earlier but isn't yet available for Windows.

Consider this code:

```
library(ncdf)
nc <- nc_open("mynetCDFfile")
myarray <- get.var.ncdf(nc, myvar)
```

In this example, all the data from the variable myvar, contained in the NetCDF file mynetCDFfile, is read and saved into an R array called myarray.

Note that both the `ncdf` and `ncdf4` packages have received major recent upgrades and may operate differently than previous versions. Additionally, function names in the two packages differ. Read the online help for details.

2.3.10   Importing data from HDF5

Hierarchical Data Format (HDF5) is a software technology suite for the management of extremely large and complex data collections. The `rhdf5` package provides an R interface for HDF5. The package is available on the Bioconductor website rather than CRAN. You can install it with the following code:

```
source("http://bioconductor.org/biocLite.R")
biocLite("rhdf5")
```

Like XML, HDF5 is beyond the scope of this book. To learn more, visit the HDF Group website (www.hdfgroup.org). There is an excellent tutorial for the `rhdf5` package by Bernd Fischer at http://mng.bz/eg6j.

2.3.11   Accessing database management systems (DBMSs)

R can interface with a wide variety of relational database management systems (DBMSs), including Microsoft SQL Server, Microsoft Access, MySQL, Oracle, PostgreSQL, DB2, Sybase, Teradata, and SQLite. Some packages provide access through native database drivers, whereas others offer access via ODBC or JDBC. Using R to access data stored in external DMBSs can be an efficient way to analyze large datasets (see appendix F) and takes advantage of the power of both SQL and R.

THE ODBC INTERFACE

Perhaps the most popular method of accessing a DBMS in R is through the RODBC package, which allows R to connect to any DBMS that has an ODBC driver. This includes all the DBMSs listed earlier.

The first step is to install and configure the appropriate ODBC driver for your platform and database (these drivers aren't part of R). If the requisite drivers aren't already installed on your machine, an internet search should provide you with options.

Once the drivers are installed and configured for the database(s) of your choice, install the RODBC package. You can do so by using the install.packages("RODBC") command. The primary functions included with RODBC are listed in table 2.3.

Table 2.3 RODBC **functions**

Function	Description
odbcConnect(*dsn*,uid="",pwd="")	Opens a connection to an ODBC database
sqlFetch(*channel*,*sqltable*)	Reads a table from an ODBC database into a data frame
sqlQuery(*channel*,*query*)	Submits a query to an ODBC database and returns the results
sqlSave(*channel*,*mydf*,tablename = *sqltable*,append=FALSE)	Writes or updates (append=TRUE) a data frame to a table in the ODBC database
sqlDrop(*channel*,*sqltable*)	Removes a table from the ODBC database
close(*channel*)	Closes the connection

The RODBC package allows two-way communication between R and an ODBC-connected SQL database. This means you can not only read data from a connected database into R, but also use R to alter the contents of the database itself. Assume that you want to import two tables (Crime and Punishment) from a DBMS into two R data frames called crimedat and pundat, respectively. You can accomplish this with code similar to the following:

```
library(RODBC)
myconn <-odbcConnect("mydsn", uid="Rob", pwd="aardvark")
crimedat <- sqlFetch(myconn, Crime)
pundat <- sqlQuery(myconn, "select * from Punishment")
close(myconn)
```

Here, you load the RODBC package and open a connection to the ODBC database through a registered data source name (mydsn) with a security UID (rob) and password (aardvark). The connection string is passed to sqlFetch(), which copies the table Crime into the R data frame crimedat. You then run the SQL select statement against the table Punishment and save the results to the data frame pundat. Finally, you close the connection.

The sqlQuery() function is powerful because any valid SQL statement can be inserted. This flexibility allows you to select specific variables, subset the data, create new variables, and recode and rename existing variables.

DBI-RELATED PACKAGES

The DBI package provides a general and consistent client-side interface to a DBMS. Building on this framework, the RJDBC package provides access to a DBMS via a JDBC driver. Be sure to install the necessary JDBC drivers for your platform and database. Other useful DBI-based packages include RMySQL, ROracle, RPostgreSQL, and RSQLite. These packages provide native database drivers for their respective databases but may not be available on all platforms. Check the documentation on CRAN (http://cran .r-project.org) for details.

2.3.12 *Importing data via Stat/Transfer*

Before we end our discussion of importing data, it's worth mentioning a commercial product that can make the task significantly easier. Stat/Transfer (www.stattransfer .com) is a standalone application that can transfer data among 34 data formats, including R (see figure 2.4).

Stat/Transfer is available for Windows, Mac, and Unix platforms. It supports the latest versions of the statistical packages we've discussed so far, as well as ODBC-accessed DBMSs such as Oracle, Sybase, Informix, and DB/2.

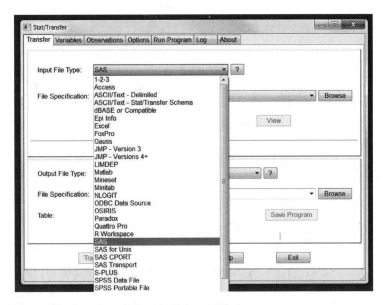

Figure 2.4   Stat/Transfer's main dialog on Windows

2.4　*Annotating datasets*

Data analysts typically annotate datasets to make the results easier to interpret. Annotating generally includes adding descriptive labels to variable names and value labels to the codes used for categorical variables. For example, for the variable age, you might want to attach the more descriptive label "Age at hospitalization (in years)." For the variable gender, coded 1 or 2, you might want to associate the labels "male" and "female."

2.4.1　*Variable labels*

Unfortunately, R's ability to handle variable labels is limited. One approach is to use the variable label as the variable's name and then refer to the variable by its position index. Consider the earlier example, where you have a data frame containing patient data. The second column, age, contains the ages at which individuals were first hospitalized. The code

```
names(patientdata)[2] <- "Age at hospitalization (in years)"
```

renames age to "Age at hospitalization (in years)". Clearly this new name is too long to type repeatedly. Instead, you can refer to this variable as patientdata[2], and the string "Age at hospitalization (in years)" will print wherever age would have originally. Obviously, this isn't an ideal approach, and you may be better off trying to come up with better variable names (for example, admissionAge).

2.4.2　*Value labels*

The factor() function can be used to create value labels for categorical variables. Continuing the example, suppose you have a variable named gender, which is coded 1 for male and 2 for female. You can create value labels with the code

```
patientdata$gender <- factor(patientdata$gender,
                             levels = c(1,2),
                             labels = c("male", "female"))
```

Here levels indicates the actual values of the variable, and labels refers to a character vector containing the desired labels.

2.5　*Useful functions for working with data objects*

We'll end this chapter with a brief summary of useful functions for working with data objects (see table 2.4).

Table 2.4　Useful functions for working with data objects

Function	Purpose
length(*object*)	Gives the number of elements/components.
dim(*object*)	Gives the dimensions of an object.
str(*object*)	Gives the structure of an object.

Table 2.4   Useful functions for working with data objects *(continued)*

Function	Purpose
`class(`*`object`*`)`	Gives the class of an object.
`mode(`*`object`*`)`	Determines how an object is stored.
`names(`*`object`*`)`	Gives the names of components in an object.
`c(`*`object, object,`*`...)`	Combines objects into a vector.
`cbind(`*`object, object,`*` ...)`	Combines objects as columns.
`rbind(`*`object, object,`*` ...)`	Combines objects as rows.
`object`	Prints an object.
`head(`*`object`*`)`	Lists the first part of an object.
`tail(object)`	Lists the last part of an object.
`ls()`	Lists current objects.
`rm(`*`object, object,`*` ...)`	Deletes one or more objects. The statement `rm(list = ls())` removes most objects from the working environment.
`newobject` `<- edit(`*`object`*`)`	Edits `object` and saves it as `newobject`.
`fix(`*`object`*`)`	Edits an object in place.

We've already discussed most of these functions. `head()` and `tail()` are useful for quickly scanning large datasets. For example, `head(patientdata)` lists the first six rows of the data frame, whereas `tail(patientdata)` lists the last six. We'll cover functions such as `length()`, `cbind()`, and `rbind()` in the next chapter; they're gathered here as a reference.

2.6   *Summary*

One of the most challenging tasks in data analysis is data preparation. We've made a good start in this chapter by outlining the various structures that R provides for holding data and the many methods available for importing data from both keyboard and external sources. In particular, we'll use the definitions of *vector, matrix, data frame,* and *list* again and again in later chapters. Your ability to specify elements of these structures via the bracket notation will be particularly important in selecting, subsetting, and transforming data.

As you've seen, R offers a wealth of functions for accessing external data. This includes data from flat files, web files, statistical packages, spreadsheets, and databases. Although the focus of this chapter has been on importing data into R, you can also export data from R into these external formats. Exporting data is covered in appendix C, and methods of working with large datasets (in the gigabyte to terabyte range) are covered in appendix F.

Once you import your datasets into R, it's likely that you'll have to manipulate them into a more conducive format (actually, I find guilt works well). In chapter 4, we'll explore ways to create new variables, transform and recode existing variables, merge datasets, and select observations.

But before turning to data-management tasks, let's spend some time with R graphics. Many readers have turned to R out of an interest in its graphing capabilities, and I don't want to make you wait any longer. In the next chapter, we'll jump directly into the creation of graphs. The emphasis will be on general methods for managing and customizing graphs that can be applied throughout the remainder of this book.

Getting started with graphs

On many occasions, I've presented clients with carefully crafted statistical results in the form of numbers and text, only to have their eyes glaze over while the chirping of crickets permeated the room. Yet those same clients had enthusiastic "Ah-ha!" moments when I presented the same information to them in the form of graphs. Often I can see patterns in data or detect anomalies in data values by looking at graphs—patterns or anomalies that I completely missed when conducting more formal statistical analyses.

Human beings are remarkably adept at discerning relationships from visual representations. A well-crafted graph can help you make meaningful comparisons among thousands of pieces of information, extracting patterns not easily found through other methods. This is one reason why advances in the field of statistical graphics have had such a major impact on data analysis. Data analysts need to *look* at their data, and this is one area where R shines.

In this chapter, we'll review general methods for working with graphs. We'll start with how to create and save graphs. Then we'll look at how to modify the features that are found in any graph. These features include graph titles, axes, labels, colors, lines, symbols, and text annotations. Our focus will be on generic techniques that apply across graphs. (In later chapters, we'll focus on specific types of graphs.) Finally, we'll investigate ways to combine multiple graphs into one overall graph.

3.1 Working with graphs

R is an amazing platform for building graphs. I'm using the term *building* intentionally. In a typical interactive session, you build a graph one statement at a time, adding features, until you have what you want.

Consider the following five lines:

```
attach(mtcars)
plot(wt, mpg)
abline(lm(mpg~wt))
title("Regression of MPG on Weight")
detach(mtcars)
```

The first statement attaches the data frame `mtcars`. The second statement opens a graphics window and generates a scatter plot between automobile weight on the horizontal axis and miles per gallon on the vertical axis. The third statement adds a line of best fit. The fourth statement adds a title. The final statement detaches the data frame. In R, graphs are typically created in this interactive fashion (see figure 3.1).

You can save your graphs via code or through GUI menus. To save a graph via code, sandwich the statements that produce the graph between a statement that sets a destination and a statement that closes that destination. For example, the following will

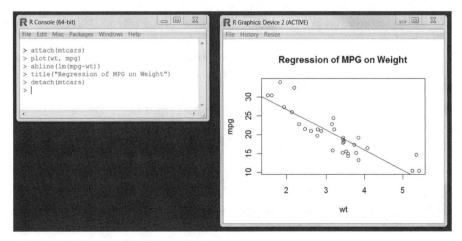

Figure 3.1   Creating a graph

save the graph as a PDF document named mygraph.pdf in the current working directory:

```
pdf("mygraph.pdf")
 attach(mtcars)
 plot(wt, mpg)
 abline(lm(mpg~wt))
 title("Regression of MPG on Weight")
 detach(mtcars)
dev.off()
```

In addition to pdf(), you can use the functions win.metafile(), png(), jpeg(), bmp(), tiff(), xfig(), and postscript() to save graphs in other formats. (Note: The Windows metafile format is only available on Windows platforms.) See chapter 1, section 1.3.4 for more details on sending graphic output to files.

Saving graphs via the GUI is platform specific. On a Windows platform, select File > Save As from the graphics window, and choose the format and location desired in the resulting dialog. On a Mac, choose File > Save As from the menu bar when the Quartz graphics window is highlighted. The only output format provided is PDF. On a Unix platform, graphs must be saved via code. In appendix A, we'll consider alternative GUIs for each platform that will give you more options.

Creating a new graph by issuing a high-level plotting command such as plot(), hist() (for histograms), or boxplot() typically overwrites a previous graph. How can you create more than one graph and still have access to each? There are several methods.

First, you can open a new graph window *before* creating a new graph:

```
dev.new()
 statements to create graph 1
dev.new()
 statements to create a graph 2
etc.
```

Each new graph will appear in the most recently opened window.

Second, you can access multiple graphs via the GUI. On a Mac platform, you can step through the graphs at any time using Back and Forward on the Quartz menu. On a Windows platform, you must use a two-step process. After opening the *first* graph window, choose History > Recording. Then use the Previous and Next menu items to step through the graphs that are created.

Finally, you can use the functions dev.new(), dev.next(), dev.prev(), dev.set(), and dev.off() to have multiple graph windows open at one time and choose which output is sent to which windows. This approach works on any platform. See help(dev.cur) for details on this approach.

R creates attractive graphs with a minimum of input on your part. But you can also use graphical parameters to specify fonts, colors, line styles, axes, reference lines, and annotations. This flexibility allows for a wide degree of customization.

In this chapter, we'll start with a simple graph and explore the ways you can modify and enhance it to meet your needs. Then we'll look at more complex examples that illustrate additional customization methods. The focus will be on techniques that you can apply to a wide range of the graphs you'll create in R. The methods discussed here will work on all the graphs described in this book, with the exception of those created with the ggplot2 package in chapter 19. (The ggplot2 package has its own methods for customizing a graph's appearance.) In other chapters, we'll explore each specific type of graph and discuss where and when each is most useful.

3.2 A simple example

Let's begin with the simple fictitious dataset given in table 3.1. It describes patient responses to two drugs at five dosage levels.

Table 3.1   Patient responses to two drugs at five dosage levels

Dosage	Response to Drug A	Response to Drug B
20	16	15
30	20	18
40	27	25
45	40	31
60	60	40

You can input this data using the following code:

```
dose  <- c(20, 30, 40, 45, 60)
drugA <- c(16, 20, 27, 40, 60)
drugB <- c(15, 18, 25, 31, 40)
```

A simple line graph relating dose to response for drug A can be created using

```
plot(dose, drugA, type="b")
```

plot() is a generic function that plots objects in R (its output varies according to the type of object being plotted). In this case, plot(*x*, *y*, type="b") places *x* on the horizontal axis and *y* on the vertical axis, plots the (*x*, *y*) data points, and connects them with line segments. The option type="b" indicates that both points and lines should be plotted. Use help(plot) to view other options. The graph is displayed in figure 3.2.

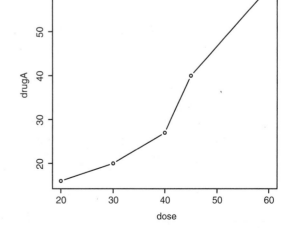

Figure 3.2   Line plot of dose vs. response for drug A

Line plots are covered in detail in chapter 11. Now let's modify the appearance of this graph.

3.3   *Graphical parameters*

You can customize many features of a graph (fonts, colors, axes, and labels) through options called *graphical parameters*. One way is to specify these options through the par() function. Values set in this manner will be in effect for the rest of the session or until they're changed. The format is par(*optionname=value, optionname=value, ...*). Specifying par() without parameters produces a list of the current graphical settings. Adding the no.readonly=TRUE option produces a list of current graphical settings that can be modified.

Continuing the example, let's say that you'd like to use a solid triangle rather than an open circle as your plotting symbol, and connect points using a dashed line rather than a solid line. You can do so with the following code:

```
opar <- par(no.readonly=TRUE)
par(lty=2, pch=17)
plot(dose, drugA, type="b")
par(opar)
```

The resulting graph is shown in figure 3.3.

The first statement makes a copy of the current settings. The second statement changes the default line type to dashed (lty=2) and the default symbol for plotting points to a solid triangle (pch=17). You then generate the plot and restore the original settings. Line types and symbols are covered in section 3.3.1.

You can have as many par() functions as desired, so par(lty=2, pch=17) could also be written as

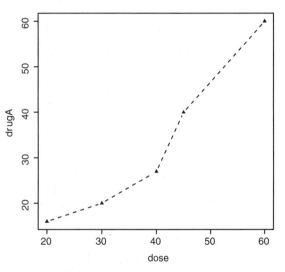

Figure 3.3   Line plot of dose vs. response for drug A with modified line type and symbol

```
par(lty=2)
par(pch=17)
```

A second way to specify graphical parameters is by providing the *optionname=value* pairs directly to a high-level plotting function. In this case, the options are only in effect for that specific graph. You could generate the same graph with this code:

```
plot(dose, drugA, type="b", lty=2, pch=17)
```

Not all high-level plotting functions allow you to specify all possible graphical parameters. See the help for a specific plotting function (such as ?plot, ?hist, or ?boxplot) to determine which graphical parameters can be set in this way. The remainder of section 3.3 describes many of the important graphical parameters that you can set.

3.3.1 Symbols and lines

As you've seen, you can use graphical parameters to specify the plotting symbols and lines used in your graphs. The relevant parameters are shown in table 3.2.

Table 3.2 Parameters for specifying symbols and lines

Parameter	Description
pch	Specifies the symbol to use when plotting points (see figure 3.4).
cex	Specifies the symbol size. cex is a number indicating the amount by which plotting symbols should be scaled relative to the default. 1 = default, 1.5 is 50% larger, 0.5 is 50% smaller, and so forth.
lty	Specifies the line type (see figure 3.5).
lwd	Specifies the line width. lwd is expressed relative to the default (1 = default). For example, lwd=2 generates a line twice as wide as the default.

The pch= option specifies the symbols to use when plotting points. Possible values are shown in figure 3.4. For symbols 21 through 25, you can also specify the border (col=) and fill (bg=) colors.

Use lty= to specify the type of line desired. The option values are shown in figure 3.5.

Taking these options together, the code

```
plot(dose, drugA, type="b", lty=3, lwd=3, pch=15, cex=2)
```

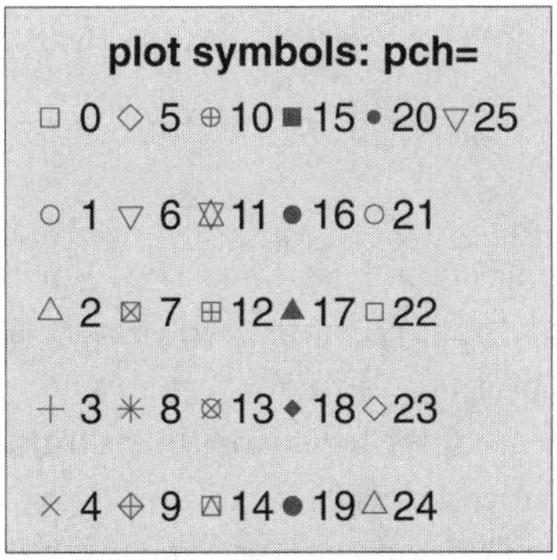

Figure 3.4 Plotting symbols specified with the pch parameter

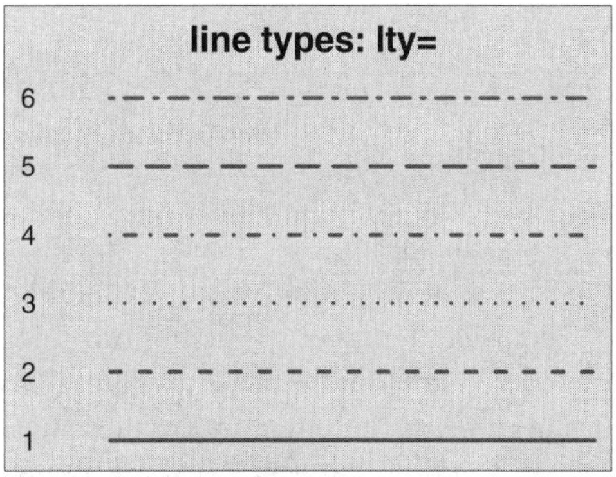

Figure 3.5 Line types specified with the lty parameter

would produce a plot with a dotted line that was three times wider than the default width, connecting points displayed as filled squares that are twice as large as the default symbol size. The results are shown in figure 3.6.

Next, let's look at specifying colors.

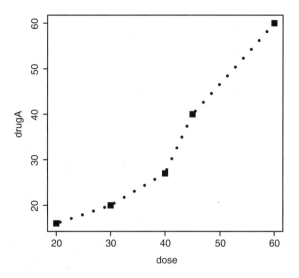

Figure 3.6   Line plot of dose vs. response for drug A with modified line type, line width, symbol, and symbol width

3.3.2 *Colors*

There are several color-related parameters in R. Table 3.3 shows some of the common ones.

Table 3.3   Parameters for specifying colors

Parameter	Description
col	Default plotting color. Some functions (such as lines and pie) accept a vector of values that are recycled. For example, if col=c("red", "blue") and three lines are plotted, the first line will be red, the second blue, and the third red.
col.axis	Color for axis text.
col.lab	Color for axis labels.
col.main	Color for titles.
col.sub	Color for subtitles.
fg	Color for the plot's foreground.
bg	Color for the plot's background.

You can specify colors in R by index, name, hexadecimal, RGB, or HSV. For example, col=1, col="white", col="#FFFFFF", col=rgb(1,1,1), and col=hsv(0,0,1) are equivalent ways of specifying the color white. The function rgb() creates colors based on red-green-blue values, whereas hsv() creates colors based on hue-saturation values. See the help feature on these functions for more details.

The function colors() returns all available color names. Earl F. Glynn has created an excellent online chart of R colors, available at http://mng.bz/9C5p. R also has a number of functions that can be used to create vectors of contiguous colors. These include rainbow(), heat.colors(), terrain.colors(), topo.colors(), and cm.colors(). For example, rainbow(10) produces 10 contiguous "rainbow" colors.

The RColorBrewer package is particularly popular for creating attractive color palettes. Be sure to download it (install.packages("RColorBrewer")) before first use. Once it's installed, use the brewer.pal(*n*, *name*) function to generate a vector of colors. For example, the code

```
library(RColorBrewer)
n <- 7
mycolors <- brewer.pal(n, "Set1")
barplot(rep(1,n), col=mycolors)
```

returns a vector of seven colors in hexadecimal format from the Set1 palette. To get a list of the available palettes, type brewer.pal.info; or type display.brewer.all() to produces a plot of each palette in a single display. See help(RColorBrewer) for more details.

Finally, gray levels are generated with the gray() function in the base installation. In this case, you specify gray levels as a vector of numbers between 0 and 1. gray(0:10/10) produces 10 gray levels. Try the following code to see how this works:

```
n <- 10
mycolors <- rainbow(n)
pie(rep(1, n), labels=mycolors, col=mycolors)
mygrays <- gray(0:n/n)
pie(rep(1, n), labels=mygrays, col=mygrays)
```

As you can see, R provides numerous methods for generating color vectors. You'll see examples that use color parameters throughout this chapter.

3.3.3 Text characteristics

Graphic parameters are also used to specify text size, font, and style. Parameters controlling text size are explained in table 3.4. Font family and style can be controlled with font options (see table 3.5).

Table 3.4 Parameters specifying text size

Parameter	Description
cex	Number indicating the amount by which plotted text should be scaled relative to the default. 1 = default, 1.5 is 50% larger, 0.5 is 50% smaller, and so on.
cex.axis	Magnification of axis text relative to cex.
cex.lab	Magnification of axis labels relative to cex.
cex.main	Magnification of titles relative to cex.
cex.sub	Magnification of subtitles relative to cex.

For example, all graphs created after the statement

```
par(font.lab=3, cex.lab=1.5, font.main=4, cex.main=2)
```

will have italic axis labels that are 1.5 times the default text size and bold italic titles that are twice the default text size.

Table 3.5   Parameters specifying font family, size, and style

Parameter	Description
font	Integer specifying the font to use for plotted text. 1 = plain, 2 = bold, 3 = italic, 4 = bold italic, and 5=symbol (in Adobe symbol encoding).
font.axis	Font for axis text.
font.lab	Font for axis labels.
font.main	Font for titles.
font.sub	Font for subtitles.
ps	Font point size (roughly 1/72 inch). The text size = ps*cex.
family	Font family for drawing text. Standard values are serif, sans, and mono.

Whereas font size and style are easily set, font family is a bit more complicated. This is because the mappings of serif, sans, and mono are device dependent. For example, on Windows platforms, mono is mapped to TT Courier New, serif is mapped to TT Times New Roman, and sans is mapped to TT Arial (TT stands for TrueType). If you're satisfied with this mapping, you can use parameters like family="serif" to get the results you want. If not, you need to create a new mapping. On Windows, you can create this mapping via the windowsFont() function. For example, after issuing this statement, you can use A, B, and C as family values:

```
windowsFonts(
  A=windowsFont("Arial Black"),
  B=windowsFont("Bookman Old Style"),
  C=windowsFont("Comic Sans MS")
)
```

In this case, par(family="A") specifies an Arial Black font. (Listing 3.2 in section 3.4.2 provides an example of modifying text parameters.) Note that the windows-Font() function only works for Windows. On a Mac, use quartzFonts() instead.

If graphs will be output in PDF or PostScript format, changing the font family is relatively straightforward. For PDFs, use names(pdfFonts()) to find out which fonts are available on your system and pdf(file="myplot.pdf", family="fontname") to generate the plots. For graphs that are output in PostScript format, use names(post-scriptFonts()) and postscript(file="myplot.ps", family="fontname"). See the online help for more information.

3.3.4   *Graph and margin dimensions*

Finally, you can control the plot dimensions and margin sizes using the parameters listed in table 3.6.

Table 3.6 Parameters for graph and margin dimensions

Parameter	Description
pin	Plot dimensions (width, height) in inches.
mai	Numerical vector indicating margin size, where c(bottom, left, top, right) is expressed in inches.
mar	Numerical vector indicating margin size, where c(bottom, left, top, right) is expressed in lines. The default is c(5, 4, 4, 2) + 0.1.

The code

```
par(pin=c(4,3), mai=c(1,.5, 1, .2))
```

produces graphs that are 4 inches wide by 3 inches tall, with a 1-inch margin on the bottom and top, a 0.5-inch margin on the left, and a 0.2-inch margin on the right. For more on margins, see Earl F. Glynn's comprehensive online tutorial (http://mng.bz/6aMp).

Let's use the options we've covered so far to enhance the simple example. The code in the following listing produces the graphs in figure 3.7.

Listing 3.1 Using graphical parameters to control graph appearance

```
dose  <- c(20, 30, 40, 45, 60)
drugA <- c(16, 20, 27, 40, 60)
drugB <- c(15, 18, 25, 31, 40)

opar <- par(no.readonly=TRUE)
par(pin=c(2, 3))
par(lwd=2, cex=1.5)
par(cex.axis=.75, font.axis=3)
plot(dose, drugA, type="b", pch=19, lty=2, col="red")
plot(dose, drugB, type="b", pch=23, lty=6, col="blue", bg="green")
par(opar)
```

First you enter your data as vectors, and then you save the current graphical parameter settings (so that you can restore them later). You modify the default graphical parameters so that graphs will be 2 inches wide by 3 inches tall. Additionally, lines will be twice the default width and symbols will be 1.5 times the default size. Axis text will be set to italic and scaled to 75% of the default. The first plot is then created using filled red circles and dashed lines. The second plot is created using filled green diamonds and a blue border and blue dashed lines. Finally, you restore the original graphical parameter settings. Note that parameters set with the par() function apply to both graphs, whereas parameters specified in the plot() functions only apply to that specific graph.

Looking at figure 3.7, you can see some limitations in the presentation. The graphs lack titles, and the vertical axes aren't on the same scale, limiting your ability to compare the two drugs directly. The axis labels could also be more informative.

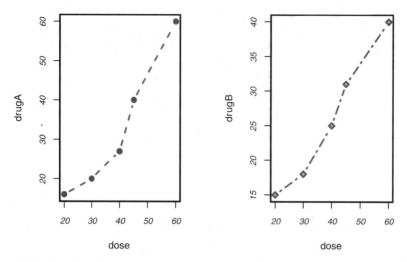

Figure 3.7   Line plot of dose vs. response for both drug A and drug B

In the next section, we'll turn to the customization of text annotations (such as titles and labels) and axes. For more information on the graphical parameters that are available, take a look at help(par).

3.4   Adding text, customized axes, and legends

Many high-level plotting functions (for example, plot, hist, and boxplot) allow you to include axis and text options, as well as graphical parameters. For example, the following adds a title (main), a subtitle (sub), axis labels (xlab, ylab), and axis ranges (xlim, ylim). The results are presented in figure 3.8:

```
plot(dose, drugA, type="b",
    col="red", lty=2, pch=2, lwd=2,
    main="Clinical Trials for Drug A",
    sub="This is hypothetical data",
    xlab="Dosage", ylab="Drug Response",
    xlim=c(0, 60), ylim=c(0, 70))
```

Again, not all functions allow you to add these options. See the help for the function of interest to see what options are accepted. For finer control and for modularization, you can use the functions described in the remainder of this section to control titles, axes, legends, and text annotations.

> **NOTE** Some high-level plotting functions include default titles and labels. You can remove them by adding ann=FALSE in the plot() statement or in a separate par() statement.

3.4.1   Titles

Use the title() function to add a title and axis labels to a plot. The format is

```
title(main="main title", sub="subtitle",
    xlab="x-axis label", ylab="y-axis label")
```

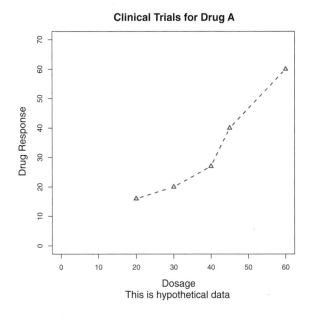

Figure 3.8   Line plot of dose vs. response for drug A with title, subtitle, and modified axes

Graphical parameters (such as text size, font, rotation, and color) can also be specified in `title()`. For example, the following code produces a red title and a blue subtitle, and creates green x and y labels that are 25% smaller than the default text size:

```
title(main="My Title", col.main="red",
      sub="My Subtitle", col.sub="blue",
      xlab="My X label", ylab="My Y label",
      col.lab="green", cex.lab=0.75)
```

The `title()` function is typically used to add information to a plot in which the default title and axis labels have been suppressed via the `ann=FALSE` option.

3.4.2   Axes

Rather than use R's default axes, you can create custom axes with the `axis()` function. The format is

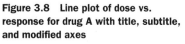

where each parameter is described in table 3.7.

Table 3.7   Axis options

Option	Description
side	Integer indicating the side of the graph on which to draw the axis (1 = bottom, 2 = left, 3 = top, and 4 = right).
at	Numeric vector indicating where tick marks should be drawn.

Table 3.7 Axis options *(continued)*

Option	Description
labels	Character vector of labels to be placed at the tick marks (if NULL, the at values are used).
pos	Coordinate at which the axis line is to be drawn (that is, the value on the other axis where it crosses).
lty	Line type.
col	Line and tick mark color.
las	Specifies that labels are parallel (= 0) or perpendicular (= 2) to the axis.
tck	Length of each tick mark as a fraction of the plotting region (a negative number is outside the graph, a positive number is inside, 0 suppresses ticks, and 1 creates gridlines). The default is –0.01.
(...)	Other graphical parameters.

When creating a custom axis, you should suppress the axis that's automatically generated by the high-level plotting function. The option axes=FALSE suppresses all axes (including all axis frame lines, unless you add the option frame.plot=TRUE). The options xaxt="n" and yaxt="n" suppress the x-axis and y-axis, respectively (leaving the frame lines, without ticks). Listing 3.2 is a somewhat silly and overblown example that demonstrates each of the features we've discussed so far. The resulting graph is presented in figure 3.9.

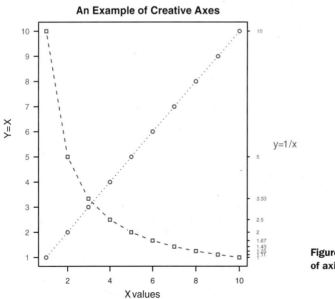

Figure 3.9 A demonstration of axis options

Listing 3.2 An example of custom axes

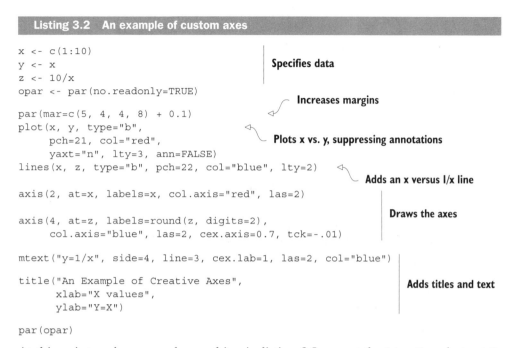

```
x <- c(1:10)
y <- x                                              Specifies data
z <- 10/x
opar <- par(no.readonly=TRUE)
                                                    Increases margins
par(mar=c(5, 4, 4, 8) + 0.1)
plot(x, y, type="b",
     pch=21, col="red",                            Plots x vs. y, suppressing annotations
     yaxt="n", lty=3, ann=FALSE)
lines(x, z, type="b", pch=22, col="blue", lty=2)    Adds an x versus l/x line

axis(2, at=x, labels=x, col.axis="red", las=2)
                                                    Draws the axes
axis(4, at=z, labels=round(z, digits=2),
     col.axis="blue", las=2, cex.axis=0.7, tck=-.01)

mtext("y=1/x", side=4, line=3, cex.lab=1, las=2, col="blue")

title("An Example of Creative Axes",
      xlab="X values",                             Adds titles and text
      ylab="Y=X")
```

```
par(opar)
```

At this point, we've covered everything in listing 3.2 except the line() and mtext() statements. A plot() statement starts a new graph. By using line() instead, you can add new graph elements to an *existing* graph. You'll use it again when you plot the response of drug A and drug B on the same graph in section 3.4.4. The mtext() function is used to add text to the margins of the plot. mtext() is covered in section 3.4.5, and line() is covered more fully in chapter 11.

Minor tick marks

Notice that each of the graphs you've created so far has major tick marks but not minor tick marks. To create minor tick marks, you need the minor.tick() function in the Hmisc package. If you don't already have Hmisc installed, be sure to install it first (see chapter 1, section 1.4.2). You can add minor tick marks with the code

```
library(Hmisc)
minor.tick(nx=n, ny=n, tick.ratio=n)
```

where nx and ny specify the number of intervals into which to divide the area between major tick marks on the x-axis and y-axis, respectively. tick.ratio is the size of the minor tick mark relative to the major tick mark. The current length of the major tick mark can be retrieved using par("tck"). For example, the following statement adds one tick mark between each major tick mark on the x-axis and two tick marks between each major tick mark on the y-axis:

```
minor.tick(nx=2, ny=3, tick.ratio=0.5)
```

These tick marks will be 50% as long as the major tick marks. An example of minor tick marks is given in section 3.4.4 (listing 3.3 and figure 3.10).

3.4.3 *Reference lines*

The `abline()` function is used to add reference lines to a graph. The format is

```
abline(h=yvalues, v=xvalues)
```

Other graphical parameters (such as line type, color, and width) can also be specified in the `abline()` function. For example

```
abline(h=c(1,5,7))
```

adds solid horizontal lines at y = 1, 5, and 7, whereas the code

```
abline(v=seq(1, 10, 2), lty=2, col="blue")
```

adds dashed blue vertical lines at x = 1, 3, 5, 7, and 9. Listing 3.3, in the next section, creates a reference line for the drug example at y = 30. The resulting graph is displayed in figure 3.10 (also in the next section).

3.4.4 *Legend*

When more than one set of data or group is incorporated into a graph, a legend can help you to identify what's being represented by each bar, pie slice, or line. A legend can be added (not surprisingly) with the `legend()` function. The format is

```
legend(location, title, legend, ...)
```

The common options are described in table 3.8.

Table 3.8 Legend options

Option	Description
`location`	There are several ways to indicate the location of the legend. You can give an x,y coordinate for its upper-left corner. You can use `locator(1)`, in which case you use the mouse to indicate the legend's location. You can also use the keyword `bottom`, `bottomleft`, `left`, `topleft`, `top`, `topright`, `right`, `bottomright`, or `center` to place the legend in the graph. If you use one of these keywords, you can also use `inset=` to specify an amount to move the legend into the graph (as a fraction of the plot region).
`title`	Character string for the legend title (optional).
`legend`	Character vector with the labels.
`...`	Other options. If the legend labels colored lines, specify `col=` and a vector of colors. If the legend labels point symbols, specify `pch=` and a vector of point symbols. If the legend labels line width or line style, use `lwd=` or `lty=` and a vector of widths or styles. To create colored boxes for the legend (common in bar, box, and pie charts), use `fill=` and a vector of colors.

Other common legend options include `bty` for box type, `bg` for background color, `cex` for size, and `text.col` for text color. Specifying `horiz=TRUE` sets the legend horizontally rather than vertically. For more on legends, see `help(legend)`. The examples in the help file are particularly informative.

Let's take a look at an example using the drug data (listing 3.3). Again, you'll use a number of the features that we've covered up to this point. The resulting graph is presented in figure 3.10.

Listing 3.3 Comparing drug A and drug B response by dose

```
dose  <- c(20, 30, 40, 45, 60)
drugA <- c(16, 20, 27, 40, 60)
drugB <- c(15, 18, 25, 31, 40)

opar <- par(no.readonly=TRUE)

par(lwd=2, cex=1.5, font.lab=2)          Increases line, text, symbol, and label size

plot(dose, drugA, type="b",
     pch=15, lty=1, col="red", ylim=c(0, 60),
     main="Drug A vs. Drug B",
     xlab="Drug Dosage", ylab="Drug Response")

lines(dose, drugB, type="b",             Generates the graph
      pch=17, lty=2, col="blue")

abline(h=c(30), lwd=1.5, lty=2, col="gray")

library(Hmisc)
minor.tick(nx=3, ny=3, tick.ratio=0.5)   Adds minor tick marks

legend("topleft", inset=.05, title="Drug Type", c("A","B")
       lty=c(1, 2), pch=c(15, 17), col=c("red", "blue"))   Adds a legend

par(opar)
```

Almost all aspects of the graph in figure 3.10 can be modified using the options discussed in this chapter. Additionally, there are many ways to specify the options desired. The final annotation to consider is the addition of text to the plot itself. This topic is covered in the next section.

3.4.5 Text annotations

Text can be added to graphs using the text() and mtext() functions. text() places text within the graph, whereas mtext() places text in one of the four margins. The formats are

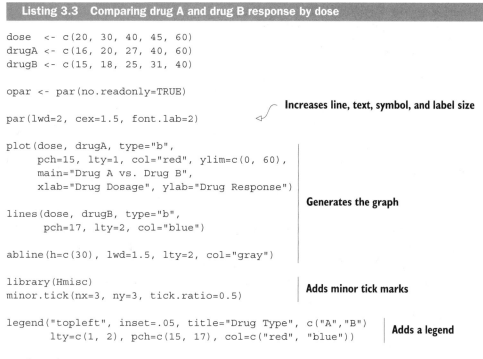

Figure 3.10 An annotated comparison of drug A and drug B

```
text(location, "text to place", pos, ...)
mtext("text to place", side, line=n, ...)
```

and the common options are described in table 3.9. Other common options are cex, col, and font (for size, color, and font style, respectively).

Table 3.9   Options for the `text()` and `mtext()` functions

Option	Description
location	Location can be an x,y coordinate. Alternatively, you can place the text interactively via mouse by specifying location as locator(1).
pos	Position relative to location. 1 = below, 2 = left, 3 = above, and 4 = right. If you specify pos, you can specify offset= as a percentage of character width.
side	Which margin to place text in, where 1 = bottom, 2 = left, 3 = top, and 4 = right. You can specify line= to indicate the line in the margin, starting with 0 (closest to the plot area) and moving out. You can also specify adj=0 for left/bottom alignment or adj=1 for top/right alignment.

The text() function is typically used for labeling points as well as for adding other text annotations. Specify location as a set of x,y coordinates, and specify the text to place as a vector of labels. The x, y, and label vectors should all be the same length. An example is given next, and the resulting graph is shown in figure 3.11:

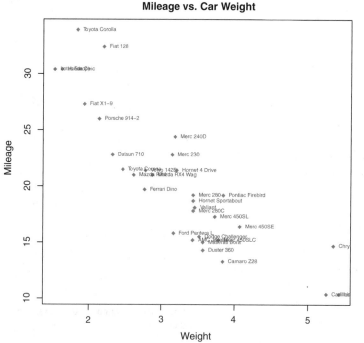

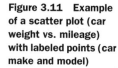

Figure 3.11   Example of a scatter plot (car weight vs. mileage) with labeled points (car make and model)

```
attach(mtcars)
plot(wt, mpg,
     main="Mileage vs. Car Weight",
     xlab="Weight", ylab="Mileage",
     pch=18, col="blue")
text(wt, mpg,
     row.names(mtcars),
     cex=0.6, pos=4, col="red")
detach(mtcars)
```

This example plots car mileage versus car weight for the 32 automobile makes provided in the `mtcars` data frame. The `text()` function is used to add the car make to the right of each data point. The point labels are shrunk by 40% and presented in red.

As a second example, the following code can be used to display font families:

```
opar <- par(no.readonly=TRUE)
par(cex=1.5)
plot(1:7,1:7,type="n")
text(3,3,"Example of default text")
text(4,4,family="mono","Example of mono-spaced text")
text(5,5,family="serif","Example of serif text")
par(opar)
```

The results, produced on a Windows platform, are shown in figure 3.12. Here the `par()` function was used to increase the font size to produce a better display.

The resulting plot will differ from platform to platform, because plain, mono, and serif text are mapped to different font families on different systems. What does it look like on yours?

3.4.6 Math annotations

Finally, you can add mathematical symbols and formulas to a graph using TeX-like rules. See `help(plotmath)` for details and examples. You can also try `demo(plotmath)`

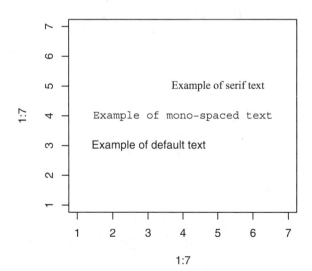

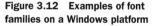

Figure 3.12 Examples of font families on a Windows platform

Arithmetic Operators		Radicals	
x + y	$x+y$	sqrt(x)	$\sqrt{x}$
x – y	$x-y$	sqrt(x, y)	$\sqrt[y]{x}$
x * y	xy	Relations	
x/y	x/y	x == y	$x=y$
x %+-% y	$x\pm y$	x != y	$x\neq y$
x%/%y	$x\div y$	x < y	$x<y$
x %*% y	$x\times y$	x <= y	$x\leq y$
x %.% y	$x\cdot y$	x > y	$x>y$
–x	$-x$	x >= y	$x\geq y$
+x	$+x$	x %~~% y	$x\approx y$
Sub/Superscripts		x %=~% y	$x\cong y$
x[i]	x_i	x %==% y	$x\equiv y$
x^2	x^2	x %prop% y	$x\propto y$
Juxtaposition		Typeface	
x * y	xy	plain(x)	x
paste(x, y, z)	xyz	italic(x)	x
Lists		bold(x)	$\mathbf{x}$
list(x, y, z)	x, y, z	bolditalic(x)	$\boldsymbol{x}$
		underline(x)	$\underline{x}$

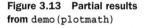

Figure 3.13   Partial results from demo(plotmath)

to see this in action. A portion of the results is presented in figure 3.13. The plotmath() function can be used to add mathematical symbols to titles, axis labels, or text annotations in the body or margins of a graph.

You can often gain greater insight into your data by comparing several graphs at one time. So, we'll end this chapter by looking at ways to combine more than one graph into a single image.

3.5   Combining graphs

R makes it easy to combine several graphs into one overall graph, using either the par() or layout() function. At this point, don't worry about the specific types of graphs being combined; our focus here is on the general methods used to combine them. The creation and interpretation of each graph type are covered in later chapters.

With the par() function, you can include the graphical parameter mfrow=c(nrows, ncols) to create a matrix of nrows × ncols plots that are filled in by row. Alternatively, you can use mfcol=c(nrows, ncols) to fill the matrix by columns.

For example, the following code creates four plots and arranges them into two rows and two columns:

```
attach(mtcars)
opar <- par(no.readonly=TRUE)
par(mfrow=c(2,2))
plot(wt,mpg, main="Scatterplot of wt vs. mpg")
plot(wt,disp, main="Scatterplot of wt vs. disp")
hist(wt, main="Histogram of wt")
boxplot(wt, main="Boxplot of wt")
par(opar)
detach(mtcars)
```

The results are presented in figure 3.14.

As a second example, let's arrange three plots in three rows and one column. Here's the code:

```
attach(mtcars)
opar <- par(no.readonly=TRUE)
par(mfrow=c(3,1))
hist(wt)
hist(mpg)
hist(disp)
par(opar)
detach(mtcars)
```

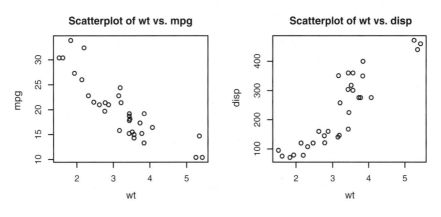
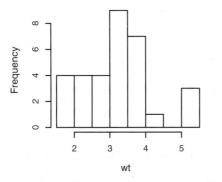

Figure 3.14 Graph combining four figures through `par(mfrow=c(2,2))`

The graph is displayed in figure 3.15. Note that the high-level function `hist()` includes a default title (use `main=""` to suppress it, or `ann=FALSE` to suppress all titles and labels).

The `layout()` function has the form `layout(mat)`, where `mat` is a matrix object specifying the location of the multiple plots to combine. In the following code, one figure is placed in row 1 and two figures are placed in row 2:

```
attach(mtcars)
layout(matrix(c(1,1,2,3), 2, 2, byrow = TRUE))
hist(wt)
hist(mpg)
hist(disp)
detach(mtcars)
```

The resulting graph is presented in figure 3.16.

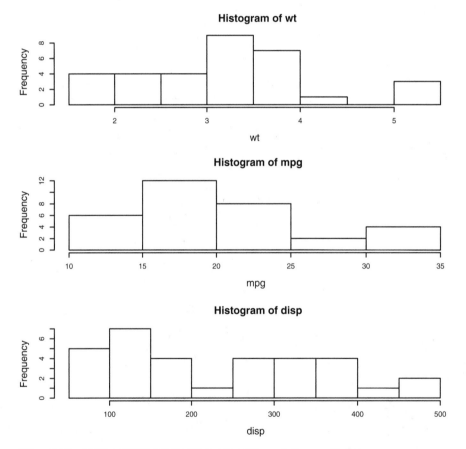

Figure 3.15 Graph combining three figures through `par(mfrow=c(3,1))`

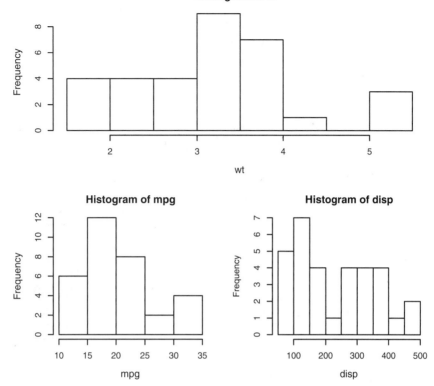

Figure 3.16   Graph combining three figures using the `layout()` **function with default widths**

Optionally, you can include `widths=` and `heights=` options in the `layout()` function to control the size of each figure more precisely. These options have the following form:

- `widths`—A vector of values for the widths of columns
- `heights`—A vector of values for the heights of rows

Relative widths are specified with numeric values. Absolute widths (in centimeters) are specified with the `lcm()` function.

In the following code, one figure is again placed in row 1 and two figures are placed in row 2. But the figure in row 1 is one-third the height of the figures in row 2. Additionally, the figure in the bottom-right cell is one-fourth the width of the figure in the bottom-left cell:

```
attach(mtcars)
layout(matrix(c(1, 1, 2, 3), 2, 2, byrow = TRUE),
       widths=c(3, 1), heights=c(1, 2))
hist(wt)
hist(mpg)
hist(disp)
detach(mtcars)
```

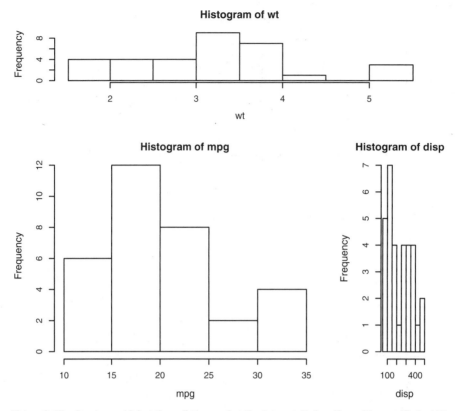

Figure 3.17   Graph combining three figures using the `layout()` function with specified widths

The graph is presented in figure 3.17.

As you can see, `layout()` gives you easy control over both the number and placement of graphs in a final image and the relative sizes of these graphs. See `help(layout)` for more details.

3.5.1   Creating a figure arrangement with fine control

There are times when you want to arrange or superimpose several figures to create a single meaningful plot. Doing so requires fine control over the placement of the figures. You can accomplish this with the `fig=` graphical parameter. In the following listing, two box plots are added to a scatter plot to create a single enhanced graph. The resulting graph is shown in figure 3.18.

Listing 3.4   Fine placement of figures in a graph

```
opar <- par(no.readonly=TRUE)
par(fig=c(0, 0.8, 0, 0.8))
plot(mtcars$wt, mtcars$mpg,
     xlab="Miles Per Gallon",                    Sets up the scatter plot
     ylab="Car Weight")
```

```
par(fig=c(0, 0.8, 0.55, 1), new=TRUE)
boxplot(mtcars$wt, horizontal=TRUE, axes=FALSE)
```
Adds a box plot above

```
par(fig=c(0.65, 1, 0, 0.8), new=TRUE)
boxplot(mtcars$mpg, axes=FALSE)
```
Adds a box plot to the right

```
mtext("Enhanced Scatterplot", side=3, outer=TRUE, line=-3)
```

```
par(opar)
```

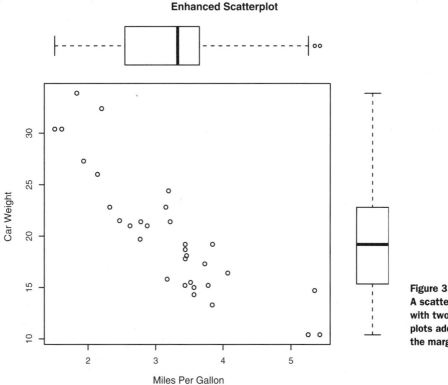

**Figure 3.18
A scatter plot
with two box
plots added to
the margins**

To understand how this graph is created, think of the full graph area as going from (0,0) in the lower-left corner to (1,1) in the upper-right corner. Figure 3.19 will help you visualize this. The format of the `fig=` parameter is a numerical vector of the form `c(x1, x2, y1, y2)`.

The first `fig=` sets up the scatter plot going from 0 to 0.8 on the x-axis and 0 to 0.8 on the y-axis. The top box

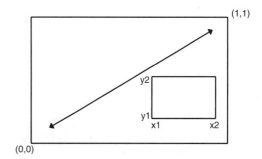

**Figure 3.19 Specifying locations using
the `fig=` graphical parameter**

plot goes from 0 to 0.8 on the x-axis and 0.55 to 1 on the y-axis. The box plot on the right goes from 0.65 to 1 on the x-axis and 0 to 0.8 on the y-axis. `fig=` starts a new plot, so when you add a figure to an existing graph, include the `new=TRUE` option.

I chose 0.55 rather than 0.8 so that the top figure would be pulled closer to the scatter plot. Similarly, I chose 0.65 to pull the box plot on the right closer to the scatter plot. You have to experiment to get the placement correct.

NOTE   The amount of space needed for individual subplots can be device dependent. If you get "Error in plot.new(): figure margins too large," try varying the area given for each portion of the overall graph.

You can use the `fig=` graphical parameter to combine several plots into any arrangement within a single graph. With a little practice, this approach gives you a great deal of flexibility when creating complex visual presentations.

3.6   *Summary*

In this chapter, we reviewed methods for creating graphs and saving them in a variety of formats. The majority of the chapter was concerned with modifying the default graphs produced by R, in order to arrive at more useful or attractive plots. You learned how to modify a graph's axes, fonts, symbols, lines, and colors, as well as how to add titles, subtitles, labels, plotted text, legends, and reference lines. You saw how to specify the size of the graph and margins, and how to combine multiple graphs into a single useful image.

Our focus in this chapter was on general techniques that you can apply to all graphs (with the exception of `ggplot2` graphs, discussed in chapter 19). Later chapters look at specific types of graphs. For example, chapter 6 covers methods for graphing a single variable. Graphing relationships between variables will be described in chapter 11. In chapter 19, we discuss advanced graphic methods, including innovative methods for displaying multivariate data.

In other chapters, we'll discuss methods of visualizing data that are particularly useful for the statistical approaches under consideration. Graphs are a central part of modern data analysis, and I'll endeavor to incorporate them into each of the statistical approaches we discuss.

In the previous chapter, we discussed a range of methods for inputting or importing data into R. Unfortunately, in the real world, your data is rarely usable in the format in which you first get it. The next chapter looks at ways to transform and massage your data into a state that's more useful and conducive to analysis.

Basic data management

In chapter 2, we covered a variety of methods for importing data into R. Unfortunately, getting your data in the rectangular arrangement of a matrix or data frame is only the first step in preparing it for analysis. To paraphrase Captain Kirk in the *Star Trek* episode "A Taste of Armageddon" (and proving my geekiness once and for all), "Data is a messy business—a very, very messy business." In my own work, as much as 60% of the time I spend on data analysis is focused on preparing the data for analysis. I'll go out a limb and say that the same is probably true in one form or another for most real-world data analysts. Let's take a look at an example.

4.1 A working example

One of the topics that I study in my current job is how men and women differ in the ways they lead their organizations. Typical questions might be

71

- Do men and women in management positions differ in the degree to which they defer to superiors?
- Does this vary from country to country, or are these gender differences universal?

One way to address these questions is to have bosses in multiple countries rate their managers on deferential behavior, using questions like the following:

This manager asks my opinion before making personnel decisions.

1	2	3	4	5
strongly disagree	disagree	neither agree nor disagree	agree	strongly agree

The resulting data might resemble that in table 4.1. Each row represents the ratings given to a manager by his or her boss.

Table 4.1　Gender differences in leadership behavior

Manager	Date	Country	Gender	Age	q1	q2	q3	q4	q5
1	10/24/14	US	M	32	5	4	5	5	5
2	10/28/14	US	F	45	3	5	2	5	5
3	10/01/14	UK	F	25	3	5	5	5	2
4	10/12/14	UK	M	39	3	3	4		
5	05/01/14	UK	F	99	2	2	1	2	1

Here, each manager is rated by their boss on five statements (q1 to q5) related to deference to authority. For example, manager 1 is a 32-year-old male working in the US and is rated deferential by his boss, whereas manager 5 is a female of unknown age (99 probably indicates that the information is missing) working in the UK and is rated low on deferential behavior. The Date column captures when the ratings were made.

Although a dataset might have dozens of variables and thousands of observations, we've included only 10 columns and 5 rows to simplify the examples. Additionally, we've limited the number of items pertaining to the managers' deferential behavior to five. In a real-world study, you'd probably use 10–20 such items to improve the reliability and validity of the results. You can create a data frame containing the data in table 4.1 using the following code.

Listing 4.1　Creating the leadership data frame

```
manager <- c(1, 2, 3, 4, 5)
date <- c("10/24/08", "10/28/08", "10/1/08", "10/12/08", "5/1/09")
country <- c("US", "US", "UK", "UK", "UK")
gender <- c("M", "F", "F", "M", "F")
```

```
age <- c(32, 45, 25, 39, 99)
q1 <- c(5, 3, 3, 3, 2)
q2 <- c(4, 5, 5, 3, 2)
q3 <- c(5, 2, 5, 4, 1)
q4 <- c(5, 5, 5, NA, 2)
q5 <- c(5, 5, 2, NA, 1)
leadership <- data.frame(manager, date, country, gender, age,
                         q1, q2, q3, q4, q5, stringsAsFactors=FALSE)
```

In order to address the questions of interest, you must first deal with several data-management issues. Here's a partial list:

- The five ratings (q1 to q5) need to be combined, yielding a single mean deferential score from each manager.
- In surveys, respondents often skip questions. For example, the boss rating manager 4 skipped questions 4 and 5. You need a method of handling incomplete data. You also need to recode values like 99 for age to *missing*.
- There may be hundreds of variables in a dataset, but you may only be interested in a few. To simplify matters, you'll want to create a new dataset with only the variables of interest.
- Past research suggests that leadership behavior may change as a function of the manager's age. To examine this, you may want to recode the current values of age into a new categorical age grouping (for example, young, middle-aged, elder).
- Leadership behavior may change over time. You might want to focus on deferential behavior during the recent global financial crisis. To do so, you may want to limit the study to data gathered during a specific period of time (say, January 1, 2009 to December 31, 2009).

We'll work through each of these issues in this chapter, as well as other basic data-management tasks such as combining and sorting datasets. Then, in chapter 5, we'll look at some advanced topics.

4.2 Creating new variables

In a typical research project, you'll need to create new variables and transform existing ones. This is accomplished with statements of the form

```
variable <- expression
```

A wide array of operators and functions can be included in the `expression` portion of the statement. Table 4.2 lists R's arithmetic operators. Arithmetic operators are used when developing formulas.

Table 4.2 Arithmetic operators

Operator	Description
+	Addition.
–	Subtraction.

Table 4.2 Arithmetic operators *(continued)*

Operator	Description
`*`	Multiplication.
`/`	Division.
`^` or `**`	Exponentiation.
`x%%y`	Modulus (x mod y): for example, `5%%2` is `1`.
`x%/%y`	Integer division: for example, `5%/%2` is `2`.

Let's say you have a data frame named `mydata`, with variables `x1` and `x2`, and you want to create a new variable `sumx` that adds these two variables and a new variable called `meanx` that averages the two variables. If you use the code

```
sumx  <-  x1 + x2
meanx <- (x1 + x2)/2
```

you'll get an error, because R doesn't know that `x1` and `x2` are from the data frame `mydata`. If you use this code instead

```
sumx  <-  mydata$x1 + mydata$x2
meanx <- (mydata$x1 + mydata$x2)/2
```

the statements will succeed but you'll end up with a data frame (`mydata`) and two separate vectors (`sumx` and `meanx`). This probably isn't the result you want. Ultimately, you want to incorporate new variables into the original data frame. The following listing provides three separate ways to accomplish this goal. The one you choose is up to you; the results will be the same.

Listing 4.2 Creating new variables

```
mydata<-data.frame(x1 = c(2, 2, 6, 4),
                   x2 = c(3, 4, 2, 8))

mydata$sumx  <-  mydata$x1 + mydata$x2
mydata$meanx <- (mydata$x1 + mydata$x2)/2

attach(mydata)
mydata$sumx  <-  x1 + x2
mydata$meanx <- (x1 + x2)/2
detach(mydata)

mydata <- transform(mydata,
                    sumx  =  x1 + x2,
                    meanx = (x1 + x2)/2)
```

Personally, I prefer the third method, exemplified by the use of the `transform()` function. It simplifies inclusion of as many new variables as desired and saves the results to the data frame.

4.3   *Recoding variables*

Recoding involves creating new values of a variable conditional on the existing values of the same and/or other variables. For example, you may want to

- Change a continuous variable into a set of categories
- Replace miscoded values with correct values
- Create a pass/fail variable based on a set of cutoff scores

To recode data, you can use one or more of R's logical operators (see table 4.3). Logical operators are expressions that return TRUE or FALSE.

Table 4.3   Logical operators

Operator	Description
<	Less than
<=	Less than or equal to
>	Greater than
>=	Greater than or equal to
==	Exactly equal to
!=	Not equal to
!x	Not x
x | y	x or y
x & y	x and y
isTRUE(x)	Tests whether x is TRUE

Let's say you want to recode the ages of the managers in the leadership dataset from the continuous variable age to the categorical variable agecat (Young, Middle Aged, Elder). First, you must recode the value 99 for age to indicate that the value is missing using code such as

```
leadership$age[leadership$age  == 99]      <- NA
```

The statement variable[condition] <- expression will only make the assignment when condition is TRUE.

Once missing values for age have been specified, you can then use the following code to create the agecat variable:

```
leadership$agecat[leadership$age  > 75]    <- "Elder"
leadership$agecat[leadership$age >= 55 &
                  leadership$age <= 75]    <- "Middle Aged"
leadership$agecat[leadership$age  < 55]    <- "Young"
```

You include the data-frame names in leadership$agecat to ensure that the new variable is saved back to the data frame. (I defined middle aged as 55 to 75 so I won't feel so old.) Note that if you hadn't recoded 99 as *missing* for age first, manager 5 would've erroneously been given the value "Elder" for `agecat`.

This code can be written more compactly as follows:

```
leadership <- within(leadership,{
                 agecat <- NA
                 agecat[age > 75]                <- "Elder"
                 agecat[age >= 55 & age <= 75] <- "Middle Aged"
                 agecat[age < 55]                <- "Young" })
```

The `within()` function is similar to the `with()` function (section 2.2.4), but it allows you to modify the data frame. First the variable `agecat` is created and set to *missing* for each row of the data frame. Then the remaining statements within the braces are executed in order. Remember that `agecat` is a character variable; you're likely to want to turn it into an ordered factor, as explained in section 2.2.5.

Several packages offer useful recoding functions; in particular, the car package's `recode()` function recodes numeric and character vectors and factors very simply. The package `doBy` offers `recodeVar()`, another popular function. Finally, R ships with `cut()`, which allows you to divide the range of a numeric variable into intervals, returning a factor.

4.4   Renaming variables

If you're not happy with your variable names, you can change them interactively or programmatically. Let's say you want to change the variable `manager` to `managerID` and `date` to `testDate`. You can use the following statement to invoke an interactive editor:

```
fix(leadership)
```

Then you click the variable names and rename them in the dialogs that are presented (see figure 4.1).

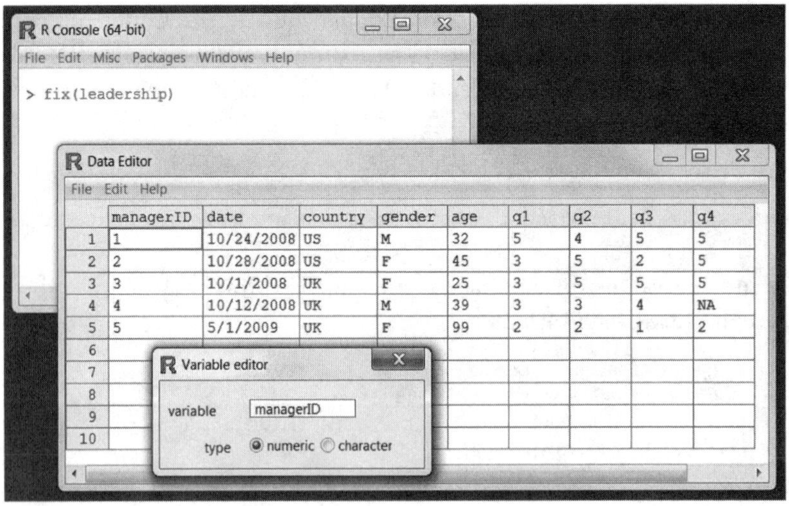

Figure 4.1   **Renaming variables interactively using the `fix()` function**

Programmatically, you can rename variables via the names() function. For example, this statement

```
names(leadership)[2] <- "testDate"
```

renames date to testDate as demonstrated in the following code:

```
> names(leadership)
 [1] "manager" "date"     "country" "gender"  "age"     "q1"      "q2"
 [8] "q3"      "q4"       "q5"
> names(leadership)[2] <- "testDate"
> leadership
  manager testDate country gender age q1 q2 q3 q4 q5
1       1 10/24/08      US      M  32  5  4  5  5  5
2       2 10/28/08      US      F  45  3  5  2  5  5
3       3 10/1/08       UK      F  25  3  5  5  5  2
4       4 10/12/08      UK      M  39  3  3  4 NA NA
5       5 5/1/09        UK      F  99  2  2  1  2  1
```

In a similar fashion, the statement

```
names(leadership)[6:10] <- c("item1", "item2", "item3", "item4", "item5")
```

renames q1 through q5 to item1 through item5.

Finally, the plyr package has a rename() function that's useful for altering the names of variables. The plyr package isn't installed by default, so you'll need to install it on first use using the install.packages("plyr") command.

The format of the rename() function is

```
rename(dataframe, c(oldname="newname", oldname="newname",...))
```

Here's an example with the leadership data:

```
library(plyr)
leadership <- rename(leadership,
                c(manager="managerID", date="testDate"))
```

The plyr package has a powerful set of functions for manipulating datasets. You can learn more about it at http://had.co.nz/plyr.

4.5   *Missing values*

In a project of any size, data is likely to be incomplete because of missed questions, faulty equipment, or improperly coded data. In R, missing values are represented by the symbol NA (not available). Unlike programs such as SAS, R uses the same missing-value symbol for character and numeric data.

R provides a number of functions for identifying observations that contain missing values. The function is.na() allows you to test for the presence of missing values. Assume that you have this vector:

```
y <- c(1, 2, 3, NA)
```

Then the following function returns c(FALSE, FALSE, FALSE, TRUE):

```
is.na(y)
```

Notice how the is.na() function works on an object. It returns an object of the same size, with the entries replaced by TRUE if the element is a missing value or FALSE if the element isn't a missing value. The following listing applies this to the leadership example.

Listing 4.3   Applying the is.na() function

```
> is.na(leadership[,6:10])
        q1    q2    q3    q4    q5
[1,] FALSE FALSE FALSE FALSE FALSE
[2,] FALSE FALSE FALSE FALSE FALSE
[3,] FALSE FALSE FALSE FALSE FALSE
[4,] FALSE FALSE FALSE  TRUE  TRUE
[5,] FALSE FALSE FALSE FALSE FALSE
```

Here, leadership[,6:10] limits the data frame to columns 6 to 10, and is.na() identifies which values are missing.

There are two important things to keep in mind when you're working with missing values in R. First, missing values are considered noncomparable, even to themselves. This means you can't use comparison operators to test for the presence of missing values. For example, the logical test myvar == NA is never TRUE. Instead, you have to use missing-value functions like is.na() to identify the missing values in R data objects.

Second, R doesn't represent infinite or impossible values as missing values. Again, this is different than the way other programs like SAS handle such data. Positive and negative infinity are represented by the symbols Inf and –Inf, respectively. Thus 5/0 returns Inf. Impossible values (for example, sin(Inf)) are represented by the symbol NaN (not a number). To identify these values, you need to use is.infinite() or is.nan().

4.5.1   Recoding values to missing

As demonstrated in section 4.3, you can use assignments to recode values to *missing*. In the leadership example, missing age values are coded as 99. Before analyzing this dataset, you must let R know that the value 99 means *missing* in this case (otherwise, the mean age for this sample of bosses will be way off!). You can accomplish this by recoding the variable:

```
leadership$age[leadership$age == 99] <- NA
```

Any value of age that's equal to 99 is changed to NA. Be sure that any missing data is properly coded as missing before you analyze the data, or the results will be meaningless.

4.5.2   Excluding missing values from analyses

Once you've identified missing values, you need to eliminate them in some way before analyzing your data further. The reason is that arithmetic expressions and functions that contain missing values yield missing values. For example, consider the following code:

```
x <- c(1, 2, NA, 3)
y <- x[1] + x[2] + x[3] + x[4]
z <- sum(x)
```

Both y and z will be NA (missing) because the third element of x is missing.

Luckily, most numeric functions have an na.rm=TRUE option that removes missing values prior to calculations and applies the function to the remaining values:

```
x <- c(1, 2, NA, 3)
y <- sum(x, na.rm=TRUE)
```

Here, y is equal to 6.

When using a function with incomplete data, be sure to check how that function handles missing data by looking at its online help (for example, help(sum)). The sum() function is only one of many functions we'll consider in chapter 5. Functions allow you to transform data with flexibility and ease.

You can remove *any* observation with missing data by using the na.omit() function. na.omit() deletes any rows with missing data. Let's apply this to the leadership dataset in the following listing.

Listing 4.4   Using `na.omit()` to delete incomplete observations

```
> leadership
  manager      date country gender age q1 q2 q3 q4 q5
1       1 10/24/08      US        M  32  5  4  5  5  5
2       2 10/28/08      US        F  40  3  5  2  5  5
3       3 10/01/08      UK        F  25  3  5  5  5  2
4       4 10/12/08      UK        M  39  3  3  4 NA NA
5       5 05/01/09      UK        F  NA  2  2  1  2  1
```
◁ **Data frame with missing data**

```
> newdata <- na.omit(leadership)
> newdata
  manager      date country gender age q1 q2 q3 q4 q5
1       1 10/24/08      US        M  32  5  4  5  5  5
2       2 10/28/08      US        F  40  3  5  2  5  5
3       3 10/01/08      UK        F  25  3  5  5  5  2
```
◁ **Data frame with complete cases only**

Any rows containing missing data are deleted from leadership before the results are saved to newdata.

Deleting all observations with missing data (called *listwise deletion*) is one of several methods of handling incomplete datasets. If there are only a few missing values or they're concentrated in a small number of observations, listwise deletion can provide a good solution to the missing-values problem. But if missing values are spread throughout the data or there's a great deal of missing data in a small number of variables, listwise deletion can exclude a substantial percentage of your data. We'll explore several more sophisticated methods of dealing with missing values in chapter 18. Next, let's look at dates.

4.6   *Date values*

Dates are typically entered into R as character strings and then translated into date variables that are stored numerically. The function as.Date() is used to make this translation. The syntax is as.Date(x, "input_format"), where x is the character data and input_format gives the appropriate format for reading the date (see table 4.4).

Table 4.4 Date formats

Symbol	Meaning	Example
%d	Day as a number (0–31)	01–31
%a	Abbreviated weekday	Mon
%A	Unabbreviated weekday	Monday
%m	Month (00–12)	00–12
%b	Abbreviated month	Jan
%B	Unabbreviated month	January
%y	Two-digit year	07
%Y	Four-digit year	2007

The default format for inputting dates is yyyy-mm-dd. The statement

```
mydates <- as.Date(c("2007-06-22", "2004-02-13"))
```

converts the character data to dates using this default format. In contrast,

```
strDates <- c("01/05/1965", "08/16/1975")
dates <- as.Date(strDates, "%m/%d/%Y")
```

reads the data using a mm/dd/yyyy format.

In the leadership dataset, date is coded as a character variable in mm/dd/yy format. Therefore:

```
myformat <- "%m/%d/%y"
leadership$date <- as.Date(leadership$date, myformat)
```

uses the specified format to read the character variable and replace it in the data frame as a date variable. Once the variable is in date format, you can analyze and plot the dates using the wide range of analytic techniques covered in later chapters.

Two functions are especially useful for time-stamping data. Sys.Date() returns today's date, and date() returns the current date and time. As I write this, it's November 27, 2014 at 1:21 pm. So executing those functions produces

```
> Sys.Date()
[1] "2014-11-27"
> date()
[1] "Fri Nov 27 13:21:54 2014"
```

You can use the format(x, format="output_format") function to output dates in a specified format and to extract portions of dates:

```
> today <- Sys.Date()
> format(today, format="%B %d %Y")
[1] "November 27 2014"
> format(today, format="%A")
[1] "Thursday"
```

The format() function takes an argument (a date in this case) and applies an output format (in this case, assembled from the symbols in table 4.4). The important result here is that there are only two more days until the weekend!

When R stores dates internally, they're represented as the number of days since January 1, 1970, with negative values for earlier dates. That means you can perform arithmetic operations on them. For example,

```
> startdate <- as.Date("2004-02-13")
> enddate   <- as.Date("2011-01-22")
> days      <- enddate - startdate
> days
Time difference of 2535 days
```

displays the number of days between February 13, 2004 and January 22, 2011.

Finally, you can also use the function difftime() to calculate a time interval and express it as seconds, minutes, hours, days, or weeks. Let's assume that I was born on October 12, 1956. How old am I?

```
> today <- Sys.Date()
> dob   <- as.Date("1956-10-12")
> difftime(today, dob, units="weeks")
Time difference of 3033 weeks
```

Apparently I am 3,033 weeks old. Who knew? Final test: On which day of the week was I born?

4.6.1 Converting dates to character variables

You can also convert date variables to character variables. Date values can be converted to character values using the as.character() function:

```
strDates <- as.character(dates)
```

The conversion allows you to apply a range of character functions to the data values (subsetting, replacement, concatenation, and so on). We'll cover character functions in detail in chapter 5.

4.6.2 Going further

To learn more about converting character data to dates, look at help(as.Date) and help(strftime). To learn more about formatting dates and times, see help(ISOdatetime). The lubridate package contains a number of functions that simplify working with dates, including functions to identify and parse date-time data, extract date-time components (for example, years, months, days, and so on), and perform arithmetic calculations on date-times. If you need to do complex calculations with dates, the timeDate package can also help. It provides a myriad of functions for dealing with dates, can handle multiple time zones at once, and provides sophisticated calendar manipulations that recognize business days, weekends, and holidays.

4.7 Type conversions

In the previous section, we discussed how to convert character data to date values, and vice versa. R provides a set of functions to identify an object's data type and convert it to a different data type.

Type conversions in R work in a similar fashion to those in other statistical programming languages. For example, adding a character string to a numeric vector converts all the elements in the vector to character values. You can use the functions listed in table 4.5 to test for a data type and to convert it to a given type.

Table 4.5   Type-conversion functions

Test	Convert
is.numeric()	as.numeric()
is.character()	as.character()
is.vector()	as.vector()
is.matrix()	as.matrix()
is.data.frame()	as.data.frame()
is.factor()	as.factor()
is.logical()	as.logical()

Functions of the form is.datatype() return TRUE or FALSE, whereas as.datatype() converts the argument to that type. The following listing provides an example.

Listing 4.5   Converting from one data type to another

```
> a <- c(1,2,3)
> a
[1] 1 2 3
> is.numeric(a)
[1] TRUE
> is.vector(a)
[1] TRUE
> a <- as.character(a)
> a
[1] "1" "2" "3"
> is.numeric(a)
[1] FALSE
> is.vector(a)
[1] TRUE
> is.character(a)
[1] TRUE
```

When combined with the flow controls (such as if-then) that we'll discuss in chapter 5, the is.datatype() function can be a powerful tool, allowing you to handle data in different ways depending on its type. Additionally, some R functions require data of a specific type (character or numeric, matrix or data frame), and as.datatype() lets you transform your data into the format required prior to analyses.

4.8   *Sorting data*

Sometimes, viewing a dataset in a sorted order can tell you quite a bit about the data. For example, which managers are most deferential? To sort a data frame in R, you use the `order()` function. By default, the sorting order is ascending. Prepend the sorting variable with a minus sign to indicate descending order. The following examples illustrate sorting with the leadership data frame.

The statement

```
newdata <- leadership[order(leadership$age),]
```

creates a new dataset containing rows sorted from youngest manager to oldest manager. The statement

```
attach(leadership)
newdata <- leadership[order(gender, age),]
detach(leadership)
```

sorts the rows into female followed by male, and youngest to oldest within each gender. Finally,

```
attach(leadership)
newdata <-leadership[order(gender, -age),]
detach(leadership)
```

sorts the rows by gender, and then from oldest to youngest manager within each gender.

4.9 Merging datasets

If your data exists in multiple locations, you'll need to combine it before moving forward. This section shows you how to add columns (variables) and rows (observations) to a data frame.

4.9.1 Adding columns to a data frame

To merge two data frames (datasets) horizontally, you use the `merge()` function. In most cases, two data frames are joined by one or more common key variables (that is, an inner join). For example,

```
total <- merge(dataframeA, dataframeB, by="ID")
```

merges `dataframeA` and `dataframeB` by ID. Similarly,

```
total <- merge(dataframeA, dataframeB, by=c("ID","Country"))
```

merges the two data frames by ID and Country. Horizontal joins like this are typically used to add variables to a data frame.

> **Horizontal concatenation with cbind()**
>
> If you're joining two matrices or data frames horizontally and don't need to specify a common key, you can use the `cbind()` function:
>
> ```
> total <- cbind(A, B)
> ```
>
> This function horizontally concatenates objects A and B. For the function to work properly, each object must have the same number of rows and be sorted in the same order.

4.9.2 Adding rows to a data frame

To join two data frames (datasets) vertically, use the `rbind()` function:

```
total <- rbind(dataframeA, dataframeB)
```

The two data frames must have the same variables, but they don't have to be in the same order. If `dataframeA` has variables that `dataframeB` doesn't, then before joining them, do one of the following:

- Delete the extra variables in `dataframeA`.
- Create the additional variables in `dataframeB`, and set them to `NA` (missing).

Vertical concatenation is typically used to add observations to a data frame.

4.10 Subsetting datasets

R has powerful indexing features for accessing the elements of an object. These features can be used to select and exclude variables, observations, or both. The following sections demonstrate several methods for keeping or deleting variables and observations.

4.10.1 Selecting (keeping) variables

It's a common practice to create a new dataset from a limited number of variables chosen from a larger dataset. In chapter 2, you saw that the elements of a data frame are accessed using the notation `dataframe[row indices, column indices]`. You can use this to select variables. For example,

```
newdata <- leadership[, c(6:10)]
```

selects variables q1, q2, q3, q4, and q5 from the `leadership` data frame and saves them to the data frame `newdata`. Leaving the row indices blank (,) selects all the rows by default.

The statements

```
myvars <- c("q1", "q2", "q3", "q4", "q5")
newdata <-leadership[myvars]
```

accomplish the same variable selection. Here, variable names (in quotes) are entered as column indices, thereby selecting the same columns.

Finally, you could use

```
myvars <- paste("q", 1:5, sep="")
newdata <- leadership[myvars]
```

This example uses the `paste()` function to create the same character vector as in the previous example. `paste()` will be covered in chapter 5.

4.10.2 Excluding (dropping) variables

There are many reasons to exclude variables. For example, if a variable has many missing values, you may want to drop it prior to further analyses. Let's look at some methods of excluding variables.

You can exclude variables q3 and q4 with these statements:

```
myvars <- names(leadership) %in% c("q3", "q4")
newdata <- leadership[!myvars]
```

In order to understand why this works, you need to break it down:

1 names(leadership) produces a character vector containing the variable names:

```
c("managerID","testDate","country","gender","age","q1","q2","q3","q4","q5")
```

2 names(leadership) %in% c("q3", "q4") returns a logical vector with TRUE for each element in names(leadership) that matches q3 or q4 and FALSE otherwise:

```
c(FALSE, FALSE, FALSE, FALSE, FALSE, FALSE, FALSE, TRUE, TRUE, FALSE)
```

3 The not (!) operator reverses the logical values:

```
c(TRUE, TRUE, TRUE, TRUE, TRUE, TRUE, TRUE, FALSE, FALSE, TRUE)
```

4 leadership[c(TRUE, TRUE, TRUE, TRUE, TRUE, TRUE, TRUE, FALSE, FALSE, TRUE)] selects columns with TRUE logical values, so q3 and q4 are excluded.

Knowing that q3 and q4 are the eighth and ninth variables, you can exclude them with the following statement:

```
newdata <- leadership[c(-8,-9)]
```

This works because prepending a column index with a minus sign (-) excludes that column.

Finally, the same deletion can be accomplished via

```
leadership$q3 <- leadership$q4 <- NULL
```

Here you set columns q3 and q4 to undefined (NULL). Note that NULL isn't the same as NA (missing).

Dropping variables is the converse of keeping variables. The choice depends on which is easier to code. If there are many variables to drop, it may be easier to keep the ones that remain, or vice versa.

4.10.3 Selecting observations

Selecting or excluding observations (rows) is typically a key aspect of successful data preparation and analysis. Several examples are given in the following listing.

Listing 4.6 Selecting observations

Asks for rows 1 through 3 (the first three observations) ⟶

```
newdata <- leadership[1:3,]

newdata <- leadership[leadership$gender=="M" &
                      leadership$age > 30,]              ❶ Selects all
                                                           men over 30

attach(leadership)                                       Uses attach() so you don't have
newdata <- leadership[gender=='M' & age > 30,]           to prepend variable names with
detach(leadership)                                       data-frame names
```

Each of these examples provides the row indices and leaves the column indices blank (therefore choosing all columns). Let's break down the line of code at ❶ in order to understand it:

1 The logical comparison `leadership$gender=="M"` produces the vector `c(TRUE, FALSE, FALSE, TRUE, FALSE)`.

2 The logical comparison `leadership$age > 30` produces the vector `c(TRUE, TRUE, FALSE, TRUE, TRUE)`.

3 The logical comparison `c(TRUE, FALSE, FALSE, TRUE, FALSE) & c(TRUE, TRUE, FALSE, TRUE, TRUE)` produces the vector `c(TRUE, FALSE, FALSE, TRUE, FALSE)`.

4 `leadership[c(TRUE, FALSE, FALSE, TRUE, FALSE),]` selects the first and fourth observations from the data frame (when the row index is TRUE, the row is included; when it's FALSE, the row is excluded). This meets the selection criteria (men over 30).

At the beginning of this chapter, I suggested that you might want to limit your analyses to observations collected between January 1, 2009 and December 31, 2009. How can you do this? Here's one solution:

Converts the date values read in originally as character values to date values using the format mm/dd/yy

```
leadership$date <- as.Date(leadership$date, "%m/%d/%y")
```

Creates starting date

```
startdate <- as.Date("2009-01-01")
enddate   <- as.Date("2009-10-31")
```

Creates ending date

```
newdata <- leadership[which(leadership$date >= startdate &
               leadership$date <= enddate),]
```

Selects cases meeting your desired criteria, as in the previous example

Note that the default for the `as.Date()` function is yyyy-mm-dd, so you don't have to supply it here.

4.10.4 *The subset() function*

The examples in the previous two sections are important because they help describe the ways in which logical vectors and comparison operators are interpreted in R. Understanding how these examples work will help you to interpret R code in general. Now that you've done things the hard way, let's look at a shortcut.

The `subset()` function is probably the easiest way to select variables and observations. Here are two examples:

```
newdata <- subset(leadership, age >= 35 | age < 24,
               select=c(q1, q2, q3, q4))
```

Selects all rows that have a value of age greater than or equal to 35 or less than 24. Keeps variables q1 through q4.

```
newdata <- subset(leadership, gender=="M" & age > 25,
               select=gender:q4)
```

Selects all men over the age of 25, and keeps variables gender through q4 (gender, q4, and all columns between them)

You saw the colon operator `from:to` in chapter 2. Here, it provides all variables in a data frame between the `from` variable and the `to` variable, inclusive.

4.10.5 *Random samples*

Sampling from larger datasets is a common practice in data mining and machine learning. For example, you may want to select two random samples, creating a predictive model from one and validating its effectiveness on the other. The `sample()` function enables you to take a random sample (with or without replacement) of size *n* from a dataset.

You could take a random sample of size 3 from the leadership dataset using the following statement:

```
mysample <- leadership[sample(1:nrow(leadership), 3, replace=FALSE),]
```

The first argument to `sample()` is a vector of elements to choose from. Here, the vector is 1 to the number of observations in the data frame. The second argument is the number of elements to be selected, and the third argument indicates sampling without replacement. `sample()` returns the randomly sampled elements, which are then used to select rows from the data frame.

R has extensive facilities for sampling, including drawing and calibrating survey samples (see the `sampling` package) and analyzing complex survey data (see the `survey` package). Other methods that rely on sampling, including bootstrapping and resampling statistics, are described in chapter 12.

4.11 *Using SQL statements to manipulate data frames*

Until now, you've been using R statements to manipulate data. But many data analysts come to R well versed in Structured Query Language (SQL). It would be a shame to lose all that accumulated knowledge. Therefore, before we end, let me briefly mention the existence of the `sqldf` package. (If you're unfamiliar with SQL, please feel free to skip this section.)

After downloading and installing the package (`install.packages("sqldf")`), you can use the `sqldf()` function to apply SQL `SELECT` statements to data frames. Two examples are given in the following listing.

Listing 4.7　Using SQL statements to manipulate data frames

> Selects all variables (columns) from data frame mtcars, keeps only automobiles
> (rows) with one carburetor (carb), sorts in ascending order by mpg, and saves
> the results as the data frame newdf. The option row.names=TRUE carries the
> row names from the original data frame over to the new one.

```
> library(sqldf)
> newdf <- sqldf("select * from mtcars where carb=1 order by mpg",
            row.names=TRUE)
> newdf
                mpg cyl  disp  hp drat   wt qsec vs am gear carb
Valiant        18.1   6 225.0 105 2.76 3.46 20.2  1  0    3    1
Hornet 4 Drive 21.4   6 258.0 110 3.08 3.21 19.4  1  0    3    1
```

```
Toyota Corona   21.5    4 120.1  97 3.70 2.46 20.0  1  0    3    1
Datsun 710      22.8    4 108.0  93 3.85 2.32 18.6  1  1    4    1
Fiat X1-9       27.3    4  79.0  66 4.08 1.94 18.9  1  1    4    1
Fiat 128        32.4    4  78.7  66 4.08 2.20 19.5  1  1    4    1
Toyota Corolla 33.9     4  71.1  65 4.22 1.83 19.9  1  1    4    1

> sqldf("select avg(mpg) as avg_mpg, avg(disp) as avg_disp, gear
            from mtcars where cyl in (4, 6) group by gear")
  avg_mpg avg_disp gear
1   20.3     201    3
2   24.5     123    4
3   25.4     120    5
```

**Prints the mean mpg and disp within
each level of gear for automobiles
with four or six cylinders (cyl)**

Experienced SQL users will find the `sqldf` package a useful adjunct to data management in R. See the project home page (http://code.google.com/p/sqldf/) for more details.

4.12   *Summary*

This chapter covered a lot of ground. First we examined how R stores missing and date values and explored various ways of handling them. Next, you learned how to determine the data type of an object and how to convert it to other types. Simple formulas were used to create new variables and recode existing variables. You learned how to sort data, rename variables, and merge data with other datasets both horizontally (adding variables) and vertically (adding observations). Finally, we discussed how to keep or drop variables and how to select observations based on a variety of criteria.

In the next chapter, we'll look at the myriad of arithmetic, character, and statistical functions that R makes available for creating and transforming variables. After exploring ways of controlling program flow, you'll see how to write your own functions. We'll also explore how you can use these functions to aggregate and summarize your data.

By the end of chapter 5, you'll have most of the tools necessary to manage complex datasets. (And you'll be the envy of data analysts everywhere!)

Advanced data management 5

This chapter covers

- Mathematical and statistical functions
- Character functions
- Looping and conditional execution
- User-written functions
- Ways to aggregate and reshape data

In chapter 4, we reviewed the basic techniques used for managing datasets in R. In this chapter, we'll focus on advanced topics. The chapter is divided into three basic parts. In the first part, we'll take a whirlwind tour of R's many functions for mathematical, statistical, and character manipulation. To give this section relevance, we begin with a data-management problem that can be solved using these functions. After covering the functions themselves, we'll look at one possible solution to the data-management problem.

Next, we cover how to write your own functions to accomplish data-management and -analysis tasks. First, we'll explore ways of controlling program flow, including looping and conditional statement execution. Then we'll investigate the structure of user-written functions and how to invoke them once created.

Then, we'll look at ways of aggregating and summarizing data, along with methods of reshaping and restructuring datasets. When aggregating data, you can specify the use of any appropriate built-in or user-written function to accomplish the summarization, so the topics you learn in the first two parts of the chapter will provide a real benefit.

5.1   A data-management challenge

To begin our discussion of numerical and character functions, let's consider a data-management problem. A group of students have taken exams in math, science, and English. You want to combine these scores in order to determine a single perfor-mance indicator for each student. Additionally, you want to assign an A to the top 20% of students, a B to the next 20%, and so on. Finally, you want to sort the students alphabetically. The data are presented in table 5.1.

Table 5.1   Student exam data

Student	Math	Science	English
John Davis	502	95	25
Angela Williams	600	99	22
Bullwinkle Moose	412	80	18
David Jones	358	82	15
Janice Markhammer	495	75	20
Cheryl Cushing	512	85	28
Reuven Ytzrhak	410	80	15
Greg Knox	625	95	30
Joel England	573	89	27
Mary Rayburn	522	86	18

Looking at this dataset, several obstacles are immediately evident. First, scores on the three exams aren't comparable. They have widely different means and standard devia-tions, so averaging them doesn't make sense. You must transform the exam scores into comparable units before combining them. Second, you'll need a method of determin-ing a student's percentile rank on this score in order to assign a grade. Third, there's a single field for names, complicating the task of sorting students. You'll need to split their names into first name and last name in order to sort them properly.

Each of these tasks can be accomplished through the judicious use of R's numeri-cal and character functions. After working through the functions described in the next section, we'll consider a possible solution to this data-management challenge.

5.2   *Numerical and character functions*

In this section, we'll review functions in R that can be used as the basic building blocks for manipulating data. They can be divided into numerical (mathematical, statistical, probability) and character functions. After we review each type, I'll show you how to apply functions to the columns (variables) and rows (observations) of matrices and data frames (see section 5.2.6).

5.2.1   *Mathematical functions*

Table 5.2 lists common mathematical functions along with short examples.

Table 5.2   Mathematical functions

Function	Description
abs(x)	Absolute value abs(-4) returns 4.
sqrt(x)	Square root sqrt(25) returns 5. This is the same as 25^(0.5).
ceiling(x)	Smallest integer not less than x ceiling(3.475) returns 4.
floor(x)	Largest integer not greater than x floor(3.475) returns 3.
trunc(x)	Integer formed by truncating values in x toward 0 trunc(5.99) returns 5.
round(x, digits=n)	Rounds x to the specified number of decimal places round(3.475, digits=2) returns 3.48.
signif(x, digits=n)	Rounds x to the specified number of significant digits signif(3.475, digits=2) returns 3.5.
cos(x), sin(x), tan(x)	Cosine, sine, and tangent cos(2) returns –0.416.
acos(x), asin(x), atan(x)	Arc-cosine, arc-sine, and arc-tangent acos(-0.416) returns 2.
cosh(x), sinh(x), tanh(x)	Hyperbolic cosine, sine, and tangent sinh(2) returns 3.627.
acosh(x), asinh(x), atanh(x)	Hyperbolic arc-cosine, arc-sine, and arc-tangent asinh(3.627) returns 2.
log(x,base=n) log(x) log10(x)	Logarithm of x to the base n For convenience: • log(x) is the natural logarithm. • log10(x) is the common logarithm. • log(10) returns 2.3026. • log10(10) returns 1.
exp(x)	Exponential function exp(2.3026) returns 10.

Data transformation is one of the primary uses for these functions. For example, you often transform positively skewed variables such as income to a log scale before further analyses. Mathematical functions are also used as components in formulas, in plotting functions (for example, x versus sin(x)), and in formatting numerical values prior to printing.

The examples in table 5.2 apply mathematical functions to *scalars* (individual numbers). When these functions are applied to numeric vectors, matrices, or data frames, they operate on each individual value. For example, sqrt(c(4, 16, 25)) returns c(2, 4, 5).

5.2.2 *Statistical functions*

Common statistical functions are presented in table 5.3. Many of these functions have optional parameters that affect the outcome. For example,

```
y <- mean(x)
```

provides the arithmetic mean of the elements in object x, and

```
z <- mean(x, trim = 0.05, na.rm=TRUE)
```

provides the trimmed mean, dropping the highest and lowest 5% of scores and any missing values. Use the help() function to learn more about each function and its arguments.

Table 5.3 Statistical functions

Function	Description
mean(*x*)	Mean mean(c(1,2,3,4)) returns 2.5.
median(*x*)	Median median(c(1,2,3,4)) returns 2.5.
sd(*x*)	Standard deviation sd(c(1,2,3,4)) returns 1.29.
var(*x*)	Variance var(c(1,2,3,4)) returns 1.67.
mad(*x*)	Median absolute deviation mad(c(1,2,3,4)) returns 1.48.
quantile(*x*, probs)	Quantiles where *x* is the numeric vector, where quantiles are desired and probs is a numeric vector with probabilities in [0,1] # 30th and 84th percentiles of x y <- quantile(x, c(.3,.84))
range(*x*)	Range x <- c(1,2,3,4) range(x) returns c(1,4). diff(range(x)) returns 3.
sum(*x*)	Sum sum(c(1,2,3,4)) returns 10.

Table 5.3 Statistical functions

Function	Description
diff(*x*, lag=*n*)	Lagged differences, with `lag` indicating which lag to use. The default lag is 1. x<- c(1, 5, 23, 29) diff(x) returns c(4, 18, 6).
min(*x*)	Minimum min(c(1,2,3,4)) returns 1.
max(*x*)	Maximum max(c(1,2,3,4)) returns 4.
scale(*x*, center=TRUE, scale=TRUE)	Column center (center=TRUE) or standardize (center=TRUE, scale=TRUE) data object *x*. An example is given in listing 5.6.

To see these functions in action, look at the next listing. This example demonstrates two ways to calculate the mean and standard deviation of a vector of numbers.

Listing 5.1 Calculating the mean and standard deviation

```
> x <- c(1,2,3,4,5,6,7,8)

> mean(x)
[1] 4.5                          Short way
> sd(x)
[1] 2.449490

> n <- length(x)
> meanx <- sum(x)/n
> css <- sum((x - meanx)^2)
> sdx <- sqrt(css / (n-1))        Long way
> meanx
[1] 4.5
> sdx
[1] 2.449490
```

It's instructive to view how the corrected sum of squares (css) is calculated in the second approach:

1. x equals c(1, 2, 3, 4, 5, 6, 7, 8), and mean x equals 4.5 (length(x) returns the number of elements in x).

2. (x – meanx) subtracts 4.5 from each element of x, resulting in

   c(-3.5, -2.5, -1.5, -0.5, 0.5, 1.5, 2.5, 3.5)

3. (x – meanx)^2 squares each element of (x - meanx), resulting in

   c(12.25, 6.25, 2.25, 0.25, 0.25, 2.25, 6.25, 12.25)

4. sum((x - meanx)^2) sums each of the elements of (x - meanx)^2, resulting in 42.

Writing formulas in R has much in common with matrix-manipulation languages such as MATLAB (we'll look more specifically at solving matrix algebra problems in appendix D).

Standardizing data

By default, the `scale()` function standardizes the specified columns of a matrix or data frame to a mean of 0 and a standard deviation of 1:

```
newdata <- scale(mydata)
```

To standardize each column to an arbitrary mean and standard deviation, you can use code similar to the following

```
newdata <- scale(mydata)*SD + M
```

where `M` is the desired mean and `SD` is the desired standard deviation. Using the `scale()` function on non-numeric columns produces an error. To standardize a specific column rather than an entire matrix or data frame, you can use code such as this:

```
newdata <- transform(mydata, myvar = scale(myvar)*10+50)
```

This code standardizes the variable `myvar` to a mean of 50 and standard deviation of 10. You'll use the `scale()` function in the solution to the data-management challenge in section 5.3.

5.2.3   *Probability functions*

You may wonder why probability functions aren't listed with the statistical functions (it was really bothering you, wasn't it?). Although probability functions are statistical by definition, they're unique enough to deserve their own section. Probability functions are often used to generate simulated data with known characteristics and to calculate probability values within user-written statistical functions.

In R, probability functions take the form

```
[dpqr]distribution_abbreviation()
```

where the first letter refers to the aspect of the *distribution* returned:

    d = density
    p = distribution function
    q = quantile function
    r = random generation (random deviates)

The common probability functions are listed in table 5.4.

Table 5.4   Probability distributions

Distribution	Abbreviation	Distribution	Abbreviation
Beta	`beta`	Logistic	`logis`
Binomial	`binom`	Multinomial	`multinom`
Cauchy	`cauchy`	Negative binomial	`nbinom`
Chi-squared (noncentral)	`chisq`	Normal	`norm`
Exponential	`exp`	Poisson	`pois`

Table 5.4 Probability distributions

Distribution	Abbreviation	Distribution	Abbreviation
F	`f`	Wilcoxon signed rank	`signrank`
Gamma	`gamma`	T	`t`
Geometric	`geom`	Uniform	`unif`
Hypergeometric	`hyper`	Weibull	`weibull`
Lognormal	`lnorm`	Wilcoxon rank sum	`wilcox`

To see how these work, let's look at functions related to the normal distribution. If you don't specify a mean and a standard deviation, the standard normal distribution is assumed (mean=0, sd=1). Examples of the density (dnorm), distribution (pnorm), quantile (qnorm), and random deviate generation (rnorm) functions are given in table 5.5.

Table 5.5 Normal distribution functions

Problem	Solution
| Plot the standard normal curve on the interval [–3,3] (see figure). | ```
x <- pretty(c(-3,3), 30)
y <- dnorm(x)
plot(x, y,
    type = "l",
    xlab = "Normal Deviate",
    ylab = "Density",
    yaxs = "i"
)
``` |
What is the area under the standard normal curve to the left of z=1.96?	`pnorm(1.96)` equals 0.975.
What is the value of the 90th percentile of a normal distribution with a mean of 500 and a standard deviation of 100?	`qnorm(.9, mean=500, sd=100)` equals 628.16.
Generate 50 random normal deviates with a mean of 50 and a standard deviation of 10.	`rnorm(50, mean=50, sd=10)`

Don't worry if the plot() function options are unfamiliar. They're covered in detail in chapter 11; pretty() is explained in table 5.7 later in this chapter.
```

SETTING THE SEED FOR RANDOM NUMBER GENERATION

Each time you generate pseudo-random deviates, a different seed, and therefore different results, are produced. To make your results reproducible, you can specify the seed explicitly, using the set.seed() function. An example is given in the next listing. Here, the runif() function is used to generate pseudo-random numbers from a uniform distribution on the interval 0 to 1.

Listing 5.2 Generating pseudo-random numbers from a uniform distribution

```
> runif(5)
[1] 0.8725344 0.3962501 0.6826534 0.3667821 0.9255909
> runif(5)
[1] 0.4273903 0.2641101 0.3550058 0.3233044 0.6584988
> set.seed(1234)
> runif(5)
[1] 0.1137034 0.6222994 0.6092747 0.6233794 0.8609154
> set.seed(1234)
> runif(5)
[1] 0.1137034 0.6222994 0.6092747 0.6233794 0.8609154
```

By setting the seed manually, you're able to reproduce your results. This ability can be helpful in creating examples you can access in the future and share with others.

GENERATING MULTIVARIATE NORMAL DATA

In simulation research and Monte Carlo studies, you often want to draw data from a multivariate normal distribution with a given mean vector and covariance matrix. The mvrnorm() function in the MASS package makes this easy. The function call is

```
mvrnorm(n, mean, sigma)
```

where *n* is the desired sample size, *mean* is the vector of means, and *sigma* is the variance-covariance (or correlation) matrix. Listing 5.3 samples 500 observations from a three-variable multivariate normal distribution for which the following are true:

Mean vector	230.7	146.7	3.6
Covariance matrix	15360.8	6721.2	-47.1
	6721.2	4700.9	-16.5
	-47.1	-16.5	0.3

Listing 5.3 Generating data from a multivariate normal distribution

```
> library(MASS)
> options(digits=3)        ❶ Sets the random number seed
> set.seed(1234)

> mean <- c(230.7, 146.7, 3.6)
> sigma <- matrix(c(15360.8, 6721.2, -47.1,
                    6721.2, 4700.9, -16.5,
                    -47.1,  -16.5,   0.3), nrow=3, ncol=3)
```

❶ Sets the random number seed

❷ Specifies the mean vector and covariance matrix

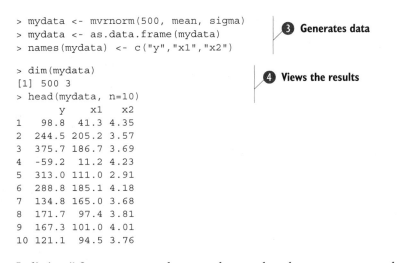

```
> mydata <- mvrnorm(500, mean, sigma)
> mydata <- as.data.frame(mydata)
> names(mydata) <- c("y","x1","x2")
```
❸ **Generates data**

```
> dim(mydata)
[1] 500 3
```
❹ **Views the results**
```
> head(mydata, n=10)
        y     x1    x2
1    98.8   41.3  4.35
2   244.5  205.2  3.57
3   375.7  186.7  3.69
4   -59.2   11.2  4.23
5   313.0  111.0  2.91
6   288.8  185.1  4.18
7   134.8  165.0  3.68
8   171.7   97.4  3.81
9   167.3  101.0  4.01
10  121.1   94.5  3.76
```

In listing 5.3, you set a random number seed so that you can reproduce the results at a later time ❶. You specify the desired mean vector and variance-covariance matrix ❷ and generate 500 pseudo-random observations ❸. For convenience, the results are converted from a matrix to a data frame, and the variables are given names. Finally, you confirm that you have 500 observations and 3 variables, and you print out the first 10 observations ❹. Note that because a correlation matrix is also a covariance matrix, you could have specified the correlation structure directly.

The probability functions in R allow you to generate simulated data, sampled from distributions with known characteristics. Statistical methods that rely on simulated data have grown exponentially in recent years, and you'll see several examples of these in later chapters.

5.2.4 Character functions

Whereas mathematical and statistical functions operate on numerical data, character functions extract information from textual data or reformat textual data for printing and reporting. For example, you may want to concatenate a person's first name and last name, ensuring that the first letter of each is capitalized. Or you may want to count the instances of obscenities in open-ended feedback. Some of the most useful character functions are listed in table 5.6.

Table 5.6 Character functions

Function	Description
`nchar(x)`	Counts the number of characters of *x*. `x <- c("ab", "cde", "fghij")` `length(x)` returns 3 (see table 5.7). `nchar(x[3])` returns 5.
`substr(x, start, stop)`	Extracts or replaces substrings in a character vector. `x <- "abcdef"` `substr(x, 2, 4)` returns bcd. `substr(x, 2, 4) <- "22222"` (x is now "a222ef").

Table 5.6   Character functions *(continued)*

Function	Description
`grep(pattern, x, ignore.case=FALSE, fixed=FALSE)`	Searches for *pattern* in *x*. If `fixed=FALSE`, then *pattern* is a regular expression. If `fixed=TRUE`, then *pattern* is a text string. Returns the matching indices. `grep("A", c("b","A","c"), fixed=TRUE)` returns 2.
`sub(pattern, replacement, x, ignore.case=FALSE, fixed=FALSE)`	Finds *pattern* in *x* and substitutes the *replacement* text. If `fixed=FALSE`, then *pattern* is a regular expression. If `fixed=TRUE`, then *pattern* is a text string. `sub("\\s",".","Hello There")` returns `Hello.There`. Note that `"\s"` is a regular expression for finding whitespace; use `"\\s"` instead, because `"\"` is R's escape character (see section 1.3.3).
`strsplit(x, split, fixed=FALSE)`	Splits the elements of character vector *x* at *split*. If `fixed=FALSE`, then *pattern* is a regular expression. If `fixed=TRUE`, then *pattern* is a text string. `y <- strsplit("abc", "")` returns a one-component, three-element list containing `"a" "b" "c"` `unlist(y)[2]` and `sapply(y, "[", 2)` both return "b".
`paste(..., sep="")`	Concatenates strings after using the *sep* string to separate them. `paste("x", 1:3, sep="")` returns `c("x1", "x2", "x3")`. `paste("x",1:3,sep="M")` returns `c("xM1","xM2" "xM3")`. `paste("Today is", date())` returns `Today is Mon Dec 28 14:17:32 2015` (I changed the date to appear more current.)
`toupper(x)`	Uppercase. `toupper("abc")` returns "ABC".
`tolower(x)`	Lowercase. `tolower("ABC")` returns "abc".

Note that the functions `grep()`, `sub()`, and `strsplit()` can search for a text string (`fixed=TRUE`) or a regular expression (`fixed=FALSE`); `FALSE` is the default. Regular expressions provide a clear and concise syntax for matching a pattern of text. For example, the regular expression

`^[hc]?at`

matches any string that starts with 0 or one occurrences of h or c, followed by at. The expression therefore matches *hat, cat,* and *at,* but not *bat.* To learn more, see the *regular expression* entry in Wikipedia.

5.2.5   *Other useful functions*

The functions in table 5.7 are also quite useful for data-management and manipulation, but they don't fit cleanly into the other categories.

Table 5.7 Other useful functions

Function	Description
length(x)	Returns the length of object x. x <- c(2, 5, 6, 9) length(x) returns 4.
seq(from, to, by)	Generates a sequence. indices <- seq(1,10,2) indices is c(1, 3, 5, 7, 9).
rep(x, n)	Repeats x n times. y <- rep(1:3, 2) y is c(1, 2, 3, 1, 2, 3).
cut(x, n)	Divides the continuous variable x into a factor with n levels. To create an ordered factor, include the option ordered_result = TRUE.
pretty(x, n)	Creates pretty breakpoints. Divides a continuous variable x into n intervals by selecting n + 1 equally spaced rounded values. Often used in plotting.
cat(... , file = "myfile", append = FALSE)	Concatenates the objects in ... and outputs them to the screen or to a file (if one is declared). name <- c("Jane") cat("Hello" , name, "\n")

The last example in the table demonstrates the use of escape characters in printing. Use \n for new lines, \t for tabs, \' for a single quote, \b for backspace, and so forth (type ?Quotes for more information). For example, the code

```
name <- "Bob"
cat( "Hello", name, "\b.\n", "Isn\'t R", "\t", "GREAT?\n")
```

produces

```
Hello Bob.
 Isn't R          GREAT?
```

Note that the second line is indented one space. When cat concatenates objects for output, it separates each by a space. That's why you include the backspace (\b) escape character before the period. Otherwise it would produce "Hello Bob ."

How you apply the functions covered so far to numbers, strings, and vectors is intuitive and straightforward, but how do you apply them to matrices and data frames? That's the subject of the next section.

5.2.6 *Applying functions to matrices and data frames*

One of the interesting features of R functions is that they can be applied to a variety of data objects (scalars, vectors, matrices, arrays, and data frames). The following listing provides an example.

Listing 5.4   Applying functions to data objects

```
> a <- 5
> sqrt(a)
[1] 2.236068
> b <- c(1.243, 5.654, 2.99)
> round(b)
[1] 1 6 3
> c <- matrix(runif(12), nrow=3)
> c
       [,1]  [,2]  [,3]  [,4]
[1,] 0.4205 0.355 0.699 0.323
[2,] 0.0270 0.601 0.181 0.926
[3,] 0.6682 0.319 0.599 0.215
> log(c)
       [,1]   [,2]   [,3]   [,4]
[1,] -0.866 -1.036 -0.358 -1.130
[2,] -3.614 -0.508 -1.711 -0.077
[3,] -0.403 -1.144 -0.513 -1.538
> mean(c)
[1] 0.444
```

Notice that the mean of matrix c in listing 5.4 results in a scalar (0.444). The mean()
function takes the average of all 12 elements in the matrix. But what if you want the
three row means or the four column means?

R provides a function, apply(), that allows you to apply an arbitrary function to any
dimension of a matrix, array, or data frame. The format for the apply() function is

```
apply(x, MARGIN, FUN, ...)
```

where *x* is the data object, *MARGIN* is the dimension index, *FUN* is a function you specify,
and . . . are any parameters you want to pass to *FUN*. In a matrix or data frame, MARGIN=1
indicates rows and MARGIN=2 indicates columns. Look at the following examples.

Listing 5.5   Applying a function to the rows (columns) of a matrix

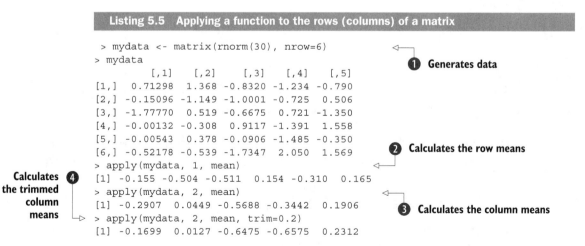

```
> mydata <- matrix(rnorm(30), nrow=6)
> mydata
           [,1]    [,2]    [,3]    [,4]    [,5]
[1,]  0.71298   1.368 -0.8320 -1.234 -0.790
[2,] -0.15096  -1.149 -1.0001 -0.725  0.506
[3,] -1.77770   0.519 -0.6675  0.721 -1.350
[4,] -0.00132  -0.308  0.9117 -1.391  1.558
[5,] -0.00543   0.378 -0.0906 -1.485 -0.350
[6,] -0.52178  -0.539 -1.7347  2.050  1.569
> apply(mydata, 1, mean)
[1] -0.155 -0.504 -0.511  0.154 -0.310  0.165
> apply(mydata, 2, mean)
[1] -0.2907  0.0449 -0.5688 -0.3442  0.1906
> apply(mydata, 2, mean, trim=0.2)
[1] -0.1699  0.0127 -0.6475 -0.6575  0.2312
```

❶ Generates data

❷ Calculates the row means

❸ Calculates the column means

Calculates ❹ the trimmed column means

You start by generating a 6 × 5 matrix containing random normal variates ❶. Then
you calculate the six row means ❷ and five column means ❸. Finally, you calculate

the trimmed column means (in this case, means based on the middle 60% of the data, with the bottom 20% and top 20% of the values discarded) ❹.

Because *FUN* can be any R function, including a function that you write yourself (see section 5.4), apply() is a powerful mechanism. Whereas apply() applies a function over the margins of an array, lapply() and sapply() apply a function over a list. You'll see an example of sapply() (which is a user-friendly version of lapply()) in the next section.

You now have all the tools you need to solve the data challenge presented in section 5.1, so let's give it a try.

5.3   A solution for the data-management challenge

Your challenge from section 5.1 is to combine subject test scores into a single performance indicator for each student, grade each student from A to F based on their relative standing (top 20%, next 20%, and so on), and sort the roster by last name followed by first name. A solution is given in the following listing.

Listing 5.6   A solution to the learning example

Step 1 ❶
```
> options(digits=2)

> Student <- c("John Davis", "Angela Williams", "Bullwinkle Moose",
              "David Jones", "Janice Markhammer", "Cheryl Cushing",
              "Reuven Ytzrhak", "Greg Knox", "Joel England",
              "Mary Rayburn")
> Math <- c(502, 600, 412, 358, 495, 512, 410, 625, 573, 522)
> Science <- c(95, 99, 80, 82, 75, 85, 80, 95, 89, 86)
> English <- c(25, 22, 18, 15, 20, 28, 15, 30, 27, 18)
> roster <- data.frame(Student, Math, Science, English,
                       stringsAsFactors=FALSE)
```

Step 2 ❷

Step 3 ❸
```
> z <- scale(roster[,2:4])
> score <- apply(z, 1, mean)        Obtains the
> roster <- cbind(roster, score)    performance scores
```

Step 4 ❹

Step 5 ❺
```
> y <- quantile(score, c(.8,.6,.4,.2))
> roster$grade[score >= y[1]] <- "A"
> roster$grade[score < y[1] & score >= y[2]] <- "B"
> roster$grade[score < y[2] & score >= y[3]] <- "C"    Grades the students
> roster$grade[score < y[3] & score >= y[4]] <- "D"
> roster$grade[score < y[4]] <- "F"
```

Step 6 ❻

Step 7 ❼
```
> name <- strsplit((roster$Student), " ")
> Lastname <- sapply(name, "[", 2)            Extracts the last
> Firstname <- sapply(name, "[", 1)           and first names
> roster <- cbind(Firstname,Lastname, roster[,-1])
```

Step 8 ❽
```
> roster <- roster[order(Lastname,Firstname),]    Sorts by last and first names

> roster
```

	Firstname	Lastname	Math	Science	English	score	grade
6	Cheryl	Cushing	512	85	28	0.35	C
1	John	Davis	502	95	25	0.56	B
9	Joel	England	573	89	27	0.70	B
4	David	Jones	358	82	15	-1.16	F
8	Greg	Knox	625	95	30	1.34	A
5	Janice	Markhammer	495	75	20	-0.63	D
3	Bullwinkle	Moose	412	80	18	-0.86	D
10	Mary	Rayburn	522	86	18	-0.18	C
2	Angela	Williams	600	99	22	0.92	A
7	Reuven	Ytzrhak	410	80	15	-1.05	F

The code is dense, so let's walk through the solution step by step.

❶ The original student roster is given. options(digits=2) limits the number of digits printed after the decimal place and makes the printouts easier to read:

```
> options(digits=2)
> roster
              Student   Math  Science  English
1          John Davis    502     95       25
2     Angela Williams    600     99       22
3    Bullwinkle Moose    412     80       18
4         David Jones    358     82       15
5   Janice Markhammer    495     75       20
6      Cheryl Cushing    512     85       28
7      Reuven Ytzrhak    410     80       15
8           Greg Knox    625     95       30
9        Joel England    573     89       27
10       Mary Rayburn    522     86       18
```

❷ Because the math, science, and English tests are reported on different scales (with widely differing means and standard deviations), you need to make them comparable before combining them. One way to do this is to standardize the variables so that each test is reported in standard-deviation units, rather than in their original scales. You can do this with the scale() function:

```
> z <- scale(roster[,2:4])
> z
        Math  Science  English
 [1,]   0.013   1.078    0.587
 [2,]   1.143   1.591    0.037
 [3,]  -1.026  -0.847   -0.697
 [4,]  -1.649  -0.590   -1.247
 [5,]  -0.068  -1.489   -0.330
 [6,]   0.128  -0.205    1.137
 [7,]  -1.049  -0.847   -1.247
 [8,]   1.432   1.078    1.504
 [9,]   0.832   0.308    0.954
[10,]   0.243  -0.077   -0.697
```

❸ You can then get a performance score for each student by calculating the row means using the mean() function and adding them to the roster using the cbind() function:

```
> score <- apply(z, 1, mean)
> roster <- cbind(roster, score)
> roster
             Student  Math  Science  English   score
1          John Davis   502      95       25   0.559
2     Angela Williams   600      99       22   0.924
3    Bullwinkle Moose   412      80       18  -0.857
4          David Jones   358      82       15  -1.162
5   Janice Markhammer   495      75       20  -0.629
6      Cheryl Cushing   512      85       28   0.353
7      Reuven Ytzrhak   410      80       15  -1.048
8           Greg Knox   625      95       30   1.338
9         Joel England   573      89       27   0.698
10        Mary Rayburn   522      86       18  -0.177
```

❹ The quantile() function gives you the percentile rank of each student's performance score. You see that the cutoff for an A is 0.74, for a B is 0.44, and so on:

```
> y <- quantile(roster$score, c(.8,.6,.4,.2))
> y
  80%   60%   40%   20%
 0.74  0.44 -0.36 -0.89
```

❺ Using logical operators, you can recode students' percentile ranks into a new categorical grade variable. This code creates the variable grade in the roster data frame:

```
> roster$grade[score >= y[1]] <- "A"
> roster$grade[score < y[1] & score >= y[2]] <- "B"
> roster$grade[score < y[2] & score >= y[3]] <- "C"
> roster$grade[score < y[3] & score >= y[4]] <- "D"
> roster$grade[score < y[4]] <- "F"
> roster
             Student  Math  Science  English   score  grade
1          John Davis   502      95       25   0.559      B
2     Angela Williams   600      99       22   0.924      A
3    Bullwinkle Moose   412      80       18  -0.857      D
4          David Jones   358      82       15  -1.162      F
5   Janice Markhammer   495      75       20  -0.629      D
6      Cheryl Cushing   512      85       28   0.353      C
7      Reuven Ytzrhak   410      80       15  -1.048      F
8           Greg Knox   625      95       30   1.338      A
9         Joel England   573      89       27   0.698      B
10        Mary Rayburn   522      86       18  -0.177      C
```

❻ You use the strsplit() function to break the student names into first name and last name at the space character. Applying strsplit() to a vector of strings returns a list:

```
> name <- strsplit((roster$Student), " ")
> name
```

```
[[1]]
[1] "John"  "Davis"

[[2]]
[1] "Angela"   "Williams"

[[3]]
[1] "Bullwinkle" "Moose"

[[4]]
[1] "David" "Jones"

[[5]]
[1] "Janice"     "Markhammer"

[[6]]
[1] "Cheryl"  "Cushing"

[[7]]
[1] "Reuven"  "Ytzrhak"

[[8]]
[1] "Greg" "Knox"

[[9]]
[1] "Joel"     "England"

[[10]]
[1] "Mary"     "Rayburn"
```

❼ You use the `sapply()` function to take the first element of each component and put it in a `Firstname` vector, and the second element of each component and put it in a `Lastname` vector. `"["` is a function that extracts part of an object—here the first or second component of the list `name`. You use `cbind()` to add these elements to the roster. Because you no longer need the `student` variable, you drop it (with the –1 in the roster index):

```
> Firstname <- sapply(name, "[", 1)
> Lastname <- sapply(name, "[", 2)
> roster <- cbind(Firstname, Lastname, roster[,-1])
> roster
       Firstname    Lastname    Math  Science  English  score  grade
1           John       Davis     502       95       25  0.559      B
2         Angela    Williams     600       99       22  0.924      A
3      Bullwinkle      Moose     412       80       18 -0.857      D
4          David       Jones     358       82       15 -1.162      F
5         Janice  Markhammer     495       75       20 -0.629      D
6         Cheryl     Cushing     512       85       28  0.353      C
7         Reuven     Ytzrhak     410       80       15 -1.048      F
8           Greg        Knox     625       95       30  1.338      A
9           Joel     England     573       89       27  0.698      B
10          Mary     Rayburn     522       86       18 -0.177      C
```

8 Finally, you sort the dataset by first and last name using the order() function:

```
> roster[order(Lastname,Firstname),]
```

	Firstname	Lastname	Math	Science	English	score	grade
6	Cheryl	Cushing	512	85	28	0.35	C
1	John	Davis	502	95	25	0.56	B
9	Joel	England	573	89	27	0.70	B
4	David	Jones	358	82	15	-1.16	F
8	Greg	Knox	625	95	30	1.34	A
5	Janice	Markhammer	495	75	20	-0.63	D
3	Bullwinkle	Moose	412	80	18	-0.86	D
10	Mary	Rayburn	522	86	18	-0.18	C
2	Angela	Williams	600	99	22	0.92	A
7	Reuven	Ytzrhak	410	80	15	-1.05	F

Voilà! Piece of cake!

There are many other ways to accomplish these tasks, but this code helps capture the flavor of these functions. Now it's time to look at control structures and user-written functions.

5.4 Control flow

In the normal course of events, the statements in an R program are executed sequentially from the top of the program to the bottom. But there are times that you'll want to execute some statements repetitively while executing other statements only if certain conditions are met. This is where control-flow constructs come in.

R has the standard control structures you'd expect to see in a modern programming language. First we'll go through the constructs used for conditional execution, followed by the constructs used for looping.

For the syntax examples throughout this section, keep the following in mind:

- *statement* is a single R statement or a compound statement (a group of R statements enclosed in curly braces {} and separated by semicolons).
- *cond* is an expression that resolves to TRUE or FALSE.
- *expr* is a statement that evaluates to a number or character string.
- *seq* is a sequence of numbers or character strings.

After we discuss control-flow constructs, you'll learn how to write your own functions.

5.4.1 Repetition and looping

Looping constructs repetitively execute a statement or series of statements until a condition isn't true. These include the for and while structures.

FOR

The for loop executes a statement repetitively until a variable's value is no longer contained in the sequence seq. The syntax is

```
for (var in seq) statement
```

In this example

```
for (i in 1:10)  print("Hello")
```

the word *Hello* is printed 10 times.

WHILE

A `while` loop executes a statement repetitively until the condition is no longer true. The syntax is

```
while (cond) statement
```

In a second example, the code

```
i <- 10
while (i > 0) {print("Hello"); i <- i - 1}
```

once again prints the word *Hello* 10 times. Make sure the statements inside the brackets modify the `while` condition so that sooner or later it's no longer true—otherwise the loop will never end! In the previous example, the statement

```
i <- i - 1
```

subtracts 1 from object `i` on each loop, so that after the tenth loop it's no longer larger than 0. If you instead added 1 on each loop, R would never stop saying hello. This is why `while` loops can be more dangerous than other looping constructs.

Looping in R can be inefficient and time consuming when you're processing the rows or columns of large datasets. Whenever possible, it's better to use R's built-in numerical and character functions in conjunction with the `apply` family of functions.

5.4.2 Conditional execution

In conditional execution, a statement or statements are executed only if a specified condition is met. These constructs include `if-else`, `ifelse`, and `switch`.

IF-ELSE

The `if-else` control structure executes a statement if a given condition is true. Optionally, a different statement is executed if the condition is false. The syntax is

```
if (cond) statement
if (cond) statement1 else statement2
```

Here are some examples:

```
if (is.character(grade)) grade <- as.factor(grade)
if (!is.factor(grade)) grade <- as.factor(grade) else print("Grade already
    is a factor")
```

In the first instance, if `grade` is a character vector, it's converted into a factor. In the second instance, one of two statements is executed. If `grade` isn't a factor (note the `!` symbol), it's turned into one. If it's a factor, then the message is printed.

IFELSE

The `ifelse` construct is a compact and vectorized version of the `if-else` construct. The syntax is

```
ifelse(cond, statement1, statement2)
```

The first statement is executed if cond is TRUE. If cond is FALSE, the second statement is executed. Here are some examples:

```
ifelse(score > 0.5, print("Passed"), print("Failed"))
outcome <- ifelse (score > 0.5, "Passed", "Failed")
```

Use `ifelse` when you want to take a binary action or when you want to input and output vectors from the construct.

SWITCH

`switch` chooses statements based on the value of an expression. The syntax is

```
switch(expr, ...)
```

where ... represents statements tied to the possible outcome values of *expr*. It's easiest to understand how `switch` works by looking at the example in the following listing.

Listing 5.7 A `switch` example

```
> feelings <- c("sad", "afraid")
> for (i in feelings)
    print(
      switch(i,
        happy  = "I am glad you are happy",
        afraid = "There is nothing to fear",
        sad    = "Cheer up",
        angry  = "Calm down now"
      )
    )

[1] "Cheer up"
[1] "There is nothing to fear"
```

This is a silly example, but it shows the main features. You'll learn how to use `switch` in user-written functions in the next section.

5.5   *User-written functions*

One of R's greatest strengths is the user's ability to add functions. In fact, many of the functions in R are functions of existing functions. The structure of a function looks like this:

```
myfunction <- function(arg1, arg2, ... ){
  statements
  return(object)
}
```

Objects in the function are local to the function. The object returned can be any data type, from scalar to list. Let's look at an example.

Say you'd like to have a function that calculates the central tendency and spread of data objects. The function should give you a choice between parametric (mean and standard deviation) and nonparametric (median and median absolute deviation) statistics. The results should be returned as a named list. Additionally, the user should have the choice of automatically printing the results or not. Unless otherwise specified, the function's default behavior should be to calculate parametric statistics and not print the results. One solution is given in the following listing.

Listing 5.8   `mystats()`: a user-written function for summary statistics

```
mystats <- function(x, parametric=TRUE, print=FALSE) {
  if (parametric) {
    center <- mean(x); spread <- sd(x)
  } else {
    center <- median(x); spread <- mad(x)
  }
  if (print & parametric) {
    cat("Mean=", center, "\n", "SD=", spread, "\n")
  } else if (print & !parametric) {
    cat("Median=", center, "\n", "MAD=", spread, "\n")
  }
  result <- list(center=center, spread=spread)
  return(result)
}
```

To see this function in action, first generate some data (a random sample of size 500 from a normal distribution):

```
set.seed(1234)
x <- rnorm(500)
```

After executing the statement

```
y <- mystats(x)
```

y$center contains the mean (0.00184) and y$spread contains the standard deviation (1.03). No output is produced. If you execute the statement

```
y <- mystats(x, parametric=FALSE, print=TRUE)
```

y$center contains the median (–0.0207) and y$spread contains the median absolute deviation (1.001). In addition, the following output is produced:

```
Median= -0.0207
MAD= 1
```

Next, let's look at a user-written function that uses the switch construct. This function gives the user a choice regarding the format of today's date. Values that are assigned to parameters in the function declaration are taken as defaults. In the mydate() function, long is the default format for dates if type isn't specified:

```
mydate <- function(type="long") {
  switch(type,
    long =  format(Sys.time(), "%A %B %d %Y"),
```

```
    short = format(Sys.time(), "%m-%d-%y"),
    cat(type, "is not a recognized type\n")
    )
}
```

Here's the function in action:

```
> mydate("long")
[1] "Monday July 14 2014"
> mydate("short")
[1] "07-14-14"
> mydate()
[1] "Monday July 14 2014"
> mydate("medium")
medium is not a recognized type
```

Note that the cat() function is executed only if the entered type doesn't match "long" or "short". It's usually a good idea to have an expression that catches user-supplied arguments that have been entered incorrectly.

Several functions are available that can help add error trapping and correction to your functions. You can use the function warning() to generate a warning message, message() to generate a diagnostic message, and stop() to stop execution of the current expression and carry out an error action. Error trapping and debugging are discussed more fully in section 20.5.

After creating your own functions, you may want to make them available in every session. Appendix B describes how to customize the R environment so that user-written functions are loaded automatically at startup. We'll look at additional examples of user-written functions in chapters 6 and 8.

You can accomplish a great deal using the basic techniques provided in this section. Control flow and other programming topics are covered in greater detail in chapter 20. Creating a package is covered in chapter 21. If you'd like to explore the subtleties of function writing, or you want to write professional-level code that you can distribute to others, I recommend reading these two chapters and then reviewing two excellent books that you'll find in the References section at the end of this book: Venables & Ripley (2000) and Chambers (2008). Together, they provide a significant level of detail and breadth of examples.

Now that we've covered user-written functions, we'll end this chapter with a discussion of data aggregation and reshaping.

5.6   *Aggregation and reshaping*

R provides a number of powerful methods for aggregating and reshaping data. When you *aggregate* data, you replace groups of observations with summary statistics based on those observations. When you *reshape* data, you alter the structure (rows and columns) determining how the data is organized. This section describes a variety of methods for accomplishing these tasks.

In the next two subsections, we'll use the mtcars data frame that's included with the base installation of R. This dataset, extracted from *Motor Trend* magazine (1974), describes the design and performance characteristics (number of cylinders, displacement, horsepower, mpg, and so on) for 34 automobiles. To learn more about the dataset, see `help(mtcars)`.

5.6.1   *Transpose*

Transposing (reversing rows and columns) is perhaps the simplest method of reshaping a dataset. Use the `t()` function to transpose a matrix or a data frame. In the latter case, row names become variable (column) names. An example is presented in the next listing.

Listing 5.9   Transposing a dataset

```
> cars <- mtcars[1:5,1:4]
> cars
                    mpg cyl disp  hp
Mazda RX4          21.0   6  160 110
Mazda RX4 Wag      21.0   6  160 110
Datsun 710         22.8   4  108  93
Hornet 4 Drive     21.4   6  258 110
Hornet Sportabout  18.7   8  360 175
> t(cars)
     Mazda RX4 Mazda RX4 Wag Datsun 710 Hornet 4 Drive Hornet Sportabout
mpg         21            21       22.8           21.4              18.7
cyl          6             6        4.0            6.0               8.0
disp       160           160      108.0          258.0             360.0
hp         110           110       93.0          110.0             175.0
```

Listing 5.9 uses a subset of the `mtcars` dataset in order to conserve space on the page. You'll see a more flexible way of transposing data when we look at the `reshape2` package later in this section.

5.6.2   *Aggregating data*

It's relatively easy to collapse data in R using one or more by variables and a defined function. The format is

```
aggregate(x, by, FUN)
```

where *x* is the data object to be collapsed, *by* is a list of variables that will be crossed to form the new observations, and *FUN* is the scalar function used to calculate summary statistics that will make up the new observation values.

As an example, let's aggregate the `mtcars` data by number of cylinders and gears, returning means for each of the numeric variables.

Listing 5.10   Aggregating data

```
> options(digits=3)
> attach(mtcars)
> aggdata <-aggregate(mtcars, by=list(cyl,gear), FUN=mean, na.rm=TRUE)
> aggdata
```

	Group.1	Group.2	mpg	cyl	disp	hp	drat	wt	qsec	vs	am	gear	carb
1	4	3	21.5	4	120	97	3.70	2.46	20.0	1.0	0.00	3	1.00
2	6	3	19.8	6	242	108	2.92	3.34	19.8	1.0	0.00	3	1.00
3	8	3	15.1	8	358	194	3.12	4.10	17.1	0.0	0.00	3	3.08
4	4	4	26.9	4	103	76	4.11	2.38	19.6	1.0	0.75	4	1.50
5	6	4	19.8	6	164	116	3.91	3.09	17.7	0.5	0.50	4	4.00
6	4	5	28.2	4	108	102	4.10	1.83	16.8	0.5	1.00	5	2.00
7	6	5	19.7	6	145	175	3.62	2.77	15.5	0.0	1.00	5	6.00
8	8	5	15.4	8	326	300	3.88	3.37	14.6	0.0	1.00	5	6.00

In these results, Group.1 represents the number of cylinders (4, 6, or 8), and Group.2 represents the number of gears (3, 4, or 5). For example, cars with 4 cylinders and 3 gears have a mean of 21.5 miles per gallon (mpg).

When you're using the aggregate() function, the *by* variables must be in a list (even if there's only one). You can declare a custom name for the groups from within the list, for instance, using by=list(Group.cyl=cyl, Group.gears=gear). The function specified can be any built-in or user-provided function. This gives the aggregate command a great deal of power. But when it comes to power, nothing beats the reshape2 package.

5.6.3 *The reshape2 package*

The reshape2 package is a tremendously versatile approach to both restructuring and aggregating datasets. Because of this versatility, it can be a bit challenging to learn. We'll go through the process slowly and use a small dataset so it's clear what's happening. Because reshape2 isn't included in the standard installation of R, you'll need to install it one time, using install.packages("reshape2").

Basically, you *melt* data so that each row is a unique ID-variable combination. Then you *cast* the melted data into any shape you desire. During the cast, you can aggregate the data with any function you wish. The dataset you'll be working with is shown in table 5.8.

Table 5.8   The original dataset (mydata)

ID	Time	X1	X2
1	1	5	6
1	2	3	5
2	1	6	1
2	2	2	4

In this dataset, the *measurements* are the values in the last two columns (5, 6, 3, 5, 6, 1, 2, and 4). Each measurement is uniquely identified by a combination of ID variables (in this case ID, Time, and whether the measurement is on X1 or X2). For example, the measured value 5 in the first row is uniquely identified by knowing that it's from observation (ID) 1, at Time 1, and on variable X1.

MELTING

When you *melt* a dataset, you restructure it into a format in which each measured variable is in its own row along with the ID variables needed to uniquely identify it. If you melt the data from table 5.8 using the following code, you end up with the structure shown in table 5.9.

```
library(reshape2)
md <- melt(mydata, id=c("ID", "Time"))
```

Table 5.9   The melted dataset

ID	Time	variable	value
1	1	X1	5
1	2	X1	3
2	1	X1	6
2	2	X1	2
1	1	X2	6
1	2	X2	5
2	1	X2	1
2	2	X2	4

Note that you must specify the variables needed to uniquely identify each measurement (ID and Time) and that the variable indicating the measurement variable names (X1 or X2) is created for you automatically.

Now that you have your data in a melted form, you can recast it into any shape, using the dcast() function.

CASTING

The dcast() function starts with a melted data frame and reshapes it into a new data frame using a formula that you provide and an (optional) function used to aggregate the data. The format is

```
newdata <- dcast(md, formula, fun.aggregate)
```

where *md* is the melted data, *formula* describes the desired end result, and *fun.aggregate* is the (optional) aggregating function. The formula takes the form

```
rowvar1 + rowvar2 + ... ~ colvar1 + colvar2 + ...
```

In this formula, rowvar1 + rowvar2 + ... defines the set of crossed variables that defines the rows, and colvar1 + colvar2 + ... defines the set of crossed variables that defines the columns. See the examples in figure 5.1.

Because the formulas on the right side (d, e, and f) don't include a function, the data is reshaped. In contrast, the examples on the left side (a, b, and c) specify the

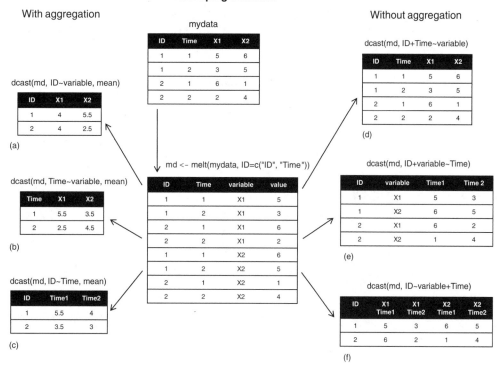

Figure 5.1 **Reshaping data with the `melt()` and `dcast()` functions**

mean as an aggregating function. Thus the data is not only reshaped but aggregated as well. For example, example a gives the means on X1 and X2 averaged over time for each observation. Example b gives the mean scores of X1 and X2 at Time 1 and Time 2, averaged over observations. In example c, you have the mean score for each observation at Time 1 and Time 2, averaged over X1 and X2.

As you can see, the flexibility provided by the `melt()` and `dcast()` functions is amazing. There are many times when you'll have to reshape or aggregate data prior to analysis. For example, you'll typically need to place your data in what's called *long format*, resembling table 5.9, when analyzing repeated-measures data (data where multiple measures are recorded for each observation). See section 9.6 for an example.

5.7 Summary

This chapter reviewed dozens of mathematical, statistical, and probability functions that are useful for manipulating data. You saw how to apply these functions to a wide range of data objects including vectors, matrices, and data frames. You learned to use control-flow constructs for looping and branching to execute some statements repetitively and execute other statements only when certain conditions are met. You then had a chance to write your own functions and apply them to data. Finally, we explored ways of collapsing, aggregating, and restructuring data.

Now that you've gathered the tools you need to get your data into shape (no pun intended), you're ready to bid part 1 goodbye and enter the exciting world of data analysis! In upcoming chapters, we'll begin to explore the many statistical and graphical methods available for turning data into information.

Part 2

Basic methods

In part 1, we explored the R environment and discussed how to input data from a wide variety of sources, combine and transform it, and prepare it for further analyses. Once your data has been input and cleaned up, the next step is typically to explore the variables one at a time. This provides you with information about the distribution of each variable, which is useful in understanding the characteristics of the sample, identifying unexpected or problematic values, and selecting appropriate statistical methods. Next, variables are typically studied two at a time. This can help you to uncover basic relationships among variables and is a useful first step in developing more complex models.

Part 2 focuses on graphical and statistical techniques for obtaining basic information about data. Chapter 6 describes methods for visualizing the distribution of individual variables. For categorical variables, this includes bar plots, pie charts, and the newer fan plot. For numeric variables, this includes histograms, density plots, box plots, dot plots, and the less well-known violin plot. Each type of graph is useful for understanding the distribution of a single variable.

Chapter 7 describes statistical methods for summarizing individual variables and bivariate relationships. The chapter starts with coverage of descriptive statistics for numerical data based on the dataset as a whole and on subgroups of interest. Next, the use of frequency tables and cross-tabulations for summarizing categorical data is described. The chapter ends by discussing basic inferential methods for understanding relationships between two variables at a time, including bivariate correlations, chi-square tests, t-tests, and nonparametric methods.

When you have finished this part of the book, you'll be able to use basic graphical and statistical methods available in R to describe your data, explore group differences, and identify significant relationships among variables.

Basic graphs

Whenever we analyze data, the first thing we should do is *look* at it. For each variable, what are the most common values? How much variability is present? Are there any unusual observations? R provides a wealth of functions for visualizing data. In this chapter, we'll look at graphs that help you understand a single categorical or continuous variable. This topic includes

- Visualizing the distribution of a variable
- Comparing groups on an outcome variable

In both cases, the variable can be continuous (for example, car mileage as miles per gallon) or categorical (for example, treatment outcome as none, some, or marked). In later chapters, we'll explore graphs that display bivariate and multivariate relationships among variables.

The following sections explore the use of bar plots, pie charts, fan charts, histograms, kernel density plots, box plots, violin plots, and dot plots. Some of these may be familiar to you, whereas others (such as fan plots or violin plots) may be new to you. The goal, as always, is to understand your data better and to communicate this understanding to others. Let's start with bar plots.

6.1 Bar plots

A bar plot displays the distribution (frequency) of a categorical variable through vertical or horizontal bars. In its simplest form, the format of the barplot() function is

```
barplot(height)
```

where *height* is a vector or matrix.

In the following examples, you'll plot the outcome of a study investigating a new treatment for rheumatoid arthritis. The data are contained in the Arthritis data frame distributed with the vcd package. This package isn't included in the default R installation, so install it before first use (install.packages("vcd")).

Note that the vcd package isn't needed to create bar plots. You're loading it in order to gain access to the Arthritis dataset. But you'll need the vcd package when creating spinograms, which are described in section 6.1.5.

6.1.1 Simple bar plots

If height is a vector, the values determine the heights of the bars in the plot, and a vertical bar plot is produced. Including the option horiz=TRUE produces a horizontal bar chart instead. You can also add annotating options. The main option adds a plot title, whereas the xlab and ylab options add x-axis and y-axis labels, respectively.

In the Arthritis study, the variable Improved records the patient outcomes for individuals receiving a placebo or drug:

```
> library(vcd)
> counts <- table(Arthritis$Improved)
> counts

  None   Some Marked
    42     14     28
```

Here, you see that 28 patients showed marked improvement, 14 showed some improvement, and 42 showed no improvement. We'll discuss the use of the table() function to obtain cell counts more fully in chapter 7.

You can graph the variable counts using a vertical or horizontal bar plot. The code is provided in the following listing, and the resulting graphs are displayed in figure 6.1.

Listing 6.1 Simple bar plots

```
barplot(counts,
        main="Simple Bar Plot",                          Simple bar plot
        xlab="Improvement", ylab="Frequency")
barplot(counts,
        main="Horizontal Bar Plot",                      Horizontal bar plot
        xlab="Frequency", ylab="Improvement",
        horiz=TRUE)
```

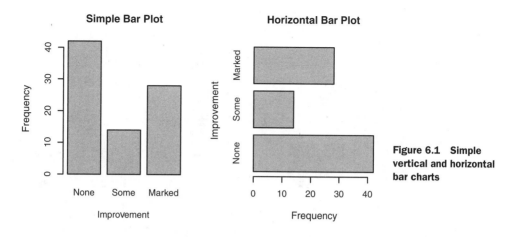

Simple Bar Plot / Horizontal Bar Plot

Figure 6.1   Simple vertical and horizontal bar charts

Creating bar plots with factor variables

If the categorical variable to be plotted is a factor or ordered factor, you can create a vertical bar plot quickly with the `plot()` function. Because `Arthritis$Improved` is a factor, the code

```
plot(Arthritis$Improved, main="Simple Bar Plot",
    xlab="Improved", ylab="Frequency")
plot(Arthritis$Improved, horiz=TRUE, main="Horizontal Bar Plot",
    xlab="Frequency", ylab="Improved")
```

will generate the same bar plots as those in listing 6.1, but without the need to tabulate values with the `table()` function.

What happens if you have long labels? In section 6.1.4, you'll see how to tweak labels so that they don't overlap.

6.1.2   Stacked and grouped bar plots

If `height` is a matrix rather than a vector, the resulting graph will be a stacked or grouped bar plot. If `beside=FALSE` (the default), then each column of the matrix produces a bar in the plot, with the values in the column giving the heights of stacked "sub-bars." If `beside=TRUE`, each column of the matrix represents a group, and the values in each column are juxtaposed rather than stacked.

Consider the cross-tabulation of treatment type and improvement status:

```
> library(vcd)
> counts <- table(Arthritis$Improved, Arthritis$Treatment)
> counts
        Treatment
Improved Placebo Treated
  None        29      13
  Some         7       7
  Marked       7      21
```

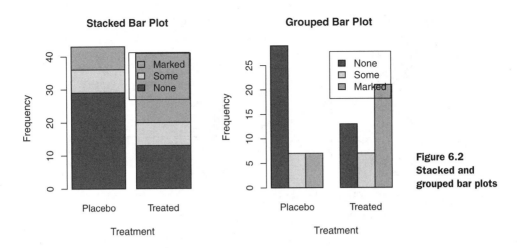

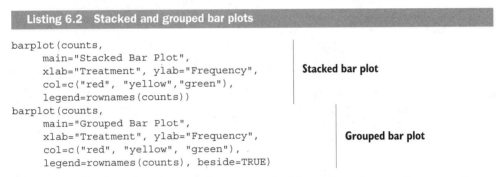

Figure 6.2
Stacked and
grouped bar plots

You can graph the results as either a stacked or a grouped bar plot (see the next list-ing). The resulting graphs are displayed in figure 6.2.

Listing 6.2   Stacked and grouped bar plots

```
barplot(counts,
    main="Stacked Bar Plot",
    xlab="Treatment", ylab="Frequency",     Stacked bar plot
    col=c("red", "yellow","green"),
    legend=rownames(counts))
barplot(counts,
    main="Grouped Bar Plot",
    xlab="Treatment", ylab="Frequency",      Grouped bar plot
    col=c("red", "yellow", "green"),
    legend=rownames(counts), beside=TRUE)
```

The first `barplot()` function produces a stacked bar plot, whereas the second pro-duces a grouped bar plot. We've also added the `col` option to add color to the bars plotted. The `legend.text` parameter provides bar labels for the legend (which are only useful when `height` is a matrix).

In chapter 3, we covered ways to format and place the legend to maximum benefit. See if you can rearrange the legend to avoid overlap with the bars.

6.1.3   *Mean bar plots*

Bar plots needn't be based on counts or frequencies. You can create bar plots that rep-resent means, medians, standard deviations, and so forth by using the aggregate func-tion and passing the results to the `barplot()` function. The following listing shows an example, which is displayed in figure 6.3.

Listing 6.3   Bar plot for sorted mean values

```
> states <- data.frame(state.region, state.x77)
> means <- aggregate(states$Illiteracy, by=list(state.region), FUN=mean)
> means
```

```
          Group.1    x
1       Northeast 1.00
2           South 1.74
3 North Central 0.70
4            West 1.02
> means <- means[order(means$x),]
> means
          Group.1    x
3 North Central 0.70
1       Northeast 1.00
4            West 1.02
2           South 1.74
> barplot(means$x, names.arg=means$Group.1)
> title("Mean Illiteracy Rate")
```

❶ Sorts means, smallest to largest

❷ Adds title

Listing 6.3 sorts the means from smallest to largest **❶**. Also note that using the title() function **❷** is equivalent to adding the main option in the plot call. means$x is the vector containing the heights of the bars, and the option names.arg=means$Group.1 is added to provide labels.

You can take this example further. The bars can be connected with straight-line segments using the lines() function. You can also create mean bar plots with superimposed confidence intervals using the barplot2() function in the gplots package. See help(barplot2) for examples.

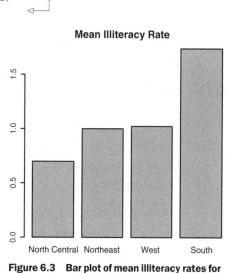

Mean Illiteracy Rate

Figure 6.3 Bar plot of mean illiteracy rates for US regions sorted by rate

6.1.4 Tweaking bar plots

There are several ways to tweak the appearance of a bar plot. For example, with many bars, bar labels may start to overlap. You can decrease the font size using the cex.names option. Specifying values smaller than 1 will shrink the size of the labels. Optionally, the names.arg argument allows you to specify a character vector of names used to label the bars. You can also use graphical parameters to help text spacing. An example is given in the following listing, with the output displayed in figure 6.4.

Listing 6.4 Fitting labels in a bar plot

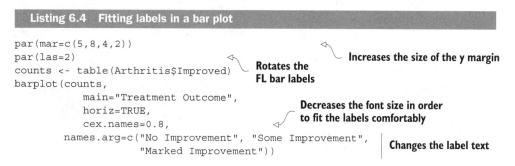

```
par(mar=c(5,8,4,2))
par(las=2)
counts <- table(Arthritis$Improved)
barplot(counts,
        main="Treatment Outcome",
        horiz=TRUE,
        cex.names=0.8,
    names.arg=c("No Improvement", "Some Improvement",
                "Marked Improvement"))
```

Increases the size of the y margin

Rotates the FL bar labels

Decreases the font size in order to fit the labels comfortably

Changes the label text

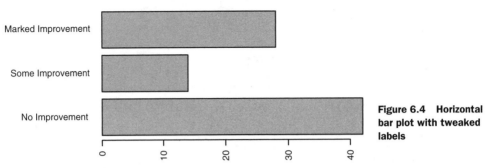

Figure 6.4   Horizontal bar plot with tweaked labels

The par() function allows you to make extensive modifications to the graphs that R produces by default. See chapter 3 for more details.

6.1.5   Spinograms

Before finishing our discussion of bar plots, let's take a look at a specialized version called a *spinogram*. In a spinogram, a stacked bar plot is rescaled so that the height of each bar is 1 and the segment heights represent proportions. Spinograms are created through the spine() function of the vcd package. The following code produces a simple spinogram:

```
library(vcd)
attach(Arthritis)
counts <- table(Treatment, Improved)
spine(counts, main="Spinogram Example")
detach(Arthritis)
```

The output is provided in figure 6.5. The larger percentage of patients with marked improvement in the Treated condition is quite evident when compared with the Placebo condition.

In addition to bar plots, pie charts are a popular vehicle for displaying the distribution of a categorical variable. We'll consider them next.

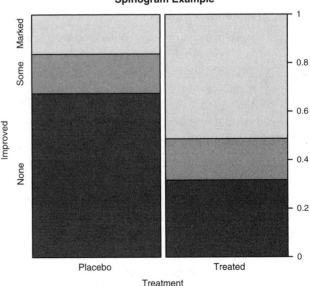

Figure 6.5   Spinogram of arthritis treatment outcome

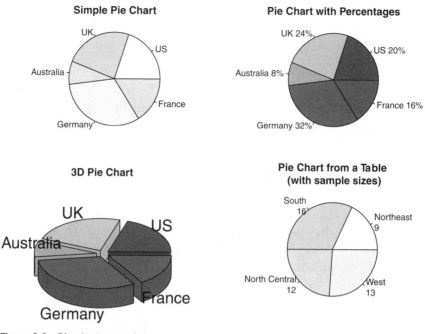

Figure 6.6   Pie chart examples

6.2   *Pie charts*

Whereas pie charts are ubiquitous in the business world, they're denigrated by most statisticians, including the authors of the R documentation. They recommend bar or dot plots over pie charts because people are able to judge length more accurately than volume. Perhaps for this reason, the pie chart options in R are limited when compared with other statistical software.

Pie charts are created with the function

```
pie(x, labels)
```

where *x* is a non-negative numeric vector indicating the area of each slice and *labels* provides a character vector of slice labels. Four examples are given in the next listing; the resulting plots are provided in figure 6.6.

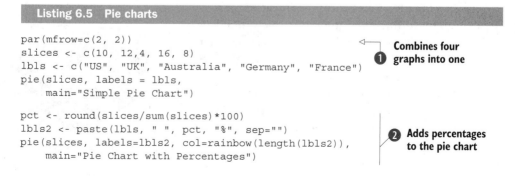

Listing 6.5   Pie charts

```
par(mfrow=c(2, 2))
slices <- c(10, 12,4, 16, 8)
lbls <- c("US", "UK", "Australia", "Germany", "France")
pie(slices, labels = lbls,
    main="Simple Pie Chart")

pct <- round(slices/sum(slices)*100)
lbls2 <- paste(lbls, " ", pct, "%", sep="")
pie(slices, labels=lbls2, col=rainbow(length(lbls2)),
    main="Pie Chart with Percentages")
```

❶ Combines four graphs into one

❷ Adds percentages to the pie chart

```
library(plotrix)
pie3D(slices, labels=lbls,explode=0.1,
      main="3D Pie Chart ")
mytable <- table(state.region)
lbls3 <- paste(names(mytable), "\n", mytable, sep="")
pie(mytable, labels = lbls3,
    main="Pie Chart from a Table\n (with sample sizes)")
```

❸ Creates a chart from the table

First you set up the plot so that four graphs are combined into one ❶. (Combining multiple graphs is covered in chapter 3.) Then you input the data that will be used for the first three graphs.

For the second pie chart ❷, you convert the sample sizes to percentages and add the information to the slice labels. The second pie chart also defines the colors of the slices using the `rainbow()` function, described in chapter 3. Here rainbow(length(lbls2)) resolves to `rainbow(5)`, providing five colors for the graph.

The third pie chart is a 3D chart created using the `pie3D()` function from the `plotrix` package. Be sure to download and install this package before using it for the first time. If statisticians dislike pie charts, they positively despise 3D pie charts (although they may secretly find them pretty). This is because the 3D effect adds no additional insight into the data and is considered distracting eye candy.

The fourth pie chart demonstrates how to create a chart from a table ❸. In this case, you count the number of states by US region and append the information to the labels before producing the plot.

Pie charts make it difficult to compare the values of the slices (unless the values are appended to the labels). For example, looking at the simple pie chart, can you tell how the US compares to Germany? (If you can, you're more perceptive than I am.) In an attempt to improve on this situation, a variation of the pie chart, called a *fan plot*, has been developed. The fan plot (Lemon & Tyagi, 2009) provides you with a way to display both relative quantities and differences. In R, it's implemented through the `fan.plot()` function in the `plotrix` package.

Consider the following code and the resulting graph (figure 6.7):

```
library(plotrix)
slices <- c(10, 12,4, 16, 8)
lbls <- c("US", "UK", "Australia", "Germany", "France")
fan.plot(slices, labels = lbls, main="Fan Plot")
```

In a fan plot, the slices are rearranged to overlap each other, and the radii are modified so that each slice is visible. Here you can see that Germany is the largest slice and that the US slice is roughly 60% as large. France appears to be half as large as Germany and twice as large as Australia. Remember that the *width* of the slice and not the radius is what's important here.

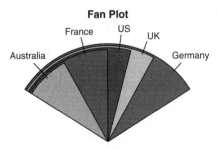

Figure 6.7   A fan plot of the country data

As you can see, it's much easier to determine the relative sizes of the slice in a fan plot than in a pie chart. Fan plots haven't caught on yet, but they're new.

Now that we've covered pie and fan charts, let's move on to histograms. Unlike bar plots and pie charts, histograms describe the distribution of a continuous variable.

6.3 Histograms

Histograms display the distribution of a continuous variable by dividing the range of scores into a specified number of bins on the x-axis and displaying the frequency of scores in each bin on the y-axis. You can create histograms with the function

```
hist(x)
```

where *x* is a numeric vector of values. The option `freq=FALSE` creates a plot based on probability densities rather than frequencies. The `breaks` option controls the number of bins. The default produces equally spaced breaks when defining the cells of the histogram. The following listing provides the code for four variations of a histogram; the results are plotted in figure 6.8.

Listing 6.6 Histograms

```
par(mfrow=c(2,2))

hist(mtcars$mpg)                                      ❶ Simple histogram

hist(mtcars$mpg,
      breaks=12,
      col="red",                                      ❷ With specified
      xlab="Miles Per Gallon",                            bins and color
      main="Colored histogram with 12 bins")

hist(mtcars$mpg,
     freq=FALSE,
     breaks=12,
     col="red",                                       ❸ With a rug plot
     xlab="Miles Per Gallon",
     main="Histogram, rug plot, density curve")
rug(jitter(mtcars$mpg))
lines(density(mtcars$mpg), col="blue", lwd=2)

x <- mtcars$mpg
h<-hist(x,
        breaks=12,
        col="red",
        xlab="Miles Per Gallon",
        main="Histogram with normal curve and box")  ❹ With a normal
xfit<-seq(min(x), max(x), length=40)                     curve and frame
yfit<-dnorm(xfit, mean=mean(x), sd=sd(x))
yfit <- yfit*diff(h$mids[1:2])*length(x)
lines(xfit, yfit, col="blue", lwd=2)
box()
```

The first histogram ❶ demonstrates the default plot when no options are specified. In this case, five bins are created, and the default axis labels and titles are printed. For the second histogram ❷, you specified 12 bins, a red fill for the bars, and more attractive and informative labels and title.

The third histogram ❸ maintains the same colors, bins, labels, and titles as the previous plot but adds a density curve and rug-plot overlay. The density curve is a kernel density estimate and is described in the next section. It provides a smoother description of the distribution of scores. You use the lines() function to overlay this curve in a blue color and a width that's twice the default thickness for lines. Finally, a *rug plot* is a one-dimensional representation of the actual data values. If there are many tied values, you can jitter the data on the rug plot using code like the following:

```
rug(jitter(mtcars$mpag, amount=0.01))
```

This adds a small random value to each data point (a uniform random variate between ±amount), in order to avoid overlapping points.

The fourth histogram ❹ is similar to the second but has a superimposed normal curve and a box around the figure. The code for superimposing the normal curve

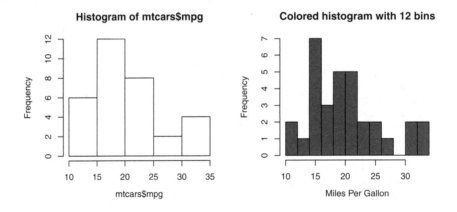

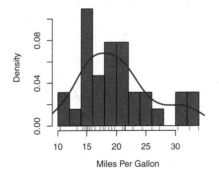

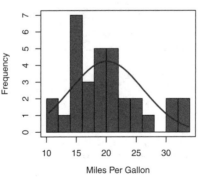

Figure 6.8   Histogram examples

comes from a suggestion posted to the R-help mailing list by Peter Dalgaard. The surrounding box is produced by the box() function.

6.4 *Kernel density plots*

In the previous section, you saw a kernel density plot superimposed on a histogram. Technically, kernel density estimation is a nonparametric method for estimating the probability density function of a random variable. Although the mathematics are beyond the scope of this text, in general, kernel density plots can be an effective way to view the distribution of a continuous variable. The format for a density plot (that's not being superimposed on another graph) is

```
plot(density(x))
```

where *x* is a numeric vector. Because the plot() function begins a new graph, use the lines() function (listing 6.6) when superimposing a density curve on an existing graph. Two kernel density examples are given in the next listing, and the results are plotted in figure 6.9.

> **Listing 6.7 Kernel density plots**

```
par(mfrow=c(2,1))
d <- density(mtcars$mpg)

plot(d)
```
Creates the minimal graph with all the defaults in place

```
d <- density(mtcars$mpg)
plot(d, main="Kernel Density of Miles Per Gallon")
polygon(d, col="red", border="blue")
rug(mtcars$mpg, col="brown")
```
Adds a title

Adds a brown rug

Colors the curve blue and fills the area under the curve with solid red

The polygon() function draws a polygon whose vertices are given by x and y. These values are provided by the density() function in this case.

Kernel density plots can be used to compare groups. This is a highly underutilized approach, probably due to a general lack of easily accessible software. Fortunately, the sm package fills this gap nicely.

Figure 6.9 Kernel density plots

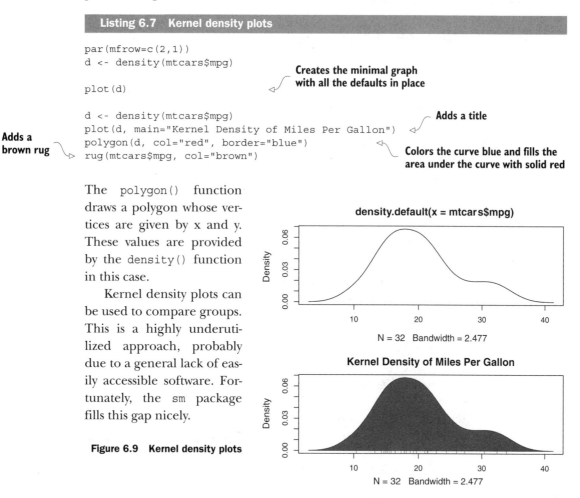

The `sm.density.compare()` function in the `sm` package allows you to superimpose the kernel density plots of two or more groups. The format is

```
sm.density.compare(x, factor)
```

where *x* is a numeric vector and *factor* is a grouping variable. Be sure to install the `sm` package before first use. An example comparing the mpg of cars with four, six, and eight cylinders is provided in the following listing.

Listing 6.8   Comparative kernel density plots

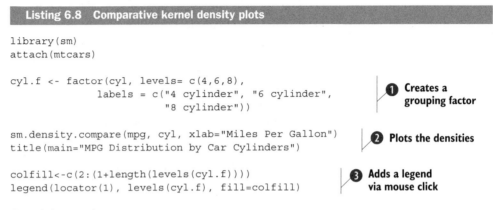

```
library(sm)
attach(mtcars)

cyl.f <- factor(cyl, levels= c(4,6,8),
          labels = c("4 cylinder", "6 cylinder",
                  "8 cylinder"))
```
❶ Creates a grouping factor

```
sm.density.compare(mpg, cyl, xlab="Miles Per Gallon")
title(main="MPG Distribution by Car Cylinders")
```
❷ Plots the densities

```
colfill<-c(2:(1+length(levels(cyl.f))))
legend(locator(1), levels(cyl.f), fill=colfill)
```
❸ Adds a legend via mouse click

```
detach(mtcars)
```

First, the `sm` package is loaded and the `mtcars` data frame is attached. In the `mtcars` data frame ❶, the variable `cyl` is a numeric variable coded 4, 6, or 8. `cyl` is transformed into a factor named `cyl.f`, in order to provide value labels for the plot. The `sm.density.compare()` function creates the plot ❷, and a `title()` statement adds a main title.

Finally, you add a legend to improve interpretability ❸. (Legends are covered in chapter 3.) A vector of colors is created; here, `colfill` is `c(2,3,4)`. Then the legend is added to the plot via the `legend()` function. The `locator(1)` option indicates that you'll place the legend interactively by clicking in the graph where you want the legend to appear. The second option provides a character vec-

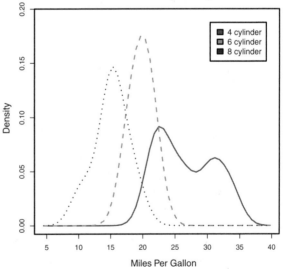

Figure 6.10   Kernel density plots of mpg by number of cylinders

tor of the labels. The third option assigns a color from the vector `colfill` to each level of `cyl.f`. The results are displayed in figure 6.10.

Overlapping kernel density plots can be a powerful way to compare groups of observations on an outcome variable. Here you can see both the shapes of the distribution of scores for each group and the amount of overlap between groups. (The moral of the story is that my next car will have four cylinders—or a battery.)

Box plots are also a wonderful (and more commonly used) graphical approach to visualizing distributions and differences among groups. We'll discuss them next.

6.5 Box plots

A *box-and-whiskers plot* describes the distribution of a continuous variable by plotting its five-number summary: the minimum, lower quartile (25th percentile), median (50th percentile), upper quartile (75th percentile), and maximum. It can also display observations that may be outliers (values outside the range of ± 1.5*IQR, where IQR is the interquartile range defined as the upper quartile minus the lower quartile). For example, this statement produces the plot shown in figure 6.11:

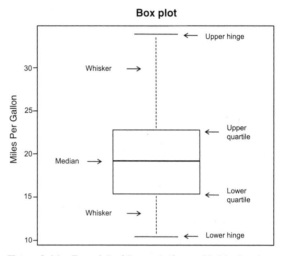

Figure 6.11 Box plot with annotations added by hand

```
boxplot(mtcars$mpg, main="Box plot", ylab="Miles per Gallon")
```

I added annotations by hand to illustrate the components.

By default, each whisker extends to the most extreme data point, which is no more than 1.5 times the interquartile range for the box. Values outside this range are depicted as dots (not shown here).

For example, in the sample of cars, the median mpg is 19.2, 50% of the scores fall between 15.3 and 22.8, the smallest value is 10.4, and the largest value is 33.9. How did I read this so precisely from the graph? Issuing `boxplot.stats(mtcars$mpg)` prints the statistics used to build the graph (in other words, I cheated). There don't appear to be any outliers, and there is a mild positive skew (the upper whisker is longer than the lower whisker).

6.5.1 Using parallel box plots to compare groups

Box plots can be created for individual variables or for variables by group. The format is

```
boxplot(formula, data=dataframe)
```

where `formula` is a formula and `dataframe` denotes the data frame (or list) providing the data. An example of a formula is y ~ A, where a separate box plot for numeric variable y is generated for each value of categorical variable A. The formula y ~ A*B would produce a box plot of numeric variable y, for each combination of levels in categorical variables A and B.

Adding the option `varwidth=TRUE` makes the box-plot widths proportional to the square root of their sample sizes. Add `horizontal=TRUE` to reverse the axis orientation.

The following code revisits the impact of four, six, and eight cylinders on auto mpg with parallel box plots. The plot is provided in figure 6.12:

```
boxplot(mpg ~ cyl, data=mtcars,
        main="Car Mileage Data",
        xlab="Number of Cylinders",
        ylab="Miles Per Gallon")
```

You can see in figure 6.12 that there's a good separation of groups based on gas mileage. You can also see that the distribution of mpg for six-cylinder cars is more symmetrical than for the other two car types. Cars with four cylinders show the greatest spread (and positive skew) of mpg scores, when compared with six- and eight-cylinder cars. There's also an outlier in the eight-cylinder group.

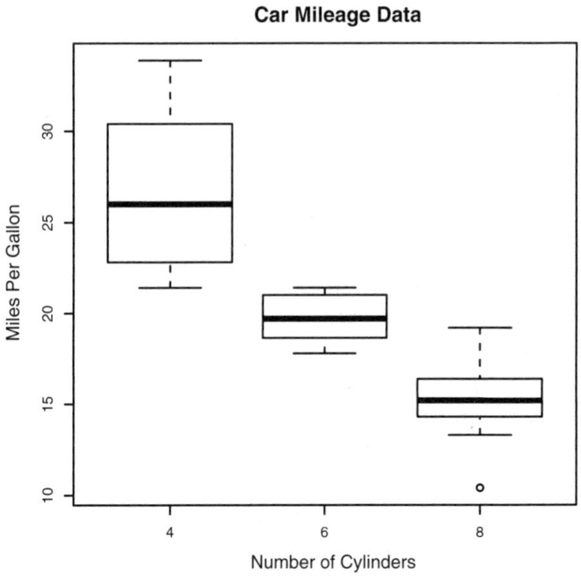

Box plots are very versatile. By adding `notch=TRUE`, you get *notched* box plots. If two boxes' notches don't overlap, there's strong evidence that their

Figure 6.12   **Box plots of car mileage vs. number of cylinders**

medians differ (Chambers et al., 1983, p. 62). The following code creates notched box plots for the mpg example:

```
boxplot(mpg ~ cyl, data=mtcars,
        notch=TRUE,
        varwidth=TRUE,
        col="red",
        main="Car Mileage Data",
        xlab="Number of Cylinders",
        ylab="Miles Per Gallon")
```

The `col` option fills the box plots with a red color, and `varwidth=TRUE` produces box plots with widths that are proportional to their sample sizes.

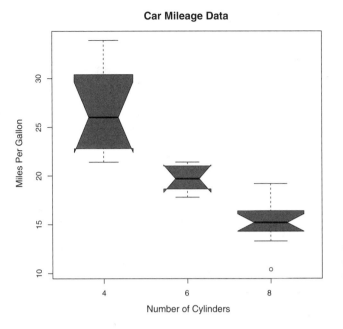

Car Mileage Data

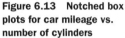

Figure 6.13 Notched box plots for car mileage vs. number of cylinders

You can see in figure 6.13 that the median car mileage for four-, six-, and eight-cylinder cars differs. Mileage clearly decreases with number of cylinders.

Finally, you can produce box plots for more than one grouping factor. Listing 6.9 provides box plots for mpg versus the number of cylinders and transmission type in an automobile (see figure 6.14). Again, you use the col option to fill the box plots with color. Note that colors recycle; in this case, there are six box plots and only two specified colors, so the colors repeat three times.

Listing 6.9 Box plots for two crossed factors

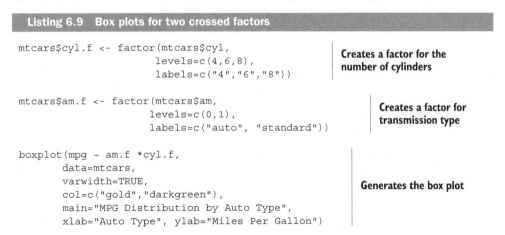

```
mtcars$cyl.f <- factor(mtcars$cyl,
                  levels=c(4,6,8),
                  labels=c("4","6","8"))
```
Creates a factor for the number of cylinders

```
mtcars$am.f <- factor(mtcars$am,
                  levels=c(0,1),
                  labels=c("auto", "standard"))
```
Creates a factor for transmission type

```
boxplot(mpg ~ am.f *cyl.f,
     data=mtcars,
     varwidth=TRUE,
     col=c("gold","darkgreen"),
     main="MPG Distribution by Auto Type",
     xlab="Auto Type", ylab="Miles Per Gallon")
```
Generates the box plot

From figure 6.14, it's again clear that median mileage decreases with number of cylinders. For four- and six-cylinder cars, mileage is higher for standard transmissions. But

MPG Distribution by Auto Type

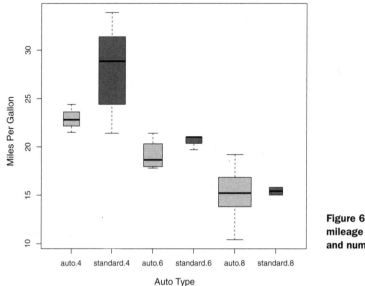

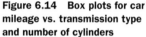

Figure 6.14   Box plots for car mileage vs. transmission type and number of cylinders

for eight-cylinder cars, there doesn't appear to be a difference. You can also see from the widths of the box plots that standard four-cylinder and automatic eight-cylinder cars are the most common in this dataset.

6.5.2   *Violin plots*

Before we end our discussion of box plots, it's worth examining a variation called a *violin plot*. A violin plot is a combination of a box plot and a kernel density plot. You can create one using the vioplot() function from the vioplot package. Be sure to install the vioplot package before first use.

The format for the vioplot() function is

```
vioplot(x1, x2, ... , names=, col=)
```

where *x1, x2, ...* represent one or more numeric vectors to be plotted (one violin plot is produced for each vector). The *names* parameter provides a character vector of labels for the violin plots, and *col* is a vector specifying the colors for each violin plot. An example is given in the following listing.

Listing 6.10   Violin plots

```
library(vioplot)
x1 <- mtcars$mpg[mtcars$cyl==4]
x2 <- mtcars$mpg[mtcars$cyl==6]
x3 <- mtcars$mpg[mtcars$cyl==8]
vioplot(x1, x2, x3,
        names=c("4 cyl", "6 cyl", "8 cyl"),
        col="gold")
```

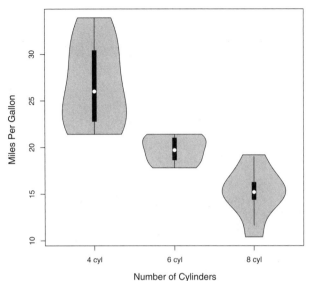

Violin Plots of Miles Per Gallon

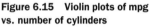

Figure 6.15   Violin plots of mpg
vs. number of cylinders

```
title("Violin Plots of Miles Per Gallon", ylab="Miles Per Gallon",
        xlab="Number of Cylinders")
```

Note that the `vioplot()` function requires you to separate the groups to be plotted into separate variables. The results are displayed in figure 6.15.

Violin plots are basically kernel density plots superimposed in a mirror-image fashion over box plots. Here, the white dot is the median, the black boxes range from the lower to the upper quartile, and the thin black lines represent the whiskers. The outer shape provides the kernel density plot. Violin plots haven't really caught on yet. Again, this may be due to a lack of easily accessible software; time will tell.

We'll end this chapter with a look at dot plots. Unlike the graphs you've seen previously, dot plots plot every value for a variable.

6.6   *Dot plots*

Dot plots provide a method of plotting a large number of labeled values on a simple horizontal scale. You create them with the `dotchart()` function, using the format

```
dotchart(x, labels=)
```

where *x* is a numeric vector and *labels* specifies a vector that labels each point. You can add a `groups` option to designate a factor specifying how the elements of *x* are grouped. If so, the option `gcolor` controls the color of the groups label, and `cex` controls the size of the labels. Here's an example with the `mtcars` dataset:

```
dotchart(mtcars$mpg, labels=row.names(mtcars), cex=.7,
        main="Gas Mileage for Car Models",
        xlab="Miles Per Gallon")
```

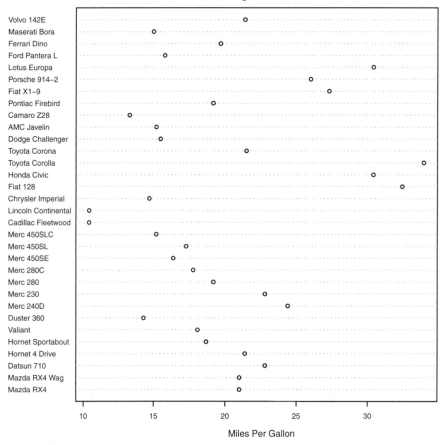

Figure 6.16   Dot plot of mpg for each car model

The resulting plot is given in figure 6.16. This graph allows you to see the mpg for each make of car on the same horizontal axis. Dot plots typically become most interesting when they're sorted and grouping factors are distinguished by symbol and color. An example is given in the following listing and shown in figure 6.17.

Listing 6.11   Dot plot grouped, sorted, and colored

Transforms
the numeric
vector cyl
into a factor

```
x <- mtcars[order(mtcars$mpg),]

x$cyl <- factor(x$cyl)

x$color[x$cyl==4] <- "red"
x$color[x$cyl==6] <- "blue"
x$color[x$cyl==8] <- "darkgreen"
```

Sorts the data frame mtcars
by mpg (lowest to highest) and
saves it as data frame x

Adds a character vector (color) to data frame
x containing the value "red", "blue", or
"darkgreen" depending on the value of cyl

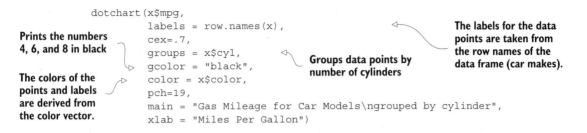

```
dotchart(x$mpg,
         labels = row.names(x),
         cex=.7,
         groups = x$cyl,
         gcolor = "black",
         color = x$color,
         pch=19,
         main = "Gas Mileage for Car Models\ngrouped by cylinder",
         xlab = "Miles Per Gallon")
```

Prints the numbers 4, 6, and 8 in black

The colors of the points and labels are derived from the color vector.

Groups data points by number of cylinders

The labels for the data points are taken from the row names of the data frame (car makes).

In figure 6.17, a number of features become evident for the first time. Again, you see an increase in gas mileage as the number of cylinders decreases. But you also see exceptions. For example, the Pontiac Firebird, with eight cylinders, gets higher gas mileage than the Mercury 280C and the Valiant, each with six cylinders. The Hornet 4 Drive, with six cylinders, gets the same miles per gallon as the Volvo 142E, which has

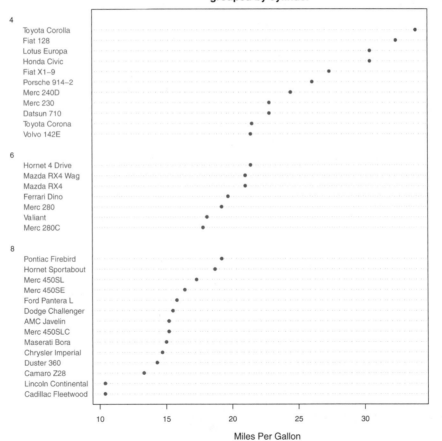

Figure 6.17   Dot plot of mpg for car models grouped by number of cylinders

four cylinders. It's also clear that the Toyota Corolla gets the best gas mileage by far, whereas the Lincoln Continental and Cadillac Fleetwood are outliers on the low end.

You can gain significant insight from a dot plot in this example because each point is labeled, the value of each point is inherently meaningful, and the points are arranged in a manner that promotes comparisons. But as the number of data points increases, the utility of the dot plot decreases.

> **NOTE** There are many variations of the dot plot. Jacoby (2006) provides a very informative discussion of the dot plot and includes R code for innovative applications. Additionally, the `Hmisc` package offers a dot-plot function (aptly named `dotchart2()`) with a number of additional features.

6.7   Summary

In this chapter, you learned how to describe continuous and categorical variables. You saw how bar plots and (to a lesser extent) pie charts can be used to gain insight into the distribution of a categorical variable, and how stacked and grouped bar charts can help you understand how groups differ on a categorical outcome. We also explored how histograms, plots, box plots, rug plots, and dot plots can help you visualize the distribution of continuous variables. Finally, we explored how overlapping kernel density plots, parallel box plots, and grouped dot plots can help you visualize group differences on a continuous outcome variable.

In later chapters, we'll extend this univariate focus to include bivariate and multivariate graphical methods. You'll see how to visually depict relationships among many variables at once using such methods as scatter plots, multigroup line plots, mosaic plots, correlograms, lattice graphs, and more.

In the next chapter, we'll look at basic statistical methods for describing distributions and bivariate relationships numerically, as well as inferential methods for evaluating whether relationships among variables exist or are due to sampling error.

Basic statistics

7

This chapter covers

- Descriptive statistics
- Frequency and contingency tables
- Correlations and covariances
- t-tests
- Nonparametric statistics

In previous chapters, you learned how to import data into R and use a variety of functions to organize and transform the data into a useful format. We then reviewed basic methods for visualizing data.

Once your data is properly organized and you've begun to explore the data visually, the next step is typically to describe the distribution of each variable numerically, followed by an exploration of the relationships among selected variables two at a time. The goal is to answer questions like these:

- What kind of mileage are cars getting these days? Specifically, what's the distribution of miles per gallon (mean, standard deviation, median, range, and so on) in a survey of automobile makes and models?

- After a new drug trial, what's the outcome (no improvement, some improvement, marked improvement) for drug versus placebo groups? Does the gender of the participants have an impact on the outcome?
- What's the correlation between income and life expectancy? Is it significantly different from zero?
- Are you more likely to receive imprisonment for a crime in different regions of the United States? Are the differences between regions statistically significant?

In this chapter, we'll review R functions for generating basic descriptive and inferential statistics. First we'll look at measures of location and scale for quantitative variables. Then you'll learn how to generate frequency and contingency tables (and associated chi-square tests) for categorical variables. Next, we'll examine the various forms of correlation coefficients available for continuous and ordinal variables. Finally, we'll turn to the study of group differences through parametric (t-tests) and nonparametric (Mann–Whitney U test, Kruskal–Wallis test) methods. Although our focus is on numerical results, we'll refer to graphical methods for visualizing these results throughout.

The statistical methods covered in this chapter are typically taught in a first-year undergraduate statistics course. If these methodologies are unfamiliar to you, two excellent references are McCall (2000) and Kirk (2007). Alternatively, many informative online resources are available (such as Wikipedia) for each of the topics covered.

7.1   *Descriptive statistics*

In this section, we'll look at measures of central tendency, variability, and distribution shape for continuous variables. For illustrative purposes, we'll use several of the variables from the Motor Trend Car Road Tests (mtcars) dataset you first saw in chapter 1. Our focus will be on miles per gallon (mpg), horsepower (hp), and weight (wt):

```
> myvars <- c("mpg", "hp", "wt")
> head(mtcars[myvars])
                   mpg   hp    wt
Mazda RX4         21.0  110  2.62
Mazda RX4 Wag     21.0  110  2.88
Datsun 710        22.8   93  2.32
Hornet 4 Drive    21.4  110  3.21
Hornet Sportabout 18.7  175  3.44
Valiant           18.1  105  3.46
```

First we'll look at descriptive statistics for all 32 cars. Then we'll examine descriptive statistics by transmission type (am) and number of cylinders (cyl). Transmission type is a dichotomous variable coded 0=automatic, 1=manual, and the number of cylinders can be 4, 5, or 6.

7.1.1   *A menagerie of methods*

When it comes to calculating descriptive statistics, R has an embarrassment of riches. Let's start with functions that are included in the base installation. Then we'll look at extensions that are available through the use of user-contributed packages.

In the base installation, you can use the summary() function to obtain descriptive statistics. An example is presented in the following listing.

Listing 7.1 Descriptive statistics via summary()

```
> myvars <- c("mpg", "hp", "wt")
> summary(mtcars[myvars])
      mpg              hp              wt
 Min.   :10.4    Min.   : 52.0    Min.   :1.51
 1st Qu.:15.4    1st Qu.: 96.5    1st Qu.:2.58
 Median :19.2    Median :123.0    Median :3.33
 Mean   :20.1    Mean   :146.7    Mean   :3.22
 3rd Qu.:22.8    3rd Qu.:180.0    3rd Qu.:3.61
 Max.   :33.9    Max.   :335.0    Max.   :5.42
```

The summary() function provides the minimum, maximum, quartiles, and mean for numerical variables and frequencies for factors and logical vectors. You can use the apply() or sapply() function from chapter 5 to provide any descriptive statistics you choose. For the sapply() function, the format is

```
sapply(x, FUN, options)
```

where x is the data frame (or matrix) and *FUN* is an arbitrary function. If *options* are present, they're passed to *FUN*. Typical functions that you can plug in here are mean(), sd(), var(), min(), max(), median(), length(), range(), and quantile(). The function fivenum() returns Tukey's five-number summary (minimum, lower-hinge, median, upper-hinge, and maximum).

Surprisingly, the base installation doesn't provide functions for skew and kurtosis, but you can add your own. The example in the next listing provides several descriptive statistics, including skew and kurtosis.

Listing 7.2 Descriptive statistics via sapply()

```
> mystats <- function(x, na.omit=FALSE){
                if (na.omit)
                    x <- x[!is.na(x)]
                m <- mean(x)
                n <- length(x)
                s <- sd(x)
                skew <- sum((x-m)^3/s^3)/n
                kurt <- sum((x-m)^4/s^4)/n - 3
                return(c(n=n, mean=m, stdev=s, skew=skew, kurtosis=kurt))
            }

> myvars <- c("mpg", "hp", "wt")
> sapply(mtcars[myvars], mystats)
              mpg        hp        wt
n          32.000    32.000    32.0000
mean       20.091   146.688     3.2172
stdev       6.027    68.563     0.9785
skew        0.611     0.726     0.4231
kurtosis   -0.373    -0.136    -0.0227
```

For cars in this sample, the mean mpg is 20.1, with a standard deviation of 6.0. The distribution is skewed to the right (+0.61) and is somewhat flatter than a normal distribution (–0.37). This is most evident if you graph the data. Note that if you wanted to omit missing values, you could use `sapply(mtcars[myvars], mystats, na.omit=TRUE)`.

7.1.2   *Even more methods*

Several user-contributed packages offer functions for descriptive statistics, including `Hmisc`, `pastecs`, and `psych`. Because these packages aren't included in the base distribution, you'll need to install them on first use (see section 1.4).

The `describe()` function in the `Hmisc` package returns the number of variables and observations, the number of missing and unique values, the mean, quantiles, and the five highest and lowest values. An example is provided in the following listing.

Listing 7.3   Descriptive statistics via `describe()` in the `Hmisc` package

```
> library(Hmisc)
> myvars <- c("mpg", "hp", "wt")
> describe(mtcars[myvars])

 3  Variables      32  Observations
-----------------------------------------------------------------------------
mpg
n missing  unique  Mean    .05    .10     .25    .50    .75     .90     .95
32      0      25   20.09  12.00  14.34  15.43  19.20  22.80  30.09  31.30

lowest : 10.4 13.3 14.3 14.7 15.0, highest: 26.0 27.3 30.4 32.4 33.9
-----------------------------------------------------------------------------
hp
n missing  unique   Mean    .05     .10    .2      .50    .75    .90      .95
32      0      22   146.7   63.65   66.00  96.50  123.00 180.00 243.50  253.55

lowest :   52  62  65  66   91, highest: 215 230 245 264 335
-----------------------------------------------------------------------------
wt
n missing  unique   Mean    .05     .10     .25     .50    .75     .90    .95
32      0      29    3.217  1.736   1.956   2.581  3.325  3.610   4.048  5.293

lowest : 1.513 1.615 1.835 1.935 2.140, highest: 3.845 4.070 5.250 5.345 5.424
-----------------------------------------------------------------------------
```

The `pastecs` package includes a function named `stat.desc()` that provides a wide range of descriptive statistics. The format is

```
stat.desc(x, basic=TRUE, desc=TRUE, norm=FALSE, p=0.95)
```

where *x* is a data frame or time series. If `basic=TRUE` (the default), the number of values, null values, missing values, minimum, maximum, range, and sum are provided. If `desc=TRUE` (also the default), the median, mean, standard error of the mean, 95% confidence interval for the mean, variance, standard deviation, and coefficient of variation are also provided. Finally, if `norm=TRUE` (not the default), normal distribution statistics are returned, including skewness and kurtosis (and their statistical significance) and the Shapiro–Wilk test of normality. A p-value option is used to calculate the confidence interval for the mean (.95 by default). The next listing gives an example.

Listing 7.4   Descriptive statistics via `stat.desc()` in the `pastecs` package

```
> library(pastecs)
> myvars <- c("mpg", "hp", "wt")
> stat.desc(mtcars[myvars])
                mpg       hp      wt
nbr.val        32.00   32.000  32.000
nbr.null        0.00    0.000   0.000
nbr.na          0.00    0.000   0.000
min            10.40   52.000   1.513
max            33.90  335.000   5.424
range          23.50  283.000   3.911
sum           642.90 4694.000 102.952
median         19.20  123.000   3.325
mean           20.09  146.688   3.217
SE.mean         1.07   12.120   0.173
CI.mean.0.95    2.17   24.720   0.353
var            36.32 4700.867   0.957
std.dev         6.03   68.563   0.978
coef.var        0.30    0.467   0.304
```

As if this isn't enough, the `psych` package also has a function called `describe()` that provides the number of nonmissing observations, mean, standard deviation, median, trimmed mean, median absolute deviation, minimum, maximum, range, skew, kurtosis, and standard error of the mean. You can see an example in the following listing.

Listing 7.5   Descriptive statistics via `describe()` in the `psych` package

```
> library(psych)
Attaching package: 'psych'
        The following object(s) are masked from package:Hmisc :
         describe
> myvars <- c("mpg", "hp", "wt")
> describe(mtcars[myvars])
     var  n   mean    sd median trimmed   mad   min    max
mpg    1 32  20.09  6.03  19.20   19.70  5.41 10.40  33.90
hp     2 32 146.69 68.56 123.00  141.19 77.10 52.00 335.00
wt     3 32   3.22  0.98   3.33    3.15  0.77  1.51   5.42
     range skew kurtosis    se
mpg  23.50 0.61    -0.37  1.07
hp  283.00 0.73    -0.14 12.12
wt    3.91 0.42    -0.02  0.17
```

I told you that it was an embarrassment of riches!

NOTE   In the previous examples, the packages `psych` and `Hmisc` both provide a function named `describe()`. How does R know which one to use? Simply put, the package last loaded takes precedence, as shown in listing 7.5. Here, `psych` is loaded after `Hmisc`, and a message is printed indicating that the `describe()` function in `Hmisc` is masked by the function in `psych`. When you type in the `describe()` function and R searches for it, R comes to the `psych` package first and executes it. If you want the `Hmisc` version instead, you can type `Hmisc::describe(mt)`. The function is still there. You have to give R more information to find it.

Now that you know how to generate descriptive statistics for the data as a whole, let's review how to obtain statistics for subgroups of the data.

7.1.3   *Descriptive statistics by group*

When comparing groups of individuals or observations, the focus is usually on the descriptive statistics of each group, rather than the total sample. Again, there are several ways to accomplish this in R. We'll start by getting descriptive statistics for each level of transmission type. In chapter 5, we discussed methods of aggregating data. You can use the `aggregate()` function (section 5.6.2) to obtain descriptive statistics by group, as shown in the following listing.

Listing 7.6   Descriptive statistics by group using `aggregate()`

```
> myvars <- c("mpg", "hp", "wt")

> aggregate(mtcars[myvars], by=list(am=mtcars$am), mean)
    am    mpg    hp    wt
1   0    17.1   160   3.77
2   1    24.4   127   2.41

> aggregate(mtcars[myvars], by=list(am=mtcars$am), sd)
    am    mpg    hp    wt
1   0    3.83   53.9  0.777
2   1    6.17   84.1  0.617
```

Note the use of `list(am=mtcars$am)`. If you used `list(mtcars$am)`, the am column would be labeled `Group.1` rather than am. You use the assignment to provide a more useful column label. If you have more than one grouping variable, you can use code like `by=list(name1=groupvar1, name2=groupvar2, ... , nameN=groupvarN)`.

Unfortunately, `aggregate()` only allows you to use single-value functions such as mean, standard deviation, and the like in each call. It won't return several statistics at once. For that task, you can use the `by()` function. The format is

```
by(data, INDICES, FUN)
```

where *data* is a data frame or matrix, *INDICES* is a factor or list of factors that defines the groups, and *FUN* is an arbitrary function that operates on all the columns of a data frame. The next listing provides an example.

Listing 7.7   Descriptive statistics by group using `by()`

```
> dstats <- function(x) sapply(x, mystats)
> myvars <- c("mpg", "hp", "wt")
> by(mtcars[myvars], mtcars$am, dstats)
```

```
mtcars$am: 0
                mpg        hp        wt
n            19.000   19.0000    19.000
mean         17.147  160.2632     3.769
stdev         3.834   53.9082     0.777
skew          0.014   -0.0142     0.976
kurtosis     -0.803   -1.2097     0.142
----------------------------------------
mtcars$am: 1
                mpg        hp        wt
n            13.0000   13.000    13.000
mean         24.3923  126.846     2.411
stdev         6.1665   84.062     0.617
skew          0.0526    1.360     0.210
kurtosis     -1.4554    0.563    -1.174
```

In this case, `dstats()` applies the `mystats()` function from listing 7.2 to each column of the data frame. Placing it in the `by()` function gives you summary statistics for each level of am.

7.1.4 Additional methods by group

The `doBy` package and the `psych` package also provide functions for descriptive statistics by group. Again, they aren't distributed in the base installation and must be installed before first use. The `summaryBy()` function in the `doBy` package has the format

```
summaryBy(formula, data=dataframe, FUN=function)
```

where the formula takes the form

```
var1 + var2 + var3 + ... + varN ~ groupvar1 + groupvar2 + ... + groupvarN
```

Variables on the left of the ~ are the numeric variables to be analyzed, and variables on the right are categorical grouping variables. The *function* can be any built-in or user-created R function. An example using the `mystats()` function created in section 7.2.1 is shown in the following listing.

> **Listing 7.8 Summary statistics by group using `summaryBy()` in the `doBy` package**

```
> library(doBy)
> summaryBy(mpg+hp+wt~am, data=mtcars, FUN=mystats)
  am  mpg.n  mpg.mean  mpg.stdev  mpg.skew  mpg.kurtosis  hp.n  hp.mean  hp.stdev
1  0     19      17.1       3.83    0.0140        -0.803    19      160      53.9
2  1     13      24.4       6.17    0.0526        -1.455    13      127      84.1
    hp.skew  hp.kurtosis  wt.n  wt.mean  wt.stdev  wt.skew  wt.kurtosis
1  -0.0142       -1.210    19     3.77     0.777    0.976        0.142
2   1.3599        0.563    13     2.41     0.617    0.210       -1.174
```

The `describeBy()` function contained in the `psych` package provides the same descriptive statistics as `describe()`, stratified by one or more grouping variables, as you can see in the following listing.

Listing 7.9 Summary statistics by group using `describe.by()` in the `psych` package

```
> library(psych)
> myvars <- c("mpg", "hp", "wt")
> describeBy(mtcars[myvars], list(am=mtcars$am))
```

am: 0

	var	n	mean	sd	median	trimmed	mad	min	max
mpg	1	19	17.15	3.83	17.30	17.12	3.11	10.40	24.40
hp	2	19	160.26	53.91	175.00	161.06	77.10	62.00	245.00
wt	3	19	3.77	0.78	3.52	3.75	0.45	2.46	5.42

	range	skew	kurtosis	se
mpg	14.00	0.01	-0.80	0.88
hp	183.00	-0.01	-1.21	12.37
wt	2.96	0.98	0.14	0.18

----

am: 1

	var	n	mean	sd	median	trimmed	mad	min	max
mpg	1	13	24.39	6.17	22.80	24.38	6.67	15.00	33.90
hp	2	13	126.85	84.06	109.00	114.73	63.75	52.00	335.00
wt	3	13	2.41	0.62	2.32	2.39	0.68	1.51	3.57

	range	skew	kurtosis	se
mpg	18.90	0.05	-1.46	1.71
hp	283.00	1.36	0.56	23.31
wt	2.06	0.21	-1.17	0.17

Unlike the previous example, the describeBy() function doesn't allow you to specify an arbitrary function, so it's less generally applicable. If there's more than one grouping variable, you can write them as list(*name1=groupvar1, name2=groupvar2, ... , nameN=groupvarN*). But this will work only if there are no empty cells when the grouping variables are crossed.

Data analysts have their own preferences for which descriptive statistics to display and how they like to see them formatted. This is probably why there are many variations available. Choose the one that works best for you, or create your own!

7.1.5 Visualizing results

Numerical summaries of a distribution's characteristics are important, but they're no substitute for a visual representation. For quantitative variables, you have histograms (section 6.3), density plots (section 6.4), box plots (section 6.5), and dot plots (section 6.6). They can provide insights that are easily missed by reliance on a small set of descriptive statistics.

The functions considered so far provide summaries of quantitative variables. The functions in the next section allow you to examine the distributions of categorical variables.

7.2 Frequency and contingency tables

In this section, we'll look at frequency and contingency tables from categorical variables, along with tests of independence, measures of association, and methods for graphically displaying results. We'll be using functions in the basic installation, along with functions from the vcd and gmodels packages. In the following examples, assume that A, B, and C represent categorical variables.

The data for this section come from the Arthritis dataset included with the vcd package. The data are from Kock & Edward (1988) and represent a double-blind clinical trial of new treatments for rheumatoid arthritis. Here are the first few observations:

```
> library(vcd)
> head(Arthritis)
    ID    Treatment    Sex    Age    Improved
1   57      Treated   Male     27        Some
2   46      Treated   Male     29        None
3   77      Treated   Male     30        None
4   17      Treated   Male     32      Marked
5   36      Treated   Male     46      Marked
6   23      Treated   Male     58      Marked
```

Treatment (Placebo, Treated), Sex (Male, Female), and Improved (None, Some, Marked) are all categorical factors. In the next section, you'll create frequency and contingency tables (cross-classifications) from the data.

7.2.1 Generating frequency tables

R provides several methods for creating frequency and contingency tables. The most important functions are listed in table 7.1.

Table 7.1   Functions for creating and manipulating contingency tables

Function	Description
table(var1, var2, ..., varN)	Creates an N-way contingency table from N categorical variables (factors)
xtabs(formula, data)	Creates an N-way contingency table based on a formula and a matrix or data frame
prop.table(table, margins)	Expresses table entries as fractions of the marginal table defined by the margins
margin.table(table, margins)	Computes the sum of table entries for a marginal table defined by the margins
addmargins(table, margins)	Puts summary margins (sums by default) on a table
ftable(table)	Creates a compact, "flat" contingency table

In the following sections, we'll use each of these functions to explore categorical variables. We'll begin with simple frequencies, followed by two-way contingency tables, and end with multiway contingency tables. The first step is to create a table using either the table() or xtabs() function and then manipulate it using the other functions.

ONE-WAY TABLES

You can generate simple frequency counts using the `table()` function. Here's an example:

```
> mytable <- with(Arthritis, table(Improved))
> mytable
Improved
  None   Some  Marked
    42     14      28
```

You can turn these frequencies into proportions with `prop.table()`

```
> prop.table(mytable)
Improved
  None   Some  Marked
 0.500  0.167   0.333
```

or into percentages using `prop.table()*100`:

```
> prop.table(mytable)*100
Improved
  None   Some  Marked
  50.0   16.7    33.3
```

Here you can see that 50% of study participants had some or marked improvement (16.7 + 33.3).

TWO-WAY TABLES

For two-way tables, the format for the `table()` function is

```
mytable <- table(A, B)
```

where *A* is the row variable and *B* is the column variable. Alternatively, the `xtabs()` function allows you to create a contingency table using formula-style input. The format is

```
mytable <- xtabs(~ A + B, data=mydata)
```

where *mydata* is a matrix or data frame. In general, the variables to be cross-classified appear on the right of the formula (that is, to the right of the ~) separated by + signs. If a variable is included on the left side of the formula, it's assumed to be a vector of frequencies (useful if the data have already been tabulated).

For the `Arthritis` data, you have

```
> mytable <- xtabs(~ Treatment+Improved, data=Arthritis)
> mytable
          Improved
Treatment  None  Some  Marked
  Placebo    29     7       7
  Treated    13     7      21
```

You can generate marginal frequencies and proportions using the `margin.table()` and `prop.table()` functions, respectively. For row sums and row proportions, you have

```
> margin.table(mytable, 1)
Treatment
Placebo Treated
      3      41
```

```
> prop.table(mytable, 1)
         Improved
Treatment   None    Some    Marked
  Placebo  0.674   0.163    0.163
  Treated  0.317   0.171    0.512
```

The index (1) refers to the first variable in the table() statement. Looking at the table, you can see that 51% of treated individuals had marked improvement, compared to 16% of those receiving a placebo.

For column sums and column proportions, you have

```
> margin.table(mytable, 2)
Improved
  None    Some   Marked
   42      14      28
> prop.table(mytable, 2)
         Improved
Treatment   None    Some    Marked
  Placebo  0.690   0.500    0.250
  Treated  0.310   0.500    0.750
```

Here, the index (2) refers to the second variable in the table() statement.

Cell proportions are obtained with this statement:

```
> prop.table(mytable)
         Improved
Treatment   None     Some     Marked
  Placebo  0.3452   0.0833   0.0833
  Treated  0.1548   0.0833   0.2500
```

You can use the addmargins() function to add marginal sums to these tables. For example, the following code adds a Sum row and column:

```
> addmargins(mytable)
         Improved
Treatment   None    Some   Marked   Sum
  Placebo    29       7       7      43
  Treated    13       7      21      41
  Sum        42      14      28      84
> addmargins(prop.table(mytable))
         Improved
Treatment   None     Some     Marked    Sum
  Placebo  0.3452   0.0833   0.0833   0.5119
  Treated  0.1548   0.0833   0.2500   0.4881
  Sum      0.5000   0.1667   0.3333   1.0000
```

When using addmargins(), the default is to create sum margins for all variables in a table. In contrast, the following code adds a Sum column alone:

```
> addmargins(prop.table(mytable, 1), 2)
         Improved
Treatment   None    Some    Marked    Sum
  Placebo  0.674   0.163    0.163    1.000
  Treated  0.317   0.171    0.512    1.000
```

Similarly, this code adds a Sum row:

```
> addmargins(prop.table(mytable, 2), 1)
          Improved
Treatment   None    Some    Marked
  Placebo   0.690   0.500   0.250
  Treated   0.310   0.500   0.750
  Sum       1.000   1.000   1.000
```

In the table, you see that 25% of those patients with marked improvement received a placebo.

> **NOTE** The `table()` function ignores missing values (NAs) by default. To include NA as a valid category in the frequency counts, include the table option `useNA="ifany"`.

A third method for creating two-way tables is the `CrossTable()` function in the `gmodels` package. The `CrossTable()` function produces two-way tables modeled after `PROC FREQ` in SAS or `CROSSTABS` in SPSS. The following listing shows an example.

Listing 7.10 Two-way table using `CrossTable`

```
> library(gmodels)
> CrossTable(Arthritis$Treatment, Arthritis$Improved)


   Cell Contents
|-------------------------|
|                       N |
| Chi-square contribution |
|           N / Row Total |
|           N / Col Total |
|         N / Table Total |
|-------------------------|


Total Observations in Table:   84


                 | Arthritis$Improved
Arthritis$Treatment |    None  |    Some  |  Marked  | Row Total |
-----------------|----------|----------|----------|-----------|
         Placebo |      29  |       7  |       7  |       43  |
                 |   2.616  |   0.004  |   3.752  |           |
                 |   0.674  |   0.163  |   0.163  |    0.512  |
                 |   0.690  |   0.500  |   0.250  |           |
                 |   0.345  |   0.083  |   0.083  |           |
-----------------|----------|----------|----------|-----------|
         Treated |      13  |       7  |      21  |       41  |
                 |   2.744  |   0.004  |   3.935  |           |
                 |   0.317  |   0.171  |   0.512  |    0.488  |
                 |   0.310  |   0.500  |   0.750  |           |
                 |   0.155  |   0.083  |   0.250  |           |
-----------------|----------|----------|----------|-----------|
    Column Total |      42  |      14  |      28  |       84  |
                 |   0.500  |   0.167  |   0.333  |           |
-----------------|----------|----------|----------|-----------|
```

The `CrossTable()` function has options to report percentages (row, column, and cell); specify decimal places; produce chi-square, Fisher, and McNemar tests of independence; report expected and residual values (Pearson, standardized, and adjusted standardized); include missing values as valid; annotate with row and column titles; and format as SAS or SPSS style output. See `help(CrossTable)` for details.

If you have more than two categorical variables, you're dealing with multidimensional tables. We'll consider these next.

MULTIDIMENSIONAL TABLES

Both `table()` and `xtabs()` can be used to generate multidimensional tables based on three or more categorical variables. The `margin.table()`, `prop.table()`, and `add-margins()` functions extend naturally to more than two dimensions. Additionally, the `ftable()` function can be used to print multidimensional tables in a compact and attractive manner. An example is given in the next listing.

Listing 7.11 Three-way contingency table

```
> mytable <- xtabs(~ Treatment+Sex+Improved, data=Arthritis)
> mytable
, , Improved = None

          Sex
Treatment Female  Male
  Placebo     19    10
  Treated      6     7

, , Improved = Some

          Sex
Treatment Female  Male
  Placebo      7     0
  Treated      5     2

, , Improved = Marked

          Sex
Treatment Female  Male
  Placebo      6     1
  Treated     16     5

> ftable(mytable)
                Sex Female Male
Treatment Improved
Placebo   None             19   10
          Some              7    0
          Marked            6    1
Treated   None              6    7
          Some              5    2
          Marked           16    5

> margin.table(mytable, 1)
```

❶ Cell frequencies

❷ Marginal frequencies

```
Treatment
Placebo Treated
     43      41
> margin.table(mytable, 2)
Sex
Female   Male
    59     25
> margin.table(mytable, 3)
Improved
  None   Some Marked
    42     14     28
> margin.table(mytable, c(1, 3))
         Improved
Treatment None Some Marked
  Placebo   29    7      7
  Treated   13    7     21
> ftable(prop.table(mytable, c(1, 2)))
                  Improved  None   Some Marked
Treatment Sex
Placebo   Female           0.594 0.219  0.188
          Male             0.909 0.000  0.091
Treated   Female           0.222 0.185  0.593
          Male             0.500 0.143  0.357

> ftable(addmargins(prop.table(mytable, c(1, 2)), 3))
                  Improved  None   Some Marked    Sum
Treatment Sex
Placebo   Female           0.594 0.219  0.188  1.000
          Male             0.909 0.000  0.091  1.000
Treated   Female           0.222 0.185  0.593  1.000
          Male             0.500 0.143  0.357  1.000
```

❸ Treatment × Improved marginal frequencies

❹ Improved proportions for Treatment × Sex

The code at ❶ produces cell frequencies for the three-way classification. The code also demonstrates how the ftable() function can be used to print a more compact and attractive version of the table.

The code at ❷ produces the marginal frequencies for Treatment, Sex, and Improved. Because you created the table with the formula ~Treatment+Sex+Improved, Treatment is referred to by index 1, Sex is referred to by index 2, and Improved is referred to by index 3.

The code at ❸ produces the marginal frequencies for the Treatment x Improved classification, summed over Sex. The proportion of patients with None, Some, and Marked improvement for each Treatment × Sex combination is provided in ❹. Here you see that 36% of treated males had marked improvement, compared to 59% of treated females. In general, the proportions will add to 1 over the indices not included in the prop.table() call (the third index, or Improved in this case). You can see this in the last example, where you add a sum margin over the third index.

If you want percentages instead of proportions, you can multiply the resulting table by 100. For example, this statement

```
ftable(addmargins(prop.table(mytable, c(1, 2)), 3)) * 100
```

produces this table:

```
                Sex Female  Male   Sum
Treatment Improved
Placebo   None         65.5  34.5 100.0
          Some        100.0   0.0 100.0
          Marked       85.7  14.3 100.0
Treated   None         46.2  53.8 100.0
          Some         71.4  28.6 100.0
          Marked       76.2  23.8 100.0
```

Contingency tables tell you the frequency or proportions of cases for each combination of the variables that make up the table, but you're probably also interested in whether the variables in the table are related or independent. Tests of independence are covered in the next section.

7.2.2 Tests of independence

R provides several methods of testing the independence of categorical variables. The three tests described in this section are the chi-square test of independence, the Fisher exact test, and the Cochran-Mantel–Haenszel test.

CHI-SQUARE TEST OF INDEPENDENCE

You can apply the function chisq.test() to a two-way table in order to produce a chi-square test of independence of the row and column variables. See the next listing for an example.

Listing 7.12 Chi-square test of independence

```
> library(vcd)
> mytable <- xtabs(~Treatment+Improved, data=Arthritis)
> chisq.test(mytable)
        Pearson's Chi-squared test
data:  mytable
 X-squared = 13.1, df = 2, p-value = 0.001463
```
❶ Treatment and Improved aren't independent.

```
> mytable <- xtabs(~Improved+Sex, data=Arthritis)
> chisq.test(mytable)
        Pearson's Chi-squared test
data:  mytable
 X-squared = 4.84, df = 2, p-value = 0.0889
```
❷ Gender and Improved are independent.

```
Warning message:
In chisq.test(mytable) : Chi-squared approximation may be incorrect
```

From the results ❶, there appears to be a relationship between treatment received and level of improvement ($p < .01$). But there doesn't appear to be a relationship ❷ between patient sex and improvement ($p > .05$). The p-values are the probability of obtaining the sampled results, assuming independence of the row and column variables in the population. Because the probability is small for ❶, you reject the hypothesis that treatment type and outcome are independent. Because the probability for ❷ isn't small, it's not unreasonable to assume that outcome and gender are independent. The warning message in listing 7.13 is produced because one of the six cells in the table (male-some improvement) has an expected value less than five, which may invalidate the chi-square approximation.

FISHER'S EXACT TEST

You can produce a Fisher's exact test via the `fisher.test()` function. Fisher's exact test evaluates the null hypothesis of independence of rows and columns in a contingency table with fixed marginals. The format is `fisher.test(mytable)`, where `mytable` is a two-way table. Here's an example:

```
> mytable <- xtabs(~Treatment+Improved, data=Arthritis)
> fisher.test(mytable)
        Fisher's Exact Test for Count Data
data:  mytable
p-value = 0.001393
alternative hypothesis: two.sided
```

In contrast to many statistical packages, the `fisher.test()` function can be applied to any two-way table with two or more rows and columns, not a 2 × 2 table.

COCHRAN–MANTEL–HAENSZEL TEST

The `mantelhaen.test()` function provides a Cochran–Mantel–Haenszel chi-square test of the null hypothesis that two nominal variables are conditionally independent in each stratum of a third variable. The following code tests the hypothesis that the Treatment and Improved variables are independent within each level for Sex. The test assumes that there's no three-way (Treatment × Improved × Sex) interaction:

```
> mytable <- xtabs(~Treatment+Improved+Sex, data=Arthritis)
> mantelhaen.test(mytable)
        Cochran-Mantel-Haenszel test
data:  mytable
Cochran-Mantel-Haenszel M^2 = 14.6, df = 2, p-value = 0.0006647
```

The results suggest that the treatment received and the improvement reported aren't independent within each level of Sex (that is, treated individuals improved more than those receiving placebos when controlling for sex).

7.2.3   *Measures of association*

The significance tests in the previous section evaluate whether sufficient evidence exists to reject a null hypothesis of independence between variables. If you can reject the null hypothesis, your interest turns naturally to measures of association in order to gauge the strength of the relationships present. The `assocstats()` function in the vcd package can be used to calculate the phi coefficient, contingency coefficient, and Cramer's V for a two-way table. An example is given in the following listing.

Listing 7.13   Measures of association for a two-way table

```
> library(vcd)
> mytable <- xtabs(~Treatment+Improved, data=Arthritis)
> assocstats(mytable)
```

```
                    X^2 df  P(> X^2)
Likelihood Ratio 13.530  2 0.0011536
Pearson          13.055  2 0.0014626

Phi-Coefficient    : 0.394
Contingency Coeff.: 0.367
Cramer's V         : 0.394
```

In general, larger magnitudes indicate stronger associations. The vcd package also provides a kappa() function that can calculate Cohen's kappa and weighted kappa for a confusion matrix (for example, the degree of agreement between two judges classifying a set of objects into categories).

7.2.4 Visualizing results

R has mechanisms for visually exploring the relationships among categorical variables that go well beyond those found in most other statistical platforms. You typically use bar charts to visualize frequencies in one dimension (see section 6.1). The vcd package has excellent functions for visualizing relationships among categorical variables in multidimensional datasets using mosaic and association plots (see section 11.4). Finally, correspondence-analysis functions in the ca package allow you to visually explore relationships between rows and columns in contingency tables using various geometric representations (Nenadic and Greenacre, 2007).

This ends the discussion of contingency tables, until we take up more advanced topics in chapters 11 and 15. Next, let's look at various types of correlation coefficients.

7.3 Correlations

Correlation coefficients are used to describe relationships among quantitative variables. The sign ± indicates the direction of the relationship (positive or inverse), and the magnitude indicates the strength of the relationship (ranging from 0 for no relationship to 1 for a perfectly predictable relationship).

In this section, we'll look at a variety of correlation coefficients, as well as tests of significance. We'll use the state.x77 dataset available in the base R installation. It provides data on the population, income, illiteracy rate, life expectancy, murder rate, and high school graduation rate for the 50 US states in 1977. There are also temperature and land-area measures, but we'll drop them to save space. Use help(state.x77) to learn more about the file. In addition to the base installation, we'll be using the psych and ggm packages.

7.3.1 Types of correlations

R can produce a variety of correlation coefficients, including Pearson, Spearman, Kendall, partial, polychoric, and polyserial. Let's look at each in turn.

PEARSON, SPEARMAN, AND KENDALL CORRELATIONS

The Pearson product-moment correlation assesses the degree of linear relationship between two quantitative variables. Spearman's rank-order correlation coefficient assesses the degree of relationship between two rank-ordered variables. Kendall's tau is also a nonparametric measure of rank correlation.

The cor() function produces all three correlation coefficients, whereas the cov() function provides covariances. There are many options, but a simplified format for producing correlations is

```
cor(x, use= , method= )
```

The options are described in table 7.2.

Table 7.2 cor/cov options

Option	Description
x	Matrix or data frame.
use	Specifies the handling of missing data. The options are all.obs (assumes no missing data—missing data will produce an error), everything (any correlation involving a case with missing values will be set to missing), complete.obs (listwise deletion), and pairwise.complete.obs (pairwise deletion).
method	Specifies the type of correlation. The options are pearson, spearman, and kendall.

The default options are use="everything" and method="pearson". You can see an example in the following listing.

Listing 7.14 Covariances and correlations

```
> states<- state.x77[,1:6]
> cov(states)
           Population Income Illiteracy Life Exp  Murder  HS Grad
Population   19931684 571230    292.868 -407.842 5663.52 -3551.51
Income         571230 377573   -163.702  280.663 -521.89  3076.77
Illiteracy        293   -164      0.372   -0.482    1.58    -3.24
Life Exp         -408    281     -0.482    1.802   -3.87     6.31
Murder           5664   -522      1.582   -3.869   13.63   -14.55
HS Grad         -3552   3077     -3.235    6.313  -14.55    65.24

> cor(states)
           Population Income Illiteracy Life Exp Murder  HS Grad
Population     1.0000  0.208      0.108   -0.068  0.344  -0.0985
Income         0.2082  1.000     -0.437    0.340 -0.230   0.6199
Illiteracy     0.1076 -0.437      1.000   -0.588  0.703  -0.6572
Life Exp      -0.0681  0.340     -0.588    1.000 -0.781   0.5822
Murder         0.3436 -0.230      0.703   -0.781  1.000  -0.4880
HS Grad       -0.0985  0.620     -0.657    0.582 -0.488   1.0000
> cor(states, method="spearman")
           Population Income Illiteracy Life Exp Murder HS Grad
Population      1.000  0.125      0.313   -0.104  0.346  -0.383
Income          0.125  1.000     -0.315    0.324 -0.217   0.510
Illiteracy      0.313 -0.315      1.000   -0.555  0.672  -0.655
Life Exp       -0.104  0.324     -0.555    1.000 -0.780   0.524
Murder          0.346 -0.217      0.672   -0.780  1.000  -0.437
HS Grad        -0.383  0.510     -0.655    0.524 -0.437   1.000
```

The first call produces the variances and covariances. The second provides Pearson product-moment correlation coefficients, and the third produces Spearman rank-order correlation coefficients. You can see, for example, that a strong positive correlation exists between income and high school graduation rate and that a strong negative correlation exists between illiteracy rates and life expectancy.

Notice that you get square matrices by default (all variables crossed with all other variables). You can also produce nonsquare matrices, as shown in the following example:

```
> x <- states[,c("Population", "Income", "Illiteracy", "HS Grad")]
> y <- states[,c("Life Exp", "Murder")]
> cor(x,y)
            Life Exp Murder
Population    -0.068  0.344
Income         0.340 -0.230
Illiteracy    -0.588  0.703
HS Grad        0.582 -0.488
```

This version of the function is particularly useful when you're interested in the relationships between one set of variables and another. Notice that the results don't tell you if the correlations differ significantly from 0 (that is, whether there's sufficient evidence based on the sample data to conclude that the population correlations differ from 0). For that, you need tests of significance (described in section 7.3.2).

PARTIAL CORRELATIONS

A *partial* correlation is a correlation between two quantitative variables, controlling for one or more other quantitative variables. You can use the pcor() function in the ggm package to provide partial correlation coefficients. The ggm package isn't installed by default, so be sure to install it on first use. The format is

```
pcor(u, S)
```

where u is a vector of numbers, with the first two numbers being the indices of the variables to be correlated, and the remaining numbers being the indices of the conditioning variables (that is, the variables being partialed out). S is the covariance matrix among the variables. An example will help clarify this:

```
> library(ggm)
> colnames(states)
[1] "Population" "Income" "Illiteracy" "Life Exp" "Murder" "HS Grad"
> pcor(c(1,5,2,3,6), cov(states))
[1] 0.346
```

In this case, 0.346 is the correlation between population (variable 1) and murder rate (variable 5), controlling for the influence of income, illiteracy rate, and high school graduation rate (variables 2, 3, and 6 respectively). The use of partial correlations is common in the social sciences.

OTHER TYPES OF CORRELATIONS

The hetcor() function in the polycor package can compute a heterogeneous correlation matrix containing Pearson product-moment correlations between numeric variables, polyserial correlations between numeric and ordinal variables, polychoric correlations between ordinal variables, and tetrachoric correlations between two dichotomous variables. Polyserial, polychoric, and tetrachoric correlations assume that the ordinal or dichotomous variables are derived from underlying normal distributions. See the documentation that accompanies this package for more information.

7.3.2 *Testing correlations for significance*

Once you've generated correlation coefficients, how do you test them for statistical significance? The typical null hypothesis is no relationship (that is, the correlation in the population is 0). You can use the `cor.test()` function to test an individual Pearson, Spearman, and Kendall correlation coefficient. A simplified format is

```
cor.test(x, y, alternative = , method = )
```

where *x* and *y* are the variables to be correlated, `alternative` specifies a two-tailed or one-tailed test (`"two.side"`, `"less"`, or `"greater"`), and `method` specifies the type of correlation (`"pearson"`, `"kendall"`, or `"spearman"`) to compute. Use `alternative ="less"` when the research hypothesis is that the population correlation is less than 0. Use `alternative="greater"` when the research hypothesis is that the population correlation is greater than 0. By default, `alternative="two.side"` (population correlation isn't equal to 0) is assumed. See the following listing for an example.

> **Listing 7.15 Testing a correlation coefficient for significance**

```
> cor.test(states[,3], states[,5])

        Pearson's product-moment correlation

data:  states[, 3] and states[, 5]
t = 6.85, df = 48, p-value = 1.258e-08
alternative hypothesis: true correlation is not equal to 0
95 percent confidence interval:
 0.528 0.821
sample estimates:
  cor
0.703
```

This code tests the null hypothesis that the Pearson correlation between life expectancy and murder rate is 0. Assuming that the population correlation is 0, you'd expect to see a sample correlation as large as 0.703 less than 1 time out of 10 million (that is, p = 1.258e-08). Given how unlikely this is, you reject the null hypothesis in favor of the research hypothesis, that the population correlation between life expectancy and murder rate is *not* 0.

Unfortunately, you can test only one correlation at a time using `cor.test()`. Luckily, the `corr.test()` function provided in the psych package allows you to go further. The `corr.test()` function produces correlations and significance levels for matrices of Pearson, Spearman, and Kendall correlations. An example is given in the following listing.

Listing 7.16 Correlation matrix and tests of significance via `corr.test()`

```
> library(psych)
> corr.test(states, use="complete")

Call:corr.test(x = states, use = "complete")
Correlation matrix
          Population Income Illiteracy Life Exp Murder HS Grad
Population      1.00   0.21       0.11    -0.07   0.34   -0.10
Income          0.21   1.00      -0.44     0.34  -0.23    0.62
Illiteracy      0.11  -0.44       1.00    -0.59   0.70   -0.66
Life Exp       -0.07   0.34      -0.59     1.00  -0.78    0.58
Murder          0.34  -0.23       0.70    -0.78   1.00   -0.49
HS Grad        -0.10   0.62      -0.66     0.58  -0.49    1.00

Sample Size
[1] 50

Probability value
          Population Income Illiteracy Life Exp Murder HS Grad
Population      0.00   0.15       0.46     0.64   0.01     0.5
Income          0.15   0.00       0.00     0.02   0.11     0.0
Illiteracy      0.46   0.00       0.00     0.00   0.00     0.0
Life Exp        0.64   0.02       0.00     0.00   0.00     0.0
Murder          0.01   0.11       0.00     0.00   0.00     0.0
HS Grad         0.50   0.00       0.00     0.00   0.00     0.0
```

The `use=` options can be `"pairwise"` or `"complete"` (for pairwise or listwise deletion of missing values, respectively). The `method=` option is `"pearson"` (the default), `"spearman"`, or `"kendall"`. Here you see that the correlation between population size and high school graduation rate (–0.10) is not significantly different from 0 ($p = 0.5$).

OTHER TESTS OF SIGNIFICANCE

In section 7.4.1, we looked at partial correlations. The `pcor.test()` function in the psych package can be used to test the conditional independence of two variables controlling for one or more additional variables, assuming multivariate normality. The format is

`pcor.test(r, q, n)`

where *r* is the partial correlation produced by the `pcor()` function, *q* is the number of variables being controlled, and *n* is the sample size.

Before leaving this topic, it should be mentioned that the `r.test()` function in the psych package also provides a number of useful significance tests. The function can be used to test the following:

- The significance of a correlation coefficient
- The difference between two independent correlations
- The difference between two dependent correlations sharing a single variable
- The difference between two dependent correlations based on completely different variables

See `help(r.test)` for details.

7.3.3   *Visualizing correlations*

The bivariate relationships underlying correlations can be visualized through scatter plots and scatter plot matrices, whereas correlograms provide a unique and powerful method for comparing a large number of correlation coefficients in a meaningful way. Each is covered in chapter 11.

7.4   *T-tests*

The most common activity in research is the comparison of two groups. Do patients receiving a new drug show greater improvement than patients using an existing medication? Does one manufacturing process produce fewer defects than another? Which of two teaching methods is most cost-effective? If your outcome variable is categorical, you can use the methods described in section 7.3. Here, we'll focus on group comparisons, where the outcome variable is continuous and assumed to be distributed normally.

For this illustration, we'll use the UScrime dataset distributed with the MASS package. It contains information about the effect of punishment regimes on crime rates in 47 US states in 1960. The outcome variables of interest will be Prob (the probability of imprisonment), U1 (the unemployment rate for urban males ages 14–24), and U2 (the unemployment rate for urban males ages 35–39). The categorical variable So (an indicator variable for Southern states) will serve as the grouping variable. The data have been rescaled by the original authors. (Note: I considered naming this section "Crime and Punishment in the Old South," but cooler heads prevailed.)

7.4.1   *Independent t-test*

Are you more likely to be imprisoned if you commit a crime in the South? The comparison of interest is Southern versus non-Southern states, and the dependent variable is the probability of incarceration. A two-group independent t-test can be used to test the hypothesis that the two population means are equal. Here, you assume that the two groups are independent and that the data is sampled from normal populations. The format is either

```
t.test(y ~ x, data)
```

where *y* is numeric and *x* is a dichotomous variable, or

```
t.test(y1, y2)
```

where *y1* and *y2* are numeric vectors (the outcome variable for each group). The optional *data* argument refers to a matrix or data frame containing the variables. In contrast to most statistical packages, the default test assumes unequal variance and applies the Welsh degrees-of-freedom modification. You can add a var.equal=TRUE option to specify equal variances and a pooled variance estimate. By default, a two-tailed alternative is assumed (that is, the means differ but the direction isn't specified). You can add the option alternative="less" or alternative="greater" to specify a directional test.

The following code compares Southern (group 1) and non-Southern (group 0) states on the probability of imprisonment using a two-tailed test without the assumption of equal variances:

```
> library(MASS)
> t.test(Prob ~ So, data=UScrime)

        Welch Two Sample t-test

data:  Prob by So
t = -3.8954, df = 24.925, p-value = 0.0006506
alternative hypothesis: true difference in means is not equal to 0
95 percent confidence interval:
 -0.03852569 -0.01187439
sample estimates:
mean in group 0 mean in group 1
    0.03851265      0.06371269
```

You can reject the hypothesis that Southern states and non-Southern states have equal probabilities of imprisonment ($p < .001$).

NOTE   Because the outcome variable is a proportion, you might try to transform it to normality before carrying out the t-test. In the current case, all reasonable transformations of the outcome variable (`Y/1-Y`, `log(Y/1-Y)`, `arcsin(Y)`, and `arcsin(sqrt(Y))`) would lead to the same conclusions. Transformations are covered in detail in chapter 8.

7.4.2   *Dependent t-test*

As a second example, you might ask if the unemployment rate for younger males (14–24) is greater than for older males (35–39). In this case, the two groups aren't independent. You wouldn't expect the unemployment rate for younger and older males in Alabama to be unrelated. When observations in the two groups are related, you have a dependent-groups design. Pre-post or repeated-measures designs also produce dependent groups.

A dependent t-test assumes that the difference between groups is normally distributed. In this case, the format is

```
t.test(y1, y2, paired=TRUE)
```

where *y1* and *y2* are the numeric vectors for the two dependent groups. The results are as follows:

```
> library(MASS)
> sapply(UScrime[c("U1","U2")], function(x)(c(mean=mean(x),sd=sd(x))))
       U1    U2
mean 95.5 33.98
sd   18.0  8.45

> with(UScrime, t.test(U1, U2, paired=TRUE))

        Paired t-test

data:  U1 and U2
```

```
t = 32.4066, df = 46, p-value < 2.2e-16
alternative hypothesis: true difference in means is not equal to 0
95 percent confidence interval:
 57.67003 65.30870
sample estimates:
mean of the differences
            61.48936
```

The mean difference (61.5) is large enough to warrant rejection of the hypothesis that the mean unemployment rate for older and younger males is the same. Younger males have a higher rate. In fact, the probability of obtaining a sample difference this large if the population means are equal is less than 0.00000000000000022 (that is, 2.2e–16).

7.4.3   When there are more than two groups

What do you do if you want to compare more than two groups? If you can assume that the data are independently sampled from normal populations, you can use analysis of variance (ANOVA). ANOVA is a comprehensive methodology that covers many experimental and quasi-experimental designs. As such, it has earned its own chapter. Feel free to abandon this section and jump to chapter 9 at any time.

7.5   Nonparametric tests of group differences

If you're unable to meet the parametric assumptions of a t-test or ANOVA, you can turn to nonparametric approaches. For example, if the outcome variables are severely skewed or ordinal in nature, you may wish to use the techniques in this section.

7.5.1   Comparing two groups

If the two groups are independent, you can use the Wilcoxon rank sum test (more popularly known as the Mann–Whitney U test) to assess whether the observations are sampled from the same probability distribution (that is, whether the probability of obtaining higher scores is greater in one population than the other). The format is either

```
wilcox.test(y ~ x, data)
```

where y is numeric and x is a dichotomous variable, or

```
wilcox.test(y1, y2)
```

where $y1$ and $y2$ are the outcome variables for each group. The optional *data* argument refers to a matrix or data frame containing the variables. The default is a two-tailed test. You can add the option `exact` to produce an exact test, and `alternative="less"` or `alternative="greater"` to specify a directional test.

    If you apply the Mann–Whitney U test to the question of incarceration rates from the previous section, you'll get these results:

```
> with(UScrime, by(Prob, So, median))

So: 0
[1] 0.0382
```

```
--------------------
So: 1
[1] 0.0556

> wilcox.test(Prob ~ So, data=UScrime)

        Wilcoxon rank sum test

data:  Prob by So
W = 81, p-value = 8.488e-05
alternative hypothesis: true location shift is not equal to 0
```

Again, you can reject the hypothesis that incarceration rates are the same in Southern and non-Southern states ($p < .001$).

The Wilcoxon signed rank test provides a nonparametric alternative to the dependent sample t-test. It's appropriate in situations where the groups are paired and the assumption of normality is unwarranted. The format is identical to the Mann–Whitney U test, but you add the `paired=TRUE` option. Let's apply it to the unemployment question from the previous section:

```
> sapply(UScrime[c("U1","U2")], median)
U1 U2
92 34

> with(UScrime, wilcox.test(U1, U2, paired=TRUE))

        Wilcoxon signed rank test with continuity correction

data:  U1 and U2
V = 1128, p-value = 2.464e-09
alternative hypothesis: true location shift is not equal to 0
```

Again, you reach the same conclusion reached with the paired t-test.

In this case, the parametric t-tests and their nonparametric equivalents reach the same conclusions. When the assumptions for the t-tests are reasonable, the parametric tests are more powerful (more likely to find a difference if it exists). The nonparametric tests are more appropriate when the assumptions are grossly unreasonable (for example, rank-ordered data).

7.5.2 Comparing more than two groups

When there are more than two groups to be compared, you must turn to other methods. Consider the `state.x77` dataset from section 7.4. It contains population, income, illiteracy rate, life expectancy, murder rate, and high school graduation rate data for US states. What if you want to compare the illiteracy rates in four regions of the country (Northeast, South, North Central, and West)? This is called a *one-way design*, and there are both parametric and nonparametric approaches available to address the question.

If you can't meet the assumptions of ANOVA designs, you can use nonparametric methods to evaluate group differences. If the groups are independent, a Kruskal–Wallis test provides a useful approach. If the groups are dependent (for example, repeated measures or randomized block design), the Friedman test is more appropriate.

The format for the Kruskal–Wallis test is

```
kruskal.test(y ~ A, data)
```

where *y* is a numeric outcome variable and A is a grouping variable with two or more levels (if there are two levels, it's equivalent to the Mann–Whitney U test). For the Friedman test, the format is

```
friedman.test(y ~ A | B, data)
```

where *y* is the numeric outcome variable, A is a grouping variable, and B is a blocking variable that identifies matched observations. In both cases, *data* is an option argument specifying a matrix or data frame containing the variables.

Let's apply the Kruskal–Wallis test to the illiteracy question. First, you'll have to add the region designations to the dataset. These are contained in the dataset `state.region` distributed with the base installation of R:

```
states <- data.frame(state.region, state.x77)
```

Now you can apply the test:

```
> kruskal.test(Illiteracy ~ state.region, data=states)
        Kruskal-Wallis rank sum test
data:  states$Illiteracy by states$state.region
Kruskal-Wallis chi-squared = 22.7, df = 3, p-value = 4.726e-05
```

The significance test suggests that the illiteracy rate isn't the same in each of the four regions of the country ($p < .001$).

Although you can reject the null hypothesis of no difference, the test doesn't tell you *which* regions differ significantly from each other. To answer this question, you could compare groups two at a time using the Wilcoxon test. A more elegant approach is to apply a multiple-comparisons procedure that computes all pairwise comparisons, while controlling the type I error rate (the probability of finding a difference that isn't there). I have created a function called wmc() that can be used for this purpose. It compares groups two at a time using the Wilcoxon test and adjusts the probability values using the p.adj() function.

To be honest, I'm stretching the definition of *basic* in the chapter title quite a bit, but because the function fits well here, I hope you'll bear with me. You can download a text file containing wmc() from www.statmethods.net/RiA/wmc.txt. The following listing uses this function to compare the illiteracy rates in the four US regions.

Listing 7.17 Nonparametric multiple comparisons

```
> source("http://www.statmethods.net/RiA/wmc.txt")          ◁──── ❶ Accesses
> states <- data.frame(state.region, state.x77)                    the function
> wmc(Illiteracy ~ state.region, data=states, method="holm")

Descriptive Statistics                                        ◁──── ❷ Basic statistics

            West North Central Northeast South
n          13.00          12.00       9.0 16.00
```

```
median  0.60        0.70        1.1  1.75
mad     0.15        0.15        0.3  0.59


Multiple Comparisons (Wilcoxon Rank Sum Tests)
Probability Adjustment = holm                              ❸ Pairwise comparisons

          Group.1       Group.2  W        p
1            West North Central 88 8.7e-01
2            West      Northeast 46 8.7e-01
3            West          South 39 1.8e-02    *
4 North Central      Northeast 20 5.4e-02    .
5 North Central          South  2 8.1e-05  ***
6      Northeast          South 18 1.2e-02    *
---
Signif. codes:  0 '***' 0.001 '**' 0.01 '*' 0.05 '.' 0.1 ' ' 1
```

The source() function downloads and executes the R script defining the wmc() function ❶. The function's format is wmc(*y ~ A, data, method*), where *y* is a numeric outcome variable, *A* is a grouping variable, *data* is the data frame containing these variables, and *method* is the approach used to limit Type I errors. Listing 7.17 uses an adjustment method developed by Holm (1979). It provides strong control of the family-wise error rate (the probability of making one or more Type I errors in a set of comparisons). See help(p.adjust) for a description of the other methods available.

The wmc() function first provides the sample sizes, medians, and median absolute deviations for each group ❷. The West has the lowest illiteracy rate, and the South has the highest. The function then generates six statistical comparisons (West versus North Central, West versus Northeast, West versus South, North Central versus Northeast, North Central versus South, and Northeast versus South) ❸. You can see from the two-sided p-values (p) that the South differs significantly from the other three regions and that the other three regions don't differ from each other at a p < .05 level.

Nonparametric multiple comparisons are a useful set of techniques that aren't easily accessible in R. In chapter 21, you'll have an opportunity to expand the wmc() function into a fully developed package that includes error checking and informative graphics.

7.6 Visualizing group differences

In sections 7.4 and 7.5, we looked at statistical methods for comparing groups. Examining group differences visually is also a crucial part of a comprehensive data-analysis strategy. It allows you to assess the magnitude of the differences, identify any distributional characteristics that influence the results (such as skew, bimodality, or outliers), and evaluate the appropriateness of the test assumptions. R provides a wide range of graphical methods for comparing groups, including box plots (simple, notched, and violin), covered in section 6.5; overlapping kernel density plots, covered in section 6.4.1; and graphical methods for visualizing outcomes in an ANOVA framework, discussed in chapter 9. Advanced methods for visualizing group differences, including grouping and faceting, are discussed in chapter 19.

7.7   Summary

In this chapter, we reviewed the functions in R that provide basic statistical summaries and tests. We looked at sample statistics and frequency tables, tests of independence and measures of association for categorical variables, correlations between quantitative variables (and their associated significance tests), and comparisons of two or more groups on a quantitative outcome variable.

In the next chapter, we'll explore simple and multiple regression, where the focus is on understanding relationships between one (simple) or more than one (multiple) predictor variables and a predicted or criterion variable. Graphical methods will help you diagnose potential problems, evaluate and improve the fit of your models, and uncover unexpected gems of information in your data.

Part 3

Intermediate methods

Whereas part 2 of this book covered basic graphical and statistical methods, part 3 discusses intermediate methods. We move from describing the relationship between two variables to, in chapter 8, using regression models to model the relationship between a numerical outcome variable and a set of numeric and/or categorical predictor variables. Modeling data is typically a complex, multistep, interactive process. Chapter 8 provides step-by-step coverage of the methods available for fitting linear models, evaluating their appropriateness, and interpreting their meaning.

Chapter 9 considers the analysis of basic experimental and quasi-experimental designs through the analysis of variance and its variants. Here we're interested in how treatment combinations or conditions affect a numerical outcome variable. The chapter introduces the functions in R that are used to perform an analysis of variance, analysis of covariance, repeated measures analysis of variance, multifactor analysis of variance, and multivariate analysis of variance. Methods for assessing the appropriateness of these analyses and visualizing the results are also discussed.

In designing experimental and quasi-experimental studies, it's important to determine whether the sample size is adequate for detecting the effects of interest (power analysis). Otherwise, why conduct the study? A detailed treatment of power analysis is provided in chapter 10. Starting with a discussion of hypothesis testing, the presentation focuses on how to use R functions to determine the sample size necessary to detect a treatment effect of a given size with a given degree of confidence. This can help you to plan studies that are likely to yield useful results.

Chapter 11 expands on the material in chapter 5 by covering the creation of graphs that help you to visualize relationships among two or more variables. This includes the various types of 2D and 3D scatter plots, scatter-plot matrices, line plots, and bubble plots. It also introduces the very useful, but less well-known, corrgrams, and mosaic plots.

The linear models described in chapters 8 and 9 assume that the outcome or response variable is not only numeric, but also randomly sampled from a normal distribution. There are situations where this distributional assumption is untenable. Chapter 12 presents analytic methods that work well in cases where data is sampled from unknown or mixed distributions, where sample sizes are small, where outliers are a problem, or where devising an appropriate test based on a theoretical distribution is mathematically intractable. They include both resampling and bootstrapping approaches—computer-intensive methods that are powerfully implemented in R. The methods described in this chapter will allow you to devise hypothesis tests for data that don't fit traditional parametric assumptions.

After completing part 3, you'll have the tools to analyze most common data-analytic problems encountered in practice. And you'll be able to create some gorgeous graphs!

Regression 8

In many ways, regression analysis lives at the heart of statistics. It's a broad term for a set of methodologies used to predict a response variable (also called a *dependent*, *criterion*, or *outcome* variable) from one or more predictor variables (also called *independent* or *explanatory* variables). In general, regression analysis can be used to *identify* the explanatory variables that are related to a response variable, to *describe* the form of the relationships involved, and to provide an equation for *predicting* the response variable from the explanatory variables.

For example, an exercise physiologist might use regression analysis to develop an equation for predicting the expected number of calories a person will burn while exercising on a treadmill. The response variable is the number of calories burned (calculated from the amount of oxygen consumed), and the predictor variables might include duration of exercise (minutes), percentage of time spent at their target heart rate, average speed (mph), age (years), gender, and body mass index (BMI).

From a theoretical point of view, the analysis will help answer such questions as these:

- What's the relationship between exercise duration and calories burned? Is it linear or curvilinear? For example, does exercise have less impact on the number of calories burned after a certain point?
- How does effort (the percentage of time at the target heart rate, the average walking speed) factor in?
- Are these relationships the same for young and old, male and female, heavy and slim?

From a practical point of view, the analysis will help answer such questions as the following:

- How many calories can a 30-year-old man with a BMI of 28.7 expect to burn if he walks for 45 minutes at an average speed of 4 miles per hour and stays within his target heart rate 80% of the time?
- What's the minimum number of variables you need to collect in order to accurately predict the number of calories a person will burn when walking?
- How accurate will your prediction tend to be?

Because regression analysis plays such a central role in modern statistics, we'll cover it in some depth in this chapter. First, we'll look at how to fit and interpret regression models. Next, we'll review a set of techniques for identifying potential problems with these models and how to deal with them. Third, we'll explore the issue of variable selection. Of all the potential predictor variables available, how do you decide which ones to include in your final model? Fourth, we'll address the question of generalizability. How well will your model work when you apply it in the real world? Finally, we'll consider relative importance. Of all the predictors in your model, which one is the most important, the second most important, and the least important?

As you can see, we're covering a lot of ground. Effective regression analysis is an interactive, holistic process with many steps, and it involves more than a little skill. Rather than break it up into multiple chapters, I've opted to present this topic in a single chapter in order to capture this flavor. As a result, this will be the longest and most involved chapter in the book. Stick with it to the end, and you'll have all the tools you need to tackle a wide variety of research questions. Promise!

8.1 *The many faces of regression*

The term *regression* can be confusing because there are so many specialized varieties (see table 8.1). In addition, R has powerful and comprehensive features for fitting regression models, and the abundance of options can be confusing as well. For example, in 2005, Vito Ricci created a list of more than 205 functions in R that are used to generate regression analyses (http://mng.bz/NJhu).

Table 8.1 Varieties of regression analysis

Type of regression	Typical use
Simple linear	Predicting a quantitative response variable from a quantitative explanatory variable.
Polynomial	Predicting a quantitative response variable from a quantitative explanatory variable, where the relationship is modeled as an nth order polynomial.
Multiple linear	Predicting a quantitative response variable from two or more explanatory variables.
Multilevel	Predicting a response variable from data that have a hierarchical structure (for example, students within classrooms within schools). Also called *hierarchical*, *nested*, or *mixed* models.
Multivariate	Predicting more than one response variable from one or more explanatory variables.
Logistic	Predicting a categorical response variable from one or more explanatory variables.
Poisson	Predicting a response variable representing counts from one or more explanatory variables.
Cox proportional hazards	Predicting time to an event (death, failure, relapse) from one or more explanatory variables.
Time-series	Modeling time-series data with correlated errors.
Nonlinear	Predicting a quantitative response variable from one or more explanatory variables, where the form of the model is nonlinear.
Nonparametric	Predicting a quantitative response variable from one or more explanatory variables, where the form of the model is derived from the data and not specified a priori.
Robust	Predicting a quantitative response variable from one or more explanatory variables using an approach that's resistant to the effect of influential observations.

In this chapter, we'll focus on regression methods that fall under the rubric of *ordinary least squares (OLS) regression*, including simple linear regression, polynomial regression, and multiple linear regression. OLS regression is the most common variety of statistical analysis today. Other types of regression models (including logistic regression and Poisson regression) will be covered in chapter 13.

8.1.1 *Scenarios for using OLS regression*

In OLS regression, a quantitative dependent variable is predicted from a weighted sum of predictor variables, where the weights are parameters estimated from the data. Let's take a look at a concrete example (no pun intended), loosely adapted from Fwa (2006).

An engineer wants to identify the most important factors related to bridge deterioration (such as age, traffic volume, bridge design, construction materials and methods, construction quality, and weather conditions) and determine the mathematical form of these relationships. She collects data on each of these variables from a representative sample of bridges and models the data using OLS regression.

The approach is highly interactive. She fits a series of models, checks their compliance with underlying statistical assumptions, explores any unexpected or aberrant findings, and finally chooses the "best" model from among many possible models. If successful, the results will help her to

- Focus on important variables, by determining which of the many collected variables are useful in predicting bridge deterioration, along with their relative importance.
- Look for bridges that are likely to be in trouble, by providing an equation that can be used to predict bridge deterioration for new cases (where the values of the predictor variables are known, but the degree of bridge deterioration isn't).
- Take advantage of serendipity, by identifying unusual bridges. If she finds that some bridges deteriorate much faster or slower than predicted by the model, a study of these outliers may yield important findings that could help her to understand the mechanisms involved in bridge deterioration.

Bridges may hold no interest for you. I'm a clinical psychologist and statistician, and I know next to nothing about civil engineering. But the general principles apply to an amazingly wide selection of problems in the physical, biological, and social sciences. Each of the following questions could also be addressed using an OLS approach:

- What's the relationship between surface stream salinity and paved road surface area (Montgomery, 2007)?
- What aspects of a user's experience contribute to the overuse of massively multiplayer online role playing games (MMORPGs) (Hsu, Wen, & Wu, 2009)?
- Which qualities of an educational environment are most strongly related to higher student achievement scores?
- What's the form of the relationship between blood pressure, salt intake, and age? Is it the same for men and women?
- What's the impact of stadiums and professional sports on metropolitan area development (Baade & Dye, 1990)?
- What factors account for interstate differences in the price of beer (Culbertson & Bradford, 1991)? (That one got your attention!)

Our primary limitation is our ability to formulate an interesting question, devise a useful response variable to measure, and gather appropriate data.

8.1.2   *What you need to know*

For the remainder of this chapter, I'll describe how to use R functions to fit OLS regression models, evaluate the fit, test assumptions, and select among competing models. I assume you've had exposure to least squares regression as typically taught in a second-semester undergraduate statistics course. But I've made efforts to keep the mathematical notation to a minimum and focus on practical rather than theoretical issues. A number of excellent texts are available that cover the statistical material outlined in this chapter. My favorites are John Fox's *Applied Regression Analysis and Generalized Linear Models* (for theory) and *An R and S-Plus Companion to Applied Regression* (for application). They both served as major sources for this chapter. A good nontechnical overview is provided by Licht (1995).

8.2 OLS regression

For most of this chapter, we'll be predicting the response variable from a set of predictor variables (also called *regressing* the response variable on the predictor variables—hence the name) using OLS. OLS regression fits models of the form

$$\hat{Y}_i = \hat{\beta}_0 + \hat{\beta}_1 X_{1i} + \ldots + \hat{\beta}_k X_{ki} \quad i = 1 \ldots n$$

where n is the number of observations and k is the number of predictor variables. (Although I've tried to keep equations out of these discussions, this is one of the few places where it simplifies things.) In this equation:

$\hat{Y}_i$ is the predicted value of the dependent variable for observation i (specifically, it's the estimated mean of the Y distribution, conditional on the set of predictor values).

X_{ji} is the jth predictor value for the ith observation.

$\hat{\beta}_0$ is the intercept (the predicted value of Y when all the predictor variables equal zero).

$\hat{\beta}_j$ is the regression coefficient for the jth predictor (slope representing the change in Y for a unit change in X_j).

Our goal is to select model parameters (intercept and slopes) that minimize the difference between actual response values and those predicted by the model. Specifically, model parameters are selected to minimize the sum of squared residuals:

$$\sum_{i=1}^{n} \left(Y_i - \hat{Y}_i \right)^2 = \sum_{i=1}^{n} \left(Y_i - \hat{\beta}_0 + \hat{\beta}_1 X_{1i} + \ldots + \hat{\beta}_k X_{ki} \right)^2 = \sum_{i=1}^{n} \varepsilon_i^2$$

To properly interpret the coefficients of the OLS model, you must satisfy a number of statistical assumptions:

- *Normality*—For fixed values of the independent variables, the dependent variable is normally distributed.
- *Independence*—The Y_i values are independent of each other.
- *Linearity*—The dependent variable is linearly related to the independent variables.

- *Homoscedasticity*—The variance of the dependent variable doesn't vary with the levels of the independent variables. (I could call this constant *variance*, but saying *homoscedasticity* makes me feel smarter.)

If you violate these assumptions, your statistical significance tests and confidence intervals may not be accurate. Note that OLS regression also assumes that the independent variables are fixed and measured without error, but this assumption is typically relaxed in practice.

8.2.1   *Fitting regression models with lm()*

In R, the basic function for fitting a linear model is `lm()`. The format is

```
myfit <- lm(formula, data)
```

where `formula` describes the model to be fit and `data` is the data frame containing the data to be used in fitting the model. The resulting object (`myfit`, in this case) is a list that contains extensive information about the fitted model. The formula is typically written as

```
Y ~ X1 + X2 + ... + Xk
```

where the ~ separates the response variable on the left from the predictor variables on the right, and the predictor variables are separated by + signs. Other symbols can be used to modify the formula in various ways (see table 8.2).

Table 8.2   Symbols commonly used in R formulas

Symbol	Usage
~	Separates response variables on the left from the explanatory variables on the right. For example, a prediction of y from x, z, and w would be coded y ~ x + z + w.
+	Separates predictor variables.
:	Denotes an interaction between predictor variables. A prediction of y from x, z, and the interaction between x and z would be coded y ~ x + z + x:z.
*	A shortcut for denoting all possible interactions. The code y ~ x * z * w expands to y ~ x + z + w + x:z + x:w + z:w + x:z:w.
^	Denotes interactions up to a specified degree. The code y ~ (x + z + w)^2 expands to y ~ x + z + w + x:z + x:w + z:w.
.	A placeholder for all other variables in the data frame except the dependent variable. For example, if a data frame contained the variables x, y, z, and w, then the code y ~ . would expand to y ~ x + z + w.
-	A minus sign removes a variable from the equation. For example, y ~ (x + z + w)^2 - x:w expands to y ~ x + z + w + x:z + z:w.
-1	Suppresses the intercept. For example, the formula y ~ x -1 fits a regression of y on x, and forces the line through the origin at x=0.

Table 8.2 Symbols commonly used in R formulas

Symbol	Usage
I()	Elements within the parentheses are interpreted arithmetically. For example, `y ~ x + (z + w)^2` would expand to `y ~ x + z + w + z:w`. In contrast, the code `y ~ x + I((z + w)^2)` would expand to `y ~ x + h`, where h is a new variable created by squaring the sum of z and w.
function	Mathematical functions can be used in formulas. For example, `log(y) ~ x + z + w` would predict `log(y)` from x, z, and w.

In addition to `lm()`, table 8.3 lists several functions that are useful when generating a simple or multiple regression analysis. Each of these functions is applied to the object returned by `lm()` in order to generate additional information based on that fitted model.

Table 8.3 Other functions that are useful when fitting linear models

Function	Action
summary()	Displays detailed results for the fitted model
coefficients()	Lists the model parameters (intercept and slopes) for the fitted model
confint()	Provides confidence intervals for the model parameters (95% by default)
fitted()	Lists the predicted values in a fitted model
residuals()	Lists the residual values in a fitted model
anova()	Generates an ANOVA table for a fitted model, or an ANOVA table comparing two or more fitted models
vcov()	Lists the covariance matrix for model parameters
AIC()	Prints Akaike's Information Criterion
plot()	Generates diagnostic plots for evaluating the fit of a model
predict()	Uses a fitted model to predict response values for a new dataset

When the regression model contains one dependent variable and one independent variable, the approach is called *simple linear regression*. When there's one predictor variable but powers of the variable are included (for example, X, X^2, X^3), it's called *polynomial regression*. When there's more than one predictor variable, it's called *multiple linear regression*. We'll start with an example of simple linear regression, then progress to examples of polynomial and multiple linear regression, and end with an example of multiple regression that includes an interaction among the predictors.

8.2.2 Simple linear regression

Let's look at the functions in table 8.3 through a simple regression example. The dataset women in the base installation provides the height and weight for a set of 15 women ages 30 to 39. Suppose you want to predict weight from height. Having an equation for predicting weight from height can help you to identify overweight or underweight individuals. The analysis is provided in the following listing, and the resulting graph is shown in figure 8.1.

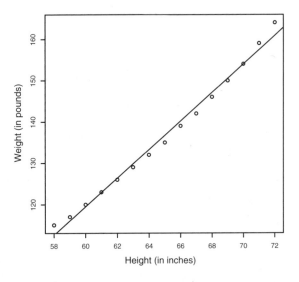

Figure 8.1 Scatter plot with regression line for weight predicted from height

Listing 8.1 Simple linear regression

```
> fit <- lm(weight ~ height, data=women)
> summary(fit)

Call:
lm(formula=weight ~ height, data=women)

Residuals:
   Min    1Q Median    3Q    Max
-1.733 -1.133 -0.383  0.742  3.117

Coefficients:
            Estimate Std. Error t value Pr(>|t|)
(Intercept) -87.5167     5.9369   -14.7  1.7e-09 ***
height        3.4500     0.0911    37.9  1.1e-14 ***
---
Signif. codes:  0 '***' 0.001 '**' 0.01 '*' 0.05 '.' 0.1 '' 1

Residual standard error: 1.53 on 13 degrees of freedom
Multiple R-squared: 0.991,      Adjusted R-squared: 0.99
F-statistic: 1.43e+03 on 1 and 13 DF,  p-value: 1.09e-14

> women$weight

 [1] 115 117 120 123 126 129 132 135 139 142 146 150 154 159 164

> fitted(fit)

      1       2       3       4       5       6       7       8       9
 112.58  116.03  119.48  122.93  126.38  129.83  133.28  136.73  140.18
     10      11      12      13      14      15
 143.63  147.08  150.53  153.98  157.43  160.88

> residuals(fit)
```

```
    1      2      3      4      5      6      7      8      9     10     11
 2.42   0.97   0.52   0.07  -0.38  -0.83  -1.28  -1.73  -1.18  -1.63  -1.08
   12     13     14     15
-0.53   0.02   1.57   3.12
```

```
> plot(women$height,women$weight,
        xlab="Height (in inches)",
        ylab="Weight (in pounds)")
> abline(fit)
```

From the output, you see that the prediction equation is

$$\widehat{\text{Weight}} = -87.52 + 3.45 \times \text{Height}$$

Because a height of 0 is impossible, you wouldn't try to give a physical interpretation to the intercept. It merely becomes an adjustment constant. From the $\Pr(>|t|)$ column, you see that the regression coefficient (3.45) is significantly different from zero ($p < 0.001$) and indicates that there's an expected increase of 3.45 pounds of weight for every 1 inch increase in height. The multiple R-squared (0.991) indicates that the model accounts for 99.1% of the variance in weights. The multiple R-squared is also the squared correlation between the actual and predicted value (that is, $R^2 = r_{\hat{y}y}$. The residual standard error (1.53 pounds) can be thought of as the average error in predicting weight from height using this model. The F statistic tests whether the predictor variables, taken together, predict the response variable above chance levels. Because there's only one predictor variable in simple regression, in this example the F test is equivalent to the t-test for the regression coefficient for height.

For demonstration purposes, we've printed out the actual, predicted, and residual values. Evidently, the largest residuals occur for low and high heights, which can also be seen in the plot (figure 8.1).

The plot suggests that you might be able to improve on the prediction by using a line with one bend. For example, a model of the form $\hat{Y}_i = \hat{\beta}_0 + \hat{\beta}_1 X + \hat{\beta}_2 X^2$ may provide a better fit to the data. Polynomial regression allows you to predict a response variable from an explanatory variable, where the form of the relationship is an *n*th-degree polynomial.

8.2.3 Polynomial regression

The plot in figure 8.1 suggests that you might be able to improve your prediction using a regression with a quadratic term (that is, X^2). You can fit a quadratic equation using the statement

```
fit2 <- lm(weight ~ height + I(height^2), data=women)
```

The new term `I(height^2)` requires explanation. `height^2` adds a height-squared term to the prediction equation. The `I` function treats the contents within the parentheses as an R regular expression. You need this because the `^` operator has a special meaning in formulas that you don't want to invoke here (see table 8.2).

The following listing shows the results of fitting the quadratic equation.

Listing 8.2   Polynomial regression

```
> fit2 <- lm(weight ~ height + I(height^2), data=women)
> summary(fit2)

Call:
lm(formula=weight ~ height + I(height^2), data=women)

Residuals:
    Min      1Q  Median      3Q     Max
-0.5094 -0.2961 -0.0094  0.2862  0.5971

Coefficients:
             Estimate Std. Error t value Pr(>|t|)
(Intercept) 261.87818   25.19677   10.39 2.4e-07 ***
height        -7.34832    0.77769   -9.45 6.6e-07 ***
I(height^2)    0.08306    0.00598   13.89 9.3e-09 ***
---
Signif. codes:  0 '***' 0.001 '**' 0.01 '*' 0.05 '.' 0.1 ' ' 1

Residual standard error: 0.384 on 12 degrees of freedom
Multiple R-squared: 0.999,      Adjusted R-squared: 0.999
F-statistic: 1.14e+04 on 2 and 12 DF,  p-value: <2e-16

> plot(women$height,women$weight,
        xlab="Height (in inches)",
        ylab="Weight (in lbs)")
> lines(women$height,fitted(fit2))
```

From this new analysis, the prediction equation is

$$\widehat{\text{Weight}} = 261.88 - 7.35 \times \text{Height} + 0.083 \times \text{Height}^2$$

and both regression coefficients are significant at the $p < 0.0001$ level. The amount of variance accounted for has increased to 99.9%. The significance of the squared term ($t = 13.89$, $p < .001$) suggests that inclusion of the quadratic term improves the model fit. If you look at the plot of fit2 (figure 8.2) you can see that the curve does indeed provide a better fit.

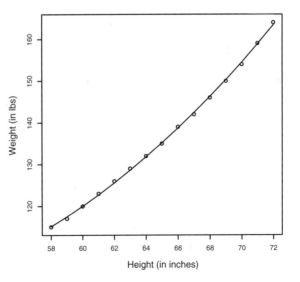

Figure 8.2   Quadratic regression for weight predicted by height

Linear vs. nonlinear models

Note that this polynomial equation still fits under the rubric of linear regression. It's linear because the equation involves a weighted sum of predictor variables (height and height-squared in this case). Even a model such as

$$\hat{Y}_i = \hat{\beta}_0 \times \log X_1 + \hat{\beta}_2 \times \sin X_2$$

would be considered a linear model (linear in terms of the parameters) and fit with the formula

```
Y ~ log(X₁) + sin(X₂)
```

In contrast, here's an example of a truly nonlinear model:

$$\hat{Y}_i = \hat{\beta}_0 + \hat{\beta}_1 \, e^{x/\beta_2}$$

Nonlinear models of this form can be fit with the `nls()` function.

In general, an nth-degree polynomial produces a curve with $n-1$ bends. To fit a cubic polynomial, you'd use

```
fit3 <- lm(weight ~ height + I(height^2) +I(height^3), data=women)
```

Although higher polynomials are possible, I've rarely found that terms higher than cubic are necessary.

Before we move on, I should mention that the `scatterplot()` function in the `car` package provides a simple and convenient method of plotting a bivariate relationship. The code

```
library(car)
scatterplot(weight ~ height, data=women,
  spread=FALSE, smoother.args=list(lty=2), pch=19,
  main="Women Age 30-39",
  xlab="Height (inches)",
  ylab="Weight (lbs.)")
```

produces the graph in figure 8.3.

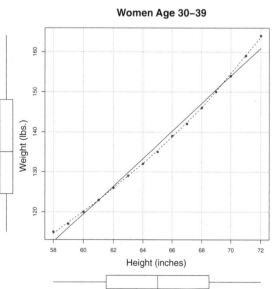

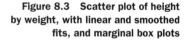

Figure 8.3 Scatter plot of height by weight, with linear and smoothed fits, and marginal box plots

This enhanced plot provides the scatter plot of weight with height, box plots for each variable in their respective margins, the linear line of best fit, and a smoothed (loess) fit line. The `spread=FALSE` options suppress spread and asymmetry information. The `smoother.args=list(lty=2)` option specifies that the loess fit be rendered as a dashed line. The `pch=19` options display points as filled circles (the default is open circles). You can tell at a glance that the two variables are roughly symmetrical and that a curved line will fit the data points better than a straight line.

8.2.4 *Multiple linear regression*

When there's more than one predictor variable, simple linear regression becomes multiple linear regression, and the analysis grows more involved. Technically, polynomial regression is a special case of multiple regression. Quadratic regression has two predictors (X and X^2), and cubic regression has three predictors (X, X^2, and X^3). Let's look at a more general example.

We'll use the `state.x77` dataset in the base package for this example. Suppose you want to explore the relationship between a state's murder rate and other characteristics of the state, including population, illiteracy rate, average income, and frost levels (mean number of days below freezing).

Because the `lm()` function requires a data frame (and the `state.x77` dataset is contained in a matrix), you can simplify your life with the following code:

```
states <- as.data.frame(state.x77[,c("Murder", "Population",
                        "Illiteracy", "Income", "Frost")])
```

This code creates a data frame called `states`, containing the variables you're interested in. You'll use this new data frame for the remainder of the chapter.

A good first step in multiple regression is to examine the relationships among the variables two at a time. The bivariate correlations are provided by the `cor()` function, and scatter plots are generated from the `scatterplotMatrix()` function in the `car` package (see the following listing and figure 8.4).

> **Listing 8.3 Examining bivariate relationships**

```
> states <- as.data.frame(state.x77[,c("Murder", "Population",
                        "Illiteracy", "Income", "Frost")])

> cor(states)
           Murder Population Illiteracy Income Frost
Murder       1.00       0.34       0.70  -0.23 -0.54
Population   0.34       1.00       0.11   0.21 -0.33
Illiteracy   0.70       0.11       1.00  -0.44 -0.67
Income      -0.23       0.21      -0.44   1.00  0.23
Frost       -0.54      -0.33      -0.67   0.23  1.00

> library(car)
> scatterplotMatrix(states, spread=FALSE, smoother.args=list(lty=2),
    main="Scatter Plot Matrix")
```

Scatterplot matrix

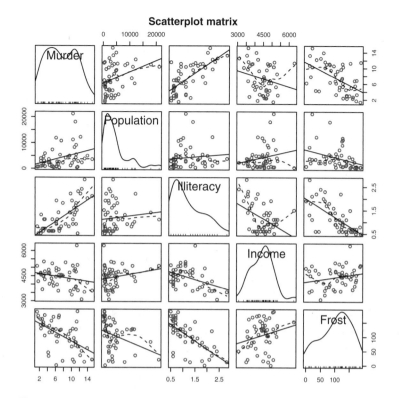

Figure 8.4 Scatter plot matrix of dependent and independent variables for the states data, including linear and smoothed fits, and marginal distributions (kernel-density plots and rug plots)

By default, the scatterplotMatrix() function provides scatter plots of the variables with each other in the off-diagonals and superimposes smoothed (loess) and linear fit lines on these plots. The principal diagonal contains density and rug plots for each variable.

You can see that murder rate may be bimodal and that each of the predictor variables is skewed to some extent. Murder rates rise with population and illiteracy, and they fall with higher income levels and frost. At the same time, colder states have lower illiteracy rates and population and higher incomes.

Now let's fit the multiple regression model with the lm() function (see the following listing).

Listing 8.4 Multiple linear regression

```
> states <- as.data.frame(state.x77[,c("Murder", "Population",
                      "Illiteracy", "Income", "Frost")])

> fit <- lm(Murder ~ Population + Illiteracy + Income + Frost,
          data=states)
> summary(fit)
```

```
Call:
lm(formula=Murder ~ Population + Illiteracy + Income + Frost,
    data=states)

Residuals:
   Min     1Q  Median     3Q    Max
-4.7960 -1.6495 -0.0811  1.4815  7.6210

Coefficients:
            Estimate Std. Error t value Pr(>|t|)
(Intercept) 1.23e+00   3.87e+00    0.32    0.751
Population  2.24e-04   9.05e-05    2.47    0.017 *
Illiteracy  4.14e+00   8.74e-01    4.74  2.2e-05 ***
Income      6.44e-05   6.84e-04    0.09    0.925
Frost       5.81e-04   1.01e-02    0.06    0.954
---
Signif. codes:  0 '***' 0.001 '**' 0.01 '*' 0.05 '.v 0.1 'v' 1

Residual standard error: 2.5 on 45 degrees of freedom
Multiple R-squared: 0.567,      Adjusted R-squared: 0.528
F-statistic: 14.7 on 4 and 45 DF,  p-value: 9.13e-08
```

When there's more than one predictor variable, the regression coefficients indicate the increase in the dependent variable for a unit change in a predictor variable, holding all other predictor variables constant. For example, the regression coefficient for Illiteracy is 4.14, suggesting that an increase of 1% in illiteracy is associated with a 4.14% increase in the murder rate, controlling for population, income, and temperature. The coefficient is significantly different from zero at the $p < .0001$ level. On the other hand, the coefficient for Frost isn't significantly different from zero ($p = 0.954$) suggesting that Frost and Murder aren't linearly related when controlling for the other predictor variables. Taken together, the predictor variables account for 57% of the variance in murder rates across states.

Up to this point, we've assumed that the predictor variables don't interact. In the next section, we'll consider a case in which they do.

8.2.5 *Multiple linear regression with interactions*

Some of the most interesting research findings are those involving interactions among predictor variables. Consider the automobile data in the mtcars data frame. Let's say that you're interested in the impact of automobile weight and horsepower on mileage. You could fit a regression model that includes both predictors, along with their interaction, as shown in the next listing.

Listing 8.5 Multiple linear regression with a significant interaction term

```
> fit <- lm(mpg ~ hp + wt + hp:wt, data=mtcars)
> summary(fit)
```

```
Call:
lm(formula=mpg ~ hp + wt + hp:wt, data=mtcars)

Residuals:
   Min    1Q Median    3Q    Max
-3.063 -1.649 -0.736  1.421  4.551

Coefficients:
            Estimate Std. Error t value Pr(>|t|)
(Intercept) 49.80842    3.60516   13.82  5.0e-14 ***
hp          -0.12010    0.02470   -4.86  4.0e-05 ***
wt          -8.21662    1.26971   -6.47  5.2e-07 ***
hp:wt        0.02785    0.00742    3.75  0.00081 ***
---
Signif. codes:  0 '***' 0.001 '**' 0.01 '*' 0.05 '.' 0.1 ' ' 1

Residual standard error: 2.1 on 28 degrees of freedom
Multiple R-squared: 0.885,     Adjusted R-squared: 0.872
F-statistic: 71.7 on 3 and 28 DF,  p-value: 2.98e-13
```

You can see from the $Pr(>|t|)$ column that the interaction between horsepower and car weight is significant. What does this mean? A significant interaction between two predictor variables tells you that the relationship between one predictor and the response variable depends on the level of the other predictor. Here it means the relationship between miles per gallon and horsepower varies by car weight.

The model for predicting mpg is $\widehat{mpg} = 49.81 - 0.12 \times hp - 8.22 \times wt + 0.03 \times hp \times wt$. To interpret the interaction, you can plug in various values of wt and simplify the equation. For example, you can try the mean of wt (3.2) and one standard deviation below and above the mean (2.2 and 4.2, respectively). For wt=2.2, the equation simplifies to $\widehat{mpg} = 49.81 - 0.12 \times hp - 8.22 \times (2.2) + 0.03 \times hp \times (2.2) = 31.41 - 0.06 \times hp$. For wt=3.2, this becomes $\widehat{mpg} = 23.37 - 0.03 \times hp$. Finally, for wt=4.2 the equation becomes $\widehat{mpg} = 15.33 - 0.003 \times hp$. You see that as weight increases (2.2, 3.2, 4.2), the expected change in mpg from a unit increase in hp decreases (0.06, 0.03, 0.003).

You can visualize interactions using the effect() function in the effects package. The format is

```
plot(effect(term, mod,, xlevels), multiline=TRUE)
```

where *term* is the quoted model term to plot, *mod* is the fitted model returned by lm(), and *xlevels* is a list specifying the variables to be set to constant values and the values to employ. The multiline=TRUE option superimposes the lines being plotted. For the previous model, this becomes

```
library(effects)
plot(effect("hp:wt", fit,, list(wt=c(2.2,3.2,4.2))), multiline=TRUE)
```

The resulting graph is displayed in figure 8.5.

You can see from this graph that as the weight of the car increases, the relationship between horsepower and miles per gallon weakens. For wt=4.2, the line is almost horizontal, indicating that as hp increases, mpg doesn't change.

Unfortunately, fitting the model is only the first step in the analysis. Once you fit a regression model, you need to evaluate whether you've met the statistical assumptions underlying your approach before you can have confidence in the inferences you draw. This is the topic of the next section.

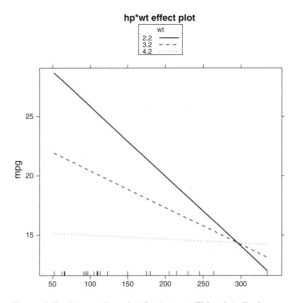

Figure 8.5 Interaction plot for hp*wt. This plot displays the relationship between mpg and hp at three values of wt.

8.3   *Regression diagnostics*

In the previous section, you used the lm() function to fit an OLS regression model and the summary() function to obtain the model parameters and summary statistics. Unfortunately, nothing in this printout tells you whether the model you've fit is appropriate. Your confidence in inferences about regression parameters depends on the degree to which you've met the statistical assumptions of the OLS model. Although the summary() function in listing 8.4 describes the model, it provides no information concerning the degree to which you've satisfied the statistical assumptions *underlying* the model.

Why is this important? Irregularities in the data or misspecifications of the relationships between the predictors and the response variable can lead you to settle on a model that's wildly inaccurate. On the one hand, you may conclude that a predictor and a response variable are unrelated when, in fact, they are. On the other hand, you may conclude that a predictor and a response variable are related when, in fact, they aren't! You may also end up with a model that makes poor predictions when applied in real-world settings, with significant and unnecessary error.

Let's look at the output from the confint() function applied to the states multiple regression problem in section 8.2.4:

```
> states <- as.data.frame(state.x77[,c("Murder", "Population",
                     "Illiteracy", "Income", "Frost")])
> fit <- lm(Murder ~ Population + Illiteracy + Income + Frost, data=states)
> confint(fit)
                2.5 %    97.5 %
(Intercept) -6.55e+00 9.021318
```

```
Population   4.14e-05 0.000406
Illiteracy   2.38e+00 5.903874
Income      -1.31e-03 0.001441
Frost       -1.97e-02 0.020830
```

The results suggest that you can be 95% confident that the interval [2.38, 5.90] contains the true change in murder rate for a 1% change in illiteracy rate. Additionally, because the confidence interval for Frost contains 0, you can conclude that a change in temperature is unrelated to murder rate, holding the other variables constant. But your faith in these results is only as strong as the evidence you have that your data satisfies the statistical assumptions underlying the model.

A set of techniques called *regression diagnostics* provides the necessary tools for evaluating the appropriateness of the regression model and can help you to uncover and correct problems. We'll start with a standard approach that uses functions that come with R's base installation. Then we'll look at newer, improved methods available through the car package.

8.3.1 A typical approach

R's base installation provides numerous methods for evaluating the statistical assumptions in a regression analysis. The most common approach is to apply the plot() function to the object returned by the lm(). Doing so produces four graphs that are useful for evaluating the model fit. Applying this approach to the simple linear regression example

```
fit <- lm(weight ~ height, data=women)
par(mfrow=c(2,2))
plot(fit)
```

produces the graphs shown in figure 8.6. The par(mfrow=c(2,2)) statement is used to combine the four plots produced by the plot() function into one large 2×2 graph. The par() function is described in chapter 3.

To understand these graphs, consider the assumptions of OLS regression:

- *Normality*—If the dependent variable is normally distributed for a fixed set of predictor values, then the residual values should be normally distributed with a mean of 0. The Normal Q-Q plot (upper right) is a probability plot of the standardized residuals against the values that would be expected under normality. If you've met the normality assumption, the points on this graph should fall on the straight 45-degree line. Because they don't, you've clearly violated the normality assumption.

- *Independence*—You can't tell if the dependent variable values are independent from these plots. You have to use your understanding of how the data was collected. There's no a priori reason to believe that one woman's weight influences another woman's weight. If you found out that the data were sampled from families, you might have to adjust your assumption of independence.

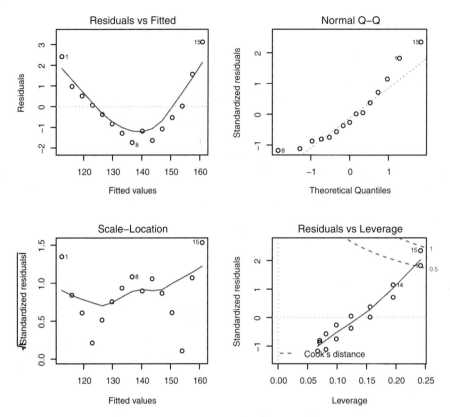

Figure 8.6   Diagnostic plots for the regression of weight on height

- *Linearity*—If the dependent variable is linearly related to the independent variables, there should be no systematic relationship between the residuals and the predicted (that is, fitted) values. In other words, the model should capture all the systematic variance present in the data, leaving nothing but random noise. In the Residuals vs. Fitted graph (upper left), you see clear evidence of a curved relationship, which suggests that you may want to add a quadratic term to the regression.

- *Homoscedasticity*—If you've met the constant variance assumption, the points in the Scale-Location graph (bottom left) should be a random band around a horizontal line. You seem to meet this assumption.

Finally, the Residuals vs. Leverage graph (bottom right) provides information about individual observations that you may wish to attend to. The graph identifies outliers, high-leverage points, and influential observations. Specifically:

- An *outlier* is an observation that isn't predicted well by the fitted regression model (that is, has a large positive or negative residual).

- An observation with a high *leverage* value has an unusual combination of predictor values. That is, it's an outlier in the predictor space. The dependent variable value isn't used to calculate an observation's leverage.
- An *influential observation* is an observation that has a disproportionate impact on the determination of the model parameters. Influential observations are identified using a statistic called *Cook's distance*, or *Cook's D*.

To be honest, I find the Residuals vs. Leverage plot difficult to read and not useful. You'll see better representations of this information in later sections.

To complete this section, let's look at the diagnostic plots for the quadratic fit. The necessary code is

```
fit2 <- lm(weight ~ height + I(height^2), data=women)
par(mfrow=c(2,2))
plot(fit2)
```

and the resulting graph is provided in figure 8.7.

This second set of plots suggests that the polynomial regression provides a better fit with regard to the linearity assumption, normality of residuals (except for observation

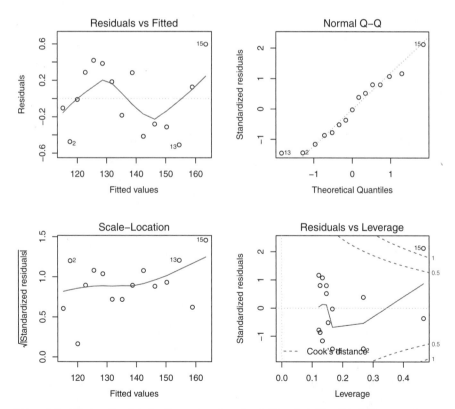

Figure 8.7 Diagnostic plots for the regression of weight on height and height-squared

13), and homoscedasticity (constant residual variance). Observation 15 appears to be influential (based on a large Cook's D value), and deleting it has an impact on the parameter estimates. In fact, dropping both observations 13 and 15 produces a better model fit. To see this, try

```
newfit <- lm(weight~ height + I(height^2), data=women[-c(13,15),])
```

for yourself. But you need to be careful when deleting data. Your models should fit your data, not the other way around!

Finally, let's apply the basic approach to the states multiple regression problem:

```
states <- as.data.frame(state.x77[,c("Murder", "Population",
                     "Illiteracy", "Income", "Frost")])
fit <- lm(Murder ~ Population + Illiteracy + Income + Frost, data=states)
par(mfrow=c(2,2))
plot(fit)
```

The results are displayed in figure 8.8. As you can see from the graph, the model assumptions appear to be well satisfied, with the exception that Nevada is an outlier.

Although these standard diagnostic plots are helpful, better tools are now available in R and I recommend their use over the plot(*fit*) approach.

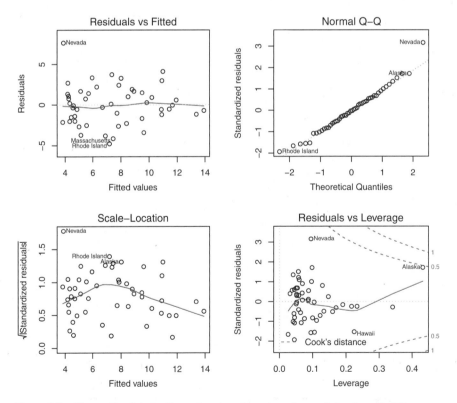

Figure 8.8 Diagnostic plots for the regression of murder rate on state characteristics

8.3.2 An enhanced approach

The car package provides a number of functions that significantly enhance your ability to fit and evaluate regression models (see table 8.4).

Table 8.4 Useful functions for regression diagnostics (car package)

Function	Purpose
qqPlot()	Quantile comparisons plot
durbinWatsonTest()	Durbin–Watson test for autocorrelated errors
crPlots()	Component plus residual plots
ncvTest()	Score test for nonconstant error variance
spreadLevelPlot()	Spread-level plots
outlierTest()	Bonferroni outlier test
avPlots()	Added variable plots
influencePlot()	Regression influence plots
scatterplot()	Enhanced scatter plots
scatterplotMatrix()	Enhanced scatter plot matrixes
vif()	Variance inflation factors

It's important to note that there are many changes between version 1.x and version 2.x of the car package, including changes in function names and behavior. This chapter is based on version 2.

In addition, the gvlma package provides a global test for linear model assumptions. Let's look at each in turn, by applying them to our multiple regression example.

NORMALITY

The qqPlot() function provides a more accurate method of assessing the normality assumption than that provided by the plot() function in the base package. It plots the *studentized residuals* (also called *studentized deleted residuals* or *jackknifed residuals*) against a *t* distribution with $n - p - 1$ degrees of freedom, where n is the sample size and p is the number of regression parameters (including the intercept). The code follows:

```
library(car)
states <- as.data.frame(state.x77[,c("Murder", "Population",
                        "Illiteracy", "Income", "Frost")])
fit <- lm(Murder ~ Population + Illiteracy + Income + Frost, data=states)
qqPlot(fit, labels=row.names(states), id.method="identify",
       simulate=TRUE, main="Q-Q Plot")
```

The `qqPlot()` function generates the probability plot displayed in figure 8.9. The option `id.method ="identify"` makes the plot interactive—after the graph is drawn, mouse clicks on points in the graph will label them with values specified in the `labels` option of the function. Pressing the Esc key, selecting Stop from the graph's drop-down menu, or right-clicking the graph turns off this interactive mode. Here, I identified Nevada. When `simulate=TRUE`, a 95% confidence envelope is produced using a parametric bootstrap. (Bootstrap methods are considered in chapter 12.)

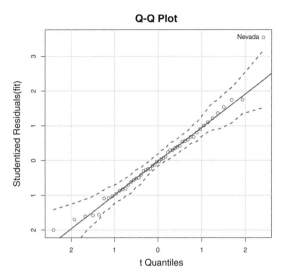

Figure 8.9   Q-Q plot for studentized residuals

With the exception of Nevada, all the points fall close to the line and are within the confidence envelope, suggesting that you've met the normality assumption fairly well. But you should definitely look at Nevada. It has a large positive residual (actual − predicted), indicating that the model underestimates the murder rate in this state. Specifically:

```
> states["Nevada",]

       Murder Population Illiteracy Income Frost
Nevada   11.5        590        0.5   5149   188

> fitted(fit)["Nevada"]

  Nevada
3.878958

> residuals(fit)["Nevada"]

  Nevada
7.621042

> rstudent(fit)["Nevada"]

  Nevada
3.542929
```

Here you see that the murder rate is 11.5%, but the model predicts a 3.9% murder rate.

The question that you need to ask is, "Why does Nevada have a higher murder rate than predicted from population, income, illiteracy, and temperature?" Anyone (who hasn't see *Goodfellas*) want to guess?

For completeness, here's another way of visualizing errors. Take a look at the code in the next listing. The `residplot()` function generates a histogram of the studentized residuals and superimposes a normal curve, kernel-density curve, and rug plot. It doesn't require the `car` package.

Listing 8.6 Function for plotting studentized residuals

```
residplot <- function(fit, nbreaks=10) {
          z <- rstudent(fit)
          hist(z, breaks=nbreaks, freq=FALSE,
              xlab="Studentized Residual",
              main="Distribution of Errors")
          rug(jitter(z), col="brown")
          curve(dnorm(x, mean=mean(z), sd=sd(z)),
              add=TRUE, col="blue", lwd=2)
          lines(density(z)$x, density(z)$y,
              col="red", lwd=2, lty=2)
          legend("topright",
              legend = c( "Normal Curve", "Kernel Density Curve"),
              lty=1:2, col=c("blue","red"), cex=.7)
    }

residplot(fit)
```

The results are displayed in figure 8.10.

As you can see, the errors follow a normal distribution quite well, with the exception of a large outlier. Although the Q-Q plot is probably more informative, I've always

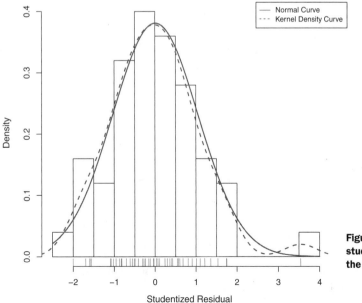

Figure 8.10 Distribution of studentized residuals using the `residplot()` function

found it easier to gauge the skew of a distribution from a histogram or density plot than from a probability plot. Why not use both?

INDEPENDENCE OF ERRORS

As indicated earlier, the best way to assess whether the dependent variable values (and thus the residuals) are independent is from your knowledge of how the data were collected. For example, time series data often display autocorrelation—observations collected closer in time are more correlated with each other than with observations distant in time. The car package provides a function for the Durbin–Watson test to detect such serially correlated errors. You can apply the Durbin–Watson test to the multiple-regression problem with the following code:

```
> durbinWatsonTest(fit)
 lag Autocorrelation D-W Statistic p-value
   1          -0.201           2.32    0.282
 Alternative hypothesis: rho != 0
```

The nonsignificant p-value (p=0.282) suggests a lack of autocorrelation and, conversely, an independence of errors. The lag value (1 in this case) indicates that each observation is being compared with the one next to it in the dataset. Although appropriate for time-dependent data, the test is less applicable for data that isn't clustered in this fashion. Note that the durbinWatsonTest() function uses bootstrapping (see chapter 12) to derive p-values. Unless you add the option simulate=FALSE, you'll get a slightly different value each time you run the test.

LINEARITY

You can look for evidence of nonlinearity in the relationship between the dependent variable and the independent variables by using *component plus residual plots* (also known as *partial residual plots*). The plot is produced by the crPlots() function in the car package. You're looking for any systematic departure from the linear model that you've specified.

To create a component plus residual plot for variable X, you plot the points

$$\varepsilon_i + (\hat{\beta}_0 + \hat{\beta}_1 \times X_{1i} + \ldots + \hat{\beta}_k \times X_{ki}) \text{ vs. } X_i$$

where the residuals are based on the full model, and $i = 1 \ldots n$. The straight line in each graph is given by $(\hat{\beta}_0 + \hat{\beta}_1 \times X_{1i} + \ldots + \hat{\beta}_k \times X_{ki})$ vs. X_i. Loess fit lines are described in chapter 11. The code to produce these plots is as follows:

```
> library(car)
> crPlots(fit)
```

The resulting plots are provided in figure 8.11. Nonlinearity in any of these plots suggests that you may not have adequately modeled the functional form of that predictor in the regression. If so, you may need to add curvilinear components such as polynomial terms, transform one or more variables (for example, use log(X) instead of X), or abandon linear regression in favor of some other regression variant. Transformations are discussed later in this chapter.

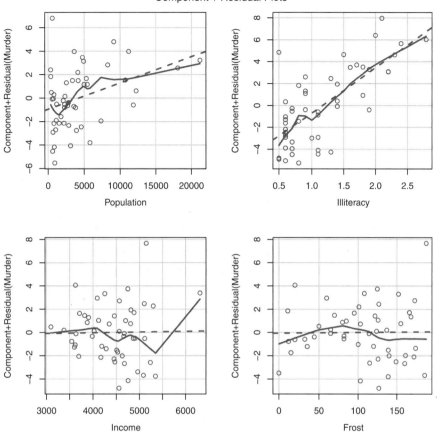

Figure 8.11   Component plus residual plots for the regression of murder rate on state characteristics

The component plus residual plots confirm that you've met the linearity assumption. The form of the linear model seems to be appropriate for this dataset.

HOMOSCEDASTICITY

The car package also provides two useful functions for identifying non-constant error variance. The ncvTest() function produces a score test of the hypothesis of constant error variance against the alternative that the error variance changes with the level of the fitted values. A significant result suggests heteroscedasticity (nonconstant error variance).

The spreadLevelPlot() function creates a scatter plot of the absolute standardized residuals versus the fitted values and superimposes a line of best fit. Both functions are demonstrated in the next listing.

Listing 8.7   Assessing homoscedasticity

```
> library(car)
> ncvTest(fit)

Non-constant Variance Score Test
Variance formula: ~ fitted.values
Chisquare=1.7     Df=1      p=0.19

> spreadLevelPlot(fit)

Suggested power transformation:  1.2
```

The score test is nonsignificant (p = 0.19), suggesting that you've met the constant variance assumption. You can also see this in the spread-level plot (figure 8.12). The points form a random horizontal band around a horizontal line of best fit. If you'd violated the assumption, you'd expect to see a nonhorizontal line. The suggested power transformation in listing 8.7 is the suggested power p (Y^p) that would stabilize the nonconstant error variance. For example, if the plot showed a nonhorizontal trend and the suggested power transformation was 0.5, then using $\sqrt{Y}$ rather than Y in the regression equation might lead to a model that satisfied homoscedasticity. If the suggested power was 0, you'd use a log transformation. In the current example, there's no evidence of heteroscedasticity, and the suggested power is close to 1 (no transformation required).

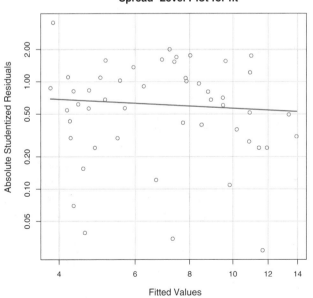

Figure 8.12   Spread-level plot for assessing constant error variance

8.3.3 *Global validation of linear model assumption*

Finally, let's examine the gvlma() function in the gvlma package. Written by Pena and Slate (2006), the gvlma() function performs a global validation of linear model assumptions as well as separate evaluations of skewness, kurtosis, and heteroscedasticity. In other words, it provides a single omnibus (go/no go) test of model assumptions. The following listing applies the test to the states data.

Listing 8.8 Global test of linear model assumptions

```
> library(gvlma)
> gvmodel <- gvlma(fit)
> summary(gvmodel)

ASSESSMENT OF THE LINEAR MODEL ASSUMPTIONS
USING THE GLOBAL TEST ON 4 DEGREES-OF-FREEDOM:
Level of Significance= 0.05

Call:
 gvlma(x=fit)

                       Value p-value                   Decision
Global Stat            2.773   0.597 Assumptions acceptable.
Skewness               1.537   0.215 Assumptions acceptable.
Kurtosis               0.638   0.425 Assumptions acceptable.
Link Function          0.115   0.734 Assumptions acceptable.
Heteroscedasticity     0.482   0.487 Assumptions acceptable.
```

You can see from the printout (the Global Stat line) that the data meet all the statistical assumptions that go with the OLS regression model ($p = 0.597$). If the decision line indicated that the assumptions were violated (say, $p < 0.05$), you'd have to explore the data using the previous methods discussed in this section to determine which assumptions were the culprit.

8.3.4 *Multicollinearity*

Before leaving this section on regression diagnostics, let's focus on a problem that's not directly related to statistical assumptions but is important in allowing you to interpret multiple regression results. Imagine you're conducting a study of grip strength. Your independent variables include date of birth (DOB) and age. You regress grip strength on DOB and age and find a significant overall F test at $p < .001$. But when you look at the individual regression coefficients for DOB and age, you find that they're both nonsignificant (that is, there's no evidence that either is related to grip strength). What happened?

The problem is that DOB and age are perfectly correlated within rounding error. A regression coefficient measures the impact of one predictor variable on the response variable, holding all other predictor variables constant. This amounts to looking at the relationship of grip strength and age, holding age constant. The problem is called *multicollinearity*. It leads to large confidence intervals for model parameters and makes the interpretation of individual coefficients difficult.

Multicollinearity can be detected using a statistic called the *variance inflation factor* (VIF). For any predictor variable, the square root of the VIF indicates the degree to which the confidence interval for that variable's regression parameter is expanded relative to a model with uncorrelated predictors (hence the name). VIF values are provided by the vif() function in the car package. As a general rule, $\sqrt{vif} > 2$ indicates a multicollinearity problem. The code is provided in the following listing. The results indicate that multicollinearity isn't a problem with these predictor variables.

Listing 8.9   Evaluating multicollinearity

```
> library(car)
> vif(fit)

Population Illiteracy      Income      Frost
      1.2         2.2         1.3         2.1

> sqrt(vif(fit)) > 2 # problem?

Population Illiteracy      Income      Frost
    FALSE       FALSE       FALSE      FALSE
```

8.4   *Unusual observations*

A comprehensive regression analysis will also include a screening for unusual observations—namely outliers, high-leverage observations, and influential observations. These are data points that warrant further investigation, either because they're different than other observations in some way, or because they exert a disproportionate amount of influence on the results. Let's look at each in turn.

8.4.1   *Outliers*

Outliers are observations that aren't predicted well by the model. They have unusually large positive or negative residuals $(Y_i - \hat{Y}_i)$. Positive residuals indicate that the model is underestimating the response value, whereas negative residuals indicate an overestimation.

You've already seen one way to identify outliers. Points in the Q-Q plot of figure 8.9 that lie outside the confidence band are considered outliers. A rough rule of thumb is that standardized residuals that are larger than 2 or less than −2 are worth attention.

The car package also provides a statistical test for outliers. The outlierTest() function reports the Bonferroni adjusted p-value for the largest absolute studentized residual:

```
> library(car)
> outlierTest(fit)

       rstudent unadjusted p-value Bonferonni p
Nevada      3.5            0.00095        0.048
```

Here, you see that Nevada is identified as an outlier ($p = 0.048$). Note that this function tests the single largest (positive or negative) residual for significance as an outlier.

If it isn't significant, there are no outliers in the dataset. If it's significant, you must delete it and rerun the test to see if others are present.

8.4.2 *High-leverage points*

Observations that have high leverage are outliers with regard to the other predictors. In other words, they have an unusual combination of predictor values. The response value isn't involved in determining leverage.

Observations with high leverage are identified through the *hat statistic*. For a given dataset, the average hat value is p/n, where p is the number of parameters estimated in the model (including the intercept) and n is the sample size. Roughly speaking, an observation with a hat value greater than 2 or 3 times the average hat value should be examined. The code that follows plots the hat values:

```
hat.plot <- function(fit) {
            p <- length(coefficients(fit))
            n <- length(fitted(fit))
            plot(hatvalues(fit), main="Index Plot of Hat Values")
            abline(h=c(2,3)*p/n, col="red", lty=2)
            identify(1:n, hatvalues(fit), names(hatvalues(fit)))
            }
hat.plot(fit)
```

The resulting graph is shown in figure 8.13.

Horizontal lines are drawn at 2 and 3 times the average hat value. The locator function places the graph in interactive mode. Clicking points of interest labels them

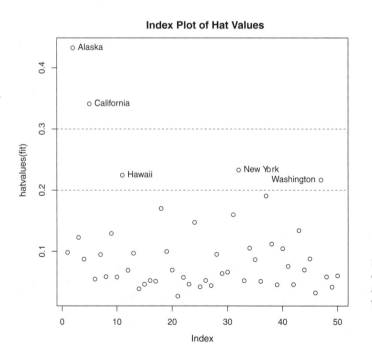

Figure 8.13 Index plot of hat values for assessing observations with high leverage

until the user presses Esc, selects Stop from the graph drop-down menu, or right-clicks the graph.

Here you see that Alaska and California are particularly unusual when it comes to their predictor values. Alaska has a much higher income than other states, while having a lower population and temperature. California has a much higher population than other states, while having a higher income and higher temperature. These states are atypical compared with the other 48 observations.

High-leverage observations may or may not be influential observations. That will depend on whether they're also outliers.

8.4.3   *Influential observations*

Influential observations have a disproportionate impact on the values of the model parameters. Imagine finding that your model changes dramatically with the removal of a single observation. It's this concern that leads you to examine your data for influential points.

There are two methods for identifying influential observations: Cook's distance (or D statistic) and *added variable* plots. Roughly speaking, Cook's D values greater than $4/(n - k - 1)$, where n is the sample size and k is the number of predictor variables, indicate influential observations. You can create a Cook's D plot (figure 8.14) with the following code:

```
cutoff <- 4/(nrow(states)-length(fit$coefficients)-2)
plot(fit, which=4, cook.levels=cutoff)
abline(h=cutoff, lty=2, col="red")
```

The graph identifies Alaska, Hawaii, and Nevada as influential observations. Deleting these states will have a notable impact on the values of the intercept and slopes in the

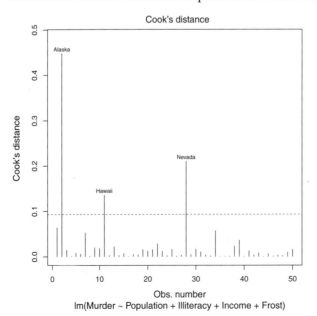

Figure 8.14   Cook's D plot for identifying influential observations

regression model. Note that although it's useful to cast a wide net when searching for influential observations, I tend to find a cutoff of 1 more generally useful than $4/(n - k - 1)$. Given a criterion of D=1, none of the observations in the dataset would appear to be influential.

Cook's D plots can help identify influential observations, but they don't provide information about how these observations affect the model. Added-variable plots can help in this regard. For one response variable and k predictor variables, you'd create k added-variable plots as follows.

For each predictor Xk, plot the residuals from regressing the response variable on the other $k - 1$ predictors versus the residuals from regressing Xk on the other $k - 1$ predictors. Added-variable plots can be created using the `avPlots()` function in the car package:

```
library(car)
avPlots(fit, ask=FALSE, id.method="identify")
```

The resulting graphs are provided in figure 8.15. The graphs are produced one at a time, and users can click points to identify them. Press Esc, choose Stop from the graph's menu, or right-click to move to the next plot. Here, I've identified Alaska in the bottom-left plot.

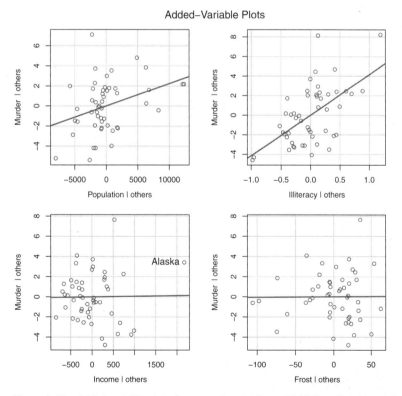

Figure 8.15 Added-variable plots for assessing the impact of influential observations

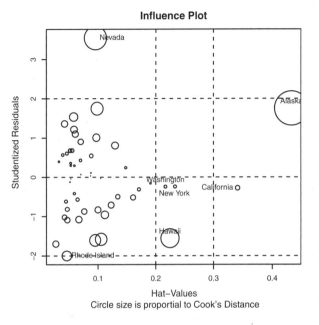

Figure 8.16   Influence plot. States above +2 or below −2 on the vertical axis are considered outliers. States above 0.2 or 0.3 on the horizontal axis have high leverage (unusual combinations of predictor values). Circle size is proportional to influence. Observations depicted by large circles may have disproportionate influence on the parameter estimates of the model.

The straight line in each plot is the actual regression coefficient for that predictor variable. You can see the impact of influential observations by imagining how the line would change if the point representing that observation was deleted. For example, look at the graph of Murder | Others versus Income | Others in the lower-left corner. You can see that eliminating the point labeled Alaska would move the line in a negative direction. In fact, deleting Alaska changes the regression coefficient for Income from positive (.00006) to negative (−.00085).

You can combine the information from outlier, leverage, and influence plots into one highly informative plot using the `influencePlot()` function from the `car` package:

```
library(car)
influencePlot(fit, id.method="identify", main="Influence Plot",
              sub="Circle size is proportional to Cook's distance")
```

The resulting plot (figure 8.16) shows that Nevada and Rhode Island are outliers; New York, California, Hawaii, and Washington have high leverage; and Nevada, Alaska, and Hawaii are influential observations.

8.5   *Corrective measures*

Having spent the last 20 pages learning about regression diagnostics, you may ask, "What do you do if you identify problems?" There are four approaches to dealing with violations of regression assumptions:

- Deleting observations
- Transforming variables

- Adding or deleting variables
- Using another regression approach

Let's look at each in turn.

8.5.1 Deleting observations

Deleting outliers can often improve a dataset's fit to the normality assumption. Influential observations are often deleted as well, because they have an inordinate impact on the results. The largest outlier or influential observation is deleted, and the model is refit. If there are still outliers or influential observations, the process is repeated until an acceptable fit is obtained.

Again, I urge caution when considering the deletion of observations. Sometimes you can determine that the observation is an outlier because of data errors in recording, or because a protocol wasn't followed, or because a test subject misunderstood instructions. In these cases, deleting the offending observation seems perfectly reasonable.

In other cases, the unusual observation may be the most interesting thing about the data you've collected. Uncovering why an observation differs from the rest can contribute great insight to the topic at hand and to other topics you might not have thought of. Some of our greatest advances have come from the serendipity of noticing that something doesn't fit our preconceptions (pardon the hyperbole).

8.5.2 Transforming variables

When models don't meet the normality, linearity, or homoscedasticity assumptions, transforming one or more variables can often improve or correct the situation. Transformations typically involve replacing a variable Y with Y^λ. Common values of λ and their interpretations are given in table 8.5. If Y is a proportion, a logit transformation [ln (Y/1-Y)] is often used.

Table 8.5 Common transformations

λ	-2	-1	-0.5	0	0.5	1	2
Transformation	$1/Y^2$	$1/Y$	$1/\sqrt{Y}$	log(Y)	$\sqrt{Y}$	None	Y^2

When the model violates the normality assumption, you typically attempt a transformation of the response variable. You can use the powerTransform() function in the car package to generate a maximum-likelihood estimation of the power λ most likely to normalize the variable X^λ. In the next listing, this is applied to the states data.

Listing 8.10 Box–Cox transformation to normality

```
> library(car)
> summary(powerTransform(states$Murder))
bcPower Transformation to Normality
```

```
                 Est.Power Std.Err. Wald Lower Bound Wald Upper Bound
states$Murder         0.6     0.26             0.088              1.1

Likelihood ratio tests about transformation parameters
                       LRT df   pval
LR test, lambda=(0)    5.7  1  0.017
LR test, lambda=(1)    2.1  1  0.145
```

The results suggest that you can normalize the variable Murder by replacing it with Murder$^{0.6}$. Because 0.6 is close to 0.5, you could try a square-root transformation to improve the model's fit to normality. But in this case, the hypothesis that $\lambda=1$ can't be rejected (p = 0.145), so there's no strong evidence that a transformation is needed in this case. This is consistent with the results of the Q-Q plot in figure 8.9.

When the assumption of linearity is violated, a transformation of the predictor variables can often help. The boxTidwell() function in the car package can be used to generate maximum-likelihood estimates of predictor powers that can improve linearity. An example of applying the Box–Tidwell transformations to a model that predicts state murder rates from their population and illiteracy rates follows:

```
> library(car)
> boxTidwell(Murder~Population+Illiteracy,data=states)

            Score Statistic p-value MLE of lambda
Population           -0.32     0.75          0.87
Illiteracy            0.62     0.54          1.36
```

The results suggest trying the transformations Population$^{.87}$ and Population$^{1.36}$ to achieve greater linearity. But the score tests for Population (p = .75) and Illiteracy (p = .54) suggest that neither variable needs to be transformed. Again, these results are consistent with the component plus residual plots in figure 8.11.

Finally, transformations of the response variable can help in situations of heteroscedasticity (nonconstant error variance). You saw in listing 8.7 that the spreadLevelPlot() function in the car package offers a power transformation for improving homoscedasticity. Again, in the case of the states example, the constant error-variance assumption is met, and no transformation is necessary.

A caution concerning transformations

There's an old joke in statistics: if you can't prove A, prove B and pretend it was A. (For statisticians, that's pretty funny.) The relevance here is that if you transform your variables, your interpretations must be based on the transformed variables, not the original variables. If the transformation makes sense, such as the log of income or the inverse of distance, the interpretation is easier. But how do you interpret the relationship between the frequency of suicidal ideation and the cube root of depression? If a transformation doesn't make sense, you should avoid it.

8.5.3   Adding or deleting variables

Changing the variables in a model will impact the fit of the model. Sometimes, adding an important variable will correct many of the problems that we've discussed. Deleting a troublesome variable can do the same thing.

Deleting variables is a particularly important approach for dealing with multicollinearity. If your only goal is to make predictions, then multicollinearity isn't a problem. But if you want to make interpretations about individual predictor variables, then you must deal with it. The most common approach is to delete one of the variables involved in the multicollinearity (that is, one of the variables with a $\sqrt{vif} > 2$). An alternative is to use ridge regression, a variant of multiple regression designed to deal with multicollinearity situations.

8.5.4   Trying a different approach

As you've just seen, one approach to dealing with multicollinearity is to fit a different type of model (ridge regression in this case). If there are outliers and/or influential observations, you can fit a robust regression model rather than an OLS regression. If you've violated the normality assumption, you can fit a nonparametric regression model. If there's significant nonlinearity, you can try a nonlinear regression model. If you've violated the assumptions of independence of errors, you can fit a model that specifically takes the error structure into account, such as time-series models or multilevel regression models. Finally, you can turn to generalized linear models to fit a wide range of models in situations where the assumptions of OLS regression don't hold.

We'll discuss some of these alternative approaches in chapter 13. The decision regarding when to try to improve the fit of an OLS regression model and when to try a different approach is a complex one. It's typically based on knowledge of the subject matter and an assessment of which approach will provide the best result.

Speaking of best results, let's turn now to the problem of deciding which predictor variables to include in a regression model.

8.6   Selecting the "best" regression model

When developing a regression equation, you're implicitly faced with a selection of many possible models. Should you include all the variables under study, or drop ones that don't make a significant contribution to prediction? Should you add polynomial and/or interaction terms to improve the fit? The selection of a final regression model always involves a compromise between predictive accuracy (a model that fits the data as well as possible) and parsimony (a simple and replicable model). All things being equal, if you have two models with approximately equal predictive accuracy, you favor the simpler one. This section describes methods for choosing among competing models. The word "best" is in quotation marks because there's no single criterion you can use to make the decision. The final decision requires judgment on the part of the investigator. (Think of it as job security.)

8.6.1 Comparing models

You can compare the fit of two nested models using the anova() function in the base installation. A *nested model* is one whose terms are completely included in the other model. In the states multiple-regression model, you found that the regression coefficients for Income and Frost were nonsignificant. You can test whether a model without these two variables predicts as well as one that includes them (see the following listing).

Listing 8.11 Comparing nested models using the anova() function

```
> states <- as.data.frame(state.x77[,c("Murder", "Population",
                          "Illiteracy", "Income", "Frost")])
> fit1 <- lm(Murder ~ Population + Illiteracy + Income + Frost,
        data=states)
> fit2 <- lm(Murder ~ Population + Illiteracy, data=states)
> anova(fit2, fit1)

Analysis of Variance Table

Model 1: Murder ~ Population + Illiteracy
Model 2: Murder ~ Population + Illiteracy + Income + Frost
  Res.Df    RSS Df  Sum of Sq      F Pr(>F)
1     47 289.246
2     45 289.167  2     0.079 0.0061    0.994
```

Here, model 1 is nested within model 2. The anova() function provides a simultaneous test that Income and Frost add to linear prediction above and beyond Population and Illiteracy. Because the test is nonsignificant (p = .994), you conclude that they don't add to the linear prediction and you're justified in dropping them from your model.

The Akaike Information Criterion (AIC) provides another method for comparing models. The index takes into account a model's statistical fit and the number of parameters needed to achieve this fit. Models with *smaller* AIC values—indicating adequate fit with fewer parameters—are preferred. The criterion is provided by the AIC() function (see the following listing).

Listing 8.12 Comparing models with the AIC

```
> fit1 <- lm(Murder ~ Population + Illiteracy + Income + Frost,
        data=states)
> fit2 <- lm(Murder ~ Population + Illiteracy, data=states)
> AIC(fit1,fit2)

     df      AIC
fit1  6 241.6429
fit2  4 237.6565
```

The AIC values suggest that the model without Income and Frost is the better model. Note that although the ANOVA approach requires nested models, the AIC approach doesn't.

Comparing two models is relatively straightforward, but what do you do when there are 4, or 10, or 100 possible models to consider? That's the topic of the next section.

8.6.2 Variable selection

Two popular approaches to selecting a final set of predictor variables from a larger pool of candidate variables are stepwise methods and all-subsets regression.

STEPWISE REGRESSION

In stepwise selection, variables are added to or deleted from a model one at a time, until some stopping criterion is reached. For example, in *forward stepwise* regression, you add predictor variables to the model one at a time, stopping when the addition of variables would no longer improve the model. In *backward stepwise* regression, you start with a model that includes all predictor variables, and then you delete them one at a time until removing variables would degrade the quality of the model. In *stepwise stepwise* regression (usually called *stepwise* to avoid sounding silly), you combine the forward and backward stepwise approaches. Variables are entered one at a time, but at each step, the variables in the model are reevaluated, and those that don't contribute to the model are deleted. A predictor variable may be added to, and deleted from, a model several times before a final solution is reached.

The implementation of stepwise regression methods varies by the criteria used to enter or remove variables. The `stepAIC()` function in the `MASS` package performs stepwise model selection (forward, backward, or stepwise) using an exact AIC criterion. The next listing applies backward stepwise regression to the multiple regression problem.

Listing 8.13 Backward stepwise selection

```
> library(MASS)
> states <- as.data.frame(state.x77[,c("Murder", "Population",
                            "Illiteracy", "Income", "Frost")])

> fit <- lm(Murder ~ Population + Illiteracy + Income + Frost,
            data=states)
> stepAIC(fit, direction="backward")

Start:  AIC=97.75
Murder ~ Population + Illiteracy + Income + Frost

              Df Sum of Sq     RSS     AIC
- Frost        1      0.02  289.19   95.75
- Income       1      0.06  289.22   95.76
<none>                      289.17   97.75
- Population   1     39.24  328.41  102.11
- Illiteracy   1    144.26  433.43  115.99


Step:  AIC=95.75
Murder ~ Population + Illiteracy + Income

              Df Sum of Sq     RSS     AIC
- Income       1      0.06  289.25   93.76
<none>                      289.19   95.75
- Population   1     43.66  332.85  100.78
- Illiteracy   1    236.20  525.38  123.61
```

```
Step:  AIC=93.76
Murder ~ Population + Illiteracy

             Df Sum of Sq    RSS    AIC
<none>                    289.25  93.76
- Population  1    48.52 337.76  99.52
- Illiteracy  1   299.65 588.89 127.31

Call:
lm(formula=Murder ~ Population + Illiteracy, data=states)

Coefficients:
(Intercept)    Population   Illiteracy
  1.6515497     0.0002242    4.0807366
```

You start with all four predictors in the model. For each step, the AIC column provides the model AIC resulting from the deletion of the variable listed in that row. The AIC value for <none> is the model AIC if no variables are removed. In the first step, Frost is removed, decreasing the AIC from 97.75 to 95.75. In the second step, Income is removed, decreasing the AIC to 93.76. Deleting any more variables would increase the AIC, so the process stops.

Stepwise regression is controversial. Although it may find a good model, there's no guarantee that it will find the "best" model. This is because not every possible model is evaluated. An approach that attempts to overcome this limitation is *all subsets regression*.

ALL SUBSETS REGRESSION

In all subsets regression, every possible model is inspected. The analyst can choose to have all possible results displayed or ask for the *nbest* models of each subset size (one predictor, two predictors, and so on). For example, if nbest=2, the two best one-predictor models are displayed, followed by the two best two-predictor models, followed by the two best three-predictor models, up to a model with all predictors.

All subsets regression is performed using the regsubsets() function from the leaps package. You can choose the R-squared, Adjusted R-squared, or Mallows Cp statistic as your criterion for reporting "best" models.

As you've seen, R-squared is the amount of variance accounted for in the response variable by the predictors variables. Adjusted R-squared is similar but takes into account the number of parameters in the model. R-squared always increases with the addition of predictors. When the number of predictors is large compared to the sample size, this can lead to significant overfitting. The Adjusted R-squared is an attempt to provide a more honest estimate of the population R-squared—one that's less likely to take advantage of chance variation in the data. The Mallows Cp statistic is also used as a stopping rule in stepwise regression. It has been widely suggested that a good model is one in which the Cp statistic is close to the number of model parameters (including the intercept).

In listing 8.14, we'll apply all subsets regression to the states data. The results can be plotted with either the plot() function in the leaps package or the subsets() function in the car package. An example of the former is provided in figure 8.17, and an example of the latter is given in figure 8.18.

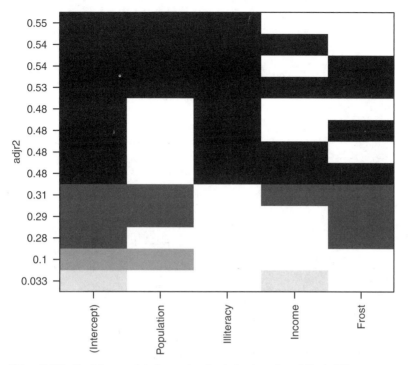

Figure 8.17   Best four models for each subset size based on Adjusted R-square

Listing 8.14   All subsets regression

```
library(leaps)
states <- as.data.frame(state.x77[,c("Murder", "Population",
        "Illiteracy", "Income", "Frost")])

leaps <-regsubsets(Murder ~ Population + Illiteracy + Income +
                  Frost, data=states, nbest=4)
plot(leaps, scale="adjr2")

library(car)
subsets(leaps, statistic="cp",
      main="Cp Plot for All Subsets Regression")
abline(1,1,lty=2,col="red")
```

Figure 8.17 can be confusing to read. Looking at the first row (starting at the bottom), you can see that a model with the intercept and Income has an adjusted R-square of 0.33. A model with the intercept and Population has an adjusted R-square of 0.1. Jumping to the 12th row, a model with the intercept, Population, Illiteracy, and Income has an adjusted R-square of 0.54, whereas one with the intercept, Population, and Illiteracy alone has an adjusted R-square of 0.55. Here you see that a model with fewer predictors has a larger adjusted R-square (something that can't happen with an unadjusted R-square). The graph suggests that the two-predictor model (Population and Illiteracy) is the best.

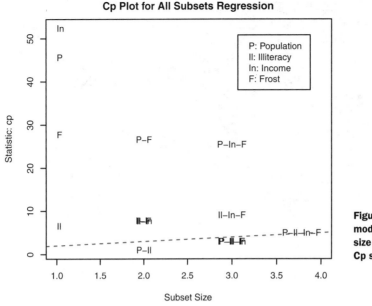

Cp Plot for All Subsets Regression

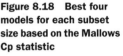

P: Population
Il: Illiteracy
In: Income
F: Frost

Figure 8.18   Best four models for each subset size based on the Mallows Cp statistic

Figure 8.18 shows the best four models for each subset size based on the Mallows Cp statistic. Better models will fall close to a line with intercept 1 and slope 1. The plot suggests that you consider a two-predictor model with Population and Illiteracy; a three-predictor model with Population, Illiteracy, and Frost, *or* Population, Illiteracy, and Income (they overlap on the graph and are hard to read); or a four-predictor model with Population, Illiteracy, Income, and Frost. You can reject the other possible models.

In most instances, all subsets regression is preferable to stepwise regression, because more models are considered. But when the number of predictors is large, the procedure can require significant computing time. In general, automated variable-selection methods should be seen as an aid rather than a directing force in model selection. A well-fitting model that doesn't make sense doesn't help you. Ultimately, it's your knowledge of the subject matter that should guide you.

8.7   *Taking the analysis further*

We'll end our discussion of regression by considering methods for assessing model generalizability and predictor relative importance.

8.7.1   *Cross-validation*

In the previous section, we examined methods for selecting the variables to include in a regression equation. When description is your primary goal, the selection and interpretation of a regression model signals the end of your labor. But when your goal is prediction, you can justifiably ask, "How well will this equation perform in the real world?"

By definition, regression techniques obtain model parameters that are optimal for a given set of data. In OLS regression, the model parameters are selected to minimize the sum of squared errors of prediction (residuals) and, conversely, maximize the amount of variance accounted for in the response variable (R-squared). Because the equation has been optimized for the given set of data, it won't perform as well with a new set of data.

We began this chapter with an example involving a research physiologist who wanted to predict the number of calories an individual will burn from the duration and intensity of their exercise, age, gender, and BMI. If you fit an OLS regression equation to this data, you'll obtain model parameters that uniquely maximize the R-squared for this *particular* set of observations. But our researcher wants to use this equation to predict the calories burned by individuals in general, not only those in the original study. You know that the equation won't perform as well with a new sample of observations, but how much will you lose? *Cross-validation* is a useful method for evaluating the generalizability of a regression equation.

In cross-validation, a portion of the data is selected as the training sample, and a portion is selected as the hold-out sample. A regression equation is developed on the training sample and then applied to the hold-out sample. Because the hold-out sample wasn't involved in the selection of the model parameters, the performance on this sample is a more accurate estimate of the operating characteristics of the model with new data.

In *k-fold cross-validation*, the sample is divided into k subsamples. Each of the k subsamples serves as a hold-out group, and the combined observations from the remaining $k - 1$ subsamples serve as the training group. The performance for the k prediction equations applied to the k hold-out samples is recorded and then averaged. (When k equals n, the total number of observations, this approach is called *jackknifing*.)

You can perform k-fold cross-validation using the `crossval()` function in the `bootstrap` package. The following listing provides a function (called `shrinkage()`) for cross-validating a model's R-square statistic using k-fold cross-validation.

Listing 8.15 Function for k-fold cross-validated R-square

```
shrinkage <- function(fit, k=10){
  require(bootstrap)

  theta.fit <- function(x,y){lsfit(x,y)}
  theta.predict <- function(fit,x){cbind(1,x)%*%fit$coef}

  x <- fit$model[,2:ncol(fit$model)]
  y <- fit$model[,1]

  results <- crossval(x, y, theta.fit, theta.predict, ngroup=k)
  r2 <- cor(y, fit$fitted.values)^2
  r2cv <- cor(y, results$cv.fit)^2
  cat("Original R-square =", r2, "\n")
  cat(k, "Fold Cross-Validated R-square =", r2cv, "\n")
  cat("Change =", r2-r2cv, "\n")
  }
```

Using this listing, you define your functions, create a matrix of predictor and predicted values, get the raw R-squared, and get the cross-validated R-squared. (Chapter 12 covers bootstrapping in detail.)

The shrinkage() function is then used to perform a 10-fold cross-validation with the states data, using a model with all four predictor variables:

```
> states .<- as.data.frame(state.x77[,c("Murder", "Population",
       "Illiteracy", "Income", "Frost")])
> fit <- lm(Murder ~ Population + Income + Illiteracy + Frost, data=states)
> shrinkage(fit)

Original R-square=0.567
10 Fold Cross-Validated R-square=0.4481
Change=0.1188
```

You can see that the R-square based on the sample (0.567) is overly optimistic. A better estimate of the amount of variance in murder rates that this model will account for with new data is the cross-validated R-square (0.448). (Note that observations are assigned to the *k* groups randomly, so you'll get a slightly different result each time you execute the shrinkage() function.)

You could use cross-validation in variable selection by choosing a model that demonstrates better generalizability. For example, a model with two predictors (Population and Illiteracy) shows less R-square shrinkage (.03 versus .12) than the full model:

```
> fit2 <- lm(Murder ~ Population + Illiteracy,data=states)
> shrinkage(fit2)

Original R-square=0.5668327
10 Fold Cross-Validated R-square=0.5346871
Change=0.03214554
```

This may make the two-predictor model a more attractive alternative.

All other things being equal, a regression equation that's based on a larger training sample and one that's more representative of the population of interest will cross-validate better. You'll get less R-squared shrinkage and make more accurate predictions.

8.7.2 *Relative importance*

Up to this point in the chapter, we've been asking, "Which variables are useful for predicting the outcome?" But often your real interest is in the question, "Which variables are *most important* in predicting the outcome?" You implicitly want to rank-order the predictors in terms of relative importance. There may be practical grounds for asking the second question. For example, if you could rank-order leadership practices by their relative importance for organizational success, you could help managers focus on the behaviors they most need to develop.

If predictor variables were uncorrelated, this would be a simple task. You would rank-order the predictor variables by their correlation with the response variable. In most cases, though, the predictors are correlated with each other, and this complicates the task significantly.

There have been many attempts to develop a means for assessing the relative importance of predictors. The simplest has been to compare standardized regression coefficients. Standardized regression coefficients describe the expected change in the response variable (expressed in standard deviation units) for a standard deviation change in a predictor variable, holding the other predictor variables constant. You can obtain the standardized regression coefficients in R by standardizing each of the variables in your dataset to a mean of 0 and standard deviation of 1 using the `scale()` function, before submitting the dataset to a regression analysis. (Note that because the `scale()` function returns a matrix and the `lm()` function requires a data frame, you convert between the two in an intermediate step.) The code and results for the multiple regression problem are shown here:

```
> states <- as.data.frame(state.x77[,c("Murder", "Population",
                         "Illiteracy", "Income", "Frost")])
> zstates <- as.data.frame(scale(states))
> zfit <- lm(Murder~Population + Income + Illiteracy + Frost, data=zstates)
> coef(zfit)


(Intercept)   Population     Income   Illiteracy       Frost
 -9.406e-17   2.705e-01   1.072e-02    6.840e-01   8.185e-03
```

Here you see that a one-standard-deviation increase in illiteracy rate yields a 0.68 standard deviation increase in murder rate, when controlling for population, income, and temperature. Using standardized regression coefficients as your guide, Illiteracy is the most important predictor and Frost is the least.

There have been many other attempts at quantifying relative importance. Relative importance can be thought of as the contribution each predictor makes to R-square, both alone and in combination with other predictors. Several possible approaches to relative importance are captured in the `relaimpo` package written by Ulrike Grömping (http://mng.bz/KDYF).

A new method called *relative weights* shows significant promise. The method closely approximates the average increase in R-square obtained by adding a predictor variable across all possible submodels (Johnson, 2004; Johnson and Lebreton, 2004; LeBreton and Tonidandel, 2008). A function for generating relative weights is provided in the next listing.

Listing 8.16 `relweights()` **for calculating relative importance of predictors**

```
relweights <- function(fit,...){
  R <- cor(fit$model)
  nvar <- ncol(R)
  rxx <- R[2:nvar, 2:nvar]
  rxy <- R[2:nvar, 1]
  svd <- eigen(rxx)
  evec <- svd$vectors
  ev <- svd$values
  delta <- diag(sqrt(ev))
  lambda <- evec %*% delta %*% t(evec)
```

```
lambdasq <- lambda ^ 2
beta <- solve(lambda) %*% rxy
rsquare <- colSums(beta ^ 2)
rawwgt <- lambdasq %*% beta ^ 2
import <- (rawwgt / rsquare) * 100
import <- as.data.frame(import)
row.names(import) <- names(fit$model[2:nvar])
names(import) <- "Weights"
import <- import[order(import),1, drop=FALSE]
dotchart(import$Weights, labels=row.names(import),
    xlab="% of R-Square", pch=19,
    main="Relative Importance of Predictor Variables",
    sub=paste("Total R-Square=", round(rsquare, digits=3)),
    ...)
return(import)
}
```

NOTE   The code in listing 8.16 is adapted from an SPSS program generously provided by Dr. Johnson. See Johnson (2000, *Multivariate Behavioral Research*, 35, 1–19) for an explanation of how the relative weights are derived.

In listing 8.17, the `relweights()` function is applied to the `states` data with murder rate predicted by the population, illiteracy, income, and temperature.

You can see from figure 8.19 that the total amount of variance accounted for by the model (R-square=0.567) has been divided among the predictor variables. Illiteracy accounts for 59% of the R-square, Frost accounts for 20.79%, and so forth. Based on

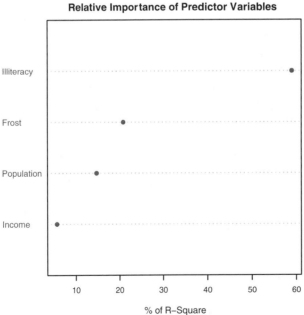

Figure 8.19 Dot chart of relative weights for the states multiple regression problem. Larger weights indicate relatively more important predictors. For example, Illiteracy accounts for 59% of the total explained variance (0.567), whereas Income only accounts for 5.49%. Thus Illiteracy has greater relative importance than Income in this model.

the method of relative weights, Illiteracy has the greatest relative importance, followed by Frost, Population, and Income, in that order.

```
> states <- as.data.frame(state.x77[,c("Murder", "Population",
        "Illiteracy", "Income", "Frost")])
> fit <- lm(Murder ~ Population + Illiteracy + Income + Frost, data=states)
> relweights(fit, col="blue")
            Weights
Income         5.49
Population    14.72
Frost         20.79
Illiteracy    59.00
```

Relative-importance measures (and, in particular, the method of relative weights) have wide applicability. They come much closer to our intuitive conception of relative importance than standardized regression coefficients do, and I expect to see their use increase dramatically in coming years.

8.8   Summary

Regression analysis is a term that covers a broad range of methodologies in statistics. You've seen that it's a highly interactive approach that involves fitting models, assessing their fit to statistical assumptions, modifying both the data and the models, and refitting to arrive at a final result. In many ways, this final result is based on art and skill as much as science.

This has been a long chapter, because regression analysis is a process with many parts. We've discussed fitting OLS regression models, using regression diagnostics to assess the data's fit to statistical assumptions, and methods for modifying the data to meet these assumptions more closely. We looked at ways of selecting a final regression model from many possible models, and you learned how to evaluate its likely performance on new samples of data. Finally, we tackled the thorny problem of variable importance: identifying which variables are the most important for predicting an outcome.

In each of the examples in this chapter, the predictor variables have been quantitative. However, there are no restrictions against using categorical variables as predictors as well. Using a categorical predictor such as gender, treatment type, or manufacturing process allows you to examine group differences on a response or outcome variable. This is the focus of our next chapter.

Analysis of variance

9

This chapter covers

- Using R to model basic experimental designs
- Fitting and interpreting ANOVA type models
- Evaluating model assumptions

In chapter 7, we looked at regression models for predicting a quantitative response variable from quantitative predictor variables. But there's no reason that we couldn't have included nominal or ordinal factors as predictors as well. When factors are included as explanatory variables, our focus usually shifts from prediction to understanding group differences, and the methodology is referred to as *analysis of variance (ANOVA)*. ANOVA methodology is used to analyze a wide variety of experimental and quasi-experimental designs. This chapter provides an overview of R functions for analyzing common research designs.

First we'll look at design terminology, followed by a general discussion of R's approach to fitting ANOVA models. Then we'll explore several examples that illustrate the analysis of common designs. Along the way, you'll treat anxiety disorders, lower blood cholesterol levels, help pregnant mice have fat babies, assure that pigs grow long in the tooth, facilitate breathing in plants, and learn which grocery shelves to avoid.

In addition to the base installation, you'll be using the `car`, `gplots`, `HH`, `rrcov`, `multicomp`, `effects`, `MASS`, and `mvoutlier` packages in the examples. Be sure to install them before trying out the sample code.

9.1 A crash course on terminology

Experimental design in general, and analysis of variance in particular, has its own language. Before discussing the analysis of these designs, we'll quickly review some important terms. We'll use a series of increasingly complex study designs to introduce the most significant concepts.

Say you're interested in studying the treatment of anxiety. Two popular therapies for anxiety are cognitive behavior therapy (CBT) and eye movement desensitization and reprocessing (EMDR). You recruit 10 anxious individuals and randomly assign half of them to receive five weeks of CBT and half to receive five weeks of EMDR. At the conclusion of therapy, each patient is asked to complete the State-Trait Anxiety Inventory (STAI), a self-report measure of anxiety. The design is outlined in table 9.1.

Table 9.1 One-way between-groups ANOVA

CBT	EMDR
s1	s6
s2	s7
s3	s8
s4	s9
s5	s10

(Treatment)

In this design, Treatment is a *between-groups* factor with two levels (CBT, EMDR). It's called a between-groups factor because patients are assigned to one and only one group. No patient receives both CBT and EMDR. The s characters represent the subjects (patients). STAI is the *dependent variable*, and Treatment is the *independent variable*. Because there is an equal number of observations in each treatment condition, you have a *balanced design*. When the sample sizes are unequal across the cells of a design, you have an *unbalanced design*.

The statistical design in table 9.1 is called a *one-way ANOVA* because there's a single classification variable. Specifically, it's a one-way between-groups ANOVA. Effects in ANOVA designs are primarily evaluated through F tests. If the F test for Treatment is significant, you can conclude that the mean STAI scores for two therapies differed after five weeks of treatment.

If you were interested in the effect of CBT on anxiety over time, you could place all 10 patients in the CBT group and assess them at the conclusion of therapy and again six months later. This design is displayed in table 9.2.

Table 9.2 One-way within-groups ANOVA

Patient	Time	
	5 weeks	6 months
s1		
s2		
s3		
s4		
s5		
s6		
s7		
s8		
s9		
s10		

Time is a *within-groups* factor with two levels (five weeks, six months). It's called a within-groups factor because each patient is measured under both levels. The statistical design is a *one-way within-groups ANOVA*. Because each subject is measured more than once, the design is also called a *repeated measures ANOVA*. If the F test for Time is significant, you can conclude that patients' mean STAI scores changed between five weeks and six months.

If you were interested in both treatment differences *and* change over time, you could combine the first two study designs and randomly assign five patients to CBT and five patients to EMDR, and assess their STAI results at the end of therapy (five weeks) and at six months (see table 9.3).

By including both Therapy and Time as factors, you're able to examine the impact of Therapy (averaged across time), Time (averaged across therapy type), and the interaction of Therapy and Time. The first two are called the *main effects*, whereas the interaction is (not surprisingly) called an *interaction effect*.

When you cross two or more factors, as is done here, you have a *factorial ANOVA* design. Crossing two factors produces a two-way ANOVA, crossing three factors produces a three-way ANOVA, and so forth. When a factorial design includes both between-groups and within-groups factors, it's also called a *mixed-model ANOVA*. The current design is a two-way mixed-model factorial ANOVA (phew!).

In this case, you'll have three F tests: one for Therapy, one for Time, and one for the Therapy × Time interaction. A significant result for Therapy indicates that CBT and EMDR differ in their impact on anxiety. A significant result for Time indicates that

Table 9.3   Two-way factorial ANOVA with one between-groups and one within-groups factor

		Patient	Time	
			5 weeks	6 months
Therapy	CBT	s1		
		s2		
		s3		
		s4		
		s5		
	EMDR	s6		
		s7		
		s8		
		s9		
		s10		

anxiety changed from week five to the six-month follow-up. A significant Therapy ×
Time interaction indicates that the two treatments for anxiety had a differential
impact over time (that is, the change in anxiety from five weeks to six months was different for the two treatments).

Now let's extend the design a bit. It's known that depression can have an impact
on therapy, and that depression and anxiety often co-occur. Even though subjects
were randomly assigned to treatment conditions, it's possible that the two therapy
groups differed in patient depression levels at the initiation of the study. Any post-
therapy differences might then be due to the preexisting depression differences and
not to your experimental manipulation. Because depression could also explain the
group differences on the dependent variable, it's a *confounding* factor. And because
you're not interested in depression, it's called a *nuisance* variable.

If you recorded depression levels using a self-report depression measure such as
the Beck Depression Inventory (BDI) when patients were recruited, you could statistically adjust for any treatment group differences in depression before assessing the
impact of therapy type. In this case, BDI would be called a *covariate*, and the design
would be called an *analysis of covariance (ANCOVA)*.

Finally, you've recorded a single dependent variable in this study (the STAI). You
could increase the validity of this study by including additional measures of anxiety
(such as family ratings, therapist ratings, and a measure assessing the impact of anxiety on their daily functioning). When there's more than one dependent variable, the
design is called a *multivariate analysis of variance (MANOVA)*. If there are covariates present, it's called a *multivariate analysis of covariance (MANCOVA)*.

Now that you have the basic terminology under your belt, you're ready to amaze
your friends, dazzle new acquaintances, and learn how to fit ANOVA/ANCOVA/
MANOVA models with R.

9.2   Fitting ANOVA models

Although ANOVA and regression methodologies developed separately, functionally
they're both special cases of the general linear model. You could analyze ANOVA models using the same `lm()` function used for regression in chapter 7. But you'll primarily
use the `aov()` function in this chapter. The results of `lm()` and `aov()` are equivalent,
but the `aov()` function presents these results in a format that's more familiar to
ANOVA methodologists. For completeness, I'll provide an example using `lm()` at the
end of this chapter.

9.2.1   The aov() function

The syntax of the `aov()` function is `aov(formula, data=dataframe)`. Table 9.4
describes special symbols that can be used in the formulas. In this table, `y` is the
dependent variable and the letters `A`, `B`, and `C` represent factors.

Table 9.4   Special symbols used in R formulas

Symbol	Usage
~	Separates response variables on the left from the explanatory variables on the right. For example, a prediction of y from A, B, and C would be coded `y ~ A + B + C`
:	Denotes an interaction between variables. A prediction of y from A, B, and the interaction between A and B would be coded `y ~ A + B + A:B`
*	Denotes the complete crossing variables. The code `y ~ A*B*C` expands to `y ~ A + B + C + A:B + A:C + B:C + A:B:C`
^	Denotes crossing to a specified degree. The code `y ~ (A+B+C)^2` expands to `y ~ A + B + C + A:B + A:C + A:B`
.	Denotes all remaining variables. The code `y ~ .` expands to `y ~ A + B + C`

Table 9.5 provides formulas for several common research designs. In this table, lower-case letters are quantitative variables, uppercase letters are grouping factors, and `Subject` is a unique identifier variable for subjects.

Table 9.5   Formulas for common research designs

Design	Formula
One-way ANOVA	`y ~ A`
One-way ANCOVA with 1 covariate	`y ~ x + A`
Two-way factorial ANOVA	`y ~ A * B`
Two-way factorial ANCOVA with 2 covariates	`y ~ x1 + x2 + A * B`
Randomized block	`y ~ B + A` (where B is a blocking factor)
One-way within-groups ANOVA	`y ~ A + Error(Subject/A)`
Repeated measures ANOVA with 1 within-groups factor (`W`) and 1 between-groups factor (`B`)	`y ~ B * W + Error(Subject/W)`

We'll explore in-depth examples of several of these designs later in this chapter.

9.2.2   *The order of formula terms*

The order in which the effects appear in a formula matters when (a) there's more than one factor and the design is unbalanced, or (b) covariates are present. When either of these two conditions is present, the variables on the right side of the equation will be correlated with each other. In this case, there's no unambiguous way to divide up their impact on the dependent variable. For example, in a two-way ANOVA with unequal numbers of observations in the treatment combinations, the model y ~ A*B *will not* produce the same results as the model y ~ B*A.

By default, R employs the Type I (sequential) approach to calculating ANOVA effects (see the sidebar "Order counts!"). The first model can be written as y ~ A + B + A:B. The resulting R ANOVA table will assess

- The impact of A on y
- The impact of B on y, controlling for A
- The interaction of A and B, controlling for the A and B main effects

---

Order counts!

When independent variables are correlated with each other or with covariates, there's no unambiguous method for assessing the independent contributions of these variables to the dependent variable. Consider an unbalanced two-way factorial design with factors A and B and dependent variable y. There are three effects in this design: the A and B main effects and the A × B interaction. Assuming that you're modeling the data using the formula

```
Y ~ A + B + A:B
```

there are three typical approaches for partitioning the variance in y among the effects on the right side of this equation.

TYPE I (SEQUENTIAL)

Effects are adjusted for those that appear earlier in the formula. A is unadjusted. B is adjusted for the A. The A:B interaction is adjusted for A and B.

TYPE II (HIERARCHICAL)

Effects are adjusted for other effects at the same or lower level. A is adjusted for B. B is adjusted for A. The A:B interaction is adjusted for both A and B.

TYPE III (MARGINAL)

Each effect is adjusted for every other effect in the model. A is adjusted for B and A:B. B is adjusted for A and A:B. The A:B interaction is adjusted for A and B.

R employs the Type I approach by default. Other programs such as SAS and SPSS employ the Type III approach by default.

The greater the imbalance in sample sizes, the greater the impact that the order of the terms will have on the results. In general, more fundamental effects should be listed earlier in the formula. In particular, covariates should be listed first, followed by main effects, followed by two-way interactions, followed by three-way interactions, and so on. For main effects, more fundamental variables should be listed first. Thus gender would be listed before treatment. Here's the bottom line: when the research design isn't orthogonal (that is, when the factors and/or covariates are correlated), be careful when specifying the order of effects.

Before moving on to specific examples, note that the Anova() function in the car package (not to be confused with the standard anova() function) provides the option of using the Type II or Type III approach, rather than the Type I approach used by the aov() function. You may want to use the Anova() function if you're concerned about matching your results to those provided by other packages such as SAS and SPSS. See help(Anova, package="car") for details.

9.3   One-way ANOVA

In a one-way ANOVA, you're interested in comparing the dependent variable means of two or more groups defined by a categorical grouping factor. This example comes from the cholesterol dataset in the multcomp package, taken from Westfall, Tobia, Rom, & Hochberg (1999). Fifty patients received one of five cholesterol-reducing drug regimens (trt). Three of the treatment conditions involved the same drug administered as 20 mg once per day (1time), 10mg twice per day (2times), or 5 mg four times per day (4times). The two remaining conditions (drugD and drugE) represented competing drugs. Which drug regimen produced the greatest cholesterol reduction (response)? The analysis is provided in the following listing.

Listing 9.1   One-way ANOVA

```
> library(multcomp)
> attach(cholesterol)
> table(trt)                            ➊ Group sample sizes
trt
 1time 2times 4times  drugD  drugE
    10     10     10     10     10

> aggregate(response, by=list(trt), FUN=mean)    ➋ Group means
  Group.1     x
1   1time  5.78
2  2times  9.22
3  4times 12.37
4   drugD 15.36
5   drugE 20.95

> aggregate(response, by=list(trt), FUN=sd)      ➌ Group standard deviations
  Group.1    x
1   1time 2.88
2  2times 3.48
3  4times 2.92
4   drugD 3.45
5   drugE 3.35

> fit <- aov(response ~ trt)            ➍ Tests for group
> summary(fit)                              differences (ANOVA)
            Df Sum Sq   Mean Sq   F value        Pr(>F)
trt          4   1351       338      32.4    9.8e-13  ***
Residuals   45    469        10
---
```

```
Signif. codes:  0 '***' 0.001 '**' 0.01 '*' 0.05 '.' 0.1 ' ' 1
```

```
> library(gplots)
> plotmeans(response ~ trt, xlab="Treatment", ylab="Response",
    main="Mean Plot\nwith 95% CI")
> detach(cholesterol)
```

❺ Plots group means and confidence intervals

Looking at the output, you can see that 10 patients received each of the drug regimens ❶. From the means, it appears that drugE produced the greatest cholesterol reduction, whereas 1time produced the least ❷. Standard deviations were relatively constant across the five groups, ranging from 2.88 to 3.48 ❸. The ANOVA F test for treatment (trt) is significant (p < .0001), providing evidence that the five treatments aren't all equally effective ❹.

The plotmeans() function in the gplots package can be used to produce a graph of group means and their confidence intervals ❺. A plot of the treat-

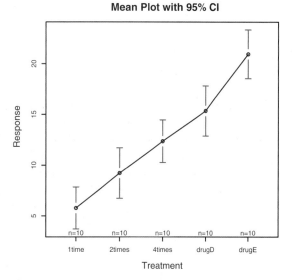

Figure 9.1 Treatment group means with 95% confidence intervals for five cholesterol-reducing drug regimens

ment means, with 95% confidence limits, is provided in figure 9.1 and allows you to clearly see these treatment differences.

9.3.1 Multiple comparisons

The ANOVA F test for treatment tells you that the five drug regimens aren't equally effective, but it doesn't tell you *which* treatments differ from one another. You can use a multiple comparison procedure to answer this question. For example, the TukeyHSD() function provides a test of all pairwise differences between group means, as shown next.

Listing 9.2 Tukey HSD pairwise group comparisons

```
> TukeyHSD(fit)
  Tukey multiple comparisons of means
    95% family-wise confidence level

Fit: aov(formula = response ~ trt)

$trt
```

```
              diff     lwr   upr p adj
2times-1time   3.44 -0.658  7.54 0.138
4times-1time   6.59  2.492 10.69 0.000
drugD-1time    9.58  5.478 13.68 0.000
drugE-1time   15.17 11.064 19.27 0.000
4times-2times  3.15 -0.951  7.25 0.205
drugD-2times   6.14  2.035 10.24 0.001
drugE-2times  11.72  7.621 15.82 0.000
drugD-4times   2.99 -1.115  7.09 0.251
drugE-4times   8.57  4.471 12.67 0.000
drugE-drugD    5.59  1.485  9.69 0.003

> par(las=2)
> par(mar=c(5,8,4,2))
> plot(TukeyHSD(fit))
```

For example, the mean cholesterol reductions for 1time and 2times aren't significantly different from each other (p = 0.138), whereas the difference between 1time and 4times is significantly different (p < .001).

The pairwise comparisons are plotted in figure 9.2. The first par statement rotates the axis labels, and the second one increases the left margin area so that the labels fit (par options are covered in chapter 3). In this graph, confidence intervals that include 0 indicate treatments that aren't significantly different (p > 0.5).

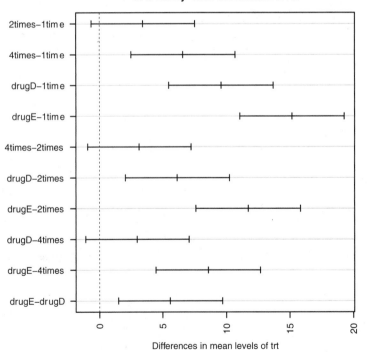

Figure 9.2   Plot of Tukey HSD pairwise mean comparisons

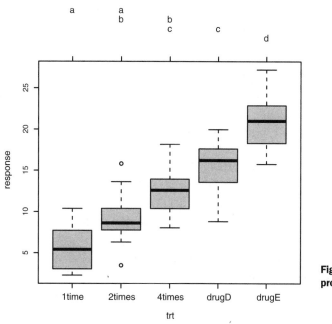

Figure 9.3   Tukey HSD tests provided by the `multcomp` **package**

The `glht()` function in the `multcomp` package provides a much more comprehensive set of methods for multiple mean comparisons that you can use for both linear models (such as those described in this chapter) and generalized linear models (covered in chapter 13). The following code reproduces the Tukey HSD test, along with a different graphical representation of the results (figure 9.3):

```
> library(multcomp)
> par(mar=c(5,4,6,2))
> tuk <- glht(fit, linfct=mcp(trt="Tukey"))
> plot(cld(tuk, level=.05),col="lightgrey")
```

In this code, the `par` statement increases the top margin to fit the letter array. The `level` option in the `cld()` function provides the significance level to use (0.05, or 95% confidence in this case).

Groups (represented by box plots) that have the same letter don't have significantly different means. You can see that 1time and 2times aren't significantly different (they both have the letter a) and that 2times and 4times aren't significantly different (they both have the letter b); but that 1time and 4times are different (they don't share a letter). Personally, I find figure 9.3 easier to read than figure 9.2. It also has the advantage of providing information on the distribution of scores within each group.

From these results, you can see that taking the cholesterol-lowering drug in 5 mg doses four times a day was better than taking a 20 mg dose once per day. The competitor drugD wasn't superior to this four-times-per-day regimen. But competitor drugE was superior to both drugD and all three dosage strategies for the focus drug.

Multiple comparisons methodology is a complex and rapidly changing area of study. To learn more, see Bretz, Hothorn, and Westfall (2010).

9.3.2   *Assessing test assumptions*

As you saw in the previous chapter, confidence in results depends on the degree to which your data satisfies the assumptions underlying the statistical tests. In a one-way ANOVA, the dependent variable is assumed to be normally distributed and have equal variance in each group. You can use a Q-Q plot to assess the normality assumption:

```
> library(car)
> qqPlot(lm(response ~ trt, data=cholesterol),
        simulate=TRUE, main="Q-Q Plot", labels=FALSE)
```

Note the qqPlot() requires an lm() fit. The graph is provided in figure 9.4. The data falls within the 95% confidence envelope, suggesting that the normality assumption has been met fairly well.

R provides several tests for the equality (homogeneity) of variances. For example, you can perform Bartlett's test with this code:

```
> bartlett.test(response ~ trt, data=cholesterol)

        Bartlett test of homogeneity of variances

data:  response by trt
Bartlett's K-squared = 0.5797, df = 4, p-value = 0.9653
```

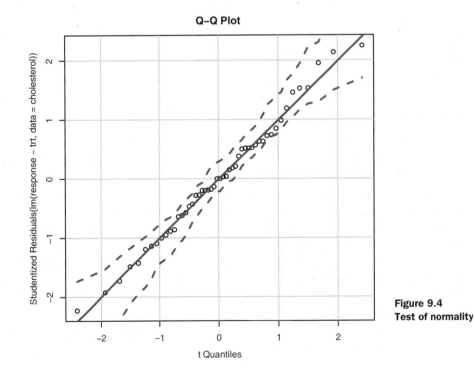

Figure 9.4
Test of normality

Bartlett's test indicates that the variances in the five groups don't differ significantly (p = 0.97). Other possible tests include the Fligner–Killeen test (provided by the `fligner.test()` function) and the Brown–Forsythe test (provided by the `hov()` function in the `HH` package). Although not shown, the other two tests reach the same conclusion.

Finally, analysis of variance methodologies can be sensitive to the presence of outliers. You can test for outliers using the `outlierTest()` function in the `car` package:

```
> library(car)
> outlierTest(fit)

No Studentized residuals with Bonferonni p < 0.05
Largest |rstudent|:
   rstudent unadjusted p-value Bonferonni p
19 2.251149          0.029422           NA
```

From the output, you can see that there's no indication of outliers in the cholesterol data (`NA` occurs when p > 1). Taking the Q-Q plot, Bartlett's test, and outlier test together, the data appear to fit the ANOVA model quite well. This, in turn, adds to your confidence in the results.

9.4 One-way ANCOVA

A one-way analysis of covariance (ANCOVA) extends the one-way ANOVA to include one or more quantitative covariates. This example comes from the `litter` dataset in the `multcomp` package (see Westfall et al., 1999). Pregnant mice were divided into four treatment groups; each group received a different dose of a drug (0, 5, 50, or 500). The mean post-birth weight for each litter was the dependent variable, and gestation time was included as a covariate. The analysis is given in the following listing.

Listing 9.3 One-way ANCOVA

```
> data(litter, package="multcomp")
> attach(litter)
> table(dose)
dose
  0   5  50 500
 20  19  18  17
> aggregate(weight, by=list(dose), FUN=mean)
  Group.1    x
1       0 32.3
2       5 29.3
3      50 29.9
4     500 29.6
> fit <- aov(weight ~ gesttime + dose)
> summary(fit)
            Df  Sum Sq Mean Sq F value   Pr(>F)
gesttime     1  134.30  134.30  8.0493 0.005971 **
dose         3  137.12   45.71  2.7394 0.049883 *
Residuals   69 1151.27   16.69
---
Signif. codes:  0 '***' 0.001 '**' 0.01 '*' 0.05 '.' 0.1 ' ' 1
```

From the table() function, you can see that there is an unequal number of litters at each dosage level, with 20 litters at zero dosage (no drug) and 17 litters at dosage 500. Based on the group means provided by the aggregate() function, the *no-drug* group had the highest mean litter weight (32.3). The ANCOVA F tests indicate that (a) gestation time was related to birth weight, and (b) drug dosage was related to birth weight after controlling for gestation time. The mean birth weight isn't the same for each of the drug dosages, after controlling for gestation time.

Because you're using a covariate, you may want to obtain adjusted group means—that is, the group means obtained after partialing out the effects of the covariate. You can use the effect() function in the effects library to calculate adjusted means:

```
> library(effects)
> effect("dose", fit)

 dose effect
dose
    0    5   50  500
32.4 28.9 30.6 29.3
```

In this case, the adjusted means are similar to the unadjusted means produced by the aggregate() function, but this won't always be the case. The effects package provides a powerful method of obtaining adjusted means for complex research designs and presenting them visually. See the package documentation on CRAN for more details.

As with the one-way ANOVA example in the last section, the F test for dose indicates that the treatments don't have the same mean birth weight, but it doesn't tell you which means differ from one another. Again you can use the multiple comparison procedures provided by the multcomp package to compute all pairwise mean comparisons. Additionally, the multcomp package can be used to test specific user-defined hypotheses about the means.

Suppose you're interested in whether the no-drug condition differs from the three-drug condition. The code in the following listing can be used to test this hypothesis.

> **Listing 9.4   Multiple comparisons employing user-supplied contrasts**

```
> library(multcomp)
> contrast <- rbind("no drug vs. drug" = c(3, -1, -1, -1))
> summary(glht(fit, linfct=mcp(dose=contrast)))

Multiple Comparisons of Means: User-defined Contrasts

Fit: aov(formula = weight ~ gesttime + dose)

Linear Hypotheses:
                     Estimate Std. Error t value Pr(>|t|)
no drug vs. drug == 0    8.284      3.209   2.581   0.0120 *
---
Signif. codes:  0 '***' 0.001 '**' 0.01 '*' 0.05 '.' 0.1 ' ' 1
```

The contrast c(3, -1, -1, -1) specifies a comparison of the first group with the average of the other three. The hypothesis is tested with a t statistic (2.581 in this case), which is significant at the p < .05 level. Therefore, you can conclude that the no-drug group has a higher birth weight than drug conditions. Other contrasts can be added to the rbind() function (see help(glht) for details).

9.4.1 Assessing test assumptions

ANCOVA designs make the same normality and homogeneity of variance assumptions described for ANOVA designs, and you can test these assumptions using the same procedures described in section 9.3.2. In addition, standard ANCOVA designs assume homogeneity of regression slopes. In this case, it's assumed that the regression slope for predicting birth weight from gestation time is the same in each of the four treatment groups. A test for the homogeneity of regression slopes can be obtained by including a gestation × dose interaction term in your ANCOVA model. A significant interaction would imply that the relationship between gestation and birth weight depends on the level of the dose variable. The code and results are provided in the following listing.

> **Listing 9.5 Testing for homogeneity of regression slopes**

```
> library(multcomp)
> fit2 <- aov(weight ~ gesttime*dose, data=litter)
> summary(fit2)
              Df Sum Sq Mean Sq F value Pr(>F)
gesttime       1    134     134    8.29 0.0054 **
dose           3    137      46    2.82 0.0456 *
gesttime:dose  3     82      27    1.68 0.1789
Residuals     66   1069      16
---
Signif. codes:  0 '***' 0.001 '**' 0.01 '*' 0.05 '.' 0.1 ' ' 1
```

The interaction is nonsignificant, supporting the assumption of equality of slopes. If the assumption is untenable, you could try transforming the covariate or dependent variable, using a model that accounts for separate slopes, or employing a nonparametric ANCOVA method that doesn't require homogeneity of regression slopes. See the sm.ancova() function in the sm package for an example of the latter.

9.4.2 Visualizing the results

The ancova() function in the HH package provides a plot of the relationship between the dependent variable, the covariate, and the factor. For example,

```
> library(HH)
> ancova(weight ~ gesttime + dose, data=litter)
```

produces the plot shown in figure 9.5. (The figure has been modified to display better in black and white and will look slightly different when you run the code yourself.)

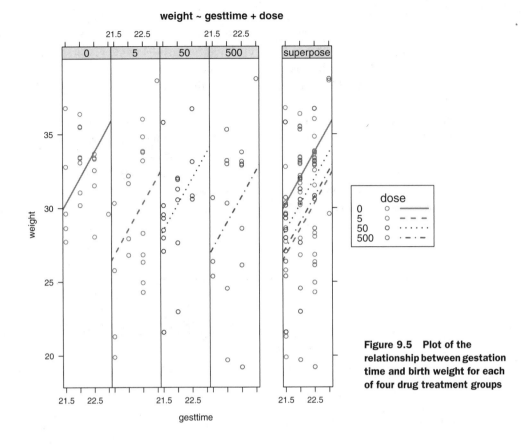

Figure 9.5   Plot of the relationship between gestation time and birth weight for each of four drug treatment groups

Here you can see that the regression lines for predicting birth weight from gestation time are parallel in each group but have different intercepts. As gestation time increases, birth weight increases. Additionally, you can see that the zero-dose group has the largest intercept and the five-dose group has the lowest intercept. The lines are parallel because they've been specified to be. If you used the statement `ancova(weight ~ gesttime*dose)` instead, you'd generate a plot that allows both the slopes and intercepts to vary by group. This approach is useful for visualizing the case where the homogeneity of regression slopes doesn't hold.

9.5   *Two-way factorial ANOVA*

In a two-way factorial ANOVA, subjects are assigned to groups that are formed from the cross-classification of two factors. This example uses the `ToothGrowth` dataset in the base installation to demonstrate a two-way between-groups ANOVA. Sixty guinea pigs are randomly assigned to receive one of three levels of ascorbic acid (0.5, 1, or 2 mg) and one of two delivery methods (orange juice or Vitamin C), under the restriction that each treatment combination has 10 guinea pigs. The dependent variable is tooth length. The following listing shows the code for the analysis.

Listing 9.6   Two-way ANOVA

```
> attach(ToothGrowth)
> table(supp, dose)
    dose
supp 0.5  1  2
  OJ  10 10 10
  VC  10 10 10

> aggregate(len, by=list(supp, dose), FUN=mean)
  Group.1 Group.2     x
1      OJ     0.5 13.23
2      VC     0.5  7.98
3      OJ     1.0 22.70
4      VC     1.0 16.77
5      OJ     2.0 26.06
6      VC     2.0 26.14

> aggregate(len, by=list(supp, dose), FUN=sd)
  Group.1 Group.2    x
1      OJ     0.5 4.46
2      VC     0.5 2.75
3      OJ     1.0 3.91
4      VC     1.0 2.52
5      OJ     2.0 2.66
6      VC     2.0 4.80

> dose <- factor(dose)
> fit <- aov(len ~ supp*dose)
> summary(fit)

            Df Sum Sq Mean Sq F value  Pr(>F)
supp         1    205     205   15.57 0.00023 ***
dose         2   2426    1213   92.00 < 2e-16 ***
supp:dose    2    108      54    4.11 0.02186 *
Residuals   54    712      13
---
Signif. codes:  0 '***' 0.001 '**' 0.01 '*' 0.05 '.' 0.1 ' ' 1

> detach(ToothGrowth)
```

The table statement indicates that you have a balanced design (equal sample sizes in each cell of the design), and the aggregate statements provide the cell means and standard deviations. The dose variable is converted to a factor so that the aov() function will treat it as a grouping variable, rather than a numeric covariate. The ANOVA table provided by the summary() function indicates that both main effects (supp and dose) and the interaction between these factors are significant.

You can visualize the results in several ways. You can use the interaction.plot() function to display the interaction in a two-way ANOVA. The code is

```
interaction.plot(dose, supp, len, type="b",
            col=c("red","blue"), pch=c(16, 18),
            main = "Interaction between Dose and Supplement Type")
```

and the resulting plot is presented in figure 9.6. The plot provides the mean tooth length for each supplement at each dosage.

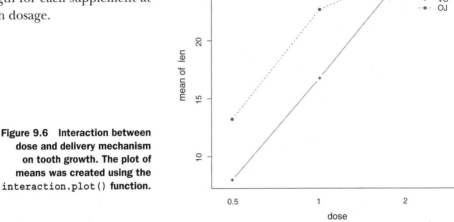

Figure 9.6 **Interaction between dose and delivery mechanism on tooth growth. The plot of means was created using the** `interaction.plot()` **function.**

With a little finesse, you can get an interaction plot out of the `plotmeans()` function in the `gplots` package. The following code produces the graph in figure 9.7:

```
library(gplots)
plotmeans(len ~ interaction(supp, dose, sep=" "),
        connect=list(c(1,3,5),c(2,4,6)),
        col=c("red", "darkgreen"),
        main = "Interaction Plot with 95% CIs",
        xlab="Treatment and Dose Combination")
```

The graph includes the means, as well as error bars (95% confidence intervals) and sample sizes.

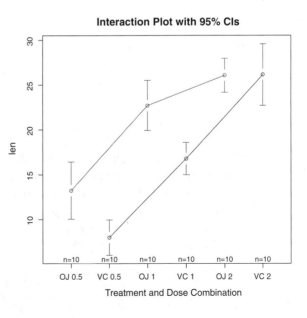

Figure 9.7 **Interaction between dose and delivery mechanism on tooth growth. The mean plot with 95% confidence intervals was created by the** `plotmeans()` **function.**

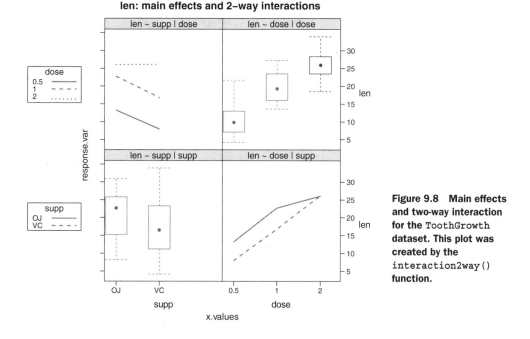

Figure 9.8 **Main effects and two-way interaction for the `ToothGrowth` dataset. This plot was created by the `interaction2way()` function.**

Finally, you can use the `interaction2wt()` function in the HH package to produce a plot of both main effects and two-way interactions for any factorial design of any order (figure 9.8):

```
library(HH)
interaction2wt(len~supp*dose)
```

Again, this figure has been modified to display more clearly in black and white and will look slightly different when you run the code yourself.

All three graphs indicate that tooth growth increases with the dose of ascorbic acid for both orange juice and Vitamin C. For the 0.5 and 1 mg doses, orange juice produced more tooth growth than Vitamin C. For 2 mg of ascorbic acid, both delivery methods produced identical growth.

Of the three plotting methods provided, I prefer the `interaction2wt()` function in the HH package. It displays both the main effects (the box plots) and the two-way interactions for designs of any complexity (two-way ANOVA, three-way ANOVA, and so on).

Although I don't cover the tests of model assumptions and mean comparison procedures, they're a natural extension of the methods you've seen so far. Additionally, the design is balanced, so you don't have to worry about the order of effects.

9.6   *Repeated measures ANOVA*

In repeated measures ANOVA, subjects are measured more than once. This section focuses on a repeated measures ANOVA with one within-groups and one between-groups factor (a common design). We'll take our example from the field of physiological ecology. Physiological ecologists study how the physiological and biochemical processes of living systems respond to variations in environmental factors (a crucial area of study given the realities of global warming). The CO2 dataset included in the base installation contains the results of a study of cold tolerance in Northern and Southern plants of the grass species *Echinochloa crus-galli* (Potvin, Lechowicz, & Tardif, 1990). The photosynthetic rates of chilled plants were compared with the photosynthetic rates of nonchilled plants at several ambient CO_2 concentrations. Half the plants were from Quebec, and half were from Mississippi.

In this example, we'll focus on chilled plants. The dependent variable is carbon dioxide uptake (uptake) in ml/L, and the independent variables are Type (Quebec versus Mississippi) and ambient CO_2 concentration (conc) with seven levels (ranging from 95 to 1000 umol/m^2 sec). Type is a between-groups factor, and conc is a within-groups factor. Type is already stored as a factor, but you'll need to convert conc to a factor before continuing. The analysis is presented in the next listing.

Listing 9.7 Repeated measures ANOVA with one between- and within-groups factor

```
> CO2$conc <- factor(CO2$conc)
> w1b1 <- subset(CO2, Treatment=='chilled')
> fit <- aov(uptake ~ conc*Type + Error(Plant/(conc)), w1b1)
> summary(fit)

Error: Plant
          Df Sum Sq Mean Sq F value Pr(>F)
Type       1   2667    2667    60.4 0.0015 **
Residuals  4    177      44
---
Signif. codes:  0 '***' 0.001 '**' 0.01 '*' 0.05 '.' 0.1 ' ' 1

Error: Plant:conc
          Df Sum Sq Mean Sq F value  Pr(>F)
conc       6   1472   245.4    52.5 1.3e-12 ***
conc:Type  6    429    71.5    15.3 3.7e-07 ***
Residuals 24    112     4.7
---
Signif. codes:  0 '***' 0.001 '**' 0.01 '*' 0.05 '.' 0.1 ' ' 1

> par(las=2)
> par(mar=c(10,4,4,2))
> with(w1b1, interaction.plot(conc,Type,uptake,
        type="b", col=c("red","blue"), pch=c(16,18),
        main="Interaction Plot for Plant Type and Concentration"))
> boxplot(uptake ~ Type*conc, data=w1b1, col=(c("gold", "green")),
        main="Chilled Quebec and Mississippi Plants",
        ylab="Carbon dioxide uptake rate (umol/m^2 sec)")
```

The ANOVA table indicates that the Type and concentration main effects and the Type × concentration interaction are all significant at the 0.01 level. The interaction is plotted via the interaction.plot() function in figure 9.9.

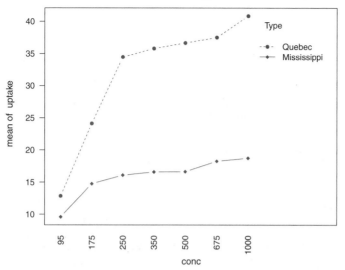

Figure 9.9 Interaction of ambient CO_2 concentration and plant type on CO_2 uptake. Graph produced by the `interaction.plot()` function.

In order to demonstrate a different presentation of the interaction, the `boxplot()` function is used to plot the same data. The results are provided in figure 9.10.

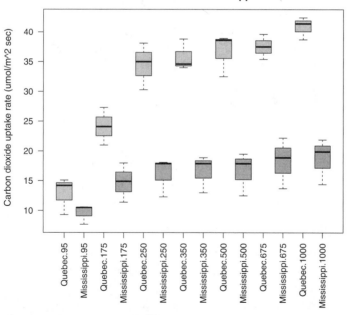

Figure 9.10 Interaction of ambient CO_2 concentration and plant type on CO_2 uptake. Graph produced by the `boxplot()` function.

From either graph, you can see that there's a greater carbon dioxide uptake in plants from Quebec compared to Mississippi. The difference is more pronounced at higher ambient CO_2 concentrations.

> **NOTE**   Datasets are typically in *wide format*, where columns are variables and rows are observations, and there's a single row for each subject. The litter data frame from section 9.4 is a good example. When dealing with repeated measures designs, you typically need the data in *long format* before fitting models. In long format, each measurement of the dependent variable is placed in its own row. The CO2 dataset follows this form. Luckily, the reshape package described in chapter 5 (section 5.6.3) can easily reorganize your data into the required format.

The many approaches to mixed-model designs

The CO_2 example in this section was analyzed using a traditional repeated measures ANOVA. The approach assumes that the covariance matrix for any within-groups factor follows a specified form known as *sphericity*. Specifically, it assumes that the variances of the differences between any two levels of the within-groups factor are equal. In real-world data, it's unlikely that this assumption will be met. This has led to a number of alternative approaches, including the following:

- Using the lmer() function in the lme4 package to fit linear mixed models (Bates, 2005)
- Using the Anova() function in the car package to adjust traditional test statistics to account for lack of sphericity (for example, the Geisser–Greenhouse correction)
- Using the gls() function in the nlme package to fit generalized least squares models with specified variance-covariance structures (UCLA, 2009)
- Using multivariate analysis of variance to model repeated measured data (Hand, 1987)

Coverage of these approaches is beyond the scope of this text. If you're interested in learning more, check out Pinheiro and Bates (2000) and Zuur et al. (2009).

Up to this point, all the methods in this chapter have assumed that there's a single dependent variable. In the next section, we'll briefly consider designs that include more than one outcome variable.

9.7   *Multivariate analysis of variance (MANOVA)*

If there's more than one dependent (outcome) variable, you can test them simultaneously using a multivariate analysis of variance (MANOVA). The following example is based on the UScereal dataset in the MASS package. The dataset comes from Venables & Ripley (1999). In this example, you're interested in whether the calories, fat, and sugar content of US cereals vary by store shelf, where 1 is the bottom shelf, 2 is the middle shelf, and 3 is the top shelf. Calories, fat, and sugars are the dependent variables, and shelf is the independent variable, with three levels (1, 2, and 3). The analysis is presented in the following listing.

Listing 9.8   One-way MANOVA

```
> library(MASS)
> attach(UScereal)
> shelf <- factor(shelf)
> y <- cbind(calories, fat, sugars)
> aggregate(y, by=list(shelf), FUN=mean)

  Group.1 calories   fat sugars
1       1      119 0.662    6.3
2       2      130 1.341   12.5
3       3      180 1.945   10.9

> cov(y)

         calories   fat sugars
calories   3895.2 60.67 180.38
fat          60.7  2.71   4.00
sugars      180.4  4.00  34.05

> fit <- manova(y ~ shelf)
> summary(fit)

          Df Pillai approx F num Df den Df Pr(>F)
shelf      2  0.402    5.12      6    122  1e-04 ***
Residuals 62
---
Signif. codes:  0 '***' 0.001 '**' 0.01 '*' 0.05 '.' 0.1 ' ' 1

> summary.aov(fit)
```

❶ **Prints univariate results**

```
Response calories :
           Df Sum Sq Mean Sq F value  Pr(>F)
shelf       2  50435   25218    7.86 0.00091 ***
Residuals  62 198860    3207
---
Signif. codes:  0 '***' 0.001 '**' 0.01 '*' 0.05 '.' 0.1 ' ' 1

 Response fat :
           Df Sum Sq Mean Sq F value Pr(>F)
shelf       2   18.4    9.22    3.68  0.031 *
Residuals  62  155.2    2.50
---
Signif. codes:  0 '***' 0.001 '**' 0.01 '*' 0.05 '.' 0.1 ' ' 1

 Response sugars :
           Df Sum Sq Mean Sq F value Pr(>F)
shelf       2    381     191    6.58 0.0026 **
Residuals  62   1798      29
---
Signif. codes:  0 '***' 0.001 '**' 0.01 '*' 0.05 '.' 0.1 ' ' 1
```

First, the shelf variable is converted to a factor so that it can represent a grouping variable in the analyses. Next, the cbind() function is used to form a matrix of the three dependent variables (calories, fat, and sugars). The aggregate() function provides the shelf means, and the cov() function provides the variance and the covariances across cereals.

The manova() function provides the multivariate test of group differences. The significant F value indicates that the three groups differ on the set of nutritional measures. Note that the shelf variable was converted to a factor so that it can represent a grouping variable.

Because the multivariate test is significant, you can use the summary.aov() function to obtain the univariate one-way ANOVAs ❶. Here, you see that the three groups differ on each nutritional measure considered separately. Finally, you can use a mean comparison procedure (such as TukeyHSD) to determine which shelves differ from each other for each of the three dependent variables (omitted here to save space).

9.7.1   *Assessing test assumptions*

The two assumptions underlying a one-way MANOVA are multivariate normality and homogeneity of variance-covariance matrices. The first assumption states that the vector of dependent variables jointly follows a multivariate normal distribution. You can use a Q-Q plot to assess this assumption (see the sidebar "A theory interlude" for a statistical explanation of how this works).

A theory interlude

If you have p × 1 multivariate normal random vector x with mean μ and covariance matrix Σ, then the squared Mahalanobis distance between x and μ is chi-square distributed with p degrees of freedom. The Q-Q plot graphs the quantiles of the chi-square distribution for the sample against the Mahalanobis D-squared values. To the degree that the points fall along a line with slope 1 and intercept 0, there's evidence that the data is multivariate normal.

The code is provided in the following listing, and the resulting graph is displayed in figure 9.11.

Listing 9.9   Assessing multivariate normality

```
> center <- colMeans(y)
> n <- nrow(y)
> p <- ncol(y)
> cov <- cov(y)
> d <- mahalanobis(y,center,cov)
> coord <- qqplot(qchisq(ppoints(n),df=p),
    d, main="Q-Q Plot Assessing Multivariate Normality",
    ylab="Mahalanobis D2")
> abline(a=0,b=1)
> identify(coord$x, coord$y, labels=row.names(UScereal))
```

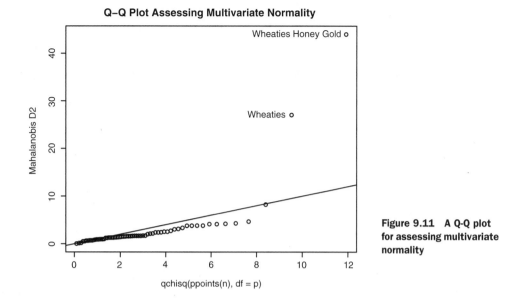

Figure 9.11 A Q-Q plot for assessing multivariate normality

If the data follow a multivariate normal distribution, then points will fall on the line. The identify() function allows you to interactively identify points in the graph. (The identify() function is covered in section 16.4.) Here, the dataset appears to violate multivariate normality, primarily due to the observations for Wheaties Honey Gold and Wheaties. You may want to delete these two cases and rerun the analyses.

The homogeneity of variance-covariance matrices assumption requires that the covariance matrix for each group is equal. The assumption is usually evaluated with a Box's M test. R doesn't include a function for Box's M, but an internet search will provide the appropriate code. Unfortunately, the test is sensitive to violations of normality, leading to rejection in most typical cases. This means that we don't yet have a good working method for evaluating this important assumption (but see Anderson [2006] and Silva et al. [2008] for interesting alternative approaches not yet available in R).

Finally, you can test for multivariate outliers using the aq.plot() function in the mvoutlier package. The code in this case looks like this:

```
library(mvoutlier)
outliers <- aq.plot(y)
outliers
```

Try it, and see what you get!

9.7.2 *Robust MANOVA*

If the assumptions of multivariate normality or homogeneity of variance-covariance matrices are untenable, or if you're concerned about multivariate outliers, you may want to consider using a robust or nonparametric version of the MANOVA test instead. A robust version of the one-way MANOVA is provided by the Wilks.test() function in the rrcov package. The `adonis()` function in the vegan package can provide the equivalent of a nonparametric MANOVA. The following listing applies `Wilks.test()` to the example.

Listing 9.10 Robust one-way MANOVA

```
library(rrcov)
> Wilks.test(y,shelf,method="mcd")

        Robust One-way MANOVA (Bartlett Chi2)

data:  x
Wilks' Lambda = 0.511, Chi2-Value = 23.96, DF = 4.98, p-value =
0.0002167
sample estimates:
  calories    fat  sugars
1      120  0.701    5.66
2      128  1.185   12.54
3      161  1.652   10.35
```

From the results, you can see that using a robust test that's insensitive to both outliers and violations of MANOVA assumptions still indicates that the cereals on the top, middle, and bottom store shelves differ in their nutritional profiles.

9.8 *ANOVA as regression*

In section 9.2, we noted that ANOVA and regression are both special cases of the same general linear model. As such, the designs in this chapter could have been analyzed using the `lm()` function. But in order to understand the output, you need to understand how R deals with categorical variables when fitting models.

Consider the one-way ANOVA problem in section 9.3, which compares the impact of five cholesterol-reducing drug regimens (trt):

```
> library(multcomp)
> levels(cholesterol$trt)

[1] "1time"  "2times"  "4times"  "drugD"  "drugE"
```

First, let's fit the model using the `aov()` function:

```
> fit.aov <- aov(response ~ trt, data=cholesterol)
> summary(fit.aov)

           Df   Sum Sq  Mean Sq  F value     Pr(>F)
trt         4  1351.37   337.84   32.433  9.819e-13 ***
Residuals  45   468.75    10.42
```

Now, let's fit the same model using `lm()`. In this case, you get the results shown in the next listing.

Listing 9.11 A regression approach to the ANOVA problem in section 9.3

```
> fit.lm <- lm(response ~ trt, data=cholesterol)
> summary(fit.lm)
```

```
Coefficients:
            Estimate Std. Error t value  Pr(>|t|)
(Intercept)    5.782      1.021   5.665  9.78e-07 ***
trt2times      3.443      1.443   2.385    0.0213 *
trt4times      6.593      1.443   4.568  3.82e-05 ***
trtdrugD       9.579      1.443   6.637  3.53e-08 ***
trtdrugE      15.166      1.443  10.507  1.08e-13 ***

Residual standard error: 3.227 on 45 degrees of freedom
Multiple R-squared: 0.7425,    Adjusted R-squared: 0.7196
F-statistic: 32.43 on 4 and 45 DF,  p-value: 9.819e-13
```

What are you looking at? Because linear models require numeric predictors, when the `lm()` function encounters a factor, it replaces that factor with a set of numeric variables representing contrasts among the levels. If the factor has k levels, $k - 1$ contrast variables are created. R provides five built-in methods for creating these contrast variables (see table 9.6). You can also create your own (we won't cover that here). By default, treatment contrasts are used for unordered factors, and orthogonal polynomials are used for ordered factors.

Table 9.6 Built-in contrasts

Contrast	Description
contr.helmert	Contrasts the second level with the first, the third level with the average of the first two, the fourth level with the average of the first three, and so on.
contr.poly	Contrasts are used for trend analysis (linear, quadratic, cubic, and so on) based on orthogonal polynomials. Use for ordered factors with equally spaced levels.
contr.sum	Contrasts are constrained to sum to zero. Also called *deviation contrasts*, they compare the mean of each level to the overall mean across levels.
contr.treatment	Contrasts each level with the baseline level (first level by default). Also called *dummy coding*.
contr.SAS	Similar to contr.treatment, but the baseline level is the last level. This produces coefficients similar to contrasts used in most SAS procedures.

With treatment contrasts, the first level of the factor becomes the reference group, and each subsequent level is compared with it. You can see the coding scheme via the `contrasts()` function:

```
> contrasts(cholesterol$trt)
        2times 4times drugD drugE
1time        0      0     0     0
2times       1      0     0     0
4times       0      1     0     0
drugD        0      0     1     0
drugE        0      0     0     1
```

If a patient is in the drugD condition, then the variable drugD equals 1, and the variables 2times, 4times, and drugE each equal zero. You don't need a variable for the first group, because a zero on each of the four indicator variables uniquely determines that the patient is in the 1times condition.

In listing 9.11, the variable trt2times represents a contrast between the levels 1time and 2time. Similarly, trt4times is a contrast between 1time and 4times, and so on. You can see from the probability values in the output that each drug condition is significantly different from the first (1time).

You can change the default contrasts used in `lm()` by specifying a `contrasts` option. For example, you can specify Helmert contrasts by using

```
fit.lm <- lm(response ~ trt, data=cholesterol, contrasts="contr.helmert")
```

You can change the default contrasts used during an R session via the `options()` function. For example,

```
options(contrasts = c("contr.SAS", "contr.helmert"))
```

would set the default contrast for unordered factors to `contr.SAS` and for ordered factors to `contr.helmert`. Although we've limited our discussion to the use of contrasts in linear models, note that they're applicable to other modeling functions in R. This includes the generalized linear models covered in chapter 13.

9.9   *Summary*

In this chapter, we reviewed the analysis of basic experimental and quasi-experimental designs using ANOVA/ANCOVA/MANOVA methodology. We reviewed the basic terminology used and looked at examples of between- and within-groups designs, including the one-way ANOVA, one-way ANCOVA, two-way factorial ANOVA, repeated measures ANOVA, and one-way MANOVA.

In addition to the basic analyses, we reviewed methods of assessing model assumptions and applying multiple comparison procedures following significant omnibus tests. Finally, we explored a wide variety of methods for displaying the results visually. If you're interested in learning more about the design of experiments (DOE) using R, be sure to see the CRAN View provided by Groemping (2009).

Chapters 8 and 9 have covered the statistical methods most often used by researchers in a wide variety of fields. In the next chapter, we'll address issues of power analysis. Power analysis helps us to determine the sample sizes needed to detect an effect of a given size with a given degree of confidence and is a crucial component of research design.

Power analysis 10

As a statistical consultant, I'm often asked, "How many subjects do I need for my study?" Sometimes the question is phrased this way: "I have *x* number of people available for this study. Is the study worth doing?" Questions like these can be answered through *power analysis*, an important set of techniques in experimental design.

Power analysis allows you to determine the sample size required to detect an effect of a given size with a given degree of confidence. Conversely, it allows you to determine the probability of detecting an effect of a given size with a given level of confidence, under sample size constraints. If the probability is unacceptably low, you'd be wise to alter or abandon the experiment.

In this chapter, you'll learn how to conduct power analyses for a variety of statistical tests, including tests of proportions, t-tests, chi-square tests, balanced one-way ANOVA, tests of correlations, and linear models. Because power analysis applies to hypothesis testing situations, we'll start with a brief review of null hypothesis significance testing (NHST). Then we'll review conducting power analyses within R, focusing primarily on the `pwr` package. Finally, we'll consider other approaches to power analysis available with R.

10.1 A quick review of hypothesis testing

To help you understand the steps in a power analysis, we'll briefly review statistical hypothesis testing in general. If you have a statistical background, feel free to skip to section 10.2.

In statistical hypothesis testing, you specify a hypothesis about a population parameter (your *null hypothesis*, or H_0). You then draw a sample from this population and calculate a statistic that's used to make inferences about the population parameter. Assuming that the null hypothesis is true, you calculate the probability of obtaining the observed sample statistic or one more extreme. If the probability is sufficiently small, you reject the null hypothesis in favor of its opposite (referred to as the *alternative* or *research hypothesis*, H_1).

An example will clarify the process. Say you're interested in evaluating the impact of cell phone use on driver reaction time. Your null hypothesis is Ho: $\mu_1 - \mu_2 = 0$, where μ_1 is the mean response time for drivers using a cell phone and μ_2 is the mean response time for drivers that are cell phone free (here, $\mu_1 - \mu_2$ is the population parameter of interest). If you reject this null hypothesis, you're left with the alternate or research hypothesis, namely H_1: $\mu_1 - \mu_2 \neq 0$. This is equivalent to $\mu_1 \neq \mu_2$, that the mean reaction times for the two conditions are not equal.

A sample of individuals is selected and randomly assigned to one of two conditions. In the first condition, participants react to a series of driving challenges in a simulator while talking on a cell phone. In the second condition, participants complete the same series of challenges but without a cell phone. Overall reaction time is assessed for each individual.

Based on the sample data, you can calculate the statistic $(\bar{X}_1 - \bar{X}_2)/(s/\sqrt{n})$, where $\bar{X}_1$ and $\bar{X}_2$ are the sample reaction time means in the two conditions, s is the pooled sample standard deviation, and n is the number of participants in each condition. If the null hypothesis is true and you can assume that reaction times are normally distributed, this sample statistic will follow a t distribution with $2n - 2$ degrees of freedom. Using this fact, you can calculate the probability of obtaining a sample statistic this large or larger. If the probability (p) is smaller than some predetermined cutoff (say $p < .05$), you reject the null hypothesis in favor of the alternate hypothesis. This predetermined cutoff (0.05) is called the *significance level* of the test.

Note that you use *sample* data to make an inference about the *population* it's drawn from. Your null hypothesis is that the mean reaction time of *all* drivers talking on cell phones isn't different from the mean reaction time of *all* drivers who aren't talking on cell phones, not just those drivers in your sample. The four possible outcomes from your decision are as follows:

- If the null hypothesis is false and the statistical test leads you to reject it, you've made a correct decision. You've correctly determined that reaction time is affected by cell phone use.

- If the null hypothesis is true and you don't reject it, again you've made a correct decision. Reaction time isn't affected by cell phone use.
- If the null hypothesis is true but you reject it, you've committed a Type I error. You've concluded that cell phone use affects reaction time when it doesn't.
- If the null hypothesis is false and you fail to reject it, you've committed a Type II error. Cell phone use affects reaction time, but you've failed to discern this.

Each of these outcomes is illustrated in the following table:

		Decision	
		Reject H_0	Fail to Reject H_0
Actual	H_0 true	Type I error	correct
	H_0 false	correct	Type II error

Controversy surrounding null hypothesis significance testing

Null hypothesis significance testing isn't without controversy; detractors have raised numerous concerns about the approach, particularly as practiced in the field of psychology. They point to a widespread misunderstanding of p values, reliance on statistical significance over practical significance, the fact that the null hypothesis is never exactly true and will always be rejected for sufficient sample sizes, and a number of logical inconsistencies in NHST practices.

An in-depth discussion of this topic is beyond the scope of this book. Interested readers are referred to Harlow, Mulaik, and Steiger (1997).

In planning research, the researcher typically pays special attention to four quantities (see figure 10.1):

- *Sample size* refers to the number of observations in each condition/group of the experimental design.
- The *significance level* (also referred to as *alpha*) is defined as the probability of making a Type I error. The significance level can also be thought of as the probability of finding an effect that is *not* there.
- *Power* is defined as one minus the probability of making a Type II error. Power can be thought of as the probability of finding an effect that *is* there.

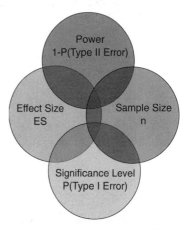

Figure 10.1 Four primary quantities considered in a study design power analysis. Given any three, you can calculate the fourth.

- *Effect size* is the magnitude of the effect under the alternate or research hypothesis. The formula for effect size depends on the statistical methodology employed in the hypothesis testing.

Although the sample size and significance level are under the direct control of the researcher, power and effect size are affected more indirectly. For example, as you relax the significance level (in other words, make it easier to reject the null hypothesis), power increases. Similarly, increasing the sample size increases power.

Your research goal is typically to maximize the power of your statistical tests while maintaining an acceptable significance level and employing as small a sample size as possible. That is, you want to maximize the chances of finding a real effect and minimize the chances of finding an effect that isn't really there, while keeping study costs within reason.

The four quantities (sample size, significance level, power, and effect size) have an intimate relationship. *Given any three, you can determine the fourth.* You'll use this fact to carry out various power analyses throughout the remainder of the chapter. In the next section, we'll look at ways of implementing power analyses using the R package `pwr`. Later, we'll briefly look at some highly specialized power functions that are used in biology and genetics.

10.2 *Implementing power analysis with the pwr package*

The `pwr` package, developed by Stéphane Champely, implements power analysis as outlined by Cohen (1988). Some of the more important functions are listed in table 10.1. For each function, you can specify three of the four quantities (sample size, significance level, power, effect size), and the fourth will be calculated.

Table 10.1 `pwr` package functions

Function	Power calculations for …
pwr.2p.test	Two proportions (equal n)
pwr.2p2n.test	Two proportions (unequal n)
pwr.anova.test	Balanced one-way ANOVA
pwr.chisq.test	Chi-square test
pwr.f2.test	General linear model
pwr.p.test	Proportion (one sample)
pwr.r.test	Correlation
pwr.t.test	t-tests (one sample, two samples, paired)
pwr.t2n.test	t-test (two samples with unequal n)

Of the four quantities, effect size is often the most difficult to specify. Calculating effect size typically requires some experience with the measures involved and knowledge of past research. But what can you do if you have no clue what effect size to expect in a given study? We'll look at this difficult question in section 10.2.7. In the remainder of this section, we'll look at the application of pwr functions to common statistical tests. Before invoking these functions, be sure to install and load the pwr package.

10.2.1 *t-tests*

When the statistical test to be used is a t-test, the pwr.t.test() function provides a number of useful power analysis options. The format is

```
pwr.t.test(n=, d=, sig.level=, power=, type=, alternative=)
```

where

- n is the sample size.
- d is the effect size defined as the standardized mean difference.

$$d = \frac{\mu_1 - \mu_2}{\sigma} \quad \text{where} \quad \begin{aligned} &\mu_1 = \text{mean of group 1} \\ &\mu_2 = \text{mean of group 2} \\ &\sigma^2 = \text{common error variance} \end{aligned}$$

- sig.level is the significance level (0.05 is the default).
- power is the power level.
- type is a two-sample t-test ("two.sample"), a one-sample t-test ("one.sample"), or a dependent sample t-test ("paired"). A two-sample test is the default.
- alternative indicates whether the statistical test is two-sided ("two.sided") or one-sided ("less" or "greater"). A two-sided test is the default.

Let's work through an example. Continuing the experiment from section 10.1 involving cell phone use and driving reaction time, assume that you'll be using a two-tailed independent sample t-test to compare the mean reaction time for participants in the cell phone condition with the mean reaction time for participants driving unencumbered.

Let's assume that you know from past experience that reaction time has a standard deviation of 1.25 seconds. Also suppose that a 1-second difference in reaction time is considered an important difference. You'd therefore like to conduct a study in which you're able to detect an effect size of d = 1/1.25 = 0.8 or larger. Additionally, you want to be 90% sure to detect such a difference if it exists, and 95% sure that you won't declare a difference to be significant when it's actually due to random variability. How many participants will you need in your study?

Entering this information in the pwr.t.test() function, you have the following:

```
> library(pwr)
> pwr.t.test(d=.8, sig.level=.05, power=.9, type="two.sample",
        alternative="two.sided")
```

```
Two-sample t test power calculation

              n = 34
              d = 0.8
      sig.level = 0.05
          power = 0.9
    alternative = two.sided
```

NOTE: n is number in *each* group

The results suggest that you need 34 participants in each group (for a total of 68 participants) in order to detect an effect size of 0.8 with 90% certainty and no more than a 5% chance of erroneously concluding that a difference exists when, in fact, it doesn't.

Let's alter the question. Assume that in comparing the two conditions you want to be able to detect a 0.5 standard deviation difference in population means. You want to limit the chances of falsely declaring the population means to be different to 1 out of 100. Additionally, you can only afford to include 40 participants in the study. What's the probability that you'll be able to detect a difference between the population means that's this large, given the constraints outlined?

Assuming that an equal number of participants will be placed in each condition, you have

```
> pwr.t.test(n=20, d=.5, sig.level=.01, type="two.sample",
             alternative="two.sided")

   Two-sample t test power calculation

              n = 20
              d = 0.5
      sig.level = 0.01
          power = 0.14
    alternative = two.sided
```

NOTE: n is number in *each* group

With 20 participants in each group, an a priori significance level of 0.01, and a dependent variable standard deviation of 1.25 seconds, you have less than a 14% chance of declaring a difference of 0.625 seconds or less significant (d = 0.5 = 0.625/1.25). Conversely, there's an 86% chance that you'll miss the effect that you're looking for. You may want to seriously rethink putting the time and effort into the study as it stands.

The previous examples assumed that there are equal sample sizes in the two groups. If the sample sizes for the two groups are unequal, the function

```
pwr.t2n.test(n1=, n2=, d=, sig.level=, power=, alternative=)
```

can be used. Here, n1 and n2 are the sample sizes, and the other parameters are the same as for pwer.t.test. Try varying the values input to the pwr.t2n.test function and see the effect on the output.

10.2.2 ANOVA

The `pwr.anova.test()` function provides power analysis options for a balanced one-way analysis of variance. The format is

```
pwr.anova.test(k=, n=, f=, sig.level=, power=)
```

where k is the number of groups and n is the common sample size in each group.

For a one-way ANOVA, effect size is measured by f,

$$f = \sqrt{\frac{\sum_{i=1}^{k} p_i \times (\mu_i - \mu)^2}{\sigma^2}}$$

where
$p_i = n_i / N$
n_i = number of observations in group i
N = total number of observations
μ_i = mean of group i
μ = grand mean
σ^2 = error variance within groups

Let's try an example. For a one-way ANOVA comparing five groups, calculate the sample size needed in each group to obtain a power of 0.80, when the effect size is 0.25 and a significance level of 0.05 is employed. The code looks like this:

```
> pwr.anova.test(k=5, f=.25, sig.level=.05, power=.8)

     Balanced one-way analysis of variance power calculation

              k = 5
              n = 39
              f = 0.25
      sig.level = 0.05
          power = 0.8

NOTE: n is number in each group
```

The total sample size is therefore 5 × 39, or 195. Note that this example requires you to estimate what the means of the five groups will be, along with the common variance. When you have no idea what to expect, the approaches described in section 10.2.7 may help.

10.2.3 Correlations

The `pwr.r.test()` function provides a power analysis for tests of correlation coefficients. The format is as follows

```
pwr.r.test(n=, r=, sig.level=, power=, alternative=)
```

where n is the number of observations, r is the effect size (as measured by a linear correlation coefficient), sig.level is the significance level, power is the power level, and alternative specifies a two-sided ("two.sided") or a one-sided ("less" or "greater") significance test.

For example, let's assume that you're studying the relationship between depression and loneliness. Your null and research hypotheses are

H_0: $\rho \leq 0.25$ versus H_1: $\rho > 0.25$

where ρ is the population correlation between these two psychological variables. You've set your significance level to 0.05, and you want to be 90% confident that you'll reject H_0 if it's false. How many observations will you need? This code provides the answer:

```
> pwr.r.test(r=.25, sig.level=.05, power=.90, alternative="greater")

     approximate correlation power calculation (arctangh transformation)

              n = 134
              r = 0.25
      sig.level = 0.05
          power = 0.9
    alternative = greater
```

Thus, you need to assess depression and loneliness in 134 participants in order to be 90% confident that you'll reject the null hypothesis if it's false.

10.2.4 *Linear models*

For linear models (such as multiple regression), the `pwr.f2.test()` function can be used to carry out a power analysis. The format is

```
pwr.f2.test(u=, v=, f2=, sig.level=, power=)
```

where u and v are the numerator and denominator degrees of freedom and f2 is the effect size.

$$f^2 = \frac{R^2}{1-R^2}$$
  where R^2 = population squared multiple correlation

$$f^2 = \frac{R_{AB}^2 - R_A^2}{1-R_{AB}^2}$$
  where R_A^2 = variance accounted for in the population by variable set A
  R_{AB}^2 = variance accounted for in the population by variable set A and B together

The first formula for f2 is appropriate when you're evaluating the impact of a set of predictors on an outcome. The second formula is appropriate when you're evaluating the impact of one set of predictors above and beyond a second set of predictors (or covariates).

Let's say you're interested in whether a boss's leadership style impacts workers' satisfaction above and beyond the salary and perks associated with the job. Leadership style is assessed by four variables, and salary and perks are associated with three variables. Past experience suggests that salary and perks account for roughly 30% of the variance in worker satisfaction. From a practical standpoint, it would be interesting if leadership style accounted for at least 5% above this figure. Assuming a significance level of 0.05, how many subjects would be needed to identify such a contribution with 90% confidence?

Here, `sig.level=0.05`, `power=0.90`, `u=3` (total number of predictors minus the number of predictors in set B), and the effect size is f2 = (.35 − .30)/(1 − .35) = 0.0769. Entering this into the function yields the following:

```
> pwr.f2.test(u=3, f2=0.0769, sig.level=0.05, power=0.90)

     Multiple regression power calculation

                u = 3
                v = 184.2426
               f2 = 0.0769
        sig.level = 0.05
            power = 0.9
```

In multiple regression, the denominator degrees of freedom equals $N - k - 1$, where N is the number of observations and k is the number of predictors. In this case, $N - 7 - 1 = 185$, which means the required sample size is $N = 185 + 7 + 1 = 193$.

10.2.5 *Tests of proportions*

The `pwr.2p.test()` function can be used to perform a power analysis when comparing two proportions. The format is

```
pwr.2p.test(h=, n=, sig.level=, power=)
```

where h is the effect size and n is the common sample size in each group. The effect size h is defined as

$$h = 2 \arcsin\left(\sqrt{p_1}\right) - 2 \arcsin\left(\sqrt{p_2}\right)$$

and can be calculated with the function `ES.h(p1, p2)`.

For unequal ns, the desired function is

```
pwr.2p2n.test(h=, n1=, n2=, sig.level=, power=)
```

The `alternative=` option can be used to specify a two-tailed (`"two.sided"`) or one-tailed (`"less"` or `"greater"`) test. A two-tailed test is the default.

Let's say that you suspect that a popular medication relieves symptoms in 60% of users. A new (and more expensive) medication will be marketed if it improves symptoms in 65% of users. How many participants will you need to include in a study comparing these two medications if you want to detect a difference this large?

Assume that you want to be 90% confident in a conclusion that the new drug is better and 95% confident that you won't reach this conclusion erroneously. You'll use a one-tailed test because you're only interested in assessing whether the new drug is better than the standard. The code looks like this:

```
> pwr.2p.test(h=ES.h(.65, .6), sig.level=.05, power=.9,
              alternative="greater")

     Difference of proportion power calculation for binomial
     distribution (arcsine transformation)
                h = 0.1033347
                n = 1604.007
        sig.level = 0.05
            power = 0.9
      alternative = greater

NOTE: same sample sizes
```

Based on these results, you'll need to conduct a study with 1,605 individuals receiving the new drug and 1,605 receiving the existing drug in order to meet the criteria.

10.2.6 *Chi-square tests*

Chi-square tests are often used to assess the relationship between two categorical variables. The null hypothesis is typically that the variables are independent versus a research hypothesis that they aren't. The `pwr.chisq.test()` function can be used to evaluate the power, effect size, or requisite sample size when employing a chi-square test. The format is

```
pwr.chisq.test(w=, N=, df=, sig.level=, power=)
```

where `w` is the effect size, `N` is the total sample size, and `df` is the degrees of freedom. Here, effect size `w` is defined as

$$w = \sqrt{\sum_{i=1}^{m} \frac{(p0_i - p1_i)^2}{p0_i}}$$

where $p0_i$ = cell probability in ith cell under H_0
$p1_i$ = cell probability in ith cell under H_1

The summation goes from 1 to *m*, where *m* is the number of cells in the contingency table. The function `ES.w2(P)` can be used to calculate the effect size corresponding to the alternative hypothesis in a two-way contingency table. Here, `P` is a hypothesized two-way probability table.

As a simple example, let's assume that you're looking at the relationship between ethnicity and promotion. You anticipate that 70% of your sample will be Caucasian, 10% will be African-American, and 20% will be Hispanic. Further, you believe that 60% of Caucasians tend to be promoted, compared with 30% for African-Americans and 50% for Hispanics. Your research hypothesis is that the probability of promotion follows the values in table 10.2.

Table 10.2   Proportion of individuals expected to be promoted based on the research hypothesis

Ethnicity	Promoted	Not promoted
Caucasian	0.42	0.28
African-American	0.03	0.07
Hispanic	0.10	0.10

For example, you expect that 42% of the population will be promoted Caucasians (.42 = .70 × .60) and 7% of the population will be nonpromoted African-Americans (.07 = .10 × .70). Let's assume a significance level of 0.05 and that the desired power level is 0.90. The degrees of freedom in a two-way contingency table are $(r-1) \times (c-1)$, where r is the number of rows and c is the number of columns. You can calculate the hypothesized effect size with the following code:

```
> prob <- matrix(c(.42, .28, .03, .07, .10, .10), byrow=TRUE, nrow=3)
> ES.w2(prob)
```

```
[1] 0.1853198
```

Using this information, you can calculate the necessary sample size like this:

```
> pwr.chisq.test(w=.1853, df=2, sig.level=.05, power=.9)
```

```
        Chi squared power calculation

              w = 0.1853
              N = 368.5317
             df = 2
      sig.level = 0.05
          power = 0.9
```

```
NOTE: N is the number of observations
```

The results suggest that a study with 369 participants will be adequate to detect a relationship between ethnicity and promotion given the effect size, power, and significance level specified.

10.2.7 Choosing an appropriate effect size in novel situations

In power analysis, the expected effect size is the most difficult parameter to determine. It typically requires that you have experience with the subject matter and the measures employed. For example, the data from past studies can be used to calculate effect sizes, which can then be used to plan future studies.

But what can you do when the research situation is completely novel and you have no past experience to call upon? In the area of behavioral sciences, Cohen (1988) attempted to provide benchmarks for "small," "medium," and "large" effect sizes for various statistical tests. These guidelines are provided in table 10.3.

Table 10.3　Cohen's effect size benchmarks

Statistical method	Effect size measures	Suggested guidelines for effect size		
		Small	*Medium*	*Large*
t-test	d	0.20	0.50	0.80
ANOVA	f	0.10	0.25	0.40
Linear models	f2	0.02	0.15	0.35
Test of proportions	h	0.20	0.50	0.80
Chi-square	w	0.10	0.30	0.50

When you have no idea what effect size may be present, this table may provide some guidance. For example, what's the probability of rejecting a false null hypothesis (that is, finding a real effect) if you're using a one-way ANOVA with 5 groups, 25 subjects per group, and a significance level of 0.05?

Using the `pwr.anova.test()` function and the suggestions in the f row of table 10.3, the power would be 0.118 for detecting a small effect, 0.574 for detecting a moderate effect, and 0.957 for detecting a large effect. Given the sample-size limitations, you're only likely to find an effect if it's large.

It's important to keep in mind that Cohen's benchmarks are just general suggestions derived from a range of social research studies and may not apply to your particular field of research. An alternative is to vary the study parameters and note the impact on such things as sample size and power. For example, again assume that you want to compare five groups using a one-way ANOVA and a 0.05 significance level. The following listing computes the sample sizes needed to detect a range of effect sizes and plots the results in figure 10.2.

Listing 10.1   Sample sizes for detecting significant effects in a one-way ANOVA

```
library(pwr)
es <- seq(.1, .5, .01)
nes <- length(es)

samsize <- NULL
for (i in 1:nes){
    result <- pwr.anova.test(k=5, f=es[i], sig.level=.05, power=.9)
    samsize[i] <- ceiling(result$n)
}

plot(samsize,es, type="l", lwd=2, col="red",
    ylab="Effect Size",
    xlab="Sample Size (per cell)",
    main="One Way ANOVA with Power=.90 and Alpha=.05")
```

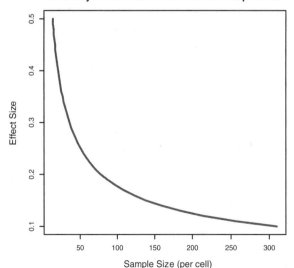

Figure 10.2   Sample size needed to detect various effect sizes in a one-way ANOVA with five groups (assuming a power of 0.90 and significance level of 0.05)

Graphs such as these can help you estimate the impact of various conditions on your experimental design. For example, there appears to be little bang for the buck in increasing the sample size above 200 observations per group. We'll look at another plotting example in the next section.

10.3 Creating power analysis plots

Before leaving the `pwr` package, let's look at a more involved graphing example. Suppose you'd like to see the sample size necessary to declare a correlation coefficient statistically significant for a range of effect sizes and power levels. You can use the `pwr.r.test()` function and `for` loops to accomplish this task, as shown in the following listing.

> **Listing 10.2 Sample-size curves for detecting correlations of various sizes**

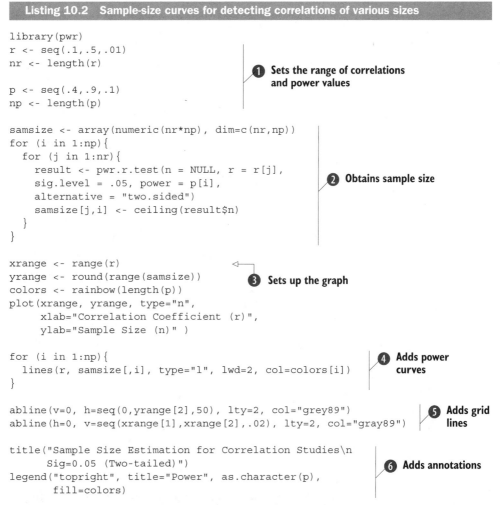

```
library(pwr)
r <- seq(.1,.5,.01)
nr <- length(r)                         ❶ Sets the range of correlations
                                          and power values
p <- seq(.4,.9,.1)
np <- length(p)

samsize <- array(numeric(nr*np), dim=c(nr,np))
for (i in 1:np){
  for (j in 1:nr){
    result <- pwr.r.test(n = NULL, r = r[j],
    sig.level = .05, power = p[i],          ❷ Obtains sample size
    alternative = "two.sided")
    samsize[j,i] <- ceiling(result$n)
  }
}

xrange <- range(r)
yrange <- round(range(samsize))         ❸ Sets up the graph
colors <- rainbow(length(p))
plot(xrange, yrange, type="n",
    xlab="Correlation Coefficient (r)",
    ylab="Sample Size (n)" )

for (i in 1:np){                        ❹ Adds power
  lines(r, samsize[,i], type="l", lwd=2, col=colors[i])   curves
}

abline(v=0, h=seq(0,yrange[2],50), lty=2, col="grey89")   ❺ Adds grid
abline(h=0, v=seq(xrange[1],xrange[2],.02), lty=2, col="gray89")  lines

title("Sample Size Estimation for Correlation Studies\n
    Sig=0.05 (Two-tailed)")           ❻ Adds annotations
legend("topright", title="Power", as.character(p),
    fill=colors)
```

Listing 10.2 uses the `seq` function to generate a range of effect sizes r (correlation coefficients under H_1) and power levels p ❶. It then uses two `for` loops to cycle

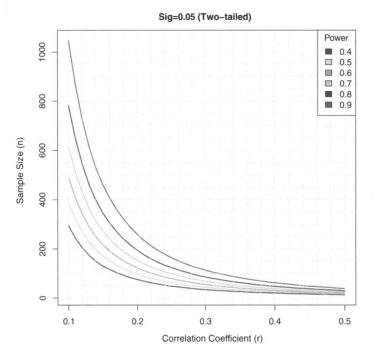

Figure 10.3   **Sample size curves for detecting a significant correlation at various power levels**

through these effect sizes and power levels, calculating the corresponding sample sizes required and saving them in the array `samsize` ❷. The graph is set up with the appropriate horizontal and vertical axes and labels ❸. Power curves are added using lines rather than points ❹. Finally, a grid ❺ and legend ❻ are added to aid in reading the graph. The resulting graph is displayed in figure 10.3.

As you can see from the graph, you'd need a sample size of approximately 75 to detect a correlation of 0.20 with 40% confidence. You'd need approximately 185 additional observations (n = 260) to detect the same correlation with 90% confidence. With simple modifications, the same approach can be used to create sample size and power curve graphs for a wide range of statistical tests.

We'll close this chapter by briefly looking at other R functions that are useful for power analysis.

10.4   *Other packages*

There are several other packages in R that can be useful in the planning stages of studies (see table 10.4). Some contain general tools, whereas some are highly specialized. The last five in the table are particularly focused on power analysis in genetic studies. Genome-wide association studies (GWAS) are studies used to identify genetic associations with observable traits. For example, these studies would focus on why some people get a specific type of heart disease.

Table 10.4 Specialized power-analysis packages

Package	Purpose
asypow	Power calculations via asymptotic likelihood ratio methods
longpower	Sample-size calculations for longitudinal data
PwrGSD	Power analysis for group sequential designs
pamm	Power analysis for random effects in mixed models
powerSurvEpi	Power and sample-size calculations for survival analysis in epidemiological studies
powerMediation	Power and sample-size calculations for mediation effects in linear, logistic, Poisson, and cox regression
powerpkg	Power analyses for the affected sib pair and the TDT (transmission disequilibrium test) design
powerGWASinteraction	Power calculations for interactions for GWAS
pedantics	Functions to facilitate power analyses for genetic studies of natural populations
gap	Functions for power and sample-size calculations in case-cohort designs
ssize.fdr	Sample-size calculations for microarray experiments

Finally, the MBESS package contains a wide range of functions that can be used for various forms of power analysis and sample size determination. The functions are particularly relevant for researchers in the behavioral, educational, and social sciences.

10.5 Summary

In chapters 7, 8, and 9, we explored a wide range of R functions for statistical hypothesis testing. In this chapter, we focused on the planning stages of such research. Power analysis helps you to determine the sample sizes needed to discern an effect of a given size with a given degree of confidence. It can also tell you the probability of detecting such an effect for a given sample size. You can directly see the tradeoff between limiting the likelihood of wrongly declaring an effect significant (a Type I error) with the likelihood of rightly identifying a real effect (power).

The bulk of this chapter has focused on the use of functions provided by the pwr package. These functions can be used to carry out power and sample-size determinations for common statistical methods (including t-tests, chi-square tests, and tests of proportions, ANOVA, and regression). Pointers to more specialized methods were provided in the final section.

Power analysis is typically an interactive process. The investigator varies the parameters of sample size, effect size, desired significance level, and desired power to observe their impact on each other. The results are used to plan studies that are more likely to yield meaningful results. Information from past research (particularly regarding effect sizes) can be used to design more effective and efficient future research.

An important side benefit of power analysis is the shift that it encourages, away from a singular focus on binary hypothesis testing (that is, does an effect exist or not), toward an appreciation of the *size* of the effect under consideration. Journal editors are increasingly requiring authors to include effect sizes as well as p values when reporting research results. This helps you to determine both the practical implications of the research and provides you with information that can be used to plan future studies.

In the next chapter, we'll look at additional and novel ways to visualize multivariate relationships. These graphic methods can complement and enhance the analytic methods that we've discussed so far and prepare you for the advanced methods covered in part 3.

Intermediate graphs

In chapter 6 (basic graphs), we considered a wide range of graph types for displaying the distribution of single categorical or continuous variables. Chapter 8 (regression) reviewed graphical methods that are useful when predicting a continuous outcome variable from a set of predictor variables. In chapter 9 (analysis of variance), we considered techniques that are particularly useful for visualizing how groups differ on a continuous outcome variable. In many ways, the current chapter is a continuation and extension of the topics covered so far.

In this chapter, we'll focus on graphical methods for displaying relationships between two variables (bivariate relationships) and between many variables (multivariate relationships). For example:

- What's the relationship between automobile mileage and car weight? Does it vary by the number of cylinders the car has?

255

- How can you picture the relationships among an automobile's mileage, weight, displacement, and rear axle ratio in a single graph?

- When plotting the relationship between two variables drawn from a large dataset (say, 10,000 observations), how can you deal with the massive overlap of data points you're likely to see? In other words, what do you do when your graph is one big smudge?

- How can you visualize the multivariate relationships among three variables at once (given a 2D computer screen or sheet of paper, and a budget slightly less than that for *Avatar*)?

- How can you display the growth of several trees over time?

- How can you visualize the correlations among a dozen variables in a single graph? How does it help you to understand the structure of your data?

- How can you visualize the relationship of class, gender, and age with passenger survival on the *Titanic*? What can you learn from such a graph?

These are the types of questions that can be answered with the methods described in this chapter. The datasets that we'll use are examples of what's possible. It's the general techniques that are most important. If the topic of automobile characteristics or tree growth isn't interesting to you, plug in your own data!

We'll start with scatter plots and scatter-plot matrices. Then, we'll explore line charts of various types. These approaches are well known and widely used in research. Next, we'll review the use of corrgrams for visualizing correlations and mosaic plots for visualizing multivariate relationships among categorical variables. These approaches are also useful but much less well known among researchers and data analysts. You'll see examples of how you can use each of these approaches to gain a better understanding of your data and communicate these findings to others.

11.1 *Scatter plots*

As you've seen in previous chapters, scatter plots describe the relationship between two continuous variables. In this section, we'll start with a depiction of a single bivariate relationship (*x* versus *y*). We'll then explore ways to enhance this plot by superimposing additional information. Next, you'll learn how to combine several scatter plots into a scatter-plot matrix so that you can view many bivariate relationships at once. We'll also review the special case where many data points overlap, limiting your ability to picture the data, and we'll discuss a number of ways around this difficulty. Finally, we'll extend the two-dimensional graph to three dimensions, with the addition of a third continuous variable. This will include 3D scatter plots and bubble plots. Each can help you understand the multivariate relationship among three variables at once.

The basic function for creating a scatter plot in R is plot(x, y), where *x* and *y* are numeric vectors denoting the (*x*, *y*) points to plot. The following listing presents an example.

Listing 11.1 A scatter plot with best-fit lines

```
attach(mtcars)
plot(wt, mpg,
     main="Basic Scatter plot of MPG vs. Weight",
     xlab="Car Weight (lbs/1000)",
     ylab="Miles Per Gallon ", pch=19)
abline(lm(mpg~wt), col="red", lwd=2, lty=1)
lines(lowess(wt,mpg), col="blue", lwd=2, lty=2)
```

The resulting graph is provided in figure 11.1.

   The code in listing 11.1 attaches the `mtcars` data frame and creates a basic scatter plot using filled circles for the plotting symbol. As expected, as car weight increases, miles per gallon decreases, although the relationship isn't perfectly linear. The `abline()` function is used to add a linear line of best fit, and the `lowess()` function is used to add a smoothed line. This smoothed line is a nonparametric fit line based on locally weighted polynomial regression. See Cleveland (1981) for details on the algorithm.

> **NOTE** R has two functions for producing lowess fits: `lowess()` and `loess()`. The `loess()` function is a newer, formula-based version of `lowess()` and is more powerful. The two functions have different defaults, so be careful not to confuse them.

The `scatterplot()` function in the `car` package offers many enhanced features and convenience functions for producing scatter plots, including fit lines, marginal box plots, confidence ellipses, plotting by subgroups, and interactive point identification.

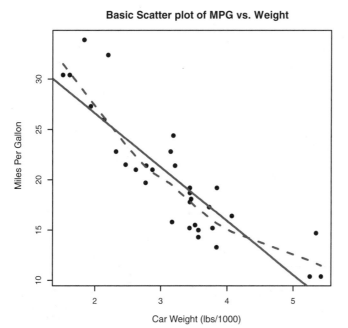

Basic Scatter plot of MPG vs. Weight

Figure 11.1 Scatter plot of car mileage vs. weight, with superimposed linear and lowess fit lines

For example, a more complex version of the previous plot is produced by the following code:

```
library(car)
scatterplot(mpg ~ wt | cyl, data=mtcars, lwd=2, span=0.75,
            main="Scatter Plot of MPG vs. Weight by # Cylinders",
            xlab="Weight of Car (lbs/1000)",
            ylab="Miles Per Gallon",
            legend.plot=TRUE,
            id.method="identify",
            labels=row.names(mtcars),
            boxplots="xy"
)
```

Here, the `scatterplot()` function is used to plot miles per gallon versus weight for automobiles that have four, six, or eight cylinders. The formula `mpg ~ wt | cyl` indicates conditioning (that is, separate plots between mpg and wt for each level of cyl). The graph is provided in figure 11.2.

By default, subgroups are differentiated by color and plotting symbol, and separate linear and loess lines are fit. The `span` parameter controls the amount of smoothing in the loess line. Larger values lead to smoother fits. The `id.method` option indicates that points will be identified interactively by mouse clicks, until you select Stop (via the Graphics or context-sensitive menu) or press the Esc key. The `labels` option indicates that points will be identified with their row names. Here you see that the Toyota Corolla and Fiat 128 have unusually good gas mileage, given their weights. The

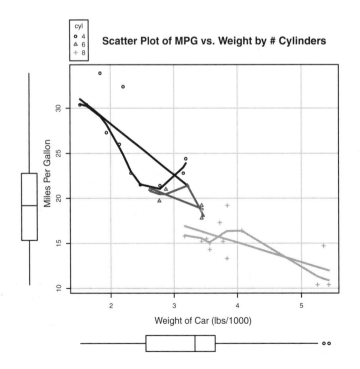

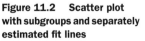

Figure 11.2   Scatter plot with subgroups and separately estimated fit lines

`legend.plot` option adds a legend to the upper-left margin, and marginal box plots for mpg and weight are requested with the `boxplots` option. The `scatterplot()` function has many features worth investigating, including robust options and data concentration ellipses not covered here. See `help(scatterplot)` for more details.

Scatter plots help you visualize relationships between quantitative variables, two at a time. But what if you wanted to look at the bivariate relationships between automobile mileage, weight, displacement (cubic inch), and rear axle ratio? One way is to arrange these six scatter plots in a matrix. When there are several quantitative variables, you can represent their relationships in a scatter-plot matrix, which is covered next.

11.1.1 Scatter-plot matrices

There are many useful functions for creating scatter-plot matrices in R. A basic scatter-plot matrix can be created with the `pairs()` function. The following code produces a scatter-plot matrix for the variables mpg, disp, drat, and wt:

```
pairs(~mpg+disp+drat+wt, data=mtcars,
    main="Basic Scatter Plot Matrix")
```

All the variables on the right of the ~ are included in the plot. The graph is provided in figure 11.3.

Here you can see the bivariate relationship among all the variables specified. For example, the scatter plot between mpg and disp is found at the row and column

Basic Scatter Plot Matrix

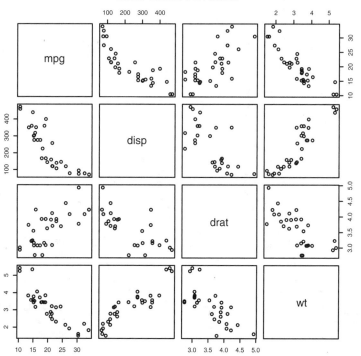

Figure 11.3 Scatter-plot matrix created by the `pairs()` function

intersection of those two variables. Note that the six scatter plots below the principal diagonal are the same as those above the diagonal. This arrangement is a matter of convenience. By adjusting the options, you could display just the lower or upper triangle. For example, the option `upper.panel=NULL` would produce a graph with just the lower triangle of plots.

The `scatterplotMatrix()` function in the `car` package can also produce scatterplot matrices and can optionally do the following:

- Condition the scatter plot matrix on a factor.
- Include linear and loess fit lines.
- Place box plots, densities, or histograms in the principal diagonal.
- Add rug plots in the margins of the cells.

Here's an example:

```
library(car)
scatterplotMatrix(~ mpg + disp + drat + wt,`data=mtcars,
                  spread=FALSE, smoother.args=list(lty=2),
                  main="Scatter Plot Matrix via car Package")
```

The graph is provided in figure 11.4. Here you can see that linear and smoothed (loess) fit lines are added by default and that kernel density and rug plots are added to the principal diagonal. The `spread=FALSE` option suppresses lines showing spread

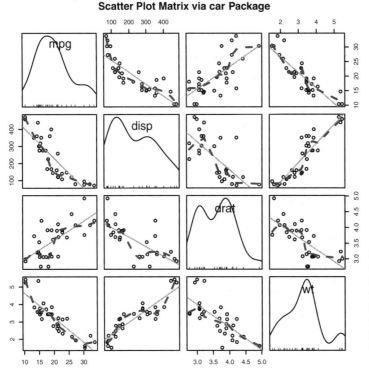

Figure 11.4 Scatter-plot matrix created with the `scatterplotMatrix()` function. The graph includes kernel density and rug plots in the principal diagonal and linear and loess fit lines.

and asymmetry, and the `smoother.args=list(lty=2)` option displays the loess fit lines using dashed rather than solid lines.

R provides many other ways to create scatter-plot matrices. You may want to explore the `cpars()` function in the `glus` package, the `pairs2()` function in the `TeachingDemos` package, the `xysplom()` function in the `HH` package, the `kepairs()` function in the `ResourceSelection` package, and `pairs.mod()` in the `SMPracticals` package. Each adds its own unique twist. Analysts must love scatter-plot matrices!

11.1.2 High-density scatter plots

When there's a significant overlap among data points, scatter plots become less useful for observing relationships. Consider the following contrived example with 10,000 observations falling into two overlapping clusters of data:

```
set.seed(1234)
n <- 10000
c1 <- matrix(rnorm(n, mean=0, sd=.5), ncol=2)
c2 <- matrix(rnorm(n, mean=3, sd=2), ncol=2)
mydata <- rbind(c1, c2)
mydata <- as.data.frame(mydata)
names(mydata) <- c("x", "y")
```

If you generate a standard scatter plot between these variables using the following code

```
with(mydata,
    plot(x, y, pch=19, main="Scatter Plot with 10,000 Observations"))
```

you'll obtain a graph like the one in figure 11.5.

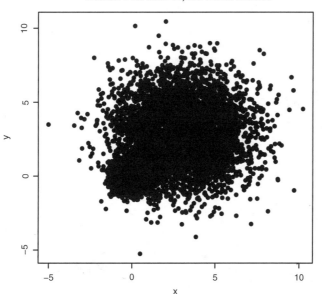

Figure 11.5 Scatter plot with 10,000 observations and significant overlap of data points. Note that the overlap of data points makes it difficult to discern where the concentration of data is greatest.

The overlap of data points in figure 11.5 makes it difficult to discern the relationship between x and y. R provides several graphical approaches that can be used when this occurs. They include the use of binning, color, and transparency to indicate the number of overprinted data points at any point on the graph.

The `smoothScatter()` function uses a kernel-density estimate to produce smoothed color density representations of the scatter plot. The following code

```
with(mydata,
     smoothScatter(x, y, main="Scatter Plot Colored by Smoothed Densities"))
```

produces the graph in figure 11.6.

Using a different approach, the `hexbin()` function in the hexbin package provides bivariate binning into hexagonal cells (it looks better than it sounds). Applying this function to the dataset

```
library(hexbin)
with(mydata, {
     bin <- hexbin(x, y, xbins=50)
     plot(bin, main="Hexagonal Binning with 10,000 Observations")
     })
```

you get the scatter plot in figure 11.7.

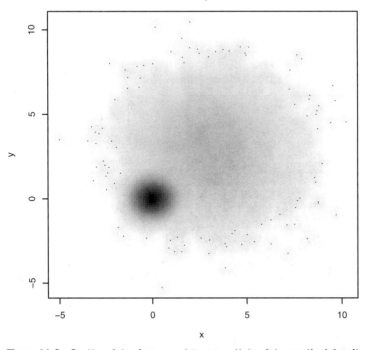

Scatter Plot Colored by Smoothed Densities

Figure 11.6   Scatter plot using `smoothScatter()` to plot smoothed density estimates. Densities are easy to read from the graph.

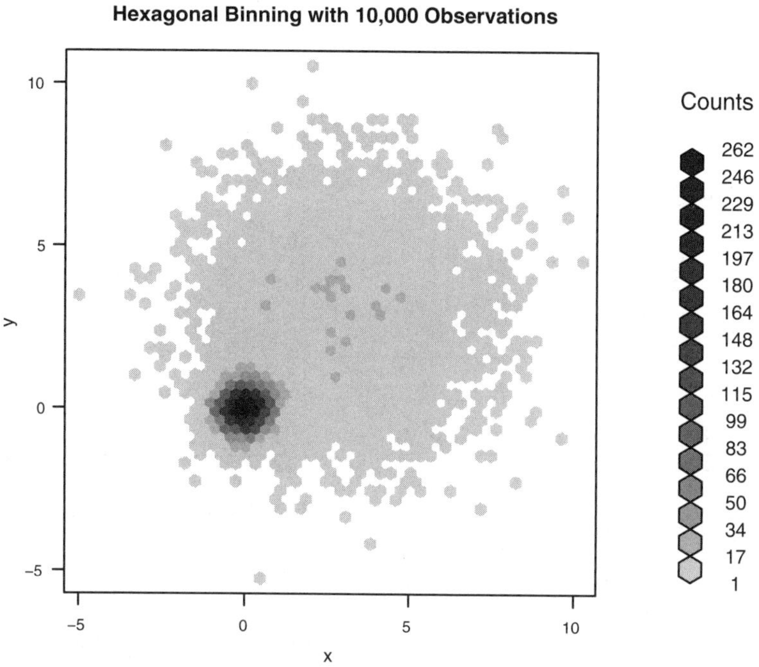

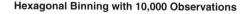

Hexagonal Binning with 10,000 Observations

Figure 11.7   Scatter plot using hexagonal binning to display the number of observations at each point. Data concentrations are easy to see, and counts can be read from the legend.

It's useful to note that the `smoothScatter()` function in the base package, along with the `ipairs()` function in the `IDPmisc` package, can be used to create readable scatter plot matrices for large datasets as well. See `?smoothScatter` and `?ipairs` for examples.

11.1.3 3D scatter plots

Scatter plots and scatter-plot matrices display bivariate relationships. What if you want to visualize the interaction of three quantitative variables at once? In this case, you can use a 3D scatter plot.

For example, say that you're interested in the relationship between automobile mileage, weight, and displacement. You can use the `scatterplot3d()` function in the `scatterplot3d` package to picture their relationship. The format is

```
scatterplot3d(x, y, z)
```

where *x* is plotted on the horizontal axis, *y* is plotted on the vertical axis, and *z* is plotted in perspective. Continuing the example,

```
library(scatterplot3d)
attach(mtcars)
scatterplot3d(wt, disp, mpg,
    main="Basic 3D Scatter Plot")
```

Basic 3D Scatter Plot

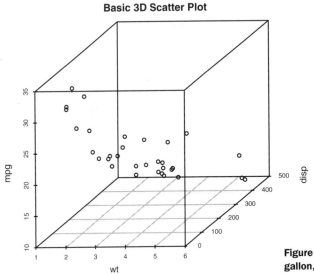

Figure 11.8   3D scatter plot of miles per gallon, auto weight, and displacement

produces the 3D scatter plot in figure 11.8.

The scatterplot3d() function offers many options, including the ability to specify symbols, axes, colors, lines, grids, highlighting, and angles. For example, the code

```
library(scatterplot3d)
attach(mtcars)
scatterplot3d(wt, disp, mpg,
              pch=16,
              highlight.3d=TRUE,
              type="h",
              main="3D Scatter Plot with Vertical Lines")
```

produces a 3D scatter plot with highlighting to enhance the impression of depth, and vertical lines connecting points to the horizontal plane (see figure 11.9).

3D Scatter Plot with Vertical Lines

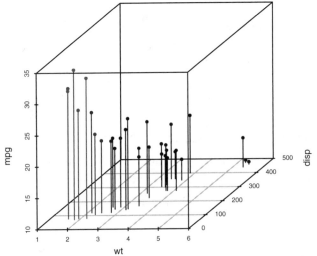

Figure 11.9   3D scatter plot with vertical lines and shading

As a final example, let's take the previous graph and add a regression plane. The necessary code is

```
library(scatterplot3d)
attach(mtcars)
s3d <-scatterplot3d(wt, disp, mpg,
     pch=16,
     highlight.3d=TRUE,
     type="h",
     main="3D Scatter Plot with Vertical Lines and Regression Plane")
fit <- lm(mpg ~ wt+disp)
s3d$plane3d(fit)
```

The resulting graph is provided in figure 11.10.

The graph allows you to visualize the prediction of miles per gallon from automobile weight and displacement using a multiple-regression equation. The plane represents the predicted values, and the points are the actual values. The vertical distances from the plane to the points are the residuals. Points that lie above the plane are under-predicted, whereas points that lie below the line are over-predicted. Multiple regression is covered in chapter 8.

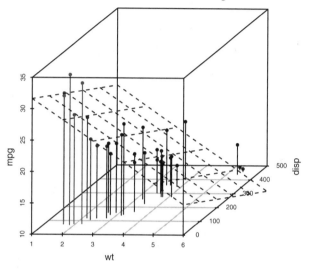

Figure 11.10   3D scatter plot with vertical lines, shading, and overlaid regression plane

11.1.4   *Spinning 3D scatter plots*

Three-dimensional scatter plots are much easier to interpret if you can interact with them. R provides several mechanisms for rotating graphs so that you can see the plotted points from more than one angle.

For example, you can create an interactive 3D scatter plot using the `plot3d()` function in the `rgl` package. It creates a spinning 3D scatter plot that can be rotated with the mouse. The format is

```
plot3d(x, y, z)
```

where *x*, *y*, and *z* are numeric vectors representing points. You can also add options like `col` and `size` to control the color and size of the points, respectively. Continuing the example, try this code:

```
library(rgl)
attach(mtcars)
plot3d(wt, disp, mpg, col="red", size=5)
```

You should get a graph like the one depicted in figure 11.11. Use the mouse to rotate the axes. I think you'll find that being able to rotate the scatter plot in three dimensions makes the graph much easier to understand.

You can perform a similar function with `scatter3d()` in the car package:

```
library(car)
with(mtcars,
     scatter3d(wt, disp, mpg))
```

The results are displayed in figure 11.12.

The `scatter3d()` function can include a variety of regression surfaces, such as linear, quadratic, smooth, and additive. The linear surface depicted is the default. Additionally, there are options for interactively identifying points. See `help(scatter3d)` for more details.

11.1.5 Bubble plots

In the previous section, you displayed the relationship between three quantitative variables using a 3D scatter plot. Another approach is to create a 2D scatter plot and use the size of the plotted point to represent the value of the third variable. This approach is referred to as a *bubble plot*.

You can create a bubble plot using the `symbols()` function. This function can be used to draw circles, squares, stars, thermometers, and box plots at a specified set of (*x*, *y*) coordinates. For plotting circles, the format is

```
symbols(x, y, circle=radius)
```

where *x*, *y*, and *radius* are vectors specifying the x and y coordinates and circle radii, respectively.

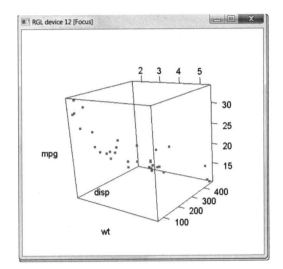

Figure 11.11   Rotating 3D scatter plot produced by the `plot3d()` function in the `rgl` package

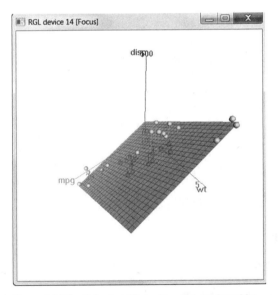

Figure 11.12   Spinning 3D scatter plot produced by the `scatter3d()` function in the `car` package

You want the areas, rather than the radii, of the circles to be proportional to the values of a third variable. Given the formula for the radius of a circle $\left(r = \sqrt{\frac{A}{\pi}}\right)$, the proper call is

```
symbols(x, y, circle=sqrt(z/pi))
```

where z is the third variable to be plotted.

Let's apply this to the `mtcars` data, plotting car weight on the x-axis, miles per gallon on the y-axis, and engine displacement as the bubble size. The following code

```
attach(mtcars)
r <- sqrt(disp/pi)
symbols(wt, mpg, circle=r, inches=0.30,
        fg="white", bg="lightblue",
        main="Bubble Plot with point size proportional to displacement",
        ylab="Miles Per Gallon",
        xlab="Weight of Car (lbs/1000)")
text(wt, mpg, rownames(mtcars), cex=0.6)
detach(mtcars)
```

produces the graph in figure 11.13. The option `inches` is a scaling factor that can be used to control the size of the circles (the default is to make the largest circle 1 inch). The `text()` function is optional. Here it is used to add the names of the cars to the plot. From the figure, you can see that increased gas mileage is associated with both decreased car weight and engine displacement.

In general, statisticians involved in the R project tend to avoid bubble plots for the same reason they avoid pie charts. Humans typically have a harder time making

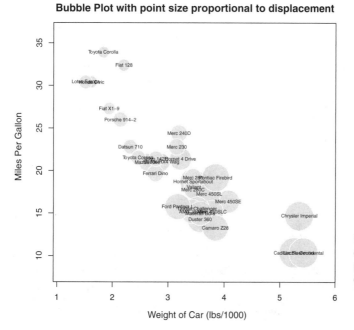

Bubble Plot with point size proportional to displacement

Miles Per Gallon

Weight of Car (lbs/1000)

Figure 11.13 Bubble plot of car weight vs. mpg, where point size is proportional to engine displacement

judgments about volume than distance. But bubble charts are popular in the business world, so I'm including them here for completeness.

I've certainly had a lot to say about scatter plots. This attention to detail is due, in part, to the central place that scatter plots hold in data analysis. Although simple, they can help you visualize your data in an immediate and straightforward manner, uncovering relationships that might otherwise be missed.

11.2 *Line charts*

If you connect the points in a scatter plot moving from left to right, you have a line plot. The dataset `Orange` that come with the base installation contains age and circumference data for five orange trees. Consider the growth of the first orange tree, depicted in figure 11.14. The plot on the left is a scatter plot, and the plot on the right is a line chart. As you can see, line charts are particularly good vehicles for conveying change. The graphs in figure 11.14 were created with the code in the following listing.

Listing 11.2 Creating side-by-side scatter and line plots

```
opar <- par(no.readonly=TRUE)
par(mfrow=c(1,2))
t1 <- subset(Orange, Tree==1)
plot(t1$age, t1$circumference,
     xlab="Age (days)",
     ylab="Circumference (mm)",
     main="Orange Tree 1 Growth")
plot(t1$age, t1$circumference,
     xlab="Age (days)",
     ylab="Circumference (mm)",
     main="Orange Tree 1 Growth",
     type="b")
par(opar)
```

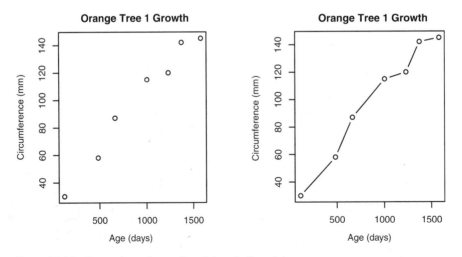

Figure 11.14 Comparison of a scatter plot and a line plot

You've seen the elements that make up this code in chapter 3, so I won't go into detail here. The main difference between the two plots in figure 11.14 is produced by the option `type="b"`. In general, line charts are created with one of the following two functions

```
plot(x, y, type=)
lines(x, y, type=)
```

where *x* and *y* are numeric vectors of (x,y) points to connect. The option `type=` can take the values described in table 11.1.

Examples of each type are given in figure 11.15. As you can see, `type="p"` produces the typical scatter plot. The option `type="b"` is the most common for line charts. The difference between `b` and `c` is whether the points appear or gaps are left instead. Both `type="s"` and `type="S"` produce stair steps (step functions). The first runs, then rises, whereas the second rises, then runs.

Table 11.1 Line chart options

Type	What is plotted
p	Points only
l	Lines only
o	Over-plotted points (that is, lines overlaid on top of points)
b, c	Points (empty if c) joined by lines
s, S	Stair steps
h	Histogram-line vertical lines
n	Doesn't produce any points or lines (used to set up the axes for later commands)

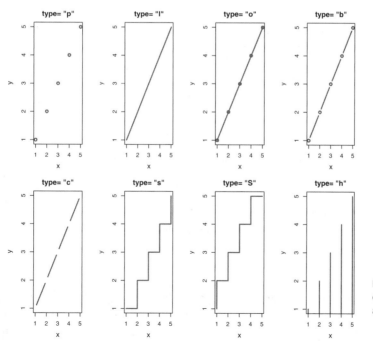

Figure 11.15 `type=` options in the `plot()` and `lines()` functions

There's an important difference between the plot() and lines() functions. The plot() function creates a new graph when invoked. The lines() function *adds* information to an existing graph but *can't* produce a graph on its own.

Because of this, the lines() function is typically used after a plot() command has produced a graph. If desired, you can use the type="n" option in the plot() function to set up the axes, titles, and other graph features, and then use the lines() function to add various lines to the plot.

To demonstrate the creation of a more complex line chart, let's plot the growth of all five orange trees over time. Each tree will have its own distinctive line. The code is shown in the next listing and the results in figure 11.16.

Listing 11.3   Line chart displaying the growth of five orange trees over time

```
Orange$Tree <- as.numeric(Orange$Tree)        Converts a factor to
ntrees <- max(Orange$Tree)                     numeric for convenience

xrange <- range(Orange$age)
yrange <- range(Orange$circumference)

plot(xrange, yrange,
    type="n",
    xlab="Age (days)",                         Sets up the plot
    ylab="Circumference (mm)"
 )

colors <- rainbow(ntrees)
linetype <- c(1:ntrees)
plotchar <- seq(18, 18+ntrees, 1)

for (i in 1:ntrees) {
    tree <- subset(Orange, Tree==i)
    lines(tree$age, tree$circumference,
        type="b",
        lwd=2,
        lty=linetype[i],                       Adds lines
        col=colors[i],
        pch=plotchar[i]
    )
}

title("Tree Growth", "example of line plot")

legend(xrange[1], yrange[2],
    1:ntrees,
    cex=0.8,
    col=colors,
    pch=plotchar,                              Adds a legend
    lty=linetype,
    title="Tree"
)
```

In listing 11.3, the plot() function is used to set up the graph and specify the axis labels and ranges but plots no actual data. The lines() function is then used to add a separate line and set of points for each orange tree. You can see that tree 4 and tree 5

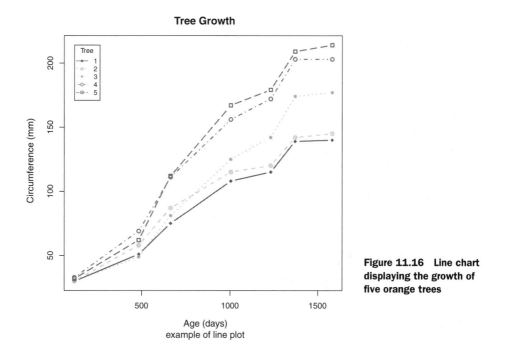

Figure 11.16   Line chart displaying the growth of five orange trees

demonstrated the greatest growth across the range of days measured, and that tree 5 overtakes tree 4 at around 664 days.

Many of the programming conventions in R that I discussed in chapters 2, 3, and 4 are used in listing 11.3. You may want to test your understanding by working through each line of code and visualizing what it's doing. If you can, you're on your way to becoming a serious R programmer (and fame and fortune is near at hand)! In the next section, you'll explore ways of examining a number of correlation coefficients at once.

11.3   *Corrgrams*

Correlation matrices are a fundamental aspect of multivariate statistics. Which variables under consideration are strongly related to each other, and which aren't? Are there clusters of variables that relate in specific ways? As the number of variables grows, such questions can be harder to answer. Corrgrams are a relatively recent tool for visualizing the data in correlation matrices.

It's easier to explain a corrgram once you've seen one. Consider the correlations among the variables in the mtcars data frame. Here you have 11 variables, each measuring some aspect of 32 automobiles. You can get the correlations using the following code:

```
> options(digits=2)
> cor(mtcars)
      mpg   cyl  disp    hp   drat    wt   qsec    vs     am  gear   carb
mpg  1.00 -0.85 -0.85 -0.78  0.681 -0.87  0.419  0.66  0.600  0.48 -0.551
cyl -0.85  1.00  0.90  0.83 -0.700  0.78 -0.591 -0.81 -0.523 -0.49  0.527
```

```
disp -0.85  0.90  1.00  0.79 -0.710  0.89 -0.434 -0.71 -0.591 -0.56  0.395
hp   -0.78  0.83  0.79  1.00 -0.449  0.66 -0.708 -0.72 -0.243 -0.13  0.750
drat  0.68 -0.70 -0.71 -0.45  1.000 -0.71  0.091  0.44  0.713  0.70 -0.091
wt   -0.87  0.78  0.89  0.66 -0.712  1.00 -0.175 -0.55 -0.692 -0.58  0.428
qsec  0.42 -0.59 -0.43 -0.71  0.091 -0.17  1.000  0.74 -0.230 -0.21 -0.656
vs    0.66 -0.81 -0.71 -0.72  0.440 -0.55  0.745  1.00  0.168  0.21 -0.570
am    0.60 -0.52 -0.59 -0.24  0.713 -0.69 -0.230  0.17  1.000  0.79  0.058
gear  0.48 -0.49 -0.56 -0.13  0.700 -0.58 -0.213  0.21  0.794  1.00  0.274
carb -0.55  0.53  0.39  0.75 -0.091  0.43 -0.656 -0.57  0.058  0.27  1.000
```

Which variables are most related? Which variables are relatively independent? Are there any patterns? It isn't that easy to tell from the correlation matrix without significant time and effort (and probably a set of colored pens to make notations).

You can display that same correlation matrix using the corrgram() function in the corrgram package (see figure 11.17). The code is

```
library(corrgram)
corrgram(mtcars, order=TRUE, lower.panel=panel.shade,
        upper.panel=panel.pie, text.panel=panel.txt,
        main="Corrgram of mtcars intercorrelations")
```

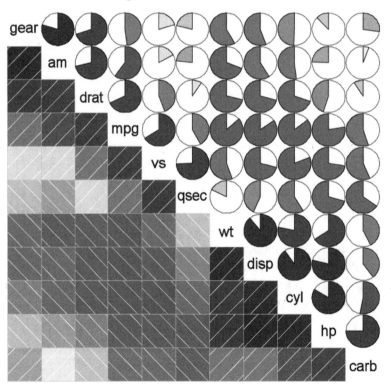

Corrgram of mtcars intercorrelations

Figure 11.17   Corrgram of the correlations among the variables in the `mtcars` data frame. Rows and columns have been reordered using principal components analysis.

To interpret this graph, start with the lower triangle of cells (the cells below the principal diagonal). By default, a blue color and hashing that goes from lower left to upper right represent a positive correlation between the two variables that meet at that cell. Conversely, a red color and hashing that goes from the upper left to lower right represent a negative correlation. The darker and more saturated the color, the greater the magnitude of the correlation. Weak correlations, near zero, appear washed out. In the current graph, the rows and columns have been reordered (using principal components analysis) to cluster variables together that have similar correlation patterns.

You can see from the shaded cells that gear, am, drat, and mpg are positively correlated with one another. You can also see that wt, disp, cyl, hp, and carb are positively correlated with one another. But the first group of variables is negatively correlated with the second group of variables. You can also see that the correlation between carb and am is weak, as is the correlation between vs and gear, vs and am, and drat and qsec.

The upper triangle of cells displays the same information using pies. Here, color plays the same role, but the strength of the correlation is displayed by the size of the filled pie slice. Positive correlations fill the pie starting at 12 o'clock and moving in a clockwise direction. Negative correlations fill the pie by moving in a counterclockwise direction.

The format of the corrgram() function is

```
corrgram(x, order=, panel=, text.panel=, diag.panel=)
```

where *x* is a data frame with one observation per row. When order=TRUE, the variables are reordered using a principal component analysis of the correlation matrix. Reordering can help make patterns of bivariate relationships more obvious.

The option panel specifies the type of off-diagonal panels to use. Alternatively, you can use the options lower.panel and upper.panel to choose different options below and above the main diagonal. The text.panel and diag.panel options refer to the main diagonal. Allowable values for panel are described in table 11.2.

Table 11.2   Panel options for the corrgram() function

Placement	Panel Option	Description
Off diagonal	panel.pie	The filled portion of the pie indicates the magnitude of the correlation.
	panel.shade	The depth of the shading indicates the magnitude of the correlation.
	panel.ellipse	Plots a confidence ellipse and smoothed line.
	panel.pts	Plots a scatter plot.
	panel.conf	Prints correlations and their confidence intervals.
Main diagonal	panel.txt	Prints the variable name.
	panel.minmax	Prints the minimum and maximum value and variable name.
	panel.density	Prints the kernel density plot and variable name.

Corrgram of mtcars data using scatter plots and ellipses

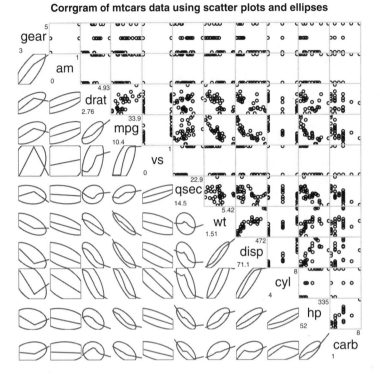

Figure 11.18 Corrgram of the correlations among the variables in the mtcars data frame. The lower triangle contains smoothed best-fit lines and confidence ellipses, and the upper triangle contains scatter plots. The diagonal panel contains minimum and maximum values. Rows and columns have been reordered using principal components analysis.

Let's try a second example. The code

```
library(corrgram)
corrgram(mtcars, order=TRUE, lower.panel=panel.ellipse,
         upper.panel=panel.pts, text.panel=panel.txt,
         diag.panel=panel.minmax,
         main="Corrgram of mtcars data using scatter plots
             and ellipses")
```

produces the graph in figure 11.18. Here you're using smoothed fit lines and confidence ellipses in the lower triangle and scatter plots in the upper triangle.

Why do the scatter plots look odd?

Several of the variables that are plotted in figure 11.18 have limited allowable values. For example, the number of gears is 3, 4, or 5. The number of cylinders is 4, 6, or 8. Both am (transmission type) and vs (V/S) are dichotomous. This explains the odd-looking scatter plots in the upper diagonal.

Always be careful that the statistical methods you choose are appropriate to the form of the data. Specifying these variables as ordered or unordered factors can serve as a useful check. When R knows that a variable is categorical or ordinal, it attempts to apply statistical methods that are appropriate to that level of measurement.

We'll finish with one more example. The code

```
library(corrgram)
corrgram(mtcars, lower.panel=panel.shade,
        upper.panel=NULL, text.panel=panel.txt,
        main="Car Mileage Data (unsorted)")
```

produces the graph in figure 11.19. Here you're using shading in the lower triangle, keeping the original variable order, and leaving the upper triangle blank.

Before moving on, I should point out that you can control the colors used by the corrgram() function. To do so, specify four colors in the colorRampPalette() function, and include the results using the col.regions option. Here's an example:

```
library(corrgram)
cols <- colorRampPalette(c("darkgoldenrod4", "burlywood1",
                          "darkkhaki", "darkgreen"))
corrgram(mtcars, order=TRUE, col.regions=cols,
        lower.panel=panel.shade,
        upper.panel=panel.conf, text.panel=panel.txt,
        main="A Corrgram (or Horse) of a Different Color")
```

Try it and see what you get.

Car Mileage Data (unsorted)

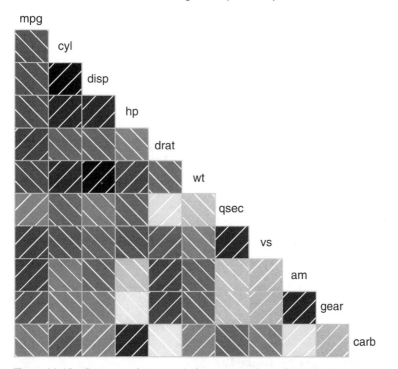

Figure 11.19 Corrgram of the correlations among the variables in the mtcars **data frame. The lower triangle is shaded to represent the magnitude and direction of the correlations. The variables are plotted in their original order.**

Corrgrams can be a useful way to examine large numbers of bivariate relationships among quantitative variables. Because they're relatively new, the greatest challenge is to educate the recipient on how to interpret them. To learn more, see Michael Friendly's article "Corrgrams: Exploratory Displays for Correlation Matrices," available at www.math.yorku.ca/SCS/Papers/corrgram.pdf.

11.4 *Mosaic plots*

Up to this point, we've been exploring methods of visualizing relationships among quantitative/continuous variables. But what if your variables are categorical? When you're looking at a single categorical variable, you can use a bar or pie chart. If there are two categorical variables, you can look at a 3D bar chart (which, by the way, is not easy to do in R). But what do you do if there are more than two categorical variables?

One approach is to use mosaic plots. In a mosaic plot, the frequencies in a multidimensional contingency table are represented by nested rectangular regions that are proportional to their cell frequency. Color and/or shading can be used to represent residuals from a fitted model. For details, see Meyer, Zeileis, and Hornick (2006), or Michael Friendly's excellent tutorial (http://mng.bz/3p0d).

Mosaic plots can be created with the mosaic() function from the vcd library (there's a mosaicplot() function in the basic installation of R, but I recommend you use the vcd package for its more extensive features). As an example, consider the *Titanic* dataset available in the base installation. It describes the number of passengers who survived or died, cross-classified by their class (1st, 2nd, 3rd, Crew), sex (Male, Female), and age (Child, Adult). This is a well-studied dataset. You can see the cross-classification using the following code:

```
> ftable(Titanic)
                   Survived  No Yes
Class Sex    Age
1st   Male   Child            0   5
             Adult          118  57
      Female Child            0   1
             Adult            4 140
2nd   Male   Child            0  11
             Adult          154  14
      Female Child            0  13
             Adult           13  80
3rd   Male   Child           35  13
             Adult          387  75
      Female Child           17  14
             Adult           89  76
Crew  Male   Child            0   0
             Adult          670 192
      Female Child            0   0
             Adult            3  20
```

The mosaic() function can be invoked as

```
mosaic(table)
```

where *table* is a contingency table in array form, or

```
mosaic(formula, data=)
```

where *formula* is a standard R formula, and `data` specifies either a data frame or a table. Adding the option `shade=TRUE` colors the figure based on Pearson residuals from a fitted model (independence by default), and the option `legend=TRUE` displays a legend for these residuals.

For example, both

```
library(vcd)
mosaic(Titanic, shade=TRUE, legend=TRUE)
```

and

```
library(vcd)
mosaic(~Class+Sex+Age+Survived, data=Titanic, shade=TRUE, legend=TRUE)
```

will produce the graph shown in figure 11.20. The formula version gives you greater control over the selection and placement of variables in the graph.

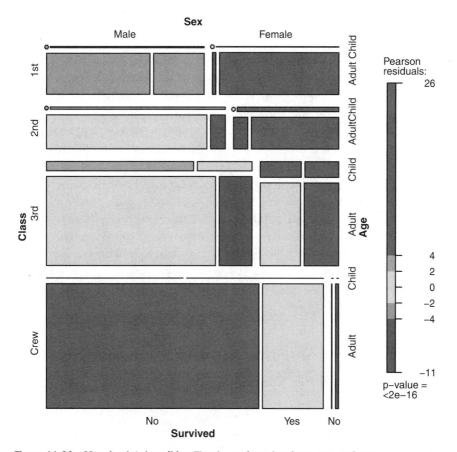

Figure 11.20 Mosaic plot describing *Titanic* survivors by class, sex, and age

A great deal of information is packed into this one picture. For example, as a person moves from crew to first class, the survival rate increases precipitously. Most children were in third and second class. Most females in first class survived, whereas only about half the females in third class survived. There were few females in the crew, causing the Survived labels (No, Yes at the bottom of the chart) to overlap for this group. Keep looking, and you'll see many more interesting facts. Remember to look at the relative widths and heights of the rectangles. What else can you learn about that night?

Extended mosaic plots add color and shading to represent the residuals from a fitted model. In this example, the blue shading indicates cross-classifications that occur more often than expected, assuming that survival is unrelated to class, gender, and age. Red shading indicates cross-classifications that occur less often than expected under the independence model. Be sure to run the example so that you can see the results in color. The graph indicates that more first-class women survived and more male crew members died than would be expected under an independence model. Fewer third-class men survived than would be expected if survival was independent of class, gender, and age. If you'd like to explore mosaic plots in greater detail, try running `example(mosaic)`.

11.5 *Summary*

In this chapter, we considered a wide range of techniques for displaying relationships among two or more variables. These included the use of 2D and 3D scatter plots, scatter-plot matrices, bubble plots, line plots, corrgrams, and mosaic plots. Some of these methods are standard techniques, where others are relatively new.

Taken together with methods that allow you to customize graphs (chapter 3), display univariate distributions (chapter 6), explore regression models (chapter 8), and visualize group differences (chapter 9), you now have a comprehensive toolbox for visualizing and extracting meaning from your data. In later chapters, you'll expand your skills with additional specialized techniques, including graphics for latent variable models (chapter 14), time series (chapter 15), clustered data (chapter 16), and techniques for creating graphs that are conditioned on one or more variables (chapter 18).

In the next chapter, we'll explore resampling statistics and bootstrapping. These are computer-intensive methods that allow you to analyze data in new and unique ways.

*Resampling statistics
and bootstrapping*

12

> **This chapter covers**
> - Understanding the logic of permutation tests
> - Applying permutation tests to linear models
> - Using bootstrapping to obtain confidence intervals

In chapters 7, 8, and 9, we reviewed statistical methods that test hypotheses and estimate confidence intervals for population parameters by assuming that the observed data is sampled from a normal distribution or some other well-known theoretical distribution. But there will be many cases in which this assumption is unwarranted. Statistical approaches based on randomization and resampling can be used in cases where the data is sampled from unknown or mixed distributions, where sample sizes are small, where outliers are a problem, or where devising an appropriate test based on a theoretical distribution is too complex and mathematically intractable.

In this chapter, we'll explore two broad statistical approaches that use randomization: permutation tests and bootstrapping. Historically, these methods were only available to experienced programmers and expert statisticians. Contributed packages in R now make them readily available to a wider audience of data analysts.

We'll also revisit problems that were initially analyzed using traditional methods (for example, t-tests, chi-square tests, ANOVA, and regression) and see how they can be approached using these robust, computer-intensive methods. To get the most out of section 12.2, be sure to read chapter 7 first. Chapters 8 and 9 serve as prerequisites for section 12.3. Other sections can be read on their own.

12.1 *Permutation tests*

Permutation tests, also called *randomization* or *re-randomization* tests, have been around for decades, but it took the advent of high-speed computers to make them practically available. To understand the logic of a permutation test, consider the following hypothetical problem. Ten subjects have been randomly assigned to one of two treatment conditions (A or B), and an outcome variable (score) has been recorded. The results of the experiment are presented in table 12.1.

The data are also displayed in the strip chart in figure 12.1. Is there enough evidence to conclude that the treatments differ in their impact?

In a parametric approach, you might assume that the data are sampled from normal populations with equal variances and apply a two-tailed independent-groups t-test. The null hypothesis is that the population mean for Treatment A is equal to the population mean for Treatment B. You'd

Table 12.1 Hypothetical two-group problem

Treatment A	Treatment B
40	57
57	64
45	55
55	62
58	65

calculate a t-statistic from the data and compare it to the theoretical distribution. If the observed t-statistic is sufficiently extreme, say outside the middle 95% of values in the theoretical distribution, you'd reject the null hypothesis and declare that the population means for the two groups are unequal at the 0.05 level of significance.

A permutation test takes a different approach. If the two treatments are truly equivalent, the label (Treatment A or Treatment B) assigned to an observed score is

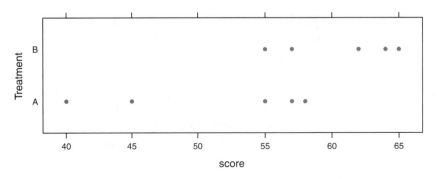

Figure 12.1 Strip chart of the hypothetical treatment data in table 12.1

arbitrary. To test for differences between the two treatments, you could follow these steps:

1. Calculate the observed t-statistic, as in the parametric approach; call this t0.
2. Place all 10 scores in a single group.
3. Randomly assign five scores to Treatment A and five scores to Treatment B.
4. Calculate and record the new observed t-statistic.
5. Repeat steps 3–4 for every possible way of assigning five scores to Treatment A and five scores to Treatment B. There are 252 such possible arrangements.
6. Arrange the 252 t-statistics in ascending order. This is the empirical distribution, based on (or conditioned on) the sample data.
7. If t0 falls outside the middle 95% of the empirical distribution, reject the null hypothesis that the population means for the two treatment groups are equal at the 0.05 level of significance.

Notice that the same t-statistic is calculated in both the permutation and parametric approaches. But instead of comparing the statistic to a theoretical distribution in order to determine if it was extreme enough to reject the null hypothesis, it's compared to an empirical distribution created from permutations of the observed data. This logic can be extended to most classical statistical tests and linear models.

In the previous example, the empirical distribution was based on all possible permutations of the data. In such cases, the permutation test is called an *exact* test. As the sample sizes increase, the time required to form all possible permutations can become prohibitive. In such cases, you can use Monte Carlo simulation to sample from all possible permutations. Doing so provides an approximate test.

If you're uncomfortable assuming that the data is normally distributed, concerned about the impact of outliers, or feel that the dataset is too small for standard parametric approaches, a permutation test provides an excellent alternative. R has some of the most comprehensive and sophisticated packages for performing permutation tests currently available. The remainder of this section focuses on two contributed packages: the `coin` package and the `lmPerm` package. The `coin` package provides a comprehensive framework for permutation tests applied to independence problems, whereas the `lmPerm` package provides permutation tests for ANOVA and regression designs. We'll consider each in turn and end the section with a quick review of other permutation packages available in R.

To install the `coin` package, use

```
install.packages(c("coin")
```

Sadly, Bob Wheeler, the author of the `lmPerm` package, passed away in 2012, and the source code has been moved into the CRAN archive for unsupported packages. Therefore, installation of the package is a bit more complicated than usual:

1. Download the file lmPerm_1.1-2.tar.gz from http://cran.r-project.org/src/contrib/Archive/lmPerm/, and save it on your hard drive.

2   MS Windows users: install `RTools` from http://cran.r-project.org/bin/windows/Rtools/. Mac and Linux users can skip this step.

3   Execute the function

```
install.packages(file.choose(), repos=NULL, type="source")
```

from within R. When a dialog box pops up, find and choose the lmPerm_1.1-2.tar.gz file. This will install the package on your machine.

Setting the random number seed

Before moving on, it's important to remember that permutation tests use pseudo-random numbers to sample from all possible permutations (when performing an approximate test). Therefore, the results will change each time the test is performed. Setting the random-number seed in R allows you to fix the random numbers generated. This is particularly useful when you want to share your examples with others, because results will always be the same if the calls are made with the same seed. Setting the random number seed to 1234 (that is, `set.seed(1234)`) will allow you to replicate the results presented in this chapter.

12.2   *Permutation tests with the coin package*

The `coin` package provides a general framework for applying permutation tests to independence problems. With this package, you can answer such questions as

- Are responses independent of group assignment?
- Are two numeric variables independent?
- Are two categorical variables independent?

Using convenience functions provided in the package (see table 12.2), you can perform permutation test equivalents for most of the traditional statistical tests covered in chapter 7.

Table 12.2   `coin` functions providing permutation test alternatives to traditional tests

Test	`coin` function
Two- and K-sample permutation test	`oneway_test( y ~ A)`
Wilcoxon–Mann–Whitney rank-sum test	`wilcox_test( y ~ A )`
Kruskal–Wallis test	`kruskal_test( y ~ A )`
Pearson's chi-square test	`chisq_test( A ~ B )`
Cochran–Mantel–Haenszel test	`cmh_test( A ~ B | C )`
Linear-by-linear association test	`lbl_test( D ~ E)`
Spearman's test	`spearman_test( y ~ x )`

Table 12.2 `coin` functions providing permutation test alternatives to traditional tests

Test	coin **function**
Friedman test	`friedman_test( y ~ A | C )`
Wilcoxon signed-rank test	`wilcoxsign_test( y1 ~ y2 )`

In the `coin` function column, `y` and `x` are numeric variables, A and B are categorical factors, C is a categorical blocking variable, D and E are ordered factors, and `y1` and `y2` are matched numeric variables.

Each of the functions listed in table 12.2 takes the form

```
function_name( formula, data, distribution= )
```

where

- *formula* describes the relationship among variables to be tested. Examples are given in the table.
- *data* identifies a data frame.
- `distribution` specifies how the empirical distribution under the null hypothesis should be derived. Possible values are `exact`, `asymptotic`, and `approximate`.

If `distribution="exact"`, the distribution under the null hypothesis is computed exactly (that is, from all possible permutations). The distribution can also be approximated by its asymptotic distribution (`distribution="asymptotic"`) or via Monte Carlo resampling (`distribution="approximate(B=#)"`), where # indicates the number of replications used to approximate the exact distribution. At present, `distribution="exact"` is only available for two-sample problems.

> **NOTE** In the `coin` package, categorical variables and ordinal variables must be coded as factors and ordered factors, respectively. Additionally, the data must be stored in a data frame.

In the remainder of this section, you'll apply several of the permutation tests described in table 12.2 to problems from previous chapters. This will allow you to compare the results to more traditional parametric and nonparametric approaches. We'll end this discussion of the `coin` package by considering advanced extensions.

12.2.1 Independent two-sample and k-sample tests

To begin, let's compare an independent samples t-test with a one-way exact test applied to the hypothetical data in table 12.2. The results are given in the following listing.

Listing 12.1 t-test vs. one-way permutation test for the hypothetical data

```
> library(coin)
> score <- c(40, 57, 45, 55, 58, 57, 64, 55, 62, 65)
> treatment <- factor(c(rep("A",5), rep("B",5)))
> mydata <- data.frame(treatment, score)
> t.test(score~treatment, data=mydata, var.equal=TRUE)
```

```
        Two Sample t-test

data:  score by treatment
t = -2.3, df = 8, p-value = 0.04705
alternative hypothesis: true difference in means is not equal to 0
95 percent confidence interval:
 -19.04  -0.16
sample estimates:
mean in group A mean in group B
           51              61


> oneway_test(score~treatment, data=mydata, distribution="exact")

        Exact 2-Sample Permutation Test

data:  score by treatment (A, B)
Z = -1.9, p-value = 0.07143
alternative hypothesis: true mu is not equal to 0
```

The traditional t-test indicates a significant group difference ($p < .05$), whereas the exact test doesn't ($p > 0.072$). With only 10 observations, I'd be more inclined to trust the results of the permutation test and attempt to collect more data before reaching a final conclusion.

Next, consider the Wilcoxon–Mann–Whitney U test. In chapter 7, we examined the difference in the probability of imprisonment in Southern versus non-Southern US states using the wilcox.test() function. Using an exact Wilcoxon rank-sum test, you'd get

```
> library(MASS)
> UScrime <- transform(UScrime, So = factor(So))
> wilcox_test(Prob ~ So, data=UScrime, distribution="exact")

        Exact Wilcoxon Mann-Whitney Rank Sum Test

data:  Prob by So (0, 1)
Z = -3.7, p-value = 8.488e-05
alternative hypothesis: true mu is not equal to 0
```

suggesting that incarceration is more likely in Southern states. Note that in the previous code, the numeric variable So was transformed into a factor. This is because the coin package requires that all categorical variables be coded as factors. Additionally, you may have noted that these results agree exactly with the results of the wilcox.test() function in chapter 7. This is because wilcox.test() also computes an exact distribution by default.

Finally, consider a k-sample test. In chapter 9, you used a one-way ANOVA to evaluate the impact of five drug regimens on cholesterol reduction in a sample of 50 patients. An approximate k-sample permutation test can be performed instead, using this code:

```
> library(multcomp)
> set.seed(1234)
> oneway_test(response~trt, data=cholesterol,
  distribution=approximate(B=9999))
```

```
          Approximative K-Sample Permutation Test

data:  response by
         trt (1time, 2times, 4times, drugD, drugE)
maxT = 4.7623, p-value < 2.2e-16
```

Here, the reference distribution is based on 9,999 permutations of the data. The random-number seed is set so that your results will be the same as mine. There's clearly a difference in response among patients in the various groups.

12.2.2 *Independence in contingency tables*

You can use permutation tests to assess the independence of two categorical variables using either the chisq_test() or cmh_test() function. The latter function is used when data is stratified on a third categorical variable. If both variables are ordinal, you can use the lbl_test() function to test for a linear trend.

In chapter 7, you applied a chi-square test to assess the relationship between arthritis treatment and improvement. Treatment had two levels (Placebo and Treated), and Improved had three levels (None, Some, and Marked). The Improved variable was encoded as an ordered factor.

If you want to perform a permutation version of the chi-square test, you can use the following code:

```
> library(coin)
> library(vcd)
> Arthritis <- transform(Arthritis,
  Improved=as.factor(as.numeric(Improved)))
> set.seed(1234)
> chisq_test(Treatment~Improved, data=Arthritis,
            distribution=approximate(B=9999))

          Approximative Pearson's Chi-Squared Test

data:  Treatment by Improved (1, 2, 3)
chi-squared = 13.055, p-value = 0.0018
```

This gives you an approximate chi-square test based on 9,999 replications. You might ask why you transformed the variable Improved from an ordered factor to a categorical factor. (Good question!) If you'd left it an ordered factor, coin() would have generated a linear × linear trend test instead of a chi-square test. Although a trend test would be a good choice in this situation, keeping it a chi-square test allows you to compare the results with those reported in chapter 7.

12.2.3 *Independence between numeric variables*

The spearman_test() function provides a permutation test of the independence of two numeric variables. In chapter 7, we examined the correlation between illiteracy rates and murder rates for US states. You can test the association via permutation, using the following code:

```
> states <- as.data.frame(state.x77)
> set.seed(1234)
```

```
> spearman_test(Illiteracy~Murder, data=states,
                distribution=approximate(B=9999))

        Approximative Spearman Correlation Test

data:  Illiteracy by Murder
Z = 4.7065, p-value < 2.2e-16
alternative hypothesis: true mu is not equal to 0
```

Based on an approximate permutation test with 9,999 replications, the hypothesis of independence can be rejected. Note that state.x77 is a matrix. It had to be converted into a data frame for use in the `coin` package.

12.2.4 *Dependent two-sample and k-sample tests*

Dependent sample tests are used when observations in different groups have been matched or when repeated measures are used. For permutation tests with two paired groups, the `wilcoxsign_test()` function can be used. For more than two groups, use the `friedman_test()` function.

In chapter 7, we compared the unemployment rate for urban males age 14–24 (U1) with urban males age 35–39 (U2). Because the two variables are reported for each of the 50 US states, you have a two-dependent groups design (state is the matching variable). You can use an exact Wilcoxon signed-rank test to see if unemployment rates for the two age groups are equal:

```
> library(coin)
> library(MASS)
> wilcoxsign_test(U1~U2, data=UScrime, distribution="exact")

        Exact Wilcoxon-Signed-Rank Test

data:  y by x (neg, pos)
        stratified by block
Z = 5.9691, p-value = 1.421e-14
alternative hypothesis: true mu is not equal to 0
```

Based on the results, you'd conclude that the unemployment rates differ.

12.2.5 *Going further*

The `coin` package provides a general framework for testing that one group of variables is independent of a second group of variables (with optional stratification on a blocking variable) against arbitrary alternatives, via approximate permutation tests. In particular, the `independence_test()` function lets you approach most traditional tests from a permutation perspective and create new and novel statistical tests for situations not covered by traditional methods. This flexibility comes at a price: a high level of statistical knowledge is required to use the function appropriately. See the vignettes that accompany the package (accessed via `vignette("coin")`) for further details.

In the next section, you'll learn about the `lmPerm` package. This package provides a permutation approach to linear models, including regression and analysis of variance.

12.3 Permutation tests with the lmPerm package

The lmPerm package provides support for a permutation approach to linear models. In particular, the lmp() and aovp() functions are the lm() and aov() functions modified to perform permutation tests rather than normal theory tests.

The parameters in the lmp() and aovp() functions are similar to those in the lm() and aov() functions, with the addition of a perm= parameter. The perm= option can take the value Exact, Prob, or SPR. Exact produces an exact test, based on all possible permutations. Prob samples from all possible permutations. Sampling continues until the estimated standard deviation falls below 0.1 of the estimated p-value. The stopping rule is controlled by an optional Ca parameter. Finally, SPR uses a sequential probability ratio test to decide when to stop sampling. Note that if the number of observations is greater than 10, perm="Exact" will automatically default to perm="Prob"; exact tests are only available for small problems.

To see how this works, you'll apply a permutation approach to simple regression, polynomial regression, multiple regression, one-way analysis of variance, one-way analysis of covariance, and a two-way factorial design.

12.3.1 Simple and polynomial regression

In chapter 8, you used linear regression to study the relationship between weight and height for a group of 15 women. Using lmp() instead of lm() generates the permutation test results shown in the following listing.

Listing 12.2 Permutation tests for simple linear regression

```
> library(lmPerm)
> set.seed(1234)
> fit <- lmp(weight~height, data=women, perm="Prob")
[1] "Settings:  unique SS : numeric variables centered"
> summary(fit)

Call:
lmp(formula = weight ~ height, data = women, perm = "Prob")

Residuals:
   Min    1Q Median    3Q    Max
-1.733 -1.133 -0.383  0.742  3.117

Coefficients:
       Estimate Iter Pr(Prob)
height     3.45 5000   <2e-16 ***
---
Signif. codes:  0 '***' 0.001 '**' 0.01 '*' 0.05 '.' 0.1 ' ' 1

Residual standard error: 1.5 on 13 degrees of freedom
Multiple R-Squared: 0.991,       Adjusted R-squared: 0.99
F-statistic: 1.43e+03 on 1 and 13 DF,  p-value: 1.09e-14
```

To fit a quadratic equation, you could use the code in this next listing.

Listing 12.3   Permutation tests for polynomial regression

```
> library(lmPerm)
> set.seed(1234)
> fit <- lmp(weight~height + I(height^2), data=women, perm="Prob")
[1] "Settings:  unique SS : numeric variables centered"
> summary(fit)

Call:
lmp(formula = weight ~ height + I(height^2), data = women, perm = "Prob")

Residuals:
    Min      1Q  Median      3Q     Max
-0.5094 -0.2961 -0.0094  0.2862  0.5971

Coefficients:
            Estimate Iter Pr(Prob)
height       -7.3483 5000   <2e-16 ***
I(height^2)   0.0831 5000   <2e-16 ***
---
Signif. codes:  0 '***' 0.001 '**' 0.01 '*' 0.05 '.' 0.1 ' ' 1

Residual standard error: 0.38 on 12 degrees of freedom
Multiple R-Squared: 0.999,      Adjusted R-squared: 0.999
F-statistic: 1.14e+04 on 2 and 12 DF,  p-value: <2e-16
```

As you can see, it's a simple matter to test these regressions using permutation tests and requires little change in the underlying code. The output is also similar to that produced by the lm() function. Note that an Iter column is added, indicating how many iterations were required to reach the stopping rule.

12.3.2 *Multiple regression*

In chapter 8, multiple regression was used to predict the murder rate based on population, illiteracy, income, and frost for 50 US states. Applying the lmp() function to this problem results in the following output.

Listing 12.4   Permutation tests for multiple regression

```
> library(lmPerm)
> set.seed(1234)
> states <- as.data.frame(state.x77)
> fit <- lmp(Murder~Population + Illiteracy+Income+Frost,
            data=states, perm="Prob")
[1] "Settings:  unique SS : numeric variables centered"
> summary(fit)

Call:
lmp(formula = Murder ~ Population + Illiteracy + Income + Frost,
    data = states, perm = "Prob")

Residuals:
     Min       1Q   Median       3Q      Max
-4.79597 -1.64946 -0.08112  1.48150  7.62104
```

```
Coefficients:
            Estimate Iter Pr(Prob)
Population 2.237e-04   51   1.0000
Illiteracy 4.143e+00 5000   0.0004 ***
Income     6.442e-05   51   1.0000
Frost      5.813e-04   51   0.8627
---
Signif. codes:  0 '***! 0.001 '**' 0.01 '*' 0.05 '. ' 0.1 ' ' 1

Residual standard error: 2.535 on 45 degrees of freedom
Multiple R-Squared: 0.567,     Adjusted R-squared: 0.5285
F-statistic: 14.73 on 4 and 45 DF,  p-value: 9.133e-08
```

Looking back to chapter 8, both Population and Illiteracy are significant ($p < 0.05$) when normal theory is used. Based on the permutation tests, the Population variable is no longer significant. When the two approaches don't agree, you should look at your data more carefully. It may be that the assumption of normality is untenable or that outliers are present.

12.3.3 One-way ANOVA and ANCOVA

Each of the analysis of variance designs discussed in chapter 9 can be performed via permutation tests. First, let's look at the one-way ANOVA problem considered in section 9.1 on the impact of treatment regimens on cholesterol reduction. The code and results are given in the next listing.

Listing 12.5   Permutation test for one-way ANOVA

```
> library(lmPerm)
> library(multcomp)
> set.seed(1234)
> fit <- aovp(response~trt, data=cholesterol, perm="Prob")
[1] "Settings:  unique SS "
> anova(fit)
Component 1 :
            Df R Sum Sq R Mean Sq Iter  Pr(Prob)
trt          4  1351.37    337.84 5000 < 2.2e-16 ***
Residuals   45   468.75     10.42
---
Signif. codes:  0 '***' 0.001 '**' 0.01 '*' 0.05 '. ' 0.1 ' ' 1
```

The results suggest that the treatment effects are not all equal.

This second example in this section applies a permutation test to a one-way analysis of covariance. The problem is from chapter 9, where you investigated the impact of four drug doses on the litter weights of rats, controlling for gestation times. The next listing shows the permutation test and results.

Listing 12.6   Permutation test for one-way ANCOVA

```
> library(lmPerm)
> set.seed(1234)
> fit <- aovp(weight ~ gesttime + dose, data=litter, perm="Prob")
```

```
[1] "Settings:  unique SS : numeric variables centered"
> anova(fit)
Component 1 :
            Df R Sum Sq R Mean Sq Iter Pr(Prob)
gesttime     1   161.49   161.493 5000   0.0006 ***
dose         3   137.12    45.708 5000   0.0392 *
Residuals   69  1151.27    16.685
---
Signif. codes:  0 '***' 0.001 '**' 0.01 '*' 0.05 '.' 0.1 ' ' 1
```

Based on the p-values, the four drug doses don't equally impact litter weights, controlling for gestation time.

12.3.4 *Two-way ANOVA*

You'll end this section by applying permutation tests to a factorial design. In chapter 9, you examined the impact of vitamin C on the tooth growth in guinea pigs. The two manipulated factors were dose (three levels) and delivery method (two levels). Ten guinea pigs were placed in each treatment combination, resulting in a balanced 3×2 factorial design. The permutation tests are provided in the next listing.

Listing 12.7 Permutation test for two-way ANOVA

```
> library(lmPerm)
> set.seed(1234)
> fit <- aovp(len~supp*dose, data=ToothGrowth, perm="Prob")
[1] "Settings:  unique SS : numeric variables centered"
> anova(fit)
Component 1 :
            Df R Sum Sq R Mean Sq Iter Pr(Prob)
supp         1   205.35    205.35 5000  < 2e-16 ***
dose         1  2224.30   2224.30 5000  < 2e-16 ***
supp:dose    1    88.92     88.92 2032  0.04724 *
Residuals   56   933.63     16.67
---
Signif. codes:  0 '***' 0.001 '**' 0.01 '*' 0.05 '.' 0.1 ' ' 1
```

At the .05 level of significance, all three effects are statistically different from zero. At the .01 level, only the main effects are significant.

It's important to note that when aovp() is applied to ANOVA designs, it defaults to unique sums of squares (also called *SAS Type III sums of squares*). Each effect is adjusted for every other effect. The default for parametric ANOVA designs in R is sequential sums of squares (*SAS Type I sums of squares*). Each effect is adjusted for those that appear *earlier* in the model. For balanced designs, the two approaches will agree, but for unbalanced designs with unequal numbers of observations per cell, they won't. The greater the imbalance, the greater the disagreement. If desired, specifying seqs=TRUE in the aovp() function will produce sequential sums of squares. For more on Type I and Type III sums of squares, see section 9.2.

12.4 Additional comments on permutation tests

R offers other permutation packages besides `coin` and `lmPerm`. The `perm` package provides some of the same functionality provided by the `coin` package and can act as an independent validation of that package. The `corrperm` package provides permutation tests of correlations with repeated measures. The `logregperm` package offers a permutation test for logistic regression. Perhaps most important, the `glmperm` package extends permutation tests to generalized linear models. Generalized linear models are described in the next chapter.

Permutation tests provide a powerful alternative to tests that rely on a knowledge of the underlying sampling distribution. In each of the permutation tests described, you were able to test statistical hypotheses without recourse to the normal, t, F, or chi-square distributions.

You may have noticed how closely the results of the tests based on normal theory agreed with the results of the permutation approach in previous sections. The data in these problems were well behaved, and the agreement between methods is a testament to how well normal-theory methods work in such cases.

Permutation tests really shine in cases where the data are clearly non-normal (for example, highly skewed), outliers are present, samples sizes are small, or no parametric tests exist. But if the original sample is a poor representation of the population of interest, no test, including permutation tests, will improve the inferences generated.

Permutation tests are primarily useful for generating p-values that can be used to test null hypotheses. They can help answer the question, "Does an effect exist?" It's more difficult to use permutation methods to obtain confidence intervals and estimates of measurement precision. Fortunately, this is an area in which bootstrapping excels.

12.5 Bootstrapping

Bootstrapping generates an empirical distribution of a test statistic or set of test statistics by repeated random sampling with replacement from the original sample. It allows you to generate confidence intervals and test statistical hypotheses without having to assume a specific underlying theoretical distribution.

It's easiest to demonstrate the logic of bootstrapping with an example. Say that you want to calculate the 95% confidence interval for a sample mean. Your sample has 10 observations, a sample mean of 40, and a sample standard deviation of 5. If you're willing to assume that the sampling distribution of the mean is normally distributed, the $(1-\alpha/2)\%$ confidence interval can be calculated using

$$\overline{X} - t\frac{s}{\sqrt{n}} < \mu < \overline{X} + t\frac{s}{\sqrt{n}}$$

where t is the upper $1-\alpha/2$ critical value for a t distribution with $n-1$ degrees of freedom. For a 95% confidence interval, you have $40 - 2.262(5/3.163) < \mu < 40 + 2.262 (5/3.162)$ or $36.424 < \mu < 43.577$. You'd expect 95% of confidence intervals created in this way to surround the true population mean.

But what if you aren't willing to assume that the sampling distribution of the mean is normally distributed? You can use a bootstrapping approach instead:

1. Randomly select 10 observations from the sample, with replacement after each selection. Some observations may be selected more than once, and some may not be selected at all.
2. Calculate and record the sample mean.
3. Repeat the first two steps 1,000 times.
4. Order the 1,000 sample means from smallest to largest.
5. Find the sample means representing the 2.5th and 97.5th percentiles. In this case, it's the 25th number from the bottom and top. These are your 95% confidence limits.

In the present case, where the sample mean is likely to be normally distributed, you gain little from the bootstrap approach. Yet there are many cases where the bootstrap approach is advantageous. What if you wanted confidence intervals for the sample median, or the difference between two sample medians? There are no simple normal-theory formulas here, and bootstrapping is the approach of choice. If the underlying distributions are unknown, if outliers are a problem, if sample sizes are small, or if parametric approaches don't exist, bootstrapping can often provide a useful method of generating confidence intervals and testing hypotheses.

12.6   *Bootstrapping with the boot package*

The `boot` package provides extensive facilities for bootstrapping and related resampling methods. You can bootstrap a single statistic (for example, a median) or a vector of statistics (for example, a set of regression coefficients). Be sure to download and install the `boot` package before first use:

```
install.packages("boot")
```

The bootstrapping process will seem complicated, but once you review the examples it should make sense.

In general, bootstrapping involves three main steps:

1. Write a function that returns the statistic or statistics of interest. If there is a single statistic (for example, a median), the function should return a number. If there is a set of statistics (for example, a set of regression coefficients), the function should return a vector.
2. Process this function through the `boot()` function in order to generate R bootstrap replications of the statistic(s).
3. Use the `boot.ci()` function to obtain confidence intervals for the statistic(s) generated in step 2.

Now to the specifics.

The main bootstrapping function is `boot()`. It has the format

```
bootobject <- boot(data=, statistic=, R=, ...)
```

The parameters are described in table 12.3.

Table 12.3 Parameters of the `boot()` **function**

Parameter	Description
data	A vector, matrix, or data frame.
statistic	A function that produces the k statistics to be bootstrapped (k=1 if bootstrapping a single statistic). The function should include an indices parameter that the `boot()` function can use to select cases for each replication (see the examples in the text).
R	Number of bootstrap replicates.
...	Additional parameters to be passed to the function that produces the statistic of interest.

The `boot()` function calls the statistic function R times. Each time, it generates a set of random indices, with replacement, from the integers `1:nrow(data)`. These indices are used in the statistic function to select a sample. The statistics are calculated on the sample, and the results are accumulated in `bootobject`. The `bootobject` structure is described in table 12.4.

Table 12.4 Elements of the object returned by the `boot()` **function**

Element	Description
t0	The observed values of k statistics applied to the original data
t	An R × k matrix, where each row is a bootstrap replicate of the k statistics

You can access these elements as `bootobject$t0` and `bootobject$t`.

Once you generate the bootstrap samples, you can use `print()` and `plot()` to examine the results. If the results look reasonable, you can use the `boot.ci()` function to obtain confidence intervals for the statistic(s). The format is

```
boot.ci(bootobject, conf=, type= )
```

The parameters are given in table 12.5.

Table 12.5 Parameters of the `boot.ci()` **function**

Parameter	Description
bootobject	The object returned by the `boot()` function.
conf	The desired confidence interval (default: `conf=0.95`).
type	The type of confidence interval returned. Possible values are `norm`, `basic`, `stud`, `perc`, `bca`, and `all` (default: `type="all"`)

The `type` parameter specifies the method for obtaining the confidence limits. The `perc` method (percentile) was demonstrated in the sample mean example. `bca` provides an interval that makes simple adjustments for bias. I find `bca` preferable in most circumstances. See Mooney and Duval (1993) for an introduction to these methods.

In the remaining sections, we'll look at bootstrapping a single statistic and a vector of statistics.

12.6.1 *Bootstrapping a single statistic*

The `mtcars` dataset contains information on 32 automobiles reported in the 1974 *Motor Trend* magazine. Suppose you're using multiple regression to predict miles per gallon from a car's weight (lb/1,000) and engine displacement (cu. in.). In addition to the standard regression statistics, you'd like to obtain a 95% confidence interval for the R-squared value (the percent of variance in the response variable explained by the predictors). The confidence interval can be obtained using nonparametric bootstrapping.

The first task is to write a function for obtaining the R-squared value:

```
rsq <- function(formula, data, indices) {
        d <- data[indices,]
        fit <- lm(formula, data=d)
        return(summary(fit)$r.square)
}
```

The function returns the R-squared value from a regression. The `d <- data[indices,]` statement is required for `boot()` to be able to select samples.

You can then draw a large number of bootstrap replications (say, 1,000) with the following code:

```
library(boot)
set.seed(1234)
results <- boot(data=mtcars, statistic=rsq,
                R=1000, formula=mpg~wt+disp)
```

The boot object can be printed using

```
> print(results)

ORDINARY NONPARAMETRIC BOOTSTRAP


Call:
boot(data = mtcars, statistic = rsq, R = 1000, formula = mpg ~
    wt + disp)


Bootstrap Statistics :
     original      bias    std. error
t1* 0.7809306  0.01333670   0.05068926
```

and plotted using `plot(results)`. The resulting graph is shown in figure 12.2.

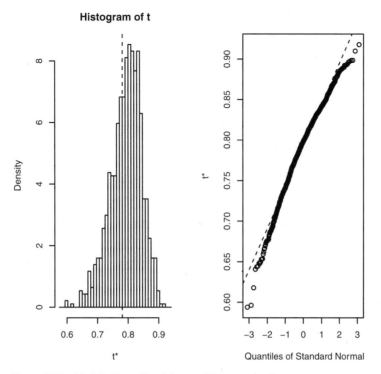

Figure 12.2 **Distribution of bootstrapped R-squared values**

In figure 12.2, you can see that the distribution of bootstrapped R-squared values isn't normally distributed. A 95% confidence interval for the R-squared values can be obtained using

```
> boot.ci(results, type=c("perc", "bca"))
BOOTSTRAP CONFIDENCE INTERVAL CALCULATIONS
Based on 1000 bootstrap replicates

CALL :
boot.ci(boot.out = results, type = c("perc", "bca"))

Intervals :
Level      Percentile             BCa
95%    ( 0.6838,  0.8833 )    ( 0.6344,  0.8549 )
Calculations and Intervals on Original Scale
Some BCa intervals may be unstable
```

You can see from this example that different approaches to generating the confidence intervals can lead to different intervals. In this case, the bias-adjusted interval is moderately different from the percentile method. In either case, the null hypothesis H^0: R-square = 0 would be rejected, because zero is outside the confidence limits.

In this section, you estimated the confidence limits of a single statistic. In the next section, you'll estimate confidence intervals for several statistics.

12.6.2   *Bootstrapping several statistics*

In the previous example, bootstrapping was used to estimate the confidence interval for a single statistic (R-squared). Continuing the example, let's obtain the 95% confidence intervals for a vector of statistics. Specifically, let's get confidence intervals for the three model regression coefficients (intercept, car weight, and engine displacement).

First, create a function that returns the vector of regression coefficients:

```
bs <- function(formula, data, indices) {
        d <- data[indices,]
        fit <- lm(formula, data=d)
        return(coef(fit))
}
```

Then use this function to bootstrap 1,000 replications:

```
library(boot)
set.seed(1234)
results <- boot(data=mtcars, statistic=bs,
                R=1000, formula=mpg~wt+disp)
> print(results)
ORDINARY NONPARAMETRIC BOOTSTRAP
Call:
boot(data = mtcars, statistic = bs, R = 1000, formula = mpg ~
    wt + disp)


Bootstrap Statistics :
     original      bias    std. error
t1*   34.9606  0.137873       2.48576
t2*   -3.3508 -0.053904       1.17043
t3*   -0.0177 -0.000121       0.00879
```

When bootstrapping multiple statistics, add an index parameter to the plot() and boot.ci() functions to indicate which column of bootobject$t to analyze. In this example, index 1 refers to the intercept, index 2 is car weight, and index 3 is the engine displacement. To plot the results for car weight, use

```
plot(results, index=2)
```

The graph is given in figure 12.3.

To get the 95% confidence intervals for car weight and engine displacement, use

```
> boot.ci(results, type="bca", index=2)
BOOTSTRAP CONFIDENCE INTERVAL CALCULATIONS
Based on 1000 bootstrap replicates

CALL :
boot.ci(boot.out = results, type = "bca", index = 2)

Intervals :
Level        BCa
95%    (-5.66, -1.19 )
Calculations and Intervals on Original Scale
```

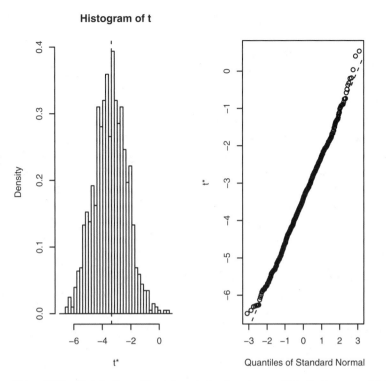

Figure 12.3   Distribution of bootstrapping regression coefficients for car weight

```
> boot.ci(results, type="bca", index=3)

BOOTSTRAP CONFIDENCE INTERVAL CALCULATIONS
Based on 1000 bootstrap replicates

CALL :
boot.ci(boot.out = results, type = "bca", index = 3)

Intervals :
Level       BCa
95%    (-0.0331,  0.0010 )
Calculations and Intervals on Original Scale
```

NOTE   The previous example resamples the entire sample of data each time. If you can assume that the predictor variables have fixed levels (typical in planned experiments), you'd do better to only resample residual terms. See Mooney and Duval (1993, pp. 16–17) for a simple explanation and algorithm.

Before we leave bootstrapping, it's worth addressing two questions that come up often:

- How large does the original sample need to be?
- How many replications are needed?

There's no simple answer to the first question. Some say that an original sample size of 20–30 is sufficient for good results, as long as the sample is representative of the population. Random sampling from the population of interest is the most trusted method for assuring the original sample's representativeness. With regard to the second question, I find that 1,000 replications are more than adequate in most cases. Computer power is cheap, and you can always increase the number of replications if desired.

There are many helpful sources of information about permutation tests and bootstrapping. An excellent starting place is an online article by Yu (2003). Good (2006) provides a comprehensive overview of resampling in general and includes R code. A good, accessible introduction to bootstrapping is provided by Mooney and Duval (1993). The definitive source on bootstrapping is Efron and Tibshirani (1998). Finally, there are a number of great online resources, including Simon (1997), Canty (2002), Shah (2005), and Fox (2002).

12.7 *Summary*

This chapter introduced a set of computer-intensive methods based on randomization and resampling that allow you to test hypotheses and form confidence intervals without reference to a known theoretical distribution. They're particularly valuable when your data comes from unknown population distributions, when there are serious outliers, when your sample sizes are small, and when there are no existing parametric methods to answer the hypotheses of interest.

The methods in this chapter are particularly exciting because they provide an avenue for answering questions when your standard data assumptions are clearly untenable or when you have no other idea how to approach the problem. Permutation tests and bootstrapping aren't panaceas, though. They can't turn bad data into good data. If your original samples aren't representative of the population of interest or are too small to accurately reflect it, then these techniques won't help.

In the next chapter, we'll consider data models for variables that follow known, but not necessarily normal, distributions.

Part 4

Advanced methods

In this part of the book, we'll consider advanced methods of statistical analysis to round out your data analysis toolkit. The methods in this part play a key role in the growing field of data mining and predictive analytics.

Chapter 13 expands on the regression methods in chapter 8 to cover parametric approaches to data that are not normally distributed. The chapter starts with a discussion of the generalized linear model and then focuses on cases where you're trying to predict an outcome variable that is either categorical (logistic regression) or a count (Poisson regression).

Dealing with a large number of variables can be challenging, due to the complexity inherent in multivariate data. Chapter 14 describes two popular methods for exploring and simplifying multivariate data. Principal components analysis can be used to transform a large number of correlated variables into a smaller set of composite variables. Factor analysis consists of a set of techniques for uncovering the latent structure underlying a given set of variables. Chapter 14 provides step-by-step instructions for carrying out each.

Chapter 15 explores time-dependent data. Analysts are frequently faced with the need to understand trends and predict future events. Chapter 15 provides a thorough introduction to the analysis of time-series data and forecasting. After describing the general characteristics of time series data, two of the most popular forecasting approaches (Exponential and ARIMA) are illustrated.

Cluster analysis is the subject of chapter 16. While principal components and factor analysis simplify multivariate data by combining individual variables into composite variables, cluster analysis attempts to simplify multivariate data by combining individual observations into subgroups called *clusters*. Clusters contain cases that are similar to each other and different from the cases in other clusters. The chapter considers methods for determining the number of clusters present in a data set and combining observations into these clusters.

Chapter 17 addresses the important topic of classification. In classification problems, the analyst attempts to develop a model for predicting the group membership of new cases (for example, good credit/bad credit risk, benign/malignant, pass/fail) from a (potentially large) set of predictor variables. A wide variety of methods are considered, including logistic regression, decision trees, random forests, and support-vector machines. Methods for assessing the efficacy of the resulting classification models are also described.

In practice, researchers must often deal with incomplete datasets. Chapter 18 considers modern approaches to the ubiquitous problem of missing data values. R supports a number of elegant approaches for analyzing datasets that are incomplete for various reasons. Several of the best are described here, along with guidance about which ones to use and which ones to avoid.

After completing part 4, you'll have the tools to manage a wide range of complex data-analysis problems. This includes modeling non-normal outcome variables, dealing with large numbers of correlated variables, reducing a large number of cases to a smaller number of homogeneous clusters, developing models to predict future values or categorical outcomes, and handling messy and incomplete data.

Generalized linear models

13

This chapter covers

- Formulating a generalized linear model
- Predicting categorical outcomes
- Modeling count data

In chapters 8 (regression) and 9 (ANOVA), we explored linear models that can be used to predict a normally distributed response variable from a set of continuous and/or categorical predictor variables. But there are many situations in which it's unreasonable to assume that the dependent variable is normally distributed (or even continuous). For example:

- The outcome variable may be categorical. Binary variables (for example, yes/no, passed/failed, lived/died) and polytomous variables (for example, poor/good/excellent, republican/democrat/independent) clearly aren't normally distributed.
- The outcome variable may be a count (for example, number of traffic accidents in a week, number of drinks per day). Such variables take on a limited number of values and are never negative. Additionally, their mean and variance are often related (which isn't true for normally distributed variables).

Generalized linear models extend the linear-model framework to include dependent variables that are decidedly non-normal.

In this chapter, we'll start with a brief overview of generalized linear models and the glm() function used to estimate them. Then we'll focus on two popular models in this framework: logistic regression (where the dependent variable is categorical) and Poisson regression (where the dependent variable is a count variable).

To motivate the discussion, you'll apply generalized linear models to two research questions that aren't easily addressed with standard linear models:

- What personal, demographic, and relationship variables predict marital infidelity? In this case, the outcome variable is binary (affair/no affair).
- What impact does a drug treatment for seizures have on the number of seizures experienced over an eight-week period? In this case, the outcome variable is a count (number of seizures).

You'll apply logistic regression to address the first question and Poison regression to address the second. Along the way, we'll consider extensions of each technique.

13.1 *Generalized linear models and the glm() function*

A wide range of popular data-analytic methods are subsumed within the framework of the generalized linear model. In this section, we'll briefly explore some of the theory behind this approach. You can safely skip this section if you like and come back to it later.

Let's say that you want to model the relationship between a response variable Y and a set of p predictor variables $X_1 \ldots X_p$. In the standard linear model, you assume that Y is normally distributed and that the form of the relationship is

$$\mu_Y = \beta_0 + \sum_{j=1}^{p} \beta_j X_j$$

This equation states that the conditional mean of the response variable is a linear combination of the predictor variables. The β_j are the parameters specifying the expected change in Y for a unit change in X_j, and β_0 is the expected value of Y when all the predictor variables are 0. You're saying that you can predict the mean of the Y distribution for observations with a given set of X values by applying the proper weights to the X variables and adding them up.

Note that you've made no distributional assumptions about the predictor variables, X_j. Unlike Y, there's no requirement that they be normally distributed. In fact, they're often categorical (for example, ANOVA designs). Additionally, nonlinear functions of the predictors are allowed. You often include such predictors as X^2 or $X_1 \times X_2$. What is important is that the equation is linear in the parameters (β_0, β_1,... β_p).

In generalized linear models, you fit models of the form

$$g(\mu_Y) = \beta_0 + \sum_{j=1}^{p} \beta_j X_j$$

where $g(\mu_Y)$ is a function of the conditional mean (called the *link function*). Additionally, you relax the assumption that Y is normally distributed. Instead, you assume that Y follows a distribution that's a member of the exponential family. You specify the link function and the probability distribution, and the parameters are derived through an iterative maximum-likelihood-estimation procedure.

13.1.1　*The glm() function*

Generalized linear models are typically fit in R through the glm() function (although other specialized functions are available). The form of the function is similar to lm() but includes additional parameters. The basic format of the function is

```
glm(formula, family=family(link=function), data=)
```

where the probability distribution (*family*) and corresponding default link function (*function*) are given in table 13.1.

Table 13.1　glm() **parameters**

Family	Default link function
binomial	(link = "logit")
gaussian	(link = "identity")
gamma	(link = "inverse")
inverse.gaussian	(link = "1/mu^2")
poisson	(link = "log")
quasi	(link = "identity", variance = "constant")
quasibinomial	(link = "logit")
quasipoisson	(link = "log")

The glm() function allows you to fit a number of popular models, including logistic regression, Poisson regression, and survival analysis (not considered here). You can demonstrate this for the first two models as follows. Assume that you have a single response variable (Y), three predictor variables (X1, X2, X3), and a data frame (mydata) containing the data.

Logistic regression is applied to situations in which the response variable is dichotomous (0 or 1). The model assumes that Y follows a binomial distribution and that you can fit a linear model of the form

$$\log_e\left(\frac{\pi}{1-\pi}\right) = \beta_0 + \sum_{j=1}^{p}\beta_j X_j$$

where $\pi = \mu_Y$ is the conditional mean of Y (that is, the probability that Y = 1 given a set of X values), $(\pi/1 - \pi)$ is the odds that Y = 1, and $\log(\pi/1 - \pi)$ is the log odds, or *logit*.

In this case, $\log(\pi/1 - \pi)$ is the link function, the probability distribution is binomial, and the logistic regression model can be fit using

```
glm(Y~X1+X2+X3, family=binomial(link="logit"), data=mydata)
```

Logistic regression is described more fully in section 13.2.

Poisson regression is applied to situations in which the response variable is the number of events to occur in a given period of time. The Poisson regression model assumes that Y follows a Poisson distribution and that you can fit a linear model of the form

$$\log_e(\lambda) = \beta_0 + \sum\nolimits_{j=1}^{p} \beta_j X_j$$

where λ is the mean (and variance) of Y. In this case, the link function is $\log(\lambda)$, the probability distribution is Poisson, and the Poisson regression model can be fit using

```
glm(Y~X1+X2+X3, family=poisson(link="log"), data=mydata)
```

Poisson regression is described in section 13.3.

It's worth noting that the standard linear model is also a special case of the generalized linear model. If you let the link function $g(\mu_Y) = \mu_Y$ or the identity function and specify that the probability distribution is normal (Gaussian), then

```
glm(Y~X1+X2+X3, family=gaussian(link="identity"), data=mydata)
```

would produce the same results as

```
lm(Y~X1+X2+X3, data=mydata)
```

To summarize, generalized linear models extend the standard linear model by fitting a *function* of the conditional mean response (rather than the conditional mean response) and assuming that the response variable follows a member of the *exponential* family of distributions (rather than being limited to the normal distribution). The parameter estimates are derived via maximum likelihood rather than least squares.

13.1.2 *Supporting functions*

Many of the functions that you used in conjunction with `lm()` when analyzing standard linear models have corresponding versions for `glm()`. Some commonly used functions are given in table 13.2.

Table 13.2 Functions that support `glm()`

Function	Description
`summary()`	Displays detailed results for the fitted model
`coefficients()`, `coef()`	Lists the model parameters (intercept and slopes) for the fitted model
`confint()`	Provides confidence intervals for the model parameters (95% by default)
`residuals()`	Lists the residual values in a fitted model
`anova()`	Generates an ANOVA table comparing two fitted models

Table 13.2 Functions that support `glm()`

Function	Description
`plot()`	Generates diagnostic plots for evaluating the fit of a model
`predict()`	Uses a fitted model to predict response values for a new dataset
`deviance()`	Deviance for the fitted model
`df.residual()`	Residual degrees of freedom for the fitted model

We'll explore examples of these functions in later sections. In the next section, we'll briefly consider the assessment of model adequacy.

13.1.3 *Model fit and regression diagnostics*

The assessment of model adequacy is as important for generalized linear models as it is for standard (OLS) linear models. Unfortunately, there's less agreement in the statistical community regarding appropriate assessment procedures. In general, you can use the techniques described in chapter 8, with the following caveats.

When assessing model adequacy, you'll typically want to plot predicted values expressed in the metric of the original response variable against residuals of the deviance type. For example, a common diagnostic plot would be

```
plot(predict(model, type="response"),
    residuals(model, type= "deviance"))
```

where `model` is the object returned by the `glm()` function.

The hat values, studentized residuals, and Cook's D statistics that R provides will be approximate values. Additionally, there's no general consensus on cutoff values for identifying problematic observations. Values have to be judged relative to each other. One approach is to create index plots for each statistic and look for unusually large values. For example, you could use the following code to create three diagnostic plots:

```
plot(hatvalues(model))
plot(rstudent(model))
plot(cooks.distance(model))
```

Alternatively, you could use the code

```
library(car)
influencePlot(model)
```

to create one omnibus plot. In the latter graph, the horizontal axis is the leverage, the vertical axis is the studentized residual, and the plotted symbol is proportional to the Cook's distance.

Diagnostic plots tend to be most helpful when the response variable takes on many values. When the response variable can only take on a limited number of values (for example, logistic regression), the utility of these plots is decreased.

For more on regression diagnostics for generalized linear models, see Fox (2008) and Faraway (2006). In the remaining portion of this chapter, we'll consider two of the most popular forms of the generalized linear model in detail: logistic regression and Poisson regression.

13.2   *Logistic regression*

Logistic regression is useful when you're predicting a binary outcome from a set of continuous and/or categorical predictor variables. To demonstrate this, let's explore the data on infidelity contained in the data frame `Affairs`, provided with the AER package. Be sure to download and install the package (using `install.pack-ages("AER")`) before first use.

The infidelity data, known as Fair's Affairs, is based on a cross-sectional survey conducted by *Psychology Today* in 1969 and is described in Greene (2003) and Fair (1978). It contains 9 variables collected on 601 participants and includes how often the respondent engaged in extramarital sexual intercourse during the past year, as well as their gender, age, years married, whether they had children, their religiousness (on a 5-point scale from 1=anti to 5=very), education, occupation (Hollingshead 7-point classification with reverse numbering), and a numeric self-rating of their marriage (from 1=very unhappy to 5=very happy).

Let's look at some descriptive statistics:

```
> data(Affairs, package="AER")
> summary(Affairs)
     affairs            gender          age          yearsmarried      children
 Min.   : 0.000   female:315   Min.   :17.50   Min.   : 0.125   no :171
 1st Qu.: 0.000   male  :286   1st Qu.:27.00   1st Qu.: 4.000   yes:430
 Median : 0.000                Median :32.00   Median : 7.000
 Mean   : 1.456                Mean   :32.49   Mean   : 8.178
 3rd Qu.: 0.000                3rd Qu.:37.00   3rd Qu.:15.000
 Max.   :12.000                Max.   :57.00   Max.   :15.000
 religiousness      education       occupation       rating
 Min.   :1.000   Min.   : 9.00   Min.   :1.000   Min.   :1.000
 1st Qu.:2.000   1st Qu.:14.00   1st Qu.:3.000   1st Qu.:3.000
 Median :3.000   Median :16.00   Median :5.000   Median :4.000
 Mean   :3.116   Mean   :16.17   Mean   :4.195   Mean   :3.932
 3rd Qu.:4.000   3rd Qu.:18.00   3rd Qu.:6.000   3rd Qu.:5.000
 Max.   :5.000   Max.   :20.00   Max.   :7.000   Max.   :5.000

> table(Affairs$affairs)
  0   1   2   3   7  12
451  34  17  19  42  38
```

From these statistics, you can see that that 52% of respondents were female, that 72% had children, and that the median age for the sample was 32 years. With regard to the response variable, 75% of respondents reported not engaging in an infidelity in the past year (451/601). The largest number of encounters reported was 12 (6%).

Although the *number* of indiscretions was recorded, your interest here is in the binary outcome (had an affair/didn't have an affair). You can transform affairs into a dichotomous factor called ynaffair with the following code.

```
> Affairs$ynaffair[Affairs$affairs  > 0]  <- 1
> Affairs$ynaffair[Affairs$affairs == 0]  <- 0
```

```
> Affairs$ynaffair <- factor(Affairs$ynaffair,
                             levels=c(0,1),
                             labels=c("No","Yes"))
> table(Affairs$ynaffair)
No Yes
451 150
```

This dichotomous factor can now be used as the outcome variable in a logistic regression model:

```
> fit.full <- glm(ynaffair ~ gender + age + yearsmarried + children +
                  religiousness + education + occupation +rating,
                  data=Affairs, family=binomial())
> summary(fit.full)

Call:
glm(formula = ynaffair ~ gender + age + yearsmarried + children +
    religiousness + education + occupation + rating, family = binomial(),
    data = Affairs)

Deviance Residuals:
   Min      1Q   Median      3Q     Max
-1.571  -0.750   -0.569  -0.254   2.519

Coefficients:
               Estimate Std. Error z value Pr(>|z|)
(Intercept)      1.3773     0.8878    1.55  0.12081
gendermale       0.2803     0.2391    1.17  0.24108
age             -0.0443     0.0182   -2.43  0.01530 *
yearsmarried     0.0948     0.0322    2.94  0.00326 **
childrenyes      0.3977     0.2915    1.36  0.17251
religiousness   -0.3247     0.0898   -3.62  0.00030 ***
education        0.0211     0.0505    0.42  0.67685
occupation       0.0309     0.0718    0.43  0.66663
rating          -0.4685     0.0909   -5.15  2.6e-07 ***
---
Signif. codes:  0 '***' 0.001 '**' 0.01 '*' 0.05 '.' 0.1 ' ' 1

(Dispersion parameter for binomial family taken to be 1)

    Null deviance: 675.38  on 600  degrees of freedom
Residual deviance: 609.51  on 592  degrees of freedom
AIC: 627.5

Number of Fisher Scoring iterations: 4
```

From the p-values for the regression coefficients (last column), you can see that gender, presence of children, education, and occupation may not make a significant contribution to the equation (you can't reject the hypothesis that the parameters are 0). Let's fit a second equation without them and test whether this reduced model fits the data as well:

```
> fit.reduced <- glm(ynaffair ~ age + yearsmarried + religiousness +
                    rating, data=Affairs, family=binomial())
> summary(fit.reduced)
```

```
Call:
glm(formula = ynaffair ~ age + yearsmarried + religiousness + rating,
    family = binomial(), data = Affairs)

Deviance Residuals:
    Min      1Q   Median      3Q      Max
 -1.628   -0.755   -0.570   -0.262    2.400

Coefficients:
              Estimate Std. Error z value Pr(>|z|)
(Intercept)     1.9308     0.6103    3.16  0.00156 **
age            -0.0353     0.0174   -2.03  0.04213 *
yearsmarried    0.1006     0.0292    3.44  0.00057 ***
religiousness  -0.3290     0.0895   -3.68  0.00023 ***
rating         -0.4614     0.0888   -5.19  2.1e-07 ***
---
Signif. codes:  0 '***' 0.001 '**' 0.01 '*' 0.05 '.' 0.1 ' ' 1

(Dispersion parameter for binomial family taken to be 1)

    Null deviance: 675.38  on 600   degrees of freedom
Residual deviance: 615.36  on 596   degrees of freedom
AIC: 625.4

Number of Fisher Scoring iterations: 4
```

Each regression coefficient in the reduced model is statistically significant ($p < .05$).
Because the two models are nested (fit.reduced is a subset of fit.full), you can use
the anova() function to compare them. For generalized linear models, you'll want a
chi-square version of this test:

```
> anova(fit.reduced, fit.full, test="Chisq")
Analysis of Deviance Table

Model 1: ynaffair ~ age + yearsmarried + religiousness + rating
Model 2: ynaffair ~ gender + age + yearsmarried + children +
    religiousness + education + occupation + rating
  Resid. Df Resid. Dev Df Deviance P(>|Chi|)
1       596        615
2       592        610  4     5.85      0.21
```

The nonsignificant chi-square value ($p = 0.21$) suggests that the reduced model with
four predictors fits as well as the full model with nine predictors, reinforcing your
belief that gender, children, education, and occupation don't add significantly to the
prediction above and beyond the other variables in the equation. Therefore, you can
base your interpretations on the simpler model.

13.2.1 *Interpreting the model parameters*

Let's look at the regression coefficients:

```
> coef(fit.reduced)
  (Intercept)           age yearsmarried religiousness       rating
        1.931        -0.035        0.101        -0.329       -0.461
```

In a logistic regression, the response being modeled is the log(odds) that Y = 1. The regression coefficients give the change in log(odds) in the response for a unit change in the predictor variable, holding all other predictor variables constant.

Because log(odds) are difficult to interpret, you can exponentiate them to put the results on an odds scale:

```
> exp(coef(fit.reduced))
  (Intercept)          age  yearsmarried religiousness        rating
        6.895        0.965         1.106         0.720         0.630
```

Now you can see that the odds of an extramarital encounter are increased by a factor of 1.106 for a one-year increase in years married (holding age, religiousness, and marital rating constant). Conversely, the odds of an extramarital affair are multiplied by a factor of 0.965 for every year increase in age. The odds of an extramarital affair increase with years married and decrease with age, religiousness, and marital rating. Because the predictor variables can't equal 0, the intercept isn't meaningful in this case.

If desired, you can use the confint() function to obtain confidence intervals for the coefficients. For example, exp(confint(fit.reduced)) would print 95% confidence intervals for each of the coefficients on an odds scale.

Finally, a one-unit change in a predictor variable may not be inherently interesting. For binary logistic regression, the change in the odds of the higher value on the response variable for an n unit change in a predictor variable is $\exp(\beta_j)^n$. If a one-year increase in years married multiplies the odds of an affair by 1.106, a 10-year increase would increase the odds by a factor of 1.106^{10}, or 2.7, holding the other predictor variables constant.

13.2.2 Assessing the impact of predictors on the probability of an outcome

For many of us, it's easier to think in terms of probabilities than odds. You can use the predict() function to observe the impact of varying the levels of a predictor variable on the probability of the outcome. The first step is to create an artificial dataset containing the values of the predictor variables you're interested in. Then you can use this artificial dataset with the predict() function to predict the probabilities of the outcome event occurring for these values.

Let's apply this strategy to assess the impact of marital ratings on the probability of having an extramarital affair. First, create an artificial dataset where age, years married, and religiousness are set to their means, and marital rating varies from 1 to 5:

```
> testdata <- data.frame(rating=c(1, 2, 3, 4, 5), age=mean(Affairs$age),
                         yearsmarried=mean(Affairs$yearsmarried),
                         religiousness=mean(Affairs$religiousness))
> testdata
  rating  age yearsmarried religiousness
1      1 32.5         8.18          3.12
2      2 32.5         8.18          3.12
3      3 32.5         8.18          3.12
4      4 32.5         8.18          3.12
5      5 32.5         8.18          3.12
```

Next, use the test dataset and prediction equation to obtain probabilities:

```
> testdata$prob <- predict(fit.reduced, newdata=testdata, type="response")
  testdata
  rating  age yearsmarried religiousness  prob
1      1 32.5         8.18          3.12 0.530
2      2 32.5         8.18          3.12 0.416
3      3 32.5         8.18          3.12 0.310
4      4 32.5         8.18          3.12 0.220
5      5 32.5         8.18          3.12 0.151
```

From these results, you see that the probability of an extramarital affair decreases from 0.53 when the marriage is rated 1=very unhappy to 0.15 when the marriage is rated 5=very happy (holding age, years married, and religiousness constant). Now look at the impact of age:

```
> testdata <- data.frame(rating=mean(Affairs$rating),
                         age=seq(17, 57, 10),
                         yearsmarried=mean(Affairs$yearsmarried),
                         religiousness=mean(Affairs$religiousness))
> testdata
  rating age yearsmarried religiousness
1   3.93  17         8.18          3.12
2   3.93  27         8.18          3.12
3   3.93  37         8.18          3.12
4   3.93  47         8.18          3.12
5   3.93  57         8.18          3.12

> testdata$prob <- predict(fit.reduced, newdata=testdata, type="response")
> testdata
  rating age yearsmarried religiousness    prob
1   3.93  17         8.18          3.12   0.335
2   3.93  27         8.18          3.12   0.262
3   3.93  37         8.18          3.12   0.199
4   3.93  47         8.18          3.12   0.149
5   3.93  57         8.18          3.12   0.109
```

Here, you see that as age increases from 17 to 57, the probability of an extramarital encounter decreases from 0.34 to 0.11, holding the other variables constant. Using this approach, you can explore the impact of each predictor variable on the outcome.

13.2.3 *Overdispersion*

The expected variance for data drawn from a binomial distribution is $\sigma^2 = n\pi(1 - \pi)$, where n is the number of observations and π is the probability of belonging to the $Y = 1$ group. *Overdispersion* occurs when the observed variance of the response variable is larger than what would be expected from a binomial distribution. Overdispersion can lead to distorted test standard errors and inaccurate tests of significance.

When overdispersion is present, you can still fit a logistic regression using the `glm()` function, but in this case, you should use the quasibinomial distribution rather than the binomial distribution.

One way to detect overdispersion is to compare the residual deviance with the residual degrees of freedom in your binomial model. If the ratio

$$\phi' = \frac{Residual\ deviance}{Residual\ df}$$

is considerably larger than 1, you have evidence of overdispersion. Applying this to the `Affairs` example, you have

```
> deviance(fit.reduced)/df.residual(fit.reduced)
[1] 1.032
```

which is close to 1, suggesting no overdispersion.

You can also test for overdispersion. To do this, you fit the model twice, but in the first instance you use `family="binomial"` and in the second instance you use `family="quasibinomial"`. If the `glm()` object returned in the first case is called `fit` and the object returned in the second case is called `fit.od`, then

```
pchisq(summary(fit.od)$dispersion * fit$df.residual,
       fit$df.residual, lower = F)
```

provides the p-value for testing the null hypothesis $H_0: \phi = 1$ versus the alternative hypothesis $H_1: \phi \neq 1$. If p is small (say, less than 0.05), you'd reject the null hypothesis.

Applying this to the `Affairs` dataset, you have

```
> fit <- glm(ynaffair ~ age + yearsmarried + religiousness +
             rating, family = binomial(), data = Affairs)
> fit.od <- glm(ynaffair ~ age + yearsmarried + religiousness +
                rating, family = quasibinomial(), data = Affairs)
> pchisq(summary(fit.od)$dispersion * fit$df.residual,
         fit$df.residual, lower = F)

[1] 0.34
```

The resulting p-value (0.34) is clearly not significant (p > 0.05), strengthening your belief that overdispersion isn't a problem. We'll return to the issue of overdispersion when we discuss Poisson regression.

13.2.4 *Extensions*

Several logistic regression extensions and variations are available in R:

- *Robust logistic regression*—The `glmRob()` function in the `robust` package can be used to fit a robust generalized linear model, including robust logistic regression. Robust logistic regression can be helpful when fitting logistic regression models to data containing outliers and influential observations.
- *Multinomial logistic regression*—If the response variable has more than two unordered categories (for example, married/widowed/divorced), you can fit a polytomous logistic regression using the `mlogit()` function in the `mlogit` package.
- *Ordinal logistic regression*—If the response variable is a set of ordered categories (for example, credit risk as poor/good/excellent), you can fit an ordinal logistic regression using the `lrm()` function in the `rms` package.

The ability to model a response variable with multiple categories (both ordered and unordered) is an important extension, but it comes at the expense of greater interpretive complexity. Assessing model fit and regression diagnostics in these cases will also be more complex.

In the Affairs example, the number of extramarital contacts was dichotomized into a yes/no response variable because our interest centered on whether respondents had an affair in the past year. If our interest had been centered on magnitude—the number of encounters in the past year—we would have analyzed the count data directly. One popular approach to analyzing count data is Poisson regression, the next topic we'll address.

13.3   *Poisson regression*

Poisson regression is useful when you're predicting an outcome variable representing counts from a set of continuous and/or categorical predictor variables. A comprehensive yet accessible introduction to Poisson regression is provided by Coxe, West, and Aiken (2009).

To illustrate the fitting of a Poisson regression model, along with some issues that can come up in the analysis, we'll use the Breslow seizure data (Breslow, 1993) provided in the robust package. Specifically, we'll consider the impact of an antiepileptic drug treatment on the number of seizures occurring over an eight-week period following the initiation of therapy. Be sure to install the robust package before continuing.

Data were collected on the age and number of seizures reported by patients suffering from simple or complex partial seizures during an eight-week period before, and eight-week period after, randomization into a drug or placebo condition. SumY (the number of seizures in the eight-week period post-randomization) is the response variable. Treatment condition (Trt), age in years (Age), and number of seizures reported in the baseline eight-week period (Base) are the predictor variables. The baseline number of seizures and age are included because of their potential effect on the response variable. We're interested in whether or not evidence exists that the drug treatment decreases the number of seizures after accounting for these covariates.

First, let's look at summary statistics for the dataset:

```
> data(breslow.dat, package="robust")
> names(breslow.dat)
 [1] "ID"    "Y1"    "Y2"    "Y3"    "Y4"    "Base"  "Age"   "Trt"   "Ysum"
[10] "sumY"  "Age10" "Base4"

> summary(breslow.dat[c(6,7,8,10)])
      Base            Age              Trt           sumY
 Min.   :  6.0   Min.   :18.0   placebo  :28   Min.   :  0.0
 1st Qu.: 12.0   1st Qu.:23.0   progabide:31   1st Qu.: 11.5
 Median : 22.0   Median :28.0                  Median : 16.0
 Mean   : 31.2   Mean   :28.3                  Mean   : 33.1
 3rd Qu.: 41.0   3rd Qu.:32.0                  3rd Qu.: 36.0
 Max.   :151.0   Max.   :42.0                  Max.   :302.0
```

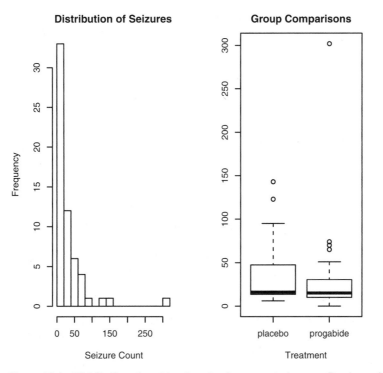

Figure 13.1   **Distribution of post-treatment seizure counts (source: Breslow seizure data)**

Note that although there are 12 variables in the dataset, we're limiting our attention to the 4 described earlier. Both the baseline and post-randomization number of seizures are highly skewed. Let's look at the response variable in more detail. The following code produces the graphs in figure 13.1:

```
opar <- par(no.readonly=TRUE)
par(mfrow=c(1,2))
attach(breslow.dat)
hist(sumY, breaks=20, xlab="Seizure Count",
    main="Distribution of Seizures")
boxplot(sumY ~ Trt, xlab="Treatment", main="Group Comparisons")
par(opar)
```

You can clearly see the skewed nature of the dependent variable and the possible presence of outliers. At first glance, the number of seizures in the drug condition appears to be smaller and has a smaller variance. (You'd expect a smaller variance to accompany a smaller mean with Poisson distributed data.) Unlike standard OLS regression, this heterogeneity of variance isn't a problem in Poisson regression.

The next step is to fit the Poisson regression:

```
> fit <- glm(sumY ~ Base + Age + Trt, data=breslow.dat, family=poisson())
> summary(fit)
```

```
Call:
glm(formula = sumY ~ Base + Age + Trt, family = poisson(), data =
    breslow.dat)

Deviance Residuals:
   Min      1Q  Median      3Q     Max
-6.057  -2.043  -0.940   0.793  11.006

Coefficients:
              Estimate Std. Error z value Pr(>|z|)
(Intercept)   1.948826   0.135619   14.37  < 2e-16 ***
Base          0.022652   0.000509   44.48  < 2e-16 ***
Age           0.022740   0.004024    5.65  1.6e-08 ***
Trtprogabide -0.152701   0.047805   -3.19   0.0014 **
---
Signif. codes:  0 '***' 0.001 '**' 0.01 '*' 0.05 '.' 0.1 ' ' 1

(Dispersion parameter for poisson family taken to be 1)

    Null deviance: 2122.73  on 58  degrees of freedom
Residual deviance:  559.44  on 55  degrees of freedom
AIC: 850.7

Number of Fisher Scoring iterations: 5
```

The output provides the deviances, regression parameters, and standard errors, and tests that these parameters are 0. Note that each of the predictor variables is significant at the p < 0.05 level.

13.3.1 *Interpreting the model parameters*

The model coefficients are obtained using the coef() function or by examining the Coefficients table in the summary() function output:

```
> coef(fit)
  (Intercept)         Base          Age Trtprogabide
       1.9488       0.0227       0.0227      -0.1527
```

In a Poisson regression, the dependent variable being modeled is the log of the conditional mean $\log_e(\lambda)$. The regression parameter 0.0227 for Age indicates that a one-year increase in age is associated with a 0.03 increase in the log mean number of seizures, holding baseline seizures and treatment condition constant. The intercept is the log mean number of seizures when each of the predictors equals 0. Because you can't have a zero age and none of the participants had a zero number of baseline seizures, the intercept isn't meaningful in this case.

It's usually much easier to interpret the regression coefficients in the original scale of the dependent variable (number of seizures, rather than log number of seizures). To accomplish this, exponentiate the coefficients:

```
> exp(coef(fit))
  (Intercept)         Base          Age Trtprogabide
        7.020        1.023        1.023        0.858
```

Now you see that a one-year increase in age *multiplies* the expected number of seizures by 1.023, holding the other variables constant. This means that increased age is associated with higher numbers of seizures. More important, a one-unit change in Trt (that is, moving from placebo to progabide) multiplies the expected number of seizures by 0.86. You'd expect a 20% decrease in the number of seizures for the drug group compared with the placebo group, holding baseline number of seizures and age constant.

It's important to remember that, like the exponentiated parameters in logistic regression, the exponentiated parameters in the Poisson model have a multiplicative rather than an additive effect on the response variable. Also, as with logistic regression, you must evaluate your model for overdispersion.

13.3.2 *Overdispersion*

In a Poisson distribution, the variance and mean are equal. Overdispersion occurs in Poisson regression when the observed variance of the response variable is larger than would be predicted by the Poisson distribution. Because overdispersion is often encountered when dealing with count data and can have a negative impact on the interpretation of the results, we'll spend some time discussing it.

There are several reasons why overdispersion may occur (Coxe et al., 2009):

- The omission of an important predictor variable can lead to overdispersion.
- Overdispersion can also be caused by a phenomenon known as *state dependence*. Within observations, each event in a count is assumed to be independent. For the seizure data, this would imply that for any patient, the probability of a seizure is independent of each other seizure. But this assumption is often untenable. For a given individual, the probability of having a first seizure is unlikely to be the same as the probability of having a 40th seizure, given that they've already had 39.
- In longitudinal studies, overdispersion can be caused by the clustering inherent in repeated measures data. We won't discuss longitudinal Poisson models here.

If overdispersion is present and you don't account for it in your model, you'll get standard errors and confidence intervals that are too small, and significance tests that are too liberal (that is, you'll find effects that aren't really there).

As with logistic regression, overdispersion is suggested if the ratio of the residual deviance to the residual degrees of freedom is much larger than 1. For the seizure data, the ratio is

```
> deviance(fit)/df.residual(fit)
[1] 10.17
```

which is clearly much larger than 1.

The qcc package provides a test for overdispersion in the Poisson case. (Be sure to download and install this package before first use.) You can test for overdispersion in the seizure data using the following code:

```
> library(qcc)
> qcc.overdispersion.test(breslow.dat$sumY, type="poisson")
```

```
Overdispersion test Obs.Var/Theor.Var Statistic p-value
        poisson data                 62.9      3646       0
```

Not surprisingly, the significance test has a p-value less than 0.05, strongly suggesting the presence of overdispersion.

You can still fit a model to your data using the glm() function, by replacing family="poisson" with family="quasipoisson". Doing so is analogous to the approach to logistic regression when overdispersion is present:

```
> fit.od <- glm(sumY ~ Base + Age + Trt, data=breslow.dat,
                family=quasipoisson())
> summary(fit.od)

Call:
glm(formula = sumY ~ Base + Age + Trt, family = quasipoisson(),
    data = breslow.dat)

Deviance Residuals:
   Min      1Q  Median      3Q     Max
-6.057  -2.043  -0.940   0.793  11.006

Coefficients:
             Estimate Std. Error t value Pr(>|t|)
(Intercept)   1.94883    0.46509    4.19  0.00010 ***
Base          0.02265    0.00175   12.97  < 2e-16 ***
Age           0.02274    0.01380    1.65  0.10509
Trtprogabide -0.15270    0.16394   -0.93  0.35570
---
Signif. codes:  0 '***' 0.001 '**' 0.01 '*' 0.05 '.' 0.1 ' ' 1

(Dispersion parameter for quasipoisson family taken to be 11.8)

    Null deviance: 2122.73  on 58  degrees of freedom
Residual deviance:  559.44  on 55  degrees of freedom
AIC: NA

Number of Fisher Scoring iterations: 5
```

Notice that the parameter estimates in the quasi-Poisson approach are identical to those produced by the Poisson approach. The standard errors are much larger, though. In this case, the larger standard errors have led to p-values for Trt (and Age) that are greater than 0.05. When you take overdispersion into account, there's insufficient evidence to declare that the drug regimen reduces seizure counts more than receiving a placebo, after controlling for baseline seizure rate and age.

Please remember that this example is used for demonstration purposes only. The results shouldn't be taken to imply anything about the efficacy of progabide in the real world. I'm not a doctor—at least not a medical doctor—and I don't even play one on TV.

We'll finish this exploration of Poisson regression with a discussion of some important variants and extensions.

13.3.3 *Extensions*

R provides several useful extensions to the basic Poisson regression model, including models that allow varying time periods, models that correct for too many zeros, and robust models that are useful when data includes outliers and influential observations. I'll describe each separately.

POISSON REGRESSION WITH VARYING TIME PERIODS

Our discussion of Poisson regression has been limited to response variables that measure a count over a fixed length of time (for example, number of seizures in an eight-week period, number of traffic accidents in the past year, or number of pro-social behaviors in a day). The length of time is constant across observations. But you can fit Poisson regression models that allow the time period to vary for each observation. In this case, the outcome variable is a rate.

To analyze rates, you must include a variable (for example, time) that records the length of time over which the count occurs for each observation. You then change the model from

$$\log_e(\lambda) = \beta_0 + \sum_{j=1}^{p} \beta_j X_j$$

to

$$\log_e\left(\frac{\lambda}{time}\right) = \beta_0 + \sum_{j=1}^{p} \beta_j X_j$$

or equivalently

$$\log_e(\lambda) = \log_e(time) + \beta_0 + \sum_{j=1}^{p} \beta_j X_j$$

To fit this new model, you use the offset option in the glm() function. For example, assume that the length of time that patients participated post-randomization in the Breslow study varied from 14 days to 60 days. You could use the rate of seizures as the dependent variable (assuming you had recorded time for each patient in days) and fit the model

```
fit <- glm(sumY ~ Base + Age + Trt, data=breslow.dat,
           offset= log(time), family=poisson)
```

where sumY is the number of seizures that occurred post-randomization for a patient during the time the patient was studied. In this case, you're assuming that rate doesn't vary over time (for example, 2 seizures in 4 days is equivalent to 10 seizures in 20 days).

ZERO-INFLATED POISSON REGRESSION

There are times when the number of zero counts in a dataset is larger than would be predicted by the Poisson model. This can occur when there's a subgroup of the population that would never engage in the behavior being counted. For example, in the Affairs dataset described in the section on logistic regression, the original outcome variable (affairs) counted the number of extramarital sexual intercourse experiences participants had in the past year. It's likely that there's a subgroup of faithful marital partners who would never have an affair, no matter how long the period of time studied. These are called *structural zeros* (primarily by the swingers in the group).

In such cases, you can analyze the data using an approach called *zero-inflated Poisson regression*. The approach fits two models simultaneously—one that predicts who would or would not have an affair, and the second that predicts how many affairs a participant would have if you excluded the permanently faithful. Think of this as a model that combines a logistic regression (for predicting structural zeros) and a Poisson regression model (that predicts counts for observations that aren't structural zeros). Zero-inflated Poisson regression can be fit using the `zeroinfl()` function in the `pscl` package.

ROBUST POISSON REGRESSION

Finally, the `glmRob()` function in the `robust` package can be used to fit a robust generalized linear model, including robust Poisson regression. As mentioned previously, this can be helpful in the presence of outliers and influential observations.

> **Going further**
>
> Generalized linear models are a complex and mathematically sophisticated subject, but many fine resources are available for learning about them. A good, short introduction to the topic is Dunteman and Ho (2006). The classic (and advanced) text on generalized linear models is provided by McCullagh and Nelder (1989). Comprehensive and accessible presentations are provided by Dobson and Barnett (2008) and Fox (2008). Faraway (2006) and Fox (2002) provide excellent introductions within the context of R.

13.4   *Summary*

In this chapter, we used generalized linear models to expand the range of approaches available for helping you to understand your data. In particular, the framework allows you to analyze response variables that are decidedly non-normal, including categorical outcomes and discrete counts. After briefly describing the general approach, we focused on logistic regression (for analyzing a dichotomous outcome) and Poisson regression (for analyzing outcomes measured as counts or rates).

We also discussed the important topic of overdispersion, including how to detect it and how to adjust for it. Finally, we looked at some of the extensions and variations that are available in R.

Each of the statistical approaches covered so far has dealt with directly observed and recorded variables. In the next chapter, we'll look at statistical models that deal with latent variables—unobserved, theoretical variables that you believe underlie and account for the behavior of the variables you do observe. In particular, you'll see how you can use factor analytic methods to detect and test hypotheses about these unobserved variables.

Principal components and factor analysis

14

This chapter covers

- Principal components analysis
- Exploratory factor analysis
- Understanding other latent variable models

One of the most challenging aspects of multivariate data is the sheer complexity of the information. If you have a dataset with 100 variables, how do you make sense of all the interrelationships present? Even with 20 variables, there are 190 pairwise correlations to consider when you're trying to understand how the individual variables relate to one another. Two related but distinct methodologies for exploring and simplifying complex multivariate data are principal components and exploratory factor analysis.

Principal components analysis (PCA) is a data-reduction technique that transforms a larger number of correlated variables into a much smaller set of uncorrelated variables called *principal components*. For example, you might use PCA to transform 30 correlated (and possibly redundant) environmental variables into 5 uncorrelated composite variables that retain as much information from the original set of variables as possible.

In contrast, *exploratory factor analysis (EFA)* is a collection of methods designed to uncover the latent structure in a given set of variables. It looks for a smaller set of underlying or latent constructs that can explain the relationships among the observed or manifest variables. For example, the dataset `Harman74.cor` contains the correlations among 24 psychological tests given to 145 seventh- and eighth-grade children. If you apply EFA to this data, the results suggest that the 276 test intercorrelations can be explained by the children's abilities on 4 underlying factors (verbal ability, processing speed, deduction, and memory).

The differences between the PCA and EFA models can be seen in figure 14.1. Principal components (PC1 and PC2) are linear combinations of the observed variables (X1 to X5). The weights used to form the linear composites are chosen to maximize the variance each principal component accounts for, while keeping the components uncorrelated.

In contrast, factors (F1 and F2) are assumed to underlie or "cause" the observed variables, rather than being linear combinations of them. The errors (e1 to e5) represent the variance in the observed variables unexplained by the factors. The circles indicate that the factors and errors aren't directly observable but are inferred from the correlations among the variables. In this example, the curved arrow between the factors indicates that they're correlated. Correlated factors are common, but not required, in the EFA model.

The methods described in this chapter require large samples to derive stable solutions. What constitutes an adequate sample size is somewhat complicated. Until recently, analysts used rules of thumb like "factor analysis requires 5–10 times as many subjects as variables." Recent studies suggest that the required sample size depends on the number of factors, the number of variables associated with each factor, and how well the set of factors explains the variance in the variables (Bandalos and Boehm-Kaufman, 2009). I'll go out on a limb and say that if you have several hundred observations, you're probably safe. In this chapter, we'll look at artificially small problems in order to keep the output (and page count) manageable.

We'll start by reviewing the functions in R that can be used to perform PCA or EFA and give a brief overview of the steps involved. Then we'll work carefully through two PCA examples, followed by an extended EFA example. A brief overview of other packages in R that can be used for fitting latent variable models is provided at the end of

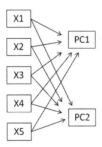

(a) Principal Components Model

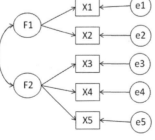

(b) Factor Analysis Model

Figure 14.1   Comparing principal components and factor analysis models. The diagrams show the observed variables (X1 to X5), the principal components (PC1, PC2), factors (F1, F2), and errors (e1 to e5).

the chapter. This discussion includes packages for confirmatory factor analysis, structural equation modeling, correspondence analysis, and latent class analysis.

14.1 Principal components and factor analysis in R

In the base installation of R, the functions for PCA and EFA are `princomp()` and `factanal()`, respectively. In this chapter, we'll focus on functions provided in the psych package. They offer many more useful options than their base counterparts. Additionally, the results are reported in a metric that will be more familiar to social scientists and more likely to match the output provided by corresponding programs in other statistical packages such as SAS and SPSS.

The psych package functions that are most relevant here are listed in table 14.1. Be sure to install the package before trying the examples in this chapter.

Table 14.1 Useful factor analytic functions in the `psych` package

Function	Description
`principal()`	Principal components analysis with optional rotation
`fa()`	Factor analysis by principal axis, minimum residual, weighted least squares, or maximum likelihood
`fa.parallel()`	Scree plots with parallel analyses
`factor.plot()`	Plot the results of a factor or principal components analysis
`fa.diagram()`	Graph factor or principal components loading matrices
`scree()`	Scree plot for factor and principal components analysis

EFA (and to a lesser degree PCA) are often confusing to new users. The reason is that they describe a wide range of approaches, and each approach requires several steps (and decisions) to achieve a final result. The most common steps are as follows:

1 *Prepare the data.* Both PCA and EFA derive their solutions from the correlations among the observed variables. You can input either the raw data matrix or the correlation matrix to the `principal()` and `fa()` functions. If raw data is input, the correlation matrix is automatically calculated. Be sure to screen the data for missing values before proceeding.

2 *Select a factor model.* Decide whether PCA (data reduction) or EFA (uncovering latent structure) is a better fit for your research goals. If you select an EFA approach, you'll also need to choose a specific factoring method (for example, maximum likelihood).

3 *Decide how many components/factors to extract.*

4 *Extract the components/factors.*

5 *Rotate the components/factors.*

6 *Interpret the results.*

7 *Compute component or factor scores.*

In the remainder of this chapter, we'll carefully consider each of the steps, starting with PCA. At the end of the chapter, you'll find a detailed flow chart of the possible steps in PCA/EFA (figure 14.7). The chart will make more sense once you've read through the intervening material.

14.2 Principal components

The goal of PCA is to replace a large number of correlated variables with a smaller number of uncorrelated variables while capturing as much information in the original variables as possible. These derived variables, called *principal components*, are linear combinations of the observed variables. Specifically, the first principal component

$$PC_1 = a_1X_1 + a_2X_2 + ... + a_kX_k$$

is the weighted combination of the k observed variables that accounts for the most variance in the original set of variables. The second principal component is the linear combination that accounts for the most variance in the original variables, under the constraint that it's *orthogonal* (uncorrelated) to the first principal component. Each subsequent component maximizes the variance accounted for, while at the same time remaining uncorrelated with all previous components. Theoretically, you can extract as many principal components as there are variables. But from a practical viewpoint, you hope that you can approximate the full set of variables with a much smaller set of components. Let's look at a simple example.

The dataset USJudgeRatings contains lawyers' ratings of state judges in the US Superior Court. The data frame contains 43 observations on 12 numeric variables. The variables are listed in table 14.2.

Table 14.2   Variables in the USJudgeRatings dataset

Variable	Description	Variable	Description
CONT	Number of contacts of lawyer with judge	PREP	Preparation for trial
INTG	Judicial integrity	FAMI	Familiarity with law
DMNR	Demeanor	ORAL	Sound oral rulings
DILG	Diligence	WRIT	Sound written rulings
CFMG	Case flow managing	PHYS	Physical ability
DECI	Prompt decisions	RTEN	Worthy of retention

From a practical point of view, can you summarize the 11 evaluative ratings (INTG to RTEN) with a smaller number of composite variables? If so, how many will you need, and how will they be defined? Because the goal is to simplify the data, you'll approach this problem using PCA. The data are in raw score format, and there are no missing values. Therefore, your next step is deciding how many principal components you'll need.

14.2.1 *Selecting the number of components to extract*

Several criteria are available for deciding how many components to retain in a PCA. They include

- Basing the number of components on prior experience and theory
- Selecting the number of components needed to account for some threshold cumulative amount of variance in the variables (for example, 80%)
- Selecting the number of components to retain by examining the eigenvalues of the $k \times k$ correlation matrix among the variables

The most common approach is based on the eigenvalues. Each component is associated with an eigenvalue of the correlation matrix. The first PC is associated with the largest eigenvalue, the second PC with the second-largest eigenvalue, and so on. The Kaiser–Harris criterion suggests retaining components with eigenvalues greater than 1. Components with eigenvalues less than 1 explain less variance than contained in a single variable. In the Cattell Scree test, the eigenvalues are plotted against their component numbers. Such plots typically demonstrate a bend or elbow, and the components above this sharp break are retained. Finally, you can run simulations, extracting eigenvalues from random data matrices of the same size as the original matrix. If an eigenvalue based on real data is larger than the average corresponding eigenvalues from a set of random data matrices, that component is retained. The approach is called *parallel analysis* (see Hayton, Allen, and Scarpello, 2004, for more details).

You can assess all three eigenvalue criteria at the same time via the `fa.parallel()` function. For the 11 ratings (dropping the CONT variable), the necessary code is as follows:

```
library(psych)
fa.parallel(USJudgeRatings[,-1], fa="pc", n.iter=100,
            show.legend=FALSE, main="Scree plot with parallel analysis")
```

This code produces the graph shown in figure 14.2. The plot displays the scree test based on the observed eigenvalues (as straight-line segments and x's), the mean eigenvalues derived from 100 random data matrices (as dashed lines), and the eigenvalues greater than 1 criteria (as a horizontal line at y=1).

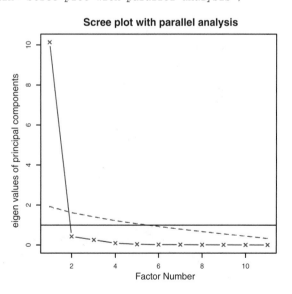

Figure 14.2 Assessing the number of principal components to retain for the `USJudgeRatings` example. A scree plot (the line with x's), eigenvalues greater than 1 criteria (horizontal line), and parallel analysis with 100 simulations (dashed line) suggest retaining a single component.

All three criteria suggest that a single component is appropriate for summarizing this dataset. Your next step is to extract the principal component using the `principal()` function.

14.2.2 Extracting principal components

As indicated earlier, the `principal()` function performs a principal components analysis starting with either a raw data matrix or a correlation matrix. The format is

```
principal(r, nfactors=, rotate=, scores=)
```

where

- `r` is a correlation matrix or a raw data matrix.
- `nfactors` specifies the number of principal components to extract (1 by default).
- `rotate` indicates the rotation to be applied (varimax by default; see section 14.2.3).
- `scores` specifies whether to calculate principal-component scores (false by default).

To extract the first principal component, you can use the code in the following listing.

Listing 14.1 Principal components analysis of `USJudgeRatings`

```
> library(psych)
> pc <- principal(USJudgeRatings[,-1], nfactors=1)
> pc

Principal Components Analysis
Call: principal(r = USJudgeRatings[, -1], nfactors=1)
Standardized loadings based upon correlation matrix
      PC1   h2    u2
INTG 0.92 0.84 0.157
DMNR 0.91 0.83 0.166
DILG 0.97 0.94 0.061
CFMG 0.96 0.93 0.072
DECI 0.96 0.92 0.076
PREP 0.98 0.97 0.030
FAMI 0.98 0.95 0.047
ORAL 1.00 0.99 0.009
WRIT 0.99 0.98 0.020
PHYS 0.89 0.80 0.201
RTEN 0.99 0.97 0.028

                 PC1
SS loadings    10.13
Proportion Var  0.92
[... additional output omitted ...]
```

Here, you're inputting the raw data without the CONT variable and specifying that one unrotated component should be extracted. (Rotation is explained in section 14.3.3.) Because PCA is performed on a correlation matrix, the raw data is automatically converted to a correlation matrix before the components are extracted.

The column labeled PC1 contains the component *loadings,* which are the correlations of the observed variables with the principal component(s). If you extracted more than one principal component, there would be columns for PC2, PC3, and so on. Component loadings are used to interpret the meaning of components. You can see that each variable correlates highly with the first component (PC1). It therefore appears to be a general evaluative dimension.

The column labeled h2 contains the component *communalities*—the amount of variance in each variable explained by the components. The u2 column contains the component *uniquenesses*—the amount of variance not accounted for by the components (or 1 – h2). For example, 80% of the variance in physical ability (PHYS) ratings is accounted for by the first PC, and 20% isn't. PHYS is the variable least well represented by a one-component solution.

The row labeled SS Loadings contains the eigenvalues associated with the components. The eigenvalues are the standardized variance associated with a particular component (in this case, the value for the first component is 10). Finally, the row labeled Proportion Var represents the amount of variance accounted for by each component. Here you see that the first principal component accounts for 92% of the variance in the 11 variables.

Let's consider a second example, one that results in a solution with more than one principal component. The dataset Harman23.cor contains data on 8 body measurements for 305 girls. In this case, the dataset consists of the correlations among the variables rather than the original data (see table 14.3).

Table 14.3 Correlations among body measurements for 305 girls (Harman23.cor)

	Height	Arm span	Forearm	Lower leg	Weight	Bitro diameter	Chest girth	Chest width
Height	1.00	0.85	0.80	0.86	0.47	0.40	0.30	0.38
Arm span	0.85	1.00	0.88	0.83	0.38	0.33	0.28	0.41
Forearm	0.80	0.88	1.00	0.80	0.38	0.32	0.24	0.34
Lower leg	0.86	0.83	0.8	1.00	0.44	0.33	0.33	0.36
Weight	0.47	0.38	0.38	0.44	1.00	0.76	0.73	0.63
Bitro diameter	0.40	0.33	0.32	0.33	0.76	1.00	0.58	0.58
Chest girth	0.30	0.28	0.24	0.33	0.73	0.58	1.00	0.54
Chest width	0.38	0.41	0.34	0.36	0.63	0.58	0.54	1.00

Source: H. H. Harman, *Modern Factor Analysis, Third Edition Revised,* University of Chicago Press, 1976, Table 2.3.

Again, you wish to replace the original physical measurements with a smaller number of derived variables. You can determine the number of components to extract using

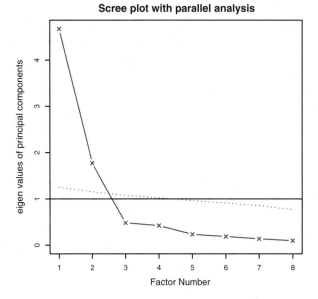

Figure 14.3 **Assessing the number of principal components to retain for the body measurements example. The scree plot (line with x's), eigenvalues greater than 1 criteria (horizontal line), and parallel analysis with 100 simulations (dashed line) suggest retaining two components.**

the following code. In this case, you need to identify the correlation matrix (the `cov` component of the `Harman23.cor` object) and specify the sample size (`n.obs`):

```
library(psych)
fa.parallel(Harman23.cor$cov, n.obs=302, fa="pc", n.iter=100,
            show.legend=FALSE, main="Scree plot with parallel analysis")
```

The resulting graph is displayed in figure 14.3.

You can see from the plot that a two-component solution is suggested. As in the first example, the Kaiser–Harris criteria, scree test, and parallel analysis agree. This won't always be the case, and you may need to extract different numbers of components and select the solution that appears most useful. The next listing extracts the first two principal components from the correlation matrix.

Listing 14.2   Principal components analysis of body measurements

```
> library(psych)
> pc <- principal(Harman23.cor$cov, nfactors=2, rotate="none")
> pc

Principal Components Analysis
Call: principal(r = Harman23.cor$cov, nfactors = 2, rotate = "none")
Standardized loadings based upon correlation matrix
                PC1    PC2   h2    u2
height          0.86 -0.37 0.88 0.123
arm.span        0.84 -0.44 0.90 0.097
forearm         0.81 -0.46 0.87 0.128
lower.leg       0.84 -0.40 0.86 0.139
weight          0.76  0.52 0.85 0.150
bitro.diameter  0.67  0.53 0.74 0.261
```

```
chest.girth    0.62  0.58 0.72 0.283
chest.width    0.67  0.42 0.62 0.375

               PC1   PC2
SS loadings    4.67 1.77
Proportion Var 0.58 0.22
Cumulative Var 0.58 0.81

[... additional output omitted ...]
```

If you examine the PC1 and PC2 columns in listing 14.2, you see that the first component accounts for 58% of the variance in the physical measurements, whereas the second component accounts for 22%. Together, the two components account for 81% of the variance. The two components together account for 88% of the variance in the height variable.

Components and factors are interpreted by examining their loadings. The first component correlates positively with each physical measure and appears to be a general size factor. The second component contrasts the first four variables (height, arm span, forearm, and lower leg), with the second four variables (weight, bitro diameter, chest girth, and chest width). It therefore appears to be a length-versus-volume factor. Conceptually, this isn't an easy construct to work with. Whenever two or more components have been extracted, you can rotate the solution to make it more interpretable. This is the topic we'll turn to next.

14.2.3 *Rotating principal components*

Rotations are a set of mathematical techniques for transforming the component loading matrix into one that's more interpretable. They do this by "purifying" the components as much as possible. Rotation methods differ with regard to whether the resulting components remain uncorrelated (*orthogonal rotation*) or are allowed to correlate (*oblique rotation*). They also differ in their definition of purifying. The most popular orthogonal rotation is the *varimax* rotation, which attempts to purify the columns of the loading matrix, so that each component is defined by a limited set of variables (that is, each column has a few large loadings and many very small loadings). Applying a varimax rotation to the body measurement data, you get the results provided in the next listing. You'll see an example of an oblique rotation in section 14.4.

> **Listing 14.3   Principal components analysis with varimax rotation**

```
> rc <- principal(Harman23.cor$cov, nfactors=2, rotate="varimax")
> rc

Principal Components Analysis
Call: principal(r = Harman23.cor$cov, nfactors = 2, rotate = "varimax")
Standardized loadings based upon correlation matrix
            RC1  RC2   h2    u2
height      0.90 0.25 0.88 0.123
arm.span    0.93 0.19 0.90 0.097
forearm     0.92 0.16 0.87 0.128
lower.leg   0.90 0.22 0.86 0.139
```

```
weight            0.26 0.88 0.85 0.150
bitro.diameter 0.19 0.84 0.74 0.261
chest.girth       0.11 0.84 0.72 0.283
chest.width       0.26 0.75 0.62 0.375

                  RC1   RC2
SS loadings       3.52 2.92
Proportion Var 0.44 0.37
Cumulative Var 0.44 0.81
```

```
[... additional output omitted ...]
```

The column names change from PC to RC to denote rotated components. Looking at the loadings in column RC1, you see that the first component is primarily defined by the first four variables (length variables). The loadings in the column RC2 indicate that the second component is primarily defined by variables 5 through 8 (volume variables). Note that the two components are still uncorrelated and that together, they still explain the variables equally well. You can see that the rotated solution explains the variables equally well because the variable communalities haven't changed. Additionally, the cumulative variance accounted for by the two-component rotated solution (81%) hasn't changed. But the proportion of variance accounted for by each individual component has changed (from 58% to 44% for component 1 and from 22% to 37% for component 2). This spreading out of the variance across components is common, and technically you should now call them components rather than principal components (because the variance-maximizing properties of individual components haven't been retained).

The ultimate goal is to replace a larger set of correlated variables with a smaller set of derived variables. To do this, you need to obtain scores for each observation on the components.

14.2.4 *Obtaining principal components scores*

In the USJudgeRatings example, you extracted a single principal component from the raw data describing lawyers' ratings on 11 variables. The principal() function makes it easy to obtain scores for each participant on this derived variable (see the next listing).

Listing 14.4   Obtaining component scores from raw data

```
> library(psych)
> pc <- principal(USJudgeRatings[,-1], nfactors=1, score=TRUE)
> head(pc$scores)
                    PC1
AARONSON,L.H.   -0.1857981
ALEXANDER,J.M.   0.7469865
ARMENTANO,A.J.   0.0704772
BERDON,R.I.      1.1358765
BRACKEN,J.J.    -2.1586211
BURNS,E.B.       0.7669406
```

The principal component scores are saved in the scores element of the object returned by the principal() function when the option scores=TRUE. If you wanted, you could now get the correlation between the number of contacts occurring between a lawyer and a judge and their evaluation of the judge using

```
> cor(USJudgeRatings$CONT, pc$score)
              PC1
[1,] -0.008815895
```

Apparently, there's no relationship between the lawyer's familiarity and their opinions!

When the principal components analysis is based on a correlation matrix and the raw data aren't available, getting principal component scores for each observation is clearly not possible. But you can get the coefficients used to calculate the principal components.

In the body measurement data, you have correlations among body measurements, but you don't have the individual measurements for these 305 girls. You can get the scoring coefficients using the code in the following listing.

Listing 14.5   Obtaining principal component scoring coefficients

```
> library(psych)
> rc <- principal(Harman23.cor$cov, nfactors=2, rotate="varimax")
> round(unclass(rc$weights), 2)
                  RC1   RC2
height           0.28 -0.05
arm.span         0.30 -0.08
forearm          0.30 -0.09
lower.leg        0.28 -0.06
weight          -0.06  0.33
bitro.diameter  -0.08  0.32
chest.girth     -0.10  0.34
chest.width     -0.04  0.27
```

The component scores are obtained using the formulas

```
PC1 = 0.28*height + 0.30*arm.span + 0.30*forearm + 0.29*lower.leg -
      0.06*weight - 0.08*bitro.diameter - 0.10*chest.girth -
      0.04*chest.width
```

and

```
PC2 = -0.05*height - 0.08*arm.span - 0.09*forearm - 0.06*lower.leg +
      0.33*weight + 0.32*bitro.diameter + 0.34*chest.girth +
      0.27*chest.width
```

These equations assume that the physical measurements have been standardized (mean = 0, sd = 1). Note that the weights for PC1 tend to be around 0.3 or 0. The same is true for PC2. As a practical matter, you could simplify your approach further by taking the first composite variable as the mean of the standardized scores for the first four variables. Similarly, you could define the second composite variable as the mean of the standardized scores for the second four variables. This is typically what I'd do in practice.

> **Little Jiffy conquers the world**
>
> There's quite a bit of confusion among data analysts regarding PCA and EFA. One reason for this is historical and can be traced back to a program called Little Jiffy (no kidding). Little Jiffy was one of the most popular early programs for factor analysis, and it defaulted to a principal components analysis, extracting components with eigenvalues greater than 1 and rotating them to a varimax solution. The program was so widely used that many social scientists came to think of this default behavior as synonymous with EFA. Many later statistical packages also incorporated these defaults in their EFA programs.
>
> As I hope you'll see in the next section, there are important and fundamental differences between PCA and EFA. To learn more about the PCA/EFA confusion, see Hayton, Allen, and Scarpello, 2004.

If your goal is to look for latent underlying variables that explain your observed variables, you can turn to factor analysis. This is the topic of the next section.

14.3 *Exploratory factor analysis*

The goal of EFA is to explain the correlations among a set of observed variables by uncovering a smaller set of more fundamental unobserved variables underlying the data. These hypothetical, unobserved variables are called *factors*. (Each factor is assumed to explain the variance shared among two or more observed variables, so technically, they're called *common factors*.)

The model can be represented as

$$X_i = a_1 F_1 + a_2 F_2 + \dots + a_p F_p + U_i$$

where X_i is the ith observed variable $(i = 1\dots k)$, F_j are the common factors $(j = 1\dots p)$, and $p < k$. U_i is the portion of variable X_i unique to that variable (not explained by the common factors). The a_i can be thought of as the degree to which each factor contributes to the composition of an observed variable. If we go back to the `Harman74.cor` example at the beginning of this chapter, we'd say that an individual's scores on each of the 24 observed psychological tests is due to a weighted combination of their ability on 4 underlying psychological constructs.

Although the PCA and EFA models differ, many of the steps appear similar. To illustrate the process, you'll apply EFA to the correlations among six psychological tests. One hundred twelve individuals were given six tests, including a nonverbal measure of general intelligence (general), a picture-completion test (picture), a block design test (blocks), a maze test (maze), a reading comprehension test (reading), and a vocabulary test (vocab). Can you explain the participants' scores on these tests with a smaller number of underlying or latent psychological constructs?

The covariance matrix among the variables is provided in the dataset `ability.cov`. You can transform this into a correlation matrix using the `cov2cor()` function:

```
> options(digits=2)
> covariances <- ability.cov$cov
> correlations <- cov2cor(covariances)
> correlations
        general picture blocks maze reading vocab
general    1.00    0.47   0.55 0.34    0.58  0.51
picture    0.47    1.00   0.57 0.19    0.26  0.24
blocks     0.55    0.57   1.00 0.45    0.35  0.36
maze       0.34    0.19   0.45 1.00    0.18  0.22
reading    0.58    0.26   0.35 0.18    1.00  0.79
vocab      0.51    0.24   0.36 0.22    0.79  1.00
```

Because you're looking for hypothetical constructs that explain the data, you'll use an EFA approach. As in PCA, the next task is to decide how many factors to extract.

14.3.1 Deciding how many common factors to extract

To decide on the number of factors to extract, turn to the fa.parallel() function:

```
> library(psych)
> covariances <- ability.cov$cov
> correlations <- cov2cor(covariances)
> fa.parallel(correlations, n.obs=112, fa="both", n.iter=100,
              main="Scree plots with parallel analysis")
```

The resulting plot is shown in figure 14.4. Notice you've requested that the function display results for both a principal-components and common-factor approach, so that you can compare them (fa = "both").

There are several things to notice in this graph. If you'd taken a PCA approach, you might have chosen one component (scree test, parallel analysis) or two components

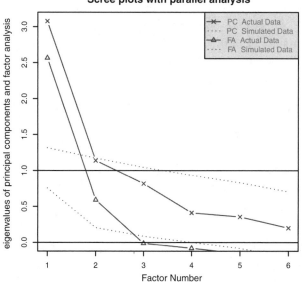

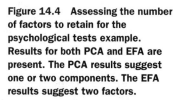

Figure 14.4 Assessing the number of factors to retain for the psychological tests example. Results for both PCA and EFA are present. The PCA results suggest one or two components. The EFA results suggest two factors.

(eigenvalues greater than 1). When in doubt, it's usually a better idea to overfactor than to underfactor. Overfactoring tends to lead to less distortion of the "true" solution.

Looking at the EFA results, a two-factor solution is clearly indicated. The first two eigenvalues (triangles) are above the bend in the scree test and also above the mean eigenvalues based on 100 simulated data matrices. For EFA, the Kaiser–Harris criterion is number of eigenvalues above 0, rather than 1. (Most people don't realize this, so it's a good way to win bets at parties.) In the present case the Kaiser–Harris criteria also suggest two factors.

14.3.2 *Extracting common factors*

Now that you've decided to extract two factors, you can use the `fa()` function to obtain your solution. The format of the `fa()` function is

```
fa(r, nfactors=, n.obs=, rotate=, scores=, fm=)
```

where

- *r* is a correlation matrix or a raw data matrix.
- `nfactors` specifies the number of factors to extract (1 by default).
- `n.obs` is the number of observations (if a correlation matrix is input).
- `rotate` indicates the rotation to be applied (oblimin by default).
- `scores` specifies whether or not to calculate factor scores (false by default).
- `fm` specifies the factoring method (minres by default).

Unlike PCA, there are many methods of extracting common factors. They include maximum likelihood (`ml`), iterated principal axis (`pa`), weighted least square (`wls`), generalized weighted least squares (`gls`), and minimum residual (`minres`). Statisticians tend to prefer the maximum likelihood approach because of its well-defined statistical model. Sometimes, this approach fails to converge, in which case the iterated principal axis option often works well. To learn more about the different approaches, see Mulaik (2009) and Gorsuch (1983).

For this example, you'll extract the unrotated factors using the iterated principal axis (`fm = "pa"`) approach. The results are given in the next listing.

Listing 14.6   Principal axis factoring without rotation

```
> fa <- fa(correlations, nfactors=2, rotate="none", fm="pa")
> fa
Factor Analysis using method =  pa
Call: fa(r = correlations, nfactors = 2, rotate = "none", fm = "pa")
Standardized loadings based upon correlation matrix
          PA1    PA2   h2    u2
general 0.75   0.07 0.57 0.43
picture 0.52   0.32 0.38 0.62
blocks  0.75   0.52 0.83 0.17
maze    0.39   0.22 0.20 0.80
reading 0.81  -0.51 0.91 0.09
vocab   0.73  -0.39 0.69 0.31
```

```
             PA1  PA2
SS loadings      2.75 0.83
Proportion Var 0.46 0.14
Cumulative Var 0.46 0.60
[... additional output deleted ...]
```

You can see that the two factors account for 60% of the variance in the six psychological tests. When you examine the loadings, though, they aren't easy to interpret. Rotating them should help.

14.3.3 Rotating factors

You can rotate the two-factor solution from section 14.3.4 using either an orthogonal rotation or an oblique rotation. Let's try both so you can see how they differ. First try an orthogonal rotation (in the next listing).

Listing 14.7 Factor extraction with orthogonal rotation

```
> fa.varimax <- fa(correlations, nfactors=2, rotate="varimax", fm="pa")
> fa.varimax
Factor Analysis using method =  pa
Call: fa(r = correlations, nfactors = 2, rotate = "varimax", fm = "pa")
Standardized loadings based upon correlation matrix
          PA1  PA2   h2   u2
general 0.49 0.57 0.57 0.43
picture 0.16 0.59 0.38 0.62
blocks  0.18 0.89 0.83 0.17
maze    0.13 0.43 0.20 0.80
reading 0.93 0.20 0.91 0.09
vocab   0.80 0.23 0.69 0.31

                PA1  PA2
SS loadings      1.83 1.75
Proportion Var 0.30 0.29
Cumulative Var 0.30 0.60

[... additional output omitted ...]
```

Looking at the factor loadings, the factors are certainly easier to interpret. Reading and vocabulary load on the first factor; and picture completion, block design, and mazes load on the second factor. The general nonverbal intelligence measure loads on both factors. This may indicate a verbal intelligence factor and a nonverbal intelligence factor.

By using an orthogonal rotation, you artificially force the two factors to be uncorrelated. What would you find if you allowed the two factors to correlate? You can try an oblique rotation such as *promax* (see the next listing).

Listing 14.8 Factor extraction with oblique rotation

```
> fa.promax <- fa(correlations, nfactors=2, rotate="promax", fm="pa")
> fa.promax
Factor Analysis using method =  pa
```

```
Call: fa(r = correlations, nfactors = 2, rotate = "promax", fm = "pa")
Standardized loadings based upon correlation matrix
          PA1   PA2   h2   u2
general   0.36  0.49 0.57 0.43
picture  -0.04  0.64 0.38 0.62
blocks   -0.12  0.98 0.83 0.17
maze     -0.01  0.45 0.20 0.80
reading   1.01 -0.11 0.91 0.09
vocab     0.84 -0.02 0.69 0.31

                 PA1   PA2
SS loadings      1.82  1.76
Proportion Var   0.30  0.29
Cumulative Var   0.30  0.60

 With factor correlations of
      PA1   PA2
PA1 1.00 0.57
PA2 0.57 1.00
[... additional output omitted ...]
```

Several differences exist between the orthogonal and oblique solutions. In an orthogonal solution, attention focuses on the *factor structure matrix* (the correlations of the variables with the factors). In an oblique solution, there are three matrices to consider: the factor structure matrix, the factor pattern matrix, and the factor intercorrelation matrix.

The *factor pattern matrix* is a matrix of standardized regression coefficients. They give the weights for predicting the variables from the factors. The *factor intercorrelation matrix* gives the correlations among the factors.

In listing 14.8, the values in the PA1 and PA2 columns constitute the factor pattern matrix. They're standardized regression coefficients rather than correlations. Examination of the columns of this matrix is still used to name the factors (although there's some controversy here). Again, you'd find a verbal and nonverbal factor.

The factor intercorrelation matrix indicates that the correlation between the two factors is 0.57. This is a hefty correlation. If the factor intercorrelations had been low, you might have gone back to an orthogonal solution to keep things simple.

The factor structure matrix (or factor loading matrix) isn't provided. But you can easily calculate it using the formula F = P*Phi, where F is the factor loading matrix, P is the factor pattern matrix, and Phi is the factor intercorrelation matrix. A simple function for carrying out the multiplication is as follows:

```
fsm <- function(oblique) {
if (class(oblique)[2]=="fa" & is.null(oblique$Phi)) {
    warning("Object doesn't look like oblique EFA")
} else {
    P <- unclass(oblique$loading)
    F <- P %*% oblique$Phi
    colnames(F) <- c("PA1", "PA2")
    return(F)
}
}
```

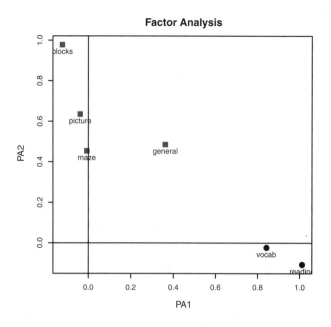

Factor Analysis

Figure 14.5 Two-factor plot for the psychological tests in ability.cov. vocab **and** reading **load on the first factor (PA1), and** blocks, picture, **and** maze **load on the second factor (PA2). The general intelligence test loads on both.**

Applying this to the example, you get

```
> fsm(fa.promax)
          PA1  PA2
general  0.64 0.69
picture  0.33 0.61
blocks   0.44 0.91
maze     0.25 0.45
reading  0.95 0.47
vocab    0.83 0.46
```

Now you can review the correlations between the variables and the factors. Comparing them to the factor loading matrix in the orthogonal solution, you see that these columns aren't as pure. This is because you've allowed the underlying factors to be correlated. Although the oblique approach is more complicated, it's often a more realistic model of the data.

You can graph an orthogonal or oblique solution using the factor.plot() or fa.diagram() function. The code

```
factor.plot(fa.promax, labels=rownames(fa.promax$loadings))
```

produces the graph in figure 14.5.

The code

```
fa.diagram(fa.promax, simple=FALSE)
```

produces the diagram in figure 14.6. If you let simple = TRUE, only the largest loading per item is displayed. It shows the largest loadings for each factor, as well as the

Factor Analysis

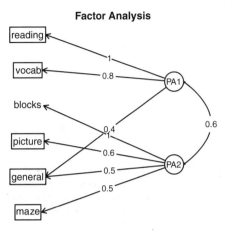

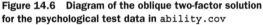

Figure 14.6   Diagram of the oblique two-factor solution for the psychological test data in `ability.cov`

correlations between the factors. This type of diagram is helpful when there are several factors.

When you're dealing with data in real life, it's unlikely that you'd apply factor analysis to a dataset with so few variables. We've done it here to keep things manageable. If you'd like to test your skills, try factor-analyzing the 24 psychological tests contained in `Harman74.cor`. The code

```
library(psych)
fa.24tests <- fa(Harman74.cor$cov, nfactors=4, rotate="promax")
```

should get you started!

14.3.4 *Factor scores*

Compared with PCA, the goal of EFA is much less likely to be the calculation of factor scores. But these scores are easily obtained from the `fa()` function by including the `score = TRUE` option (when raw data are available). Additionally, the scoring coefficients (standardized regression weights) are available in the `weights` element of the object returned.

For the `ability.cov` dataset, you can obtain the beta weights for calculating the factor score estimates for the two-factor oblique solution using

```
> fa.promax$weights
          [,1]  [,2]
general 0.080 0.210
picture 0.021 0.090
blocks  0.044 0.695
maze    0.027 0.035
reading 0.739 0.044
vocab   0.176 0.039
```

Unlike component scores, which are calculated exactly, factor scores can only be estimated. Several methods exist. The `fa()` function uses the regression approach. To learn more about factor scores, see DiStefano, Zhu, and Mîndrilă, (2009).

Before moving on, let's briefly review other R packages that are useful for exploratory factor analysis.

14.3.5 *Other EFA-related packages*

R contains a number of other contributed packages that are useful for conducting factor analyses. The FactoMineR package provides methods for PCA and EFA, as well as other latent variable models. It provides many options that we haven't considered here, including the use of both numeric and categorical variables. The FAiR package estimates factor analysis models using a genetic algorithm that permits the ability to impose inequality restrictions on model parameters. The GPArotation package offers many additional factor rotation methods. Finally, the nFactors package offers sophisticated techniques for determining the number of factors underlying data.

14.4 *Other latent variable models*

EFA is only one of a wide range of latent variable models used in statistics. We'll end this chapter with a brief description of other models that can be fit within R. These include models that test a priori theories, that can handle mixed data types (numeric and categorical), or that are based solely on categorical multiway tables.

In EFA, you allow the data to determine the number of factors to be extracted and their meaning. But you could start with a theory about how many factors underlie a set of variables, how the variables load on those factors, and how the factors correlate with one another. You could then test this theory against a set of collected data. The approach is called *confirmatory factor analysis (CFA)*.

CFA is a subset of a methodology called *structural equation modeling (SEM)*. SEM allows you to posit not only the number and composition of underlying factors but also how these factors impact one another. You can think of SEM as a combination of confirmatory factor analyses (for the variables) and regression analyses (for the factors). The resulting output includes statistical tests and fit indices. There are several excellent packages for CFA and SEM in R. They include sem, OpenMx, and lavaan.

The ltm package can be used to fit latent models to the items contained in tests and questionnaires. The methodology is often used to create large-scale standardized tests. Examples include the Scholastic Aptitude Test (SAT) and the Graduate Record Exam (GRE).

Latent class models (where the underlying factors are assumed to be categorical rather than continuous) can be fit with the FlexMix, lcmm, randomLCA, and poLCA packages. The lcda package performs latent class discriminant analysis, and the lsa package performs latent semantic analysis, a methodology used in natural language processing.

The ca package provides functions for simple and multiple correspondence analysis. These methods allow you to explore the structure of categorical variables in two-way and multiway tables, respectively.

Finally, R contains numerous methods for *multidimensional scaling (MDS)*. MDS is designed to detect underlying dimensions that explain the similarities and distances between a set of measured objects (for example, countries). The cmdscale() function in the base installation performs a classical MDS, whereas the isoMDS() function in the MASS package performs a nonmetric MDS. The vegan package also contains functions for classical and nonmetric MDS.

14.5   Summary

In this chapter, we reviewed methods for principal components (PCA) analysis and exploratory factor analysis (EFA). PCA is a useful data-reduction method that can replace a large number of correlated variables with a smaller number of uncorrelated variables, simplifying the analyses. EFA contains a broad range of methods for identifying latent or unobserved constructs (factors) that may underlie a set of observed or manifest variables.

Whereas the goal of PCA is typically to summarize the data and reduce its dimensionality, EFA can be used as a hypothesis-generating tool, useful when you're trying to

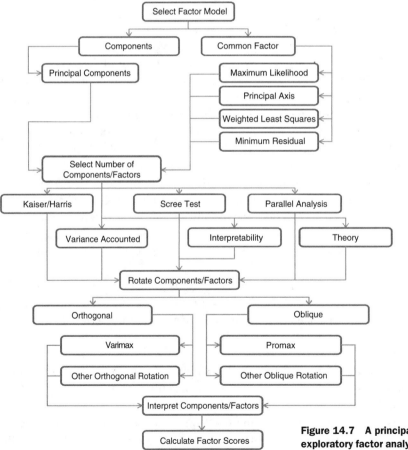

Figure 14.7   A principal components/exploratory factor analysis decision chart

understand the relationships between a large number of variables. It's often used in the social sciences for theory development.

Although there are many superficial similarities between the two approaches, important differences exist as well. In this chapter, we considered the models underlying each, methods for selecting the number of components/factors to extract, methods for extracting components/factors and rotating (transforming) them to enhance interpretability, and techniques for obtaining component or factor scores. The steps in a PCA or EFA are summarized in figure 14.7. We ended the chapter with a brief discussion of other latent variable methods available in R.

In the next chapter, we'll consider methods for working with time-series data.

Time series

15

This chapter covers

- Creating a time series
- Decomposing a time series into components
- Developing predictive models
- Forecasting future values

How fast is global warming occurring, and what will the impact be in 10 years? With the exception of repeated measures ANOVA in section 9.6, each of the preceding chapters has focused on *cross-sectional* data. In a cross-sectional dataset, variables are measured at a single point in time. In contrast, *longitudinal* data involves measuring variables repeatedly over time. By following a phenomenon over time, it's possible to learn a great deal about it.

In this chapter, we'll examine observations that have been recorded at regularly spaced time intervals for a given span of time. We can arrange observations such as these into a *time series* of the form Y_1, Y_2, Y_3, ... , $Y_{t, ...}$, Y_T, where Y_t represents the value of Y at time t and T is the total number of observations in the series.

Consider two very different time series displayed in figure 15.1. The series on the left contains the quarterly earnings (dollars) per Johnson & Johnson share between 1960 and 1980. There are 84 observations: one for each quarter over 21

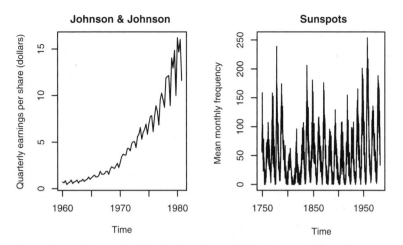

Figure 15.1   Time series plots for (a) Johnson & Johnson quarterly earnings per share (in dollars) from 1960 to 1980, and (b) the monthly mean relative sunspot numbers recorded from 1749 to 1983

years. The series on the right describes the monthly mean relative sunspot numbers from 1749 to 1983 recorded by the Swiss Federal Observatory and the Tokyo Astronomical Observatory. The sunspots time series is much longer, with 2,820 observations—1 per month for 235 years.

Studies of time-series data involve two fundamental questions: what happened (description), and what will happen next (forecasting)? For the Johnson & Johnson data, you might ask

- Is the price of Johnson & Johnson shares changing over time?
- Are there quarterly effects, with share prices rising and falling in a regular fashion throughout the year?
- Can you forecast what future share prices will be and, if so, to what degree of accuracy?

For the sunspot data, you might ask

- What statistical models best describe sunspot activity?
- Do some models fit the data better than others?
- Are the number of sunspots at a given time predictable and, if so, to what degree?

The ability to accurately predict stock prices has relevance for my (hopefully) early retirement to a tropical island, whereas the ability to predict sunspot activity has relevance for my cell phone reception on said island.

Predicting future values of a time series, or *forecasting*, is a fundamental human activity, and studies of time series data have important real-world applications. Economists use time-series data in an attempt to understand and predict what will happen in financial markets. City planners use time-series data to predict future transportation demands. Climate scientists use time-series data to study global climate change. Corporations use time series to predict product demand and future sales. Healthcare officials use time-series data to study the spread of disease and to predict the number of future cases in a given region. Seismologists study times-series data in order to predict earthquakes. In each case, the study of historical time series is an indispensable part of the process. Because different approaches may work best with different types of time series, we'll investigate many examples in this chapter.

There is a wide range of methods for describing time-series data and forecasting future values. If you work with time-series data, you'll find that R has some of the most comprehensive analytic capabilities available anywhere. This chapter explores some of the most common descriptive and forecasting approaches and the R functions used to perform them. The functions are listed in table 15.1 in their order of appearance in the chapter.

Table 15.1   Functions for time-series analysis

Function	Package	Use
ts()	stats	Creates a time-series object.
plot()	graphics	Plots a time series.
start()	stats	Returns the starting time of a time series.
end()	stats	Returns the ending time of a time series.
frequency()	stats	Returns the period of a time series.
window()	stats	Subsets a time-series object.
ma()	forecast	Fits a simple moving-average model.
stl()	stats	Decomposes a time series into seasonal, trend, and irregular components using loess.
monthplot()	stats	Plots the seasonal components of a time series.
seasonplot()	forecast	Generates a season plot.
HoltWinters()	stats	Fits an exponential smoothing model.
forecast()	forecast	Forecasts future values of a time series.
accuracy()	forecast	Reports fit measures for a time-series model.
ets()	forecast	Fits an exponential smoothing model. Includes the ability to automate the selection of a model.
lag()	stats	Returns a lagged version of a time series.
Acf()	forecast	Estimates the autocorrelation function.
Pacf()	forecast	Estimates the partial autocorrelation function.
diff()	base	Returns lagged and iterated differences.

Table 15.1 Functions for time-series analysis

Function	Package	Use
ndiffs()	forecast	Determines the level of differencing needed to remove trends in a time series.
adf.test()	tseries	Computes an Augmented Dickey–Fuller test that a time series is stationary.
arima()	stats	Fits autoregressive integrated moving-average models.
Box.test()	stats	Computes a Ljung–Box test that the residuals of a time series are independent.
bds.test()	tseries	Computes the BDS test that a series consists of independent, identically distributed random variables.
auto.arima()	forecast	Automates the selection of an ARIMA model.

Table 15.2 lists the time-series data that you'll analyze. They're available with the base installation of R. The datasets vary greatly in their characteristics and the models that fit them best.

Table 15.2 Datasets used in this chapter

Time series	Description
AirPassengers	Monthly airline passenger numbers from 1949–1960
JohnsonJohnson	Quarterly earnings per Johnson & Johnson share
nhtemp	Average yearly temperatures in New Haven, Connecticut, from 1912–1971
Nile	Flow of the river Nile
sunspots	Monthly sunspot numbers from 1749–1983

We'll start with methods for creating and manipulating time series, describing and plotting them, and decomposing them into level, trend, seasonal, and irregular (error) components. Then we'll turn to forecasting, starting with popular exponential modeling approaches that use weighted averages of time-series values to predict future values. Next we'll consider a set of forecasting techniques called *autoregressive integrated moving averages (ARIMA) models* that use correlations among recent data points and among recent prediction errors to make future forecasts. Throughout, we'll consider methods of evaluating the fit of models and the accuracy of their predictions. The chapter ends with a description of resources available for learning more about these topics.

15.1 Creating a time-series object in R

In order to work with a time series in R, you have to place it into a *time-series object*—an R structure that contains the observations, the starting and ending time of the series, and information about its periodicity (for example, monthly, quarterly, or annual data). Once the data are in a time-series object, you can use numerous functions to manipulate, model, and plot the data.

A vector of numbers, or a column in a data frame, can be saved as a time-series object using the ts() function. The format is

```
myseries <- ts(data, start=, end=, frequency=)
```

where myseries is the time-series object, data is a numeric vector containing the observations, start specifies the series start time, end specifies the end time (optional), and frequency indicates the number of observations per unit time (for example, frequency=1 for annual data, frequency=12 for monthly data, and frequency=4 for quarterly data).

An example is given in the following listing. The data consist of monthly sales figures for two years, starting in January 2003.

Listing 15.1   Creating a time-series object

```
> sales <- c(18, 33, 41,  7, 34, 35, 24, 25, 24, 21, 25, 20,
             22, 31, 40, 29, 25, 21, 22, 54, 31, 25, 26, 35)

> tsales <- ts(sales, start=c(2003, 1), frequency=12)        ◁─┐  Creates a
> tsales                                                         time-series
                                                            ❶   object
     Jan Feb Mar Apr May Jun Jul Aug Sep Oct Nov Dec
2003  18  33  41   7  34  35  24  25  24  21  25  20
2004  22  31  40  29  25  21  22  54  31  25  26  35

> plot(tsales)
> start(tsales)                       ◁─┐  Gets information
                                      ❷  about the object
[1] 2003    1

> end(tsales)

[1] 2004   12

> frequency(tsales)
                                                          Subsets the object ❸
[1] 12

> tsales.subset <- window(tsales, start=c(2003, 5), end=c(2004, 6))   ◁─┘
> tsales.subset

     Jan Feb Mar Apr May Jun Jul Aug Sep Oct Nov Dec
2003                  34  35  24  25  24  21  25  20
2004  22  31  40  29  25  21
```

In this listing, the ts() function is used to create the time-series object ❶. Once it's created, you can print and plot it; the plot is given in figure 15.2. You can modify the plot using the techniques described in chapter 3. For example, plot(tsales, type="o", pch=19) would create a time-series plot with connected, solid-filled circles.

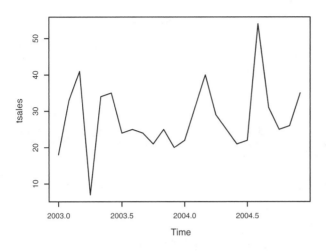

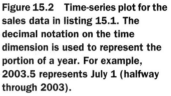

Figure 15.2 Time-series plot for the sales data in listing 15.1. The decimal notation on the time dimension is used to represent the portion of a year. For example, 2003.5 represents July 1 (halfway through 2003).

Once you've created the time-series object, you can use functions like `start()`, `end()`, and `frequency()` to return its properties ❷. You can also use the `window()` function to create a new time series that's a subset of the original ❸.

15.2 Smoothing and seasonal decomposition

Just as analysts explore a dataset with descriptive statistics and graphs before attempting to model the data, describing a time series numerically and visually should be the first step before attempting to build complex models. In this section, we'll look at smoothing a time series to clarify its general trend, and decomposing a time series in order to observe any seasonal effects.

15.2.1 Smoothing with simple moving averages

The first step when investigating a time series is to plot it, as in listing 15.1. Consider the `Nile` time series. It records the annual flow of the river Nile at Ashwan from 1871–1970. A plot of the series can be seen in the upper-left panel of figure 15.3. The time series appears to be decreasing, but there is a great deal of variation from year to year.

Time series typically have a significant irregular or error component. In order to discern any patterns in the data, you'll frequently want to plot a smoothed curve that damps down these fluctuations. One of the simplest methods of smoothing a time series is to use simple moving averages. For example, each data point can be replaced with the mean of that observation and one observation before and after it. This is called a *centered moving average*. A centered moving average is defined as

$$S_t = (Y_{t-q} + \ldots + Y_t + \ldots + Y_{t+q}) / (2q + 1)$$

where S_t is the smoothed value at time t and $k = 2q + 1$ is the number of observations that are averaged. The k value is usually chosen to be an odd number (3 in this example). By necessity, when using a centered moving average, you lose the $(k - 1) / 2$ observations at each end of the series.

Several functions in R can provide a simple moving average, including SMA() in the TTR package, rollmean() in the zoo package, and ma() in the forecast package. Here, you'll use the ma() function to smooth the Nile time series that comes with the base R installation.

The code in the next listing plots the raw time series and smoothed versions using k equal to 3, 7, and 15. The plots are given in figure 15.3.

Listing 15.2 Simple moving averages

```
library(forecast)
opar <- par(no.readonly=TRUE)
par(mfrow=c(2,2))
ylim <- c(min(Nile), max(Nile))
plot(Nile, main="Raw time series")
plot(ma(Nile, 3), main="Simple Moving Averages (k=3)", ylim=ylim)
plot(ma(Nile, 7), main="Simple Moving Averages (k=7)", ylim=ylim)
plot(ma(Nile, 15), main="Simple Moving Averages (k=15)", ylim=ylim)
par(opar)
```

As k increases, the plot becomes increasingly smoothed. The challenge is to find the value of k that highlights the major patterns in the data, without under- or over-smoothing. This is more art than science, and you'll probably want to try several values of k before settling on one. From the plots in figure 15.3, there certainly appears to have been a drop in river flow between 1892 and 1900. Other changes are open to interpretation. For example, there may have been a small increasing trend between 1941 and 1961, but this could also have been a random variation.

For time-series data with a periodicity greater than one (that is, with a seasonal component), you'll want to go beyond a description of the overall trend. Seasonal decomposition can be used to examine both seasonal and general trends.

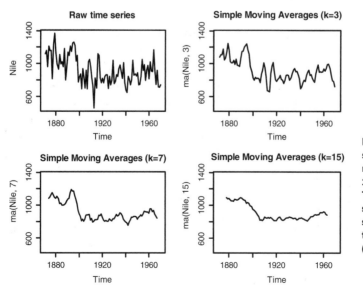

Figure 15.3 The Nile time series measuring annual river flow at Ashwan from 1871–1970 (upper left). The other plots are smoothed versions using simple moving averages at three smoothing levels (k=3, 7, and 15).

15.2.2 *Seasonal decomposition*

Time-series data that have a seasonal aspect (such as monthly or quarterly data) can be decomposed into a trend component, a seasonal component, and an irregular component. The *trend component* captures changes in level over time. The *seasonal component* captures cyclical effects due to the time of year. The *irregular* (or *error*) *component* captures those influences not described by the trend and seasonal effects.

The decomposition can be additive or multiplicative. In an additive model, the components sum to give the values of the time series. Specifically,

$$Y_t = \text{Trend}_t + \text{Seasonal}_t + \text{Irregular}_t$$

where the observation at time t is the sum of the contributions of the trend at time t, the seasonal effect at time t, and an irregular effect at time t.

In a multiplicative model, given by the equation

$$Y_t = \text{Trend}_t * \text{Seasonal}_t * \text{Irregular}_t$$

the trend, seasonal, and irregular influences are multiplied. Examples are given in figure 15.4.

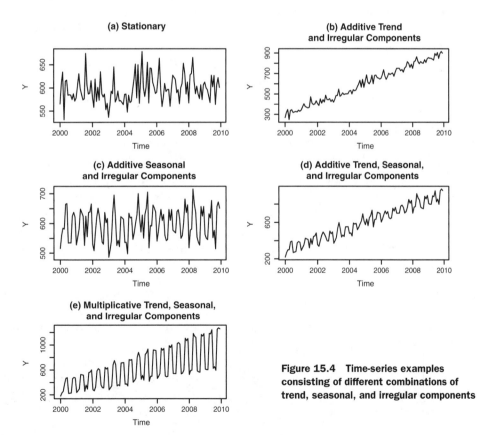

Figure 15.4 Time-series examples consisting of different combinations of trend, seasonal, and irregular components

In the first plot (a), there is neither a trend nor a seasonal component. The only influence is a random fluctuation around a given level. In the second plot (b), there is an upward trend over time, as well as random fluctuations. In the third plot (c), there are seasonal effects and random fluctuations, but no overall trend away from a horizontal line. In the fourth plot (d), all three components are present: an upward trend, seasonal effects, and random fluctuations. You also see all three components in the final plot (e), but here they combine in a multiplicative way. Notice how the variability is proportional to the level: as the level increases, so does the variability. This amplification (or possible damping) based on the current level of the series strongly suggests a multiplicative model.

An example may make the difference between additive and multiplicative models clearer. Consider a time series that records the monthly sales of motorcycles over a 10-year period. In a model with an additive seasonal effect, the number of motorcycles sold tends to increase by 500 in November and December (due to the Christmas rush) and decrease by 200 in January (when sales tend to be down). The seasonal increase or decrease is independent of the current sales volume.

In a model with a multiplicative seasonal effect, motorcycle sales in November and December tend to increase by 20% and decrease in January by 10%. In the multiplicative case, the impact of the seasonal effect is proportional to the current sales volume. This isn't the case in an additive model. In many instances, the multiplicative model is more realistic.

A popular method for decomposing a time series into trend, seasonal, and irregular components is seasonal decomposition by loess smoothing. In R, this can be accomplished with the `stl()` function. The format is

```
stl(ts, s.window=, t.window=)
```

where `ts` is the time series to be decomposed, `s.window` controls how fast the seasonal effects can change over time, and `t.window` controls how fast the trend can change over time. Smaller values allow more rapid change. Setting `s.window="periodic"` forces seasonal effects to be identical across years. Only the `ts` and `s.window` parameters are required. See `help(stl)` for details.

The `stl()` function can only handle additive models, but this isn't a serious limitation. Multiplicative models can be transformed into additive models using a log transformation:

```
log(Yₜ) = log(Trendₜ * Seasonalₜ * Irregularₜ)
        = log(Trendₜ) + log(Seasonalₜ) + log(Irregularₜ)
```

After fitting the additive model to the log transformed series, the results can be back-transformed to the original scale. Let's look at an example.

The time series `AirPassengers` comes with a base R installation and describes the monthly totals (in thousands) of international airline passengers between 1949 and 1960. A plot of the data is given in the top of figure 15.5. From the graph, it appears that variability of the series increases with the level, suggesting a multiplicative model.

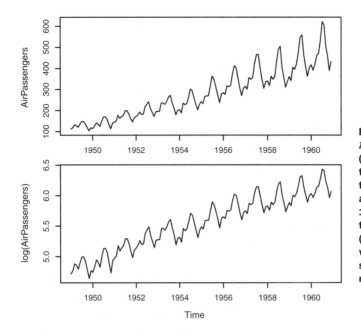

Figure 15.5 Plot of the
`AirPassengers` time series
(top). The time series contains
the monthly totals (in
thousands) of international
airline passengers between
1949 and 1960. The log-
transformed time series
(bottom) stabilizes the
variance and fits an additive
seasonal decomposition
model better.

The plot in the lower portion of figure 15.5 displays the time series created by taking the log of each observation. The variance has stabilized, and the logged series looks like an appropriate candidate for an additive decomposition. This is carried out using the `stl()` function in the following listing.

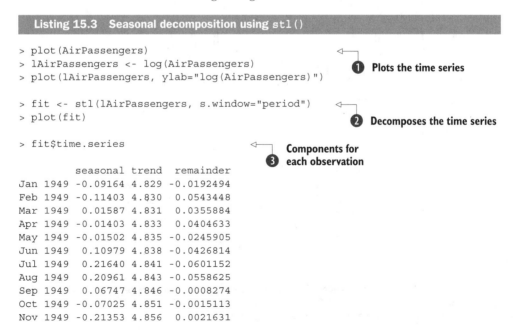

Listing 15.3   Seasonal decomposition using `stl()`

```
> plot(AirPassengers)                                         ◁───┐
> lAirPassengers <- log(AirPassengers)                            ❶ Plots the time series
> plot(lAirPassengers, ylab="log(AirPassengers)")


> fit <- stl(lAirPassengers, s.window="period")              ◁──┐
> plot(fit)                                                      ❷ Decomposes the time series

> fit$time.series                                            ◁──┐ Components for
                                                                 ❸ each observation
          seasonal trend   remainder
Jan 1949 -0.09164 4.829 -0.0192494
Feb 1949 -0.11403 4.830  0.0543448
Mar 1949  0.01587 4.831  0.0355884
Apr 1949 -0.01403 4.833  0.0404633
May 1949 -0.01502 4.835 -0.0245905
Jun 1949  0.10979 4.838 -0.0426814
Jul 1949  0.21640 4.841 -0.0601152
Aug 1949  0.20961 4.843 -0.0558625
Sep 1949  0.06747 4.846 -0.0008274
Oct 1949 -0.07025 4.851 -0.0015113
Nov 1949 -0.21353 4.856  0.0021631
```

```
Dec 1949 -0.10064 4.865  0.0067347
... output omitted ...

> exp(fit$time.series)

          seasonal trend remainder
Jan 1949    0.9124 125.1    0.9809
Feb 1949    0.8922 125.3    1.0558
Mar 1949    1.0160 125.4    1.0362
Apr 1949    0.9861 125.6    1.0413
May 1949    0.9851 125.9    0.9757
Jun 1949    1.1160 126.2    0.9582
Jul 1949    1.2416 126.6    0.9417
Aug 1949    1.2332 126.9    0.9457
Sep 1949    1.0698 127.2    0.9992
Oct 1949    0.9322 127.9    0.9985
Nov 1949    0.8077 128.5    1.0022
Dec 1949    0.9043 129.6    1.0068
... output omitted ...
```

First, the time series is plotted and transformed ❶. A seasonal decomposition is performed and saved in an object called fit ❷. Plotting the results gives the graph in figure 15.6. The graph shows the time series, seasonal, trend, and irregular components from 1949 to 1960. Note that the seasonal components have been constrained to

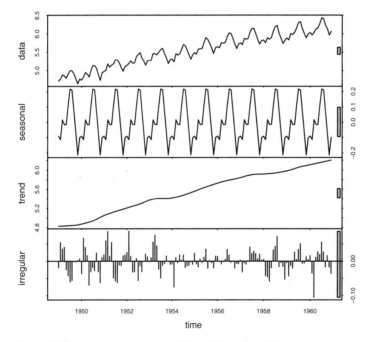

**Figure 15.6   A seasonal decomposition of the logged `AirPassengers`
time series using the `stl()` function. The time series (data) is
decomposed into seasonal, trend, and irregular components.**

remain the same across each year (using the s.window="period" option). The trend is monotonically increasing, and the seasonal effect suggests more passengers in the summer (perhaps during vacations). The grey bars on the right are magnitude guides—each bar represents the same magnitude. This is useful because the y-axes are different for each graph.

The object returned by the stl() function contains a component called time.series that contains the trend, season, and irregular portion of each observation ❸. In this case, fit$time.series is based on the logged time series. exp(fit$time.series) converts the decomposition back to the original metric. Examining the seasonal effects suggests that the number of passengers increased by 24% in July (a multiplier of 1.24) and decreased by 20% in November (with a multiplier of .80).

Two additional graphs can help to visualize a seasonal decomposition. They're created by the monthplot() function that comes with base R and the seasonplot() function provided in the forecast package. The code

```
par(mfrow=c(2,1))
library(forecast)
monthplot(AirPassengers, xlab="",  ylab="")
seasonplot(AirPassengers, year.labels="TRUE", main="")
```

produces the graphs in figure 15.7.

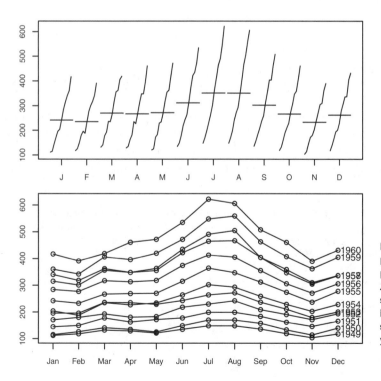

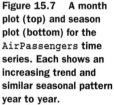

Figure 15.7 A month plot (top) and season plot (bottom) for the AirPassengers time series. Each shows an increasing trend and similar seasonal pattern year to year.

The month plot (top figure) displays the subseries for each month (all January values connected, all February values connected, and so on), along with the average of each subseries. From this graph, it appears that the trend is increasing for each month in a roughly uniform way. Additionally, the greatest number of passengers occurs in July and August. The season plot (lower figure) displays the subseries by year. Again you see a similar pattern, with increases in passengers each year, and the same seasonal pattern.

Note that although you've described the time series, you haven't predicted any future values. In the next section, we'll consider the use of exponential models for forecasting beyond the available data.

15.3 *Exponential forecasting models*

Exponential models are some of the most popular approaches to forecasting the future values of a time series. They're simpler than many other types of models, but they can yield good short-term predictions in a wide range of applications. They differ from each other in the components of the time series that are modeled. A simple exponential model (also called a *single exponential model*) fits a time series that has a constant level and an irregular component at time *i* but has neither a trend nor a seasonal component. A *double exponential model* (also called a *Holt exponential smoothing*) fits a time series with both a level and a trend. Finally, a *triple exponential model* (also called a *Holt-Winters exponential smoothing*) fits a time series with level, trend, and seasonal components.

Exponential models can be fit with either the HoltWinters() function in the base installation or the ets() function that comes with the forecast package. The ets() function has more options and is generally more powerful. We'll focus on the ets() function in this section.

The format of the ets() function is

```
ets(ts, model="ZZZ")
```

where *ts* is a time series and the model is specified by three letters. The first letter denotes the error type, the second letter denotes the trend type, and the third letter denotes the seasonal type. Allowable letters are *A* for additive, *M* for multiplicative, *N* for none, and *Z* for automatically selected. Examples of common models are given in table 15.3.

Table 15.3 Functions for fitting simple, double, and triple exponential forecasting models

Type	Parameters fit	Functions
simple	level	ets(ts, model="ANN") ses(ts)
double	level, slope	ets(ts, model="AAN") holt(ts)
triple	level, slope, seasonal	ets(ts, model="AAA") hw(ts)

The ses(), holt(), and hw() functions are convenience wrappers to the ets() function with prespecified defaults.

First we'll look at the most basic exponential model: simple exponential smoothing. Be sure to install the forecast package (install.packages("forecast")) before proceeding.

15.3.1 *Simple exponential smoothing*

Simple exponential smoothing uses a weighted average of existing time-series values to make a short-term prediction of future values. The weights are chosen so that observations have an exponentially decreasing impact on the average as you go back in time.

The simple exponential smoothing model assumes that an observation in the time series can be described by

$$Y_t = \text{level} + \text{irregular}_t$$

The prediction at time Y_{t+1} (called the *1-step ahead forecast*) is written as

$$Y_{t+1} = c_0 Y_t + c_1 Y_{t-1} + c_2 Y_{t-2} + c_2 Y_{t-2} + \dots$$

where $c_i = \alpha(1-\alpha)^i$, $i = 0, 1, 2, \dots$ and $0 \leq \alpha \leq 1$. The c_i weights sum to one, and the 1-step ahead forecast can be seen to be a weighted average of the current value and all past values of the time series. The alpha (α) parameter controls the rate of decay for the weights. The closer alpha is to 1, the more weight is given to recent observations. The closer alpha is to 0, the more weight is given to past observations. The actual value of alpha is usually chosen by computer in order to optimize a fit criterion. A common fit criterion is the sum of squared errors between the actual and predicted values. An example will help clarify these ideas.

The nhtemp time series contains the mean annual temperature in degrees Fahrenheit in New Haven, Connecticut, from 1912 to 1971. A plot of the time series can be seen as the line in figure 15.8.

There is no obvious trend, and the yearly data lack a seasonal component, so the simple exponential model is a reasonable place to start. The code for making a 1-step ahead forecast using the ses() function is given next.

Listing 15.4 Simple exponential smoothing

```
> library(forecast)
> fit <- ets(nhtemp, model="ANN")          ① Fits the model
> fit

ETS(A,N,N)

Call:
 ets(y = nhtemp, model = "ANN")

  Smoothing parameters:
    alpha = 0.182

  Initial states:
    l = 50.2759
```

```
    sigma:  1.126

  AIC  AICc   BIC
263.9 264.1 268.1
```

2 **1-step ahead forecast**

```
> forecast(fit, 1)
```

```
      Point Forecast Lo 80 Hi 80 Lo 95 Hi 95
1972           51.87 50.43 53.31 49.66 54.08
```

```
> plot(forecast(fit, 1), xlab="Year",
    ylab=expression(paste("Temperature (", degree*F,")"),)),
    main="New Haven Annual Mean Temperature")
```

```
> accuracy(fit)
```

3 **Prints accuracy measures**

```
              ME  RMSE    MAE    MPE  MAPE   MASE
Training set 0.146 1.126 0.8951 0.2419 1.749 0.9228
```

The ets(mode="ANN") statement fits the simple exponential model to the nhtemp time series **1**. The A indicates that the errors are additive, and the NN indicates that there is no trend and no seasonal component. The relatively low value of alpha (0.18) indicates that distant as well as recent observations are being considered in the forecast. This value is automatically chosen to maximize the fit of the model to the given dataset.

The forecast() function is used to predict the time series *k* steps into the future. The format is forecast(*fit, k*). The 1-step ahead forecast for this series is 51.9°F with a 95% confidence interval (49.7°F to 54.1°F) **2**. The time series, the forecasted value, and the 80% and 95% confidence intervals are plotted in figure 15.8 **3**.

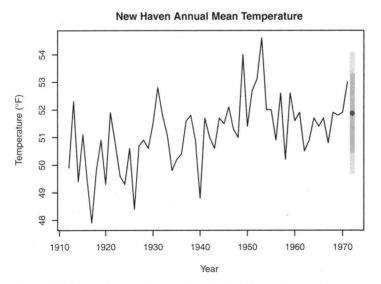

New Haven Annual Mean Temperature

Figure 15.8   Average yearly temperatures in New Haven, Connecticut; and a 1-step ahead prediction from a simple exponential forecast using the ets() function

The forecast package also provides an accuracy() function that displays the most popular predictive accuracy measures for time-series forecasts ❸. A description of each is given in table 15.4. The e_t represent the error or irregular component of each observation $(Y_t - \hat{Y}_i)$.

Table 15.4 Predictive accuracy measures

Measure	Abbreviation	Definition
Mean error	ME	mean(e_t)
Root mean squared error	RMSE	sqrt(mean(e_t^2))
Mean absolute error	MAE	mean($\mid e_t \mid$)
Mean percentage error	MPE	mean($100 * e_t / Y_t$)
Mean absolute percentage error	MAPE	mean($\mid 100 * e_t / Y_t \mid$)
Mean absolute scaled error	MASE	mean($\mid q_t \mid$) where $q_t = e_t / (1/(T\text{-}1) * \text{sum}(\mid y_t - y_{t\text{-}1} \mid))$, T is the number of observations, and the sum goes from t=2 to t=T

The mean error and mean percentage error may not be that useful, because positive and negative errors can cancel out. The RMSE gives the square root of the mean square error, which in this case is 1.13°F. The mean absolute percentage error reports the error as a percentage of the time-series values. It's unit-less and can be used to compare prediction accuracy across time series. But it assumes a measurement scale with a true zero point (for example, number of passengers per day). Because the Fahrenheit scale has no true zero, you can't use it here. The mean absolute scaled error is the most recent accuracy measure and is used to compare the forecast accuracy across time series on different scales. There is no one best measure of predictive accuracy. The RMSE is certainly the best known and often cited.

Simple exponential smoothing assumes the absence of trend or seasonal components. The next section considers exponential models that can accommodate both.

15.3.2 *Holt and Holt-Winters exponential smoothing*

The Holt exponential smoothing approach can fit a time series that has an overall level and a trend (slope). The model for an observation at time *t* is

Y_t = level + slope*t + irregular$_t$

An alpha smoothing parameter controls the exponential decay for the level, and a beta smoothing parameter controls the exponential decay for the slope. Again, each parameter ranges from 0 to 1, with larger values giving more weight to recent observations.

The Holt-Winters exponential smoothing approach can be used to fit a time series that has an overall level, a trend, and a seasonal component. Here, the model is

Y_t = level + slope*t + s$_t$ + irregular$_t$

where s_t represents the seasonal influence at time t. In addition to alpha and beta parameters, a gamma smoothing parameter controls the exponential decay of the seasonal component. Like the others, it ranges from 0 to 1, and larger values give more weight to recent observations in calculating the seasonal effect.

In section 15.2, you decomposed a time series describing the monthly totals (in log thousands) of international airline passengers into additive trend, seasonal, and irregular components. Let's use an exponential model to predict future travel. Again, you'll use log values so that an additive model fits the data. The code in the following listing applies the Holt-Winters exponential smoothing approach to predicting the next five values of the AirPassengers time series.

Listing 15.5   Exponential smoothing with level, slope, and seasonal components

```
> library(forecast)
> fit <- ets(log(AirPassengers), model="AAA")
> fit

ETS(A,A,A)

Call:
 ets(y = log(AirPassengers), model = "AAA")

  Smoothing parameters:
    alpha = 0.8528
    beta  = 4e-04
    gamma = 0.0121

  Initial states:
    l = 4.8362
    b = 0.0097
    s=-0.1137 -0.2251 -0.0756 0.0623 0.2079 0.2222
          0.1235 -0.009 0 0.0203 -0.1203 -0.0925

  sigma:  0.0367

   AIC    AICc    BIC
-204.1 -199.8 -156.5

>accuracy(fit)

                   ME     RMSE     MAE      MPE    MAPE    MASE
Training set -0.0003695 0.03672 0.02835 -0.007882 0.5206 0.07532

> pred <- forecast(fit, 5)
> pred
          Point Forecast Lo 80 Hi 80 Lo 95 Hi 95
Jan 1961          6.101 6.054 6.148 6.029 6.173
Feb 1961          6.084 6.022 6.146 5.989 6.179
Mar 1961          6.233 6.159 6.307 6.120 6.346
Apr 1961          6.222 6.138 6.306 6.093 6.350
May 1961          6.225 6.131 6.318 6.082 6.367

> plot(pred, main="Forecast for Air Travel",
    ylab="Log(AirPassengers)", xlab="Time")
```

❶ Smoothing parameters

❷ Future forecasts

```
> pred$mean <- exp(pred$mean)
> pred$lower <- exp(pred$lower)
> pred$upper <- exp(pred$upper)
> p <- cbind(pred$mean, pred$lower, pred$upper)
> dimnames(p)[[2]] <- c("mean", "Lo 80", "Lo 95", "Hi 80", "Hi 95")
> p
```

❸ Makes forecasts in the original scale

```
          mean Lo 80 Lo 95 Hi 80 Hi 95
Jan 1961 446.3 425.8 415.3 467.8 479.6
Feb 1961 438.8 412.5 399.2 466.8 482.3
Mar 1961 509.2 473.0 454.9 548.2 570.0
Apr 1961 503.6 463.0 442.9 547.7 572.6
May 1961 505.0 460.1 437.9 554.3 582.3
```

The smoothing parameters for the level (.82), trend (.0004), and seasonal components (.012) are given in ❶. The low value for the trend (.0004) doesn't mean there is no slope; it indicates that the slope estimated from early observations didn't need to be updated.

The forecast() function produces forecasts for the next five months ❷ and is plotted in figure 15.9. Because the predictions are on a log scale, exponentiation is used to get the predictions in the original metric: numbers (in thousands) of passengers ❸. The matrix pred$mean contains the point forecasts, and the matrices pred$lower and pred$upper contain the 80% and 95% lower and upper confidence limits, respectively. The exp() function is used to return the predictions to the original scale, and cbind() creates a single table. Thus the model predicts 509,200 passengers in March, with a 95% confidence band ranging from 454,900 to 570,000.

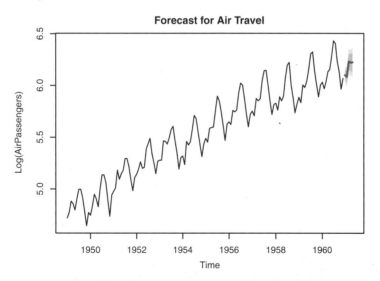

Figure 15.9 Five-year forecast of log(number of international airline passengers in thousands) based on a Holt-Winters exponential smoothing model. Data are from the AirPassengers time series.

15.3.3 *The ets() function and automated forecasting*

The ets() function has additional capabilities. You can use it to fit exponential models that have multiplicative components, add a dampening component, and perform automated forecasts. Let's consider each in turn.

In the previous section, you fit an additive exponential model to the log of the AirPassengers time series. Alternatively, you could fit a multiplicative model to the original data. The function call would be either ets(AirPassengers, model="MAM") or the equivalent hw(AirPassengers, seasonal="multiplicative"). The trend remains additive, but the seasonal and irregular components are assumed to be multiplicative. By using a multiplicative model in this case, the accuracy statistics and forecasted values are reported in the original metric (thousands of passengers)—a decided advantage.

The ets() function can also fit a damping component. Time-series predictions often assume that a trend will continue up forever (housing market, anyone?). A damping component forces the trend to a horizontal asymptote over a period of time. In many cases, a damped model makes more realistic predictions.

Finally, you can invoke the ets() function to automatically select a best-fitting model for the data. Let's fit an automated exponential model to the Johnson & Johnson data described in the introduction to this chapter. The following code allows the software to select a best-fitting model.

> **Listing 15.6 Automatic exponential forecasting with ets()**

```
> library(forecast)
> fit <- ets(JohnsonJohnson)
> fit

ETS(M,M,M)

Call:
 ets(y = JohnsonJohnson)

  Smoothing parameters:
    alpha = 0.2328
    beta  = 0.0367
    gamma = 0.5261

  Initial states:
    l = 0.625
    b = 1.0286
    s=0.6916 1.2639 0.9724 1.0721

  sigma:  0.0863

     AIC      AICc      BIC
162.4737 164.3937 181.9203

> plot(forecast(fit), main="Johnson & Johnson Forecasts",
    ylab="Quarterly Earnings (Dollars)", xlab="Time", flty=2)
```

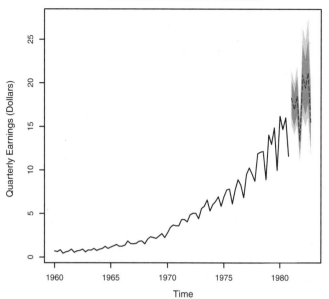

Johnson & Johnson Forecasts

Figure 15.10   Multiplicative exponential smoothing forecast with trend and seasonal components. The forecasts are a dashed line, and the 80% and 95% confidence intervals are provided in light and dark gray, respectively.

Because no model is specified, the software performs a search over a wide array of models to find one that minimizes the fit criterion (log-likelihood by default). The selected model is one that has multiplicative trend, seasonal, and error components. The plot, along with forecasts for the next eight quarters (the default in this case), is given in figure 15.10. The `flty` parameter sets the line type for the forecast line (dashed in this case).

As stated earlier, exponential time-series modeling is popular because it can give good short-term forecasts in many situations. A second approach that is also popular is the Box-Jenkins methodology, commonly referred to as ARIMA models. These are described in the next section.

15.4   ARIMA forecasting models

In the *autoregressive integrated moving average (ARIMA)* approach to forecasting, predicted values are a linear function of recent actual values and recent errors of prediction (residuals). ARIMA is a complex approach to forecasting. In this section, we'll limit discussion to ARIMA models for non-seasonal time series.

Before describing ARIMA models, a number of terms need to be defined, including lags, autocorrelation, partial autocorrelation, differencing, and stationarity. Each is considered in the next section.

15.4.1   Prerequisite concepts

When you *lag* a time series, you shift it back by a given number of observations. Consider the first few observations from the `Nile` time series, displayed in table 15.5. Lag 0 is the unshifted time series. Lag 1 is the time series shifted one position to the left. Lag 2 shifts the time series two positions to the left, and so on. Time series can be lagged using the function lag(*ts*,*k*), where *ts* is the time series and *k* is the number of lags.

Table 15.5 The Nile time series at various lags

Lag	1869	1870	1871	1872	1873	1874	1875	...
0			1120	1160	963	1210	1160	...
1		1120	1160	963	1210	1160	1160	...
2	1120	1160	963	1210	1160	1160	813	...

Autocorrelation measures the way observations in a time series relate to each other. AC_k is the correlation between a set of observations (Y_t) and observations k periods earlier (Y_{t-k}). So AC_1 is the correlation between the Lag 1 and Lag 0 time series, AC_2 is the correlation between the Lag 2 and Lag 0 time series, and so on. Plotting these correlations (AC_1, AC_2, ..., AC_k) produces an *autocorrelation function (ACF) plot*. The ACF plot is used to select appropriate parameters for the ARIMA model and to assess the fit of the final model.

An ACF plot can be produced with the acf() function in the stats package or the Acf() function in the forecast package. Here, the Acf() function is used because it produces a plot that is somewhat easier to read. The format is Acf(*ts*), where *ts* is the original time series. The ACF plot for the Nile time series, with *k*=1 to 18, is provided a little later, in the top half of figure 15.12.

A *partial autocorrelation* is the correlation between Y_t and Y_{t-k} with the effects of all Y values between the two (Y_{t-1}, Y_{t-2}, ..., Y_{t-k+1}) removed. Partial autocorrelations can also be plotted for multiple values of *k*. The PACF plot can be generated with either the pacf() function in the stats package or the Pacf() function in the forecast package. Again, the Pacf() function is preferred due to its formatting. The function call is Pacf(*ts*), where *ts* is the time series to be assessed. The PACF plot is also used to determine the most appropriate parameters for the ARIMA model. The results for the Nile time series are given in the bottom half of figure 15.12.

ARIMA models are designed to fit *stationary* time series (or time series that can be made stationary). In a stationary time series, the statistical properties of the series don't change over time. For example, the mean and variance of Y_t are constant. Additionally, the autocorrelations for any lag *k* don't change with time.

It may be necessary to transform the values of a time series in order to achieve constant variance before proceeding to fitting an ARIMA model. The log transformation is often useful here, as you saw in section 15.1.3. Other transformations, such as the Box-Cox transformation described in section 8.5.2, may also be helpful.

Because stationary time series are assumed to have constant means, they can't have a trend component. Many non-stationary time series can be made stationary through *differencing.* In differencing, each value of a time series Y_t is replaced with $Y_{t-1} - Y_t$. Differencing a time series once removes a linear trend. Differencing it a second time removes a quadratic trend. A third time removes a cubic trend. It's rarely necessary to difference more than twice.

You can difference a time series with the `diff()` function. The format is `diff(ts, differences=d)`, where d indicates the number of times the time series `ts` is differenced. The default is d=1. The `ndiffs()` function in the `forecast` package can be used to help determine the best value of d. The format is `ndiffs(ts)`.

Stationarity is often evaluated with a visual inspection of a time-series plot. If the variance isn't constant, the data are transformed. If there are trends, the data are differenced. You can also use a statistical procedure called the *Augmented Dickey-Fuller (ADF) test* to evaluate the assumption of stationarity. In R, the function `adf.test()` in the `tseries` package performs the test. The format is `adf.test(ts)`, where `ts` is the time series to be evaluated. A significant result suggests stationarity.

To summarize, ACF and PCF plots are used to determine the parameters of ARIMA models. Stationarity is an important assumption, and transformations and differencing are used to help achieve stationarity. With these concepts in hand, we can now turn to fitting models with an autoregressive (AR) component, a moving averages (MA) component, or both components (ARMA). Finally, we'll examine ARIMA models that include ARMA components and differencing to achieve stationarity (Integration).

15.4.2 *ARMA and ARIMA models*

In an *autoregressive* model of order p, each value in a time series is predicted from a linear combination of the previous p values

$$AR(p): Y_t = \mu + \beta_1 Y_{t-1} + \beta_2 Y_{t-2} + \ldots + \beta_p Y_{t-p} + \varepsilon_t$$

where Y_t is a given value of the series, μ is the mean of the series, the βs are the weights, and ε_t is the irregular component. In a *moving average* model of order q, each value in the time series is predicted from a linear combination of q previous errors. In this case

$$MA(q): Y_t = \mu - \theta_1 \varepsilon_{t-1} - \theta_2 \varepsilon_{t-2} \ldots - \theta_q \varepsilon_{t-q} + \varepsilon_t$$

where the εs are the errors of prediction and the θs are the weights. (It's important to note that the moving averages described here aren't the simple moving averages described in section 15.1.2.)

Combining the two approaches yields an ARMA(p, q) model of the form

$$Y_t = \mu + \beta_1 Y_{t-1} + \beta_2 Y_{t-2} + \ldots + \beta_p Y_{t-p} - \theta_1 \varepsilon_{t-1} - \theta_2 \varepsilon_{t-2} \ldots - \theta_q \varepsilon_{t-q} + \varepsilon_t$$

that predicts each value of the time series from the past p values and q residuals.

An ARIMA(p, d, q) model is a model in which the time series has been differenced d times, and the resulting values are predicted from the previous p actual values and q previous errors. The predictions are "un-differenced" or *integrated* to achieve the final prediction.

The steps in ARIMA modeling are as follows:

1 Ensure that the time series is stationary.
2 Identify a reasonable model or models (possible values of p and q).
3 Fit the model.
4 Evaluate the model's fit, including statistical assumptions and predictive accuracy.
5 Make forecasts.

Let's apply each step in turn to fit an ARIMA model to the `Nile` time series.

ENSURING THAT THE TIME SERIES IS STATIONARY

First you plot the time series and assess its stationarity (see listing 15.7 and the top half of figure 15.11). The variance appears to be stable across the years observed, so there's no need for a transformation. There may be a trend, which is supported by the results of the `ndiffs()` function.

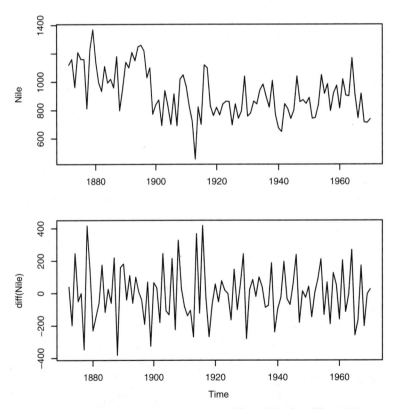

Figure 15.11   Time series displaying the annual flow of the river Nile at Ashwan from 1871 to 1970 (top) along with the times series differenced once (bottom). The differencing removes the decreasing trend evident in the original plot.

Listing 15.7 Transforming the time series and assessing stationarity

```
> library(forecast)
> library(tseries)
> plot(Nile)
> ndiffs(Nile)

[1] 1

> dNile <- diff(Nile)
> plot(dNile)
> adf.test(dNile)

    Augmented Dickey-Fuller Test

data:  dNile
Dickey-Fuller = -6.5924, Lag order = 4, p-value = 0.01
alternative hypothesis: stationary
```

The series is differenced once (lag=1 is the default) and saved as dNile. The differenced time series is plotted in the bottom half of figure 15.11 and certainly looks more stationary. Applying the ADF test to the differenced series suggest that it's now stationary, so you can proceed to the next step.

IDENTIFYING ONE OR MORE REASONABLE MODELS

Possible models are selected based on the ACF and PACF plots:

```
Acf(dNile)
Pacf(dNile)
```

The resulting plots are given in figure 15.12.

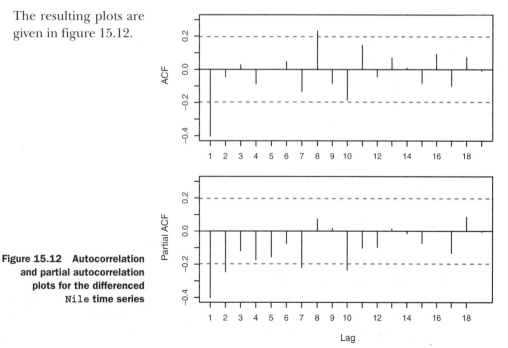

Figure 15.12 Autocorrelation and partial autocorrelation plots for the differenced Nile time series

The goal is to identify the parameters p, d, and q. You already know that d=1 from the previous section. You get p and q by comparing the ACF and PACF plots with the guidelines given in table 15.6.

Table 15.6   Guidelines for selecting an ARIMA model

Model	ACF	PACF
Box-Jenkins methodology	Trails off to zero	Zero after lag p
Box-Jenkins methodology	Zero after lag q	Trails off to zero
Box-Jenkins methodology	Trails off to zero	Trails off to zero

The results in table 15.6 are theoretical, and the actual ACF and PACF may not match this exactly. But they can be used to give a rough guide of reasonable models to try. For the `Nile` time series in figure 15.12, there appears to be one large autocorrelation at lag 1, and the partial autocorrelations trail off to zero as the lags get bigger. This suggests trying an ARIMA(0, 1, 1) model.

FITTING THE MODEL(S)

The ARIMA model is fit with the `arima()` function. The format is `arima(ts, order=c(q, d, q))`. The result of fitting an ARIMA(0, 1, 1) model to the `Nile` time series is given in the following listing.

Listing 15.8   Fitting an ARIMA model

```
> library(forecast)
> fit <- arima(Nile, order=c(0,1,1))
> fit

Series: Nile
ARIMA(0,1,1)

Coefficients:
         ma1
      -0.7329
s.e.   0.1143

sigma^2 estimated as 20600:  log likelihood=-632.55
AIC=1269.09   AICc=1269.22   BIC=1274.28

> accuracy(fit)

               ME  RMSE   MAE    MPE  MAPE   MASE
Training set -11.94 142.8 112.2 -3.575 12.94 0.8089
```

Note that you apply the model to the original time series. By specifying d=1, it calculates first differences for you. The coefficient for the moving averages (-0.73) is provided along with the AIC. If you fit other models, the AIC can help you choose which one is most reasonable. Smaller AIC values suggest better models. The accuracy measures can help you determine whether the model fits with sufficient accuracy. Here the mean absolute percent error is 13% of the river level.

EVALUATING MODEL FIT

If the model is appropriate, the residuals should be normally distributed with mean zero, and the autocorrelations should be zero for every possible lag. In other words, the residuals should be normally and independently distributed (no relationship between them). The assumptions can be evaluated with the following code.

Listing 15.9   Evaluating the model fit

```
> qqnorm(fit$residuals)
> qqline(fit$residuals)
> Box.test(fit$residuals, type="Ljung-Box")

    Box-Ljung test

data:  fit$residuals
X-squared = 1.3711, df = 1, p-value = 0.2416
```

The qqnorm() and qqline() functions produce the plot in figure 15.13. Normally distributed data should fall along the line. In this case, the results look good.

The Box.test() function provides a test that the autocorrelations are all zero. The results aren't significant, suggesting that the autocorrelations don't differ from zero. This ARIMA model appears to fit the data well.

MAKING FORECASTS

If the model hadn't met the assumptions of normal residuals and zero autocorrelations, it would have been necessary to alter the model, add parameters, or try a different approach. Once a final model has been chosen, it can be used to make predictions of future values. In the next listing, the forecast() function from the forecast package is used to predict three years ahead.

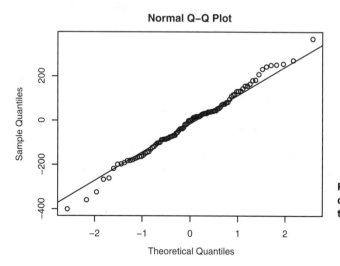

Figure 15.13   Normal Q-Q plot for determining the normality of the time-series residuals

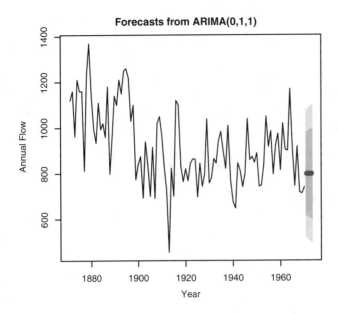

Forecasts from ARIMA(0,1,1)

Figure 15.14   Three-year forecast for the `Nile` time series from a fitted ARIMA(0,1,1) model. Blue dots represent point estimates, and the light and dark gray bands represent the 80% and 95% confidence bands limits, respectively.

Listing 15.10   Forecasting with an ARIMA model

```
> forecast(fit, 3)

     Point Forecast     Lo 80     Hi 80     Lo 95     Hi 95
1971       798.3673  614.4307  982.3040  517.0605  1079.674
1972       798.3673  607.9845  988.7502  507.2019  1089.533
1973       798.3673  601.7495  994.9851  497.6663  1099.068

> plot(forecast(fit, 3), xlab="Year", ylab="Annual Flow")
```

The plot() function is used to plot the forecast in figure 15.14. Point estimates are given by the blue dots, and 80% and 95% confidence bands are represented by dark and light bands, respectively.

15.4.3 *Automated ARIMA forecasting*

In section 15.2.3, you used the ets() function in the forecast package to automate the selection of a best exponential model. The package also provides an auto.arima() function to select a best ARIMA model. The next listing applies this approach to the sunspots time series described in the chapter introduction.

Listing 15.11   Automated ARIMA forecasting

```
> library(forecast)
> fit <- auto.arima(sunspots)
> fit
Series: sunspots
ARIMA(2,1,2)
```

```
Coefficients:
         ar1      ar2     ma1     ma2
        1.35   -0.396   -1.77   0.810
s.e.    0.03    0.029    0.02   0.019

sigma^2 estimated as 243:  log likelihood=-11746
AIC=23501    AICc=23501    BIC=23531

> forecast(fit, 3)


         Point Forecast        Lo 80      Hi 80        Lo 95      Hi 95
Jan 1984       40.437722   20.4412613   60.43418     9.855774   71.01967
Feb 1984       41.352897   18.2795867   64.42621     6.065314   76.64048
Mar 1984       39.796425   15.2537785   64.33907     2.261686   77.33116

> accuracy(fit)
                   ME RMSE    MAE MPE MAPE MASE
Training set -0.02673 15.6  11.03 NaN  Inf 0.32
```

The function selects an ARIMA model with p=2, d=1, and q=2. These are values that minimize the AIC criterion over a large number of possible models. The MPE and MAPE accuracy blow up because there are zero values in the series (a drawback of these two statistics). Plotting the results and evaluating the fit are left for you as an exercise.

15.5 *Going further*

There are many good books on time-series analysis and forecasting. If you're new to the subject, I suggest starting with the book *Time Series* (Open University, 2006). Although it doesn't include R code, it provides a very understandable and intuitive introduction. *A Little Book of R for Time Series* by Avril Coghlan (http://mng.bz/8fz0, 2010) pairs well with the Open University text and includes R code and examples.

Forecasting: Principles and Practice (http://otexts.com/fpp, 2013) is a clear and concise online textbook written by Rob Hyndman and George Athanasopoulos; it includes R code throughout. I highly recommend it. Additionally, Cowpertwait & Metcalfe (2009) have written an excellent text on analyzing time series with R. A more advanced treatment that also includes R code can be found in Shumway & Stoffer (2010).

Finally, you can consult the CRAN Task View on Time Series Analysis (http://cran.r-project.org/web/views/TimeSeries.html). It contains a comprehensive summary of all of R's time-series capabilities.

15.6 *Summary*

Forecasting has a long and varied history, from early shamans predicting the weather to modern data scientists predicting the results of recent elections. Prediction is fundamental to both science and human nature. In this chapter, we've looked at how to create time series in R, assess trends, and examine seasonal effects. Then we considered two of the most popular approaches to forecasting: exponential models and ARIMA models.

Although these methodologies can be crucial in understanding and predicting a wide variety of phenomena, it's important to remember that they each entail extrapolation—going beyond the data. They assume that future conditions mirror current conditions. Financial predictions made in 2007 assumed continued economic growth in 2008 and beyond. As we all know now, that isn't exactly how things turned out. Significant events can change the trend and pattern in a time series, and the farther out you try to predict, the greater the uncertainty.

In the next chapter, we'll shift gears and look at methodologies that are important to anyone trying to classify individuals or observations into discrete groups.

Cluster analysis

This chapter covers
- Identifying cohesive subgroups (clusters) of observations
- Determining the number of clusters present
- Obtaining a nested hierarchy of clusters
- Obtaining discrete clusters

Cluster analysis is a data-reduction technique designed to uncover subgroups of observations within a dataset. It allows you to reduce a large number of observations to a much smaller number of clusters or types. A *cluster* is defined as a group of observations that are more similar to each other than they are to the observations in other groups. This isn't a precise definition, and that fact has led to an enormous variety of clustering methods.

Cluster analysis is widely used in the biological and behavioral sciences, marketing, and medical research. For example, a psychological researcher might cluster data on the symptoms and demographics of depressed patients, seeking to uncover subtypes of depression. The hope would be that finding such subtypes might lead to more targeted and effective treatments and a better understanding of the disorder. Marketing researchers use cluster analysis as a customer-segmentation strategy.

Customers are arranged into clusters based on the similarity of their demographics and buying behaviors. Marketing campaigns are then tailored to appeal to one or more of these subgroups. Medical researchers use cluster analysis to help catalog gene-expression patterns obtained from DNA microarray data. This can help them to understand normal growth and development and the underlying causes of many human diseases.

The two most popular clustering approaches are *hierarchical agglomerative clustering* and *partitioning clustering*. In agglomerative hierarchical clustering, each observation starts as its own cluster. Clusters are then combined, two at a time, until all clusters are merged into a single cluster. In the partitioning approach, you specify *K*: the number of clusters sought. Observations are then randomly divided into *K* groups and reshuffled to form cohesive clusters.

Within each of these broad approaches, there are many clustering algorithms to choose from. For hierarchical clustering, the most popular are single linkage, complete linkage, average linkage, centroid, and Ward's method. For partitioning, the two most popular are k-means and partitioning around medoids (PAM). Each clustering method has advantages and disadvantages, which we'll discuss.

The examples in this chapter focus on food and wine (I suspect my friends aren't surprised). Hierarchical clustering is applied to the `nutrient` dataset contained in the `flexclust` package to answer the following questions:

- What are the similarities and differences among 27 types of fish, fowl, and meat, based on 5 nutrient measures?
- Is there a smaller number of groups into which these foods can be meaningfully clustered?

Partitioning methods will be used to evaluate 13 chemical analyses of 178 Italian wine samples. The data are contained in the `wine` dataset available with the `rattle` package. Here, the questions are as follows:

- Are there subtypes of wine in the data?
- If so, how many subtypes are there, and what are their characteristics?

In fact, the wine samples represent three varietals (recorded as Type). This will allow you to evaluate how well the cluster analysis recovers the underlying structure.

Although there are many approaches to cluster analysis, they usually follow a similar set of steps. These common steps are described in section 16.1. Hierarchical agglomerative clustering is described in section 16.2, and partitioning methods are covered in section 16.3. Some final advice and cautionary statements are provided in section 16.4. In order to run the examples in this chapter, be sure to install the `cluster`, `NbClust`, `flexclust`, `fMultivar`, `ggplot2`, and `rattle` packages. The `rattle` package will also be used in chapter 17.

16.1   *Common steps in cluster analysis*

Like factor analysis (chapter 14), an effective cluster analysis is a multistep process with numerous decision points. Each decision can affect the quality and usefulness of the results. This section describes the 11 typical steps in a comprehensive cluster analysis:

1 *Choose appropriate attributes.* The first (and perhaps most important) step is to select variables that you feel may be important for identifying and understanding differences among groups of observations within the data. For example, in a study of depression, you might want to assess one or more of the following: psychological symptoms; physical symptoms; age at onset; number, duration, and timing of episodes; number of hospitalizations; functional status with regard to self-care; social and work history; current age; gender; ethnicity; socioeconomic status; marital status; family medical history; and response to previous treatments. A sophisticated cluster analysis can't compensate for a poor choice of variables.

2 *Scale the data.* If the variables in the analysis vary in range, the variables with the largest range will have the greatest impact on the results. This is often undesirable, and analysts scale the data before continuing. The most popular approach is to standardize each variable to a mean of 0 and a standard deviation of 1. Other alternatives include dividing each variable by its maximum value or subtracting the variable's mean and dividing by the variable's median absolute deviation. The three approaches are illustrated with the following code snippets:

```
df1 <- apply(mydata, 2, function(x){(x-mean(x))/sd(x)})
df2 <- apply(mydata, 2, function(x){x/max(x)})
df3 <- apply(mydata, 2, function(x){(x - mean(x))/mad(x)})
```

In this chapter, you'll use the scale() function to standardize the variables to a mean of 0 and a standard deviation of 1. This is equivalent to the first code snippet (df1).

3 *Screen for outliers.* Many clustering techniques are sensitive to outliers, distorting the cluster solutions obtained. You can screen for (and remove) univariate outliers using functions from the outliers package. The mvoutlier package contains functions that can be used to identify multivariate outliers. An alternative is to use a clustering method that is robust to the presence of outliers. Partitioning around medoids (section 16.3.2) is an example of the latter approach.

4 *Calculate distances.* Although clustering algorithms vary widely, they typically require a measure of the distance among the entities to be clustered. The most popular measure of the distance between two observations is the Euclidean distance, but the Manhattan, Canberra, asymmetric binary, maximum, and Minkowski distance measures are also available (see ?dist for details). In this chapter, the Euclidean distance is used throughout. Calculating Euclidean distances is covered in section 16.1.1.

5 *Select a clustering algorithm.* Next, you select a method of clustering the data. Hierarchical clustering is useful for smaller problems (say, 150 observations or less) and where a nested hierarchy of groupings is desired. The partitioning method can handle much larger problems but requires that the number of clusters be specified in advance.

Once you've chosen the hierarchical or partitioning approach, you must select a specific clustering algorithm. Again, each has advantages and disadvantages. The most popular methods are described in sections 16.2 and 16.3. You may wish to try more than one algorithm to see how robust the results are to the choice of methods.

6   *Obtain one or more cluster solutions.* This step uses the method(s) selected in step 5.

7   *Determine the number of clusters present.* In order to obtain a final cluster solution, you must decide how many clusters are present in the data. This is a thorny problem, and many approaches have been proposed. It usually involves extracting various numbers of clusters (say, 2 to *K*) and comparing the quality of the solutions. The NbClust() function in the NBClust package provides 30 different indices to help you make this decision (elegantly demonstrating how unresolved this issue is). NbClust is used throughout this chapter.

8   *Obtain a final clustering solution.* Once the number of clusters has been determined, a final clustering is performed to extract that number of subgroups.

9   *Visualize the results.* Visualization can help you determine the meaning and usefulness of the cluster solution. The results of a hierarchical clustering are usually presented as a dendrogram. Partitioning results are typically visualized using a bivariate cluster plot.

10   *Interpret the clusters.* Once a cluster solution has been obtained, you must interpret (and possibly name) the clusters. What do the observations in a cluster have in common? How do they differ from the observations in other clusters? This step is typically accomplished by obtaining summary statistics for each variable by cluster. For continuous data, the mean or median for each variable within each cluster is calculated. For mixed data (data that contain categorical variables), the summary statistics will also include modes or category distributions.

11   *Validate the results.* Validating the cluster solution involves asking the question, "Are these groupings in some sense real, and not a manifestation of unique aspects of this dataset or statistical technique?" If a different cluster method or different sample is employed, would the same clusters be obtained? The fpc, clv, and clValid packages each contain functions for evaluating the stability of a clustering solution.

Because the calculations of distances between observations is such an integral part of cluster analysis, it's described next and in some detail.

16.2 *Calculating distances*

Every cluster analysis begins with the calculation of a distance, dissimilarity, or proximity between each entity to be clustered. The Euclidean distance between two observations is given by

$$d_{ij} = \sqrt{\sum_{p=1}^{p} (x_{ip} - x_{jp})^2}$$

where *i* and *j* are observations and *P* is the number of variables.

Consider the `nutrient` dataset provided with the `flexclust` package. The dataset contains measurements on the nutrients of 27 types of meat, fish, and fowl. The first few observations are given by

```
> data(nutrient, package="flexclust")
> head(nutrient, 4)

             energy protein fat calcium iron
BEEF BRAISED    340      20  28       9  2.6
HAMBURGER       245      21  17       9  2.7
BEEF ROAST      420      15  39       7  2.0
BEEF STEAK      375      19  32       9  2.6
```

and the Euclidean distance between the first two (beef braised and hamburger) is

$$d = \sqrt{(340 - 245)^2 + (20 - 21)^2 + (28 - 17)^2 + (9 - 9)^2 + (26 - 27)^2} = 95.64$$

The `dist()` function in the base R installation can be used to calculate the distances between all rows (observations) of a matrix or data frame. The format is `dist(x, method=)`, where *x* is the input data and `method="euclidean"` by default. The function returns a lower triangle matrix by default, but the `as.matrix()` function can be used to access the distances using standard bracket notation. For the `nutrient` data frame,

```
> d <- dist(nutrient)
> as.matrix(d)[1:4,1:4]

             BEEF BRAISED HAMBURGER BEEF ROAST BEEF STEAK
BEEF BRAISED          0.0      95.6       80.9       35.2
HAMBURGER            95.6       0.0      176.5      130.9
BEEF ROAST           80.9     176.5        0.0       45.8
BEEF STEAK           35.2     130.9       45.8        0.0
```

Larger distances indicate larger dissimilarities between observations. The distance between an observation and itself is 0. As expected, the `dist()` function provides the same distance between beef braised and hamburger as the hand calculations.

Cluster analysis with mixed data types

Euclidean distances are usually the distance measure of choice for continuous data. But if other variable types are present, alternative dissimilarity measures are required. You can use the `daisy()` function in the `cluster` package to obtain a dissimilarity matrix among observations that have any combination of binary, nominal, ordinal, and continuous attributes. Other functions in the `cluster` package can use these dissimilarities to carry out a cluster analysis. For example, `agnes()` offers agglomerative hierarchical clustering, and `pam()` provides partitioning around medoids.

Note that distances in the `nutrient` data frame are heavily dominated by the contribution of the energy variable, which has a much larger range. Scaling the data will help to equalize the impact of each variable. In the next section, you'll apply hierarchical cluster analysis to this dataset.

16.3 *Hierarchical cluster analysis*

As stated previously, in agglomerative hierarchical clustering, each case or observation starts as its own cluster. Clusters are then combined two at a time until all clusters are merged into a single cluster. The algorithm is as follows:

1 Define each observation (row, case) as a cluster.
2 Calculate the distances between every cluster and every other cluster.
3 Combine the two clusters that have the smallest distance. This reduces the number of clusters by one.
4 Repeat steps 2 and 3 until all clusters have been merged into a single cluster containing all observations.

The primary difference among hierarchical clustering algorithms is their definitions of cluster distances (step 2). Five of the most common hierarchical clustering methods and their definitions of the distance between two clusters are given in table 16.1.

Table 16.1   Hierarchical clustering methods

Cluster method	Definition of the distance between two clusters
Single linkage	Shortest distance between a point in one cluster and a point in the other cluster.
Complete linkage	Longest distance between a point in one cluster and a point in the other cluster.
Average linkage	Average distance between each point in one cluster and each point in the other cluster (also called UPGMA [unweighted pair group mean averaging]).
Centroid	Distance between the centroids (vector of variable means) of the two clusters. For a single observation, the centroid is the variable's values.
Ward	The ANOVA sum of squares between the two clusters added up over all the variables.

Single-linkage clustering tends to find elongated, cigar-shaped clusters. It also commonly displays a phenomenon called *chaining*—dissimilar observations are joined into the same cluster because they're similar to intermediate observations between them. Complete-linkage clustering tends to find compact clusters of approximately equal diameter. It can also be sensitive to outliers. Average-linkage clustering offers a compromise between the two. It's less likely to chain and is less susceptible to outliers. It also has a tendency to join clusters with small variances.

Ward's method tends to join clusters with small numbers of observations and tends to produce clusters with roughly equal numbers of observations. It can also be sensitive to outliers. The centroid method offers an attractive alternative due to its simple and easily understood definition of cluster distances. It's also less sensitive to outliers than other hierarchical methods. But it may not perform as well as the average-linkage or Ward method.

Hierarchical clustering can be accomplished with the `hclust()` function. The format is `hclust(d, method=)`, where *d* is a distance matrix produced by the `dist()` function and methods include `"single"`, `"complete"`, `"average"`, `"centroid"`, and `"ward"`.

In this section, you'll apply average-linkage clustering to the `nutrient` data introduced from section 16.1.1. The goal is to identify similarities, differences, and groupings among 27 food types based on nutritional information. The code for carrying out the clustering is provided in the following listing.

Listing 16.1   Average-linkage clustering of the nutrient data

```
data(nutrient, package="flexclust")
row.names(nutrient) <- tolower(row.names(nutrient))
nutrient.scaled <- scale(nutrient)

d <- dist(nutrient.scaled)

fit.average <- hclust(d, method="average")
plot(fit.average, hang=-1, cex=.8, main="Average Linkage Clustering")
```

First the data are imported, and the row names are set to lowercase (because I hate UPPERCASE LABELS). Because the variables differ widely in range, they're standardized to a mean of 0 and a standard deviation of 1. Euclidean distances between each of the 27 food types are calculated, and an average-linkage clustering is performed. Finally, the results are plotted as a dendrogram (see figure 16.1). The `hang` option in the `plot()` function justifies the observation labels (causing them to hang down from 0).

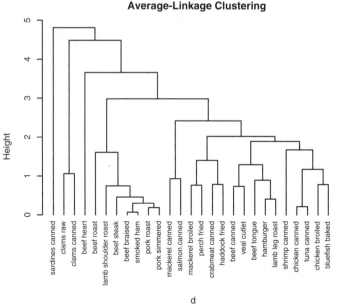

Figure 16.1   Average-linkage clustering of nutrient data

The dendrogram displays how items are combined into clusters and is read from the bottom up. Each observation starts as its own cluster. Then the two observations that are closest (beef braised and smoked ham) are combined. Next, pork roast and pork simmered are combined, followed by chicken canned and tuna canned. In the fourth step, the beef braised/smoked ham cluster and the pork roast/pork simmered clusters are combined (and the cluster now contains four food items). This continues until all observations are combined into a single cluster. The height dimension indicates the criterion value at which clusters are joined. For average-linkage clustering, this criterion is the average distance between each point in one cluster and each point in the other cluster.

If your goal is to understand how food types are similar or different with regard to their nutrients, then figure 16.1 may be sufficient. It creates a hierarchical view of the similarity/dissimilarity among the 27 items. Canned tuna and chicken are similar, and both differ greatly from canned clams. But if the end goal is to assign these foods to a smaller number of (hopefully meaningful) groups, additional analyses are required to select an appropriate number of clusters.

The NbClust package offers numerous indices for determining the best number of clusters in a cluster analysis. There is no guarantee that they will agree with each other. In fact, they probably won't. But the results can be used as a guide for selecting possible candidate values for *K*, the number of clusters. Input to the NbClust() function includes the matrix or data frame to be clustered, the distance measure and clustering method to employ, and the minimum and maximum number of clusters to consider. It returns each of the clustering indices, along with the best number of clusters proposed by each. The next listing applies this approach to the average-linkage clustering of the nutrient data.

Listing 16.2   Selecting the number of clusters

```
> library(NbClust)
> devAskNewPage(ask=TRUE)
> nc <- NbClust(nutrient.scaled, distance="euclidean",
                min.nc=2, max.nc=15, method="average")
> table(nc$Best.n[1,])

 0  2  3  4  5  9 10 13 14 15
 2  4  4  3  4  1  1  2  1  4

> barplot(table(nc$Best.n[1,]),
        xlab="Numer of Clusters", ylab="Number of Criteria",
        main="Number of Clusters Chosen by 26 Criteria")
```

Here, four criteria each favor two clusters, four criteria favor three clusters, and so on. The results are plotted in figure 16.2.

You could try the number of clusters (2, 3, 5, and 15) with the most "votes" and select the one that makes the most interpretive sense. The following listing explores the five-cluster solution.

Number of Clusters Chosen by 26 Criteria

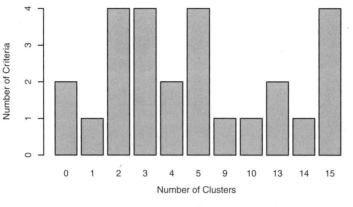

Figure 16.2 Recommended number of clusters using 26 criteria provided by the `NbClust` package

---

Listing 16.3 Obtaining the final cluster solution

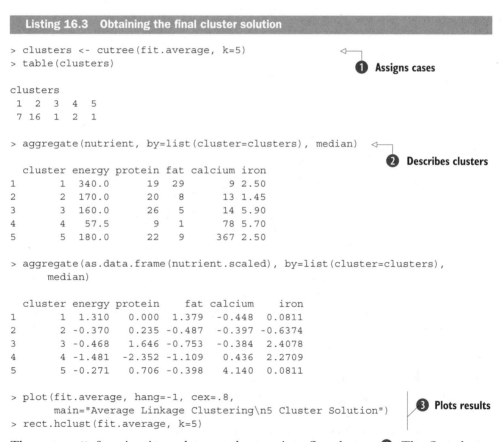

```
> clusters <- cutree(fit.average, k=5)
> table(clusters)
                                                          ❶ Assigns cases

clusters
 1  2  3  4  5
 7 16  1  2  1

> aggregate(nutrient, by=list(cluster=clusters), median)
                                                          ❷ Describes clusters

  cluster energy protein fat calcium iron
1       1  340.0      19  29       9 2.50
2       2  170.0      20   8      13 1.45
3       3  160.0      26   5      14 5.90
4       4   57.5       9   1      78 5.70
5       5  180.0      22   9     367 2.50

> aggregate(as.data.frame(nutrient.scaled), by=list(cluster=clusters),
      median)

  cluster energy protein    fat calcium    iron
1       1  1.310   0.000  1.379  -0.448  0.0811
2       2 -0.370   0.235 -0.487  -0.397 -0.6374
3       3 -0.468   1.646 -0.753  -0.384  2.4078
4       4 -1.481  -2.352 -1.109   0.436  2.2709
5       5 -0.271   0.706 -0.398   4.140  0.0811

> plot(fit.average, hang=-1, cex=.8,
      main="Average Linkage Clustering\n5 Cluster Solution")    ❸ Plots results
> rect.hclust(fit.average, k=5)
```

The `cutree()` function is used to cut the tree into five clusters ❶. The first cluster has 7 observations, the second cluster has 16 observations, and so on. The `aggregate()` function is then used to obtain the median profile for each cluster ❷. The results are reported in both the original metric and in standardized form. Finally, the

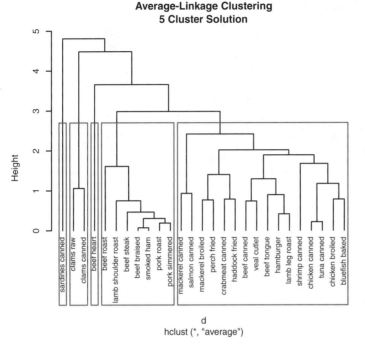

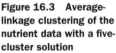

Figure 16.3 Average-linkage clustering of the nutrient data with a five-cluster solution

dendrogram is replotted, and the `rect.hclust()` function is used to superimpose the five-cluster solution ❸. The results are displayed in figure 16.3.

Sardines form their own cluster and are much higher in calcium than the other food groups. Beef heart is also a singleton and is high in protein and iron. The clam cluster is low in protein and high in iron. The items in the cluster containing beef roast to pork simmered are high in energy and fat. Finally, the largest group (mackerel to bluefish) is relatively low in iron.

Hierarchical clustering can be particularly useful when you expect nested clustering and a meaningful hierarchy. This is often the case in the biological sciences. But the hierarchical algorithms are greedy in the sense that once an observation is assigned to a cluster, it can't be reassigned later in the process. Additionally, hierarchical clustering is difficult to apply in large samples, where there may be hundreds or even thousands of observations. Partitioning methods can work well in these situations.

16.4 *Partitioning cluster analysis*

In the partitioning approach, observations are divided into *K* groups and reshuffled to form the most cohesive clusters possible according to a given criterion. This section considers two methods: k-means and partitioning around medoids (PAM).

16.4.1 *K-means clustering*

The most common partitioning method is the k-means cluster analysis. Conceptually, the k-means algorithm is as follows:

1 Select *K* centroids (*K* rows chosen at random).

2 Assign each data point to its closest centroid.

3 Recalculate the centroids as the average of all data points in a cluster (that is, the centroids are *p*-length mean vectors, where *p* is the number of variables).

4 Assign data points to their closest centroids.

5 Continue steps 3 and 4 until the observations aren't reassigned or the maximum number of iterations (R uses 10 as a default) is reached.

Implementation details for this approach can vary.

R uses an efficient algorithm by Hartigan and Wong (1979) that partitions the observations into *k* groups such that the sum of squares of the observations to their assigned cluster centers is a minimum. This means, in steps 2 and 4, each observation is assigned to the cluster with the smallest value of

$$ss(k) = \sum_{i=1}^{n} \sum_{j=0}^{p} (x_{ij} - \bar{x}_{kj})^2$$

where *k* is the cluster, x_{ij} is the value of the jth variable for the ith observation, $\bar{x}_{kj}$ is the mean of the jth variable for the kth cluster, and *p* is the number of variables.

K-means clustering can handle larger datasets than hierarchical cluster approaches. Additionally, observations aren't permanently committed to a cluster. They're moved when doing so improves the overall solution. But the use of means implies that all variables must be continuous, and the approach can be severely affected by outliers. It also performs poorly in the presence of non-convex (for example, U-shaped) clusters.

The format of the k-means function in R is `kmeans(x, centers)`, where *x* is a numeric dataset (matrix or data frame) and `centers` is the number of clusters to extract. The function returns the cluster memberships, centroids, sums of squares (within, between, total), and cluster sizes.

Because k-means cluster analysis starts with *k* randomly chosen centroids, a different solution can be obtained each time the function is invoked. Use the `set.seed()` function to guarantee that the results are reproducible. Additionally, this clustering approach can be sensitive to the initial selection of centroids. The `kmeans()` function has an `nstart` option that attempts multiple initial configurations and reports on the best one. For example, adding `nstart=25` generates 25 initial configurations. This approach is often recommended.

Unlike hierarchical clustering, k-means clustering requires that you specify in advance the number of clusters to extract. Again, the `NbClust` package can be used as a guide. Additionally, a plot of the total within-groups sums of squares against the number of clusters in a k-means solution can be helpful. A bend in the graph (similar to the bend in the Scree test described in section 14.2.1) can suggest the appropriate number of clusters.

The graph can be produced with the following function:

```
wssplot <- function(data, nc=15, seed=1234){
        wss <- (nrow(data)-1)*sum(apply(data,2,var))
```

```
      for (i in 2:nc){
          set.seed(seed)
          wss[i] <- sum(kmeans(data, centers=i)$withinss)}
      plot(1:nc, wss, type="b", xlab="Number of Clusters",
          ylab="Within groups sum of squares")}
```

The data parameter is the numeric dataset to be analyzed, nc is the maximum number of clusters to consider, and seed is a random-number seed.

Let's apply k-means clustering to a dataset containing 13 chemical measurements on 178 Italian wine samples. The data originally come from the UCI Machine Learning Repository (www.ics.uci.edu/~mlearn/MLRepository.html), but you'll access them here via the rattle package. In this dataset, the observations represent three wine varietals, as indicated by the first variable (Type). You'll drop this variable, perform the cluster analysis, and see if you can recover the known structure.

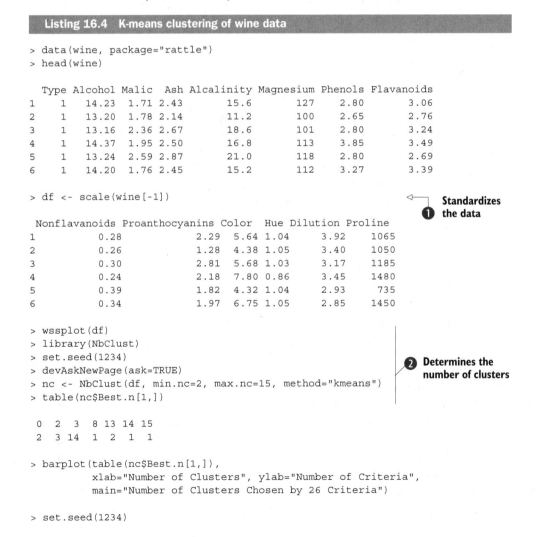

Listing 16.4   K-means clustering of wine data

```
> data(wine, package="rattle")
> head(wine)

  Type Alcohol Malic  Ash Alcalinity Magnesium Phenols Flavanoids
1    1   14.23  1.71 2.43       15.6       127    2.80       3.06
2    1   13.20  1.78 2.14       11.2       100    2.65       2.76
3    1   13.16  2.36 2.67       18.6       101    2.80       3.24
4    1   14.37  1.95 2.50       16.8       113    3.85       3.49
5    1   13.24  2.59 2.87       21.0       118    2.80       2.69
6    1   14.20  1.76 2.45       15.2       112    3.27       3.39

> df <- scale(wine[-1])
```

❶ Standardizes the data

```
  Nonflavanoids Proanthocyanins Color  Hue Dilution Proline
1          0.28            2.29  5.64 1.04     3.92    1065
2          0.26            1.28  4.38 1.05     3.40    1050
3          0.30            2.81  5.68 1.03     3.17    1185
4          0.24            2.18  7.80 0.86     3.45    1480
5          0.39            1.82  4.32 1.04     2.93     735
6          0.34            1.97  6.75 1.05     2.85    1450

> wssplot(df)
> library(NbClust)
> set.seed(1234)
> devAskNewPage(ask=TRUE)
> nc <- NbClust(df, min.nc=2, max.nc=15, method="kmeans")
> table(nc$Best.n[1,])
```

❷ Determines the number of clusters

```
 0  2  3  8 13 14 15
 2  3 14  1  2  1  1

> barplot(table(nc$Best.n[1,]),
        xlab="Number of Clusters", ylab="Number of Criteria",
        main="Number of Clusters Chosen by 26 Criteria")

> set.seed(1234)
```

```
> fit.km <- kmeans(df, 3, nstart=25)
> fit.km$size
```

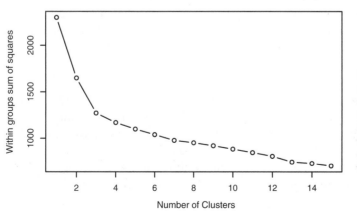

Performs the k-means cluster analysis ❸

```
[1] 62 65 51
```

```
> fit.km$centers
```

	Alcohol	Malic	Ash	Alcalinity	Magnesium	Phenols	Flavanoids	Nonflavanoids
1	0.83	-0.30	0.36	-0.61	0.576	0.883	0.975	-0.561
2	-0.92	-0.39	-0.49	0.17	-0.490	-0.076	0.021	-0.033
3	0.16	0.87	0.19	0.52	-0.075	-0.977	-1.212	0.724

	Proanthocyanins	Color	Hue	Dilution	Proline
1	0.579	0.17	0.47	0.78	1.12
2	0.058	-0.90	0.46	0.27	-0.75
3	-0.778	0.94	-1.16	-1.29	-0.41

```
> aggregate(wine[-1], by=list(cluster=fit.km$cluster), mean)
```

	cluster	Alcohol	Malic	Ash	Alcalinity	Magnesium	Phenols	Flavanoids
1	1	14	1.8	2.4	17	106	2.8	3.0
2	2	12	1.6	2.2	20	88	2.2	2.0
3	3	13	3.3	2.4	21	97	1.6	0.7

	Nonflavanoids	Proanthocyanins	Color	Hue	Dilution	Proline
1	0.29	1.9	5.4	1.07	3.2	1072
2	0.35	1.6	2.9	1.04	2.8	495
3	0.47	1.1	7.3	0.67	1.7	620

Because the variables vary in range, they're standardized prior to clustering ❶. Next, the number of clusters is determined using the wssplot() and NbClust() functions ❷. Figure 16.4 indicates that there is a distinct drop in the within-groups sum of squares when moving from one to three clusters. After three clusters, this decrease drops off, suggesting that a three-cluster solution may be a good fit to the data. In figure 16.5, 14 of 24 criteria provided by the NbClust package suggest a three-cluster solution. Note that not all 30 criteria can be calculated for every dataset.

A final cluster solution is obtained with the kmeans() function, and the cluster centroids are printed ❸. Because the centroids provided by the function are based on

Figure 16.4 Plotting the within-groups sums of squares vs. the number of clusters extracted. The sharp decreases from one to three clusters (with little decrease after) suggests a three-cluster solution.

Number of Clusters Chosen by 26 Criteria

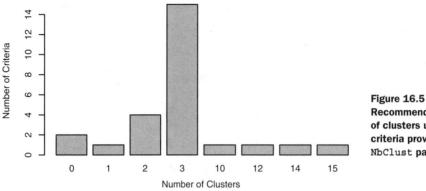

Figure 16.5
Recommended number
of clusters using 26
criteria provided by the
NbClust package

standardized data, the `aggregate()` function is used along with the cluster member-ships to determine variable means for each cluster in the original metric.

How well did k-means clustering uncover the actual structure of the data con-tained in the Type variable? A cross-tabulation of Type (wine varietal) and cluster membership is given by

```
> ct.km <- table(wine$Type, fit.km$cluster)
> ct.km

      1  2  3
  1  59  0  0
  2   3 65  3
  3   0  0 48
```

You can quantify the agreement between type and cluster using an adjusted Rand index, provided by the `flexclust` package:

```
> library(flexclust)
> randIndex(ct.km)
[1] 0.897
```

The adjusted Rand index provides a measure of the agreement between two parti-tions, adjusted for chance. It ranges from -1 (no agreement) to 1 (perfect agree-ment). Agreement between the wine varietal type and the cluster solution is 0.9. Not bad—shall we have some wine?

16.4.2 *Partitioning around medoids*

Because it's based on means, the k-means clustering approach can be sensitive to out-liers. A more robust solution is provided by partitioning around medoids (PAM). Rather than representing each cluster using a centroid (a vector of variable means), each cluster is identified by its most representative observation (called a *medoid*). Whereas k-means uses Euclidean distances, PAM can be based on any distance mea-sure. It can therefore accommodate mixed data types and isn't limited to continuous variables.

The PAM algorithm is as follows:

1 Randomly select K observations (call each a medoid).
2 Calculate the distance/dissimilarity of every observation to each medoid.
3 Assign each observation to its closest medoid.
4 Calculate the sum of the distances of each observation from its medoid (total cost).
5 Select a point that isn't a medoid, and swap it with its medoid.
6 Reassign every point to its closest medoid.
7 Calculate the total cost.
8 If this total cost is smaller, keep the new point as a medoid.
9 Repeat steps 5–8 until the medoids don't change.

A good worked example of the underlying math in the PAM approach can be found at http://en.wikipedia.org/wiki/k-medoids (I don't usually cite Wikipedia, but this is a great example).

You can use the pam() function in the cluster package to partition around medoids. The format is pam(x, k, metric="euclidean", stand=FALSE), where x is a data matrix or data frame, k is the number of clusters, metric is the type of distance/ dissimilarity measure to use, and stand is a logical value indicating whether the variables should be standardized before calculating this metric. PAM is applied to the wine data in the following listing; see figure 16.6.

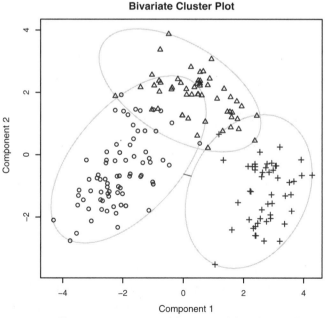

Bivariate Cluster Plot

These two components explain 55.41 % of the point variability.

Figure 16.6 Cluster plot for the three-group PAM clustering of the Italian wine data

Listing 16.5 Partitioning around medoids for the wine data

```
> library(cluster)
> set.seed(1234)
> fit.pam <- pam(wine[-1], k=3, stand=TRUE)
> fit.pam$medoids
```

Clusters standardized data

Prints the medoids

```
      Alcohol Malic  Ash Alcalinity Magnesium Phenols Flavanoids
[1,]    13.5  1.81 2.41       20.5       100    2.70       2.98
[2,]    12.2  1.73 2.12       19.0        80    1.65       2.03
[3,]    13.4  3.91 2.48       23.0       102    1.80       0.75
      Nonflavanoids Proanthocyanins Color  Hue Dilution Proline
[1,]           0.26            1.86   5.1 1.04     3.47     920
[2,]           0.37            1.63   3.4 1.00     3.17     510
[3,]           0.43            1.41   7.3 0.70     1.56     750
```

Plots the cluster solution

```
> clusplot(fit.pam, main="Bivariate Cluster Plot")
```

Note that the medoids are actual observations contained in the wine dataset. In this case, they're observations 36, 107, and 175, and they have been chosen to represent the three clusters. The bivariate plot is created by plotting the coordinates of each observation on the first two principal components (see chapter 14) derived from the 13 assay variables. Each cluster is represented by an ellipse with the smallest area containing all its points.

Also note that PAM didn't perform as well as k-means in this instance:

```
> ct.pam <- table(wine$Type, fit.pam$clustering)

     1  2  3
  1 59  0  0
  2 16 53  2
  3  0  1 47

> randIndex(ct.pam)
[1] 0.699
```

The adjusted Rand index has decreased from 0.9 (for k-means) to 0.7.

16.5 *Avoiding nonexistent clusters*

Before I finish this discussion, a word of caution is in order. Cluster analysis is a methodology designed to identify cohesive subgroups in a dataset. It's very good at doing this. In fact, it's so good, it can find clusters where none exist.

Consider the following code:

```
library(fMultivar)
set.seed(1234)
df <- rnorm2d(1000, rho=.5)
df <- as.data.frame(df)
plot(df, main="Bivariate Normal Distribution with rho=0.5")
```

The rnorm2d() function in the fMultivar package is used to sample 1,000 observations from a bivariate normal distribution with a correlation of 0.5. The resulting graph is displayed in figure 16.7. Clearly there are no clusters in this data.

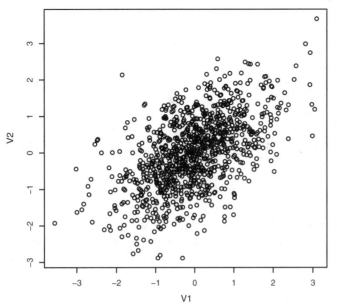

Bivariate Normal Distribution with rho=0.5

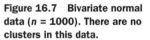

Figure 16.7 Bivariate normal data (*n* = 1000). There are no clusters in this data.

The `wssplot()` and `NbClust()` functions are then used to determine the number of clusters present:

```
wssplot(df)
library(NbClust)
nc <- NbClust(df, min.nc=2, max.nc=15, method="kmeans")
dev.new()
barplot(table(nc$Best.n[1,]),
        xlab="Number of Clusters", ylab="Number of Criteria",
        main="Number of Clusters Chosen by 26 Criteria")
```

The results are plotted in figures 16.8 and 16.9.

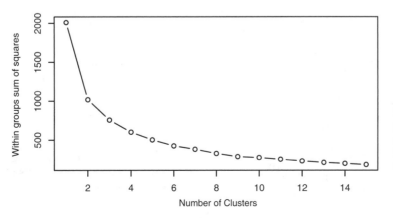

Figure 16.8 Plot of within-groups sums of squares vs. number of k-means clusters for bivariate normal data

Number of Clusters Chosen by 26 Criteria

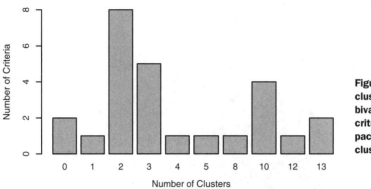

Figure 16.9   Number of
clusters recommended for
bivariate normal data by
criteria in the NbClust
package. Two or three
clusters are suggested.

The `wssplot()` function suggest that there are three clusters, whereas many of the criteria returned by `NbClust()` suggest between two and three clusters. If you carry out a two-cluster analysis with PAM,

```
library(ggplot2)
library(cluster)
fit <- pam(df, k=2)
df$clustering <- factor(fit$clustering)
ggplot(data=df, aes(x=V1, y=V2, color=clustering, shape=clustering)) +
    geom_point() + ggtitle("Clustering of Bivariate Normal Data")
```

you get the two-cluster plot shown in figure 16.10. (The `ggplot()` statement is part of the comprehensive graphics package `ggplot2`. Chapter 19 covers `ggplot2` in detail.)

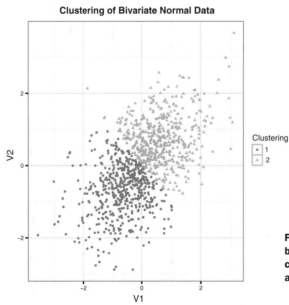

Figure 16.10   PAM cluster analysis of
bivariate normal data, extracting two
clusters. Note that the clusters are an
arbitrary division of the data.

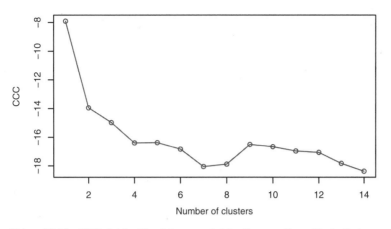

Figure 16.11 CCC plot for bivariate normal data. It correctly suggests that no clusters are present.

Clearly the partitioning is artificial. There are no real clusters here. How can you avoid this mistake? Although it isn't foolproof, I have found that the Cubic Cluster Criteria (CCC) reported by `NbClust` can often help to uncover situations where no structure exists. The code is

```
plot(nc$All.index[,4], type="o", ylab="CCC",
    xlab="Number of clusters", col="blue")
```

and the resulting graph is displayed in figure 16.11. When the CCC values are all negative and decreasing for two or more clusters, the distribution is typically unimodal.

The ability of cluster analysis (or your interpretation of it) to find erroneous clusters makes the validation step of cluster analysis important. If you're trying to identify clusters that are "real" in some sense (rather than a convenient partitioning), be sure the results are robust and repeatable. Try different clustering methods, and replicate the findings with new samples. If the same clusters are consistently recovered, you can be more confident in the results.

16.6 *Summary*

In this chapter, we reviewed some of the most common approaches to clustering observations into cohesive groups. First we reviewed the general steps for a comprehensive cluster analysis. Next, common methods for hierarchical and partitioning clustering were described. Finally, I reinforced the need to validate the resulting clusters in situations where you seek more than convenient partitioning.

Cluster analysis is a broad topic, and R has some of the most comprehensive facilities for applying this methodology currently available. To learn more about these capabilities, see the CRAN Task View for Cluster Analysis & Finite Mixture Models (http://cran.r-project.org/web/views/Cluster.html). Additionally, Tan, Steinbach, & Kumar (2006) have an excellent book on data-mining techniques. It contains a lucid chapter on cluster analysis that you can freely downloaded (www-users.cs.umn.edu/ ~kumar/dmbook/ch8.pdf). Finally, Everitt, Landau, Leese, & Stahl (2011) have written a practical and highly regarded textbook on this subject.

Cluster analysis is a methodology for discovering cohesive subgroups of observations in a dataset. In the next chapter, we'll consider situations where the groups have already been defined and your goal is to find an accurate method of classifying observations into them.

Classification

17

Data analysts are frequently faced with the need to predict a categorical outcome from a set of predictor variables. Some examples include

- Predicting whether an individual will repay a loan, given their demographics and financial history
- Determining whether an ER patient is having a heart attack, based on their symptoms and vital signs
- Deciding whether an email is spam, given the presence of key words, images, hypertext, header information, and origin

Each of these cases involves the prediction of a binary categorical outcome (good credit risk/bad credit risk, heart attack/no heart attack, spam/not spam) from a set of predictors (also called *features*). The goal is to find an accurate method of classifying new cases into one of the two groups.

The field of supervised machine learning offers numerous classification methods that can be used to predict categorical outcomes, including logistic regression, decision trees, random forests, support vector machines, and neural networks. The first four are discussed in this chapter. Neural networks are beyond the scope of this book.

Supervised learning starts with a set of observations containing values for both the predictor variables and the outcome. The dataset is then divided into a training sample and a validation sample. A predictive model is developed using the data in the training sample and tested for accuracy using the data in the validation sample. Both samples are needed because classification techniques maximize prediction for a given set of data. Estimates of their effectiveness will be overly optimistic if they're evaluated using the same data that generated the model. By applying the classification rules developed on a training sample to a separate validation sample, you can obtain a more realistic accuracy estimate. Once you've created an effective predictive model, you can use it to predict outcomes in situations where only the predictor variables are known.

In this chapter, you'll use the `rpart`, `rpart.plot`, and `party` packages to create and visualize decision trees; the `randomForest` package to fit random forests; and the `e1071` package to build support vector machines. Logistic regression will be fit with the `glm()` function in the base R installation. Before starting, be sure to install the necessary packages:

```
pkgs <- c("rpart", "rpart.plot", "party",
          "randomForest", "e1071")
install.packages(pkgs, depend=TRUE)
```

The primary example used in this chapter comes from the Wisconsin Breast Cancer data originally posted to the UCI Machine Learning Repository. The goal will be to develop a model for predicting whether a patient has breast cancer from the characteristics of a fine-needle tissue aspiration (a tissue sample taken with a thin hollow needle from a lump or mass just under the skin).

17.1   *Preparing the data*

The Wisconsin Breast Cancer dataset is available as a comma-delimited text file on the UCI Machine Learning Server (http://archive.ics.uci.edu/ml). The dataset contains 699 fine-needle aspirate samples, where 458 (65.5%) are benign and 241 (34.5%) are malignant. The dataset contains a total of 11 variables and doesn't include the variable names in the file. Sixteen samples have missing data and are coded in the text file with a question mark (?).

The variables are as follows:

- ID
- Clump thickness
- Uniformity of cell size
- Uniformity of cell shape
- Marginal adhesion

- Single epithelial cell size
- Bare nuclei
- Bland chromatin
- Normal nucleoli
- Mitoses
- Class

The first variable is an ID variable (which you'll drop), and the last variable (class) contains the outcome (coded 2=benign, 4=malignant).

For each sample, nine cytological characteristics previously found to correlate with malignancy are also recorded. These variables are each scored from 1 (closest to benign) to 10 (most anaplastic). But no one predictor alone can distinguish between benign and malignant samples. The challenge is to find a set of classification rules that can be used to accurately predict malignancy from some combination of these nine cell characteristics. See Mangasarian and Wolberg (1990) for details.

In the following listing, the comma-delimited text file containing the data is downloaded from the UCI repository and randomly divided into a training sample (70%) and a validation sample (30%).

Listing 17.1 Preparing the breast cancer data

```
loc <- "http://archive.ics.uci.edu/ml/machine-learning-databases/"
ds  <- "breast-cancer-wisconsin/breast-cancer-wisconsin.data"
url <- paste(loc, ds, sep="")

breast <- read.table(url, sep=",", header=FALSE, na.strings="?")
names(breast) <- c("ID", "clumpThickness", "sizeUniformity",
                   "shapeUniformity", "maginalAdhesion",
                   "singleEpithelialCellSize", "bareNuclei",
                   "blandChromatin", "normalNucleoli", "mitosis", "class")

df <- breast[-1]
df$class <- factor(df$class, levels=c(2,4),
                   labels=c("benign", "malignant"))

set.seed(1234)
train <- sample(nrow(df), 0.7*nrow(df))
df.train <- df[train,]
df.validate <- df[-train,]
table(df.train$class)
table(df.validate$class)
```

The training sample has 499 cases (329 benign, 160 malignant), and the validation sample has 210 cases (129 benign, 81 malignant).

The training sample will be used to create classification schemes using logistic regression, a decision tree, a conditional decision tree, a random forest, and a support vector machine. The validation sample will be used to evaluate the effectiveness of these schemes. By using the same example throughout the chapter, you can compare the results of each approach.

17.2   *Logistic regression*

Logistic regression is a type of generalized linear model that is often used to predict a binary outcome from a set of numeric variables (see section 13.2 for details). The glm() function in the base R installation is used for fitting the model. Categorical predictors (factors) are automatically replaced with a set of dummy coded variables. All the predictors in the Wisconsin Breast Cancer data are numeric, so dummy coding is unnecessary. The next listing provides a logistic regression analysis of the data.

Listing 17.2   Logistic regression with glm()

```
> fit.logit <- glm(class~., data=df.train, family=binomial())        ← ❶ Fits the logistic
> summary(fit.logit)       ←                                               regression
                              ❷ Examines the model
Call:
glm(formula = class ~ ., family = binomial(), data = df.train)

Deviance Residuals:
    Min        1Q    Median        3Q       Max
-2.7581   -0.1060   -0.0568    0.0124    2.6432

Coefficients:
                         Estimate Std. Error z value Pr(>|z|)
(Intercept)              -10.4276     1.4760   -7.06  1.6e-12 ***
clumpThickness             0.5243     0.1595    3.29   0.0010 **
sizeUniformity            -0.0481     0.2571   -0.19   0.8517
shapeUniformity            0.4231     0.2677    1.58   0.1141
maginalAdhesion            0.2924     0.1469    1.99   0.0465 *
singleEpithelialCellSize   0.1105     0.1798    0.61   0.5387
bareNuclei                 0.3357     0.1072    3.13   0.0017 **
blandChromatin             0.4235     0.2067    2.05   0.0405 *
normalNucleoli             0.2889     0.1399    2.06   0.0390 *
mitosis                    0.6906     0.3983    1.73   0.0829 .
---
Signif. codes:  0 '***' 0.001 '**' 0.01 '*' 0.05 '.' 0.1 ' ' 1

> prob <- predict(fit.logit, df.validate, type="response")
> logit.pred <- factor(prob > .5, levels=c(FALSE, TRUE),            ❸ Classifies
                 labels=c("benign", "malignant"))                      new cases
> logit.perf <- table(df.validate$class, logit.pred,          ❹ Evaluates the
                 dnn=c("Actual", "Predicted"))                    predictive accuracy
> logit.perf


           Predicted
Actual     benign malignant
   benign      118         2
   malignant     4        76
```

First, a logistic regression model is fit using class as the dependent variable and the remaining variables as predictors ❶. The model is based on the cases in the df.train data frame. The coefficients for the model are displayed next ❷. Section 13.2 provides guidelines for interpreting logistic model coefficients.

Next, the prediction equation developed on the df.train dataset is used to classify cases in the df.validate dataset. By default, the predict() function predicts the log odds of having a malignant outcome. By using the type="response" option, the probability of obtaining a malignant classification is returned instead ❸. In the next line, cases with probabilities greater than 0.5 are classified into the malignant group and cases with probabilities less than or equal to 0.5 are classified as benign.

Finally, a cross-tabulation of actual status and predicted status (called a *confusion matrix*) is printed ❹. It shows that 118 cases that were benign were classified as benign, and 76 cases that were malignant were classified as malignant. Ten cases in the df.validate data frame had missing predictor data and could not be included in the evaluation.

The total number of cases correctly classified (also called the *accuracy*) was (76 + 118) / 200 or 97% in the validation sample. Statistics for evaluating the accuracy of a classification scheme are discussed more fully in section 17.4.

Before moving on, note that three of the predictor variables (sizeUniformity, shapeUniformity, and singleEpithelialCellSize) have coefficients that don't differ from zero at the p < .10 level. What, if anything, should you do with predictor variables that have nonsignificant coefficients?

In a prediction context, it's often useful to remove such variables from the final model. This is especially important in situations where a large number of non-informative predictor variables are adding what is essentially noise to the system.

In this case, stepwise logistic regression can be used to generate a smaller model with fewer variables. Predictor variables are added or removed in order to obtain a model with a smaller AIC value. In the current context, you could use

```
logit.fit.reduced <- step(fit.logit)
```

to obtain a more parsimonious model. The reduced model excludes the three variables mentioned previously. When used to predict outcomes in the validation dataset, this reduced model makes fewer errors. Try it out.

The next approach we'll consider involves the creation of decision or classification trees.

17.3 Decision trees

Decision trees are popular in data-mining contexts. They involve creating a set of binary splits on the predictor variables in order to create a tree that can be used to classify new observations into one of two groups. In this section, we'll look at two types of decision trees: classical trees and conditional inference trees.

17.3.1 Classical decision trees

The process of building a classical decision tree starts with a binary outcome variable (benign/malignant in this case) and a set of predictor variables (the nine cytology measurements). The algorithm is as follows:

1 Choose the predictor variable that best splits the data into two groups such that the purity (homogeneity) of the outcome in the two groups is maximized (that

is, as many benign cases in one group and malignant cases in the other as possible). If the predictor is continuous, choose a cut-point that maximizes purity for the two groups created. If the predictor variable is categorical (not applicable in this case), combine the categories to obtain two groups with maximum purity.

2 Separate the data into these two groups, and continue the process for each subgroup.

3 Repeat steps 1 and 2 until a subgroup contains fewer than a minimum number of observations or no splits decrease the impurity beyond a specified threshold.

The subgroups in the final set are called *terminal nodes*. Each terminal node is classified as one category of the outcome or the other based on the most frequent value of the outcome for the sample in that node.

4 To classify a case, run it down the tree to a terminal node, and assign it the modal outcome value assigned in step 3.

Unfortunately, this process tends to produce a tree that is too large and suffers from overfitting. As a result, new cases aren't classified well. To compensate, you can prune back the tree by choosing the tree with the lowest 10-fold cross-validated prediction error. This pruned tree is then used for future predictions.

In R, decision trees can be grown and pruned using the `rpart()` and `prune()` functions in the `rpart` package. The following listing creates a decision tree for classifying the cell data as benign or malignant.

Listing 17.3   Creating a classical decision tree with `rpart()`

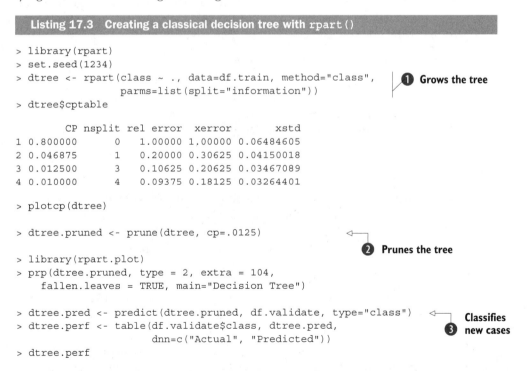

```
> library(rpart)
> set.seed(1234)
> dtree <- rpart(class ~ ., data=df.train, method="class",     ❶ Grows the tree
                 parms=list(split="information"))
> dtree$cptable

        CP nsplit rel error  xerror       xstd
1 0.800000      0   1.00000 1.00000 0.06484605
2 0.046875      1   0.20000 0.30625 0.04150018
3 0.012500      3   0.10625 0.20625 0.03467089
4 0.010000      4   0.09375 0.18125 0.03264401

> plotcp(dtree)

> dtree.pruned <- prune(dtree, cp=.0125)
                                                      ❷ Prunes the tree
> library(rpart.plot)
> prp(dtree.pruned, type = 2, extra = 104,
    fallen.leaves = TRUE, main="Decision Tree")

> dtree.pred <- predict(dtree.pruned, df.validate, type="class")    Classifies
> dtree.perf <- table(df.validate$class, dtree.pred,               ❸ new cases
                 dnn=c("Actual", "Predicted"))
> dtree.perf
```

```
          Predicted
Actual       benign malignant
  benign         122        7
  malignant        2       79
```

First the tree is grown using the `rpart()` function **❶**. You can use `print(dtree)` and `summary(dtree)` to examine the fitted model (not shown here). The tree may be too large and need to be pruned.

In order to choose a final tree size, examine the `cptable` component of the list returned by `rpart()`. It contains data about the prediction error for various tree sizes. The complexity parameter (`cp`) is used to penalize larger trees. Tree size is defined by the number of branch splits (`nsplit`). A tree with *n* splits has *n* + 1 terminal nodes. The `rel error` column contains the error rate for a tree of a given size in the training sample. The cross-validated error (`xerror`) is based on 10-fold cross validation (also using the training sample). The `xstd` column contains the standard error of the cross-validation error.

The `plotcp()` function plots the cross-validated error against the complexity parameter (see figure 17.1). A good choice for the final tree size is the smallest tree whose cross-validated error is within one standard error of the minimum cross-validated error value.

The minimum cross-validated error is 0.18 with a standard error of 0.0326. In this case, the smallest tree with a cross-validated error within 0.18 ± 0.0326 (that is, between 0.15 and 0.21) is selected. Looking at the `cptable` table in listing 17.3, a tree with three splits (cross-validated error = 0.20625) fits this requirement. Equivalently,

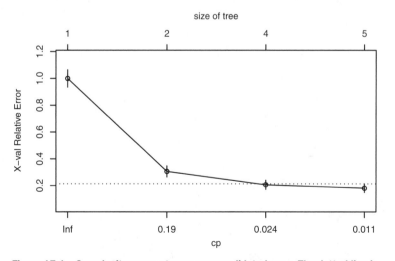

Figure 17.1 Complexity parameter vs. cross-validated error. The dotted line is the upper limit of the one standard deviation rule (0.18 + 1 * 0.0326 = .21). The plot suggests selecting the tree with the leftmost `cp` value below the line.

you can select the tree size associated with the largest complexity parameter below the line in figure 17.1. Results again suggest a tree with three splits (four terminal nodes).

The prune() function uses the complexity parameter to cut back a tree to the desired size. It takes the full tree and snips off the least important splits based on the desired complexity parameter. From the cptable in listing 17.3, a tree with three splits has a complexity parameter of 0.0125, so the statement prune(dtree, cp=0.0125) returns a tree with the desired size ❷.

The prp() function in the rpart.plot package is used to draw an attractive plot of the final decision tree (see figure 17.2). The prp() function has many options (see ?prp for details). The type=2 option draws the split labels below each node. The extra=104 parameter includes the probabilities for each class, along with the percentage of observations in each node. The fallen.leaves=TRUE option displays the terminal nodes at the bottom of the graph. To classify an observation, start at the top of the tree, moving to the left branch if a condition is true or to the right otherwise. Continue moving down the tree until you hit a terminal node. Classify the observation using the label of the node.

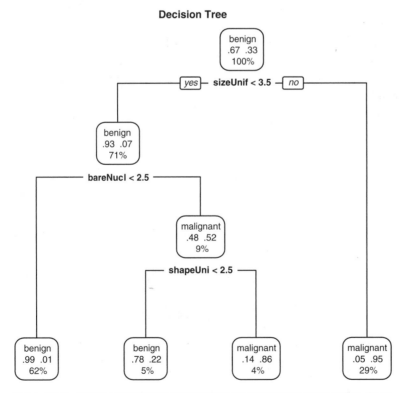

Figure 17.2   Traditional (pruned) decision tree for predicting cancer status. Start at the top of the tree, moving left if a condition is true or right otherwise. When an observation hits a terminal node, it's classified. Each node contains the probability of the classes in that node, along with the percentage of the sample.

Finally, the `predict()` function is used to classify each observation in the validation sample ❸. A cross-tabulation of the actual status against the predicted status is
provided. The overall accuracy was 96% in the validation sample. Unlike the logistic
regression example, all 210 cases in the validation sample could be classified by the
final tree. Note that decision trees can be biased toward selecting predictors that have
many levels or many missing values.

17.3.2 *Conditional inference trees*

Before moving on to random forests, let's look at an important variant of the traditional decision tree called a *conditional inference tree*. Conditional inference trees are
similar to traditional trees, but variables and splits are selected based on significance
tests rather than purity/homogeneity measures. The significance tests are permutation tests (discussed in chapter 12).

In this case, the algorithm is as follows:

1 Calculate p-values for the relationship between each predictor and the outcome
   variable.
2 Select the predictor with the lowest p-value.
3 Explore all possible binary splits on the chosen predictor and dependent variable (using permutation tests), and pick the most significant split.
4 Separate the data into these two groups, and continue the process for each
   subgroup.
5 Continue until splits are no longer significant or the minimum node size is
   reached.

Conditional inference trees are provided by the `ctree()` function in the `party` package. In the next listing, a conditional inference tree is grown for the breast cancer
data.

Listing 17.4 Creating a conditional inference tree with `ctree()`

```
library(party)
fit.ctree <- ctree(class~., data=df.train)
plot(fit.ctree, main="Conditional Inference Tree")

> ctree.pred <- predict(fit.ctree, df.validate, type="response")
> ctree.perf <- table(df.validate$class, ctree.pred,
                       dnn=c("Actual", "Predicted"))
> ctree.perf

          Predicted
Actual      benign malignant
  benign       122         7
  malignant      3        78
```

Note that pruning isn't required for conditional inference trees, and the process is
somewhat more automated. Additionally, the `party` package has attractive plotting

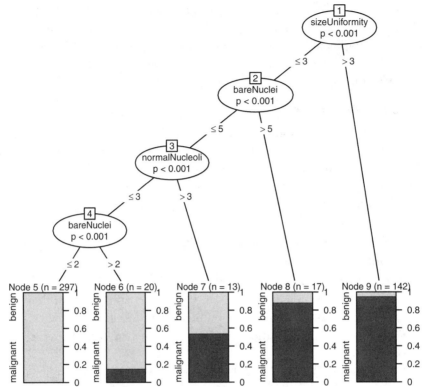

Figure 17.3   **Conditional inference tree for the breast cancer data**

options. The conditional inference tree is plotted in figure 17.3. The shaded area of each node represents the proportion of malignant cases in that node.

Displaying an rpart() tree with a ctree()-like graph

If you create a classical decision tree using `rpart()`, but you'd like to display the resulting tree using a plot like the one in figure 17.3, the `partykit` package can help. After installing and loading the package, you can use the statement `plot(as.party(an.rpart.tree))` to create the desired graph. For example, try creating a graph like figure 17.3 using the `dtree.pruned` object created in listing 17.3, and compare the results to the plot presented in figure 17.2.

The decision trees grown by the traditional and conditional methods can differ substantially. In the current example, the accuracy of each is similar. In the next section, a large number of decision trees are grown and combined in order to classify cases into groups.

17.4   *Random forests*

A *random forest* is an ensemble learning approach to supervised learning. Multiple predictive models are developed, and the results are aggregated to improve classification rates. You can find a comprehensive introduction to random forests, written by Leo Breiman and Adele Cutler, at http://mng.bz/7Nul.

The algorithm for a random forest involves sampling cases and variables to create a large number of decision trees. Each case is classified by each decision tree. The most common classification for that case is then used as the outcome.

Assume that N is the number of cases in the training sample and M is the number of variables. Then the algorithm is as follows:

1. Grow a large number of decision trees by sampling N cases with replacement from the training set.
2. Sample $m < M$ variables at each node. These variables are considered candidates for splitting in that node. The value m is the same for each node.
3. Grow each tree fully without pruning (the minimum node size is set to 1).
4. Terminal nodes are assigned to a class based on the mode of cases in that node.
5. Classify new cases by sending them down all the trees and taking a vote—majority rules.

An out-of-bag (OOB) error estimate is obtained by classifying the cases that aren't selected when building a tree, using that tree. This is an advantage when a validation sample is unavailable. Random forests also provide a natural measure of variable importance, as you'll see.

Random forests are grown using the `randomForest()` function in the `random-Forest` package. The default number of trees is 500, the default number of variables sampled at each node is `sqrt(M)`, and the minimum node size is 1.

The following listing provides the code and results for predicting malignancy status in the breast cancer data.

Listing 17.5   Random forest

```
> library(randomForest)
> set.seed(1234)
> fit.forest <- randomForest(class~., data=df.train,          ① Grows the forest
                             na.action=na.roughfix,
                             importance=TRUE)
> fit.forest

Call:
 randomForest(formula = class ~ ., data = df.train,
             importance = TRUE,      na.action = na.roughfix)
               Type of random forest: classification
                     Number of trees: 500
No. of variables tried at each split: 3

        OOB estimate of  error rate: 3.68%
```

```
Confusion matrix:
         benign malignant class.error
benign      319        10      0.0304
malignant     8       152      0.0500

> importance(fit.forest, type=2)
```

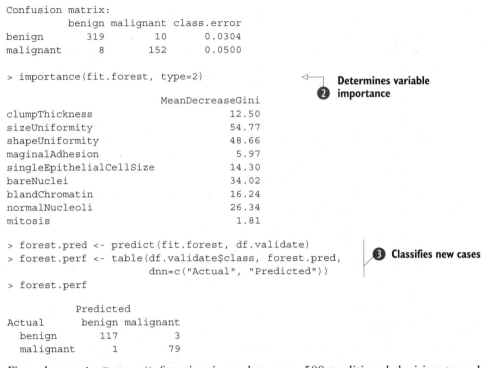

Determines variable importance ❷

```
                          MeanDecreaseGini
clumpThickness                       12.50
sizeUniformity                       54.77
shapeUniformity                      48.66
maginalAdhesion                       5.97
singleEpithelialCellSize             14.30
bareNuclei                           34.02
blandChromatin                       16.24
normalNucleoli                       26.34
mitosis                               1.81

> forest.pred <- predict(fit.forest, df.validate)
> forest.perf <- table(df.validate$class, forest.pred,
                  dnn=c("Actual", "Predicted"))
> forest.perf
```

Classifies new cases ❸

```
           Predicted
Actual     benign malignant
  benign      117         3
  malignant     1        79
```

First, the randomForest() function is used to grow 500 traditional decision trees by sampling 489 observations with replacement from the training sample and sampling 3 variables at each node of each tree ❶. The na.action=na.roughfix option replaces missing values on numeric variables with column medians, and missing values on categorical variables with the modal category for that variable (breaking ties at random).

Random forests can provide a natural measure of variable importance, requested with the information=TRUE option, and printed with the importance() function ❷. The relative importance measure specified by the type=2 option is the total decrease in node impurities (heterogeneity) from splitting on that variable, averaged over all trees. Node impurity is measured with the Gini coefficient. sizeUniformity is the most important variable and mitosis is the least important.

Finally, the validation sample is classified using the random forest and the predictive accuracy is calculated ❸. Note that cases with missing values in the validation sample aren't classified. The prediction accuracy (98% overall) is good.

Whereas the randomForest package provides forests based on traditional decision trees, the cforest() function in the party package can be used to generate random forests based on conditional inference trees. If predictor variables are highly correlated, a random forest using conditional inference trees may provide better predictions.

Random forests tend to be very accurate compared with other classification methods. Additionally, they can handle large problems (many observations and variables), can handle large amounts of missing data in the training set, and can handle cases in which the number of variables is much greater than the number of observations. The provision of OOB error rates and measures of variable importance are also significant advantages.

A significant disadvantage is that it's difficult to understand the classification rules (there are 500 trees!) and communicate them to others. Additionally, you need to store the entire forest in order to classify new cases.

The final classification model we'll consider here is the support vector machine, described next.

17.5 *Support vector machines*

Support vector machines (SVMs) are a group of supervised machine-learning models that can be used for classification and regression. They're popular at present, in part because of their success in developing accurate prediction models, and in part because of the elegant mathematics that underlie the approach. We'll focus on the use of SVMs for binary classification.

SVMs seek an optimal hyperplane for separating two classes in a multidimensional space. The hyperplane is chosen to maximize the *margin* between the two classes' closest points. The points on the boundary of the margin are called *support vectors* (they help define the margin), and the middle of the margin is the separating hyperplane.

For an *N*-dimensional space (that is, with *N* predictor variables), the optimal hyperplane (also called a *linear decision surface*) has $N - 1$ dimensions. If there are two variables, the surface is a line. For three variables, the surface is a plane. For 10 variables, the surface is a 9-dimensional hyperplane. Trying to picture it will give you headache.

Consider the two-dimensional example shown in figure 17.4. Circles and triangles represent the two groups. The *margin* is the gap, represented by the distance between

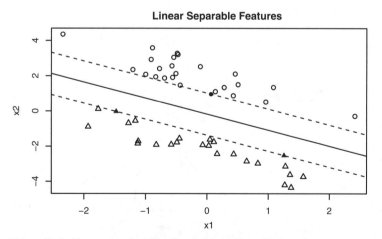

Figure 17.4   Two-group classification problem where the two groups are linearly separable. The separating hyperplane is indicated by the solid black line. The margin is the distance from the line to the dashed line on either side. The filled circles and triangles are the support vectors.

the two dashed lines. The points on the dashed lines (filled circles and triangles) are the support vectors. In the two-dimensional case, the optimal hyperplane is the black line in the middle of the gap. In this idealized example, the two groups are linearly separable—the line can completely separate the two groups without errors.

The optimal hyperplane is identified using quadratic programming to optimize the margin under the constraint that the data points on one side have an outcome value of +1 and the data on the other side has an outcome value of -1. If the data points are "almost" separable (not all the points are on one side or the other), a penalizing term is added to the optimization in order to account for errors, and "soft" margins are produced.

But the data may be fundamentally nonlinear. Consider the example in figure 17.5. There is no line that can correctly separate the circles and triangles. SVMs use kernel functions to transform the data into higher dimensions, in the hope that they will become more linearly separable. Imagine transforming the data in figure 17.5 in such a way that the circles lift off the page. One way to do this is to transform the two-dimensional data into three dimensions using

$$(X, Y) \rightarrow (X^2, \sqrt{2}\, XY, Y^2) \rightarrow (Z_1, Z_2, Z_2)$$

Then you can separate the triangles from the circles using a rigid sheet of paper (that is, a two-dimensional plane in what is now a three-dimensional space).

The mathematics of SVMs is complex and well beyond the scope of this book. Statnikov, Aliferis, Hardin, & Guyon (2011) offer a lucid and intuitive presentation of SVMs that goes into quite a bit of conceptual detail without getting bogged down in higher math.

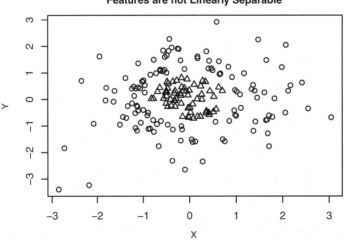

Figure 17.5   Two-group classification problem where the two groups aren't linearly separable. The groups can't be separated with a hyperplane (line).

SVMs are available in R using the `ksvm()` function in the `kernlab` package and the `svm()` function in the `e1071` package. The former is more powerful, but the latter is a bit easier to use. The example in the next listing uses the latter (easy is good) to develop an SVM for the Wisconsin breast cancer data.

Listing 17.6 A support vector machine

```
> library(e1071)
> set.seed(1234)
> fit.svm <- svm(class~., data=df.train)
> fit.svm

Call:
svm(formula = class ~ ., data = df.train)


Parameters:
   SVM-Type:  C-classification
 SVM-Kernel:  radial
       cost:  1
      gamma:  0.1111

Number of Support Vectors:  76

> svm.pred <- predict(fit.svm, na.omit(df.validate))
> svm.perf <- table(na.omit(df.validate)$class,
                svm.pred, dnn=c("Actual", "Predicted"))
> svm.perf

          Predicted
Actual     benign malignant
  benign      116         4
  malignant     3        77
```

Because predictor variables with larger variances typically have a greater influence on the development of SVMs, the `svm()` function scales each variable to a mean of 0 and standard deviation of 1 before fitting the model by default. As you can see, the predictive accuracy is good, but not quite as good as that found for the random forest approach in section 17.2. Unlike the random forest approach, the SVM is also unable to accommodate missing predictor values when classifying new cases.

17.5.1 *Tuning an SVM*

By default, the `svm()` function uses a *radial basis function* (RBF) to map samples into a higher-dimensional space (the kernel trick). The RBF kernel is often a good choice because it's a nonlinear mapping that can handle relations between class labels and predictors that are nonlinear.

When fitting an SVM with the RBF kernel, two parameters can affect the results: *gamma* and *cost*. Gamma is a kernel parameter that controls the shape of the separating hyperplane. Larger values of gamma typically result in a larger number of support vectors. Gamma can also be thought of as a parameter that controls how widely a training sample "reaches," with larger values meaning far and smaller values meaning close. Gamma must be greater than zero.

The cost parameter represents the cost of making errors. A large value severely penalizes errors and leads to a more complex classification boundary. There will be less misclassifications in the training sample, but over-fitting may result in poor predictive ability in new samples. Smaller values lead to a flatter classification boundary but may result in under-fitting. Like gamma, cost is always positive.

By default, the `svm()` function sets gamma to 1 / (number of predictors) and cost to 1. But a different combination of gamma and cost may lead to a more effective model. You can try fitting SVMs by varying parameter values one at a time, but a grid search is more efficient. You can specify a range of values for each parameter using the `tune.svm()` function. `tune.svm()` fits every combination of values and reports on the performance of each. An example is given next.

Listing 17.7 Tuning an RBF support vector machine

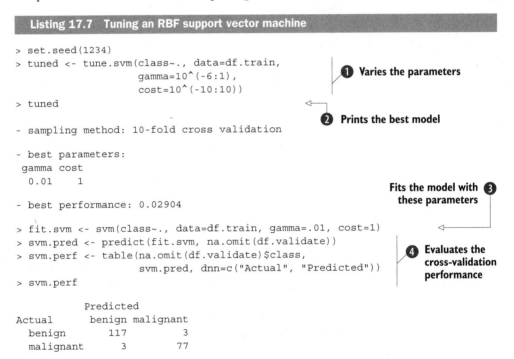

```
> set.seed(1234)
> tuned <- tune.svm(class~., data=df.train,           ❶ Varies the parameters
                gamma=10^(-6:1),
                cost=10^(-10:10))
> tuned                                                 ❷ Prints the best model

- sampling method: 10-fold cross validation

- best parameters:
 gamma cost
  0.01    1
                                                        ❸ Fits the model with
                                                           these parameters
- best performance: 0.02904

> fit.svm <- svm(class~., data=df.train, gamma=.01, cost=1)
> svm.pred <- predict(fit.svm, na.omit(df.validate))    ❹ Evaluates the
> svm.perf <- table(na.omit(df.validate)$class,            cross-validation
                svm.pred, dnn=c("Actual", "Predicted"))    performance
> svm.perf

          Predicted
Actual      benign malignant
  benign       117         3
  malignant      3        77
```

First, an SVM model is fit with an RBF kernel and varying values of gamma and cost ❶. Eight values of gamma (ranging from 0.000001 to 10) and 21 values of cost (ranging from .01 to 10000000000) are specified. In all, 168 models (8 × 21) are fit and compared. The model with the fewest 10-fold cross validated errors in the training sample has gamma = 0.01 and cost = 1.

Using these parameter values, a new SVM is fit to the training sample ❸. The model is then used to predict outcomes in the validation sample ❹, and the number of errors is displayed. Tuning the model ❷ decreased the number of errors slightly (from seven to six). In many cases, tuning the SVM parameters will lead to greater gains.

As stated previously, SVMs are popular because they work well in many situations. They can also handle situations in which the number of variables is much larger than the number of observations. This has made them popular in the field of biomedicine, where the number of variables collected in a typical DNA microarray study of gene expressions may be one or two orders of magnitude larger than the number of cases available.

One drawback of SVMs is that, like random forests, the resulting classification rules are difficult to understand and communicate. They're essentially a black box. Additionally, SVMs don't scale as well as random forests when building models from large training samples. But once a successful model is built, classifying new observations does scale well.

17.6 *Choosing a best predictive solution*

In sections 17.1 through 17.3, fine-needle aspiration samples were classified as malignant or benign using several supervised machine-learning techniques. Which approach was most accurate? To answer this question, we need to define the term *accurate* in a binary classification context.

The most commonly reported statistic is the *accuracy*, or how often the classifier is correct. Although informative, the accuracy is insufficient by itself. Additional information is also needed to evaluate the utility of a classification scheme.

Consider a set of rules for classifying individuals as schizophrenic or non-schizophrenic. Schizophrenia is a rare disorder, with a prevalence of roughly 1% in the general population. If you classify everyone as non-schizophrenic, you'll be right 99% of time. But this isn't a good classifier because it will also misclassify every schizophrenic as non-schizophrenic. In addition to the accuracy, you should ask these questions:

- What percentage of schizophrenics are correctly identified?
- What percentage of non-schizophrenics are correctly identified?
- If a person is classified as schizophrenic, how likely is it that this classification will be correct?
- If a person is classified as non-schizophrenic, how likely is it that this classification is correct?

These are questions pertaining to a classifier's sensitivity, specificity, positive predictive power, and negative predictive power. Each is defined in table 17.1.

Table 17.1 Measures of predictive accuracy

Statistic	Interpretation
Sensitivity	Probability of getting a positive classification when the true outcome is positive (also called *true positive rate or recall*)
Specificity	Probability of getting a negative classification when the true outcome is negative (also called *true negative rate*)

Table 17.1   Measures of predictive accuracy *(continued)*

Statistic	Interpretation
Positive predictive value	Probability that an observation with a positive classification is correctly identified as positive (also called *precision*)
Negative predictive value	Probability that an observation with a negative classification is correctly identified as negative
Accuracy	Proportion of observations correctly identified (also called *ACC*)

A function for calculating these statistics is provided next.

Listing 17.8   Function for assessing binary classification accuracy

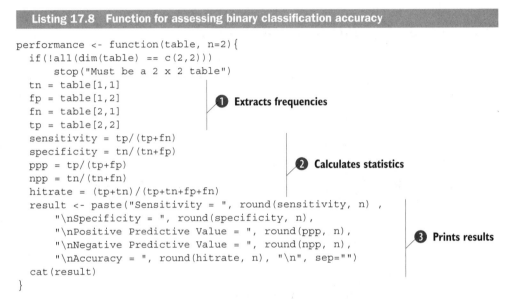

```
performance <- function(table, n=2){
  if(!all(dim(table) == c(2,2)))
      stop("Must be a 2 x 2 table")
  tn = table[1,1]
  fp = table[1,2]                      ❶ Extracts frequencies
  fn = table[2,1]
  tp = table[2,2]
  sensitivity = tp/(tp+fn)
  specificity = tn/(tn+fp)
  ppp = tp/(tp+fp)                     ❷ Calculates statistics
  npp = tn/(tn+fn)
  hitrate = (tp+tn)/(tp+tn+fp+fn)
  result <- paste("Sensitivity = ", round(sensitivity, n) ,
      "\nSpecificity = ", round(specificity, n),
      "\nPositive Predictive Value = ", round(ppp, n),
      "\nNegative Predictive Value = ", round(npp, n),    ❸ Prints results
      "\nAccuracy = ", round(hitrate, n), "\n", sep="")
  cat(result)
}
```

The `performance()` function takes a table containing the true outcome (rows) and predicted outcome (columns) and returns the five accuracy measures. First, the number of *true negatives* (benign tissue identified as benign), *false positives* (benign tissue identified as malignant), *false negatives* (malignant tissue identified as benign), and *true positives* (malignant tissue identified as malignant) are extracted ❶. Next, these counts are used to calculate the sensitivity, specificity, positive and negative predictive values, and accuracy ❷. Finally, the results are formatted and printed ❸.

In the following listing, the `performance()` function is applied to each of the five classifiers developed in this chapter.

Listing 17.9   Performance of breast cancer data classifiers

```
> performance(logit.perf)
Sensitivity = 0.95
Specificity = 0.98
Positive Predictive Value = 0.97
```

```
Negative Predictive Value = 0.97
Accuracy = 0.97

> performance(dtree.perf)
Sensitivity = 0.98
Specificity = 0.95
Positive Predictive Power = 0.92
Negative Predictive Power = 0.98
Accuracy = 0.96

> performance(ctree.perf)
Sensitivity = 0.96
Specificity = 0.95
Positive Predictive Value = 0.92
Negative Predictive Value = 0.98
Accuracy = 0.95

> performance(forest.perf)
Sensitivity = 0.99
Specificity = 0.98
Positive Predictive Value = 0.96
Negative Predictive Value = 0.99
Accuracy = 0.98

> performance(svm.perf)
Sensitivity = 0.96
Specificity = 0.98
Positive Predictive Value = 0.96
Negative Predictive Value = 0.98
Accuracy = 0.97
```

Each of these classifiers (logistic regression, traditional decision tree, conditional inference tree, random forest, and support vector machine) performed exceedingly well on each of the accuracy measures. This won't always be the case!

In this particular instance, the award appears to go to the random forest model (although the differences are so small, they may be due to chance). For the random forest model, 99% of malignancies were correctly identified, 98% of benign samples were correctly identified, and the overall percent of correct classifications is 99%. A diagnosis of malignancy was correct 96% of the time (for a 4% false positive rate), and a benign diagnosis was correct 99% of the time (for a 1% false negative rate). For diagnoses of cancer, the specificity (proportion of malignant samples correctly identified as malignant) is particularly important.

Although it's beyond the scope of this chapter, you can often improve a classification system by trading specificity for sensitivity and vice versa. In the logistic regression model, predict() was used to estimate the probability that a case belonged in the malignant group. If the probability was greater than 0.5, the case was assigned to that group. The 0.5 value is called the *threshold* or *cutoff value*. If you vary this threshold, you can increase the sensitivity of the classification model at the expense of its specificity. predict() can generate probabilities for decision trees, random forests, and SVMs as well (although the syntax varies by method).

The impact of varying the threshold value is typically assessed using a receiver operating characteristic (ROC) curve. A ROC curve plots sensitivity versus specificity for a range of threshold values. You can then select a threshold with the best balance of sensitivity and specificity for a given problem. Many R packages generate ROC curves, including ROCR and pROC. Analytic functions in these packages can help you to select the best threshold values for a given scenario or to compare the ROC curves produced by different classification algorithms in order to choose the most useful approach. To learn more, see Kuhn & Johnson (2013). A more advanced discussion is offered by Fawcett (2005).

Until now, each classification technique has been applied to data by writing and executing code. In the next section, we'll look at a graphical user interface that lets you develop and deploy predictive models using a visual interface.

17.7   *Using the rattle package for data mining*

Rattle (R Analytic Tool to Learn Easily) offers a graphic user interface (GUI) for data mining in R. It gives the user point-and-click access to many of the R functions you've been using in this chapter, as well as other unsupervised and supervised data models not covered here. Rattle also supports the ability to transform and score data, and it offers a number of data-visualization tools for evaluating models.

You can install the `rattle` package from CRAN using

```
install.packages("rattle")
```

This installs the `rattle` package, along with several additional packages. A full installation of Rattle and all the packages it can access would require downloading and installing hundreds of packages. To save time and space, a basic set of packages is installed by default. Other packages are installed when you first request an analysis that requires them. In this case, you'll be prompted to install the missing package(s), and if you reply `Yes`, the required package will be downloaded and installed from CRAN.

Depending on your operating system and current software, you may have to install additional software. In particular, Rattle requires access to the GTK+ Toolkit. If you have difficulty, follow the OS-specific installation directions and troubleshooting suggestions offered at http://rattle.togaware.com.

Once `rattle` is installed, launch the interface using

```
library(rattle)
rattle()
```

The GUI (see figure 17.6) should open on top of the R console.

In this section, you'll use Rattle to develop a conditional inference tree for predicting diabetes. The data also comes from the UCI Machine Learning Repository. The Pima Indians Diabetes dataset contains 768 cases originally collected by the National Institute of Diabetes and Digestive and Kidney Disease. The variables are as follows:

- Number of times pregnant
- Plasma glucose concentration at 2 hours in an oral glucose tolerance test

- Diastolic blood pressure (mm Hg)
- Triceps skin fold thickness (mm)
- 2-hour serum insulin (mu U/ml)
- Body mass index (weight in kg/(height in m)^2)
- Diabetes pedigree function
- Age (years)
- Class variable (0 = non-diabetic or 1 = diabetic)

Thirty-four percent of the sample was diagnosed with diabetes.

To access this data in Rattle, use the following code:

```
loc <- "http://archive.ics.uci.edu/ml/machine-learning-databases/"
ds <- "pima-indians-diabetes/pima-indians-diabetes.data"
url <- paste(loc, ds, sep="")
diabetes <- read.table(url, sep=",", header=FALSE)
names(diabetes) <- c("npregant", "plasma", "bp", "triceps",
                     "insulin", "bmi", "pedigree", "age", "class")
diabetes$class <- factor(diabetes$class, levels=c(0,1),
                         labels=c("normal", "diabetic"))
library(rattle)
rattle()
```

This downloads the data from the UCI repository, names the variables, adds labels to the outcome variable, and opens Rattle. You should be presented with the tabbed dialog box in figure 17.6.

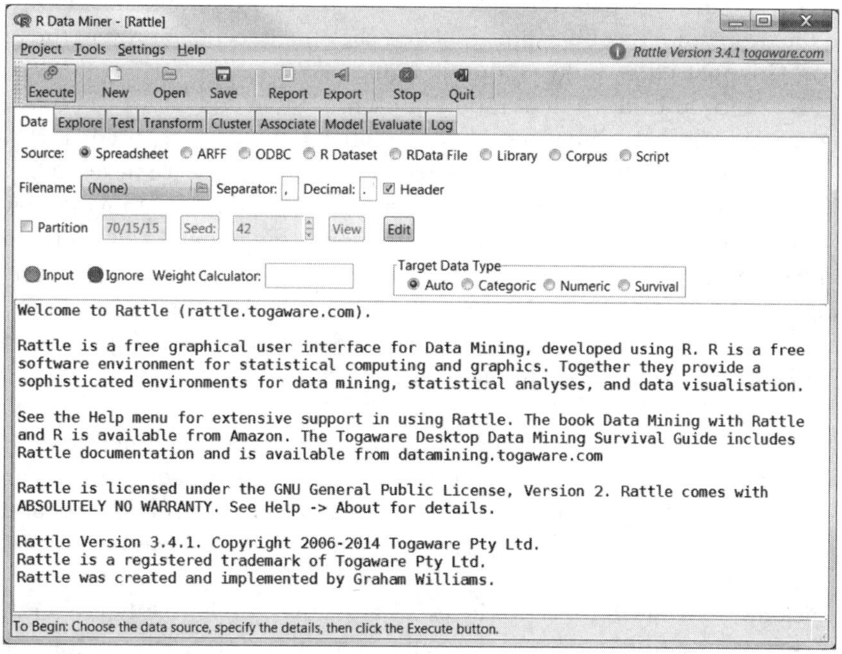

Figure 17.6   Opening Rattle screen

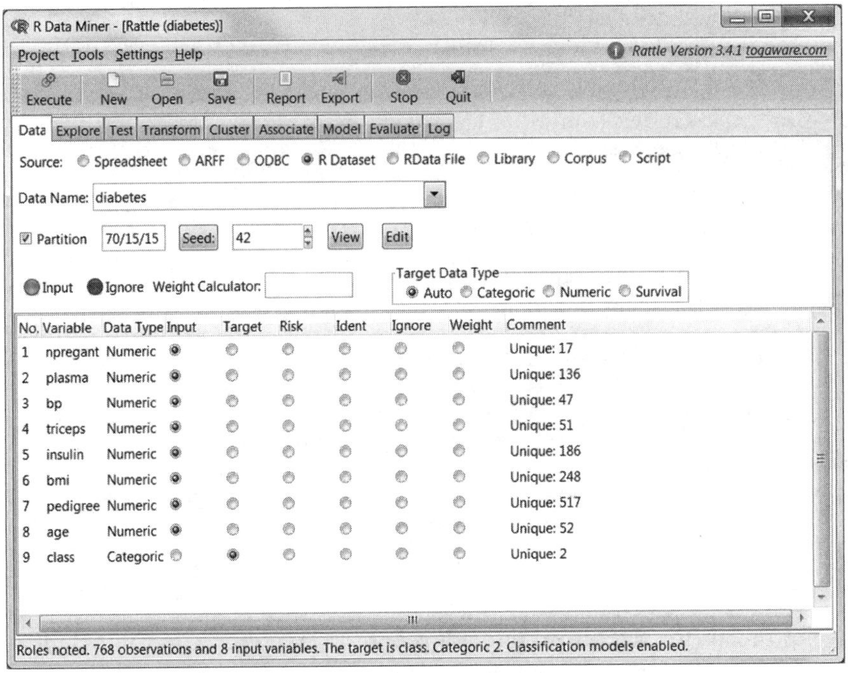

Figure 17.7   Data tab with options to specify the role of each variable

To access the diabetes dataset, click the R Dataset radio button, and select Diabetes from the drop-down box that appears. Then click the Execute button in the upper-left corner. This opens the window shown in figure 17.7.

This window provides a description of each variable and allows you to specify the role each will play in the analyses. Here, variables 1–9 are input (predictor) variables, and class is the target (or predicted) outcome, so no changes are necessary.

You can also specify the percentage of cases to be used as a training sample, validation sample, and testing sample. Analysts frequently build models with a training sample, fine-tune parameters with a validation sample, and evaluate the results with a testing sample. By default, Rattle uses a 70/15/15 split and a seed value of 42.

You'll divide the data into training and validation samples, skipping the test sample. Therefore, enter `70/30/0` in the Partition text box and `1234` in the Seed text box, and click Execute again.

Now let's fit a prediction model. To generate a conditional inference tree, select the Model tab. Be sure the Tree radio button is selected (the default); and for Algorithm, choose the Conditional radio button. Clicking Execute builds the model using the `ctree()` function in the `party` package and displays the results in the bottom of the window (see figure 17.8).

Clicking the Draw button produces an attractive graph (see figure 17.9). (Hint: specifying Use Cairo Graphics in the Settings menu before clicking Draw often produces a more attractive plot.)

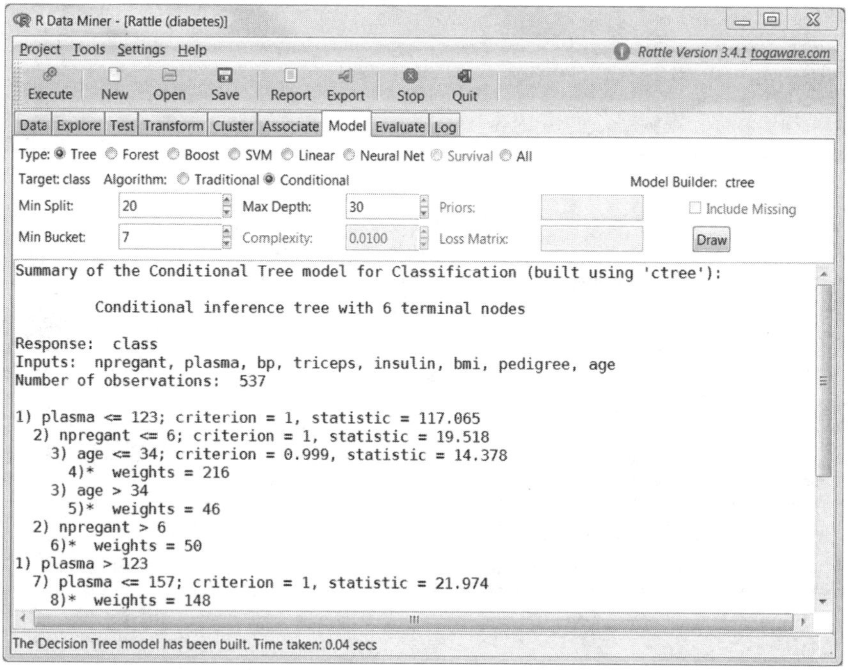

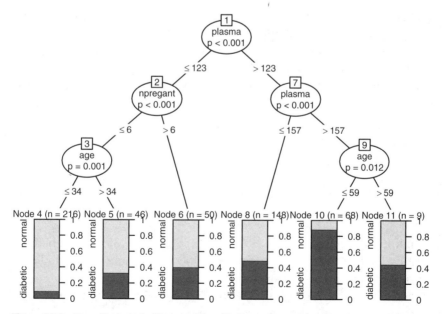

Figure 17.8   Model tab with options to build decision trees, random forests, support vector machines, and more. Here, a conditional inference tree has been fitted to the training data.

Figure 17.9   Tree diagram for the conditional inference tree using the diabetes training sample

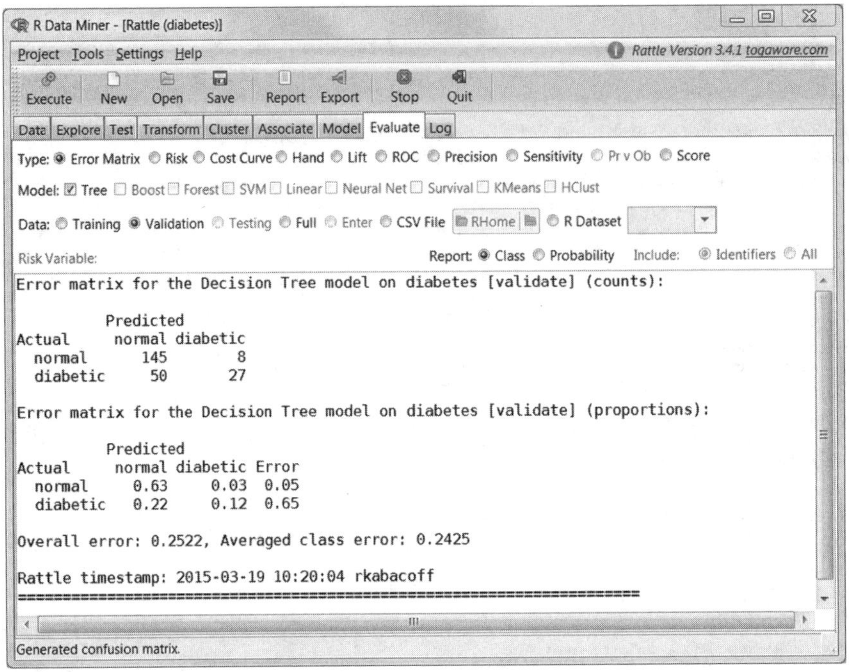

Figure 17.10   Evaluation tab with the error matrix for the conditional inference tree calculated on the validation sample

To evaluate the fitted model, select the Evaluate tab. Here you can specify a number of evaluative criteria and the sample (training, validation) to use. By default, the error matrix (also called a *confusion matrix* in this chapter) is selected. Clicking Execute produces the results shown in figure 17.10.

You can import the error matrix into the `performance()` function to obtain the accuracy statistics:

```
> cv <- matrix(c(145, 50, 8, 27), nrow=2)
> performance(as.table(cv))

Sensitivity = 0.35
Specificity = 0.95
Positive Predictive Value = 0.77
Negative Predictive Value = 0.74
Accuracy = 0.75
```

Although the overall accuracy (75%) isn't terrible, only 35% of diabetics were correctly identified. Try to develop a better classification scheme using random forests or support vector machines—it can be done.

A significant advantage of using Rattle is the ability to fit multiple models to the same dataset and compare each model directly on the Evaluate tab. Check each method on this tab that you want to compare, and click Execute. Additionally, all the

R code executed during the data-mining session can be viewed in the Log tab and exported to a text file for reuse.

To learn more, visit the Rattle homepage (http://rattle.togaware.com/), and see Graham J. Williams' overview article in the R journal (http://mng.bz/D16Q). *Data Mining with Rattle and R*, also by Williams (2011), is the definitive book on Rattle.

17.8 Summary

This chapter presented a number of machine-learning techniques for classifying observations into one of two groups. First, the use of logistic regression as a classification tool was described. Next, traditional decision trees were described, followed by conditional inference trees. The ensemble random forest approach was considered next. Finally, the increasingly popular support vector machine approach was described. The last section introduced Rattle, a graphic user interface for data mining, which allows the user point-and-click access to these functions. Rattle can be particularly useful for comparing the results of various classification techniques. Because it generates reusable R code in a log file, it can also be a useful tool for learning the syntax of many of R's predictive analytics functions.

The techniques described in this chapter vary in complexity. Data miners typically try some of the simpler approaches (logistic regression, decision trees) and more complex, black-box approaches (random forests, support vector machines). If the black-box approaches don't provide a significant improvement over the simpler methods, the simpler methods are usually selected for deployment.

The examples in this chapter (cancer and diabetes diagnosis) both came from the field of medicine, but classification techniques are used widely in other disciplines, including computer science, marketing, finance, economics, and the behavioral sciences. Although the examples involved a binary classification (malignant/benign, diabetic/non-diabetic), modifications are available that allow these techniques to be used with multigroup classification problems.

To learn more about the functions in R that support classification, look in the CRAN Task View for Machine Learning and Statistical Learning (http://mng.bz/I1Lm). Other good resources include books by Kuhn & Johnson (2013) and Torgo (2010).

18
Advanced methods
for missing data

This chapter covers

- Identifying missing data
- Visualizing missing data patterns
- Complete-case analysis
- Multiple imputation of missing data

In previous chapters, we focused on analyzing complete datasets (that is, datasets without missing values). Although doing so helps simplify the presentation of statistical and graphical methods, in the real world, missing data are ubiquitous.

In some ways, the impact of missing data is a subject that most of us want to avoid. Statistics books may not mention it or may limit discussion to a few paragraphs. Statistical packages offer automatic handling of missing data using methods that may not be optimal. Even though most data analyses (at least in social sciences) involve missing data, this topic is rarely mentioned in the methods and results sections of journal articles. Given how often missing values occur, and the degree to which their presence can invalidate study results, it's fair to say that the subject has received insufficient attention outside of specialized books and courses.

Data can be missing for many reasons. Survey participants may forget to answer one or more questions, refuse to answer sensitive questions, or grow fatigued and fail to complete a long questionnaire. Study participants may miss appointments or drop out of a study prematurely. Recording equipment may fail, internet connections may be lost, or data may be miscoded. Analysts may even plan for some data to be missing. For example, to increase study efficiency or reduce costs, you may choose not to collect all data from all participants. Finally, data may be lost for reasons that you're never able to ascertain.

Unfortunately, most statistical methods assume that you're working with complete matrices, vectors, and data frames. In most cases, you have to eliminate missing data before you address the substantive questions that led you to collect the data. You can eliminate missing data by (1) removing cases with missing data or (2) replacing missing data with reasonable substitute values. In either case, the end result is a dataset without missing values.

In this chapter, we'll look at both traditional and modern approaches for dealing with missing data. We'll primarily use the VIM and mice packages. The command `install.packages(c("VIM", "mice"))` will download and install both.

To motivate the discussion, we'll look at the mammal sleep dataset (sleep) provided in the VIM package (not to be confused with the sleep dataset describing the impact of drugs on sleep provided in the base installation). The data come from a study by Allison and Chichetti (1976) that examined the relationship between sleep and ecological and constitutional variables for 62 mammal species. The authors were interested in why animals' sleep requirements vary from species to species. The sleep variables served as the dependent variables, whereas the ecological and constitutional variables served as the independent or predictor variables.

Sleep variables included length of dreaming sleep (Dream), nondreaming sleep (NonD), and their sum (Sleep). The constitutional variables included body weight in kilograms (BodyWgt), brain weight in grams (BrainWgt), life span in years (Span), and gestation time in days (Gest). The ecological variables included degree to which species were preyed upon (Pred), degree of their exposure while sleeping (Exp), and overall danger (Danger) faced. The ecological variables were measured on 5-point rating scales that ranged from 1 (low) to 5 (high).

In their original article, Allison and Chichetti limited their analyses to the species that had complete data. We'll go further, analyzing all 62 cases using a multiple imputation approach.

18.1 Steps in dealing with missing data

If you're new to the study of missing data, you'll find a bewildering array of approaches, critiques, and methodologies. The classic text in this area is Little and Rubin (2002). Excellent, accessible reviews can be found in Allison (2001); Schafer and Graham (2002); and Schlomer, Bauman, and Card (2010). A comprehensive approach usually includes the following steps:

1 Identify the missing data.
2 Examine the causes of the missing data.
3 Delete the cases containing missing data, or replace (impute) the missing values with reasonable alternative data values.

Unfortunately, identifying missing data is usually the only unambiguous step. Learning why data are missing depends on your understanding of the processes that generated the data. Deciding how to treat missing values will depend on your estimation of which procedures will produce the most reliable and accurate results.

A classification system for missing data

Statisticians typically classify missing data into one of three types. These types are usually described in probabilistic terms, but the underlying ideas are straightforward. We'll use the measurement of dreaming in the `sleep` study (where 12 animals have missing values) to illustrate each type in turn:

- *Missing completely at random*—If the presence of missing data on a variable is unrelated to any other observed or unobserved variable, then the data are missing completely at random (MCAR). If there's no systematic reason why dream sleep is missing for these 12 animals, the data are said to be MCAR. Note that if every variable with missing data is MCAR, you can consider the complete cases to be a simple random sample from the larger dataset.
- *Missing at random*—If the presence of missing data on a variable is related to other observed variables but *not* to its own unobserved value, the data are missing at random (MAR). For example, if animals with smaller body weights are more likely to have missing values for dream sleep (perhaps because it's harder to observe smaller animals), and the "missingness" is unrelated to an animal's time spent dreaming, the data are considered MAR. In this case, the presence or absence of dream sleep data is random, once you control for body weight.
- *Not missing at random*—If the missing data for a variable are neither MCAR nor MAR, the data are not missing at random (NMAR). For example, if animals that spend less time dreaming are also more likely to have a missing dream value (perhaps because it's harder to measure shorter events), the data are considered NMAR.

Most approaches to missing data assume that the data are either MCAR or MAR. In this case, you can ignore the mechanism producing the missing data and (after replacing or deleting the missing data) model the relationships of interest directly.

Data that are NMAR can be difficult to analyze properly. When data are NMAR, you have to model the mechanisms that produced the missing values, as well as the relationships of interest. (Current approaches to analyzing NMAR data include the use of selection models and pattern mixtures. The analysis of NMAR data can be complex and is beyond the scope of this book.)

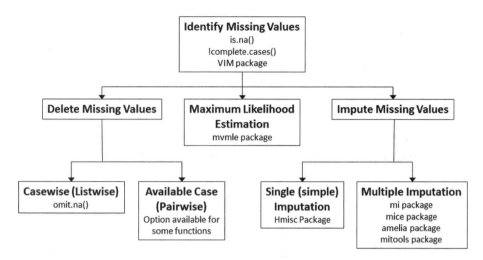

Figure 18.1 Methods for handling incomplete data, along with the R packages that support them

There are *many* methods for dealing with missing data—and no guarantee that they'll produce the same results. Figure 18.1 describes an array of methods used for handling incomplete data and the R packages that support them.

A complete review of missing-data methodologies would require a book in itself. In this chapter, we'll review methods for exploring missing-values patterns and focus on the three most popular methods for dealing with incomplete data (a rational approach, listwise deletion, and multiple imputation). We'll end the chapter with a brief discussion of other methods, including those that are useful in special circumstances.

18.2 *Identifying missing values*

To begin, let's review the material introduced in section 4.5, and expand on it. R represents missing values using the symbol NA (not available) and impossible values using the symbol NaN (not a number). In addition, the symbols Inf and -Inf represent positive infinity and negative infinity, respectively. The functions is.na(), is.nan(), and is.infinite() can be used to identify missing, impossible, and infinite values, respectively. Each returns either TRUE or FALSE. Examples are given in table 18.1.

Table 18.1 Examples of return values for the is.na(), is.nan(), and is.infinite() functions

x	is.na(x)	is.nan(x)	is.infinite(x)
x <- NA	TRUE	FALSE	FALSE
x <- 0 / 0	TRUE	TRUE	FALSE
x <- 1 / 0	FALSE	FALSE	TRUE

These functions return an object that's the same size as its argument, with each element replaced by TRUE if the element is of the type being tested or FALSE otherwise. For example, let y <- c(1, 2, 3, NA). Then is.na(y) will return the vector c(FALSE, FALSE, FALSE, TRUE).

The function complete.cases() can be used to identify the rows in a matrix or data frame that don't contain missing data. It returns a logical vector with TRUE for every row that contains complete cases and FALSE for every row that has one or more missing values.

Let's apply this to the sleep dataset:

```
# load the dataset
data(sleep, package="VIM")

# list the rows that do not have missing values
sleep[complete.cases(sleep),]

# list the rows that have one or more missing values
sleep[!complete.cases(sleep),]
```

Examining the output reveals that 42 cases have complete data and 20 cases have one or more missing values.

Because the logical values TRUE and FALSE are equivalent to the numeric values 1 and 0, the sum() and mean() functions can be used to obtain useful information about missing data. Consider the following:

```
> sum(is.na(sleep$Dream))
[1] 12
> mean(is.na(sleep$Dream))
[1] 0.19
> mean(!complete.cases(sleep))
[1] 0.32
```

The results indicate that 12 values are missing for the variable Dream. Nineteen percent of the cases have a missing value on this variable. In addition, 32% of the cases in the dataset have one or more missing values.

There are two things to keep in mind when identifying missing values. First, the complete.cases() function only identifies NA and NaN as missing. Infinite values (Inf and -Inf) are treated as valid values. Second, you must use missing-values functions, like those in this section, to identify the missing values in R data objects. Logical comparisons such as myvar == NA are never true.

Now that you know how to identify missing values programmatically, let's look at tools that help you explore possible *patterns* in the occurrence of missing data.

18.3   *Exploring missing-values patterns*

Before deciding how to deal with missing data, you'll find it useful to determine which variables have missing values, in what amounts, and in what combinations. In this section, we'll review tabular, graphical, and correlational methods for exploring missing values patterns. Ultimately, you want to understand *why* the data are missing. The answer will have implications for how you proceed with further analyses.

18.3.1 Tabulating missing values

You've already seen a rudimentary approach to identifying missing values. You can use the complete.cases() function from section 18.2 to list cases that are complete or, conversely, list cases that have one or more missing values. As the size of a dataset grows, though, it becomes a less attractive approach. In this case, you can turn to other R functions.

The md.pattern() function in the mice package produces a tabulation of the missing data patterns in a matrix or data frame. Applying this function to the sleep dataset, you get the following:

```
> library(mice)
> data(sleep, package="VIM")
> md.pattern(sleep)
   BodyWgt BrainWgt Pred Exp Danger Sleep Span Gest Dream NonD
42       1        1    1   1      1     1    1    1     1    1   0
 2       1        1    1   1      1     1    0    1     1    1   1
 3       1        1    1   1      1     1    1    0     1    1   1
 9       1        1    1   1      1     1    1    1     0    0   2
 2       1        1    1   1      1     0    1    1     1    0   2
 1       1        1    1   1      1     1    0    0     1    1   2
 2       1        1    1   1      1     0    1    1     0    0   3
 1       1        1    1   1      1     1    0    1     0    0   3
         0        0    0   0      0     4    4    4    12   14  38
```

The 1s and 0s in the body of the table indicate the missing-values patterns, with a 0 indicating a missing value for a given column variable and a 1 indicating a non-missing value. The first row describes the pattern of "no missing values" (all elements are 1). The second row describes the pattern "no missing values except for Span." The first column indicates the number of cases in each missing data pattern, and the last column indicates the number of variables with missing values present in each pattern. Here you can see that there are 42 cases without missing data and 2 cases that are missing Span alone. Nine cases are missing both NonD and Dream values. The dataset has a total of $(42 \times 0) + (2 \times 1) + \ldots + (1 \times 3) = 38$ missing values. The last row gives the total number of missing values on each variable.

18.3.2 Exploring missing data visually

Although the tabular output from the md.pattern() function is compact, I often find it easier to discern patterns visually. Luckily, the VIM package provides numerous functions for visualizing missing-values patterns in datasets. In this section, we'll review several, including aggr(), matrixplot(), and scattMiss().

The aggr() function plots the number of missing values for each variable alone and for each combination of variables. For example, the code

```
library("VIM")
aggr(sleep, prop=FALSE, numbers=TRUE)
```

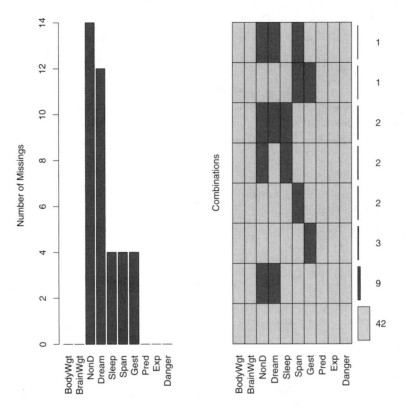

Figure 18.2 `aggr()`-produced plot of missing-values patterns for the sleep dataset

produces the graph in figure 18.2. (The VIM package opens a GUI interface. You can close it; you'll be using code to accomplish the tasks in this chapter.)

You can see that the variable NonD has the largest number of missing values (14), and that two mammals are missing NonD, Dream, and Sleep scores. Forty-two mammals have no missing data.

The statement `aggr(sleep, prop=TRUE, numbers=TRUE)` produces the same plot, but proportions are displayed instead of counts. The option `numbers=FALSE` (the default) suppresses the numeric labels.

The `matrixplot()` function produces a plot displaying the data for each case. A graph created using `matrixplot(sleep)` is displayed in figure 18.3. Here, the numeric data are rescaled to the interval [0, 1] and represented by grayscale colors, with lighter colors representing lower values and darker colors representing larger values. By default, missing values are represented in red. Note that in figure 18.3, red has been replaced with crosshatching by hand, so that the missing values are viewable in grayscale. It will look different when you create the graph yourself.

The graph is interactive: clicking a column re-sorts the matrix by that variable. The rows in figure 18.3 are sorted in descending order by BodyWgt. A matrix plot allows

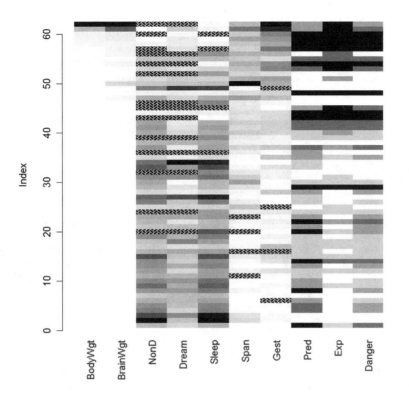

Figure 18.3 Matrix plot of actual and missing values by case (row) for the sleep dataset. The matrix is sorted by BodyWgt.

you to see if the fact that values are missing on one or more variables is related to the actual values of other variables. Here, you can see that there are no missing values on sleep variables (Dream, NonD, Sleep) for low values of body or brain weight (Body-Wgt, BrainWgt).

The `marginplot()` function produces a scatter plot between two variables with information about missing values shown in the plot's margins. Consider the relationship between the amount of dream sleep and the length of a mammal's gestation. The statement

```
marginplot(sleep[c("Gest","Dream")], pch=c(20),
           col=c("darkgray", "red", "blue"))
```

produces the graph in figure 18.4. The `pch` and `col` parameters are optional and provide control over the plotting symbols and colors used.

The body of the graph displays the scatter plot between Gest and Dream (based on complete cases for the two variables). In the left margin, box plots display the distribution of Dream for mammals with (dark gray) and without (red) Gest values. (Note that in grayscale, red is the darker shade.) Four red dots represent the values of Dream for mammals missing Gest scores. In the bottom margin, the roles of Gest and `Dream` are

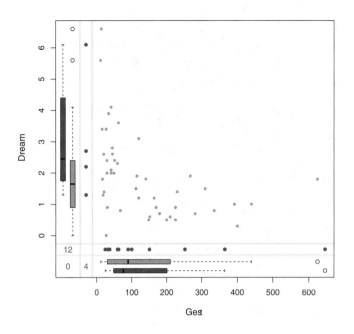

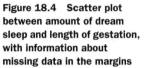

Figure 18.4 Scatter plot between amount of dream sleep and length of gestation, with information about missing data in the margins

reversed. You can see that a negative relationship exists between length of gestation and dream sleep and that dream sleep tends to be higher for mammals that are missing a gestation score. The number of observations missing values on both variables at the same time is printed in blue at the intersection of both margins (bottom left).

The VIM package has many graphs that can help you understand the role of missing data in a dataset and is well worth exploring. There are functions to produce scatter plots, box plots, histograms, scatter plot matrices, parallel plots, rug plots, and bubble plots that incorporate information about missing values.

18.3.3 *Using correlations to explore missing values*

Before moving on, there's one more approach worth noting. You can replace the data in a dataset with indicator variables, coded 1 for missing and 0 for present. The resulting matrix is sometimes called a *shadow matrix*. Correlating these indicator variables with each other and with the original (observed) variables can help you to see which variables tend to be missing together, as well as relationships between a variable's "missingness" and the values of the other variables.

Consider the following code:

```
x <- as.data.frame(abs(is.na(sleep)))
```

The elements of data frame x are 1 if the corresponding element of sleep is missing and 0 otherwise. You can see this by viewing the first few rows of each:

```
> head(sleep, n=5)
   BodyWgt BrainWgt NonD Dream Sleep Span Gest Pred Exp Danger
1 6654.000   5712.0   NA    NA   3.3 38.6  645    3   5      3
```

```
2    1.000      6.6  6.3   2.0   8.3  4.5   42   3   1    3
3    3.385     44.5   NA    NA  12.5 14.0   60   1   1    1
4    0.920      5.7   NA    NA  16.5   NA   25   5   2    3
5 2547.000   4603.0  2.1   1.8   3.9 69.0  624   3   5    4

> head(x, n=5)
  BodyWgt BrainWgt NonD Dream Sleep Span Gest Pred Exp Danger
1       0        0    1     1     0    0    0    0   0      0
2       0        0    0     0     0    0    0    0   0      0
3       0        0    1     1     0    0    0    0   0      0
4       0        0    1     1     0    1    0    0   0      0
5       0        0    0     0     0    0    0    0   0      0
```

The statement

```
y <- x[which(apply(x,2,sum)>0)]
```

extracts the variables that have some (but not all) missing values, and

```
cor(y)
```

gives you the correlations among these indicator variables:

```
        NonD  Dream  Sleep    Span   Gest
NonD   1.000  0.907  0.486   0.015 -0.142
Dream  0.907  1.000  0.204   0.038 -0.129
Sleep  0.486  0.204  1.000  -0.069 -0.069
Span   0.015  0.038 -0.069   1.000  0.198
Gest  -0.142 -0.129 -0.069   0.198  1.000
```

Here, you can see that Dream and NonD tend to be missing together (r = 0.91). To a lesser extent, Sleep and NonD tend to be missing together (r = 0.49) and Sleep and Dream tend to be missing together (r = 0.20).

Finally, you can look at the relationship between missing values in a variable and the observed values on other variables:

```
> cor(sleep, y, use="pairwise.complete.obs")
            NonD   Dream   Sleep    Span    Gest
BodyWgt    0.227   0.223  0.0017  -0.058  -0.054
BrainWgt   0.179   0.163  0.0079  -0.079  -0.073
NonD          NA      NA      NA  -0.043  -0.046
Dream     -0.189      NA -0.1890   0.117   0.228
Sleep     -0.080  -0.080      NA   0.096   0.040
Span       0.083   0.060  0.0052      NA  -0.065
Gest       0.202   0.051  0.1597  -0.175      NA
Pred       0.048  -0.068  0.2025   0.023  -0.201
Exp        0.245   0.127  0.2608  -0.193  -0.193
Danger     0.065  -0.067  0.2089  -0.067  -0.204
Warning message:
In cor(sleep, y, use = "pairwise.complete.obs") :
  the standard deviation is zero
```

In this correlation matrix, the rows are observed variables, and the columns are indicator variables representing missingness. You can ignore the warning message and NA values in the correlation matrix; they're artifacts of our approach.

From the first column of the correlation matrix, you can see that nondreaming sleep scores are more likely to be missing for mammals with higher body weight ($r = 0.227$), gestation period ($r = 0.202$), and sleeping exposure ($r = 0.245$). Other columns are read in a similar fashion. None of the correlations in this table are particularly large or striking, which suggests that the data deviate minimally from MCAR and may be MAR.

Note that you can never rule out the possibility that the data are NMAR, because you don't know what the values would have been for data that are missing. For example, you don't know if there's a relationship between the amount of dreaming a mammal engages in and the probability of a value being missing on this variable. In the absence of strong external evidence to the contrary, we typically assume that data are either MCAR or MAR.

18.4   *Understanding the sources and impact of missing data*

You can identify the amount, distribution, and pattern of missing data in order to evaluate the potential mechanisms leading to the missing data and the impact of the missing data on your ability to answer substantive questions. In particular, you want to answer the following questions:

- What percentage of the data is missing?
- Are the missing data concentrated in a few variables or widely distributed?
- Do the missing values appear to be random?
- Does the covariation of missing data with each other or with observed data suggest a possible mechanism that's producing the missing values?

Answers to these questions help determine which statistical methods are most appropriate for analyzing your data. For example, if the missing data are concentrated in a few relatively unimportant variables, you may be able to delete these variables and continue your analyses normally. If a small amount of data (say, less than 10%) is randomly distributed throughout the dataset (MCAR), you may be able to limit your analyses to cases with complete data and still get reliable and valid results. If you can assume that the data are either MCAR or MAR, you may be able to apply multiple imputation methods to arrive at valid conclusions. If the data are NMAR, you can turn to specialized methods, collect new data, or go into an easier and more rewarding profession.

Here are some examples:

- In a recent survey employing paper questionnaires, I found that several items tended to be missing together. It became apparent that these items clustered together because participants didn't realize that the third page of the questionnaire had a reverse side—which contained the items. In this case, the data could be considered MCAR.
- In another study, an education variable was frequently missing in a global survey of leadership styles. Investigation revealed that European participants were more likely to leave this item blank. It turned out that the categories didn't

make sense for participants in certain countries. In this case, the data were most likely MAR.

- Finally, I was involved in a study of depression in which older patients were more likely to omit items describing depressed mood when compared with younger patients. Interviews revealed that older patients were loath to admit to such symptoms because doing so violated their values about keeping a "stiff upper lip." Unfortunately, it was also determined that severely depressed patients were more likely to omit these items due to a sense of hopelessness and difficulties with concentration. In this case, the data had to be considered NMAR.

As you can see, identifying patterns is only the first step. You need to bring your understanding of the research subject matter and the data collection process to bear in order to determine the source of the missing values.

Now that we've considered the source and impact of missing data, let's see how standard statistical approaches can be altered to accommodate them. We'll focus on three popular approaches: a rational approach for recovering data, a traditional approach that involves deleting missing data, and a modern approach that uses simulation. Along the way, we'll briefly look at methods for specialized situations and methods that have become obsolete and should be retired. The goal will remain constant: to answer, as accurately as possible, the substantive questions that led you to collect the data, given the absence of complete information.

18.5 *Rational approaches for dealing with incomplete data*

In a rational approach, you use mathematical or logical relationships among variables to attempt to fill in or recover missing values. A few examples will help clarify this approach.

In the sleep dataset, the variable Sleep is the sum of the Dream and NonD variables. If you know a mammal's scores on any two, you can derive the third. Thus, if some observations were missing only one of the three variables, you could recover the missing information through addition or subtraction.

As a second example, consider research that focuses on work/life balance differences between generational cohorts (for example, Silents, Early Boomers, Late Boomers, Xers, Millennials), where cohorts are defined by their birth year. Participants are asked both their date of birth and their age. If date of birth is missing, you can recover their birth year (and therefore their generational cohort) by knowing their age and the date they completed the survey.

An example that uses logical relationships to recover missing data comes from a set of leadership studies in which participants were asked if they were a manager (yes/no) and the number of their direct reports (integer). If they left the manager question blank but indicated that they had one or more direct reports, it would be reasonable to infer that they were a manager.

As a final example, I frequently engage in gender research that compares the leadership styles and effectiveness of men and women. Participants complete surveys that include their name (first and last), their gender, and a detailed assessment of their leadership approach and impact. If participants leave the gender question blank, I have to impute the value in order to include them in the research. In one recent study of 66,000 managers, 11,000 (17%) were missing a value for gender.

To remedy the situation, I employed the following rational process. First, I cross-tabulated first name with gender. Some first names were associated with males, some with females, and some with both. For example, "William" appeared 417 times and was always a male. Conversely, the name "Chris" appeared 237 times but was some-times a male (86%) and sometimes a female (14%). If a first name appeared more than 20 times in the dataset and was always associated with males or with females (but never both), I assumed that the name represented a single gender. I used this assump-tion to create a gender-lookup table for gender-specific first names. Using this lookup table for participants with missing gender values, I was able to recover 7,000 cases (63% of the missing responses).

A rational approach typically requires creativity and thoughtfulness, along with a degree of data-management skill. Data recovery may be exact (as in the sleep exam-ple) or approximate (as in the gender example). In the next section, we'll explore an approach that creates complete datasets by removing observations.

18.6   *Complete-case analysis (listwise deletion)*

In complete-case analysis, only observations containing valid data values on every vari-able are retained for further analysis. Practically, this involves deleting any row with one or more missing values, and is also known as *listwise*, or *case-wise*, deletion. Most popular statistical packages employ listwise deletion as the default approach for han-dling missing data. In fact, it's so common that many analysts carrying out analyses like regression or ANOVA may not even realize that there's a "missing-values problem" to be dealt with!

The function complete.cases() can be used to save the cases (rows) of a matrix or data frame without missing data:

```
newdata <- mydata[complete.cases(mydata),]
```

The same result can be accomplished with the na.omit function:

```
newdata <- na.omit(mydata)
```

In both statements, any rows that are missing data are deleted from mydata before the results are saved to newdata.

Suppose you're interested in the correlations among the variables in the sleep study. Applying listwise deletion, you'd delete all mammals with missing data prior to calculating the correlations:

```
> options(digits=1)
> cor(na.omit(sleep))
         BodyWgt BrainWgt NonD Dream Sleep  Span  Gest   Pred Exp Danger
BodyWgt     1.00     0.96 -0.4 -0.07  -0.3  0.47  0.71   0.10 0.4   0.26
BrainWgt    0.96     1.00 -0.4 -0.07  -0.3  0.63  0.73  -0.02 0.3   0.15
```

NonD	-0.39	-0.39	1.0	0.52	1.0	-0.37	-0.61	-0.35	-0.6	-0.53
Dream	-0.07	-0.07	0.5	1.00	0.7	-0.27	-0.41	-0.40	-0.5	-0.57
Sleep	-0.34	-0.34	1.0	0.72	1.0	-0.38	-0.61	-0.40	-0.6	-0.60
Span	0.47	0.63	-0.4	-0.27	-0.4	1.00	0.65	-0.17	0.3	0.01
Gest	0.71	0.73	-0.6	-0.41	-0.6	0.65	1.00	0.09	0.6	0.31
Pred	0.10	-0.02	-0.4	-0.40	-0.4	-0.17	0.09	1.00	0.6	0.93
Exp	0.41	0.32	-0.6	-0.50	-0.6	0.32	0.57	0.63	1.0	0.79
Danger	0.26	0.15	-0.5	-0.57	-0.6	0.01	0.31	0.93	0.8	1.00

The correlations in this table are based solely on the 42 mammals that have complete data on all variables. (Note that the statement cor(sleep, use="complete.obs") would have produced the same results.)

If you wanted to study the impact of life span and length of gestation on the amount of dream sleep, you could employ linear regression with listwise deletion:

```
> fit <- lm(Dream ~ Span + Gest, data=na.omit(sleep))
> summary(fit)

Call:
lm(formula = Dream ~ Span + Gest, data = na.omit(sleep))

Residuals:
   Min    1Q Median    3Q    Max
-2.333 -0.915 -0.221  0.382  4.183

Coefficients:
             Estimate Std. Error t value Pr(>|t|)
(Intercept)  2.480122   0.298476    8.31 3.7e-10 ***
Span        -0.000472   0.013130   -0.04   0.971
Gest        -0.004394   0.002081   -2.11   0.041 *
---
Signif. codes:  0 '***' 0.001 '**' 0.01 '*' 0.05 '.' 0.1 ' ' 1

Residual standard error: 1 on 39 degrees of freedom
Multiple R-squared: 0.167,      Adjusted R-squared: 0.125
F-statistic: 3.92 on 2 and 39 DF,  p-value: 0.0282
```

Here you see that mammals with shorter gestation periods have more dream sleep (controlling for life span) and that life span is unrelated to dream sleep when controlling for gestation period. The analysis is based on 42 cases with complete data.

In the previous example, what would have happened if data=na.omit(sleep) had been replaced with data=sleep? Like many R functions, lm() uses a limited definition of listwise deletion. Cases with any missing data on the variables fitted by the function (Dream, Span, and Gest in this case) would have been deleted. The analysis would have been based on 44 cases.

Listwise deletion assumes that the data are MCAR (that is, the complete observations are a random subsample of the full dataset). In the current example, we've assumed that the 42 mammals used are a random subsample of the 62 mammals collected. To the degree that the MCAR assumption is violated, the resulting regression parameters will be biased. Deleting all observations with missing data can also reduce statistical power by reducing the available sample size. In the current example, listwise deletion reduced the sample size by 32%. Next, we'll consider an approach that employs the entire dataset (including cases with missing data).

18.7   *Multiple imputation*

Multiple imputation (MI) provides an approach to missing values that's based on repeated simulations. MI is frequently the method of choice for complex missing-values problems. In MI, a set of complete datasets (typically 3 to 10) is generated from an existing dataset that's missing values. Monte Carlo methods are used to fill in the missing data in each of the simulated datasets. Standard statistical methods are applied to each of the simulated datasets, and the outcomes are combined to provide estimated results and confidence intervals that take into account the uncertainty introduced by the missing values. Good implementations are available in R through the Amelia, mice, and mi packages.

In this section, we'll focus on the approach provided by the mice (multivariate imputation by chained equations) package. To understand how the mice package operates, consider the diagram in figure 18.5.

The function mice() starts with a data frame that's missing data and returns an object containing several

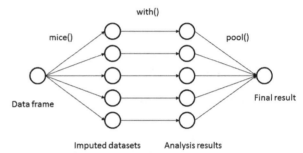

Figure 18.5   Steps in applying multiple imputation to missing data via the mice approach

complete datasets (the default is five). Each complete dataset is created by imputing values for the missing data in the original data frame. There's a random component to the imputations, so each complete dataset is slightly different. The with() function is then used to apply a statistical model (for example, a linear or generalized linear model) to each complete dataset in turn. Finally, the pool() function combines the results of these separate analyses into a single set of results. The standard errors and p-values in this final model correctly reflect the uncertainty produced by both the missing values and the multiple imputations.

How does the mice() function impute missing values?

Missing values are imputed by *Gibbs sampling*. By default, each variable with missing values is predicted from all other variables in the dataset. These prediction equations are used to impute plausible values for the missing data. The process iterates until convergence over the missing values is achieved. For each variable, you can choose the form of the prediction model (called an *elementary imputation method*) and the variables entered into it.

By default, predictive mean matching is used to replace missing data on continuous variables, whereas logistic or polytomous logistic regression is used for target variables that are *dichotomous* (factors with two levels) or *polytomous* (factors with more than two levels), respectively. Other elementary imputation methods include Bayesian linear regression, discriminant function analysis, two-level normal imputation, and random sampling from observed values. You can supply your own methods as well.

An analysis based on the `mice` package typically conforms to the following structure

```
library(mice)
imp <- mice(data, m)
fit <- with(imp, analysis)
pooled <- pool(fit)
summary(pooled)
```

where

- *data* is a matrix or data frame containing missing values.
- imp is a list object containing the *m* imputed datasets, along with information on how the imputations were accomplished. By default, *m* = 5.
- *analysis* is a formula object specifying the statistical analysis to be applied to each of the *m* imputed datasets. Examples include `lm()` for linear regression models, `glm()` for generalized linear models, `gam()` for generalized additive models, and `nbrm()` for negative binomial models. Formulas within the parentheses give the response variables on the left of the ~ and the predictor variables (separated by + signs) on the right.
- fit is a list object containing the results of the *m* separate statistical analyses.
- pooled is a list object containing the averaged results of these *m* statistical analyses.

Let's apply multiple imputation to the `sleep` dataset. You'll repeat the analysis from section 18.6, but this time use all 62 mammals. Set the seed value for the random number generator to 1,234 so that your results will match the following:

```
> library(mice)
> data(sleep, package="VIM")
> imp <- mice(sleep, seed=1234)

 [...output deleted to save space...]

> fit <- with(imp, lm(Dream ~ Span + Gest))
> pooled <- pool(fit)
> summary(pooled)
                 est       se       t    df  Pr(>|t|)      lo 95
(Intercept)  2.58858  0.27552   9.395  52.1  8.34e-13    2.03576
Span        -0.00276  0.01295  -0.213  52.9  8.32e-01   -0.02874
Gest        -0.00421  0.00157  -2.671  55.6  9.91e-03   -0.00736
               hi 95 nmis    fmi
(Intercept)  3.14141   NA 0.0870
Span         0.02322    4 0.0806
Gest        -0.00105    4 0.0537
```

Here, you see that the regression coefficient for Span isn't significant ($p \cong 0.08$), and the coefficient for Gest is significant at the $p < 0.01$ level. If you compare these results with those produced by a complete case analysis (section 18.6), you see that you'd come to the same conclusions in this instance. Length of gestation has a (statistically) significant, negative relationship with amount of dream sleep, controlling for life span. Although the complete-case analysis was based on the 42 mammals with complete data, the current analysis is based on information gathered from the full set of 62 mammals. By the way, the `fmi` column reports the fraction of missing information (that is, the proportion of variability that is attributable to the uncertainty introduced by the missing data).

You can access more information about the imputation by examining the objects created in the analysis. For example, let's view a summary of the `imp` object:

```
> imp

Multiply imputed data set
Call:
mice(data = sleep, seed = 1234)
Number of multiple imputations:  5
Missing cells per column:
  BodyWgt BrainWgt    NonD    Dream    Sleep     Span     Gest    Pred
        0        0      14       12        4        4        4       0
      Exp   Danger
        0        0
Imputation methods:
  BodyWgt BrainWgt    NonD    Dream    Sleep     Span     Gest    Pred
       ""       ""   "pmm"    "pmm"    "pmm"    "pmm"    "pmm"      ""
      Exp   Danger
       ""       ""
VisitSequence:
 NonD Dream Sleep  Span  Gest
    3     4     5     6     7
PredictorMatrix:
          BodyWgt BrainWgt NonD Dream Sleep Span Gest Pred Exp Danger
BodyWgt         0        0    0     0     0    0    0    0   0      0
BrainWgt        0        0    0     0     0    0    0    0   0      0
NonD            1        1    0     1     1    1    1    1   1      1
Dream           1        1    1     0     1    1    1    1   1      1
Sleep           1        1    1     1     0    1    1    1   1      1
Span            1        1    1     1     1    0    1    1   1      1
Gest            1        1    1     1     1    1    0    1   1      1
Pred            0        0    0     0     0    0    0    0   0      0
Exp             0        0    0     0     0    0    0    0   0      0
Danger          0        0    0     0     0    0    0    0   0      0
Random generator seed value:  1234
```

From the resulting output, you can see that five synthetic datasets were created and that the predictive mean matching (pmm) method was used for each variable with missing data. No imputation ("") was needed for BodyWgt, BrainWgt, Pred, Exp, or Danger, because they had no missing values. The visit sequence tells you that variables were imputed from right to left, starting with NonD and ending with Gest. Finally, the predictor matrix indicates that each variable with missing data was imputed using all the other variables in the dataset. (In this matrix, the rows represent the variables being imputed, the columns represent the variables used for the imputation, and 1s/0s indicate used/not used).

You can view the imputations by looking at subcomponents of the imp object. For example,

```
> imp$imp$Dream
      1   2   3   4   5
1   0.5 0.5 0.5 0.5 0.0
3   2.3 2.4 1.9 1.5 2.4
4   1.2 1.3 5.6 2.3 1.3
14  0.6 1.0 0.0 0.3 0.5
24  1.2 1.0 5.6 1.0 6.6
26  1.9 6.6 0.9 2.2 2.0
30  1.0 1.2 2.6 2.3 1.4
31  5.6 0.5 1.2 0.5 1.4
47  0.7 0.6 1.4 1.8 3.6
53  0.7 0.5 0.7 0.5 0.5
55  0.5 2.4 0.7 2.6 2.6
62  1.9 1.4 3.6 5.6 6.6
```

displays the 5 imputed values for each of the 12 mammals with missing data on the Dream variable. A review of these matrices helps you determine whether the imputed values are reasonable. A negative value for length of sleep might give you pause (or nightmares).

You can view each of the *m* imputed datasets via the complete() function. The format is

```
complete(imp, action=#)
```

where *#* specifies one of the *m* synthetically complete datasets. For example,

```
> dataset3 <- complete(imp, action=3)
> dataset3
  BodyWgt BrainWgt NonD Dream Sleep Span Gest Pred Exp Danger
1 6654.00   5712.0  2.1   0.5   3.3 38.6  645    3   5      3
2    1.00      6.6  6.3   2.0   8.3  4.5   42    3   1      3
3    3.38     44.5 10.6   1.9  12.5 14.0   60    1   1      1
4    0.92      5.7 11.0   5.6  16.5  4.7   25    5   2      3
5 2547.00   4603.0  2.1   1.8   3.9 69.0  624    3   5      4
6   10.55    179.5  9.1   0.7   9.8 27.0  180    4   4      4
[...output deleted to save space...]
```

displays the third (out of five) complete dataset created by the multiple imputation process.

Due to space limitations, we've only briefly considered the MI implementation provided in the mice package. The mi and Amelia packages also contain valuable approaches. If you're interested in the multiple imputation approach to missing data, I recommend the following resources:

- The multiple imputation FAQ page (www.stat.psu.edu/~jls/mifaq.html)
- Articles by Van Buuren and Groothuis-Oudshoorn (2010) and Yu-Sung, Gelman, Hill, and Yajima (2010)
- Amelia II: A Program for Missing Data (http://gking.harvard.edu/amelia)

Each can help to reinforce and extend your understanding of this important, but underutilized, methodology.

18.8 *Other approaches to missing data*

R supports several other approaches for dealing with missing data. Although not as broadly applicable as the methods described thus far, the packages described in table 18.2 offer functions that can be useful in specialized circumstances.

Table 18.2 Specialized methods for dealing with missing data

Package	Description
mvnmle	Maximum-likelihood estimation for multivariate normal data with missing values
cat	Analysis of categorical-variable datasets with missing values
arrayImpute, arrayMissPattern, and SeqKnn	Useful functions for dealing with missing microarray data
longitudinalData	Utility functions, including interpolation routines for imputing missing time-series values
kmi	Kaplan-Meier multiple imputation for survival analysis with missing data
mix	Multiple imputation for mixed categorical and continuous data
pan	Multiple imputation for multivariate panel or clustered data

Finally, there are two methods for dealing with missing data that are still in use but should be considered obsolete: pairwise deletion and simple imputation.

18.8.1 *Pairwise deletion*

Pairwise deletion is often considered an alternative to listwise deletion when working with datasets that are missing values. In pairwise deletion, observations are deleted only if they're missing data for the variables involved in a specific analysis. Consider the following code:

```
> cor(sleep, use="pairwise.complete.obs")
         BodyWgt BrainWgt NonD Dream Sleep  Span Gest  Pred Exp Danger
BodyWgt     1.00     0.93 -0.4  -0.1  -0.3  0.30  0.7  0.06 0.3   0.13
BrainWgt    0.93     1.00 -0.4  -0.1  -0.4  0.51  0.7  0.03 0.4   0.15
```

NonD	-0.38	-0.37	1.0	0.5	1.0	-0.38	-0.6	-0.32	-0.5	-0.48
Dream	-0.11	-0.11	0.5	1.0	0.7	-0.30	-0.5	-0.45	-0.5	-0.58
Sleep	-0.31	-0.36	1.0	0.7	1.0	-0.41	-0.6	-0.40	-0.6	-0.59
Span	0.30	0.51	-0.4	-0.3	-0.4	1.00	0.6	-0.10	0.4	0.06
Gest	0.65	0.75	-0.6	-0.5	-0.6	0.61	1.0	0.20	0.6	0.38
Pred	0.06	0.03	-0.3	-0.4	-0.4	-0.10	0.2	1.00	0.6	0.92
Exp	0.34	0.37	-0.5	-0.5	-0.6	0.36	0.6	0.62	1.0	0.79
Danger	0.13	0.15	-0.5	-0.6	-0.6	0.06	0.4	0.92	0.8	1.00

In this example, correlations between any two variables use all available observations for those two variables (ignoring the other variables). The correlation between Kaplan-Meier multiple is based on all 62 mammals (the number of mammals with data on both variables). The correlation between Kaplan-Meier multiple is based on 42 mammals, and the correlation between Kaplan-Meier multiple is based on 46 mammals.

Although pairwise deletion appears to use all available data, in fact each calculation is based on a different subset of the data. This can lead to distorted and difficult-to-interpret results. I recommend staying away from this approach.

18.8.2 *Simple (nonstochastic) imputation*

In simple imputation, the missing values in a variable are replaced with a single value (for example, mean, median, or mode). Using *mean substitution*, you could replace missing values on Kaplan-Meier multiple with the value 1.97 and missing values on Kaplan-Meier multiple with the value 8.67 (the means on Kaplan-Meier multiple, respectively). Note that the substitution is *nonstochastic*, meaning that random error isn't introduced (unlike with multiple imputation).

An advantage of simple imputation is that it solves the missing-values problem without reducing the sample size available for analyses. Simple imputation is, well, simple, but it produces biased results for data that isn't MCAR. If moderate to large amounts of data are missing, simple imputation is likely to underestimate standard errors, distort correlations among variables, and produce incorrect p-values in statistical tests. Like pairwise deletion, I recommend avoiding this approach for most missing-data problems.

18.9 *Summary*

Most statistical methods assume that the input data are complete and don't include missing values (such as, `NA`, `NaN`, or `Inf`). But most datasets in real-world settings contain missing values. Therefore, you must either delete the missing values or replace them with reasonable substitute values before continuing with the desired analyses. Often, statistical packages provide default methods for handling missing data, but these approaches may not be optimal. Therefore, it's important that you understand the various approaches available and the ramifications of using each.

In this chapter, we examined methods for identifying missing values and exploring patterns of missing data. The goal was to understand the mechanisms that led to the missing data and their possible impact on subsequent analyses. We then reviewed three popular methods for dealing with missing data: a rational approach, listwise deletion, and the use of multiple imputation.

Rational approaches can be used to recover missing values when there are redundancies in the data or when external information can be brought to bear on the problem. The listwise deletion of missing data is useful if the data are MCAR and the subsequent sample size reduction doesn't seriously impact the power of statistical tests. Multiple imputation is rapidly becoming the method of choice for complex missing-data problems when you can assume that the data are MCAR or MAR. Although many analysts may be unfamiliar with multiple imputation strategies, user-contributed packages (mice, mi, and Amelia) make them readily accessible. I believe we'll see rapid growth in their use over the next few years.

I ended the chapter by briefly mentioning R packages that provide specialized approaches for dealing with missing data, and singled out general approaches for handling missing data (pairwise deletion, simple imputation) that should be avoided.

In the next chapter, we'll explore advanced graphical methods, using the ggplot2 package to create innovative multivariate plots.

Part 5

Expanding your skills

In this final section, we consider advanced topics that will enhance your skills as an R programmer. Chapter 19 completes our discussion of graphics with a presentation of one of R's most powerful approaches to visualizing data. Based on a comprehensive grammar of graphics, the ggplot2 package provides a set of tools that allow you visualize complex data sets in new and creative ways. You'll be able to easily create attractive and informative graphs that would be difficult or impossible to create using R's base graphics system.

Chapter 20 provides a review of the R language at a deeper level. This includes a discussion of R's object-oriented programming features, working with environments, and advanced function writing. Tips for writing efficient code and debugging programs are also described. Although chapter 20 is more technical than the other chapters in this book, it provides extensive practical advice for developing more useful programs.

Throughout this book, you've used packages to get work done. In chapter 21, you'll learn to write your *own* packages. This can help you organize and document your work, create more complex and comprehensive software solutions, and share your creations with others. Sharing a useful package of functions with others can also be a wonderful way to give back to the R community (while spreading your fame far and wide).

Chapter 22 is all about report writing. R provides compressive facilities for generating attractive reports dynamically from data. In this last chapter, you'll learn how to create reports as web pages, PDF documents, and word processor documents (including Microsoft Word documents).

After completing part 5, you'll have a much deeper appreciation of how R works and the tools it offers for creating more sophisticated graphics, software, and reports.

*Advanced graphics
with ggplot2*

19

This chapter covers

- An introduction to the `ggplot2` package
- Using shape, color, and size to visualize multivariate data
- Comparing groups with faceted graphs
- Customizing `ggplot2` plots

In previous chapters, you created a wide variety of general and specialized graphs (and had lots of fun in the process). Most were produced using R's base graphics system. Given the diversity of methods available in R, it may not surprise you to learn that four separate and complete graphics systems are currently available.

In addition to base graphics, graphics systems are provided by the `grid`, `lattice`, and `ggplot2` packages. Each is designed to expand on the capabilities of, and correct for deficiencies in, R's base graphics system.

The `grid` graphics system provides low-level access to graphic primitives, giving programmers a great deal of flexibility in the creation of graphic output. The `lattice` package provides an intuitive approach for examining multivariate relationships through conditional one-, two-, or three-dimensional graphs called *trellis graphs*. The ggplot2 package provides a method of creating innovative graphs based on a comprehensive graphical "grammar."

In this chapter, we'll start with a brief overview of the four graphic systems. Then we'll focus on graphs that can be generated with the ggplot2 package. ggplot2 greatly expands the range and quality of the graphs you can produce in R. It allows you to visualize datasets with many variables using a comprehensive and consistent syntax, and easily generate graphs that would be difficult to create using base R graphics.

19.1   *The four graphics systems in R*

As stated earlier, there are currently four graphical systems available in R. The base graphics system, written by Ross Ihaka, is included in every R installation. Most of the graphs produced in previous chapters rely on base graphics functions.

The grid graphics system, written by Paul Murrell (2011), is implemented through the grid package. grid graphics offer a lower-level alternative to the standard graphics system. The user can create arbitrary rectangular regions on graphics devices, define coordinate systems for each region, and use a rich set of drawing primitives to control the arrangement and appearance of graphic elements.

This flexibility makes grid graphics a valuable tool for software developers. But the grid package doesn't provide functions for producing statistical graphics or complete plots. Because of this, the package is rarely used directly by data analysts and won't be discussed further. If you're interested in learning more about grid, visit Dr. Murrell's Grid website (http://mng.bz/C86p) for details.

The lattice package, written by Deepayan Sarkar (2008), implements *trellis* graphs, as outlined by Cleveland (1985, 1993). Basically, trellis graphs display the distribution of a variable or the relationship between variables, separately for each level of one or more other variables. Built using the grid package, the lattice package has grown beyond Cleveland's original approach to visualizing multivariate data and now provides a comprehensive alternative system for creating statistical graphics in R. A number of packages described in this book (effects, flexclust, Hmisc, mice, and odfWeave) use functions in the lattice package to produce graphs.

Finally, the ggplot2 package, written by Hadley Wickham (2009a), provides a system for creating graphs based on the grammar of graphics described by Wilkinson (2005) and expanded by Wickham (2009b). The intention of the ggplot2 package is to provide a comprehensive, grammar-based system for generating graphs in a unified and coherent manner, allowing users to create new and innovative data visualizations. The power of this approach has led ggplot2 to become an important tool for visualizing data using R.

Access to the four systems differs, as outlined in table 19.1. Base graphic functions are automatically available. To access grid and lattice functions, you must load the appropriate package explicitly (for example, library(lattice)). To access ggplot2 functions, you have to download and install the package (install.packages ("ggplot2")) before first use and then load it (library(ggplot2)).

Table 19.1   Access to graphic systems

System	Included in base installation?	Must be explicitly loaded?
base	Yes	No
grid	Yes	Yes
lattice	Yes	Yes
ggplot2	No	Yes

The lattice and ggplot2 packages overlap in functionality but approach the creation of graphs differently. Analysts tend to rely on one package or the other when plotting multivariate data. Given its power and popularity, the remainder of this chapter will focus on ggplot2. If you would like to learn more about the lattice package, I've created a supplementary chapter that you can download (www.statmethods .net/RiA/lattice.pdf) or from the publisher's website at www.manning.com/ RinActionSecondEdition.

This chapter uses three datasets to illustrate the use of ggplot2. The first is a data frame called singer that comes from the lattice package; it contains the heights and voice parts of singers in the New York Choral Society. The second is the mtcars data frame that you've used throughout this book; it contains automotive details on 32 automobiles. The final data frame is called Salaries and is included with the car package described in chapter 8. Salaries contains salary information for university professors and was collected to explore gender discrepancies in income. Together, these datasets offer a variety of visualization challenges.

Before continuing, be sure the ggplot2 and car packages are installed. You'll also want to install the gridExtra package. It allows you to place multiple ggplot2 graphs into a single plot (see section 19.7.4).

19.2   *An introduction to the ggplot2 package*

The ggplot2 package implements a system for creating graphics in R based on a comprehensive and coherent grammar. This provides a consistency to graph creation that's often lacking in R and allows you to create graph types that are innovative and novel. In this section, we'll start with an overview of ggplot2 grammar; subsequent sections dive into the details.

In ggplot2, plots are created by chaining together functions using the plus (+) sign. Each function modifies the plot created up to that point. It's easiest to see with an example (the graph is given in figure 19.1):

```
library(ggplot2)
ggplot(data=mtcars, aes(x=wt, y=mpg)) +
   geom_point() +
   labs(title="Automobile Data", x="Weight", y="Miles Per Gallon")
```

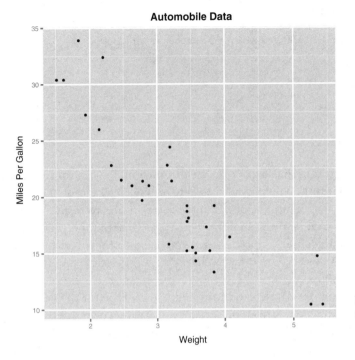

Figure 19.1   Scatterplot of automobile weight by mileage

Let's break down how the plot was produced. The ggplot() function initializes the plot and specifies the data source (mtcars) and variables (wt, mpg) to be used. The options in the aes() function specify what role each variable will play. (aes stands for *aesthetics,* or how information is represented visually.) Here, the wt values are mapped to distances along the x-axis, and mpg values are mapped to distances along the y-axis.

The ggplot() function sets up the graph but produces no visual output on its own. Geometric objects (called *geoms* for short), which include points, lines, bars, box plots, and shaded regions, are added to the graph using one or more *geom functions.* In this example, the geom_point() function draws points on the graph, creating a scatter-plot. The labs() function is optional and adds *annotations* (axis labels and a title).

There are many functions in ggplot2, and most can include optional parameters. Expanding on the previous example, the code

```
library(ggplot2)
ggplot(data=mtcars, aes(x=wt, y=mpg)) +
    geom_point(pch=17, color="blue", size=2) +
    geom_smooth(method="lm", color="red", linetype=2) +
    labs(title="Automobile Data", x="Weight", y="Miles Per Gallon")
```

produces the graph in figure 19.2.

Options to geom_point() set the point shape to triangles (pch=17), double the points' size (size=2), and render them in blue (color="blue"). The geom_smooth() function adds a "smoothed" line. Here a linear fit is requested (method="lm") and a red

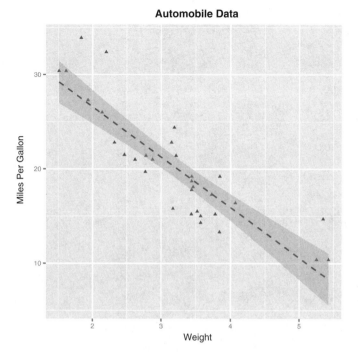

Automobile Data

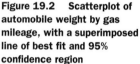

Figure 19.2　Scatterplot of automobile weight by gas mileage, with a superimposed line of best fit and 95% confidence region

(color="red") dashed (linetype=2) line of size 1 (size=1) is produced. By default, the line includes 95% confidence intervals (the darker band). We'll go into more detail about modeling relationships with linear and nonlinear fits in section 19.6.

The ggplot2 package provides methods for grouping and faceting. *Grouping* displays two or more groups of observations in a single plot. Groups are usually differentiated by color, shape, or shading. *Faceting* displays groups of observations in separate, side-by-side plots. The ggplot2 package uses factors when defining groups or facets.

You can see both grouping and faceting with the mtcars data frame. First, transform the am, vs, and cyl variables into factors:

```
mtcars$am <- factor(mtcars$am, levels=c(0,1),
                    labels=c("Automatic", "Manual"))
mtcars$vs <- factor(mtcars$vs, levels=c(0,1),
                    labels=c("V-Engine", "Straight Engine"))
mtcars$cyl <- factor(mtcars$cyl)
```

Next, generate a plot using the following code:

```
library(ggplot2)
ggplot(data=mtcars, aes(x=hp, y=mpg,
       shape=cyl, color=cyl)) +
       geom_point(size=3) +
       facet_grid(am~vs) +
       labs(title="Automobile Data by Engine Type",
            x="Horsepower", y="Miles Per Gallon")
```

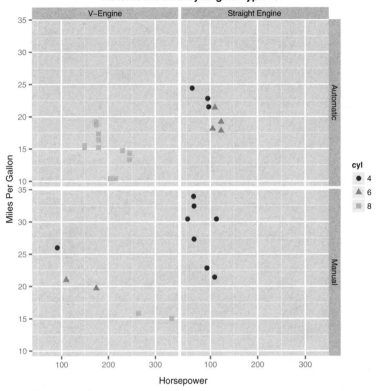

Figure 19.3   A scatterplot showing the relationship between horsepower and gas mileage separately for transmission and engine type. The number of cylinders in each automobile engine is represented by both shape and color.

The resulting graph (see figure 19.3) contains separate scatterplots for each combination of transmission type (automatic vs. manual) and engine arrangement (V-engine vs. straight engine). The color and shape of each point indicates the number of engine cylinders in that car. In this case, am and vs are the faceting variables, and cyl is the grouping variable.

The ggplot2 package is powerful and can be used to create a wide array of informative graphs. It's popular among seasoned R analysts and programmers; and, based on postings in R blogs and discussion groups, that popularity is growing.

Unfortunately, with power comes complexity. Unlike other R packages, ggplot2 can be thought of as a comprehensive graphical programming language in its own right. It has its own learning curve, and at times that curve can be steep. Hang in there—the effort is worth it. Luckily, there are function defaults and language simplifications designed to make your introduction to this package easier. With practice, you'll be able to create a wide variety of interesting and useful plots with just a few lines of code.

Let's start with a description of geom functions and the type of graphs they can create. Then we'll look at the aes() function in more detail and how you can use it to group data. Next, we'll consider faceting and the creation of trellis graphs. Finally, we'll look at ways to tweak the appearance of ggplot2 graphs, including modifying axes and legends, changing color schemes, and adding annotations. The chapter will end with pointers to resources that can help you master the ggplot2 approach more fully.

19.3 Specifying the plot type with geoms

Whereas the ggplot() function specifies the data source and variables to be plotted, the geom functions specify how these variables are to be visually represented (using points, bars, lines, and shaded regions). Currently, 37 geoms are available. Table 19.2 lists the more common ones, along with frequently used options. The options are described more fully in table 19.3.

Table 19.2 Geom functions

Function	Adds	Options
geom_bar()	Bar chart	color, fill, alpha
geom_boxplot()	Box plot	color, fill, alpha, notch, width
geom_density()	Density plot	color, fill, alpha, linetype
geom_histogram()	Histogram	color, fill, alpha, linetype, binwidth
geom_hline()	Horizontal lines	color, alpha, linetype, size
geom_jitter()	Jittered points	color, size, alpha, shape
geom_line()	Line graph	colorvalpha, linetype, size
geom_point()	Scatterplot	color, alpha, shape, size
geom_rug()	Rug plot	color, side
geom_smooth()	Fitted line	method, formula, color, fill, linetype, size
geom_text()	Text annotations	Many; see the help for this function
geom_violin()	Violin plot	color, fill, alpha, linetype
geom_vline()	Vertical lines	color, alpha, linetype, size

Most of the graphs described in this book can be created using the geoms in table 19.2. For example, the code

```
data(singer, package="lattice")
ggplot(singer, aes(x=height)) + geom_histogram()
```

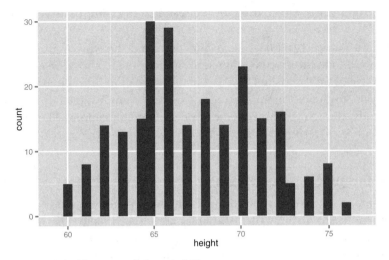

Figure 19.4   Histogram of singer heights

produces the histogram in figure 19.4, and

```
ggplot(singer, aes(x=voice.part, y=height)) + geom_boxplot()
```

produces the box plot in figure 19.5.

From figure 19.5, it appears that basses tend to be taller and sopranos tend to be shorter. Although gender wasn't measured, it probably accounts for much of the variation you see.

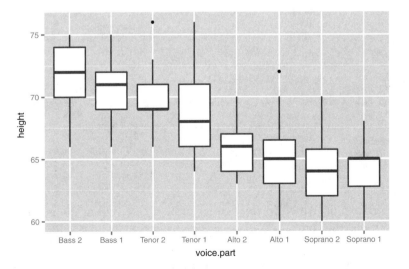

Figure 19.5   Box plot of singer heights by voice part

Note that only the x variable was specified when creating a histogram, but both an x and a y variable were specified for the box plot. The geom_histogram() function defaults to counts on the y-axis when no y variable is specified. See the documentation for each function for details and additional examples.

Each geom function has a set of options that can be used to modify its representation. Common options are listed in table 19.3.

Table 19.3 Common options for geom functions

Option	Specifies
color	Color of points, lines, and borders around filled regions.
fill	Color of filled areas such as bars and density regions.
alpha	Transparency of colors, ranging from 0 (fully transparent) to 1 (opaque).
linetype	Pattern for lines (1 = solid, 2 = dashed, 3 = dotted, 4 = dotdash, 5 = longdash, 6 = twodash).
size	Point size and line width.
shape	Point shapes (same as pch, with 0 = open square, 1 = open circle, 2 = open triangle, and so on). See figure 3.4 for examples.
position	Position of plotted objects such as bars and points. For bars, "dodge" places grouped bar charts side by side, "stacked" vertically stacks grouped bar charts, and "fill" vertically stacks grouped bar charts and standardizes their heights to be equal. For points, "jitter" reduces point overlap.
binwidth	Bin width for histograms.
notch	Indicates whether box plots should be notched (TRUE/FALSE).
sides	Placement of rug plots on the graph ("b" = bottom, "l" = left, "t" = top, "r" = right, "bl" = both bottom and left, and so on).
width	Width of box plots.

You can examine the use of many of these options using the Salaries dataset. The code

```
data(Salaries, package="car")
library(ggplot2)
ggplot(Salaries, aes(x=rank, y=salary)) +
      geom_boxplot(fill="cornflowerblue",
      color="black", notch=TRUE) +
      geom_point(position="jitter", color="blue", alpha=.5) +
      geom_rug(side="l", color="black")
```

produces the plot in figure 19.6. The figure displays notched box plots of salary by academic rank. The actual observations (teachers) are overlaid and given some transparency so they don't obscure the box plots. They're also jittered to reduce their overlap. Finally, a rug plot is provided on the left to indicate the general spread of salaries.

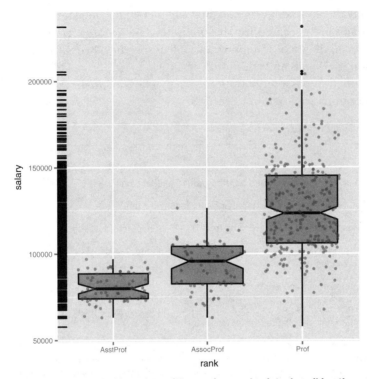

Figure 19.6   Notched box plots with superimposed points describing the salaries of college professors by rank. A rug plot is provided on the vertical axis.

From figure 19.6, you can see that the salaries of assistant, associate, and full professors differ significantly from each other (there is no overlap in the box plot notches). Additionally, the variance in salaries increases with greater rank, with a large range of salaries for full professors. In fact, at least one full professor earns less than assistant professors. There are also three full professors whose salaries are so large as to make them outliers (as indicated by the black dots in the Prof box plot). Having been a full professor earlier in my career, the data suggests to me that I was *clearly* underpaid.

The real power of the `ggplot2` package is realized when geoms are combined to form new types of plots. Returning to the `singer` dataset, the code

```
library(ggplot2)
data(singer, package="lattice")
ggplot(singer, aes(x=voice.part, y=height)) +
       geom_violin(fill="lightblue") +
       geom_boxplot(fill="lightgreen", width=.2)
```

combines box plots with violin plots to create a new type of graph (displayed in figure 19.7). The box plots show the 25th, 50th, and 75th percentile scores for each voice part in the `singer` dataframe, along with any outliers. The violin plots provide more visual cues as to the distribution of scores over the range of heights for each voice part.

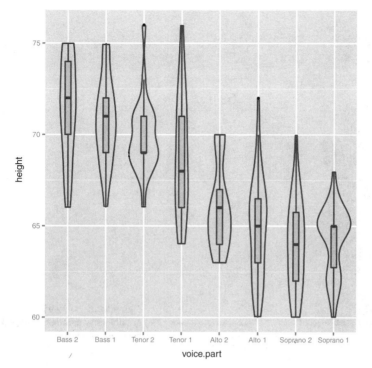

Figure 19.7 A combined violin and box plot graph of singer heights by voice part

In the remainder of this chapter, you'll use geoms to create a wide range of graph types. Let's start with grouping—the representation of more than one group of observations in a single graph.

19.4 Grouping

In order to understand data, it's often helpful to plot two or more groups of observations on the same graph. In R, the groups are usually defined as the levels of a categorical variable (factor). Grouping is accomplished in `ggplot2` graphs by associating one or more grouping variables with visual characteristics such as shape, color, fill, size, and line type. The `aes()` function in the `ggplot()` statement assigns variables to roles (visual characteristics of the plot), so this is a natural place to assign grouping variables.

Let's use grouping to explore the `Salaries` dataset. The dataframe contains information on the salaries of university professors collected during the 2008–2009 academic year. Variables include rank (AsstProf, AssocProf, Prof), sex (Female, Male), yrs.since.phd (years since Ph.D.), yrs.service (years of service), and salary (nine-month salary in dollars).

First, you can ask how salaries vary by academic rank. The code

```
data(Salaries, package="car")
library(ggplot2)
ggplot(data=Salaries, aes(x=salary, fill=rank)) +
    geom_density(alpha=.3)
```

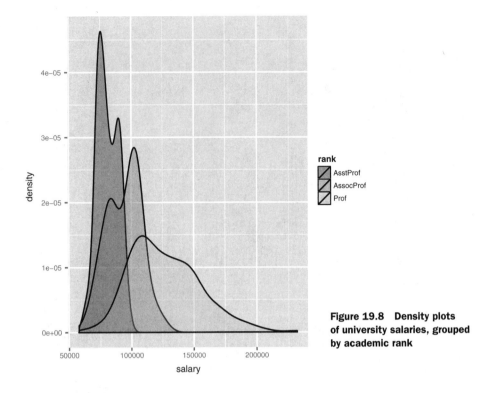

Figure 19.8   **Density plots of university salaries, grouped by academic rank**

plots three density curves in the same graph (one for each level of academic rank) and distinguishes them by fill color. The fills are set to be somewhat transparent (alpha) so that the overlapping curves don't obscure each other. The colors also combine to improve visualization in join areas. The plot is given is figure 19.8. Note that a legend is produced automatically. In section 19.7.2, you'll learn how to customize the legend generated for grouped data.

Salary increases by rank, but there is significant overlap, with some associate and full professors earning the same as assistant professors. As rank increases, so does the range of salaries. This is especially true for full professors, who have wide variation in their incomes. Placing all three distributions in the same graph facilitates comparisons among the groups.

Next, let's plot the relationship between years since Ph.D. and salary, grouping by sex and rank:

```
ggplot(Salaries, aes(x=yrs.since.phd, y=salary, color=rank,
       shape=sex)) + geom_point()
```

In the resulting graph (figure 19.9), academic rank is represented by point color (assistant professors in red, associate professors in green, and full professors in blue). Additionally, sex is indicated by point shape (circles are females and triangles are men). If you're looking at a greyscale image, the color differences can be difficult to see; try running the code yourself. Note that reasonable legends are again produced

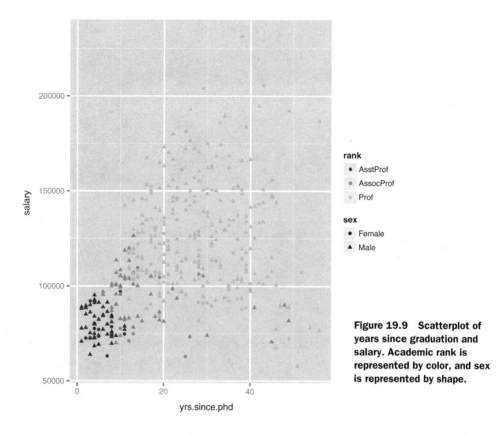

Figure 19.9 Scatterplot of years since graduation and salary. Academic rank is represented by color, and sex is represented by shape.

automatically. Here you can see that income increases with years since graduation, but the relationship is by no means linear.

Finally, you can visualize the number of professors by rank and sex using a grouped bar chart. The following code provides three bar-chart variations, displayed in figure 19.10:

```
ggplot(Salaries, aes(x=rank, fill=sex)) +
    geom_bar(position="stack") + labs(title='position="stack"')

ggplot(Salaries, aes(x=rank, fill=sex)) +
    geom_bar(position="dodge") + labs(title='position="dodge"')

ggplot(Salaries, aes(x=rank, fill=sex)) +
    geom_bar(position="fill") + labs(title='position="fill"')
```

Each of the plots in figure 19.10 emphasizes different aspects of the data. It's clear from the first two graphs that there are many more full professors than members of other ranks. Additionally, there are more female full professors than female assistant or associate professors. The third graph indicates that the relative percentage of women to men in the full-professor group is *less* than in the other two groups, even though the total *number* of women is greater.

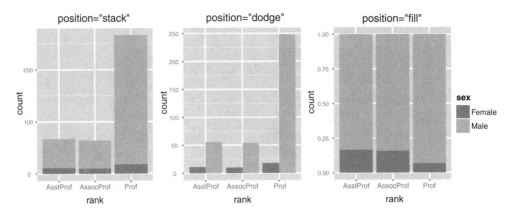

Figure 19.10   Three versions of a grouped bar chart. Each displays the number of professors by academic rank and sex.

Note that the label on the y-axis for the third graph isn't correct. It should say *Proportion* rather than *count*. You can correct this by adding `y="Proportion"` to the `labs()` function.

Options can be used in different ways, depending on whether they occur inside or outside the `aes()` function. Look at the following examples and try to guess what they do:

```
ggplot(Salaries, aes(x=rank, fill=sex))+ geom_bar()
ggplot(Salaries, aes(x=rank)) + geom_bar(fill="red")
ggplot(Salaries, aes(x=rank, fill="red")) + geom_bar()
```

In the first example, sex is a variable represented by fill color in the bar graph. In the second example, each bar is filled with the color red. In the third example, `ggplot2` assumes that `"red"` is the name of a variable, and you get unexpected (and undesirable) results. In general, variables should go inside `aes()`, and assigned constants should go outside `aes()`.

19.5   *Faceting*

Sometimes relationships are clearer if groups appear in side-by-side graphs rather than overlapping in a single graph. You can create trellis graphs (called *faceted graphs* in `ggplot2`) using the `facet_wrap()` and `facet_grid()` functions. The syntax is given in table 19.4, where *var*, *rowvar*, and *colvar* are factors.

Table 19.4   `ggplot2` facet functions

Syntax	Results
`facet_wrap(~var, ncol=n)`	Separate plots for each level of *var* arranged into *n* columns
`facet_wrap(~var, nrow=n)`	Separate plots for each level of *var* arranged into *n* rows

Table 19.4 ggplot2 facet functions

Syntax	Results
`facet_grid(`*`rowvar~colvar`*`)`	Separate plots for each combination of *`rowvar`* and *`colvar`*, where *`rowvar`* represents rows and *`colvar`* represents columns
`facet_grid(`*`rowvar~.`*`)`	Separate plots for each level of *`rowvar`*, arranged as a single column
`facet_grid(`*`.~colvar`*`)`	Separate plots for each level of *`colvar`*, arranged as a single row

Going back to the choral example, you can a faceted graph using the following code:

```
data(singer, package="lattice")
library(ggplot2)
ggplot(data=singer, aes(x=height)) +
      geom_histogram() +
      facet_wrap(~voice.part, nrow=4)
```

The resulting plot (figure 19.11) displays the distribution of singer heights by voice part. Separating the eight distributions into their own small, side-by-side plots makes them easier to compare.

As a second example, let's create a graph that has faceting and grouping:

```
library(ggplot2)
ggplot(Salaries, aes(x=yrs.since.phd, y=salary, color=rank,
      shape=rank)) + geom_point() + facet_grid(.~sex)
```

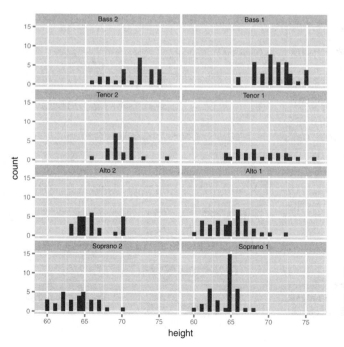

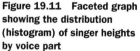
Figure 19.11 Faceted graph showing the distribution (histogram) of singer heights by voice part

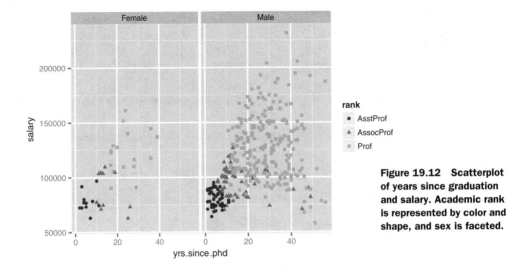

Figure 19.12   Scatterplot of years since graduation and salary. Academic rank is represented by color and shape, and sex is faceted.

The resulting graph is presented in 19.12. It contains the same information, but separating the plot into facets makes it somewhat easier to read.

Finally, try displaying the height distribution of choral members in the `singer` dataset separately for each voice part, using kernel-density plots arranged horizontally. Give each a different color. One solution is as follows:

```
data(singer, package="lattice")
library(ggplot2)
ggplot(data=singer, aes(x=height, fill=voice.part)) +
        geom_density() +
        facet_grid(voice.part~.)
```

The result is displayed in figure 19.13.

Note that the horizontal arrangement facilitates comparisons among the groups. The colors aren't strictly necessary, but they can aid in distinguishing the plots. (If you're viewing this in greyscale, be sure to try the example yourself.)

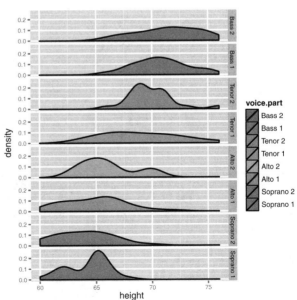

Figure 19.13   Faceted density plots for singer heights by voice part

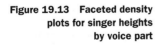

NOTE You may wonder why the legend for the density plots includes a black diagonal line through each box. Because you can control both the fill color of the density plots and their border colors (black by default), the legend displays both.

19.6 Adding smoothed lines

The ggplot2 package contains a wide range of functions for calculating statistical summaries that can be added to graphs. These include functions for binning data and calculating densities, contours, and quantiles. This section looks at methods for adding smoothed lines (linear, nonlinear, and nonparametric) to scatter plots.

You can use the geom_smooth() function to add a variety of smoothed lines and confidence regions. An example of a linear regression with confidence limits was given in figure 19.2. The parameters for the function are given in table 19.5.

Table 19.5 geom_smooth() options

Option	Description
method=	Smoothing function to use. Allowable values include lm, glm, smooth, rlm, and gam, for linear, generalized linear, loess, robust linear, and generalized additive modeling, respectively. smooth is the default.
formula=	Formula to use in the smoothing function. Examples include y~x (the default), y~log(x), y~poly(x,n) for an nth degree polynomial fit, and y~ns(x,n) for a spline fit with n degrees of freedom.
se	Plots confidence intervals (TRUE/FALSE). TRUE is the default.
level	Level of confidence interval to use (95% by default).
fullrange	Specifies whether the fit should span the full range of the plot (TRUE) or just the data (FALSE). FALSE is the default.

Using the Salaries dataset, let's first examine the relationship between years since obtaining a Ph.D. and faculty salaries. In this example, you'll use a nonparametric smoothed line (loess) with 95% confidence limits. Ignore sex and rank for now. The code is as follows, and the graph is shown in figure 19.14:

```
data(Salaries, package="car")
library(ggplot2)
ggplot(data=Salaries, aes(x=yrs.since.phd, y=salary)) +
    geom_smooth() + geom_point()
```

The plot suggests that the relationship between experience and salary isn't linear, at least when considering faculty who graduated many years ago.

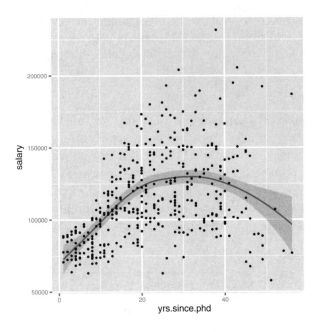

Figure 19.14   Scatterplot of years since doctorate and current faculty salary. A fitted loess smoothed line with 95% confidence limits has been added.

Next, let's fit a quadratic polynomial regression (one bend) separately by gender:

```
ggplot(data=Salaries, aes(x=yrs.since.phd, y=salary,
                    linetype=sex, shape=sex, color=sex)) +
    geom_smooth(method=lm, formula=y~poly(x,2),
              se=FALSE, size=1) +
    geom_point(size=2)
```

The confidence limits are suppressed to simplify the graph (se=FALSE). Genders are differentiated by color, symbol shape, and line type. The plot is displayed in figure 19.15.

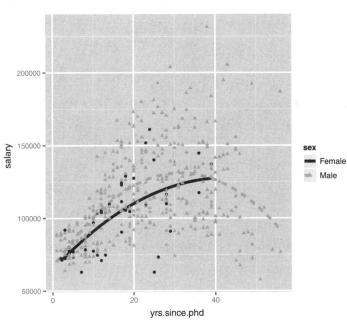

Figure 19.15   Scatterplot of years since graduation vs. salary with separate fitted quadratic regression lines for men and women

The curve for males appears to increase from 0 to about 30 years and then decrease. The curve for women rises from 0 to 40 years. No women in the dataset received their degree more than 40 years ago. For most of the range where both genders have data, men have received higher salaries.

Stat functions

In this section, you've added smoothed lines to scatter plots. The ggplot2 package contains a wide range of statistical functions (called *stat* functions) for calculating the quantities necessary to produce a variety of data visualizations. Typically, geom functions call the stat functions implicitly, and you won't need to deal with them directly. But it's useful to know they exist. Each stat function has help pages that can aid you in understanding how the geoms work.

For example, the geom_smooth() function relies on the stat_smooth() function to calculate the quantities needed to plot a fitted line and its confidence limits. The help page for geom_smooth() is sparse, but the help page for stat_smooth() contains a wealth of useful information. When exploring how a geom works and what options are available, be sure to check out both the geom function and its related stat function(s).

19.7 Modifying the appearance of ggplot2 graphs

In chapter 3, you saw how to customize base graphics using graphical parameters placed in the par() function or specific plotting functions. Unfortunately, changing base graphics parameters has no effect on ggplot2 graphs. Instead, the ggplot2 package offers specific functions for changing the appearance of its graphs.

In this section, we'll look at several functions that allow you to customize the appearance of ggplot2 graphs. You'll learn how to customize the appearance of axes (limits, tick marks, and tick mark labels), the placement and content of legends, and the colors used to represent variable values. You'll also learn how to create custom themes (allowing you to add a consistent look and feel to your graphs) and arrange several plots into a single graph.

19.7.1 Axes

The ggplot2 package automatically creates plot axes with tick marks, tick mark labels, and axis labels. Often they look fine, but occasionally you'll want to take greater control over their appearance. You've already seen how to use the labs() function to add a title and change the axis labels. In this section, you'll customize the axes themselves. Table 19.6 contains functions that are useful for customizing axes.

Table 19.6 Functions that control the appearance of axes and tick marks

Function	Options
scale_x_continuous(), scale_y_continuous()	breaks= specifies tick marks, labels= specifies labels for tick marks, and limits= controls the range of the values displayed.

Table 19.6 Functions that control the appearance of axes and tick marks (*continued*)

Function	Options
`scale_x_discrete()`, `scale_y_discrete()`	`breaks=` places and orders the levels of a factor, `labels=` specifies the labels for these levels, and `limits=` indicates which levels should be displayed.
`coord_flip()`	Reverses the x and y axes.

As you can see, `ggplot2` functions distinguish between the x- and y-axes and whether an axis represents a continuous or discrete (factor) variable.

Let's apply these functions to a graph with grouped box plots for faculty salaries by rank and sex. The code is as follows:

```
data(Salaries,package="car")
library(ggplot2)
ggplot(data=Salaries, aes(x=rank, y=salary, fill=sex)) +
    geom_boxplot() +
    scale_x_discrete(breaks=c("AsstProf", "AssocProf", "Prof"),
                     labels=c("Assistant\nProfessor",
                              "Associate\nProfessor",
                              "Full\nProfessor")) +
    scale_y_continuous(breaks=c(50000, 100000, 150000, 200000),
                       labels=c("$50K", "$100K", "$150K", "$200K")) +
    labs(title="Faculty Salary by Rank and Sex", x="", y="")
```

The resulting graph is provided in figure 19.16.

Clearly, average income goes up with rank, and men make more than women within each teaching rank. (For a more complete picture, try controlling for years since Ph.D.)

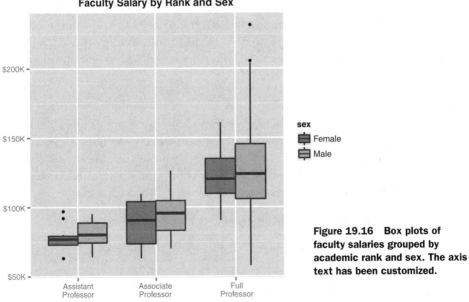

Figure 19.16 Box plots of faculty salaries grouped by academic rank and sex. The axis text has been customized.

19.7.2 Legends

Legends are guides that indicate how visual characteristics like color, shape, and size represent qualities of the data. The ggplot2 package generates legends automatically, and in many cases they suffice quite well. At other times, you may want to customize them. The title and placement are the most commonly customized characteristics.

When modifying a legend's title, you have to take into account whether the legend is based on color, fill, size, shape, or a combination. In figure 19.16, the legend represents the fill aesthetic (as you can see in the aes() function), so you can change the title by adding fill="mytitle" to the labs() function.

The placement of the legend is controlled by the legend.position option in the theme() function. Possible values include "left", "top", "right" (the default), and "bottom". Alternatively, you can specify a two-element vector that gives the position within the graph. Let's modify the graph in figure 19.16 so that the legend appears in the upper-left corner and the title is changed from *sex* to *Gender*. This can be accomplished with the following code:

```
data(Salaries,package="car")
library(ggplot2)
ggplot(data=Salaries, aes(x=rank, y=salary, fill=sex)) +
    geom_boxplot() +
    scale_x_discrete(breaks=c("AsstProf", "AssocProf", "Prof"),
                labels=c("Assistant\nProfessor",
                         "Associate\nProfessor",
                         "Full\nProfessor")) +
    scale_y_continuous(breaks=c(50000, 100000, 150000, 200000),
                labels=c("$50K", "$100K", "$150K", "$200K")) +
    labs(title="Faculty Salary by Rank and Gender",
        x="", y="", fill="Gender") +
    theme(legend.position=c(.1,.8))
```

The results are shown in figure 19.17.

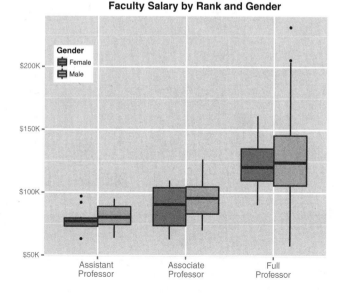

Figure 19.17 Box plots of faculty salaries grouped by academic rank. The axis text has been customized, along with the legend title and position.

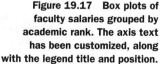

In this example, the upper-left corner of the legend was placed 10% from the left edge and 80% from the bottom edge of the graph. If you want to omit the legend, use `legend.position="none"`. The `theme()` function can change many aspects of a ggplot2 graph's appearance; other examples are given in section 19.7.4.

19.7.3 Scales

The ggplot2 package uses *scales* to map observations from the data space to the visual space. Scales apply to both continuous and discrete variables. In figure 19.15, a continuous scale was used to map the numeric values of the `yrs.since.phd` variable to distances along the x-axis and map the numeric values of the `salary` variable to distances along the y-axis.

Continuous scales can map numeric variables to other characteristics of the plot. Consider the following code:

```
ggplot(mtcars, aes(x=wt, y=mpg, size=disp)) +
      geom_point(shape=21, color="black", fill="cornsilk") +
        labs(x="Weight", y="Miles Per Gallon",
            title="Bubble Chart", size="Engine\nDisplacement")
```

The `aes()` parameter `size=disp` generates a scale for the continuous variable `disp` (engine displacement) and uses it to control the size of the points. The result is the bubble chart presented in figure 19.18. The graph shows that auto mileage decreases with both weight and engine displacement.

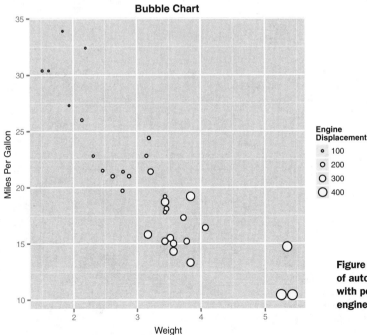

Figure 19.18 Bubble chart of auto weight by mileage, with point size representing engine displacement

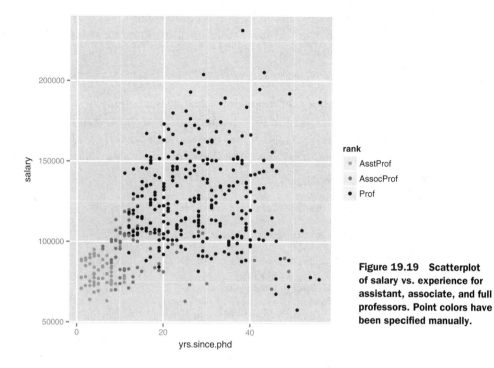

Figure 19.19 Scatterplot of salary vs. experience for assistant, associate, and full professors. Point colors have been specified manually.

In the discrete case, you can use a scale to associate visual cues (for example, color, shape, line type, size, and transparency) with the levels of a factor. The code

```
data(Salaries, package="car")
ggplot(data=Salaries, aes(x=yrs.since.phd, y=salary, color=rank)) +
    scale_color_manual(values=c("orange", "olivedrab", "navy")) +
    geom_point(size=2)
```

uses the `scale_color_manual()` function to set the point colors for the three academic ranks. The results are displayed in figure 19.19.

If you're color challenged like I am (does purple go with orange?), you can use color presets via the `scale_color_brewer()` and `scale_fill_brewer()` functions to specify attractive color sets. For example, try the code

```
ggplot(data=Salaries, aes(x=yrs.since.phd, y=salary, color=rank)) +
    scale_color_brewer(palette="Set1") + geom_point(size=2)
```

and see what you get. Replacing `palette="Set1"` with another value (such as `"Set2"`, `"Set3"`, `"Pastel1"`, `"Pastel2"`, `"Paired"`, `"Dark2"`, or `"Accent"`) will result in a different color scheme. To see the available color sets, use

```
library(RColorBrewer)
display.brewer.all()
```

to generate a display. For more information, see `help(scale_color_brewer)` and the ColorBrewer homepage (http://colorbrewer2.org).

The concept of scales is general in ggplot2. Although we won't cover this further, you can control the characteristics of scales. See the functions that have scale_ in their name for more details.

19.7.4   *Themes*

You've seen several methods for modifying specific visual elements of ggplot2 graphs. Themes allow you to control the overall appearance of these graphs. Options in the theme() function let you change fonts, backgrounds, colors, gridlines, and more. Themes can be used once or saved and applied to many graphs. Consider the following:

```
data(Salaries, package="car")
library(ggplot2)
mytheme <- theme(plot.title=element_text(face="bold.italic",
                 size="14", color="brown"),
                 axis.title=element_text(face="bold.italic",
                     size=10, color="brown"),
                 axis.text=element_text(face="bold", size=9,
                     color="darkblue"),
                 panel.background=element_rect(fill="white",
                     color="darkblue"),
                 panel.grid.major.y=element_line(color="grey",
                     linetype=1),
                 panel.grid.minor.y=element_line(color="grey",
                     linetype=2),
                 panel.grid.minor.x=element_blank(),
                 legend.position="top")

ggplot(Salaries, aes(x=rank, y=salary, fill=sex)) +
       geom_boxplot() +
       labs(title="Salary by Rank and Sex", x="Rank", y="Salary") +
       mytheme
```

Adding + mytheme to the plotting statements generates the graph shown in figure 19.20.

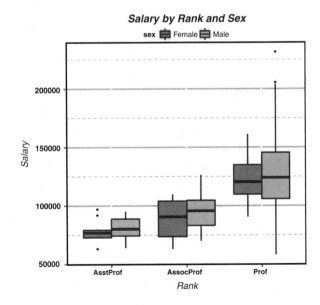

Figure 19.20   Box plots with a customized theme

The theme, mytheme, specifies that plot titles should be printed in brown, 14-point, bold italics; axis titles should be printed in brown, 10-point, bold italics; axis labels should be printed in dark blue, 9-point bold; the plot area should have a white fill and dark blue borders; major horizontal grids should be gray solid lines; minor horizontal grids should be grey dashed lines; vertical grids should be suppressed; and the legend should appear at the top of the graph. The theme() function gives you great control over the look of the finished product. See help(theme) to learn more about these options.

19.7.5 *Multiple graphs per page*

In section 3.5, you used the graphic parameter mfrow and the base function layout() to combine two or more base graphs into a single plot. Again, this approach won't work with plots created with the ggplot2 package. The easiest way to place multiple ggplot2 graphs in a single figure is to use the grid.arrange() function in the gridExtra package. You'll need to install it (install.packages(gridExtra)) before first use.

Let's create three ggplot2 graphs and place them in a single graph. The code is given in the following listing:

```
data(Salaries, package="car")
library(ggplot2)
p1 <- ggplot(data=Salaries, aes(x=rank)) + geom_bar()
p2 <- ggplot(data=Salaries, aes(x=sex)) + geom_bar()
p3 <- ggplot(data=Salaries, aes(x=yrs.since.phd, y=salary)) + geom_point()

library(gridExtra)
grid.arrange(p1, p2, p3, ncol=3)
```

The resulting graph is shown in figure 19.21. Each graph is saved as an object and then arranged into a single plot with the grid.arrange() function.

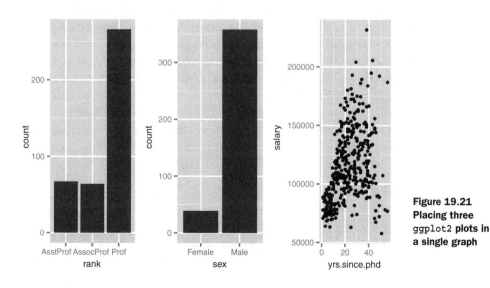

Figure 19.21 Placing three ggplot2 plots in a single graph

Note the difference between faceting and multiple graphs. Faceting creates an array of plots based on one or more categorical variables. In this section, you're arranging completely independent plots into a single graph.

19.8   Saving graphs

You can save the graphs created by ggplot2 using the standard methods discussed in section 1.3.4. But a convenience function named ggsave() can be particularly useful. Options include which plot to save, where to save it, and in what format. For example,

```
myplot <- ggplot(data=mtcars, aes(x=mpg)) + geom_histogram()
ggsave(file="mygraph.png", plot=myplot, width=5, height=4)
```

saves myplot as a 5-inch by 4-inch PNG file named mygraph.png in the current working directory. You can save the graph in a different format by setting the file extension to ps, tex, jpeg, pdf, jpeg, tiff, png, bmp, svg, or wmf. The wmf format is only available on Windows machines.

If you omit the plot= option, the most recently created graph is saved. The code

```
ggplot(data=mtcars, aes(x=mpg)) + geom_histogram()
ggsave(file="mygraph.pdf")
```

is valid and saves the graph to disk. See help(ggsave) for additional details.

19.9   Summary

This chapter reviewed the ggplot2 package, which provides advanced graphical methods based on a comprehensive grammar of graphics. The package is designed to provide you with a complete and comprehensive alternative to the native graphics provided with R. It offers methods for creating attractive and meaningful visualizations of data that are difficult to generate in other ways.

The ggplot2 package can be difficult to learn, but a wealth of material is available to help you on your journey (I promised myself that I would never use that word, but learning ggplot2 can certainly feel like one). A list of all ggplot2 functions, along with examples, can be found at http://docs.ggplot2.org. To learn about the theory underlying ggplot2, see the original book by Wickham (2009). Finally, Chang (2013) has written a very practical book, chock full of useful examples. Chang's book is definitely where I would start.

You should now have a firm grasp of the many ways that R allows you to create visual representations of data. If a picture is worth a thousand words, and R provides a thousand ways to create a picture, then R must be worth a million words (or something to that effect). In the next chapter two chapters, you'll delve deeper into R as a programming language.

Advanced programming

20

This chapter covers

- A deeper dive into the R language
- Using R's OOP features to create generic functions
- Tweaking code to run more efficiently
- Finding and correcting programming errors

Previous chapters introduced various topics that are important for application development, including data types (section 2.2), control flow (section 5.4), and function creation (section 5.5). This chapter will review these aspects of R as a programming language—but from a more advanced and detailed perspective. By the end of this chapter, you'll have a better idea of how the R language works.

We'll start with a review of objects, data types, and control flow before moving on to details of function creation, including the role of scope and environments. The chapter introduces R's approach to object-oriented programming and discusses the creation of generic functions. Finally, we'll go over tips for writing efficient code-generating and debugging applications. A mastery of these topics will help you to understand the code in other people's applications and aid you in creating new applications. In chapter 21, you'll have an opportunity to put these skills into practice by creating a useful package from start to finish.

20.1   *A review of the language*

R is an object-oriented, functional, array programming language in which objects are specialized data structures, stored in RAM, and accessed via names or symbols. Names of objects consist of uppercase and lowercase letters, the digits 0–9, the period, and the underscore. Names are case-sensitive and can't start with a digit, and a period is treated as a simple character without special meaning.

Unlike in languages such as C and C++, you can't access memory locations directly. Data, functions, and just about everything else that can be stored and named are objects. Additionally, the names and symbols themselves are objects that can be manipulated. All objects are stored in RAM during program execution, which has significant implications for the analysis of massive datasets.

Every object has *attributes*: meta-information describing the characteristics of the object. Attributes can be listed with the `attributes()` function and set with the `attr()` function. A key attribute is an object's *class*. R functions use information about an object's class in order to determine how the object should be handled. The class of an object can be read and set with the `class()` function. Examples will be given throughout this chapter and the next.

20.1.1   *Data types*

There are two fundamental data types: *atomic vectors* and *generic vectors*. Atomic vectors are arrays that contain a single data type. Generic vectors, also called *lists*, are collections of atomic vectors. Lists are recursive in that they can also contain other lists. This section considers both types in some detail.

Unlike in many languages, you don't have to declare an object's data type or allocate space for it. The type is determined implicitly from the object's contents, and the size grows or shrinks automatically depending on the type and number of elements the object contains.

ATOMIC VECTORS

Atomic vectors are arrays that contain a single data type (logical, real, complex, character, or raw). For example, each of the following is a one-dimensional atomic vector:

```
passed <- c(TRUE, TRUE, FALSE, TRUE)
ages <- c(15, 18, 25, 14, 19)
cmplxNums <- c(1+2i, 0+1i, 39+3i, 12+2i)
names <- c("Bob", "Ted", "Carol", "Alice")
```

Vectors of type "raw" hold raw bytes and aren't discussed here.

Many R data types are atomic vectors with special attributes. For example, R doesn't have a scalar type. A *scalar* is an atomic vector with a single element. So `k <- 2` is a shortcut for `k <- c(2)`.

A *matrix* is an atomic vector that has a dimension attribute, dim, containing two elements (number of rows and number of columns). For example, start with a one-dimensional numeric vector x:

```
> x <- c(1,2,3,4,5,6,7,8)
> class(x)
[1] "numeric"
> print(x)
{1] 1 2 3 4 5 6 7 8
```

Then add a dim attribute:

```
> attr(x, "dim") <- c(2,4)
```

The object x is now a 2 × 3 matrix of class matrix:

```
> print(x)
     [,1] [,2] [,3] [,4]
[1,]    1    3    5    7
[2,]    2    4    6    8

> class(x)
[1] "matrix"
> attributes(x)
$dim
[1] 2 2
```

Row and column names can be attached by adding a dimnames attribute:

```
> attr(x, "dimnames") <- list(c("A1", "A2"),
                              c("B1", "B2", "B3", "B4"))
> print(x)
   B1 B2 B3 B4
A1  1  3  5  7
A2  2  4  6  8
```

Finally, the matrix can be returned to a one-dimensional vector by removing the dim attribute:

```
> attr(x, "dim") <- NULL
> class(x)
[1] "numeric"
> print(x)
[1] 1 2 3 4 5 6 7 8
```

An *array* is an atomic vector with a dim attribute that has three or more elements. Again, you set the dimensions with the dim attribute, and you can attach labels with the dimnames attribute. Like one-dimensional vectors, matrices and arrays can be of type logical, numeric, character, complex, or raw. But you can't mix types in a single matrix or array.

The attr() function allows you to create arbitrary attributes and associate them with an object. Attributes store additional information about an object and can be used by functions to determine how they're processed.

There are a number of special functions for setting attributes, including `dim()`, `dimnames()`, `names()`, `row.names()`, `class()`, and `tsp()`. The latter is used to create time series objects. These special functions have restrictions on the values that can be set. Unless you're creating custom attributes, it's always a good idea to use these special functions. Their restrictions and the error messages they produce make coding errors less likely and more obvious.

GENERIC VECTORS OR LISTS

Lists are collections of atomic vectors and/or other lists. Data frames are a special type of list, where each atomic vector in the collection has the same length. Consider the `iris` data frame that comes with the base R installation. It describes four physical measures taken on each of 150 plants, along with their species (setosa, versicolor, or virginica):

```
> head(iris)
  Sepal.Length Sepal.Width Petal.Length Petal.Width Species
1          5.1         3.5          1.4         0.2  setosa
2          4.9         3.0          1.4         0.2  setosa
3          4.7         3.2          1.3         0.2  setosa
4          4.6         3.1          1.5         0.2  setosa
5          5.0         3.6          1.4         0.2  setosa
6          5.4         3.9          1.7         0.4  setosa
```

This data frame is actually a list containing five atomic vectors. It has a `names` attribute (a character vector of variable names), a `row.names` attribute (a numeric vector identifying individual plants), and a `class` attribute with the value `"data.frame"`. Each vector represents a column (variable) in the data frame. This can be easily seen by printing the data frame with the `unclass()` function and obtaining the attributes with the `attributes()` function:

```
unclass(iris)
attributes(iris)
```

The output is omitted here to save space.

It's important to understand lists because R functions frequently return them as values. Let's look at an example using a cluster-analysis technique from chapter 16. Cluster analysis uses a family of methods to identify naturally occurring groupings of observations.

You'll apply k-means cluster analysis (section 16.3.1) to the `iris` data. Assume that there are three clusters present in the data, and observe how the observations (rows) become grouped. You'll ignore the species variable and use only the physical measures of each plant to form the clusters. The required code is

```
set.seed(1234)
fit <- kmeans(iris[1:4], 3)
```

What information is contained in the object `fit`? The help page for `kmeans()` indicates that the function returns a list with seven components. The `str()` function displays the object's structure, and the `unclass()` function can be used to examine the object's contents directly. The `length()` function indicates how many components the object contains, and the `names()` function provides the names of these components. You can use the `attributes()` function to examine the attributes of the object. The contents of the object returned by `kmeans()` are explored here:

```
> names(fit)
[1] "cluster"      "centers"     "totss"        "withinss"
[5] "tot.withinss" "betweenss"   "size"         "iter"
[9] "ifault"

> unclass(fit)
$cluster
  [1] 1 1 1 1 1 1 1 1 1 1 1 1 1 1 1 1 1 1 1 1 1 1 1 1 1 1 1 1
 [29] 1 1 1 1 1 1 1 1 1 1 1 1 1 1 1 1 1 1 1 1 1 1 2 2 3 2 2 2
 [57] 2 2 2 2 2 2 2 2 2 2 2 2 2 2 2 2 2 2 2 2 3 2 2 2 2 2 2 2
 [85] 2 2 2 2 2 2 2 2 2 2 2 2 2 2 3 2 3 3 3 3 2 3 3 3 3 3 3 3
[113] 3 2 2 3 3 3 3 2 3 2 3 2 3 3 2 2 3 3 3 3 3 2 3 3 3 3 2 3
[141] 3 3 2 3 3 3 2 3 3 2

$centers
  Sepal.Length Sepal.Width Petal.Length Petal.Width
1        5.006       3.428        1.462       0.246
2        5.902       2.748        4.394       1.434
3        6.850       3.074        5.742       2.071

$totss
[1] 681.4

$withinss
[1] 15.15 39.82 23.88

$tot.withinss
[1] 78.85

$betweenss
[1] 602.5

$size
[1] 50 62 38

$iter
[1] 2

$ifault
[1] 0
```

Executing `sapply(fit, class)` returns the class of each component in the object:

```
> sapply(fit, class)
      cluster       centers         totss      withinss tot.withinss
    "integer"      "matrix"     "numeric"     "numeric"    "numeric"
    betweenss          size          iter        ifault
    "numeric"     "integer"     "integer"     "integer"
```

In this example, `cluster` is an integer vector containing the cluster memberships, and `centers` is a matrix containing the cluster centroids (means on each variable for each cluster). The size component is an integer vector containing the number of plants in each of the three clusters. To learn about the other components, see the Value section of help(kmeans).

INDEXING

Learning to unpack the information in a list is a critical R programming skill. The elements of any data object can be extracted via indexing. Before diving into a list, let's look at extracting elements from an atomic vector.

Elements are extracted using *object*[*index*], where *object* is the vector and *index* is an integer vector. If the elements of the atomic vector have been named, *index* can also be a character vector with these names. Note that in R, indices start with 1, not 0 as in many other languages.

Here is an example, using this approach for an atomic vector without named elements:

```
> x <- c(20, 30, 40)
> x[3]
[1] 40
> x[c(2,3)]
[1] 30 40
```

For an atomic vector with named elements, you could use

```
> x <- c(A=20, B=30, C=40)
> x[c(2,3)]
 B  C
30 40
> x[c("B", "C")]
 B  C
30 40
```

For lists, *components* (atomic vectors or other lists) can be extracted using *object*[*index*], where *index* is an integer vector. The following uses the fit object from the kmeans example that appears a little later, in listing 20.1:

```
> fit[c(2,7)]
$centers
  Sepal.Length Sepal.Width Petal.Length Petal.Width
1        5.006       3.428        1.462       0.246
2        5.902       2.748        4.394       1.434
3        6.850       3.074        5.742       2.071

$size
[1] 50 62 38
```

Note that components are returned as a list.

To get just the elements in the component, use *object*[[*integer*]]:

```
> fit[2]
$centers
  Sepal.Length Sepal.Width Petal.Length Petal.Width
1        5.006       3.428        1.462       0.246
2        5.902       2.748        4.394       1.434
3        6.850       3.074        5.742       2.071
```

```
> fit[[2]]
  Sepal.Length Sepal.Width Petal.Length Petal.Width
1        5.006       3.428        1.462       0.246
2        5.902       2.748        4.394       1.434
3        6.850       3.074        5.742       2.071
```

In the first case, a list is returned. In second case, a matrix is returned. The difference can be important, depending on what you do with the results. If you want to pass the results to a function that requires a matrix as input, you would want to use the double-bracket notation.

To extract a single named component, you can use the $ notation. In this case, *object[[integer]]* and *object$name* are equivalent:

```
> fit$centers
  Sepal.Length Sepal.Width Petal.Length Petal.Width
1        5.006       3.428        1.462       0.246
2        5.902       2.748        4.394       1.434
3        6.850       3.074        5.742       2.071
```

This also explains why the $ notation works with data frames. Consider the iris data frame. The data frame is a special case of a list, where each variable is represented as a component. This is why iris$Sepal.Length returns the 150-element vector of sepal lengths.

Notations can be combined to obtain the elements within components. For example,

```
> fit[[2]][1,]
Sepal.Length  Sepal.Width Petal.Length  Petal.Width
       5.006        3.428        1.462        0.246
```

extracts the second component of fit (a matrix of means) and returns the first row (the means for the first cluster on each of the four variables).

By extracting the components and elements of lists returned by functions, you can take the results and go further. For example, to plot the cluster centroids with a line graph, you can use the following code.

Listing 20.1 Plotting the centroids from a k-means cluster analysis

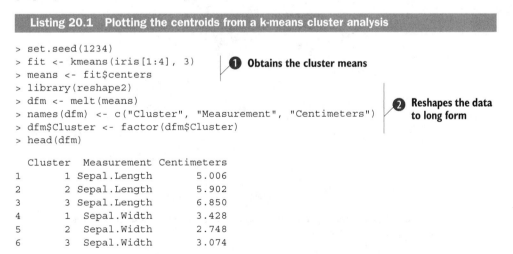

```
> set.seed(1234)
> fit <- kmeans(iris[1:4], 3)            ❶ Obtains the cluster means
> means <- fit$centers
> library(reshape2)
> dfm <- melt(means)
> names(dfm) <- c("Cluster", "Measurement", "Centimeters")     ❷ Reshapes the data
> dfm$Cluster <- factor(dfm$Cluster)                              to long form
> head(dfm)

  Cluster  Measurement Centimeters
1       1 Sepal.Length       5.006
2       2 Sepal.Length       5.902
3       3 Sepal.Length       6.850
4       1  Sepal.Width       3.428
5       2  Sepal.Width       2.748
6       3  Sepal.Width       3.074
```

```
library(ggplot2)
ggplot(data=dfm,
       aes(x=Measurement, y=Centimeters, group=Cluster)) +
       geom_point(size=3, aes(shape=Cluster, color=Cluster)) +
       geom_line(size=1, aes(color=Cluster)) +
       ggtitle("Profiles for Iris Clusters")
```

❸ Plots a line graph

First, the matrix of cluster centroids is extracted (rows are clusters, and columns are variable means) ❶. The matrix is then reshaped into long format using the reshape package (see section 5.6.2) ❷. Finally the data is plotted using the ggplot2 package (see section 18.3) ❸. The resulting graph is displayed in figure 20.1.

This type of graph is possible because all the variables plotted use the same units of measurement (centimeters). If the cluster analysis involved variables on different scales, you would need to standardize the data before plotting and label the y-axis something like Standardized Scores. See section 16.1 for details.

Now that you can represent data in structures and unpack the results, let's look at flow control.

20.1.2   Control structures

When the R interpreter processes code, it reads sequentially, line by line. If a line isn't a complete statement, it reads additional lines until a fully formed statement can be constructed. For example, if you wanted to add $3 + 2 + 5$,

```
> 3 + 2 + 5
[1] 10
```

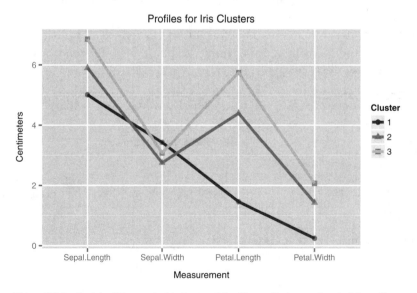

Figure 20.1   A plot of the centroids (means) for three clusters extracted from the Iris dataset using k-means clustering

will work. So will

```
>  3 + 2 +
   5
[1]  10
```

The + sign at the end of the first line indicates that the statement isn't complete. But

```
>  3 + 2
[1]  5
>  + 5
[1]  5
```

obviously doesn't work, because 3 + 2 is interpreted as a complete statement.

Sometimes you need to process code nonsequentially. You may want to execute code conditionally or repeat one or more statements multiple times. This section describes three control-flow functions that are particularly useful in writing functions: for(), if(), and ifelse().

FOR LOOPS

The for() function allows you to execute a statement repeatedly. The syntax is

```
for(var in seq){
    statements
}
```

where *var* is a variable name and *seq* is an expression that evaluates to a vector. If there is only one statement, the curly braces are optional:

```
> for(i in 1:5) print(1:i)
[1]  1
[1]  1 2
[1]  1 2 3
[1]  1 2 3 4
[1]  1 2 3 4 5

> for(i in 5:1)print(1:i)
[1]  1 2 3 4 5
[1]  1 2 3 4
[1]  1 2 3
[1]  1 2
[1]  1
```

Note that *var* continues to exist after the function exits. Here, i equals 1.

IF() AND ELSE

The if() function allows you to execute statements conditionally. The syntax for the if() construct is

```
if(condition){
    statements
} else {
    statements
}
```

The condition should be a one-element logical vector (TRUE or FALSE) and can't be missing (NA). The else portion is optional. If there is only one statement, the curly braces are also optional.

As an example, consider the following code fragment:

```
if(interactive()){
    plot(x, y)
} else {
    png("myplot.png")
    plot(x, y)
    dev.off()
}
```

If the code is being run interactively, the interactive() function returns TRUE and a plot is sent to the screen. Otherwise, the plot is saved to disk. You'll use the if() function extensively in chapter 21.

IFELSE()

The ifelse() function is a *vectorized* version of if(). Vectorization allows a function to process objects without explicit looping. The format of ifelse() is

```
ifelse(test, yes, no)
```

where *test* is an object that has been coerced to logical mode, *yes* returns values for true elements of *test*, and *no* returns values for false elements of *test*.

Let's say that you have a vector of p-values that you have extracted from a statistical analysis that involved six statistical tests, and you want to flag the tests that are significant at the $p < .05$ level. This can be accomplished with the following code:

```
> pvalues <- c(.0867, .0018, .0054, .1572, .0183, .5386)
> results <- ifelse(pvalues <.05, "Significant", "Not Significant")
> results

[1] "Not Significant" "Significant"     "Significant"
[4] "Not Significant" "Significant"     "Not Significant"
```

The ifelse() function loops through the vector pvalues and returns a character vector containing the value "Significant" or "Not Significant" depending on whether the corresponding element of pvalues is greater than .05.

The same result can be accomplished with explicit loops using

```
pvalues <- c(.0867, .0018, .0054, .1572, .0183, .5386)
results <- vector(mode="character", length=length(pvalues))
for(i in 1:length(pvalues)){
   if (pvalues[i] < .05) results[i] <- "Significant"
   else results[i] <- "Not Significant"
}
```

The vectorized version is faster and more efficient.

There are other control structures, including while(), repeat(), and switch(), but the ones presented here are the most commonly used. Now that you have data structures and control structures, we can talk about creating functions.

20.1.3 Creating functions

Almost everything in R is a function. Even arithmetic operators like +, -, /, and * are actually functions. For example, `2 + 2` is equivalent to `"+"(2, 2)`. This section describes function syntax. Scope is considered in section 20.2.

FUNCTION SYNTAX

The syntax of a function is

```
functionname <- function(parameters){
                    statements
                    return(value)
}
```

If there is more than one parameter, the parameters are separated by commas.

Parameters can be passed by keyword, by position, or both. Additionally, parameters can have default values. Consider the following function:

```
f <- function(x, y, z=1){
    result <- x + (2*y) + (3*z)
    return(result)
}

> f(2,3,4)
[1] 20
> f(2,3)
[1] 11
> f(x=2, y=3)
[1] 11
> f(z=4, y=2, 3)
[1] 19
```

In the first case, the parameters are passed by position (x = 2, y = 3, z = 4). In the second case, the parameters are passed by position, and z defaults to 1. In the third case, the parameters are passed by keyword, and z again defaults to 1. In the final case, y and z are passed by keyword, and x is assumed to be the first parameter not explicitly specified (x = 3). This also demonstrates that parameters passed by keyword can appear in any order.

Parameters are optional, but you must include the parentheses even if no values are being passed. The `return()` function returns the object produced by the function. It's also optional, and if it's missing, the results of the last statement in the function are returned.

You can use the `args()` function to view the parameter names and default values:

```
> args(f)
function (x, y, z = 0)
NULL
```

The `args()` function is designed for interactive viewing. If you need to obtain the parameter names and default values programmatically, use the `formals()` function. It returns a list with the necessary information.

Parameters are passed by value, not by reference. Consider this function statement:

```
result <- lm(height ~ weight, data=women)
```

The dataset women isn't accessed directly. A copy is made and passed to the function. If the women dataset was very large, RAM could be used up quickly. This can become an issue when you're dealing with *big* data problems, and you may need to use special techniques (see appendix G).

OBJECT SCOPE

The scope of the objects in R (how names are resolved to produce contents) is a complex topic. In the typical case,

- Objects created outside of any function are global (can be resolved within any function). Objects created within a function are local (available only within the function).
- Local objects are discarded at the end of function execution. Only objects passed back via the return() function (or assigned using an operator like <<-) are accessible after the function finishes executing.
- Global objects can be accessed (read) from within a function but not altered (again, unless the <<- operator is used).
- Objects passed to a function through parameters aren't altered by the function. Copies of the objects are passed, not the objects themselves.

Here is a simple example:

```
> x <- 2
> y <- 3
> z <- 4
> f <- function(w) {
        z <- 2
        x <- w*y*z
        return(x)
  }
> f(x)
[1] 12
> x
[1] 2
> y
[1] 3
> z
[1] 4
```

In this example, a copy of x is passed to the function f(), but the original isn't altered. The value of y is obtained from the environment. Even though z exists in the environment, the value set in the function is used and doesn't alter the value in the environment.

To understand scoping rules better, we need to discuss environments.

20.2 *Working with environments*

An *environment* in R consists of a frame and enclosure. A *frame* is set of symbol-value pairs (object names and their contents), and an *enclosure* is a pointer to an enclosing environment. The enclosing environment is also called the *parent environment*. R allows you to manipulate environments from within the language, resulting in fine-grained control over scope and the segregation of functions and data.

In an interactive session, when you first see the R prompt, you're in the global environment. You can create a new environment with the new.env() function and create assignments in that environment with the assign() function. Object values can be retrieved from an environment using the get() function. Here's an example:

```
> x <- 5
> myenv <- new.env()
> assign("x", "Homer", env=myenv)
> ls()
[1] "myenv" "x"
> ls(myenv)
[1] "x"
> x
[1] 5
> get("x", env=myenv)
[1] "Homer"
```

An object called x exists in the global environment and has the value 5. An object also called x exists in the environment myenv and has the value "Homer".

In addition to using the assign() and get() functions, you can use the $ notation. For example,

```
> myenv <- new.env()
> myenv$x <- "Homer"
> myenv$x
[1] "Homer"
```

produces the same results.

The parent.env() function displays the parent environment. Continuing the example, the parent environment for myenv is the global environment:

```
> parent.env(myenv)
<environment: R_GlobalEnv>
```

The parent environment for the global environment is the empty environment. See help(environment) for details.

Because functions are objects, they also have environments. This is important when considering *function closures* (functions that are packaged with the state that existed when they were created). Consider a function that is created by another function:

```
trim <- function(p){
    trimit <- function(x){
        n <- length(x)
        lo <- floor(n*p) + 1
```

```
        hi <- n + 1 - lo
        x <- sort.int(x, partial = unique(c(lo, hi)))[lo:hi]
    }
    trimit
}
```

The `trim(p)` function returns a function that trims *p* percent of the high and low values from a vector:

```
> x <- 1:10
> trim10pct <- trim(.1)
> y <- trim10pct(x)
> y
[1] 2 3 4 5 6 7 8 9
> trim20pct <- trim(.2)
> y <- trim20pct(x)
> y
  [1] 3 4 5 6 7 8
```

This works because the value of *p* is in the environment of the `trimit()` function and is saved with the function:

```
> ls(environment(trim10pct))
[1] "p"        "trimit"
> get("p", env=environment(trim10pct))
[1] 0.1
```

The lesson here is that, in R, functions include the objects that existed in their environment when they were created. This fact helps to explain the following behavior:

```
> makeFunction <- function(k){
      f <- function(x){
        print(x + k)
      }
  }

> g <- makeFunction(10)
> g(4)
[1] 14
> k <- 2
> g(5)
[1] 15
```

The `g()` function uses k=3 no matter what value k has in the global environment, because k equaled 3 when the function was created. Again, you can see this with

```
> ls(environment(g))
[1] "f" "k"
> environment(g)$k
[1] 10
```

In general, the value of an object is obtained from its local environment. If the object isn't found in its local environment, R searches in the parent environment, then the parent's parent environment, and so on, until the object is found. If R reaches the empty environment and still hasn't found the object, it throws an error. This is called *lexical* scoping.

To learn more about environments and lexical scoping, see "Environments in R" by Christopher Bare (http://mng.bz/uPYM) and "Lexical Scope and Function Closures in R" by Darren Wilkinson (http://mng.bz/R286).

20.3 Object-oriented programming

R is an object-oriented programming (OOP) language that's based on the use of generic functions. Each object has a class attribute that is used to determine what code to run when a copy of the object is passed to a generic function such as `print()`, `plot()`, or `summary()`.

R has two separate OOP models. The S3 model is older, simpler, and less structured. The S4 model is newer and more structured. The S3 approach is easier to use, and most applications in R use this model. We'll primarily focus on the S3 model here. The section ends with a brief discussion of the limitations of the S3 model and how the S4 model attempts to address them.

20.3.1 Generic functions

R uses the class of an object to determine what action to take when a generic function is called. Consider the following code:

```
summary(women)
fit <- lm(weight ~ height, data=women)
summary(fit)
```

In the first instance, the `summary()` function produces descriptive statistics for each variable in the data frame women. In the second instance, `summary()` produces a description of a linear regression model. How does this happen?

Let's look at the code for `summary()`:

```
> summary
function (object, ...) UseMethod("summary")
```

Now let's look at the class for the women data frame and the fit object:

```
> class(women)
[1] "data.frame"
> class(fit)
[1] "lm"
```

The function call `summary(women)` executes the function `summary.data.frame(women)` if it exists, or `summary.default(women)` otherwise. Similarly, `summary(fit)` executes the function `summary.lm(fit)` if it exists, or `summary.default(fit)` otherwise. The `UseMethod()` function *dispatches* the object to the generic function that has an extension matching the object's class.

To list all S3 generic functions available, use the `methods()` function:

```
> methods(summary)
 [1] summary.aov              summary.aovlist
 [3] summary.aspell*          summary.connection
 [5] summary.data.frame       summary.Date
```

```
 [7] summary.default          summary.ecdf*
                    ...output omitted...
[31] summary.table            summary.tukeysmooth*
[33] summary.wmc*
```

```
Non-visible functions are asterisked
```

The number of functions returned depends on the packages you have installed on your machine. On my computer, separate `summary()` functions have been defined for 33 classes!

You can view the code for the functions in the previous example by typing their names without the parentheses (`summary.data.frame`, `summary.lm`, and `summary.default`). Non-visible functions (functions in the methods list followed by asterisks) can't be viewed this way. In these cases, you can use the `getAnywhere()` function to view their code. To see the code for `summary.ecdf()`, type `getAnywhere(summary.ecdf)`. Viewing existing code is a great way to get ideas for your own functions.

You've seen classes such as `numeric`, `matrix`, `data.frame`, `array`, `lm`, `glm`, and `table`, but the class of an object can be any arbitrary string. Additionally, a generic function doesn't have to be `print()`, `plot()`, or `summary()`. Any function can be generic. The following listing defines a generic function called `mymethod()`.

Listing 20.2   An example of an arbitrary generic function

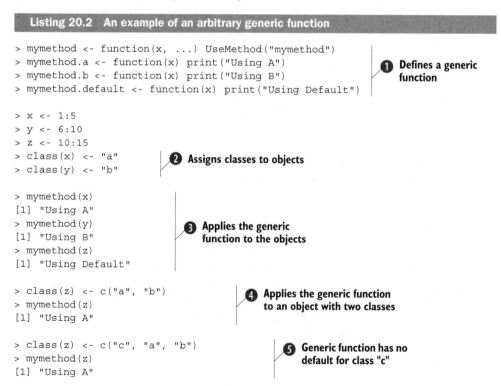

```
> mymethod <- function(x, ...) UseMethod("mymethod")
> mymethod.a <- function(x) print("Using A")
> mymethod.b <- function(x) print("Using B")
> mymethod.default <- function(x) print("Using Default")
```
❶ Defines a generic function

```
> x <- 1:5
> y <- 6:10
> z <- 10:15
> class(x) <- "a"
> class(y) <- "b"
```
❷ Assigns classes to objects

```
> mymethod(x)
[1] "Using A"
> mymethod(y)
[1] "Using B"
> mymethod(z)
[1] "Using Default"
```
❸ Applies the generic function to the objects

```
> class(z) <- c("a", "b")
> mymethod(z)
[1] "Using A"
```
❹ Applies the generic function to an object with two classes

```
> class(z) <- c("c", "a", "b")
> mymethod(z)
[1] "Using A"
```
❺ Generic function has no default for class "c"

In this example, `mymethod()` generic functions are defined for objects of classes a and b. A `default()` function is also defined ❶. The objects x, y, and z are then defined, and a class is assigned to x and y ❷. Next, `mymethod()` is applied to each object, and the appropriate function is called ❸. The default method is used for object z because the object has class `integer` and no `mymethod.integer()` function has been defined.

An object can be assigned to more than one class (for example, `building`, `residential`, and `commercial`). How does R determine which generic function to call in such a case? When z is assigned two classes ❹, the first class is used to determine which generic function to call. In the final example ❺, there is no `mymethod.c()` function, so the next class in line (a) is used. R searches the class list from left to right, looking for the first available generic function.

20.3.2 Limitations of the S3 model

The primarily limitation of the S3 object model is the fact that any class can be assigned to any object. There are no integrity checks. In this example,

```
> class(women) <- "lm"
> summary(women)
Error in if (p == 0) { : argument is of length zero
```

the data frame `women` is assigned class `lm`, which is nonsensical and leads to errors.

The S4 OOP model is more formal and rigorous and designed to avoid the difficulties raised by the S3 method's less structured approach. In the S4 approach, classes are defined as abstract objects that have slots containing specific types of information (that is, typed variables). Object and method construction are formally defined, with rules that are enforced. But programming using the S4 model is more complex and less interactive. To learn more about the S4 OOP model, see "A (Not So) Short Introduction to S4" by Chistophe Genolini (http://mng.bz/1VkD).

20.4 Writing efficient code

There is a saying among programmers: "A power user is someone who spends an hour tweaking their code so that it runs a second faster." R is a spritely language, and most R users don't have to worry about writing efficient code. The easiest way to make your code run faster is to beef up your hardware (RAM, processor speed, and so on). As a general rule, it's more important to write code that is understandable and easy to maintain than it is to optimize its speed. But when you're working with large datasets or highly repetitive tasks, speed can become an issue.

Several coding techniques can help to make your programs more efficient:

- Read in only the data you need.
- Use vectorization rather than loops whenever possible.
- Create objects of the correct size, rather than resizing repeatedly.
- Use parallelization for repetitive, independent tasks.

Let's look at each one in turn.

EFFICIENT DATA INPUT

When you're reading data from a delimited text file via the `read.table()` function, you can achieve significant speed gains by specifying which variables are needed and their types. This can be accomplished by including a `colClasses` parameter. For example, suppose you want to access 3 numeric variables and 2 character variables in a comma-delimited file with 10 variables per line. The numeric variables are in positions 1, 2, and 5, and the character variables are in positions 3 and 7. In this case, the code

```
my.data.frame <- read.table(mytextfile, header=TRUE, sep=',',
                colClasses=c("numeric", "numeric", "character",
                NULL, "numeric", NULL, "character", NULL,
                NULL, NULL))
```

will run faster than

```
my.data.frame <- read.table(mytextfile, header=TRUE, sep=',')
```

Variables associated with a `NULL` `colClasses` value are skipped. As the number of rows and columns in the text file increases, the speed gain becomes more significant.

VECTORIZATION

Use vectorization rather than loops whenever possible. Here, *vectorization* means using R functions that are designed to process vectors in a highly optimized manner. Examples in the base installation include `ifelse()`, `colSums()`, `colMeans()`, `rowSums()`, and `rowMeans()`. The `matrixStats` package offers optimized functions for many additional calculations, including counts, sums, products, measures of central tendency and dispersion, quantiles, ranks, and binning. Packages such as `plyr`, `dplyr`, `reshape2`, and `data.table` also provide functions that are highly optimized.

Consider a matrix with 1 million rows and 10 columns. Let's calculate the column sums using loops and again using the `colSums()` function. First, create the matrix:

```
set.seed(1234)
mymatrix <- matrix(rnorm(10000000), ncol=10)
```

Next, create a function called `accum()` that uses `for` loops to obtain the column sums:

```
accum <- function(x){
    sums <- numeric(ncol(x))
    for (i in 1:ncol(x)){
        for(j in 1:nrow(x)){
            sums[i] <- sums[i] + x[j,i]
        }
    }
}
```

The `system.time()` function can be used to determine the amount of CPU and real time needed to run the function:

```
> system.time(accum(mymatrix))
   user  system elapsed
  25.67    0.01   25.75
```

Calculating the same sums using the `colSums()` function produces

```
> system.time(colSums(mymatrix))
    user  system elapsed
   0.02    0.00    0.02
```

On my machine, the vectorized function ran more than 1,200 times faster. Your mileage may vary.

CORRECTLY SIZING OBJECTS

It's more efficient to initialize objects to their required final size and fill in the values than it is to start with a smaller object and grow it by appending values. Let's say you have a vector x with 100,000 numeric values. You want to obtain a vector y with the squares of these values:

```
> set.seed(1234)
> k <- 100000
  > x <- rnorm(k)
```

One approach is as follows:

```
>  y <- 0
>  system.time(for (i in 1:length(x)) y[i] <- x[i]^2)
   user  system elapsed
   10.03    0.00    10.03
```

y starts as a one-element vector and grows to be a 100,000-element vector containing the squared values of x. It takes about 10 seconds on my machine.

If you first initialize y to be a vector with 100,000 elements,

```
>  y <- numeric(length=k)
>  system.time(for (i in 1:k) y[i] <- x[i]^2)
   user  system elapsed
   0.23    0.00    0.24
```

the same calculations take less than a second. You avoid the considerable time it takes R to continually resize the object.

If you use vectorization,

```
> y <- numeric(length=k)
> system.time(y <- x^2)
   user  system elapsed
      0       0       0
```

the process is even faster. Note that operations like exponentiation, addition, multiplication, and the like are also vectorized functions.

PARALLELIZATION

Parallelization involves chunking up a task, running the chunks simultaneously on two or more cores, and combining the results. The cores might be on the same computer or on different machines in a cluster. Tasks that require the repeated independent execution of a numerically intensive function are likely to benefit from parallelization. This includes many Monte Carlo methods, including bootstrapping.

Many packages in R support parallelization (see "CRAN Task View: High-Performance and Parallel Computing with R" by Dirk Eddelbuettel, http://mng.bz/65sT). In this section, you'll use the foreach and doParallel packages to see parallelization on a single computer. The foreach package supports the foreach looping construct (iterating over the elements in a collection) and facilitates executing loops in parallel. The doParallel package provides a parallel back end for the foreach package.

In principal components and factor analysis, a critical step is identifying the appropriate number of components or factors to extract from the data (see section 14.2.1). One approach involves repeatedly performing an *eigenanalysis* of correlation matrices derived from random data that have the same number of rows and columns as the original data. The analysis is demonstrated in listing 20.3. Parallel and non-parallel versions of this analysis are compared in the listing. To execute this code, you'll need to install both packages and know how many cores your computer has.

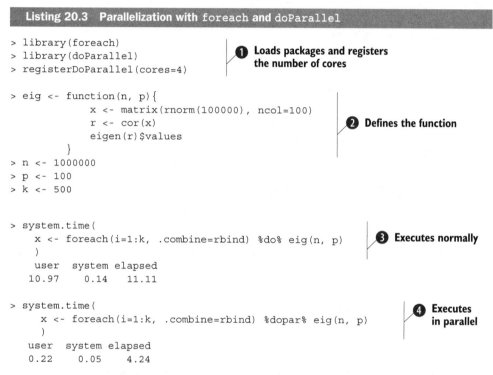

Listing 20.3   Parallelization with foreach and doParallel

```
> library(foreach)
> library(doParallel)                    ❶ Loads packages and registers
> registerDoParallel(cores=4)              the number of cores

> eig <- function(n, p){
            x <- matrix(rnorm(100000), ncol=100)
            r <- cor(x)                   ❷ Defines the function
            eigen(r)$values
        }
> n <- 1000000
> p <- 100
> k <- 500

> system.time(
    x <- foreach(i=1:k, .combine=rbind) %do% eig(n, p)   ❸ Executes normally
    )
  user   system elapsed
 10.97    0.14   11.11

> system.time(                                           ❹ Executes
    x <- foreach(i=1:k, .combine=rbind) %dopar% eig(n, p)   in parallel
    )
  user   system elapsed
  0.22    0.05    4.24
```

First the packages are loaded and the number of cores (four on my machine) is registered ❶. Next, the function for the eigenanalysis is defined ❷. Here 100,000 × 100 random data matrices are analyzed ❷. The eig() function is executed 500 times using foreach and %do% ❸. The %do% operator runs the function sequentially, and the .combine=rbind option appends the results to object x as rows. Finally, the function is run in parallel using the %dopar% operator ❹. In this case, parallel execution was about 2.5 times faster than sequential execution.

In this example, each iteration of the eig() function was numerically intensive, didn't require access to other iterations, and didn't involve disk I/O. This is the type of situation that benefits the most from parallelization. The downside of parallelization is that it can make the code less portable—there is no guarantee that others will have the same hardware configuration that you do.

The four efficiency measures described in this section can help with everyday coding problems. But they only go so far in helping you to process really large datasets (for example, datasets in the terabyte range). When you're working with *big* datasets, methods like those described in appendix G are required.

> **Locating bottlenecks**
>
> "Why is my code taking so long?" R provides tools for profiling programs in order to identify the most time-consuming functions. Place the code to be profiled between `Rprof()` and `Rprof(NULL)`. Then execute `summaryRprof()` to get a summary of the time spent executing each function. See `?Rprof` and `?summaryRprof` for details.

Efficiency is little comfort when a program won't execute or gives nonsensical results. Methods for uncovering programming errors are considered next.

20.5   *Debugging*

Debugging is the process of finding and reducing the number of errors or defects in a program. It would be wonderful if programs worked the first time. It would also be wonderful if unicorns lived in my neighborhood. In all but the simplest programs, errors occur. Determining the cause of these errors and fixing them is a time-consuming process. In this section, we'll look at common sources of error and tools that can help to uncover errors.

20.5.1   *Common sources of errors*

The following are some common reasons functions fail in R:

- An object name is misspelled, or the object doesn't exist.
- There is a misspecification of the parameters in a function call.
- The contents of an object aren't what the user expects. In particular, errors are often caused by passing objects that are NULL or contain NaN or NA values to a function that can't handle them.

The third reason is more common than you may think. It results from R's terse approach to errors and warnings.

Consider the following example. For the `mtcars` dataset in the base installation, you want to provide the variable `am` (transmission type) with a more informative title and labels. Next, you want to compare the gas mileage of cars with automatic transmissions to those with manual transmissions:

```
> mtcars$Transmission <- factor(mtcars$a,
                                  levels=c(1,2),
                                  labels=c("Automatic", "Manual"))
> aov(mpg ~ Transmission, data=mtcars)
Error in `contrasts<-`(`*tmp*`, value = contr.funs[1 + isOF[nn]]) :
  contrasts can be applied only to factors with 2 or more levels
```

Yikes! (Embarrassing, but this is actually what I said.) What happened?

You didn't get an "Object xxx not found" error, so you probably didn't misspell a function, data frame, or variable name. Let's look at the data that was passed to the aov() function:

```
> head(mtcars[c("mpg", "Transmission")])
                      mpg Transmission
Mazda RX4            21.0    Automatic
Mazda RX4 Wag        21.0    Automatic
Datsun 710           22.8    Automatic
Hornet 4 Drive       21.4         <NA>
Hornet Sportabout    18.7         <NA>
Valiant              18.1         <NA>

> table(mtcars$Transmission)

Automatic    Manual
       13         0
```

There are no cars with a manual transmission. Looking back at the original dataset, the variable am is coded 0=automatic, 1=manual (not 1=automatic, 2=manual).

The factor() function happily did what you asked without warnings or errors. It set all cars with manual transmissions to automatic and all cars with automatic transmissions to missing. With only one group available, the analysis of variance failed. Confirming that each input to a function contains the expected data can save you hours of frustrating detective work.

20.5.2 *Debugging tools*

Although examining object names, function parameters, and function inputs will uncover many sources of error, sometimes you have to delve into the inner workings of functions and functions that call functions. In these cases, the internal debugger that comes with R can be useful. Some helpful debugging functions are listed table 20.1.

Table 20.1   Built-in debugging functions

Function	Action
debug()	Marks a function for debugging.
undebug()	Unmarks a function for debugging.
browser()	Allows single-stepping through the execution of a function. While you're debugging, typing n or pressing <RET> (the Enter key) executes the current statement and moves on to the next. Typing c continues execution to the end of the function without single-stepping. Typing where displays the call stack, and Q halts execution and jumps to the top level immediately. Other R commands like ls(), print(), and assignment statements can also be submitted at the debugger prompt.
trace()	Modifies a function to allow debug code to be temporarily inserted.
untrace()	Cancels tracing and removes the temporary code.
traceback()	Prints the sequence of function calls that led to the last uncaught error.

The debug() function marks a function for debugging. When the function is executed, the browser() function is called and allows you to step through the function's execution one line at a time. The undebug() function turns this off, allowing the function to execute normally. You can temporarily insert debugging code into a function with the trace() function. This is particularly useful when you're debugging base functions and CRAN-contributed functions that can't be edited directly.

If a function calls other functions, it can be hard to determine where an error has occurred. In this case, executing the traceback() function immediately after an error will list the sequence of function calls that led to the error. The last call is the one that produced the error.

Let's look at an example. The mad() function calculates the median absolute deviation for a numeric vector. You'll use debug() to explore how this function works. The debugging session is displayed in the following listing.

Listing 20.4 A sample debugging session

```
> args(mad)                                              ①  Views the formal
function (x, center = median(x), constant = 1.4826,          arguments
    na.rm = FALSE, low = FALSE, high = FALSE)
NULL
> debug(mad)                                             ②  Sets the function
> mad(1:10)                                                  to debug
debugging in: mad(x)
debug: {
    if (na.rm)
        x <- x[!is.na(x)]
    n <- length(x)
    constant * if ((low || high) && n%%2 == 0) {
        if (low && high)
            stop("'low' and 'high' cannot be both TRUE")
        n2 <- n%/%2 + as.integer(high)
        sort(abs(x - center), partial = n2)[n2]
    }
    else median(abs(x - center))
}                                                        ③  Lists objects
Browse[2]> ls()
[1] "center"    "constant" "high"      "low"       "na.rm"    "x"
Browse[2]> center
[1] 5.5
Browse[2]> constant
[1] 1.4826
Browse[2]> na.rm
[1] FALSE
Browse[2]> x
 [1]  1  2  3  4  5  6  7  8  9 10
Browse[2]> n                                             ④  Single-steps
debug: if (na.rm) x <- x[!is.na(x)]                          through the code
Browse[2]> n
debug: n <- length(x)
Browse[2]> n
debug: constant * if ((low || high) && n%%2 == 0) {
```

```
    if (low && high)
        stop("'low' and 'high' cannot be both TRUE")
    n2 <- n%/%2 + as.integer(high)
    sort(abs(x - center), partial = n2)[n2]
} else median(abs(x - center))
Browse[2]> print(n)
[1] 10
Browse[2]> where
where 1: mad(x)
Browse[2]> c
exiting from: mad(x)
[1] 3.7065
> undebug(mad)
```

⑤ Resumes continuous execution

First, the arg() function is used to display the argument names and default values for the mad() function ❶. The debug flag is then set using debug(mad) ❷. Now, whenever mad() is called, the browser() function is executed, allowing you to step through the function a line at a time.

When mad() is called, the session goes into browser() mode. The code for the function is listed but not executed. Additionally, the prompt changes to Browse[*n*]>, where *n* indicates the *browser level*. The number increments with each recursive call.

In browser() mode, other R commands can be executed. For example, ls() lists the objects in existence at a given point during the function's execution ❸. Typing an object's name displays its contents. If an object is named n, c, or Q, you must use print(n), print(c), or print(Q) to view its contents. You can change the values of objects by typing assignment statements.

You step through the function and execute the statements one at a time by entering the letter n or pressing the Return or Enter key ❹. The where statement indicates where you are in the stack of function calls being executed. With a single function, this isn't very interesting; but if you have functions that call other functions, it can be helpful.

Typing c moves out of single-step mode and executes the remainder of the current function ❺. Typing Q exits the function and returns you to the R prompt.

The debug() function is useful when you have loops and want to see how values are changing. You can also embed the browser() function directly in code in order to help locate a problem. Let's say that you have a variable X that should never be negative. Adding the code

```
if (X < 0) browser()
```

allows you to explore the current state of the function when the problem occurs. You can take out the extra code when the function is sufficiently debugged. (I originally wrote "fully debugged," but this almost never happens, so I changed it to "sufficiently debugged" to reflect a programmer's reality.)

20.5.3   *Session options that support debugging*

When you have functions that call functions, two session options can help in the debugging process. Normally, when R encounters an error, it prints an error message and exits the function. Setting `options(error=traceback)` prints the *call stack* (the sequence of function calls that led to the error) as soon as an error occurs. This can help you to determine which function generated the error.

Setting `options(error=recover)` also prints the call stack when an error occurs. In addition, it prompts you to select one of the functions on the list and then invokes `browser()` in the corresponding environment. Typing c returns you to the list, and typing 0 quits back to the R prompt.

Using this `recover()` mode lets you explore the contents of any object in any function chosen from the sequence of functions called. By selectively viewing the contents of objects, you can frequently determine the origin of the problem. To return to R's default state, set `options(error=NULL)`. A toy example is given next.

Listing 20.5 Sample debugging session with `recover()`

```
f <- function(x, y){
        z <- x + y                          Creates functions
        g(z)
}
g <- function(x){
        z <- round(x)
        h(z)
}
h <- function(x){
        set.seed(1234)
        z <- rnorm(x)
        print(z)
}
> options(error=recover)
> f(2,3)
[1] -1.207  0.277  1.084 -2.346  0.429
> f(2, -3)                                Enters values
Error in rnorm(x) : invalid arguments     that cause an error

Enter a frame number, or 0 to exit

1: f(2, -3)
2: #3: g(z)
3: #3: h(z)
4: #3: rnorm(x)

Selection: 4
Called from: rnorm(x)                     Examines rnorm()
Browse[1]> ls()
[1] "mean" "n"     "sd"
Browse[1]> mean
[1] 0
Browse[1]> print(n)
[1] -1
Browse[1]> c

Enter a frame number, or 0 to exit
```

```
1: f(2, -3)
2: #3: g(z)
3: #3: h(z)
4: #3: rnorm(x)

Selection: 3
Called from: h(z)
Browse[1]> ls()
[1] "x"
Browse[1]> x
[1] -1
Browse[1]> c
```

Examines h(z)

```
Enter a frame number, or 0 to exit

1: f(2, -3)
2: #3: g(z)
3: #3: h(z)
4: #3: rnorm(x)

Selection: 2
Called from: g(z)
Browse[1]> ls()
[1] "x" "z"
Browse[1]> x
[1] -1
Browse[1]> z
[1] -1
Browse[1]> c
```

Examines g(z)

```
Enter a frame number, or 0 to exit

1: f(2, -3)
2: #3: g(z)
3: #3: h(z)
4: #3: rnorm(x)

Selection: 1
Called from: f(2, -3)
Browse[1]> ls()
[1] "x" "y" "z"
Browse[1]> x
[1] 2
Browse[1]> y
[1] -3
Browse[1]> z
[1] -1
Browse[1]> print(f)
function(x, y){
    z <- x + y
    g(z)
}
Browse[1]> c
```

Examines f(2, -3)

```
Enter a frame number, or 0 to exit
```

```
1: f(2, -3)
2: #3: g(z)
3: #3: h(z)
4: #3: rnorm(x)

Selection: 0

> options(error=NULL)
```

The code first creates a series of functions. Function f() calls function g(). Function g() calls function h(). Executing f(2, 3) works fine, but f(2, -3) throws an error. Because of options(error=recover), the interactive session is immediately moved into recover mode. The function call stack is listed, and you can choose which function to examine in browser() mode.

Typing 4 moves you into the rnorm() function, where ls() lists the objects; you can see that n = -1, which isn't allowed in rnorm(). This is clearly the problem, but to see how n became -1, you move up the stack.

Typing c returns you to the menu, and typing 3 moves you into the h(z) function, where x = -1. Typing c and 2 moves you into the g(z) function. Here both x and z are -1. Finally, moving up to the f(2, -3) function reveals that z is -1 because x = 2 and y = -3.

Note the use of print() to view the function code. This is useful when you're debugging code that you didn't write. Normally you can type the function name to view the code. In this example, f is a reserved word in browser mode that means "finish execution of the current loop or function"; the print() function is used explicitly to escape this special meaning.

Finally, c takes you back to the menu and 0 returns you to the normal R prompt. Alternatively, typing Q at any time returns you to the R prompt.

To learn more debugging in general and recover mode in particular, see Roger Peng's excellent "An Introduction to the Interactive Debugging Tools in R" (http://mng.bz/GPR6).

20.6   *Going further*

There are a number of excellent sources of information on advanced programming in R. The R Language Definition (http://mng.bz/U4Cm) is a good place to start. "Frames, Environments, and Scope in R and S-PLUS" by John Fox (http://mng.bz/Kkbi) is a great article for gaining a better understanding of scope. "How R Searches and Finds Stuff," by Suraj Gupta (http://mng.bz/2o5B), is a blog article that can help you understand just what the title implies. To learn more about efficient coding, see "FasteR! HigheR! StrongeR!—A Guide to Speeding Up R Code for Busy People," by Noam Ross (http://mng.bz/Iq3i). Finally, *R Programming for Bioinformatics* (2009) by Robert Gentleman is a comprehensive yet highly accessible text for programmers that want to look under the hood. I highly recommend it for anyone who wants to become a more effective R programmer.

20.7   *Summary*

In this chapter, we've taken a deeper dive into the R language from a programmer's point of view. Objects, data types, functions, environments, and scope were each described in greater detail. You learned about the S3 object-oriented approach along with its primary limitation. Finally, methods for writing efficient code and debugging troublesome programs were illustrated.

At this point you have all the tools you need to create a more complex application. In the next chapter, you'll have an opportunity to build a package from start to finish. Packages allow you to organize your programs and share them with others.

Creating a package

21

This chapter covers
- Creating the functions for a package
- Adding package documentation
- Building the package and sharing it with others

In previous chapters, you completed most tasks by using functions that were provided by others. The functions came from packages in the base R installation or from contributed packages downloaded from CRAN.

Installing a new package extends R's functionality. For example, installing the mice package provides you with new ways of dealing with missing data. Installing the ggplot2 packages provides you with new ways of visualizing data. Many of R's most powerful capabilities come from contributed packages.

Technically, a package is simply a set of functions, documentation, and data, saved in a standardized format. A package allows you to organize your functions in a well-defined and fully documented manner and facilitates sharing your programs with others.

There are several reasons why you might want to create a package:

- To make a set of frequently used functions easily accessible, along with the documentation on how to use them

491

- To create a set of examples and datasets that can be distributed to students in a classroom
- To create a program (a set of interrelated functions) that can be used to solve a significant analytic problem (such as imputing missing values)

Creating a useful package is also a great way of introducing yourself to others and giving back to the R community. Packages can be shared directly or through online repositories such as CRAN and GitHub.

In this chapter, you'll have an opportunity to develop a package from start to finish. By the end of the chapter, you'll be able to build your own R packages (and enjoy the smug self-satisfaction and bragging rights that attend such a feat).

The package you'll develop is called npar. It provides functions for nonparametric group comparisons. This is a set of analytic techniques that can be used to compare two or more groups on an outcome variable that's not normally distributed, or in situations where the variance of the outcome variable differs markedly across groups. This is a common problem facing analysts.

Before continuing, install the package using the following code:

```
pkg <- "npar_1.0.tar.gz"
loc <- "http://www.statmethods.net/RiA"
url <- paste(loc, pkg, sep="/")
download.file(url, pkg)
install.packages(pkg, repos=NULL, type="source")
```

This downloads the package from the statmethods.net website and saves it in your current working directory. It then installs the package in your default R library.

In section 21.1, you'll take the npar package for a test drive. Its features and functions are described and demonstrated. Then in section 22.2, you'll build the package from scratch.

21.1   *Nonparametric analysis and the npar package*

Nonparametric methods are a data-analytic approach that is particularly useful when the assumptions of traditional parametric methods (such as normality and constant variance) can't be met. Here, we'll focus on methods for comparing two or more independent groups on a numeric outcome variable.

Consider the life dataset that comes with the npar package. It contains the healthy life expectancy (HLE), or the estimated number of years of healthy living remaining, at age 65, for each American state from 2007 to 2009. Estimates are reported separately for men (hlem) and women (hlef). The HLE data were obtained from a Centers for Disease Control and Prevention publication (http://mng.bz/HTGD).

The dataset also contains a variable named region, dividing the states into Northeast, North Central, South, and West. I added this variable from the state.region data frame included in the base R installation.

Suppose you wanted to know whether HLE estimates for women vary significantly by region. One approach would be to use a one-way analysis of variance (ANOVA) as

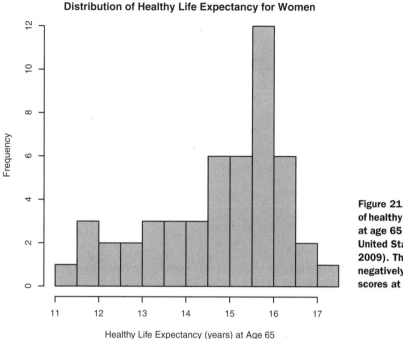

Figure 21.1 Distribution of healthy life expectancies at age 65 for women in the United States (2007–2009). The scores are negatively skewed (fewer scores at the low end).

described in chapter 9. But ANOVA assumes that the outcome variable is normally distributed and has a constant variance across each of the four country regions. Let's examine both assumptions.

The distribution of HLE scores for women can be visualized using a histogram:

```
library(npar)
hist(life$hlef, xlab="Healthy Life Expectancy (years) at Age 65",
    main="Distribution of Healthy Life Expectancy for Women",
    col="grey", breaks=10)
```

The plot is displayed in figure 21.1. Clearly the outcome variable is negatively skewed, with fewer scores at the low end.

The variance of HLE scores across regions can be visualized using a side-by-side dot chart (see chapter 19 for details):

```
library(ggplot2)
ggplot(data=life, aes(x=region, y=hlef)) +
    geom_point(size=3, color="darkgrey") +
    labs(title="Distribution of HLE Estimates by Region",
        x="US Region", y="Healthy Life Expectancy at Age 65") +
    theme_bw()
```

The results are displayed in figure 21.2, where each dot represents a state. Variances differ by region, with the greatest differences occurring between the Northeast and South.

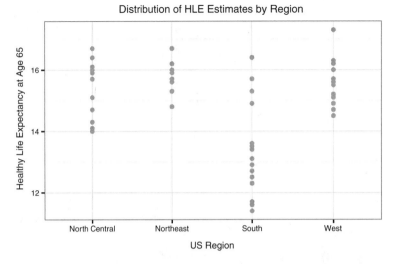

Figure 21.2   Dot chart of healthy life expectancies by region. The variability of HLE estimates differs across the four regions (compare the Northeast with the South).

Because the data violates two important ANOVA assumptions (normality and homogeneity of variance), you need a different approach. Unlike ANOVA, nonparametric methods don't assume normality or equal variances. In the current case, you would only need to assume that the data are ordinal—that higher scores indicate greater healthy life expectancy. This makes a nonparametric approach a reasonable alternative for the current problem.

21.1.1 Comparing groups with the npar package

You can use the npar package to compare independent groups on a numeric outcome variable that is at least ordinal. Given a numerical dependent variable and a categorical grouping variable, it provides

- An omnibus Kruskal–Wallis test that the groups don't differ.
- Descriptive statistics for each group.
- Post-hoc comparisons (Wilcoxon rank-sum tests) comparing groups two at a time. The test p-values can be adjusted to take multiple testing into account.
- Annotated side-by-side box plots for visualizing group differences.

The following listing demonstrates use of the npar package with the HLE estimates by region for women.

Listing 21.1   Comparison of HLE estimates with the npar package

```
> library(npar)
> results <- oneway(hlef ~ region, life)
> summary(results)
```

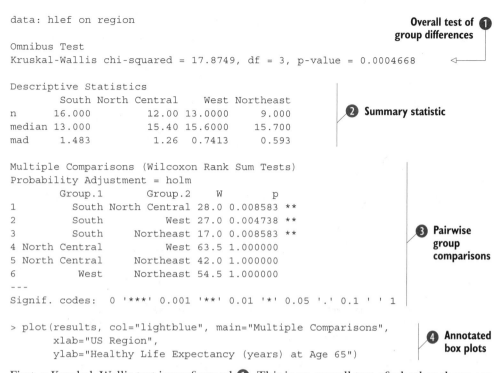

```
data: hlef on region                                      Overall test of  ①
                                                          group differences

Omnibus Test
Kruskal-Wallis chi-squared = 17.8749, df = 3, p-value = 0.0004668   ◁

Descriptive Statistics
          South North Central    West Northeast
n        16.000        12.00 13.0000    9.000        ② Summary statistic
median   13.000        15.40 15.6000   15.700
mad       1.483         1.26  0.7413    0.593

Multiple Comparisons (Wilcoxon Rank Sum Tests)
Probability Adjustment = holm
          Group.1       Group.2    W        p
1          South North Central 28.0 0.008583 **
2          South          West 27.0 0.004738 **
3          South      Northeast 17.0 0.008583 **       ③ Pairwise
4 North Central          West 63.5 1.000000              group
5 North Central      Northeast 42.0 1.000000             comparisons
6          West      Northeast 54.5 1.000000
---
Signif. codes:  0 '***' 0.001 '**' 0.01 '*' 0.05 '.' 0.1 ' ' 1

> plot(results, col="lightblue", main="Multiple Comparisons",
       xlab="US Region",                                ④ Annotated
       ylab="Healthy Life Expectancy (years) at Age 65")   box plots
```

First, a Kruskal–Wallis test is performed ①. This is an overall test of whether there are HLE differences between the regions. The small p-value (.00005) suggests that there are.

Next, descriptive statistics (sample size, median, and median absolute deviation) are provided for each region ②. The HLE estimates are highest for the Northeast (median = 15.7 years) and lowest for the South (median = 13.0 years). The smallest variability among the states occurs in the Northeast (mad = 0.59), and the largest occurs in the South (mad = 1.48).

Although the Kruskal–Wallis test indicates that there are HLE differences among the regions, it doesn't indicate where the differences lie. To determine this, you compare the groups two at a time using a Wilcoxon rank-sum test ③. With four groups, there are $4 \times (4 - 1) / 2$ or 6 pairwise comparisons.

The difference between the South and the North Central regions is statistically significant (p = 0.009), whereas the difference between the Northeast and North Central regions isn't (p = 1.0). In fact, the South differs from each of the other regions, but the other regions don't differ from each other.

When computing multiple comparisons, you have to be concerned with *alpha inflation*: an increase in the probability of declaring groups to be significantly different when in fact they aren't. For six independent comparisons, the chances of finding at least one erroneous difference by chance is $1 - (1 - .05)^6$ or 0.26.

With a chance of finding at least one false pairwise difference hovering around one in four, you'll want to adjust the p-value for each comparison upward (make each test more stringent and less likely to declare a difference). Doing so keeps the overall

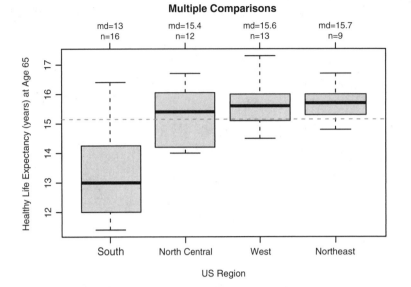

Figure 21.3   Annotated box plots displaying group differences. The plot is annotated with the medians and sample sizes for each group. The dotted vertical line represents the overall median.

family-wise error rate (the probability of finding one or more erroneous differences in a set of comparisons) at a reasonable level (say, .05).

The oneway() function accomplishes this by calling the p.adjust() function in the base R installation. The p.adjust() function adjusts p-values to account for multiple comparisons using one of several methods. The Bonferonni correction is perhaps the most well-known, but the Holm correction is more powerful and thus set as the default.

Differences among the groups are easiest to see with a graph. The plot() statement ❹ produces the side-by-side box plots in figure 21.3. The plot is annotated with a key that indicates the median and sample size for each group. A dotted horizontal line indicates the overall median for all observations combined.

It's clear from these analyses that women in the South can expect fewer years of health past age 65. This has implications for the distribution and focus of health services. You might want to analyze the HLE estimates for males and see if you reach a similar conclusion.

The next section describes the code files for the npar package. You can download them (and save yourself some typing) from www.statmethods.net/RiA/nparFiles.zip.

21.2 *Developing the package*

The npar package consists of four functions: oneway(), print.oneway(), summary .oneway(), and plot.oneway(). The first is the primary function that computes the statistics, and the others are S3 object-oriented generic functions (see section 20.3.1) used to print and plot the results. Here, oneway indicates that there is a single grouping factor.

It's a good idea to place each function in a separate text file with a .R extension. This isn't strictly necessary, but it makes organizing the work easier. Additionally, it isn't necessary for the names of the functions and the names of the files to match, but again, it's good coding practice. The files are provided in listings 21.2 through 21.5.

Each file has a header consisting of a set of comments that start with the characters #'. The R interpreter ignores these lines, but you'll use the roxygen2 package to turn the comments into your package documentation. These header comments will be discussed in section 21.3.

The oneway() function computes the statistics, and the print(), summary(), and plot() functions display the results. In the next section, you'll develop the oneway() function.

21.2.1 Computing the statistics

The oneway() function in the oneway.R text file performs all the statistical computations required.

Listing 21.2 Contents of the oneway.R file

```
#' @title Nonparametric group comparisons
#'
#' @description
#' \code{oneway} computes nonparametric group comparisons, including an
#' omnibus test and post-hoc pairwise group comparisons.
#'
#' @details
#' This function computes an omnibus Kruskal-Wallis test that the
#' groups are equal, followed by all pairwise comparisons using
#' Wilcoxon Rank Sum tests. Exact Wilcoxon tests can be requested if
#' there are no ties on the dependent variable. The p-values are
#' adjusted for multiple comparisons using the \code{\link{p.adjust}}
#' function.
#'
#' @param formula an object of class formula, relating the dependent
#' variable to the grouping variable.
#' @param data a data frame containing the variables in the model.
#' @param exact logical. If \code{TRUE}, calculate exact Wilcoxon tests.
#' @param sort logical. If \code{TRUE}, sort groups by median dependent
#' variable values.
#' @param method method for correcting p-values for multiple comparisons.
#' @export
#' @return a list with 7 elements:
#' \item{CALL}{function call}
#' \item{data}{data frame containing the depending and grouping variable}
#' \item{sumstats}{data frame with descriptive statistics by group}
#' \item{kw}{results of the Kruskal-Wallis test}
#' \item{method}{method used to adjust p-values}
#' \item{wmc}{data frame containing the multiple comparisons}
#' \item{vnames}{variable names}
#' @author Rob Kabacoff <rkabacoff@@statmethods.net>
```

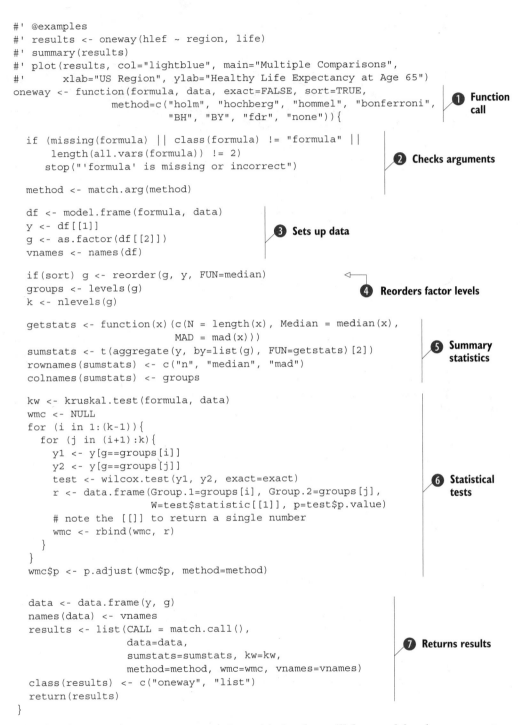

```
#' @examples
#' results <- oneway(hlef ~ region, life)
#' summary(results)
#' plot(results, col="lightblue", main="Multiple Comparisons",
#'      xlab="US Region", ylab="Healthy Life Expectancy at Age 65")
oneway <- function(formula, data, exact=FALSE, sort=TRUE,                    ❶ Function
                  method=c("holm", "hochberg", "hommel", "bonferroni",          call
                            "BH", "BY", "fdr", "none")){

  if (missing(formula) || class(formula) != "formula" ||
      length(all.vars(formula)) != 2)                                        ❷ Checks arguments
    stop("'formula' is missing or incorrect")

  method <- match.arg(method)

  df <- model.frame(formula, data)
  y <- df[[1]]
  g <- as.factor(df[[2]])                                                   ❸ Sets up data
  vnames <- names(df)

  if(sort) g <- reorder(g, y, FUN=median)
  groups <- levels(g)                                                       ❹ Reorders factor levels
  k <- nlevels(g)

  getstats <- function(x)(c(N = length(x), Median = median(x),
                          MAD = mad(x)))                                     ❺ Summary
  sumstats <- t(aggregate(y, by=list(g), FUN=getstats)[2])                     statistics
  rownames(sumstats) <- c("n", "median", "mad")
  colnames(sumstats) <- groups

  kw <- kruskal.test(formula, data)
  wmc <- NULL
  for (i in 1:(k-1)){
    for (j in (i+1):k){
      y1 <- y[g==groups[i]]
      y2 <- y[g==groups[j]]
      test <- wilcox.test(y1, y2, exact=exact)                              ❻ Statistical
      r <- data.frame(Group.1=groups[i], Group.2=groups[j],                   tests
                      W=test$statistic[[1]], p=test$p.value)
      # note the [[]] to return a single number
      wmc <- rbind(wmc, r)
    }
  }
  wmc$p <- p.adjust(wmc$p, method=method)


  data <- data.frame(y, g)
  names(data) <- vnames
  results <- list(CALL = match.call(),
                  data=data,
                  sumstats=sumstats, kw=kw,                                 ❼ Returns results
                  method=method, wmc=wmc, vnames=vnames)
  class(results) <- c("oneway", "list")
  return(results)
}
```

The header contains comments starting with #' that will be used by the roxygen2 package to create package documentation (see section 21.3). Next you see the function argument list ❶. The user provides a formula of the form *dependent variable~grouping variable* and a data frame containing the data. By default, approximate p-values are computed, and the groups are ordered by their median dependent variable values. The user can choose from among eight adjustment methods, with the `holm` method (the first option in the list) chosen by default.

Once the user enters the arguments, they're scanned for errors ❷. The `if()` function tests that the formula isn't missing, that it's a formula (*variables* ~ variables), and that there is only one variable on each side of the tilde (~). If any of these three conditions isn't true, the `stop()` function halts execution, prints an error message, and returns the user to the R prompt. For debugging purposes, you can alter the error action with the `options(error=)` function. See section 20.5.3 for details.

The `match.arg(arg, choices)` function ensures that the user has entered an argument that matches one of the strings in the *choices* character vector. If a match isn't found, an error is thrown, and, again, `oneway()` exits.

Next, the `model.frame()` function is used to create a data frame containing the dependent variable as the first column and the grouping variable as the second column ❸. In general, `model.frame()` returns a data frame containing all the variables in a formula. From this data frame, you create a numeric vector (y) containing the dependent variable and a factor vector (g) containing the grouping variable. The character vector vnames contains the variable names.

If sort=TRUE, you use the `reorder()` function to reorder the levels of the grouping variable g by the median dependent variable values y ❹. This is the default. The character vector groups contains the names of the groups, and the value k contains the number of groups.

Next, a numeric matrix (sumstats) is created, containing the sample size, median, and median absolute deviation for each group ❺. The `aggregate()` function uses the `getstats()` function to calculate the summary statistics, and the remaining code formats the table so that groups are columns and statistics are rows (I thought this was more attractive).

The statistical tests are then computed ❻. The results of the Kruskal–Wallis test are saved to a list called kw. The `for()` functions calculate every pairwise Wilcoxon test. The results of these pairwise tests are saved in the wmc data frame:

```
          Group.1       Group.2   W          p
1         South  North Central  28.0  0.008583
2         South          West  27.0  0.004738
3         South      Northeast  17.0  0.008583
4 North Central          West  63.5  1.000000
5 North Central      Northeast  42.0  1.000000
6          West      Northeast  54.5  1.000000
```

Here, Group.1 and Group.2 indicate the groups being compared to each other, W is the Wilcoxon statistic, and p is the (adjusted) p-value for each comparison.

Finally, the results are bundled up and returned as a list ❼. The list contains seven components, which are summarized in table 21.1. Additionally, you set the class of the list to `c("wmc", "list")`. This is a critical step in creating generic functions for handling the object.

Table 21.1 List object returned by the `wmc()` function

Component	Description
CALL	Function call
data	Data frame containing the dependent and grouping variable
sumstats	Data frame with groups as columns and n, median, and mad as rows
kw	Five-component list containing the results of the Kruskal–Wallis test
method	One-element character vector containing the method used to adjust p-values for multiple comparisons
wmc	Four-column data frame containing the multiple comparisons
vnames	Variable names

Although the list provides all the information required, you'd rarely access the components directly. Instead, you can create generic `print()`, `summary()`, and `plot()` functions to present this information in more concise and meaningful ways. These generic functions are considered next.

21.2.2 *Printing the results*

Most analytic functions of any breadth come with generic `print()` and `summary()` functions. `print()` provides basic or raw information about an object, and `summary()` provides more detailed or processed (summarized) information. A `plot()` function is frequently included when a plot makes sense in the given context.

Following the S3 OOP guidelines described in section 20.3.1, if an object has the class attribute `"foo"`, then `print(x)` executes `print.foo(x)` if it exists or `print.default(x)` otherwise. The same goes for `summary()` and `plot()`. Because the `oneway()` function returns an object of class `"oneway"`, you need to define `print.oneway()`, `summary.oneway()`, and `plot.oneway()` functions. The `print.oneway()` function is given in listing 21.3.

For the `life` data, `print(results)` produces basic information about the multiple comparisons:

```
data: hlef by region

Multiple Comparisons (Wilcoxon Rank Sum Tests)
Probability Adjustment = holm
        Group.1       Group.2    W        p
1        South   North Central 28.0  0.008583
2        South            West 27.0  0.004738
3        South       Northeast 17.0  0.008583
4 North Central          West 63.5  1.000000
5 North Central     Northeast 42.0  1.000000
6         West       Northeast 54.5  1.000000
```

An informative header is printed, followed by Wilcoxon statistics and adjusted p-values for each pair of groups (Group.1 with Group.2).

Listing 21.3 Contents of the print.R file

```
#' @title Print multiple comparisons
#'
#' @description
#' \code{print.oneway} prints pairwise group comparisons.
#'
#' @details
#' This function prints Wilcoxon pairwise multiple comparisons created
#' by the \code{\link{oneway}} function.
#'
#' @param x an object of class \code{oneway}.
#' @param ... additional arguments passed to the function.
#' @method print oneway
#' @export
#' @return the input object is returned silently.
#' @author Rob Kabacoff <rkabacoff@@statmethods.net>
#' @examples
#' results <- oneway(hlef ~ region, life)
#' print(results)
print.oneway <- function(x, ...){
  if (!inherits(x, "oneway"))                         ❶ Checks input
    stop("Object must be of class 'oneway'")

  cat("data:", x$vnames[1], "by", x$vnames[2], "\n\n")
  cat("Multiple Comparisons (Wilcoxon Rank Sum Tests)\n")   ❷ Prints the
  cat(paste("Probability Adjustment = ", x$method, "\n", sep=""))   header

  print(x$wmc,  ...)         ❸ Prints the table
}
```

The header contains comments starting with #' that will be used by the roxygen2 package to create package documentation (see section 21.3). The inherits() function is used to make sure the submitted object has class "oneway" ❶. A set of cat() functions prints a description of the analysis ❷. (This could have been written as a single cat() function, but I thought the current code was easier to read.) Finally, print.default() is called to print the multiple comparisons ❸. The summary .oneway() function is considered next.

21.2.3 *Summarizing the results*

The summary() function produces more comprehensive and processed output than the print() function. For the healthy life-expectancy data, the summary(results) statement produces the following:

```
data: hlef on region

Omnibus Test
Kruskal-Wallis chi-squared = 17.8749, df = 3, p-value = 0.0004668
```

```
Descriptive Statistics
        South North Central   West Northeast
n       16.000           12.00 13.0000    9.000
median 13.000            15.40 15.6000   15.700
mad     1.483             1.26  0.7413    0.593

Multiple Comparisons (Wilcoxon Rank Sum Tests)
Probability Adjustment = holm
          Group.1        Group.2    W        p
1          South  North Central  28.0 0.008583 **
2          South           West  27.0 0.004738 **
3          South       Northeast 17.0 0.008583 **
4  North Central          West  63.5 1.000000
5  North Central      Northeast 42.0 1.000000
6           West       Northeast 54.5 1.000000
---
Signif. codes:  0 '***' 0.001 '**' 0.01 '*' 0.05 '.' 0.1 ' ' 1
```

The output includes the results of the Kruskal–Wallis test, descriptive statistics (sample sizes, median, and median absolute deviations) for each group, and the multiple comparisons. In addition, the multiple-comparison table is annotated with stars to highlight significant results. The code for the summary.oneway() function is given in the following listing.

Listing 21.4   Contents of the summary.R file

```
#' @title Summarize oneway nonparametric analyses
#'
#' @description
#' \code{summary.oneway} summarizes the results of a oneway
#' nonparametric analysis.
#'
#' @details
#' This function prints a summary of analyses produced by
#' the \code{\link{oneway}} function. This includes descriptive
#' statistics by group, an omnibus Kruskal-Wallis test, and
#' Wilcoxon pairwise multiple comparisons.
#'
#' @param object an object of class \code{oneway}.
#' @param ... additional parameters.
#' @method summary oneway
#' @export
#' @return the input object is returned silently.
#' @author Rob Kabacoff <rkabacoff@@statmethods.net>
#' @examples
#' results <- oneway(hlef ~ region, life)
#' summary(results)
summary.oneway <- function(object, ...){
  if (!inherits(object, "oneway"))
    stop("Object must be of class 'oneway'")

  if(!exists("digits")) digits <- 4L

  kw <- object$kw
  wmc <- object$wmc
```

```
        cat("data:", object$vnames[1], "on", object$vnames[2], "\n\n")

        cat("Omnibus Test\n")
        cat(paste("Kruskal-Wallis chi-squared = ",
                round(kw$statistic,4),
                ", df = ", round(kw$parameter, 3),
                ", p-value = ",
                   format.pval(kw$p.value, digits = digits),
                "\n\n", sep=""))
```
① Kruskal–Wallis test

```
        cat("Descriptive Statistics\n")
        print(object$sumstats, ...)
```
② Descriptive statistics

```
        wmc$stars <- " "
        wmc$stars[wmc$p <    .1] <- "."
        wmc$stars[wmc$p <    .05] <- "*"
        wmc$stars[wmc$p <    .01] <- "**"
        wmc$stars[wmc$p < .001] <- "***"
        names(wmc)[which(names(wmc)=="stars")] <- " "
```
③ Table annotation

Pairwise multiple comparisons **④**
```
        cat("\nMultiple Comparisons (Wilcoxon Rank Sum Tests)\n")
        cat(paste("Probability Adjustment = ", object$method, "\n", sep=""))
        print(wmc, ...)
        cat("---\nSignif. codes:  0 '***' 0.001 '**' 0.01 '*' 0.05 '.' 0.1 ' '
           1\n")
        }
```

The class of the object passed to the function must be "oneway" or an error is thrown. Notice that the input parameter in the print.oneway() function is called x, but in the summary() function it's called object. I chose these names to be consistent with the argument names in the print.default() and summary.default() functions provided by the base R installation. After the informational details, the results of the Kruskal–Wallis test are printed **①**. The format.pval() function formats the p-value in the output.

Next, you print the descriptive statistics (n, median, mad) for each group **②**. Before printing the data frame of pairwise multiple comparisons, a column of stars is added **③**. This column serves as an annotation for the table and indicates the level of significance each test would achieve (.1, .05, .01, or .001). Nonsignificant results are represented by a blank (empty string). The statement

```
names(wmc)[which(names(wmc)=="stars")] <- " "
```

removes the column name for the annotation column. You could have used the statement

```
names(wmc)[5] <- " "
```

but that would break if the column order was changed in the future. The annotated results are printed **④**, and a key describing the meaning of the annotations is printed below the table.

21.2.4 *Plotting the results*

The final function, plot(), visualizes the results returned by the oneway() function:

```
plot(results, col="lightblue", main="Multiple Comparisons",
     xlab="US Region",
     ylab="Healthy Life Expectancy (years) at Age 65")
```

The resulting plot is provided in figure 21.3.

Unlike standard box plots, this plot provides annotations that indicate the median and sample size for each group, and a dashed line indicating the overall group median. The code for the plot.oneway() function is given next.

Listing 21.5   Contents of the plot.R file

```
#' @title Plot nonparametric group comparisons
#'
#' @description
#' \code{plot.oneway} plots nonparametric group comparisons.
#'
#' @details
#' This function plots nonparametric group comparisons
#' created by the \code{\link{oneway}} function using
#' annotated side by side boxplots. Medians and
#' sample sizes are placed at the top of the chart.
#' The overall median is represented by a horizontal
#' dashed line.
#'
#' @param x an object of class \code{oneway}.
#' @param ... additional arguments passed to the
#' \code{\link{boxplot}} function.
#' @method plot oneway
#' @export
#' @return NULL
#' @author Rob Kabacoff <rkabacoff@@statmethods.net>
#' @examples
#' results <- oneway(hlef ~ region, life)
#' plot(results, col="lightblue", main="Multiple Comparisons",
#'      xlab="US Region", ylab="Healthy Life Expectancy at Age 65")
plot.oneway <- function(x, ...){

  if (!inherits(x, "oneway"))                           ❶ Checks input
    stop("Object must be of class 'oneway'")
  data <- x$data
  y <- data[,1]
  g <- data[,2]
  stats <- x$sumstats                                   ❷ Generates the
  lbl <- paste("md=", stats[2,], "\nn=", stats[1,], sep="")    box plots
  opar <- par(no.readonly=TRUE)
  par(mar=c(5,4,8,2))
  boxplot(y~g,  ...)
  abline(h=median(y), lty=2, col="darkgrey")            ❸ Annotates the plot
  axis(3, at=1:length(lbl), labels=lbl, cex.axis=.9)
  par(opar)
}
```

Again, you check the class of the object passed to the function **❶**. Next, the original data are extracted and the box plots are produced **❷**. Annotations (medians, sample sizes, overall median line) are then added **❸**. You use the abline() function to add the overall median line and the axis() function to add the medians and sample sizes at the top of the graph.

Now that the functions have been created, it's time to add data to test them.

21.2.5 *Adding sample data to the package*

When you're creating a package, it's a good idea to include one or more datasets that can be used to try out the included functions. For the npar package, this involves adding the life data frame, as shown in the next listing. You add data frames to a package as .rda files.

Listing 21.6   Creating the life data frame

```
region <- c(rep("North Central", 12), rep("Northeast", 9),
            rep("South", 16), rep("West", 13))
state <- c("IL","IN","IA","KS","MI","MN","MO","NE","ND","OH","SD","WI",
           "CT","ME","MA","NH","NJ","NY","PA","RI","VT","AL","AR","DE",
           "FL","GA","KY","LA","MD","MS","NC","OK","SC","TN","TX","VA",
           "WV","AK","AZ","CA","CO","HI","ID","MT","NV","NM","OR","UT",
           "WA","WY")
hlem <- c(12.6,12.2,13.4,13.1,12.8,14.3,11.7,13.1,12.9,12.2,13.3,13.4,
          14.3,13.5,13.8,14,12.9,13.6,12.8,13.1,13.9,10.3,11.6,13.5,
          14.3,11.6,10.2,11.6,13.3,10.1,11.7,10.8,12,11.2,12.2,13.3,
          10.3,13.3,13.7,13.8,14.3,15,13.1,13.4,12.8,13.1,13.9,14.3,14,
          13.7)
hlef <- c(14.3,14.1,15.9,15.1,14.7,16.7,14,15.7,16,14,16.4,16.1,16.7,
          15.7,15.9,16,14.8,15.3,14.8,15.6,16.2,11.7,12.7,15.7,16.4,
          13.1,11.6,12.3,15.3,11.4,13.5,12.9,13.6,12.5,13.4,14.9,11.6,
          14.9,16.3,15.5,16.2,17.3,15.1,15.6,14.5,14.7,16,15.7,16,15.2)

life <- data.frame(region=factor(region), state=factor(state), hlem, hlef)

save(life, file='life.rda')
```

The save() function saves the data frame life.rda in the current working directory. When you build the final package in section 21.4, you'll move this file to a data subdirectory in the package file tree.

You also need to create a .R file that documents the data frame. The code is given next.

Listing 21.7   Contents of the life.R file

```
#' @title Healthy Life Expectancy at Age 65
#'
#' @description A dataset containing the healthy life expectancy (expected
#' years of life in good health) at age 65, by US state in 2007-2009.
#' Estimates are reported separately for men and women.
#'
#' @docType data
```

```
#' @keywords datasets
#' @name life
#' @usage life
#' @format A data frame with 50 rows and 4 variables. The variables
#' are as follows:
#' \describe{
#'   \item{region}{A factor with 4 levels (North Central, Northeast,
#'                  South, West)}
#'   \item{state}{A factor with the 2-letter ISO codes for the 50 US
#'                 states}
#'   \item{hlem}{Healthy life expectancy for men in years}
#'   \item{hlef}{Healthy life expectancy for women in years}
#' }
#' @source The \code{hlem} and \code{hlef} data were obtained from
#' the Center for Disease Control and Prevention
#' \emph{Morbidity and Mortality Weekly Report} at \url{
#' http://www.cdc.gov/mmwr/preview/mmwrhtml/mm6228a1.htm?s_cid=mm6228a1_w}.
#' The \code{region} variable was added from the
#' \code{\link[datasets]{state.region}} dataset.
NULL
```

Note that the code in listing 21.7 consists entirely of comments. In the next section, you'll process all the comments in the .R files in this section to create the package's documentation. R requires that rigorous and structured documentation be included with any package.

21.3   *Creating the package documentation*

Every R package follows the same set of enforced guidelines for documentation. Each function in a package must be documented in the same fashion using LaTeX, a document markup language and typesetting system. Each function is placed in a separate .R file, and the documentation for that function (written in LaTeX) is placed in a .Rd file. Both the .R and .Rd files are text files.

There are two limitations to this approach. First, the documentation is stored separately from the functions it describes. If you change the function code, you have to search out the documentation and change it as well. Second, the user has to learn LaTeX. If you thought R has a steep learning curve, wait until you start working with LaTeX!

The roxygen2 package can dramatically simplify the creation of documentation. You place comments in the head of each .R file that will serve as the function's documentation. Then, the documentation is created using a simple markup language. When the file is processed by Roxygen2, lines that start with #' are used to generate the LaTeX documentation (.Rd file) automatically.

Look at the file contents in listings 21.4–21.7. The comments at the head of each file use the tags described in table 21.2. The tags (called *roclets*) are fundamental to how Roxygen2 creates LaTeX documentation.

To see what the resulting documentation looks like, be sure the npar package has been loaded, and request help on each of the functions (help(oneway), help (print.oneway), help(summary.oneway), and help(plot.oneway)). The help(life) statement should provide information about the dataset. See `help(rd_roclet)` for more details about these tags.

Table 21.2 Tags for use with Roxygen2

Tag	Description
`@title`	Function title
`@description`	One-line function description
`@details`	Multiline function description (indent after the first line)
`@parm`	Function parameter
`@export`	Adds the function to the NAMESPACE
`@method generic class`	Documents a generic S3 method
`@return`	Value returned by the function
`@author`	Author(s) and contact address(es)
`@examples`	Examples using the function
`@note`	Any notes about the operation of the function
`@aliases`	Additional aliases through which users can find documentation
`@references`	References concerning the methodology employed by function

A few additional markup elements are useful to know as you create documentation. The tag \code{*text*} prints *text* in code font, and \link{*function*} generates a hypertext link to an R function in the current package or elsewhere. Finally, \item{*text*} generates an itemized list. This is particularly useful for describing the results returned by a function.

There is a documentation task that is optional, but useful. As described so far, when a user installs the npar package, no help is available for ?npar. How is the user to know what functions are available? One way would be to type `help(package="npar")`, but you can make it easier for them by adding another file to the documentation; see the following listing.

Listing 21.8 Contents of the npar.R file

```
#' Functions for nonparametric group comparisons.
#'
#' npar provides tools for calculating and visualizing
#' nonparametric differences among groups.
#'
#' @docType package
#' @name npar-package
#' @aliases npar
NULL
... this file must end with a blank line after the NULL...
```

Note that the last line of this file must be blank. When the package is built, a call to ?npar will now produce a description of the package, with a clickable link to an index of functions.

Finally, create a text file named DESCRIPTION that describes the package. Following is a sample.

> **Listing 21.9   Contents of the DESCRIPTION file**

```
Package: npar
Type: Package
Title: Nonparametric group comparisons
Version: 1.0
Date: 2015-01-26
Author: Rob Kabacoff
Maintainer: Robert Kabacoff <robk@statmethods.net>
Description: This package assesses group differences using nonparametric
    statistics. Currently a one-way layout is supported. Kruskal-Wallis
    test followed by pairwise Wilcoxon tests are provided. p-values are
    adjusted for multiple comparisons using the p.adjust() function.
    Results are plotted via annotated boxplots.
LazyData: yes
License: GPL-3
```

The Description: section can be span several lines but must be indented after the first line. The LazyData: yes statement indicates that the datasets in the package (life, in this case) should be available as soon as the package is loaded. If this was set to no, the user would have to use data(life) to access the dataset.

The final line indicates the license under which the package is being released. Common license types include MIT, GPL-2, and GPL-3. See www.r-project.org/Licenses for license descriptions. Of course, when creating your own package, don't use my name (unless the package is really good!).

The roxygen2 package will be used in the next section, when you build the final npar package. To learn more about roxygen2, see Hadley Wickham's description at http://mng.bz/K26J.

21.4   *Building the package*

It's finally time to build the package. (Really, I promise.) The developer's bible for creating packages is *Writing R Extensions* by the R Core Team (http://cran.r-project.org/doc/manuals/R-exts.pdf). Friedrich Leischn also has produced a nice tutorial on creating packages (http://mng.bz/Ks84).

In this section, you'll follow a streamlined process for building a package. Specifically, you'll use Hadley Wickham's roxygen2 package to simplify documentation creation. I'm building the package on a Windows machine, but the steps will work on Mac and Linux platforms as well:

1   *Install the necessary tools.* Download and install the roxygen2 packages using install.packages("roxygen2", depend=TRUE). If you're using a Windows platform, you'll also need to install Rtools.exe (http://cran.r-project.org/bin/

windows/Rtools) and MiKTeX (http://miktex.org). If you're using a Mac, install
MacTeX (www.tug.org/mactex). Rtools, MiKTeX, and MacTeX are applications
rather than packages. Therefore, you'll need to install them outside of R.

2 *Set up the directories.* In your home
directory (the current working directory when you start R), create a subdirectory named npar. In this directory,
create two subdirectories named R
and data (see figure 21.4). Place the
DESCRIPTION file in the npar directory and the source files (oneway.R,
print.R, summary.R, plot.R, life.R,
and npar.R) in the R subdirectory.
Place the life.rda file in the data subdirectory. Your setup should look like
figure 21.4.

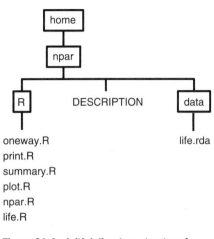

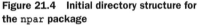

oneway.R   life.rda
print.R
summary.R
plot.R
npar.R
life.R

**Figure 21.4 Initial directory structure for
the npar package**

From this point on, I'll assume
that you're in your R home directory.
If not, enter the full path to the package (for example, c:/applications/
npar) instead of just its name (npar).

3 *Generate the documentation.* Load the roxygen2 package, and use the roxygen-
ize() function to process the documentation headers in each code file:

```
> library(roxygen2)
> roxygenize("npar")

Updating namespace directives
Writing oneway.Rd
Writing plot.oneway.Rd
Writing print.oneway.Rd
Writing summary.oneway.Rd
Writing life.Rd
Writing npar-package.Rd
```

The roxygenize() function creates a new subdirectory, called man, that contains the .Rd documentation file for each function. The markup from the comments at the top of each code file is used to build these documentation files.
roxygenize() also adds information to the DESCRIPTION file and creates a
NAMESPACE file. The NAMESPACE file that is created for npar is as follows.

Listing 21.10 Contents of the NAMESPACE file

```
S3method(plot,oneway)
S3method(print,oneway)
S3method(summary,oneway)
export(oneway)
```

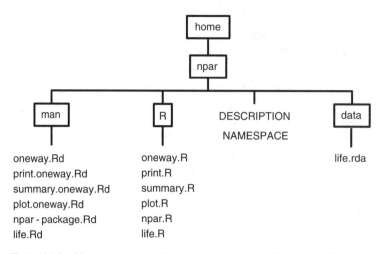

Figure 21.5 Directory structure for the `npar` package after running the `roxygenize()` function

The NAMESPACE file controls the visibility of your functions (are all functions available to the package user directly, or are some used internally by other functions?). In the current case, all functions are available to the user. To learn more about namespaces, see http://adv-r.had.co.nz/Namespaces.html.

The new directory structure is given in figure 21.5.

4   *Build the package.* Build the package using the following system commands:

```
> system("R CMD build npar")
... informational messages omitted ...
```

This creates the file npar_1.0.tar.gz in the current working directory. The version number in the name is taken from the DESCRIPTION file. The package is now in a format that can be distributed to others.

To create a binary .zip file for use on Windows platforms, execute this code:

```
> system("Rcmd INSTALL --build npar")
... informational messages omitted ...
packaged installation of 'npar' as npar_1.0.zip
* DONE (npar)
```

This creates the npar_1.0.zip file in the current working directory. Note that you can only create a Windows binary file this way if you're working on a Windows platform. If you want to build a binary file for Windows but you don't have access to a Windows machine running R, you can use the online service provided at http://win-builder.r-project.org/.

5   *Check the package (optional).* To run extensive consistency checks on the package, execute this statement:

```
system("R CMD check npar")
```

This creates a folder call npar.Rcheck in the current working directory. The folder contains the file 00.check.log, which describes the results of the checks. There must be no errors or warnings if you want to contribute the package to CRAN.

The directory also contains a file called npar-EX.R containing the code from any examples listed in the documentation. The text output produced by executing the example code is contained in the file npar-EX.out. If the examples created graphs (true in this case), they're placed in npar-Ex.pdf.

6 *Create a PDF manual (optional).* Executing the statement

```
system("R CMD Rd2pdf npar")
```

generates a PDF reference manual like those you see on CRAN. If you ran step 5, you already have this document in the npar.Rcheck folder.

7 *Install the package locally (optional).* Executing

```
system("R CMD INSTALL npar")
```

installs the package on your machine and makes it available for use. Another way to install the package locally is to use

```
install.packages(paste(getwd(),"/npar_1.0.tar.gz",sep=""),
                 repos=NULL, type="source")
```

You can see that the package has been installed by typing `library()`. After you type `library(npar)`, the package will be available for use.

During the development cycle, you may want to delete a package from your local machine so that you can install a new version. In this case, use

```
detach(package:npar, unload=TRUE)
remove.packages("npar")
```

to get a fresh start.

8 *Upload the package to CRAN (optional).* If you would like to share your package with others by adding it to the CRAN repository, follow these three steps:

- Read the CRAN Repository Policy (http://cran.r-project.org/web/packages/policies.html).
- Make sure the package passes all checks in step 5 without errors or warnings. Otherwise the package will be rejected.
- Submit the package. To do so via web form, use the submission form at http://cran.r-project.org/submit.html. You'll be sent an automated confirmation email that needs to be accepted.

  To do so via FTP, upload the *packageName_version*.tar.gz file via anonymous FTP to ftp://cran.r-Project.org/incoming. Then send a plain-text email to CRAN@R-project.org from the maintainer email address listed in the package. Use the subject line "CRAN submission *PACKAGE VERSION*" without the quotes, where *PACKAGE* and *VERSION* are the package name and the version, respectively. For new submissions, confirm in the body of the email that you have read and agree to CRAN's policies.

But please don't upload the npar package you just created to CRAN! You now have the tools to create your own packages.

21.5   *Going further*

In this chapter, all the code used to create the npar package was R code. In fact, most packages contain code that is written entirely in R. But you can also call compiled C, C++, Fortran, and Java code from R. External code is typically included when doing so will improve execution speed or when the author wants to use existing external libraries from within their R code.

There are several methods for including compiled external code. Useful functions include .C(), .Fortran(), .External(), and .Call(). Several packages have also been written to facilitate the process, including inline (C, C++, Fortran), Rcpp (C++), and rJava (Java).

Adding external compiled code to an R package is beyond the scope of this book. The *Writing R Extensions* manual (http://cran.r-project.org/doc/manuals/R-exts .html), along with the help files for these functions and packages, should provide you with enough details to get started. Stack Overflow (http://stackoverflow.com) is a great place to ask questions if you get stuck.

21.6   *Summary*

R packages are a great way to organize your frequently used functions, develop complete applications, and share your results with others. In this chapter, you created a complete R package that can be used for carrying out nonparametric group comparisons. These object-oriented techniques can be applied to many other data-management and data-analytic tasks. Although packages seem complicated at first, they're pretty easy to create once you have the process down. Now, get to work! And remember, have fun out there.

Creating dynamic reports

Welcome to the final chapter! You've accessed your data, cleaned it up, described its characteristics, modeled the relationships, and visualized the results. The next step is to

   A Relax and perhaps go to Disney World.

   B Communicate the results to others.

If you chose A, please take me with you. If you chose B, welcome to the real world.

Research doesn't end when the last statistical analysis or graph is finished. You'll almost always have to communicate the results to others. This means incorporating the analyses into a report of some kind.

There are three common report scenarios. In the first, you create a report that includes your code and the results, so that you can remember what you did six months from now. It's easier to reconstruct what was done from a single comprehensive document than from a set of related files.

In the second scenario, you have to generate a report for a teacher, a supervisor, a client, a government agency, an internet audience, or a journal editor. Clarity and attractiveness matter, and the report may only need to be created once.

In the third scenario, you need to generate a specific type of report on a regular basis. It may be a monthly report on product or resource usage, a weekly financial analysis, or a report on web traffic that's updated hourly. In any case, the data changes, but the analyses and the structure of the report remain the same.

One approach to incorporating R output into a report involves running the analyses, cutting and pasting each graph and text table into a word-processing document, and reformatting the results. This approach is usually time consuming, inefficient, and frustrating. Although R creates state-of-the-art graphics, its text output is woefully retro—tables of monospaced text with columns lined up using spaces. Reformatting them is no easy task. And if the data changes, you have to go through the entire process again!

Given these limitations, you may feel that R won't work for you. Have no fear. (OK, have a little fear—it's an important survival mechanism.) R offers several elegant solutions for incorporating R code and results into reports. Additionally, the data can be tied to the report so that changing the data changes the report. These dynamic reports can be saved as

- Web pages
- Microsoft Word documents
- Open Document files
- Publication-ready PDF or PostScript documents

For example, say you're using regression analysis to study the relationship between weight and height in a sample of women. R allows you to take the monospaced output generated by the lm() function

```
> lm(weight ~ height, data=women)

Call:
lm(formula = weight ~ height, data = women)

Residuals:
    Min      1Q  Median      3Q     Max
-1.7333 -1.1333 -0.3833  0.7417  3.1167

Coefficients:
            Estimate Std. Error t value Pr(>|t|)
(Intercept) -87.51667    5.93694  -14.74 1.71e-09 ***
height        3.45000    0.09114   37.85 1.09e-14 ***
---
Signif. codes:  0 '***' 0.001 '**' 0.01 '*' 0.05 '.' 0.1 ' ' 1
Residual standard error: 1.525 on 13 degrees of freedom
Multiple R-squared:  0.991,     Adjusted R-squared:  0.9903
F-statistic:  1433 on 1 and 13 DF,  p-value: 1.091e-14
```

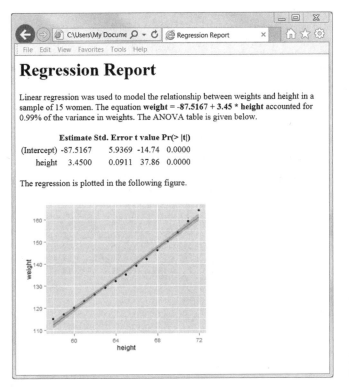

Figure 22.1 Regression analysis saved to a web page

and turn it into a web page like the one in figure 22.1. In this chapter, you'll learn how.

Dynamic documents and reproducible research

There is a powerful movement growing within the academic community in support of *reproducible research*. The goal of reproducible research is to facilitate the replication of scientific findings by including the data and software code necessary to reproduce findings with the publications that report them. This allows readers to verify the findings for themselves and gives them an opportunity to build on the results more directly in their own work. The techniques described in this chapter, including the embedding of data and source code with documents, directly support this effort.

22.1 A template approach to reports

The majority of this chapter employs a template approach to report generation. A report starts with a template file. The template contains the report text, formatting syntax, and R code chunks.

The template file is processed, the R code is run, the formatting syntax is applied, and a report is generated. How R output is included in the report is controlled by

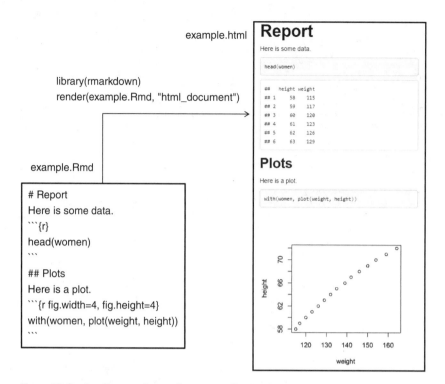

Figure 22.2   Creating a web page from a text file that includes Markdown syntax, report text, and R code chunks

options. A simple example using an R Markdown template to create a web page is given in figure 22.2.

The template file (example.Rmd) is a plain text file containing three components:

- *Report text*—Any explanatory phrases and text. Here, the report text is *Report, Here is some data, Plots*, and *Here is a plot*.

- *Formatting syntax*—The tags that control report formatting. In this file, Markdown tags are used to format the results. Markdown is a simple markup language than can be used to convert plain text files to structurally valid HTML or XHTML. The pound symbol # in the first line isn't a comment. It produces a level-1 header. ## produces a level-2 header, and so on.

- *R code*—R statements to be executed. In R Markdown documents, R code chunks are surrounded by ```` ```{r} ```` and ```` ``` ````. The first code chunk lists the first six rows of the dataset, and the second code chunk produces a scatter plot. In this example, both the code and the results are output to the report, but options allow you to control what's printed on a chunk-by-chunk basis.

The template file is passed to the render() function in the rmarkdown package, and a web page named example.html is created. The web page contains both the report text and R results.

The examples in this chapter are based on descriptive statistics, regression, and ANOVA problems. None of them represent full analyses of the data. The goal in this chapter is to learn how to incorporate the R results into various types of reports. Feel free to jump around in this chapter, reading the sections that are most relevant to you.

Depending on the template file you start with and the functions used to process it, different report formats (HTML web pages, Microsoft Word documents, OpenOffice Writer documents, PDF reports, articles, and books) are created. The reports are dynamic in the sense that changing the data and reprocessing the template file will result in a new report.

In this chapter, you'll work with four types of templates: an R Markdown template, an ODT template, a DOCX template, and a LaTeX template. R Markdown templates can be used to create HTML, PDF, and MS Word documents. ODT and DOCX templates are used to create Open Document and Microsoft Word documents, respectively. LaTeX templates are used to create publication-quality PDF documents, including reports, articles, and books. Let's consider each in turn.

22.2 Creating dynamic reports with R and Markdown

In this section, you'll use the `rmarkdown` package to create documents generated from Markdown syntax and R code. When the document is processed, the R code is executed, and the output is formatted and embedded in the finished document. You can use this approach to generate reports as HTML, Word, or PDF documents. Here are the steps:

1. Install the `rmarkdown` package (`install.packages("rmarkdown")`). This will install several other packages including `knitr`. If you're using a recent version of RStudio, you can skip this step because you already have the necessary packages.
2. Install the `xtable` package (`install.packages("xtable")`). The `xtable()` function in this package attractively formats data frames and matrices for inclusion in reports. `xtable()` can also format objects produced by the `lm()`, `glm()`, `aov()`, `table()`, `ts()`, and `coxph()` functions. After loading the package, use `methods(xtable)` to view a comprehensive list of the objects it can format.
3. Install Pandoc (http://johnmacfarlane.net/pandoc/index.html). Pandoc is a free application available for Windows, Mac OS X, and Linux. It converts files from one markup format to another. Again, RStudio users can skip this step.
4. If you want to create PDF documents, install a LaTeX compiler. A LaTeX compiler converts a LaTeX document into a high-quality typeset PDF document. I recommend MiKTeX (www.miktex.org) for Windows, MacTeX for Macs (http://tug.org/mactex), and TeX Live for Linux (www.tug.org/texlive).

With the software set up, you're ready to go.

To incorporate R output (values, tables, graphs) in a document using Markdown syntax, first create a text document that contains

- Report text
- Markdown syntax
- R code chunks (R code surrounded by delimiters)

By convention, the text file has the filename extension .Rmd.

A sample file (named women.Rmd) is provided in listing 22.1. To generate an HTML document, process this file using

```
library(rmarkdown)
render("women.Rmd", "html_document")
```

The results are displayed in figure 22.1.

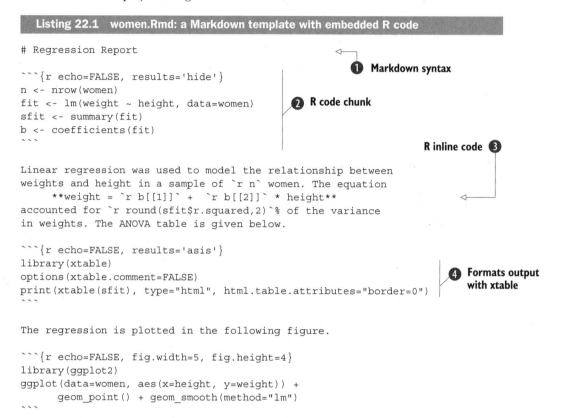

Listing 22.1   women.Rmd: a Markdown template with embedded R code

```
# Regression Report

```{r echo=FALSE, results='hide'}
n <- nrow(women)
fit <- lm(weight ~ height, data=women)
sfit <- summary(fit)
b <- coefficients(fit)
```

Linear regression was used to model the relationship between
weights and height in a sample of `r n` women. The equation
    weight = `r b[[1]]` + `r b[[2]]` * height
accounted for `r round(sfit$r.squared,2)`% of the variance
in weights. The ANOVA table is given below.

```{r echo=FALSE, results='asis'}
library(xtable)
options(xtable.comment=FALSE)
print(xtable(sfit), type="html", html.table.attributes="border=0")
```

The regression is plotted in the following figure.

```{r echo=FALSE, fig.width=5, fig.height=4}
library(ggplot2)
ggplot(data=women, aes(x=height, y=weight)) +
    geom_point() + geom_smooth(method="lm")
```
```

❶ Markdown syntax

❷ R code chunk

❸ R inline code

❹ Formats output with xtable

The report starts with a first-level header ❶. It indicates that "Regression Report" should be printed in a large, bold font. Examples of other Markdown syntax are given in table 22.1.

Table 22.1   Markdown code and the resulting output

Markdown syntax	Resulting HTML output
# Heading 1 ## Heading 2 ... ###### Heading 6	\<h1\>Heading 1\</h1\> \<h2\>Heading 2\</h2\> ... \<h6\>Heading 2\</h6\>
One or more blank lines between text	Separates text into paragraphs

Table 22.1   **Markdown code and the resulting output**

Markdown syntax	Resulting HTML output
Two or more spaces at the end of a line	Adds a line break
`*I mean it*`	`<em>I mean it</em>`
`**I really mean it**`	`<strong>I really mean it</strong>`

`* item 1`
`* item 2`
	`<ul>`
	`<li> item 1 </li>`
	`<li> item 2 </li>`
	`</ul>`

`1. item 1`
`2. item 2`
	`<ol>`
	`<li> item 1 </li>`
	`<li> item 2 </li>`
	`</ol>`

`[Google](http://google.com)`	`<a href="http://google.com">Google</a>`
`![My text](path to image)`	`<img src="path to image", alt="My text">`

Next comes an R code chunk. R code in Markdown documents is delimited by ` ```{r options} ` and ` ``` ` ❷. When the file is processed, the R code is executed and the results are inserted. Code chunk options are described in table 22.2.

Table 22.2   **Code chunk options**

Option	Description
`echo`	Whether to include the R source code in the output (`TRUE`) or not (`FALSE`)
`results`	Whether to output raw results (`asis`) or hide the results (`hide`)
`warning`	Whether to include warnings in the output (`TRUE`) or not (`FALSE`)
`message`	Whether to include informational messages in the output (`TRUE`) or not (`FALSE`)
`error`	Whether to include error messages in in the output (`TRUE`) or not (`FALSE`)
`fig.width`	Figure width for plots (inches)
`fig.height`	Figure height for plots (inches)

Simple R output (a number or string) can also be placed directly within report text. This inline R code allows you to customize the text in individual sentences. Inline code is placed between `` `r `` and `` ` `` tags ❸. In the regression example, the sample size, prediction equation, and R-squared value are embedded in the first paragraph.

Finally, you use the `xtable()` function to format the regression results ❹. The statement `options(xtable.comment=FALSE)` suppresses superfluous messages. The `type="html"` option in the `print()` function outputs the `xtable` object as an HTML table. By default, this table has an unattractive 1-pixel border that's removed by adding `html.table.attributes="border=0"`. See `help(print.xtable)` for additional formatting options.

To render the file as a PDF document, you only have to make one change. Replace

```
print(xtable(sfit), type="html", html.table.attributes="border=0")
```

with

```
print(xtable(sfit), type="latex")
```

Then process the file using

```
library(rmarkdown)
render("women.Rmd", "pdf_document")
```

to get a nicely formatted PDF document.

Unfortunately, the `xtable()` function doesn't work for Word documents. You'll have to get a bit more creative to render statistical output in an attractive fashion. One possibility is to replace `xtable()` with the `kable()` function in the `knitr` package. It can render matrices and data frames in a simple and appealing manner.

Replace

```
library(xtable)
options(xtable.comment=FALSE)
print(xtable(sfit), type="html", html.table.attributes="border=0")
```

with

```
library(knitr)
kable(sfit$coefficients)
```

Then render the file using

```
library(rmarkdown)
render("women.Rmd", "word_document")
```

The result is an attractive Word document that you can edit using Word. Note that you had to replace the `sfit` object with `sfit$coefficients`. The `xtable()` function can handle `lm()` objects, but the `kable()` function can only handle matrices and data frames. Therefore, you have to extract the parts you want to print from more complicated objects. See `help(kable)` for more details.

Using RStudio to create and process R Markdown documents

Throughout this book, I've tried to keep the presentation independent of the interface used to access R. Each of the techniques described will work in the basic R Console. But there are several other options, including RStudio (see appendix A). RStudio makes it particularly easy to render reports from Markdown documents.

If you choose File > New File > R Markdown from the GUI menu, you'll see the dialog box shown next.

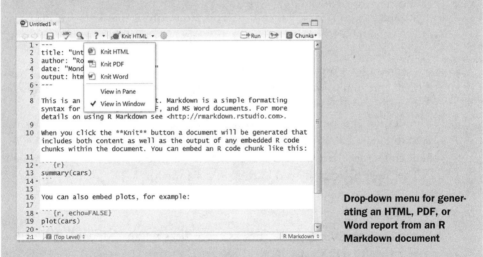

Dialog box for creating a new R Markdown document in RStudio

Choose the type of report you want to generate, and RStudio will create a skeleton file for you. Edit it with your text and code, and then select the rendering option from the Knit drop-down list. That's it!

Drop-down menu for generating an HTML, PDF, or Word report from an R Markdown document

RStudio has many useful features for programmers. It's by far my favorite way to work in R.

Markdown syntax is convenient for creating simple documents quickly. To learn more about Markdown, visit the homepage at http://daringfireball.net/projects/markdown and the `rmarkdown` documentation at http://rmarkdown.rstudio.com. If you want to create complex documents such as publication-quality articles and books, then you may want to look at using LaTeX as your markup language. In the next section, you'll use LaTeX and the `knitr` package to create high-quality typeset documents.

22.3 *Creating dynamic reports with R and LaTeX*

LaTeX is a document-preparation system for high-quality typesetting that's freely available for Windows, Mac, and Linux platforms. LaTeX allows you to create beautiful, complex, multipart documents, and it can convert from one type of document (such as an article) to another type of document (such as a report) by changing just a few lines of code. It's extraordinarily powerful software and, as such, has a significant learning curve.

If you're unfamiliar with LaTeX, you may want to read "The Not So Short Introduction to LaTeX 2e" by Tobias Oetiker et al. (http://mng.bz/45vP) or LaTeX Tutorials: A Primer by the Indian TEX Users Group (http://mng.bz/2c0O) before continuing. The language is definitely worth learning, but it will take some time and patience to master. Once you're familiar with LaTeX, creating a dynamic report is a straightforward process.

The `knitr` package allows you to embed R code within the LaTeX document using techniques that are analogous to the ones used previously for creating web pages. If you installed `rmarkdown` or are using RStudio, you already have `knitr`. If not, install it now (`install.packages("knitr")`). Additionally, you'll need a LaTeX compiler; see section 22.2 for details.

In this section, you'll create a report describing patients' reactions to various drugs, using data from the `multcomp` package. If you didn't install it in chapter 9, be sure to run `install.packages("multcomp")` before continuing.

To generate a report using R and LaTeX, you first create a text file (typically with the filename extension .Rnw) containing the report text, LaTeX markup code, and R code chunks. An example is given in listing 22.2. Each R code chunk starts with the delimiter `<<options>>=` and ends with the delimiter `@`. The code chunk options are listed in table 22.3. Inline R code is included using the `\Sexpr{R code}` syntax. When the R code is evaluated, the number or string is inserted at that point in the text.

The file is then processed by the `knit()` function:

```
library(knitr)
knit("drugs.Rnw")
```

During this step, the R code chunks are processed and, depending on the options, replaced with LaTeX-formatted R code and output. By default, `knit("drugs.Rnw")` inputs the file drugs.Rnw and outputs the file drugs.tex. The .tex file is then run through a LaTeX compiler, creating a PDF, PostScript, or DVI file.

As a simpler alternative, you can use the `knit2pdf()` helper function in the `knitr` package:

```
library(knitr)
knit2pdf("drugs.Rnw")
```

The function generates the .tex file and converts it to a finished PDF document named drugs.pdf. The resulting PDF document is displayed in figure 22.3.

Listing 22.2 drugs.Rnw: a sample LaTeX template with embedded R code

```
\documentclass[11pt]{article}
\title{Sample Report}
\author{Robert I. Kabacoff, Ph.D.}
\usepackage{float}
\usepackage[top=.5in, bottom=.5in, left=1in, right=1in]{geometry}
\begin{document}
\maketitle
<<echo=FALSE, results='hide', message=FALSE>>=
library(multcomp)
library(xtable)
df <- cholesterol
@

\section{Results}

Cholesterol reduction was assessed in a study
that randomized \Sexpr{nrow(df)} patients
to one of \Sexpr{length(unique(df$trt))} treatments.
Summary statistics are provided in
Table \ref{table:descriptives}.

<<echo=FALSE, results='asis'>>=
descTable <- data.frame("Treatment" = sort(unique(df$trt)),
    "N"    = as.vector(table(df$trt)),
    "Mean" = tapply(df$response, list(df$trt), mean, na.rm=TRUE),
    "SD"   = tapply(df$response, list(df$trt), sd, na.rm=TRUE)
 )
print(xtable(descTable, caption = "Descriptive statistics
for each treatment group", label = "table:descriptives"),
caption.placement = "top", include.rownames = FALSE)
@

The analysis of variance is provided in Table \ref{table:anova}.

<<echo=FALSE, results='asis'>>=
fit <- aov(response ~ trt, data=df)
print(xtable(fit, caption = "Analysis of variance",
    label = "table:anova"), caption.placement = "top")
@

\noindent and group differences are plotted in Figure \ref{figure:tukey}.

\begin{figure}[H]\label{figure:tukey}
\begin{center}

<<echo=FALSE, fig.width=4, fig.height=3>>=
par(mar=c(3,3,1,3))
boxplot(response ~ trt, data=df, col="lightgrey",
        xlab="Treatment", ylab="Response")
@

\caption{Distribution of response times by treatment.}
\end{center}
\end{figure}
\end{document}
```

Sample Report

Robert I. Kabacoff, Ph.D.

March 23, 2015

1   Results

Cholesterol reduction was assessed in a study that randomized 50 patients to one of 5 treatments. Summary statistics are provided in Table 1.

Table 1: Descriptive statistics for each treatment group

Treatment	N	Mean	SD
1time	10	5.78	2.88
2times	10	9.22	3.48
4times	10	12.37	2.92
drugD	10	15.36	3.45
drugE	10	20.95	3.35

The analysis of variance is provided in Table 2.

Table 2: Analysis of variance

	Df	Sum Sq	Mean Sq	F value	Pr(> F)
trt	4	1351.37	337.84	32.43	0.0000
Residuals	45	468.75	10.42		

and group differences are plotted in Figure 1.

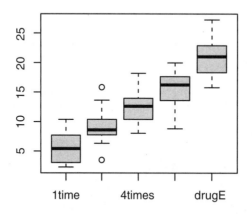

Figure 1: Distribution of response times by treatment.

1

Figure 22.3   The text file drugs.Rnw is processed through the `knit2pdf()` function, resulting in a typeset PDF document (drugs.pdf).

The knitr package is documented at http://yihui.name/knitr and in Yihui Xie's book *Dynamic Documents with R and knitr* (Chapman and Hall/CRC, 2013). To learn more about LaTeX, check out the tutorials mentioned earlier and visit www.latex-project.org.

22.4 *Creating dynamic reports with R and Open Document*

Although LaTeX is powerful, it requires significant study to use effectively and creates documents in formats (PDF, DVI, PS) that can't be edited. You can also output R results to a word-processing document. Two of the most popular formats are Microsoft Word (.docx) and Open Document (.odf).

Open Document Format for Office Applications (ODF) is an open source, XML-based file format that's compatible with many software suites. Two popular and freely available office suites are OpenOffice (www.openoffice.org) and LibreOffice (www.libreoffice.org). Both are available for Windows, Mac OS X, and Linux environments, and either can be used in this section.

The odfWeave package provides a mechanism for embedding R code and output in an Open Document file. In this section, you'll create a report exploring salary differences between male and female professors.

After installing OpenOffice (or LibreOffice) and the odfWeave package, create a document named salaryTemplate.odt (see figure 22.4). The document contains formatted text and R code chunks. The text is formatted using the OpenOffice (or LibreOffice) GUI. The code chunks are delimited as follows:

```
<<options>>=
R statements
@
```

Code chunk options are given in table 22.3. Inline R code results (numbers or strings) are included using \Sexpr{R code}.

Table 22.3   R code chunk options in odfWeave

Option	Action
echo	Includes R code in the output file (TRUE/FALSE)
results	Outputs results as is (verbatim), as XML code (xml), or suppress output (hide)
fig	Code chunk produces graphical output (TRUE/FALSE)

Once the document is saved, process it using odfWeave() in the odfWeave package:

```
library(odfWeave)
infile <- "salaryTemplate.odt"
outfile <- "salaryReport.odf"
odfWeave(infile, outfile)
```

This takes the salaryTemplate.odt file displayed in figure 22.4 and produces the salaryReport.odf file displayed in figure 22.5.

My Sample Report

Robert I. Kabacoff, Ph.D.

```
<<echo=FALSE, results=hide>>=
library(car)
df <- Salaries
percentiles <- function(x, y){
    P0   <- aggregate(x, by=list(y), FUN=quantile,   0)
    P25  <- aggregate(x, by=list(y), FUN=quantile, .25)
    P50  <- aggregate(x, by=list(y), FUN=quantile,  .5)
    P75  <- aggregate(x, by=list(y), FUN=quantile, .75)
    P100 <- aggregate(x, by=list(y), FUN=quantile,   1)
    qT <- data.frame(P0, P25[2], P50[2], P75[2], P100[2])
    names(qT) <- c("Group", "0%", "25%", "50%", "75%", "100%")
    return(qT)
3
quantTable<- percentiles(df$salary, df$sex)
5
```

1 The study

The salaries of \Sexpr{nrow(df)} male and female college professors were studied to assess possible gender discrimination. Summary statistics are provide in Table 1.

Table 1. Salary quantiles for male and female professors
```
<<echo=FALSE, results=xml>>=
odfTable(quantTable, useRowNames=FALSE)
5
```

The distributions are plotted in Figure 1.

```
<<fig=TRUE, echo=FALSE>>=
boxplot(df$salary ~ df$sex, col="lightgrey", ylab="Annual Salary
(dollars)")
5
```
Figure 1. Distribution of salaries by gender.

Figure 22.4
OpenOffice Writer file (salaryTemplate.odt) with embedded R code chunks. After the file is processed by the `odfWeave()` function, the report in figure 22.7 (salaryReport.odf) is produced.

My Sample Report

Robert I. Kabacoff, Ph.D.

1 The study

The salaries of 397 male and female college professors were studied to assess possible gender discrimination. Summary statistics are provide in Table 1.

Table 1. Salary quantiles for male and female professors

Group	0%	25%	50%	75%	100%
Female	62884	77250	103750	117003	161101
Male	57800	92000	108043	134864	231545

The distributions are plotted in Figure 1.

Figure 1. Distribution of salaries by gender.

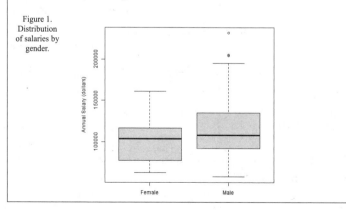

Figure 22.5 Final report in ODF format (salaryReport.odf)

By default, odfWeave renders data frames, matrices, and vectors in an attractive table format. The odfTable() function can be used to format tables with a higher degree of precision and control. The function produces XML code, so be sure to specify result=xml in code chunks employing this function. Unfortunately, the xtable() function doesn't work with odfWeave.

Once you have your report in ODF format, you can continue to edit it, tighten up the formatting, and save the results to the ODT, HTML, DOC, or DOCX file format. To learn more, read the odfWeave manual and vignette. Additional information, including a tutorial on document formatting with odfWeave, can be found in the Examples folder installed in the odfWeave directory in your R library. (The function .libPaths() will display your library location.)

22.5 *Creating dynamic reports with R and Microsoft Word*

For good or ill, Microsoft Word is the standard for report writing in corporate settings. You've already seen how to create a Word document from a Markdown file using rmarkdown (section 22.2). In this section, we'll look at a method for creating dynamic reports by embedding R code directly into Word documents using the R2wd package. The methods in the section will only work on Windows platforms (sorry, Mac and Linux users).

To follow the examples in this section, you'll need to install the R2wd package (install.packages("R2wd")). R2wd also requires the RDCOMClient package, available from the Omega Project for Statistical Computing.

At the time of this writing, RDCOMClient must be installed from source. First be sure Rtools is installed (http://cran.r-project.org/bin/windows/Rtools). Next, download the source file (RDCOMClient_0.93-0.tar.gz) from www.omegahat.org/RDCOMClient. Note that the version numbers are likely to change over time. Finally, install the package using

```
install.packages(RDCOMClient_0.93-0.tar.gz, repos = NULL, type = "source")
```

The R2wd package provides functions that allow you to create a blank Word document; insert sections and titles; insert text, tables, and graphs; add formatting; and save the results. Although the package is versatile, building and formatting Word documents programmatically can be time-consuming.

The easiest way to create a dynamic report in Word using the R2wd package is a two-step process:

1　Create a Word document that contains bookmarks indicating where you want your R results to be placed.
2　Create an R script that inserts the results in the Word document at the bookmarked locations and saves the finished document.

Let's try this approach.

Open a new Word document, and call it salaryTemplate2.docx. Add the text and bookmarks displayed in figure 22.6. (In reality, the bookmarks in figure 22.6 aren't

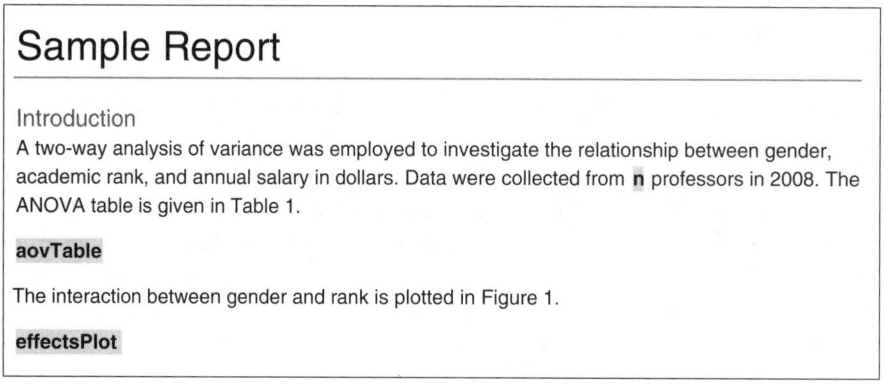

Sample Report

Introduction

A two-way analysis of variance was employed to investigate the relationship between gender, academic rank, and annual salary in dollars. Data were collected from **n** professors in 2008. The ANOVA table is given in Table 1.

aovTable

The interaction between gender and rank is plotted in Figure 1.

effectsPlot

Figure 22.6   A Microsoft Word document named salaryTemplate2.docx containing text and bookmarks. The file is processed by the script salary.R (listing 22.3), results are inserted at the bookmark locations, and the document is saved as salaryReport2.docx (figure 22.7). Note that the bookmarks (in bold shaded text) aren't actually visible on the page; the image has been annotated so that you can see where to place them.

visible. I've annotated the image, adding the bookmark names with a bold colored background, so that you can see where each should go.)

To insert a bookmark, place the cursor where you want the bookmark, choose Insert > Bookmark, give the bookmark a name, and click Add. The bookmarks in this example are named n, aovTable, and effectsPlot.

> **TIP**   Selecting Options > Advanced > Show Bookmarks in Microsoft Word will help you see where bookmarks are placed.

Next, create the R script given in listing 22.3. When the script is executed, it produces the necessary analyses, inserts them into the Word document, and saves the final document to disk. The script uses the functions listed in table 22.4.

Table 22.4   R2wd functions

Function	Use
wdGet()	Returns a handle to a Word document. If Word isn't running, it's started, a blank document is opened, and a handle is returned.
wdGoToBookmark()	Places the cursor at a bookmark.
wdWrite()	Writes text at the cursor.
wdTable()	Writes a data frame or an array as a Word table at the current cursor location.
wdPlot()	Creates an R plot, and pastes it into Word at the current cursor location.
wdSave()	Saves the Word document. If no file name is given, Word prompts the user for one.
wdQuit()	Closes Word, and removes the handle.

Listing 22.3 salary.R: R script for inserting results in salary.docx

```
require(R2wd)
require(car)

df <- Salaries
n <- nrow(df)
fit <- lm(salary ~ rank*sex, data=df)
aovTable <- Anova(fit, type=3)
aovTable <- round(as.data.frame(aovTable), 3)
aovTable[is.na(aovTable)] <- ""
```
❶ Opens the document
```
wdGet("salaryTemplate2.docx", method="RDCOMClient")
wdGoToBookmark("n")
wdWrite(n)
```
❷ Inserts text
```
wdGoToBookmark("aovTable")
wdTable(aovTable, caption="Two-way Analysis of Variance",
   caption.pos="above", pointsize=12, autoformat=4)
```
❸ Inserts a table
```
wdGoToBookmark("effectsPlot")
myplot <- function(){
      require(effects)
      par(mar=c(2,2,2,2))
      plot(allEffects(fit), main="")
}
wdPlot(plotfun=myplot, caption="Mean Effects Plot",
```
❹ Inserts a plot
```
      height=4, width=5, method="metafile")
wdSave("SalaryReport2.docx")
wdQuit()
```
❺ Saves and quits

First, the salary2Template.docx file is opened. If Word isn't running, it's automatically launched ❶. Next, the data analyses are performed. The cursor then is moved to the bookmark named n, and the sample size is inserted ❷.

Next, the cursor is moved to the bookmark named `aovTable` and the ANOVA results are inserted as a Word table ❸. Because R2wd doesn't support the `xtable()` function, it's important that the table be an R data frame, a matrix, or an array. Options can control the text and location of the table caption, font size, and table formatting. Try autoformat = 1, 2, 3, and so on, to see the various formats available. Currently there is no way to suppress the caption.

Two of the statements in the ANOVA code require additional explanation. The `aovTable` object is a data frame containing the two-way ANOVA results. The `round()` function is used to limit the number of decimal places printed in the table. The statement

```
aovTable[is.na(aovTable)] <- ""
```

is a trick that replaces NAs with blanks. This is necessary because there are no values in the F and Pr(>F) columns for the Residuals row, and you don't want NA to print in these cells of the table.

The cursor next moves to the bookmark named `effectsPlot`. The `wdPlot()` function requires that the user specify a plotting function. Here, the `myplot()` function produces an effects plot via the `allEffects()` function in the `effects` package ❹.

The `wdPlot()` function supports `method="bitmap"` and `method="metafile"`. Use `metafile` whenever possible—it looks better in a Word document. Unfortunately, the `metafile` option doesn't support transparency, so you have to use the `bitmap` option when transparency is present. You're most likely to encounter transparency when using the `ggplot2` package to produce graphs.

When the code in salary.R is executed, it runs the R code, inserts the results into salaryTemplate2.docx, and saves the finished Word document as salaryReport2.docx ❺. Then the Microsoft Word application quits. The resulting document is displayed in figure 22.7.

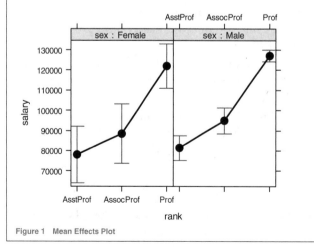

Sample Report

Introduction

A two-way analysis of variance was employed to investigate the relationship between gender, academic rank, and annual salary in dollars. Data were collected from 397 professors in 2008. The ANOVA table is given in Table 1.

Table 1   Two-way Analysis of Variance

	Sum Sq	Df	F value	Pr(>F)
(Intercept)	67009671400	1	119.538	0
rank	15266607695	2	13.617	0
sex	97803720	1	0.174	0.676
rank:sex	43603063	2	0.039	0.962
Residuals	219184457146	391		

The interaction between gender and rank is plotted in Figure 1.

Figure 1   Mean Effects Plot

Figure 22.7   Final report in DOCX format (salaryReport2.docx)

Note that unlike previous approaches, this approach to dynamic report generation involves two files—the Word template and an R script. The R code isn't directly embedded in the Word document.

In this section, you've used the R2wd package, but others are available. The ReporteRs package (http://davidgohel.github.io/ReporteRs) is a serious contender for dynamically creating Microsoft Office documents from R. In general, technologies that connect R with Microsoft Office are developing rapidly, so you can expect new options in the future.

22.6 *Summary*

In this chapter, you've seen several ways that R results can be incorporated into reports. The reports are dynamic in the sense that changing the data and reprocessing the code results in an updated report. You learned methods for creating web pages, typeset documents, Open Document Format reports, and Microsoft Word documents.

There are several advantages to the template approach described in this chapter. By embedding the code needed to perform statistical analyses directly into the report template, you can see exactly how the results were calculated. Six months from now, you can easily see what was done. You can also modify the statistical analyses or add new data and immediately regenerate the report with minimum effort. Additionally, you avoid the need to cut and paste and reformat the results. This by itself is worth the price of admission.

The templates in this chapter are static in the sense that their structure is fixed. Although not covered here, you can also use these methods to create a variety of expert reporting systems. For example, the output of an R code chunk can depend on the data submitted. If numeric variables are submitted, a scatterplot matrix can be produced. Alternatively, if categorical variables are submitted, a mosaic plot can be produced. In a similar fashion, the explanatory text that is generated can depend on the results of the analyses. Using R's if/then construct makes the possibilities for customization endless. You can use this approach to create a sophisticated expert system.

In this book, we've talked about getting your data into R, cleaning it up, analyzing it, graphing it, and presenting it to others. We've discussed a great many topics. The afterword considers where you may want to go next.

afterword
Into the rabbit hole

We've covered a broad range of topics in the book, including major ones like the R development environment, data management, traditional statistical models, and statistical graphics. We've also examined hidden gems like resampling statistics, missing values imputation, and interactive graphics. The great (or perhaps infuriating) thing about R is that there's always more to learn.

R is a large, robust, and evolving statistical platform and programming language. With so many new packages, frequent updates, and new directions, how can you stay current? Happily, many websites support this active community and provide coverage of platform and package changes, new methodologies, and a wealth of tutorials. I've listed some of my favorite sites next:

- *The R Project (www.r-project.org)*
  The official R website and your first stop for all things R. The site includes extensive documentation, including "An Introduction to R," "The R Language Definition," "Writing R Extensions," "R Data Import/Export," "R Installation and Administration," and "The R FAQ."

- *The R Journal (http://journal.r-project.org)*
  A freely accessible, refereed journal containing articles on the R project and contributed packages.

- *R Bloggers (www.r-bloggers.com)*
  A central hub (blog aggregator) that collects content from bloggers writing about R. It contains new articles daily. I'm addicted to it.

- *Planet R (http://planetr.stderr.org)*
  Another good site aggregator, including information from a wide range of sources. Updated daily.

- *CRANberries (http://dirk.eddelbuettel.com/cranberries)*
  A site that aggregates information about new and updated packages and contains links to CRAN for each.
- *Journal of Statistical Software (www.jstatsoft.org)*
  A freely accessible, refereed journal containing articles, book reviews, and code snippets on statistical computing. Contains frequent articles about R.
- *Revolutions (http://blog.revolution-computing.com)*
  A popular, well-organized blog dedicated to news and information about R.
- *CRAN Task Views (http://cran.r-project.org/web/views)*
  Task views are guides to the use of R in different academic and research fields. They include a description of the packages and methods available for a given area. Currently, 33 task views are available (see the following table).

CRAN task views	
Bayesian Inference	Natural Language Processing
Chemometrics and Computational Physics	Numerical Mathematics
Clinical Trial Design, Monitoring, and Analysis	Official Statistics & Survey Methodology
Cluster Analysis & Finite Mixture Models	Optimization and Mathematical Programming
Differential Equations	Analysis of Pharmacokinetic Data
Probability Distributions	Phylogenetics, Especially Comparative Methods
Computational Econometrics	Psychometric Models and Methods
Analysis of Ecological and Environmental Data	Reproducible Research
Design of Experiments (DoE) & Analysis of Experimental Data	Robust Statistical Methods
Empirical Finance	Statistics for the Social Sciences
Statistical Genetics	Analysis of Spatial Data
Graphic Displays & Dynamic Graphics & Graphic Devices & Visualization	Handling and Analyzing Spatio-Temporal Data
High-Performance and Parallel Computing with R	Survival Analysis
Machine Learning & Statistical Learning	Time Series Analysis
Medical Image Analysis	Web Technologies and Services
Meta-Analysis	gRaphical Models in R
Multivariate Statistics	

- *R-Help main R mailing list (https://stat.ethz.ch/mailman/listinfo/r-help)*
  This electronic mailing list is the best place to ask questions about R. The archives are also searchable. Be sure to read the FAQ before posting questions.

- *Cross Validated (http://stats.stackexchange.com)*
  A question and answer site for people interested in statistics and data science. This is a good place to post questions about R and see what other people are asking.

- *Quick-R (www.statmethods.net)*
  This is my R website. It's stocked with more than 80 brief tutorials on R topics. False modesty forbids me from saying more.

The R community is a helpful, vibrant, and exciting lot. Welcome to Wonderland.

appendix A
Graphical user interfaces

You turned here first, didn't you? By default, R provides a simple command-line interface (CLI). The user enters statements at a command-line prompt (> by default), and each command is executed one at a time. For many data analysts, the CLI is one of R's most significant limitations.

There have been a number of attempts to create more graphical interfaces, ranging from code editors that interact with R (such as RStudio), to GUIs for specific functions or packages (such as BiplotGUI), to full-blown GUIs that allow you to construct analyses through interactions with menus and dialog boxes (such as R Commander).

Several of the more useful code editors are listed in table A.1.

Table A.1 Integrated development environments and syntax editors

Name	URL
RStudio	www.rstudio.com/products/RStudio
Eclipse with StatET plug-in	www.eclipse.org and www.walware.de/goto/statet
Architect	www.openanalytics.eu/architect
ESS (Emacs Speaks Statistics)	http://ess.r-project.org
JGR	http://jgr.markushelbig.org/JGR.html
Tinn-R (Windows only)	http://nbcgib.uesc.br/lec/software/editores/tinn-r/en
Notepad++ with NppToR (Windows only)	http://notepad-plus-plus.org and http://sourceforge.net/projects/npptor

These code editors let you edit and execute R code and include syntax highlighting, statement completion, object exploration, project organization, and online help. A screenshot of RStudio is shown in figure A.1.

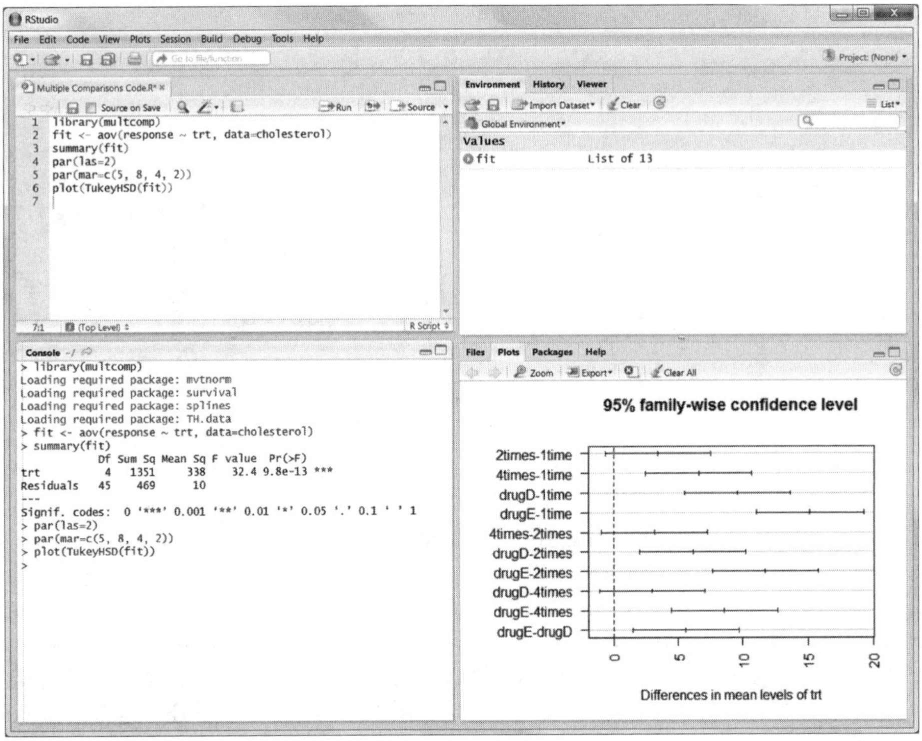

Figure A.1   RStudio IDE

Several promising, full-blown GUIs for R are listed in table A.2. The GUIs available for R are less comprehensive and mature than those offered by SAS or IBM SPSS, but they're developing rapidly.

Table A.2   Comprehensive GUIs for R

Name	URL
JGR/Deducer	www.deducer.org
R Analytic Flow	www.ef-prime.com/products/ranalyticflow_en
Rattle (for data mining)	http://rattle.togaware.com
R Commander	http://socserv.mcmaster.ca/jfox/Misc/Rcmdr
Rkward	http://rkward.sourceforge.net

My favorite GUI for introductory statistics courses is R Commander (shown in figure A.2).

Finally, a number of applications allow you to create GUI wrappers for R functions (including user-written functions). These include the R GUI Generator (RGG)

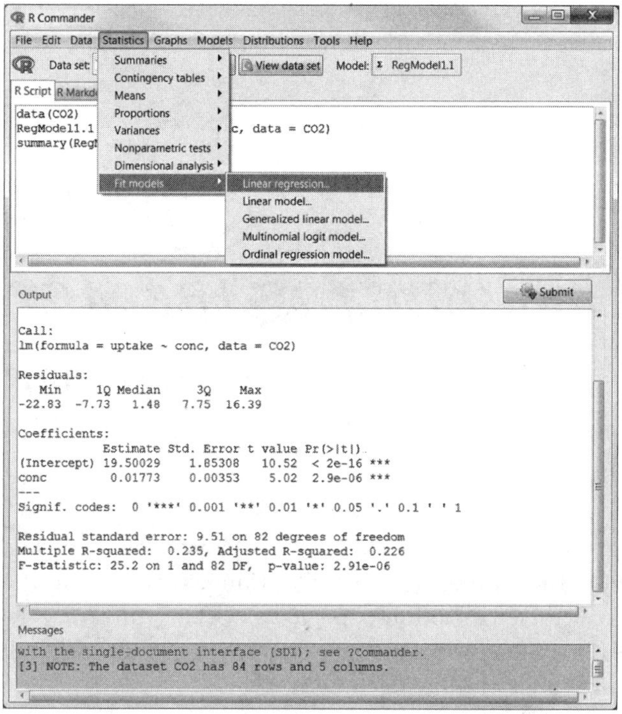

Figure A.2   R Commander GUI

(http://rgg.r-forge.r-project.org) and the `fgui` and `twiddler` packages available from CRAN. The most comprehensive approach is currently `Shiny` (http://shiny.rstudio .com/). `Shiny` lets you easily create web applications with interactive access to R functions.

appendix B
Customizing the startup environment

One of the first things that programmers like to do is customize their startup environment to conform to their preferred way of working. Customizing the startup environment allows you to set R options, specify a working directory, load commonly used packages, load user-written functions, set a default CRAN download site, and perform any number of housekeeping tasks.

You can customize the R environment through either a site-initialization file (Rprofile.site) or a directory-initialization file (.Rprofile). These are text files containing R code to be executed at startup.

At startup, R will source the file Rprofile.site from the R_HOME/etc directory, where R_HOME is an environment value. It will then look for an .Rprofile file to source in the current working directory. If R doesn't find this file, it will look for it in the user's home directory. You can use Sys.getenv("R_HOME"), Sys.getenv ("HOME"), and getwd() to identify the location of R_HOME, HOME, and current working directory, respectively.

You can place two special functions in these files. The .First() function is executed at the start of each R session, and the .Last() function is executed at the end of each session. An example of an Rprofile.site file is shown in listing B.1.

Listing B.1 Sample Rprofile.site file

```
options(papersize="a4")
options(editor="notepad")
options(tab.width = 2)
options(width = 130)                        Sets common options
options(digits=4)
options(stringsAsFactors=FALSE)
options(show.signif.stars=FALSE)
```

Sets path for local library →

```
grDevices::windows.options(record=TRUE)
options(prompt="> ")
options(continue="+ ")
.libPaths("C:/my_R_library")
local({r <- getOption("repos")
       r["CRAN"] <- "http://cran.case.edu/"
       options(repos=r)})

.First <- function(){
library(lattice)
library(Hmisc)
source("C:/mydir/myfunctions.R")
cat("\nWelcome at", date(), "\n")
}
.Last <- function(){
cat("\nGoodbye at ", date(), "\n")
}
```

Sets R interactive prompt

Sets CRAN mirror default

Startup function

Session end function

There are several things you should note about this file:

- Setting a .libPaths value allows you to create a local library for packages outside of the R directory tree. This can be useful for retaining packages during an upgrade.

- Setting a default CRAN mirror site frees you from having to choose one each time you issue an install.packages() command.

- The .First() function is an excellent place to load libraries that you use often, as well as source text files containing user-written functions that you apply frequently.

- The .Last() function is an excellent place for any cleanup activities, including archiving command histories, program output, and data files.

There are other ways to customize the startup environment, including the use of command-line options and environment variables. See help(Startup) and appendix B in the "Introduction to R" manual (http://cran.r-project.org/doc/manuals/R-intro.pdf) for more details.

appendix C
Exporting data from R

In chapter 2, we reviewed a wide range of methods for importing data into R. But sometimes you'll want to go the other way—exporting data from R—so that data can be archived or imported into external applications. In this appendix, you'll learn how to output an R object to a delimited text file, an Excel spreadsheet, or a statistical application (such as SPSS, SAS, or Stata).

Delimited text file

You can use the `write.table()` function to output an R object to a delimited text file. The format is

```
write.table(x, outfile, sep=delimiter, quote=TRUE, na="NA")
```

where *x* is the object and *outfile* is the target file. For example, the statement

```
write.table(mydata, "mydata.txt", sep=",")
```

saves the dataset `mydata` to a comma-delimited file named mydata.txt in the current working directory. Include a path (for example, `"c:/myprojects/mydata.txt"`) to save the output file elsewhere. Replacing `sep=","` with `sep="\t"` saves the data in a tab-delimited file. By default, strings are enclosed in quotes (`""`) and missing values are written as `NA`.

Excel spreadsheet

The `write.xlsx()` function in the `xlsx` package can be used to save an R data frame to an Excel 2007 workbook. The format is

```
library(xlsx)
write.xlsx(x, outfile, col.Names=TRUE, row.names=TRUE,
           sheetName="Sheet 1", append=FALSE)
```

For example, the statements

```
library(xlsx)
write.xlsx(mydata, "mydata.xlsx")
```

export the data frame `mydata` to a worksheet (Sheet 1 by default) in an Excel workbook named mydata.xlsx in the current working directory. By default, the variable names in the dataset are used to create column headings in the spreadsheet, and row names are placed in the first column of the spreadsheet. If mydata.xlsx already exists, it's overwritten.

The `xlsx` package is a powerful tool for manipulating Excel 2007 workbooks. See the package documentation for more details.

Statistical applications

The `write.foreign()` function in the `foreign` package can be used to export a data frame to an external statistical application. Two files are created: a free-format text file containing the data, and a code file containing instructions for reading the data into the external statistical application. The format is

```
write.foreign(dataframe, datafile, codefile, package=package)
```

For example, the code

```
library(foreign)
write.foreign(mydata, "mydata.txt", "mycode.sps", package="SPSS")
```

exports the dataframe `mydata` into a free-format text file named mydata.txt in the current working directory and an SPSS program named mycode.sps that can be used to read the text file. Other values of *package* include `"SAS"` and `"Stata"`.

To learn more about exporting data from R, see the "R Data Import/Export" documentation, available from http://cran.r-project.org/doc/manuals/R-data.pdf.

appendix D
Matrix algebra in R

Many of the functions described in this book operate on matrices. The manipulation of matrices is built deeply into the R language. Table D.1 describes operators and functions that are particularly important for solving linear algebra problems. In the table, A and B are matrices, x and b are vectors, and k is a scalar.

Table D.1 R functions and operators for matrix algebra

Operator or function	Description
+ - * / ^	Element-wise addition, subtraction, multiplication, division, and exponentiation, respectively.
A %*% B	Matrix multiplication.
A %o% B	Outer product: AB'.
cbind(A, B, …)	Combines matrices or vectors horizontally. Returns a matrix.
chol(A)	Choleski factorization of A. If R <- chol(A), then chol(A) contains the upper triangular factor, such that R'R = A.
colMeans(A)	Returns a vector containing the column means of A.
crossprod(A)	Returns A'A.
crossprod(A,B)	Returns A'B.
colSums(A)	Returns a vector containing the column sums of A.
diag(A)	Returns a vector containing the elements of the principal diagonal.
diag(x)	Creates a diagonal matrix with elements of x in the principal diagonal.
diag(k)	If k is a scalar, this creates a k × k identity matrix. Go figure.
eigen(A)	Eigenvalues and eigenvectors of A. If y <- eigen(A) then • y$val are the eigenvalues of A. • y$vec are the eigenvectors of A.

Table D.1 R functions and operators for matrix algebra

Operator or function	Description
`ginv(A)`	Moore-Penrose Generalized Inverse of A. (Requires the MASS package.)
`qr(A)`	QR decomposition of A. If `y <- qr(A)`, then • `y$qr` has an upper triangle that contains the decomposition and a lower triangle that contains information on the decomposition. • `y$rank` is the rank of A. • `y$qraux` is a vector which contains additional information on Q. • `y$pivot` contains information on the pivoting strategy used.
`rbind(A, B, …)`	Combines matrices or vectors vertically. Returns a matrix.
`rowMeans(A)`	Returns a vector containing the row means of A.
`rowSums(A)`	Returns a vector containing the row sums of A.
`solve(A)`	Inverse of A where A is a square matrix.
`solve(A, b)`	Solves for vector x in the equation b = Ax.
`svd(A)`	Single-value decomposition of A. If `y <- svd(A)`, then • `y$d` is a vector containing the singular values of A. • `y$u` is a matrix with columns containing the left singular vectors of A. • `y$v` is a matrix with columns containing the right singular vectors of A.
`t(A)`	Transpose of A.

Several user-contributed packages are particularly useful for matrix algebra. The `matlab` package contains wrapper functions and variables used to replicate MATLAB function calls as closely as possible. These functions can help you port MATLAB applications and code to R. There's also a useful cheat sheet for converting MATLAB statements to R statements at http://mathesaurus.sourceforge.net/octave-r.html.

The `Matrix` package contains functions that extend R in order to support highly dense or sparse matrices. It provides efficient access to BLAS (Basic Linear Algebra Subroutines), Lapack (dense matrix), TAUCS (sparse matrix), and UMFPACK (sparse matrix) routines.

Finally, the `matrixStats` package provides methods for operating on the rows and columns of matrices, including functions that calculate counts, sums, products, central tendency, dispersion, and more. Each is optimized for speed and efficient memory use.

appendix E
Packages used in this book

R derives much of its breadth and power from the contributions of selfless authors. Table E.1 lists the user-contributed packages described in this book, along with the chapter(s) in which they appear.

Table E.1   Contributed packages used in this book

Package	Authors	Description	Chapter(s)
AER	Christian Kleiber and Achim Zeileis	Functions, data sets, examples, demos, and vignettes from the book *Applied Econometrics with R* by Christian Kleiber and Achim Zeileis (Springer, 2008)	13
Amelia	James Honaker, Gary King, and Matthew Blackwell	Amelia II: a program for missing data via multiple imputation	18
arrayImpute	Eun-kyung Lee, Dankyu Yoon, and Taesung Park	Missing imputation for microarray data	18
arrayMiss-Pattern	Eun-kyung Lee and Taesung Park	Exploratory analysis of missing patterns for microarray data	18
boot	S original by Angelo Canty. R port by Brian Ripley	Bootstrap functions	12
ca	Michael Greenacre and Oleg Nenadic	Simple, multiple, and joint correspondence analysis	7
car	John Fox and Sanford Weisberg	Companion to Applied Regression	1, 8, 9, 10, 11, 19, 22
cat	Ported to R by Ted Harding and Fernando Tusell; original by Joseph L. Schafer	Analysis of categorical-variable datasets with missing values	15

Table E.1 Contributed packages used in this book *(continued)*

Package	Authors	Description	Chapter(s)
coin	Torsten Hothorn, Kurt Hornik, Mark A. van de Wiel, and Achim Zeileis	Conditional inference procedures in a permutation test framework	12
corrgram	Kevin Wright	Plots a corrgram	11
corrperm	Douglas M. Potter	Permutation tests of correlation with repeated measurements	12
doBy	Søren Højsgaard with contributions from Kevin Wright and Alessandro A. Leidi	Group-wise computations of summary statistics, general linear contrasts and other utilities	7
doParallel	Revolution Analytics, Steve Weston	foreach parallel adaptor for the parallel package	20
effects	John Fox and Jangman Hong	Effect displays for linear, generalized linear, multinomial-logit, and proportional-odds logit models	8, 9
FactoMineR	Francois Husson, Julie Josse, Sebastien Le, and Jeremy Mazet	Multivariate exploratory data analysis and data mining with R	14
FAiR	Ben Goodrich	Factor analysis using a genetic algorithm	14
fCalendar	Diethelm Wuertz and Yohan Chalabi	Functions for chronological and calendrical objects	4
flexclust	Friedrich Leish and Evgenia Dimnitriadou	Flexible cluster algorithms	16
forecast	Rob J. Hyndman with contributions from George Athanasopoulos, Slava Razbash, Drew Schmidt, Zhenyu Zhou, Yousaf Khan, Christoph Bergmeir, and Earo Wang	Methods and tools for displaying and analyzing univariate time series forecasts, including exponential smoothing via state space models and automatic ARIMA modeling	15
foreach	Revolution Analytics, Steve Weston	foreach looping construct for R	20
foreign	R Core members Saikat DebRoy, Roger Bivand, and others	Reads data stored by Minitab, S, SAS, SPSS, Stata, Systat, dBase, and others	2
gclus	Catherine Hurley	Clustering graphics	1, 11
ggplot2	Hadley Wickam	An implementation of the Grammar of Graphics	19, 20
glmPerm	Wiebke Werft and Douglas M. Potter	Permutation test for inference in generalized linear models	12

Table E.1 Contributed packages used in this book (*continued*)

Package	Authors	Description	Chapter(s)
gmodels	Gregory R. Warnes. Includes R source code and/or documentation contributed by Ben Bolker, Thomas Lumley, and Randall C. Johnson. Contributions from Randall C. Johnson are copyright (2005) SAIC-Frederick, Inc.	Various R programming tools for model fitting	7
gplots	Gregory R. Warnes. Includes R source code and/or documentation contributed by Ben Bolker, Lodewijk Bonebakker, Robert Gentleman, Wolfgang Huber, Andy Liaw, Thomas Lumley, Martin Maechler, Arni Magnusson, Steffen Moeller, Marc Schwartz, and Bill Venables.	Various R programming tools for plotting data	6, 9
grid	Paul Murrell	A rewrite of the graphics layout capabilities, plus some support for interaction	19
gridExtra	Baptiste Auguie	Functions for grid graphics	19
gvlma	Edsel A. Pena and Elizabeth H. Slate	Global validation of linear models assumptions	8
rhdf5	Bernd Fisher and Gregoire Paue	Interface to the NCSA HDF5 library	2
roxygen2	Hadley Wickham	A Doxygen-like in-source documentation system	21
hexbin	Dan Carr, ported by Nicholas Lewin-Koh and Martin Maechler	Hexagonal binning routines	11
HH	Richard M. Heiberger	Support software for *Statistical Analysis and Data Display* by Heiberger and Holland (Springer, 2004)	9
kernlab	Alexandros Karatzoglou, Alex Smola, and Kurt Hornik	Kernel-based machine learning lab	17
knitr	Yihui Xie	A general-purpose package for dynamic report generation in R	22
Hmisc	Frank E. Harrell Jr., with contributions from many other users	Harrell miscellaneous functions for data analysis, high-level graphics, utility operations, and more	2, 3, 7
kmi	Arthur Allignol	Kaplan-Meier multiple imputation for the analysis of cumulative incidence functions in the competing risks setting	18

Table E.1   Contributed packages used in this book *(continued)*

Package	Authors	Description	Chapter(s)
lattice	Deepayan Sarkar	Lattice graphics	19
lavaan	Yves Rosseel	Functions for latent variable models, including confirmatory factor analysis, structural equation modeling, and latent growth-curve models	14
lcda	Michael Buecker	Latent class-discriminant analysis	14
leaps	Thomas Lumley, using Fortran code by Alan Miller	Regression subset selection, including exhaustive search	8
lmPerm	Bob Wheeler	Permutation tests for linear models	12
logregperm	Douglas M. Potter	Permutation test for inference in logistic regression	12
longitudinal-Data	Christophe Genolini	Tools for longitudinal data	18
lsa	Fridolin Wild	Latent semantic analysis	14
ltm	Dimitris Rizopoulos	Latent trait models under item response theory	14
lubridate	Garrett Grolemund and Hadley Wickham	Functions to identify and parse date-time data, extract and modify components of a date-time, perform accurate math on date-times, and handle time zones and Daylight Savings Time	4
MASS	S original by Venables and Ripley. R port by Brian Ripley, following earlier work by Kurt Hornik and Albrecht Gebhardt.	Functions and datasets to support Venables' and Ripley's *Modern Applied Statistics with S*, 4th edition (Springer, 2003)	4, 5, 7, 8, 9, 12
mlogit	Yves Croissant	Estimation of the multinomial logit model	13
multcomp	Torsten Hothorn, Frank Bretz, Peter Westfall, Richard M. Heiberger, and Andre Schuetzenmeister	Simultaneous tests and confidence intervals for general linear hypotheses in parametric models, including linear, generalized linear, linear mixed effects, and survival models	9, 12
mvnmle	Kevin Gross, with help from Douglas Bates	ML estimation for multivariate normal data with missing values	18
mvoutlier	Moritz Gschwandtner and Peter Filzmoser	Multivariate outlier detection based on robust methods	9

Table E.1   Contributed packages used in this book *(continued)*

Package	Authors	Description	Chapter(s)
NbClustv	Malika Charrad, Nadia Ghazzali, Veronique Boiteau, and Azam Niknafs	An examination of indices for determining the number of clusters	16
ncdf, ncdf4	David Pierce	Interface to Unidata netCDF data files	2
nFactors	Gilles Raiche	Parallel analysis and non-graphical solutions to the Cattell scree test	14
OpenMx	Steven Boker, Michael Neale, Hermine Maes, Michael Wilde, Michael Spiegel, Timothy R. Brick, Jeffrey Spies, Ryne Estabrook, Sarah Kenny, Timothy Bates, Paras Mehta, and John Fox	Advanced structural equation modeling.	14
odfWeave	Max Kuhn, with contributions from Steve Weston, Nathan Coulter, Patrick Lenon, Zekai Otles, and the R Core Team	Sweave processing of Open Document Format (ODF) files	22
pastecs	Frederic Ibanez, Philippe Grosjean, and Michele Etienne	Package for the analysis of space-time ecological series	7
party	Torsten Hothorn, Kurt Hornik, Carolin Strobl, and Achim Zeileis	A laboratory for recursive partitioning	17
poLCA	Drew Linzer and Jeffrey Lewis	Polytomous variable latent-class analysis	14
psych	William Revelle	Procedures for psychological, psychometric, and personality research	7, 14
pwr	Stephane Champely	Basic functions for power analysis	10
qcc	Luca Scrucca	Quality-control charts	13
randomLCA	Ken Beath	Random effects latent-class analysis	14
randomForest	Fortran original by Leo Breiman and Adele Cutler, R port by Andy Liaw and Matthew Wiener	Breiman and Cutler's random forests for classification and regression	17
R2wd	Christian Ritter	Writes MS-Word documents from R	22
rattle	Graham Williams, Mark Vere Culp, Ed Cox, Anthony Nolan, Denis White, Daniele Medri, Akbar Waljee (OOB AUC for Random Forest), and Brian Ripley (original author of print.summary.nnet)	Graphical user interface for data mining in R	16, 17

Table E.1 Contributed packages used in this book *(continued)*

Package	Authors	Description	Chapter(s)
Rcmdr	John Fox, with contributions from Liviu Andronic, Michael Ash, Theophilius Boye, Stefano Calza, Andy Chang, Philippe Grosjean, Richard Heiberger, G. Jay Kerns, Renaud Lancelot, Matthieu Lesnoff, Uwe Ligges, Samir Messad, Martin Maechler, Robert Muenchen, Duncan Murdoch, Erich Neuwirth, Dan Putler, Brian Ripley, Miroslav Ristic, and Peter Wolf	R Commander, a platform-independent, basic-statistics graphical user interface for R, based on the `tcltk` package	Appendix A
reshape2	Hadley Wickham	Flexibly reshape data	4, 5, 7, 20
rgl	Daniel Adler and Duncan Murdoch	3D visualization device system (OpenGL)	11
RJDBC	Simon Urbanek	Provides access to databases through the JDBC interface	2
rms	Frank E. Harrell, Jr.	Regression modeling strategies: about 225 functions that assist with and streamline regression modeling, testing, estimations, validation, graphics, prediction, and typesetting	13
robust	Jiahui Wang, Ruben Zamar, Alfio Marazzi, Victor Yohai, Matias Salibian-Barrera, Ricardo Maronna, Eric Zivot, David Rocke, Doug Martin, Martin Maechler, and Kjell Konis	A package of robust methods	13
RODBC	Brian Ripley and Michael Lapsley	ODBC database access	2
rpart	Terry Therneau, Beth Atkinson, and Brian Ripley (author of the initial R port)	Recursive partitioning and regression trees	17
ROracle	David A. James and Jake Luciani	Oracle database interface for R	2
rrcov	Valentin Todorov	Robust location and scatter estimation, and robust multivariate analysis with a high breakdown point	9
sampling	Yves Tillé and Alina Matei	Functions for drawing and calibrating samples	4
scatterplot3d	Uwe Ligges	Plots a three-dimensional (3D) point cloud	11

Table E.1   Contributed packages used in this book *(continued)*

Package	Authors	Description	Chapter(s)
sem	John Fox, with contributions from Adam Kramer and Michael Friendly	Structural equation models	14
SeqKnn	Ki-Yeol Kim and Gwan-Su Yi, CSBio lab, Information and Communications University	Sequential KNN imputation method	18
sm	Adrian Bowman and Adelchi Azzalini. Ported to R by B. D. Ripley up to version 2.0, version 2.1 by Adrian Bowman and Adelchi Azzalini, version 2.2 by Adrian Bowman.	Smoothing methods for nonparametric regression and density estimation	6, 9
vcd	David Meyer, Achim Zeileis, and Kurt Hornik	Functions for visualizing categorical data	1, 6, 7, 11, 12
vegan	Jari Oksanen, F. Guillaume Blanchet, Roeland Kindt, Pierre Legendre, R. B. O'Hara, Gavin L. Simpson, Peter Solymos, M. Henry, H. Stevens, and Helene Wagner	Ordination methods, diversity analysis, and other functions for community and vegetation ecologists	9
VIM	Matthias Templ, Andreas Alfons, and Alexander Kowarik	Visualization and imputation of missing values	18
xlsx	Adrian A. Dragulescu	Reads, writes, and formats Excel 2007 (.xlsx) files	2
XML	Duncan Temple Lang	Tools for parsing and generating XML in R and S-Plus	2

appendix F
Working with large datasets

R holds all of its objects in virtual memory. For most of us, this design decision has led to a zippy interactive experience, but for analysts working with large datasets, it can lead to slow program execution and memory-related errors.

Memory limits depend primarily on the R build (32- versus 64-bit) and the OS version involved. Error messages starting with "cannot allocate vector of size" typically indicate a failure to obtain sufficient contiguous memory, whereas error messages starting with "cannot allocate vector of length" indicate that an address limit has been exceeded. When working with large datasets, try to use a 64-bit build if at all possible. See ?Memory for more information.

There are three issues to consider when working with large datasets: efficient programming to speed execution, storing data externally to limit memory issues, and using specialized statistical routines designed to efficiently analyze massive amounts of data. First we'll consider simple solutions for each. Then we'll turn to more comprehensive (and complex) solutions for working with *big* data.

F.1   Efficient programming

A number of programming tips can help you improve performance when working with large datasets:

- Vectorize calculations when possible. Use R's built-in functions for manipulating vectors, matrices, and lists (for example, ifelse, colMeans, and row-Sums), and avoid loops (for and while) when feasible.
- Use matrices rather than data frames (they have less overhead).
- When using the read.table() family of functions to input external data into data frames, specify the colClasses and nrows options explicitly, set comment.char = "", and specify "NULL" for columns that aren't needed. This will decrease memory usage and speed up processing considerably. When reading external data into a matrix, use the scan() function instead.

- Correctly size objects initially, rather than growing them from smaller objects by appending values.
- Use parallelization for repetitive, independent, and numerically intensive tasks.
- Test programs on a sample of the data, in order to optimize code and remove bugs, before attempting a run on the full dataset.
- Delete temporary objects and objects that are no longer needed. The call `rm(list=ls())` removes all objects from memory, providing a clean slate. Specific objects can be removed with `rm(object)`. After removing large objects, a call to `gc()` will initiate garbage collection, ensuring that the objects are removed from memory.
- Use the function `.ls.objects()` described in Jeromy Anglim's blog entry "Memory Management in R: A Few Tips and Tricks" (jeromyanglim.blogspot .com) to list all workspace objects sorted by size (MB). This function will help you find and deal with memory hogs.
- Profile your programs to see how much time is being spent in each function. You can accomplish this with the `Rprof()` and `summaryRprof()` functions. The `system.time()` function can also help. The `profr` and `prooftools` packages provide functions that can help in analyzing profiling output.
- Use compiled external routines to speed up program execution. You can use the `Rcpp` package to transfer R objects to C++ functions and back when more optimized subroutines are needed.

Section 20.4 offers examples of vectorization, efficient data input, correctly sizing objects, and parallelization.

With large datasets, increasing code efficiency will only get you so far. When you bump up against memory limits, you can also store your data externally and use specialized analysis routines.

F.2   *Storing data outside of RAM*

Several packages are available for storing data outside of R's main memory. The strategy involves storing data in external databases or in binary flat files on disk and then accessing portions as needed. Several useful packages are described in table F.1.

Table F.1   R packages for accessing large datasets

Package	Description
bigmemory	Supports the creation, storage, access, and manipulation of massive matrices. Matrices are allocated to shared memory and memory-mapped files.
ff	Provides data structures that are stored on disk but behave as if they're in RAM.
filehash	Implements a simple key-value database where character string keys are associated with data values stored on disk.

Table F.1 R packages for accessing large datasets

Package	Description
`ncdf, ncdf4`	Provide an interface to Unidata netCDF data files.
`RODBC, RMySQL, ROracle, RPostgreSQL, RSQLite`	Each provides access to external relational database management systems.

These packages help overcome R's memory limits on data storage. But you also need specialized methods when you attempt to analyze large datasets in a reasonable length of time. Some of the most useful are described next.

F.3 *Analytic packages for out-of-memory data*

R provides several packages for the analysis of large datasets:

- The `biglm` and `speedglm` packages fit linear and generalized linear models to large datasets in a memory-efficient manner. This offers `lm()` and `glm()` type functionality when dealing with massive datasets.
- Several packages offer analytic functions for working with the massive matrices produced by the `bigmemory` package. The `biganalytics` package offers k-means clustering, column statistics, and a wrapper to `biglm`. The `bigrf` package can be used to fit classification and regression forests. The `bigtabulate` package provides `table()`, `split()`, and `tapply()` functionality, and the `bigalgebra` package provides advanced linear algebra functions.
- The `biglars` package offers least-angle regression, lasso, and stepwise regression for datasets that are too large to be held in memory, when used in conjunction with the `ff` package.
- The `data.table` package provides an enhanced version of `data.frame` that includes faster aggregation; faster ordered and overlapping range joins; and faster column addition, modification, and deletion by reference by group (without copies). You can use the `data.table` structure with large datasets (for example, 100 GB in RAM), and it's compatible with any R function expecting a data frame.

Each of these packages accommodates large datasets for specific purposes and is relatively easy to use. More comprehensive solutions for analyzing data in the terabyte range are described next.

F.4 *Comprehensive solutions for working with enormous datasets*

At least five projects have been designed to facilitate the use of R with terabyte-class datasets. Three are free and open source (RHIPE, RHadoop, and pbdr), and two are commercial products (Revolution R Enterprise with RevoScaleR and Oracle R Enterprise). Each requires some familiarity with high-performance computing.

The RHIPE package (www.datadr.org/) provides a programming environment that deeply integrates R and Hadoop (a free Java-based software framework for the processing of large datasets in a distributed computing environment). Additional software from the same authors provides "divide and recombine" methods and data visualization for very large datasets.

The RHadoop project offers a collection of R packages for managing and analyzing data with Hadoop. The `rmr` package provides Hadoop MapReduce functionality from within R, and the `rhdfs` and `rhbase` packages support access to HDFS file systems and HBASE datastores. A Wiki (https://github.com/RevolutionAnalytics/RHadoop/wiki) describes the project and provides tutorials. Note that RHadoop packages must be installed from GitHub rather than CRAN.

The pbdR (Programming with Big Data in R) project enables high-level data parallelism in R through a simple interface to scalable, high-performance libraries (such as MPI, ScaLAPACK, and netCDF4). The pbdR software also supports the single program, multiple data (SPMD) model on large-scale computing clusters. See http://r-pbd.org/ for details.

Revolution R Enterprise (www.revolutionanalytics.com) is a commercial version of R that includes `RevoScaleR`, a package supporting scalable data analyses and high-performance computing. `RevoScaleR` uses a binary XDF data file format to optimize streaming data from disk to memory, and it provides a series of big-data algorithms for common statistical analyses. You can perform data-management tasks and obtain summary statistics, cross tabulations, correlations and covariances, nonparametric statistics, linear and generalized linear regression, stepwise regression, k-means clustering, and classification and regression trees on terabyte-sized datasets. Additionally, Revolution R Enterprise can be integrated with Hadoop (via RHadoop packages) and IBM Netezza (via a plug-in for IBM PureData System for Analytics). At the time of this writing, students and professors in academic settings can obtain a free software subscription (excluding the IBM components).

Finally, Oracle R Enterprise (www.oracle.com) is a commercial product that makes the R environment available for use with massive datasets stored in Oracle databases and Hadoop. Oracle R Enterprise is part of Oracle Advanced Analytics, and it requires an installation of Oracle Database Enterprise Edition. Virtually all of R's functionality, including the thousands of contributed packages, can be applied to terabyte-sized data problems using the Oracle R Enterprise interface. This is a relatively expensive but comprehensive solution, and it will appeal primarily to large organizations with deep pockets.

Working with datasets in the gigabyte-to-terabyte range can be challenging in any language. Each of these approaches comes with a significant learning curve. Of the four, RevoScaleR is perhaps the easiest to learn and install. (Important disclaimer: I teach Revolution R courses as an adjunct instructor and may be biased.)

Additional information on the analysis of large datasets is available in the CRAN task view "High-Performance and Parallel Computing with R" (http://cran.r-project.org/web/views). This is an area of rapid change and development, so be sure to check back often.

appendix G
Updating an R installation

As consumers, we take for granted that we can update a piece of software via a Check for Updates option. In chapter 1, I noted that the update.packages() function can be used to download and install the most recent version of a contributed package. Unfortunately, updating the R installation itself can be more complicated.

If you want to update an R installation from version 5.1.0 to 6.1.1, you must get creative. (As I write this, the current version is actually 3.1.1, but I want this book to appear hip and current for years to come.) Two methods are described here: an automated method using the installr package and a manual method that works on all platforms.

G.1   *Automated installation (Windows only)*

If you're a Windows user, you can use the installr package to update an R installation. First install the package and load it:

```
install.packages("installr")
library(installr)
```

This adds an Update menu to the RGui (see figure G.1).

The menu allows you to install a new version of R, update existing packages, and install other useful software produces (such as RStudio). Currently, the

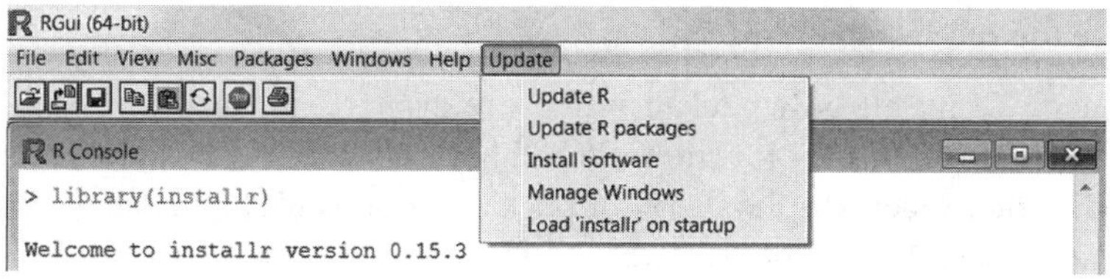

Figure G.1   Update menu added to Windows RGui by the installr package

`installr` package is only available for Windows platforms. For Mac users, or Windows users that don't want to use `installr`, updating R is usually a manual process.

G.2   *Manual installation (Windows and Mac OS X)*

Downloading and installing the latest version of R from CRAN (http://cran.r-project .org/bin) is relatively straightforward. The complicating factor is that customizations (including previously installed contributed packages) aren't included in the new installation. In my current setup, I have more than 500 contributed packages installed. I really don't want to have to write down their names and reinstall them by hand the next time I upgrade my R installation!

There has been much discussion on the web concerning the most elegant and efficient way to update an R installation. The method described here is neither elegant nor efficient, but I find that it works well on both Windows and Mac platforms.

In this approach, you use the `installed.packages()` function to save a list of packages to a location outside of the R directory tree, and then you use the list with the `install.packages()` function to download and install the latest contributed packages into the new R installation. Here are the steps:

1 If you have a customized Rprofile.site file (see appendix B), save a copy outside of R.

2 Launch your current version of R, and issue the following statements

```
oldip <- installed.packages()[,1]
save(oldip, file="path/installedPackages.Rdata")
```

where *path* is a directory outside of R.

3 Download and install the newer version of R.

4 If you saved a customized version of the Rprofile.site file in step 1, copy it into the new installation.

5 Launch the new version of R, and issue the following statements

```
load("path/installedPackages.Rdata")
newip <- installed.packages()[,1]
for(i in setdiff(oldip, newip)){
   install.packages(i)
}
```

where *path* is the location specified in step 2.

6 Delete the old installation (optional).

This approach will install only packages that are available from CRAN. It won't find packages obtained from other locations. You'll have to find and download these separately. Luckily, the process displays a list of packages that can't be installed. During my last installation, `globaltest` and `Biobase` couldn't be found. Because I got them from the Bioconductor site, I was able to install them via this code:

```
source("http://bioconductor.org/biocLite.R")
biocLite("globaltest")
biocLite("Biobase")
```

Step 6 involves the optional deletion of the old installation. On a Windows machine, more than one version of R can be installed at a time. If desired, uninstall the older version via Start > Control Panel > Uninstall a Program. On Mac platforms, the new version of R will overwrite the older version. To delete any remnants on a Mac, use the Finder to go to the /Library/Frameworks/R.frameworks/versions/ directory, and delete the folder representing the older version.

Clearly, manually updating an existing version of R is more involved than is desirable for such a sophisticated piece of software. I'm hopeful that someday this appendix will simply say "Select the Check for Updates option" to update an R installation.

G.3 *Updating an R installation (Linux)*

The process of updating an R installation on a Linux platform is quite different from the process used on Windows and Mac OS X machines. Additionally, it varies by Linux distribution (Debian, Red Hat, SUSE, or Ubuntu). See http://cran.r-project.org/bin/linux for details.

Allison, P. 2001. *Missing Data.* Thousand Oaks, CA: Sage.

Allison, T. and D. Chichetti. 1976. "Sleep in Mammals: Ecological and Constitutional Correlates." *Science* 194 (4266): 732–734.

Anderson, M. J. 2006. "Distance-Based Tests for Homogeneity of Multivariate Dispersions." *Biometrics* 62:245–253.

Baade, R. and R. Dye. 1990. "The Impact of Stadiums and Professional Sports on Metropolitan Area Development." *Growth and Change* 21:1–14.

Bandalos, D. L. and M. R. Boehm-Kaufman. 2009. "Four Common Misconceptions in Exploratory Factor Analysis." In *Statistical and Methodological Myths and Urban Legends*, edited by C. E. Lance and R. J. Vandenberg, 61–87. New York: Routledge.

Bates, D. 2005. "Fitting Linear Mixed Models in R." *R News* 5 (1): 27–30. www.r-project.org/doc/Rnews/Rnews_2005-1.pdf.

Breslow, N. and D. Clayton. 1993. "Approximate Inference in Generalized Linear Mixed Models." *Journal of the American Statistical Association* 88:9–25.

Bretz, F., T. Hothorn, and P. Westfall. 2010. *Multiple Comparisons Using R.* Boca Raton, FL: Chapman & Hall.

Canty, A. J. 2002. "Resampling Methods in R: The boot Package." *R News* 2 (3): 2–7. www.r-project.org/doc/Rnews/Rnews_2002-3.pdf.

Chambers, J. M. 2008. *Software for Data Analysis: Programming with R.* New York: Springer.

Chang, W. 2013. *R Graphics Cookbook.* Sebastopol, California: O'Reilly.

Cleveland, W. 1981. "LOWESS: A Program for Smoothing Scatter Plots by Robust Locally Weighted Regression." *The American Statistician* 35:54.

_____. 1994. *The Elements of Graphing Data.* Monterey, CA: Wadsworth.

_____. 1993. *Visualizing Data.* Summit, NJ: Hobart Press.

Cohen, J. 1988. *Statistical Power Analysis for the Behavioral Sciences*, 2nd ed. Hillsdale, NJ: Lawrence Erlbaum.

Cowpertwait, P. S. and A. V. Metcalfe. 2009. *Introductory Time Series with R.* Auckland, New Zealand: Springer.

Coxe, S., S. West, and L. Aiken. 2009. "The Analysis of Count Data: A Gentle Introduction to Poisson Regression and Its Alternatives." *Journal of Personality Assessment* 91:121–136.

Culbertson, W. and D. Bradford. 1991. "The Price of Beer: Some Evidence for Interstate Comparisons." *International Journal of Industrial Organization* 9:275–289.

DiStefano, C., M. Zhu, and D. Mîndrilă. 2009. "Understanding and Using Factor Scores: Considerations for the Applied Researcher." *Practical Assessment, Research & Evaluation* 14 (20). http://pareonline .net/pdf/v14n20.pdf.

Dobson, A. and A. Barnett. 2008. *An Introduction to Generalized Linear Models*, 3rd ed. Boca Raton, FL: Chapman & Hall.

Dunteman, G. and M-H Ho. 2006. *An Introduction to Generalized Linear Models*. Thousand Oaks, CA: Sage.

Efron, B. and R. Tibshirani. 1998. *An Introduction to the Bootstrap*. New York: Chapman & Hall.

Everitt, B. S., S. Landau, M. Leese, and D. Stahl. 2011. *Cluster Analysis*, 5th ed. London: Wiley.

Fair, R. C. 1978. "A Theory of Extramarital Affairs." *Journal of Political Economy* 86:45–61.

Faraway, J. 2006. *Extending the Linear Model with R: Generalized Linear, Mixed Effects and Nonparametric Regression Models*. Boca Raton, FL: Chapman & Hall.

Fawcett, T. 2005. "An Introduction to ROC Analysis." *Pattern Recognition Letters* 27:861–874.

Fox, J. 2002. *An R and S-Plus Companion to Applied Regression*. Thousand Oaks, CA: Sage.

———. 2002. "Bootstrapping Regression Models." http://mng.bz/pY9m.

———. 2008. *Applied Regression Analysis and Generalized Linear Models*. Thousand Oaks, CA: Sage.

Fwa, T., ed. 2006. *The Handbook of Highway Engineering*, 2nd ed. Boca Raton, FL: CRC Press.

Gentleman, R. 2009. *R Programming for Bioinformatics*. Boca Raton, FL: Chapman &Hall/CRC.

Good, P. 2006. *Resampling Methods: A Practical Guide to Data Analysis*, 3rd ed. Boston: Birkhäuser.

Gorsuch, R. L. 1983. *Factor Analysis*, 2nd ed. Hillsdale, NJ: Lawrence Erlbaum.

Greene, W. H. 2003. *Econometric Analysis*, 5th ed. Upper Saddle River, NJ: Prentice Hall.

Grissom, R. and J. Kim. 2005. *Effect Sizes for Research: A Broad Practical Approach*. Mahwah, NJ: Lawrence Erlbaum.

Groemping, U. 2009. "CRAN Task View: Design of Experiments (DoE) and Analysis of Experimental Data." http://cran.r-project.org/web/views/ExperimentalDesign.html.

Hand, D. J. and C. C. Taylor. 1987. *Multivariate Analysis of Variance and Repeated Measures*. London: Chapman & Hall.

Harlow, L., S. Mulaik, and J. Steiger. 1997. *What If There Were No Significance Tests?* Mahwah, NJ: Lawrence Erlbaum.

Hartigan, J. A. and M. A. Wong. 1979. "A K-Means Clustering Algorithm." *Applied Statistics* 28:100–108.

Hayton, J. C., D. G. Allen, and V. Scarpello. 2004. "Factor Retention Decisions in Exploratory Factor Analysis: A Tutorial on Parallel Analysis." *Organizational Research Methods* 7:191–204.

Hsu, S., M. Wen, and M. Wu. 2009. "Exploring User Experiences as Predictors of MMORPG Addiction." *Computers and Education* 53:990–999.

Jacoby, W. G. 2006. "The Dot Plot: A Graphical Display for Labeled Quantitative Values." *Political Methodologist* 14:6–14.

Johnson, J. 2004. "Factors Affecting Relative Weights: The Influence of Sample and Measurement Error." *Organizational Research Methods* 7:283–299.

Johnson, J. and J. Lebreton. 2004. "History and Use of Relative Importance Indices in Organizational Research." *Organizational Research Methods* 7:238–257.

Koch, G. and S. Edwards. 1988. "Clinical Efficiency Trials with Categorical Data." In *Statistical Analysis with Missing Data*, 2nd ed., by R. J. A. Little and D. Rubin. Hoboken, NJ: John Wiley & Sons, 2002.

Kuhn, M. and K. Johnson. 2013. *Applied Predictive Modeling*. New York: Springer.

LeBreton, J. M and S. Tonidandel. 2008. "Multivariate Relative Importance: Extending Relative Weight Analysis to Multivariate Criterion Spaces." *Journal of Applied Psychology* 93:329–345.

Lemon, J. and A. Tyagi. 2009. "The Fan Plot: A Technique for Displaying Relative Quantities and Differences." *Statistical Computing and Graphics Newsletter* 20:8–10. http://stat-computing.org/newsletter/issues/scgn-20-1.pdf.

Licht, M. 1995. "Multiple Regression and Correlation." In *Reading and Understanding Multivariate Statistics*, edited by L. Grimm and P. Yarnold. Washington, DC: American Psychological Association, 19–64.

Mangasarian, O. L. and W. H. Wolberg. 1990. "Cancer Diagnosis via Linear Programming." *SIAM News*, 23:1–18.

McCall, R. B. 2000. *Fundamental Statistics for the Behavioral Sciences*, 8th ed. New York: Wadsworth.

McCullagh, P. and J. Nelder. 1989. *Generalized Linear Models*, 2nd ed. Boca Raton, FL: Chapman & Hall.

Meyer, D., A. Zeileis, and K. Hornick. 2006. "The Strucplot Framework: Visualizing Multi-way Contingency Tables with vcd." *Journal of Statistical Software* 17 (3):1–48. www.jstatsoft.org/v17/i03/paper.

Montgomery, D. C. 2007. *Engineering Statistics*. Hoboken, NJ: John Wiley & Sons.

Mooney, C. and R. Duval. 1993. *Bootstrapping: A Nonparametric Approach to Statistical Inference*. Monterey, CA: Sage.

Mulaik, S. 2009. *Foundations of Factor Analysis*, 2nd ed. Boca Raton, FL: Chapman & Hall.

Murrell, P. 2011. *R Graphics*, 2nd ed. Boca Raton, FL: Chapman & Hall/CRC.

Nenadić, O. and M. Greenacre. 2007. "Correspondence Analysis in R, with Two- and Three-Dimensional Graphics: The ca Package." *Journal of Statistical Software* 20 (3). www.jstatsoft.org/v20/i03/paper.

Peace, K. E., ed. 1987. *Biopharmaceutical Statistics for Drug Development*. New York: Marcel Dekker, 403–451.

Pena, E. and E. Slate. 2006. "Global Validation of Linear Model Assumptions." *Journal of the American Statistical Association* 101:341–354.

Pinheiro, J. C. and D. M. Bates. 2000. *Mixed-Effects Models in S and S-PLUS*. New York: Springer.

Potvin, C., M. J. Lechowicz, and S. Tardif. 1990. "The Statistical Analysis of Ecophysiological Response Curves Obtained from Experiments Involving Repeated Measures." *Ecology* 71:1389–1400.

Rosenthal, R., R. Rosnow, and D. Rubin. 2000. *Contrasts and Effect Sizes in Behavioral Research: A Correlational Approach*. Cambridge, UK: Cambridge University Press.

Sarkar, D. 2008. *Lattice: Multivariate Data Visualization with R*. New York: Springer.

Schafer, J. and J. Graham. 2002. "Missing Data: Our View of the State of the Art." *Psychological Methods* 7:147–177.

Schlomer, G., S. Bauman, and N. Card. 2010. "Best Practices for Missing Data Management in Counseling Psychology." *Journal of Counseling Psychology* 57:1–10.

Shah, A. 2005. "Getting Started with the boot Package in R for Statistical Inference." www.mayin.org/ajayshah/KB/R/documents/boot.html.

Shumway, R. H. and D. S. Stoffer. 2010. *Time Series Analysis and Its Applications*. New York: Springer.

Silva, R. B., D. F. Ferreirra, and D. A. Nogueira. 2008. "Robustness of Asymptotic and Bootstrap Tests for Multivariate Homogeneity of Covariance Matrices." *Ciênc. agrotec.* 32:157–166.

Simon, J. 1997. "Resampling: The New Statistics." www.resample.com/intro-text-online/.

Snedecor, G. W. and W. G. Cochran. 1988. *Statistical Methods*, 8th ed. Ames, IA: Iowa State University Press.

Statnikov, A., C. F. Aliferis, D. P. Hardin, and I. Guyon. 2011. *A Gentle Introduction to Support Vector Machines in Biomedicine* (vol. 1: *Theory and Methods*). Hackensack, NJ: World Scientific Publishing.

Torgo, L. 2010. *Data Mining with R: Learning with Case Studies*. Boca Raton, Florida: Chapman & Hall/CRC.

UCLA: Academic Technology Services, Statistical Consulting Group. 2009. "Repeated Measures Analysis with R." http://mng.bz/a9c7.

van Buuren, S. and K. Groothuis-Oudshoorn. 2010. "MICE: Multivariate Imputation by Chained Equations in R." *Journal of Statistical Software*, forthcoming. http://mng.bz/3EH5.

Venables, W. N. and B. D. Ripley. 1999. *Modern Applied Statistics with S-PLUS*, 3rd ed. New York: Springer.

_____. 2000. *S Programming*. New York: Springer.

Westfall, P. H., Y. Hochberg, D. Rom, R. Wolfinger, and R. Tobias. 1999. *Multiple Comparisons and Multiple Tests Using the SAS System*. Cary, NC: SAS Institute.

Wickham, H. 2009a. *ggplot2: Elegant Graphics for Data Analysis*. New York: Springer.

_____. 2009b. "A Layered Grammar of Graphics." *Journal of Computational and Graphical Statistics* 19:3–28.

Williams, G. 2011. *Data Mining with Rattle and R*. New York: Springer.

Wilkinson, L. 2005. *The Grammar of Graphics*. New York: Springer-Verlag.

Yu, C. H. 2003. "Resampling Methods: Concepts, Applications, and Justification." *Practical Assessment, Research & Evaluation*, 8 (19). http://pareonline.net/getvn.asp?v=8&n=19.

Yu-Sung, S., A. Gelman, J. Hill, and M. Yajima. 2011. "Multiple Imputation with Diagnostics (mi) in R: Opening Windows into the Black Box." *Journal of Statistical Software* 45 (2). www.jstatsoft.org/v45/i02/paper.

Zuur, A. F., E. Ieno, N. Walker, A. A. Saveliev, and G. M. Smith. 2009. *Mixed Effects Models and Extensions in Ecology with R*. New York: Springer.

index

RELATED MANNING TITLES

Practical Data Science with R
by Nina Zumel and John Mount

ISBN: 9781617291562
416 pages, $49.99
March 2014

Big Data
Principles and best practices of scalable realtime data systems
by Nathan Marz with James Warren

ISBN: 9781617290343
328 pages, $49.99
April 2015

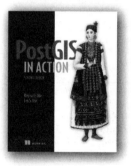

PostGIS in Action, Second Edition
by Regina O. Obe and Leo S. Hsu

ISBN: 9781617291395
600 pages, $49.99
April 2015

Gnuplot in Action, Second Edition
by Philipp K. Janert

ISBN: 9781633430181
425 pages, $44.99
October 2015

For ordering information go to www.manning.com